AMERICAN
SOCIETY, INC.

AMERICAN
SOCIETY, INC.

Studies of the Social Structure
and Political Economy of the United States

edited by

MAURICE ZEITLIN
University of Wisconsin

MARKHAM PUBLISHING COMPANY
Chicago

MARKHAM SOCIOLOGY SERIES
ROBERT W. HODGE, Editor

ADAMS, *Kinship in an Urban Setting*

FARLEY, *Growth of the Black Population: A Study of Demographic Trends*

FILSTEAD, ed., *Qualitative Methodology: Firsthand Involvement with the Social World*

ZEITLIN, ed., *American Society, Inc.: Studies of the Social Structure and Political Economy of the United States*

To the Memory of My Mother,
Rose Zeitlin

INTRODUCTION

The studies in this volume are about fundamental features of the social structure and political economy of the United States. In one way or another they are related to the question: whither America? They deal with the shape and movement of the country's social structure and they focus on the interaction between economic and political forces. The question raised six decades ago by Max Weber, the great German social scientist, is the question asked most frequently in this volume:

> It is utterly ridiculous to see any connection between the high capitalism of today [1906] . . . as it exists in America, and democracy or freedom in any sense of these words. Yet this capitalism is an unavoidable result of our economic development. The question is: *How are freedom and democracy in the long run at all possible under the domination of highly developed capitalism?* [*From Max Weber*, edited by H. Gerth and C. W. Mills (New York: Oxford University Press, 1946), p. 71, italics added; translation slightly reworded.]

The studies in this volume generally utilize social scientific reasoning and evidence to deal with one or another of the aspects of this larger question. Writers of varying and often opposing views deal with a range of controversial issues concerning the nature of our country. These issues are controversial politically, and—it should be emphasized—*controversial within the field of social science.* They are issues on which there is little agreement (although there is a dominant view about most of them among American academics); interpretations vary and even the "evidence" itself is often called into question and debated.

Some of the major questions raised in this volume are:

What is the shape of the economic structure of the United States, and what are the major tendencies of development within it? What relationships are there between the largest corporations and banks, and to what extent and in what ways are they interlocked by common owners, officers, and directors? What are the political and economic consequences of the ascendancy of the large corporations?

To what extent is wealth concentrated in American society, and how has this been changing in the past quarter of a century or more? How do the trends in the distribution of personal and national income compare to the distribution of wealth?

Is poverty in the United States a mass phenomenon, or is it an insular and case phenomenon? How widespread is poverty and how, indeed, is it measured? How does poverty affect the relative "life chances" of the poor? What are the major causes of poverty —are they essentially flaws in the individual character and capacity of the poor, or are they rooted in the social structure and political economy of capitalism?

Have power and property become separated from each other in the United States, and have the requirements of technology and size created a new factor of production in the "organized intelligence" or "technostructure" of the large corporation? How are innovation and efficiency related to the domination of most industries by a few large corporations? Are ownership and control of the large corporations separated from each other, and what implications does this have for their conduct? How does a capitalist economy dominated by a few hundred very large corporations behave compared to a competitive capitalist economy? Does such an economy have a tendency to produce investment funds in excess of the volume that can be absorbed by available outlets in the private sector? Is a tendency toward an increasing surplus, economic stagnation, and war inherent in contemporary capitalism, or has the "new capitalism" solved the problems of its predecessor?

How, by whom, and for what ends is power in America exercised? Is the national power structure characterized by multiple influences, interest groups, and overlapping memberships whose interplay results in an essentially pluralistic governmental process, or may it best be characterized as a "power elite" or ruling class? Does the political economy itself impose limits on and shape the conduct of men of power irrespective of their social origins, concrete interests, and personal predilections? Does contemporary advanced industrial society in the United States tend, in fact, toward a new totalitarianism in which even the very awareness of oppression is eliminated by new forms of social control?

How does this affect the struggle for power in America? What relationship is there between the Negro "riots" and the military ascendancy in our country? Are American workers integrated into the status quo, lacking in class consciousness, and cynical about movements for social reform? Are there worker revolts which go unnoticed and unreported and are there even deeper stirrings among blacks and whites which portend profound changes in American society?

Rarely do American social scientists try to answer such socially relevant and historically significant questions. Their studies too frequently are concerned with trivial and peripheral aspects of our society. In their rush to "generalize," most social scientists ignore analysis of the historically specific social structure and political economy of contemporary America. This structure is usually accepted as a given, while movement around and within it, and its consequences for individual behavior, are explored. The social structure itself is not questioned; the causes of its development, its inner tendencies, and the forces within it that may lead to its transformation are scarcely studied. There is a kind of conservative metaphysic underlying much of current academic social science. It is assumed, unconsciously or not, that the social order in the United States is harmonious and timeless rather than historically changing, temporal, and as likely as other such orders to be transformed by emerging social forces within it.

This is not to say that such analysis is either easy or undemanding, or that it does not pose exceptional difficulties and require both imagination and disciplined research. Mastery of a variety of quantitative techniques may be useful to such analysis; but these techniques do not provide a conceptual framework nor do they broach the important questions. Of course, this is true of all social analysis, but it is possible to do insignificant research by simple emulation of earlier work on meaningless questions, by replication of what was not worth doing in the first place, by impressing one's colleagues and students with one's technical virtuosity. *Important* questions cannot be dealt with adequately in this fashion. There is an understandable reluctance on the part of even the most capable social scientists to take on analysis of such complex and transcendental questions, where the evidence is often elusive, and reasoning and analysis must play a primary role in discovery. Neither the training nor the experience of most social scientists prepares them to grapple with such questions, even if they have the inclination and desire to do so.   Moreover, like other members of their society, they are also limited and constricted by the norms, values, and socially determined perceptions of that society, with the result that such questions often do not even occur to them.   They are not able—so to speak—to stand outside their society and see it as a historical whole: to search for its conflicts and contradictions; to locate its central tendencies; to focus on the national rather than on the local scene; to raise such questions as who owns and controls its economy and how this determines the distribution of wealth, income, and life chances; who rules, and how and why; what forces within are undermining and subverting it; which social relations are emergent and ascendant and which fading; and what the morrow will bring.

These difficult-to-answer questions are rarely asked in social science research and writing about American society, whether the authors be sociologists or economists, historians or political scientists.   In fact, the academic division of labor along bureaucratically determined lines between "disciplines" that separate the major aspects of social reality from one another and force students to see only within such "departmental" boundaries is both cause and consequence of the limitations of contemporary academic social science.   This volume recognizes no such boundaries. Trained incapacity and professional psychosis are far more significant obstacles to relevant social research than the government contracts, grants, and consultantships which are the current targets of "radical caucuses" within the various social sciences— although such pressures and rewards undoubtedly also play a role in steering social research away from *verboten* topics.   Whatever the authors' intentions may be, social research and writing on the United States by the most academic of men typically contains considerable ideological content that serves to rationalize the existing social structure and political economy, rather than to go to the root of things and lay them bare.

Few of the writers whose studies appear here are immune to the critical remarks I've made, but all of them do try to answer fundamental questions about our society.   Most importantly, because this volume juxtaposes articles of contrary and colliding interpretations and findings concerning the same realities, I think that these studies will enlighten us more about such questions than they would if read as isolated reports.   Their analytical gaps and inadequacies and their ideological content, as well as their insights and contributions to our understanding, will be more readily seen in this context of comparison and contrast.   Further, by putting these studies together, I hope to enable the reader to see the interrelationships of the questions and issues brought up by the studies.   Perhaps, then, the reader will be encouraged to try to synthesize his own answers to these questions; an adequate theory of American society requires such a synthesis.   This volume is unique, I believe, in posing such questions simultaneously, thus forcing a confrontation between thinkers of divergent views.

This book is not only for undergraduate college students, although I think it will serve them well.   I am convinced that readers with advanced training and a high level of sophistication in the field of social science (including "professional" social scientists) also will learn much from a close reading of this volume of studies of the social structure and political economy of the United States.

M. Z.

October, 1969
Madison, Wisconsin

CONTENTS

Part One

OWNERSHIP AND CONTROL

MEANS HAS STUDIED ECONOMIC CONCENTRATION FOR THIRTY YEARS, *beginning with research reported in his classic work with Adolph Berle, Jr.,* The Modern Corporation and Private Property. *He argues that by 1929 the American economy had been transformed from the pre-Civil War economy in which flexible prices were determined by the interaction of buyers and sellers within a competitive economy, into one dominated by mass production and the administered prices of the large corporations.*

In 1929 the 200 largest corporations had legal *control (actual control being greater) of 58 percent of the reported net capital assets of all nonfinancial corporations. This proportion is larger today. Three major periods of mergers brought the greatest increases in manufacturing concentration, but internal growth was also a major factor in increased concentration. By 1929 the 100 largest manufacturing corporations had legal control of 44 percent of the net capital assets of all manufacturing corporations. Means tentatively estimates that by 1962 the 100 largest manufacturing corporations controlled at least 58 percent of the net capital assets—net land, buildings, and equipment—of all manufacturing corporations. These are minimal estimates that do not take account of actual control exercised with stock ownership below the level necessary for legal control. Thus, it can be seen that there has been a very considerable increase in manufacturing concentration during this 23-year period.*

1

ECONOMIC CONCENTRATION

Gardiner C. Means

Bigness in business can serve the public interest or run counter to the public interest depending largely on the public policies which condition its activity. Bigness in business creates problems of economic policy which do not arise with small business. I believe these problems should be the focus of your attention.

Economic concentration is a subject in which I have done much pioneering work. More than 30 years ago I made the first statistical measurements of the long-term trend of concentration. The results of this measurement were presented in *The Modern Corporation and Private Property* which I authored jointly with Adolf Berle.[1] I continued this analysis of overall trends when I was with the National Resources Committee which published the findings in *The Structure of the American Economy*.[2] There we published—also for the first time—what have come to be called "concentration ratios" for the various industries based on the reports to the Bureau of the Census.

This morning my testimony will continue this exploration. It will start with a discussion of concentration for the American economy as a whole; it will then focus on concentration in manufacturing which is your committee's most immediate concern;

Reprinted from Gardiner C. Means, *Economic Concentration* in *Hearings before the Subcommittee on Antitrust and Monopoly of the Committee on the Judiciary, United States Senate, 88th Cong., 2nd Sess., persuant to S. Res. 262. Part 1: Overall and Conglomerate Aspects* (Washington, D.C.: U.S. Government Printing Office, July 1964), pp. 8–19. Footnotes have been renumbered.

[1] Adolf A. Berle, Jr., and Gardiner C. Means (New York: Macmillan, 1933).
[2] National Resources Committee (Washington, D.C.: 1939).

and finally it will discuss the importance of concentration and the problems of policy it engenders.

CONCENTRATION IN THE ECONOMY AS A WHOLE

Let me take you back a century to the economic conditions which prevailed just before the Civil War.   Then there was little concentration.   Two-thirds of the labor force was engaged in agriculture where the family farm was the usual form of organization and flexible farm prices were determined by the interaction of a considerable number of buyers and sellers in the market.   There were no telephones or electric power companies then and the railroads were just beginning to be consolidated.   In 1853 the New York Central was formed by consolidating the 10 short sections of railway, mostly end-to-end, which spanned the 300-mile distance between Albany and Buffalo.   At that time, according to Professor Ripley, a railroad ". . . 100 miles in length constituted the maximum for efficient operation."[3]   And little railroad mileage had been built beyond the Mississippi.

Likewise, with manufacturing, most production was in small local plants or in small shops.   The clothing industry was just coming out of the home with the invention of the sewing machine. The shoe industry was just being brought into factories and shoes were still made by handsewing or by pegging.   American ironmasters had only just shifted from the old method of hammering out bar iron in a forge fired by charcoal to the newer methods of rolling.   The Bessemer steel furnace, invented in 1856, had not yet been put into practical operation and the open-hearth furnace was still to be developed.

At that time, ours was indeed an economy of small-scale enterprise.   For practical purposes there was little concentration.   For theoretical purposes even such concentration, as existed, could be disregarded.   National economic policy could be decided on the basis of a body of economic theory which assumed that all production was carried on under conditions of classical competition; that is, competition in which no producer or consumer had significant pricing power; one in which the laws of supply and demand determined prices; and one in which most prices could not be

[3] William Z. Ripley, "Railroads" (New York: Longmans, Green, 1915), p. 456.   The largest railroad in 1860 was the recently created Illinois Central Railroad with a total of 700 miles of track.

administered and such administered prices as existed were not significant.

The next 70 years saw a complete change in the character of our economy. Mass production and big corporate enterprises took over much of manufacturing; the railroads were consolidated into a few great systems; public utility empires and the big telephone system developed; and, even in merchandising, the big corporation played a part.

By 1929, the economy of this country had become one in which the big modern corporation was the outstanding characteristic. Only a fifth of the labor force was engaged in agriculture. Railroads, public utilities, over 90 percent of manufacturing, and much of merchandising was conducted by corporations. In the year 1929, the 200 largest corporations legally controlled 48 percent of the assets of all nonfinancial corporations, that is, of all corporations other than banks, insurance companies, and similar financial companies. If we focus on land, buildings, and equipment—the instruments of physical production—the 200 largest corporations had legal control of 58 percent of the net capital assets reported by all nonfinancial corporations. Thus, by 1929, the dominantly small-enterprise economy which prevailed in 1860 had been largely replaced by one in which the huge corporation was the most characteristic feature.

I emphasize 1929 for three reasons:

First, it is a prosperous year for which we have unusually reliable estimates of corporate concentration.

Second, at that time economic policy was still dominated by the 19th century economic theories which applied only to an economy of small-scale enterprise and flexible prices. In 1929, those theories were still taught as gospel in the universities. There was no other body of economic theory for guiding the operation of a free enterprise system.

My third reason for emphasizing 1929 is that it saw the beginning of the great depression which brought a clear rejection by Government of 19th century economic theory as the basis for overall economic policy.

Since 1929, there have been forces working both against and for greater concentration in the American economy as a whole. In the 1930's, legislation against holding companies was passed and many of the big utility systems were broken up or forced to reorganize; further concentration in railroading was kept to a minimum; and the automobile, bus, and truck, took business away from the railroads so that, today, transportation, as a whole, is probably less concentrated than in 1929; in manufacturing, there was greater resistance to mergers among big companies than prevailed in the 1920's; and a larger proportion of national effort has gone into producing services such as health and recreation, which tend to be less concentrated activities.   All of these tend to reduce or limit concentration.

On the other hand, there have been developments which have tended to increase the degree of concentration.   Today, less than 7 percent of the gainfully employed are engaged in agriculture as compared with 20 percent in 1929; manufacturing is more concentrated than it was in 1929; the chain supermarket and other chain stores have increased in relative importance.

Without making a major study, it would be difficult to say just how concentration for the economy, as a whole, compares today with concentration in 1929.   The main source of data for the economy, as a whole, is that derived from corporate income tax returns.   But the income tax compilations made public by the Bureau of Internal Revenue give a very incomplete picture of concentration.   This is because many companies legally controlled by the big corporations file separate tax returns and are thus treated by the Bureau as independent companies.   The importance of this for estimates of concentration is shown by the fact that in 1960, while nonfinancial corporations distributed $13.7 billion in dividends, they received $1.4 billion of dividends distributed by domestic corporations or more than a tenth as much as they paid out.   Also the large corporations with a quarter of a billion assets or more received two-thirds of these dividends and three-quarters of the dividends from foreign corporations.   An important part of these dividends is from subsidiaries or legally controlled companies which are not consolidated in the returns filed for income tax purposes.   Just how much difference the complete consolidation would make is very difficult to tell.   But that it would make a big difference was indicated in the 1929 study in which we were able to go back of the published data and take account of the unconsolidated subsidiaries.   I am sure this would still be true.

I have tried to make an estimate of the proportion of corporate assets legally controlled by the 200 largest corporations comparable to that we made for 1929.   The results are too crude to be worth publishing but they suggest that if a careful study were made based on the tax returns in the Bureau files—and I strongly recommend this be done—it would show the 200 corporations legally controlled somewhat more than the 58 percent of the net capital assets controlled by the 200 that were largest in 1929.[4] However, the most that I can say with reasonable certainty is that concentration for the economy as a whole is not significantly less than it was in 1929.

What is more important for national economic policy is the fact that both in 1929 and today the atomistic economy around which 19th century economic theory was built has ceased to exist. Policy must deal with an economy in which big corporations and inflexible administered prices play a major role. How this affects economic policy, I will discuss after I have examined concentration in the more limited field of manufacturing.

CONCENTRATION IN MANUFACTURING

Though manufacturing employs less than a quarter of the gainfully employed persons in this country, it is the field in which unregulated competition has been, *par excellence*, the instrument relied on to convert the actions of self-seeking individuals into actions which serve the public interest. It is the field with which this committee is most immediately and quite properly concerned. What has been the trend of concentration in manufacturing?

I have already pointed out that, in 1860, most of manufacturing was carried on in small-scale unincorporated enterprises. In the major industrial center of Pittsburgh with 17 foundries, 21 rolling mills, 76 glass factories, and 47 other manufactures, not a single manufacturing enterprise was incorporated. The only industry in which the modern type of corporation played an important role was the cotton textile industry. The big integrated cotton mills of Lowell, Lawrence, and some other New

---

[4] The BIR compilations show net capital assets of $240.3 billion for all non-financial corporations in 1960 and $139.2 billion reported by 267 nonfinancial corporations or 58 percent of the total. Since consolidation was allowed only if 80 percent or more of a subsidiary's stock was controlled by the parent and not all allowable consolidations were made, many legally controlled companies were not consolidated. This 58-percent figure, therefore, substantially underrepresents the proportion of the net capital assets legally controlled by the 267 largest and a significant number of the latter are likely to be legally controlled by others in the group. It seems almost certain that a complete consolidation would show the largest 200 nonfinancial corporations with more than 58 percent of the net capital assets of all nonfinancial corporations. BIR data do not allow even a rough approximation to a complete consolidation.

England towns were incorporated with characteristics that today look quite modern.   Indeed, they were known throughout New England as "the corporations."[5]   But apart from these cotton mills, big corporate business was almost nonexistent in manufacturing before the Civl War.   Altogether it is doubtful if as much as 6 or 8 percent of manufacturing activity at that time was carried on by corporations and a much smaller proportion by what could be called in these days big corporations.

Between the Civil War and the turn of the century, there was a great increase in corporate manufacturing so that by 1900, close to two-thirds of manufacturing output was produced by corporations.[6]

Also toward the end of the century there was the first great merger movement culminating in the formation of the United States Steel Corp. as a merger of mergers in 1901.   The pattern of mergers in this period is shown in Figure 1 which indicates the number of mergers reported in the *Commercial and Financial Chronicle* year by year from 1895 to 1914.   It does not include all the mergers but presumably includes all the important mergers.

As you can see, there was a great burst of mergers from 1898 to 1902.   All of this led to a great increase in manufacturing concentration even though a third of manufacturing output was still produced by unincorporated enterprises.

A very sharp peak in 1899, a heavy volume of mergers in 1900, 1901, and 1902, and then a fall off.

But the drive for monopoly created a strong public reaction. When Theodore Roosevelt became President in 1901, he was responsible for vigorous enforcement of the Sherman Act.   The *Northern Securities* decision by the Supreme Court in 1904 outlawed the holding company as a device for achieving monopoly and other cases were brought which led to the breakup of the Standard Oil monopoly and the Tobacco Trust.   Also some of the early combinations proved to be less successful than had been expected.   As Figure 1 shows, the wave of mergers came to an end as the goal of monopoly was clearly established as illegal. Between 1902 and the First World War, reported mergers averaged only a hundred a year.   Whether there was an actual decline in manufacturing concentration in this period or a very slow growth is far from clear.

A second merger movement occurred after World War I, cul-

[5] *The Modern Corporation and Private Property, op. cit.*, pp. 11, 12.
[6] U.S. Bureau of Census, Historical Statistics of the United States (Washington, D.C.: U.S. Government Printing Office, 1960), p. 413.

**Figure 1. Recorded Mergers in Manufacturing and Mining
1895–1914**

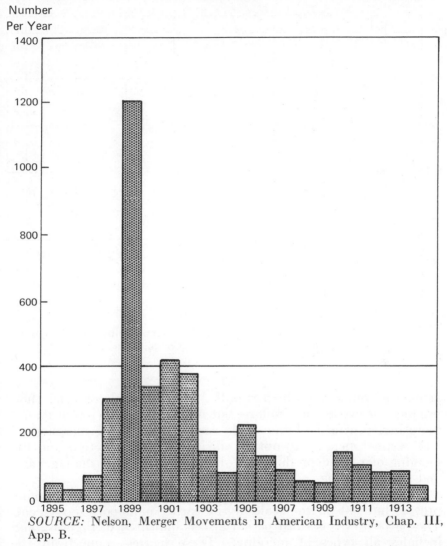

SOURCE: Nelson, Merger Movements in American Industry, Chap. III,
App. B.

minated in 1929, and was followed after the great depression by
a quiescent period under a second President Roosevelt. This
pattern of mergers is shown in Figure 2.

In this second merger movement, the aim of combination
appears to have been quite different from that in the first. Particular big companies sought to strengthen their organization by

Figure 2. Number of Mergers and Acquisitions in Manufacturing and Mining, 1919–1961

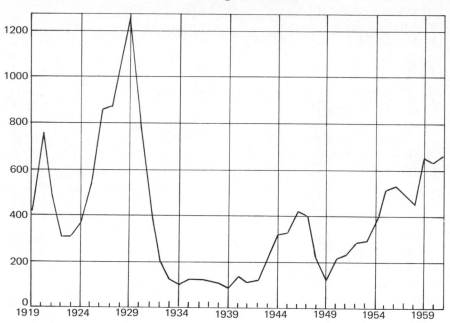

SOURCE: 1919–1939, Temporary National Economic Committee, Monograph No. 27 ; 1940–1961, Federal Trade Commission.

acquiring companies which supplied raw materials or used their products or carried on similar—but not identical—types of manufacturing. Instead of monopoly-seeking horizontal merging we had vertical merging to obtain efficiencies in production and the merging of related products to obtain economies in management and merchandising.

Since World War II, there has been a renewal of the merging process but not on the scale of the earlier monopoly movement. The pattern of this third period also is indicated in Figure 2 and includes all types of merging. These figures come from the Federal Trade Commission and are more comprehensive in their coverage than those covered by the first figure, but probably fail to include a significant number of small mergers. However, their inclusion would not change the general pattern though they would alter the actual number of mergers in particular years.

It is fair to assume that the greatest increases in manufacturing concentration have come in the three periods of greatest mergering. But increased concentration can also come from internal growth either through the reinvestment of earnings or from the sale of new securities provided, of course, that the growth from these sources is more rapid for larger companies than for smaller companies. In a 6-year period in the 1920's more than four-fifths of the growth of large companies came from internal growth and only a fifth from mergers.[7] Presumably the present day concentration has come partly from mergers and partly from more rapid internal growth.

What has been the actual trend of manufacturing concentration and how far has concentration progressed?

Clearly a peak in the rate of concentration was reached just after 1900. It would be nice if we had reliable concentration data for that period but we don't. Certainly some lines of manufacturing such as steel were more concentrated at the turn of the century than they are today and some product lines such as cotton textiles are more concentrated today. But this is not the issue when we are considering concentration for manufacturing as a whole since mergers have been to a much greater extent either vertical or conglomerate and their effect on concentration is not fully reflected in separate product or narrow industry figures. Much careful research will be needed before we can determine the relative change in manufacturing concentration since 1900. And in this connection it is important to remember that, in 1900, only about two-thirds of manufacturing was carried on by corporations while today, 95 percent is corporate.[8]

The most reliable figures we have on concentration in manufacturing are those reported in the study made by the National Resources Committee for 1929. Among the 200 largest corporations in that year, the Resources Committee report included 82 manufacturing corporations. It included the Western Electric Co. along with the assets of its parent, the American Telephone & Telegraph Co., and it presented unconsolidated data for 107 large industrial corporations for 1935. From these data I have derived two concentration estimates for the 100 largest manufacturing corporation in 1929. According to these figures, 100 large companies in 1929 had legal control of approximately 40 percent of the

[7] *The Modern Corporation and Private Property, op. cit.*, p. 43.

[8] U.S. Bureau of Census, *Historical Statistics of the United States* (Washington, D.C.: U.S. Government Printing Office, 1960), p. 413.

total assets of all manufacturing corporations and 44 percent of their net capital assets.[9]

Let me explain just what these figures mean. The figures for legal control by the 100 largest mean that these companies either own the assets directly or control them through owning or controlling more than 50 percent of the stock of the corporations that do own the assets.[10]

By restricting the figures to legal control, the practical degree of concentration tends to be somewhat understated, partly because the figures exclude joint ventures in which each of two or more of the big companies owns 50 percent or less of a smaller company but in combination have legal control and partly because practical or working control of one company can often be exercised with a holding of stock which is not sufficient to give legal control.

The figures for "total assets" include total current assets such as inventories, accounts receivable, and government securities and

[9] Estimate for 100 largest manufacturing corporations in 1929:

	Total consolidated assets (millions)	Ratio to all manufac- turing (percent)	Net capital assets (millions)	Ratio to all manufac- turing (percent)
82 largest (excluding Western Electric)	$23,641	37.0	$11,803	41.4
Western Electric	309	.5	70	.2
17 next largest	1,350	2.1	605	2.1
100 largest manufac- turing corporations	25,300	39.6	12,478	43.7
All manufacturing corpo- rations (including Western Electric)	63,955	100.0	28,531	100.0

SOURCE: For 82 largest, *The Structure of the American Economy*, op. cit., p. 285. For Western Electric, *Moody's Manual*. For total consolidated assets of 17 next largest, the partially consolidated figures given in the *Structure of the American Economy*, pp. 274–275—complete consolidation might increase the figures slightly. For net capital assets of 17 next largest, the ratio of net capital assets to total assets for all corporations (44.8 percent), was applied to the total assets of the 17 next largest. For all manufacturing corporations, *The Structure of the American Economy*, p. 285 plus Western Electric.

[10] Where 2 or more of the 100 largest corporations have a combined stock holdings of more than 50 percent in another corporation which would otherwise be included in the 100 largest, its assets are combined with the assets of the 100 largest as if it were legally controlled by 1 of them.

the fixed assets such as land, buildings and equipment after depreciation and depletion but exclude the estimated holdings of securities of other corporations. The latter are excluded since they represent, in large degree, double counting. This still leaves some duplication in the figures due to intercorporate debt between parent and subsidiary but complete consolidation would probably not affect the concentration percentages significantly.

The figures for net capital assets include only the net property—the land, buildings, and equipment less depreciation and depletion. They constitute the instruments of production and provide the material basis for corporate power. A corporation is not industrially powerful because it has a large amount of bills receivable. It is not industrially powerful because it has large inventories. It is not industrially powerful because it has large holdings of government securities. Its industrial power must rest on its control of factories or natural resources. For this reason, the 44 percent of net capital assets legally controlled by the 100 largest manufacturing corporations in 1929 would appear to be a more significant figure of concentration than the 40 percent of total assets held by the 100 largest. It has the added advantage that the figures for net capital assets do not involve any double counting.

Whether we consider total assets or net capital assets, the 40 percent or more controlled by the largest 100 corporations indicates that a very considerable degree of concentration existed in manufacturing in 1929.

What has happened since 1929? We have no figures for manufacturing concentration which are as reliable as those for 1929. However, I have attempted to make estimates for concentration in 1962 as nearly comparable with the 1929 figures as published data will allow. Because these estimates are less reliable, I want to indicate just how they were made.

The big problem in making such estimates arises from incomplete consolidation in the published figures of the large corporations. A few, like Standard Oil of New Jersey, publish balance sheets in which they consolidate the assets of all corporations in which they control more than 50 percent of the voting stock. More often corporations consolidate only those subsidiaries in which they have a 95 to 100 percent stock interest, reporting the stocks of corporations over which they have legal control by a smaller percent as "investments in subsidiaries" or in the larger category of "other noncurrent assets." As a result, the assets over which they have legal control exceed the assets reported in their balance sheets to the extent that the assets of controlled companies exceed the value of their stocks on the books of the controlling company.   To get a clear picture of concentration, it is necessary to approximate a more complete consolidation.   In making the study for 1929 back in the 1930's, a small staff and I were sworn into the Bureau of Internal Revenue and had direct access to the actual tax returns of corporations.   We selected what appeared to be the biggest 200 companies and then for all other corporations with 14 million assets or more and for a sample of still smaller companies, several thousand companies in total, we searched the standard reference books to discover all cases in which more than 50 percent of the stock was controlled by one of the big companies.   While we undoubtedly missed some subsidiaries, we probably picked up most of the important ones.   The exact methods and the detailed results were set forth in a 20-page appendix to the structure report. . . .[11]

Today much more information is publicly available than in 1929 but it would still be necessary to go into the detailed information in the hands of Government to make an estimate as reliable as that which we made in 1929.   For my present estimates I have done the best I could with the information that has been made public. . . . I [have compiled a list of] what appear to be the 100 largest manufacturing corporations in 1962, giving their total assets, including investments, and their net capital assets. . . [I have also adjusted] the total assets and property of these 100 companies for intercorporate stockholding, [comparing] the result with the adjusted assets of all manufacturing corporations to [obtain] ratios of concentration comparable to those for 1929.

On this basis, I estimate that the 100 largest manufacturing corporations in 1962 controlled at least 49 percent of the assets of all manufacturing corporations (excluding stocks in other corporations) and 58 percent of the net capital assets—the net land, buildings, and equipment—of all manufacturing corporations.

These estimates, though less reliable than those for 1929, suggest that there has been a very considerable increase in concentration in manufacturing as a whole in the last 33 years.   The difference is shown in Figure 3 which compares the estimates for the 2 years.

[11] *Op. cit.*, app. 11, pp. 277–97.   [*This report is printed as an appendix to Mr. Means' testimony*, Hearings . . . , *Part 1, pp. 285ff.*—M.Z.]

**Figure 3. Increase in Manufacturing Concentration Measured
by Assets 1929–1962**

PROPORTION OF ASSETS
OF ALL MANUFACTURING CORPORATIONS
LEGALLY CONTROLLED BY THE 100 LARGEST
MANUFACTURING CORPORATIONS

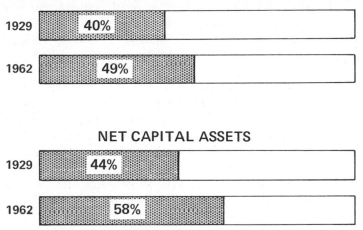

TOTAL ASSETS LESS STOCKS OF OTHER CORPORATIONS

1929   40%

1962   49%

NET CAPITAL ASSETS

1929   44%

1962   58%

The top panel shows the increase in the proportion of total
assets held by the 100 largest from 40 to 49 percent, the area in
black. The lower panel shows the corresponding increase for
net capital assets from 44 to 58 percent.* This is a very sizable
increase in concentration since 1929.

Just when this increase in concentration took place is debatable. There is little question that there was a considerable

* *"The difference in the two figures grows out of the inclusion or the exclusion of
bills receivable and current assets. Big corporations tend to be in industries in
which a very large amount of capital per worker is used as compared with the less
concentrated industries. This means that when you just look at the physical capital
assets, the land, buildings, and equipment net, big corporations have a larger proportion
of total manufacturing corporations assets of that sort than they have for all assets,
which includes the current assets . . . . It is the last figure which seems to me the
more important." From Means' testimony, p. 25.—*M.Z.

increase in concentration from 1929 to 1933 as business activity declined in the great depression. How much of this was a temporary depression effect which would be reversed with recovery and how much it was a part of the long run trend in manufacturing concentration is not clear. Certainly some of it was reversible. The net capital assets of the big companies declined only 6 percent in that period while the net capital assets of smaller companies declined 24 percent. Some of this was the result of big companies acquiring the assets of smaller companies. But to a greater extent it reflected the simple closing down of many smaller companies which would be reopened or replaced in the period of recovery. In measuring trends in concentration as in measuring trends in so many other economic factors, I believe the only valid comparisons are between years which are reasonably comparable in the rate of business activity.

The question of whether—and the extent to which—events during and after World War II contributed to this overall increase is a subject on which I am not commenting here but I hope that this question will be examined by the subcommiteee during the course of these hearings. What I can testify to is that manufacturing concentration, whether measured by total assets or by net capital assets, has increased greatly since 1929 and that, without taking account of joint ventures or companies controlled through less than a majority ownership, somewhere in the close vicinity of 58 percent of the net capital assets of manufacturing are controlled by 100 companies. This concentration, along with concentration in other aspects of the economy, presents a set of problems in economic policy which need more intense attention.

MUELLER, DIRECTOR OF THE FEDERAL TRADE COMMISSION'S *Bureau of Economics, presents data on industrial concentration using such measures as total assets, net capital assets, net income, net profits, and net sales. He makes no adjustments, however, as Means did to some extent, to consolidate companies under common ownership. So these are* underestimates.

In 1962 there were 180,000 corporations and 240,000 partnerships and proprietorships constituting the population of all manufacturing enterprises, 98 percent of whose assets were held by the corporations. The 20 largest manufacturing corporations held an estimated 25 percent of all assets of manufacturing companies. The 50 largest held 36 percent, the 100 largest 46 percent, and the 200 largest 56 percent. The 419,000 smallest companies held only 25 percent of the total manufacturing assets. Thus, the total assets of the 20 largest manufacturing corporations were about the same as those of the 419,000 smallest companies.

Concentration measured by net profits is even greater: The 20 largest manufacturing corporations held 31 percent of total net capital assets and received 38 percent of all profits after taxes. The net profits of the 5 largest corporations were nearly twice as large as those of the approximately 178,000 smallest corporations.

Regardless of the measure used, it is obvious that a relatively few immense corporations hold the great bulk of the financial resources of American manufacturing. Similar degrees of concentration exist in each of 28 selected industry groups. In fact, concentration in manufacturing has increased substantially since 1950. In just 12 years, the share of all manufacturing assets held by the 200 largest corporations increased by about 17 percent.

American industry is going through another great wave of mergers, with over 60 large mergers (among the 2,000 companies with at least $10 million in assets) each year since 1959. Since the end of 1950, one in five of the 1,000 largest manufacturing companies have disappeared because of mergers. Very few of them were losing money before being acquired. Many of the acquired companies were very profitable enterprises which could have offered effective competition to the large corporations if they had not been acquired by them.

2

RECENT CHANGES IN INDUSTRIAL CONCENTRATION, AND THE CURRENT MERGER MOVEMENT

Willard F. Mueller

I. THE MEASUREMENT OF INDUSTRIAL CONCENTRATION

There is no doubt that large U.S. manufacturing corporations have been growing at a rapid rate in recent years, both in terms of number and assets. In 1947, there were 113 corporations with assets of $100 million or more; by the end of 1962 their number had more than tripled to about 370. This substantial and rapid growth, by itself, is not to be equated with increases in industrial concentration. Increases in concentration occur only when growth is not distributed proportionately among companies.

This, then, is the distinction between increasing bigness and increasing concentration.

Reprinted from Willard F. Mueller, *Economic Concentration* in *Hearings before the Subcommittee on Antitrust and Monopoly of the Committee on the Judiciary, United States Senate, 88th Cong., 2nd sess., persuant to S. Res. 262. Part 1: Overall and Conglomerate Aspects* (Washington, D.C.: U.S. Government Printing Office, July 1964), pp. 111–29. Footnotes and tables have been renumbered.

Concentration refers to:

the ownership or control of a large proportion of some aggregate of economic resources or activity by a small proportion of the units which own or control the aggregate, or by a small absolute number of such units.[1]

Concentration may be measured in a variety of different economic sectors; the universe selected for measurement is largely a question of what is being analyzed.   For example the *degree* of concentration may be measured for nonfinancial companies, all manufacturing companies, companies in identical "industries," or companies producing identical "products."   The broader and more heterogeneous the universe, the more general the measure; the narrower and more homogeneous the universe, the more specific the measure. In one instance, the degree of concentration measures the control over the assets, income, or output of perhaps all manufacturing corporations; in another, only the control over the output of outboard motors.   Thus, the terms "general" or "specific" refer to the universe being measured rather than the method of measurement employed or the variables selected for measurement.

Many methods have been developed to measure concentration. But all have essentially the same purpose: to measure the extent to which a small absolute or relative number of firms account for a large proportion of assets, income, or output.

Approximately a half dozen variables have been employed to measure concentration.   These include total assets, net capital assets, sales, value added by manufacture, value of shipments, income and employment.

Total Assets and Net Capital Assets.   Assets, both total and net capital assets (property, plant, and equipment less depreciation), have been widely used to measure economic concentration. Assets fairly accurately reflect the productive resources and financial strength of a corporation.   The advantages and disadvantages of this measure have been discussed at considerable length.[2]

An advantage of using *total assets* is that they include financial

---

[1] J. S. Bain, *Industrial Organization* (1959).

[2] See, for example, *The Concentration of Productive Facilities* (Federal Trade Commission, 1949), 6, 7; M. A. Adelman, "The Measurement of Industrial Concentration."   *The Review of Economics and Statistics* (November 1951), 272–73; John M. Blair, "The Measurement of Industrial Concentration: A Reply," *The Review of Economics and Statistics*, Vol. 52 (1952), 343–55.

as well as physical productive resources. On the other hand, *net capital assets* probably do a better job of taking into account the extent to which firms are vertically integrated. This may be one of the reasons the degree of concentration as measured by net capital assets and by net income differs by less than the degree of concentration as measured by total assets and net income. Another advantage of using net capital assets rather than total assets is that the former exclude intercorporate obligations and investment.[3]

Sales. Sales data are readily available for most companies. However, as most critics of this measure have pointed out, it disregards the extent to which firms are vertically integrated.[4] Although this is not a particular problem when measuring a firm's share of a given product, it makes this measure all but useless in measuring overall concentration of productive and financial resources in broad sectors of the economy; for example, all manufacturing.

Income Generated. Adelman suggests "income generated," which he considers to be "almost identical with that of the Census 'value added by manufacture,'" is the most appropriate single measure of economic size.[5] Profits represent another form of income generated. Net profits constitute one of the most important indicators of the financial strength of a business enterprise. Therefore, in many respects it serves as a useful proxy of the concentration of economic power.

In the following section we shall use most of the above measures: (1) Total assets are used in measuring the extent of concentration in all manufacturing in 1962 (Table 1). (2) Total assets, net capital assets, and net income are used in measuring concentration among manufacturing corporations in 1962 (Table 2). (3) Total assets, net capital assets, net profits, and sales are used to measure concentration in 28 broad industry groups (Tables 3 and 4). (4) Total assets are used in measuring the share of assets held by the 200 largest manufacturing corporations in 1950 and 1962, and in measuring the share of assets held by the 113 largest manufacturing corporations in 1947, 1950, and 1962 (Tables 5 and 6).

---

[3] *The Concentration of Productive Facilities* (Federal Trade Commission, 1949), 6.

[4] *Ibid.*, 5, and Adelman, *op. cit.*, 222.

[5] Adelman, *op. cit.*, 272.

II. CONCENTRATION IN
AMERICAN MANUFACTURING

Introduction

The data on manufacturing corporations for the fourth quarter of the year 1962 are based on information submitted to the Securities and Exchange Commission and the Federal Trade Commission and used in the preparation by these agencies of the Quarterly Financial Report for Manufacturing Corporations.[6]

In a few instances, these special tabulations have been adjusted to include certain items which some companies omitted from their quarterly reports but which they included in their annual consolidated income and operating statements. No adjustments have been made in these preliminary figures which would consolidate companies under common ownership.

I would like to say that the following data on concentration have not adjusted in the same fashion as those of Gardiner Means; namely, of consolidating certain companies under common ownership. This is one of the reasons for the differences in our data on concentration and those presented by Dr. Means.

Also, the data which I shall summarize do not consolidate the assets of joint ventures. A brief examination of the largest manufacturing corporations indicates that, at a minimum, 15 joint ventures with combined assets of almost $900 million are included among the 1,000 largest U.S. manufacturing corporations. Thus, the following preliminary asset concentration figures under-estimate the degree of concentration actually present in American manufacturing. Throughout this statement newspapers are not included among manufacturing companies.

Concentration of Assets in Total Manufacturing

In 1962, the population of American manufacturing enterprises consisted of about 180,000 corporations and 240,000 partnerships and proprietorships. These approximately 420,000 business units had combined assets of about $296 billion as of the fourth quarter of 1962. About 98.4 percent of these assets were held by corporations.

Table 1 and Figure 1 show the ownership distribution of

---

[6] A discussion of the history, sampling methods, and limitations of these data appears in each issue of these quarterly reports.

Table 1. Concentration of Total Manufacturing Assets, 4th Quarter 1962

Corporate size group	Assets (millions)	All manu- facturing (percent)	Corpora- tions only (percent)
5 largest	$ 36,447	12.3%	12.5%
10 largest	54,353	18.4	18.7
20 largest	74,825	25.0	25.4
50 largest	105,421	35.7	36.2
100 largest	136,222	46.1	46.8
200 largest	165,328	55.9	56.8
500 largest	199,894	67.6	68.7
1,000 largest	221,279	74.8	76.0
Corporations with assets over $10,000,000[a]	237,410	80.3	81.6
All corporations[b]	291,022	98.4	100.0
Total manufacturing business[c]	295,690	100.0	—

SOURCE: Bureau of Economics, Federal Trade Commission.

[a] There were 2,041 manufacturing corporations in operation the first quarter of 1963.

[b] This group includes about 180,000 manufacturing corporations.

[c] Includes asset estimates for approximately 240,000 manufacturing proprietorships and partnerships.

Figure 1. Percent of Total Manufacturing Assets Accounted for by Various Groups of Firms: 1962

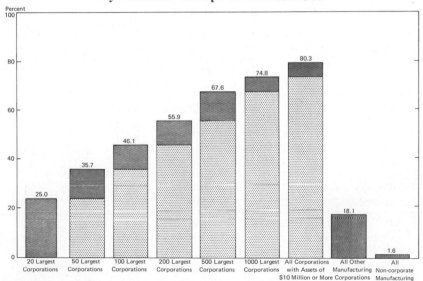

SOURCE: Table 1.

manufacturing assets.   The 20 largest manufacturing corporations (all of which had assets of more than $1.5 billion in assets, or an estimated 25 percent of the total assets of *all* U.S. manufacturing companies.   The 50 largest corporations accounted for 35.7 percent, the 100 largest for 46.1 percent, the 200 largest for 55.9 percent, and the 1,000 largest for almost three-fourths (74.8 percent) of the total assets of all manufacturing companies.   These data demonstrate quite clearly the high degree of concentration in American manufacturing.   In fact, whereas the 20 largest companies held 25 percent and the 1,000 largest held 74.8 percent of all manufacturing assets, the 419,000 smallest companies accounted for only 25.2 percent of total manufacturing assets.   Thus, the total assets of the 20 largest manufacturing corporations were approximately the same as those of the 419,000 smallest.

Asset and Profit Concentration Among Manufacturing Corporations, 1962

Three financial items were used to measure concentration among manufacturing corporations: total assets, net capital assets, and net income.   The results of these comparisons are shown in Table 2 and Figure 2.

Table 2. Concentration of Assets and Income All Manufacturing Corporations, 4th Quarter 1962

Corporate size group	Total assets		Net capital assets		Profit after taxes	
	Millions	Percent	Millions	Percent	Millions	Percent
5 largest	$ 36,447	12.5	$ 17,502	15.3	$ 957	19.8
10 largest	54,353	18.7	27,783	24.3	1,434	29.6
20 largest	73,825	25.4	35,840	31.3	1,839	38.0
50 largest	105,421	36.2	51,057	44.6	2,315	47.9
100 largest	136,222	46.8	63,128	55.1	2,788	57.6
200 largest	165,328	56.8	73,447	64.1	3,265	67.5
500 largest	199,894	68.9	86,818	75.8	3,821	79.0
1000 largest	221,279	76.0	94,178	82.2	4,178	86.4
All over $10,000,000[a]	237,409	81.6	99,443	86.8	4,321	89.3
All corporations[b]	291,022[c]	100.0	114,589	100.0	4,837	100.0

SOURCE: Bureau of Economics, Federal Trade Commission.

[a] There were 2,041 corporations in this size class the 1st quarter of 1963. *Quarterly Financial Report*, 1963, p. 61.

[b] There were approximately 180,000 manufacturing corporations at the end of 1962.

[c] Adjusted.   See text for explanation of adjustment.

Figure 2. Concentration of Manufacturing Corporations Assets and Income: 1962

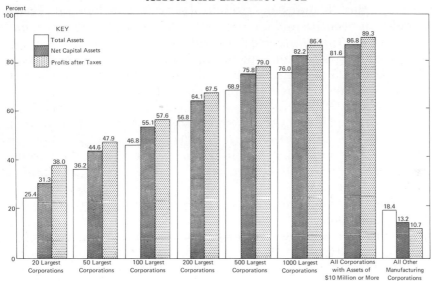

SOURCE: Table 2.

When concentration is measured in terms of net capital assets, it is greater than when total assets are used. Concentration measured in terms of net profits is greater than when either asset measure is used. For example, the 20 largest manufacturing corporations, with 25.4 percent of total corporate assets, accounted for 31.3 percent of total net capital assets and 38 percent of profits after taxes. The 100 largest manufacturing corporations in 1962 accounted for 57.6 percent of net profits, compared with 55.1 percent of net capital assets and 46.8 percent of total assets. The 1,000 largest corporations accounted for 86.4 percent of profits after taxes, 82.2 percent of net capital assets and 76 percent of total assets.

The approximately 2,041 corporations with assets of $10 million or more earned 89.3 percent of all corporate profits whereas the about 178,000 remaining corporations earned 10.7 percent. Also of significance, the net profits of the 5 largest corporations were nearly twice as large as those of the about 178,000 smallest corporations.

These data indicate unmistakably that, regardless of the measure used, a relatively few immense corporations hold the great bulk of the financial resources of American manufacturing.

Concentration in 28 Industry Groups, 1962

These are the 28 industries which appear in the Federal Trade Commission-Security and Exchange Commission's *Quarterly Financial Report on Manufacturing Corporations.*

The 20 largest manufacturing corporations, at year-end 1962, accounted for 25 percent of the total assets, 31 percent of the net capital assets and 38 percent of profits after taxes of all manufacturing businesses.   While these data demonstrate that there is a high degree of concentration of economic resources, they tell us little of the degree of concentration in individual industries.   To enlarge this area of the analysis, concentration measures have been computed for 28 individual industry groups.   Table 3 contains estimates of the share of each industry group's sales, total assets, net capital assets and income after taxes that are held by the 4 and 20 largest companies.

These data, while for broader industry groups than generally used to measure product concentration, do provide interesting insights into relative strength of the major producers in each industry group.   Most major producers confront their competitors in a number of different related industries and produce a large

Table 3. Concentration of Sales, Total Assets, Net Capital Assets, and Profits After Taxes, for 27 Selected Industry Groups, 4th Quarter 1962[a]

	Number of industries							
	Sales		Total assets		Net capital assets		Profits after taxes	
Percent of industry	4 larg- est	20[b] larg- est	4 larg- est	20[b] larg- est	4 larg- est	20[b] larg- est	4 larg- est	20[b] larg- est
90 to 100	—	4	—	4	—	4	—	5
80 to 89	1	1	—	3	1	5	1	6
70 to 79	1	2	2	4	—	3	2	2
60 to 69	—	4	—	4	1	4	1	7
50 to 59	1	5	2	2	3	5	6	—
40 to 49	6	2	8	6	7	3	4	5
30 to 39	5	5	5	2	9	1	5	—
20 to 29	6	2	4	1	1	2	4	2
10 to 19	5	2	4	1	4	—	2	—
Less than 10	2	—	2	—	1	—	2	—

SOURCE: Bureau of Economics, Federal Trade Commission.

   [a] Based on the data appearing in Table 4 except that textile products are not included.

   [b] Includes 2 industry groups with less than 20 companies.

number of common products. Also, while almost all of the companies covered by this analysis are diversified to some extent, the bulk of the diversification of these companies has been into related product areas.[7]

Table 3 provides a brief summary of . . . individual industry group data. . . .* Again, as in Table 2, the degree of concentration in each industry group may vary depending upon the financial variable employed   These data, like those in Table 2, reveal that profits and net capital assets are more concentrated than total assets. In every industry group, sales are the least concentrated. Regardless of the variable selected, however, in more than half the industry groups the 20 largest companies account for 50 percent or more of total sales, total assets, net capital assets, or profits after taxes.

In 23 of the 28 industry groups (about 82 percent), profits after taxes show either the highest concentration or concentration within 1 percentage point of the highest figure. In 20 of the industry groups, the 20 top companies earned over 60 percent of industry profits.

Considerable variations in the degree of concentration exist among industry groups. For example, the four largest producers of motor vehicles and parts accounted for 79.7 percent of that industry's total assets and 89.1 percent of its net profits; the four largest producers of tobacco products accounted for 72.7 percent of total assets and 72.5 percent of total net profits of that industry group. Both industries are highly concentrated and there is

---

[7] A preliminary tabulation was made of the number of 2-, 3-, 4-, and 5-digit classifications in which each of the 1,000 largest manufacturing corporations appeared, as reported in *Fortune's* 1963 *Plant and Product Directory*. This tabulation indicates a high degree of diversification at the narrow 5-digit product level, but a substantially smaller degree at the broader 2-digit industry group level. (Examples of 5-digit product classifications are margarine, roasted coffee, lace goods, and softwood plywood; examples of 2-digit industry groups are food and kindred products, chemicals, and transportation equipment.)

These data indicate that while less than 5 percent of the 1,000 largest manufacturing companies are engaged in the production of goods confined to a single 5-digit product class, over 25 percent manufacture products included entirely in a single 2-digit industry group; and that only 21 percent of these companies were engaged in the production of as few as four 5-digit products, but that 73 percent of the 1,000 largest companies accounted for their total output in 4 or less 2-digit industry groups. Therefore, the above data, while not providing a precise picture of the structure of narrowly defined industries, have the virtue of showing concentration in a number of more or less closely related industries.

* *A table in the original showing concentration in 28 selected industry groups has been omitted here.*—M.Z.

considerable disparity between the size of the four largest and all other producers of these products.

Rather high degrees of concentration also exist in rubber and miscellaneous plastic products, dairy products, primary iron and steel, alcoholic beverages, petroleum refining, industrial chemicals, other transportation equipment, and instruments and related products. In each one of these relatively broad industry groups, the four largest companies accounted for more than 40 percent of the total assets and more than 50 percent of the profits after taxes.

On the other hand, there are seven industry groups in which the four largest companies accounted for less than 20 percent of total assets. These include stone, clay, and glass products, fabricated metal products, textile products, metalworking machinery, other food products (except alcoholic beverages, dairy and bakery products), furniture and fixtures, and apparel. However, in all but 2 of the above industry groups the 20 largest companies in each group accounted for 40 percent or more of the profits after taxes.[8]

Concentration in Manufacturing, 1950 and 1962

In addition to the above estimates of concentration in 1962, we have prepared estimates of the share of total manufacturing assets held by the 200 largest manufacturing corporations in 1950 (Table 4). These data show that between 1950 and 1962 a substantial increase in total manufacturing assets occurred in this country.[9] During the period, the total assets of all manufacturing businesses increased by 106 percent and the total assets of all manufacturing corporations grew by 111 percent. However, the assets of the 200 largest manufacturing corporations increased by 141.3 percent during the same period.

The data presented in Table 4 reflect the relatively more rapid growth of the 200 largest American manufacturing corporations (all with assets of $200 million or more in 1962). In 1950, for example, the 20 largest companies accounted for 21.5 percent of

---

[8] [S]ales concentration figures for each industry group . . . were not included in the above comparisons because of the limited usefulness for the analysis of broad industry groups.

[9] The 1950 and 1952 data presented in this section were taken from corporation annual reports and *Moody's Industrial Manual*. Therefore, the 1962 figures contained in Table 4 are slightly lower than those contained in Tables 1 and 2.

Table 4. Concentration of Total Assets, 200 Largest Manufacturing Corporations, 1950 and 1962

Corporate size group	1950, total assets (millions)[a]	Percent of total All corpo- rations	Percent of total All manufac- turing	1962, total assets (millions)[a]	Percent of total All corpo- rations	Percent of total All manufac- turing
5 largest	$ 13,711	10.0	9.6	$ 35,299	12.3	11.9
10 largest	20,759	15.7	14.5	52,924	18.9	17.9
20 largest	29,682	21.5	20.7	72,179	24.8	24.4
50 largest	43,353	31.8	30.2	103,560	35.8	35.0
100 largest	55,388	40.2	38.6	133,000	45.7	45.0
200 largest	66,931	48.9	46.7	161,531	55.0	54.6
All corporations	137,719[b]	—	—	291,022[b]	—	—
All manufacturing	143,396[c]	—	—	295,690[c]	—	—

SOURCE: Bureau of Economics, Federal Trade Commission.

[a] These asset figures differ from those appearing in Tables 1 and 2 because the asset data used here are those reported in *Moody's Industrial Manual* rather than those reported in the *FTC-SEC Quarterly Financial Report.*

[b] Estimate. (See text for explanation for basis of estimates.)

[c] Estimate of the total assets of all incorporated and unincorporated manufacturing corporations. (See text for explanation of basis of estimates.)

total *corporate* assets. By 1962, the 20 largest companies' share had grown to 24.8 percent—an increase of 3.3 percentage points. The share of the 100 largest companies increased from 40.2 percent in 1950 to 45.7 percent in 1962—an increase of 5.5 percentage points, while that of the 200 largest companies increased from 48.9 percent in 1950 to 55 percent in 1962—an increase of 6.1 percentage points. These data show that concentration in manufacturing has increased substantially since 1959.

When noncorporate manufacturing companies are included in the comparison, the increase in concentration is even more pronounced. Whereas in 1950 the largest corporations held 38.6 percent of all manufacturing assets, by 1962 they held 45 percent of such assets—an increase of 6.4 percentage points. The share of the 200 largest companies increased from 46.7 to 54.6 percent, an increase of 7.9 percentage points. Hence, in just 12 years, their share of all manufacturing assets grew by about 17 percent.

Moreover, it must be recalled that this may well represent a minimum estimate of the actual increase in concentration of the period. As noted earlier, the assets of a number of joint ventures have not been credited to their parents.

Concentration in Manufacturing, 1947, 1950, and 1962

In 1950 the Federal Trade Commission published concentration estimates for the 113 largest manufacturing corporations of 1947 with assets of $100 million or more.[10]   That study showed that in 1947 the 113 largest manufacturing corporations controlled 40 percent of the total assets and 46.1 percent of the net capital assets of all U.S. manufacturing businesses.

Table 5 presents estimates of the share of all manufacturing assets held by the 133 largest manufacturing corporations in each of the years 1947, 1950, and 1962.   Considerable care should be taken in drawing any precise comparisons between these estimates. In 1951 substantial changes were made in the sample design of the *Quarterly Financial Report* program; therefore, we have adjusted the 1950 asset data on the basis of the 1951 change.   However, we have no logical basis on which to make a similar adjustment in the 1947 data.

These data show that between 1947 and 1950 the share of all manufacturing assets held by the 113 largest companies increased from 40 to 43.5 percent (the 1950 unadjusted figure).   It is further shown that between 1950 and 1962 the 113 largest increased their share from 40 (adjusted 1950 figure) to 46.6 percent.   While the data for the 3 years are not directly comparable, they show quite clearly that between 1947 and 1962 the share of all manufacturing assets held by the 113 largest manufacturing corporations *probably* increased by about 10 percentage points, or by about 25 percent. . . .

The data contained in Tables 4 and 5 show that over the past 15 years the degree of concentration in the manufacturing segment of our economy increased at a rate comparable to increases in concentration which occurred in the 1920's.[11]   At this time we have no data which indicates that this growth is subsiding.   In fact, according to the latest copy of *Fortune* magazine which came to my attention yesterday, between 1962 and 1963 the assets of the 500 largest industrial corporations as measured by *Fortune* grew more rapidly than did all manufacturing assets during that

[10] *The Concentration of Productive Facilities* (Federal Trade Commission, 1947, 1950).

[11] N. R. Collins and Lee E. Preston, "The Size Structure of the Largest Industrial Firms, 1909–58," *The American Economic Review* (December 1962), 987, Table 1.

Table 5. Concentration of Total Assets, 113 Largest Manufacturing Corporations, 1947, 1950, and 1960[a]

Year	Total manufacturing assets (millions)[b]	113 largest corporations Total assets (millions)	113 largest corporations Percent of total manufacturing
1947[c]	$105,369	$ 42,197	40.0
1950	132,032[d]	57,430[e]	43.5
1950	143,396[f]	57,430[e]	40.0
1962	295,690	137,786[e]	46.6

SOURCE: Bureau of Economics, Federal Trade Commission.

[a] The data for the 3 years may not be compared directly because of the noncomparability of the total asset figures due to differences in sampling procedures. However, substantial comparability exists between the 1947 and the 1950 (unadjusted) figures, and between the 1950 (adjusted) and the 1962 figures.

[b] Includes estimates of unincorporated manufacturing firms.

[c] Federal Trade Commission, *Report on the Concentration of Productive Facilities, 1947,* 1949 p. 16.

[d] Unadjusted

[e] *Moody's Industrial Manual.*

[f] 1950 data adjusted to allow for 1951 change in sample design.

period, suggesting that an additional increase in concentration occurred between 1962 and 1963. . . .

III. THE SCOPE OF THE CURRENT MERGER MOVEMENT

American industry is undergoing another important merger movement, and I am reasonably confident that this movement has played a major role in the post-World War II increases in overall concentration discussed earlier. I regret that we are unable, today, to provide you with very complete information of the scope and comparative significance of this movement. We are currently in the process of compiling and summarizing the merger information in our files. Although we have not completed this compilation, the information developed to date indicates some of the important dimensions of the current merger movement. . . .

Acquisitions of Large Manufacturing and Mining Concerns

As we pointed out earlier (Table 2), in 1962 the approximately 2,000 manufacturing corporations with assets of $10 million or more held about 81.6 percent of the total assets and 89.3 percent of the total profits of all manufacturing corporations.

This, then, is really the heart of American manufacturing— about 2,000 companies with assets of over $10 million. Consequently, substantial merger activity among firms in this size class could have a significant impact upon the structure of the American economy.

Table 6 summarizes the total number and value of assets for manufacturing and mining acquisitions occurring since 1948 in

Table 6. Acquisitions of Mining and Manufacturing Corporations with Assets of $10,000,000 and over, 1948–1963

Year	Number of acquisitions[a]	Total assets of acquired corporations (millions)[b]
1948	2	$ 39.6
1949	1	21.5
1950	3	135.7
1951	12	257.3
1952	12	313.8
1953	24	713.6
1954	30	1,165.4
1955	66	2,202.1
1956	53	2,052.9
1957	44	1,304.1
1958	33	943.1
1959	61	1,790.7
1960	61	1,861.0
1961	66	2,569.3
1962	61	1,651.6
1963	62	2,490.5
Total[c]	591	$19,512.2

SOURCE: Bureau of Economics, Federal Trade Commission.

[a] See App. A for sources of merger data.

[b] Includes consideration paid, when asset data not available.

[c] Total does not include 10 nonmining and nonmanufacturing acquisitions with total assets of $265,700,000.

which the acquired concern had assets of $10 million or more in the year prior to acquisition. Although these "large" acquisitions represented only about 6 percent of all acquisitions recorded by the Federal Trade Commission since 1948, they very likely accounted for well over half of the value of assets of all recorded acquisitions.[12]

The first point to be noted from these statistics is the rising tide of merger activity among large concerns following 1948–50. From a low of under 10 per year during 1948–50, mergers moved upward, reaching a postwar peak of 66 in 1955; they then declined to 33 in the recession year of 1958. Beginning with 1959, there were over 60 large mergers each year.

During the entire 1948–63 period at least 591 manufacturing and mining corporations with assets of $10 million or more merged or were acquired. These merged[13] corporations had total assets of $19.5 billion in the year prior to acquisition (Table 6).

One way to gauge the magnitude of these mergers is to compare them with the total number and assets of firms in this size class. Had these "large" firms not been acquired, and had they continued to operate in this size class in 1963, there would have been at least 26 percent more firms[14] in this size class in 1963 than there actually were (about 2,230).[15]

More significant, during each of the last 5 years, over 60 "large" firms were acquired each year. Whether or not this is a high merger rate is a question of judgment; but certainly, compared to the recorded wartime and immediate postwar merger rates, this

[12] In 1963 the Federal Trade Commission recorded 1,018 manufacturing and mining acquisitions. The 62 of these with assets of $10 million or more had combined assets of $2.5 billion; 198 other acquisitions for which asset information could be obtained, or could be estimated, had combined assets of about $500 million.

[13] Throughout this discussion the terms "merger" and "acquisition" are used interchangeably to mean the disappearance of the whole or substantial part of a previously independent business entity, or a stock acquisition involving purchase by one company of over 50 percent of the stock of another company.

[14] Of course, had they not been acquired, some of the firms may well have dropped from this size class because they failed or declined in size after 1948. On the other hand, an unknown—but perhaps larger—number of firms (not included in this count) with assets under $10 million when acquired, would have been in the $10 million class by 1963 had they not been acquired in the meantime.

[15] There were in this size class 2,041 manufacturing corporations in the first quarter of 1963 (*Quarterly Financial Report*, FTC–SEC, *op. cit.*, 61) and 189 mining corporations in fiscal 1961–62, the last year for which the Internal Revenue Service has such information.

is a high rate.   During 1940–47, 81 concerns with assets of $10 million or more were acquired,[16] and during 1948–50 only 6 additional firms of this size class were acquired (Table 6).   Clearly, the annual rate of the 1940–50 period fell far short of current levels.[17]

The total value of assets acquired during 1948–63 was equal to about 22 percent of total manufacturing and mining assets in 1948 and 8 percent of such assets in 1963.

Perhaps the most meaningful measure of the relative magnitude of these mergers is to compare them with the assets of all firms in the size class of firms with assets of between $10 and $250 million, since all but three of the acquired concerns fell in this size class.[18]   Such a comparison reveals that the assets of acquired concerns were 20 percent as great as the assets of all firms in the $10 to $250 million size class in 1963.   And in recent years, the merger mortality rate (measured by assets) among firms in this size class exceeded 2 percent annually.

Acquisitions Involving the 1,000 Largest Manufacturing Corporations of 1950

Another indication of the relative volume of large mergers is the number of the 1,000 largest manufacturing corporations of 1950 which have disappeared because of mergers.   Since December 31, 1950, at least 216, or over 1 in 5, of the 1,000 largest manufacturing corporations of 1950 have merged or been acquired (Table 7).[19] These merger-caused disappearances were especially heavy among the companies ranking in the 501 to 1,000 largest class.   A total of 139 corporations, or 27.8 percent, of those in this class were

[16] *Report of the Federal Trade Commission on the Merger Movement* (1948), 27. Lintner and Butters place the number of such acquisitions at 58.   Lintner and Butters, "Effect of Mergers on Industrial Concentrations, 1940–47," *Review of Economics and Statistics* (February 1950), 38.

[17] During 1940–47, 139 manufacturing and mining corporations with assets of $5 million or more were acquired.   *Report of the Federal Trade Commission on the Merger Movement* (1948), 27.   Since there were in 1947 about the same number of corporations with assets of $5 million or more as there were corporations with $10 million or more in 1963, the current merger rate among "large" firms clearly in higher than during the wartime merger movement.

[18] Three acquired concerns had assets of over $250 million in the year prior to being acquired.   The total assets of these three concerns were $839.5 million.

[19] Kottke analyzed the number of acquisitions involving these concerns during the 1951–59 period.   Kottke, "Mergers of Large Manufacturing Companies, 1951–59," *The Review of Economics and Statistics* (November 1959).

Table 7. Companies Ranked among the 1,000 Largest
Manufacturing Companies in 1950 Disappearing
through Mergers during 1951–1963

Nature of acquiring company	Total	Rank of acquired company, 1950		
		1 to 200	201 to 500	501 to 1,000
Company rank in 1950:				
1 to 200	82	8	35	39
201 to 500	52	4	12	36
501 to 1,000	29	1	6	22
Total by 1,000 largest of 1950	163	13	53	97
Other manufacturing companies	37	2	6	29
Companies not principally engaged in manufacturing	16	—	3	13
Total number of disappearances	216	15	62	139

SOURCE: Bureau of Economics, Federal Trade Commission.

acquired. The comparable percentages for the 201 to 500 class were 20.7 percent, and for the top 200 class, 7.5 percent. These tabulations further reveal that over one-third of the disappearing companies were acquired by companies which ranked among the 200 largest corporations in 1950. The assets of the firms acquired by these 200 corporations represented about 66 percent of the total assets of all acquisitions involving the 1,000 largest corporations of 1950.

Finally I would like to discuss the pattern of acquisitions made by the 200 largest manufacturing corporations of 1962.

Acquisitions of the 200 Largest Corporations

Between January 1, 1951, and the end of 1963, the 200 largest manufacturing corporations made at least 1,956 acquisitions (Table 8). Asset estimates could be made for 1,080 (55 percent) of these; we believe that most of the 876 for which no asset estimates have been made were very small.

Of those acquisitions for which we have asset estimates, 308 (28 percent) had assets below $1 million and 611 (56 percent) had assets below $5 million; these 611 acquired units involved assets of about $875 million. On the other hand, the 339 acquired units with assets of $10 million or more involved total assets of over $13

**Table 8. Size of Acquisitions Made between 1951 and 1963 by the
200 Largest Manufacturing Corporations of 1962**

Asset size of acquired units (in millions)	Number of acquisitions	Total acquired assets (in millions)[a]	Percent of total
Unknown	876	—	—
Under 1	308	$ 100.7	0.7
1 to 4.9	303	773.9	5.1
5 to 9.9	130	918.9	6.1
10 to 24.9	183	2,799.4	18.5
25 to 49	85	3,006.4	19.9
50 to 99.9	45	3,176.1	21.0
100 to 249.9	23	3,479.7	23.1
250 to 1,000	3	839.5	5.6
Total	1,956	$15,094.6	100.0

SOURCE: Bureau of Economics, Federal Trade Commission.
[a] These figures include all acquisitions (including partial acquisitions) made by the acquiring companies during the period 1951–1963 and are not limited to acquisitions of mining and manufacturing companies.   In instances where asset data were unavailable, consideration paid has been used.   See App. A for sources of merger data.

billion, or about 88 percent of all assets acquired between 1951 and 1963 by the 200 largest manufacturing corporations.

Table 9 summarizes the asset values of acquisitions made by the 200 largest manufacturing corporations and compares the acquired assets with the 1950 and 1962 assets of the acquiring corporations, as well as with the growth in their assets between 1950 and 1962.

Firms in all size classes made a substantial volume of acquisitions (measured in assets) during the period (Table 9).   The 10 largest corporations acquired the greatest volume of assets per firm, averaging about $143 million each; and as a group their acquired assets totaled $1,436 million.

The contribution of assets to the asset growth of the 200 largest firms varied, generally being relatively more important to firms in the smaller size classes.   For example, acquired assets were equal to 2.8 percent of the asset growth of the 5 largest corporations and over 20 percent of the asset growth of the 51st to 200th largest corporation (last column, Table 9).

As shown earlier (Table 4), between 1950 and 1962 the 200

Table 9. Acquisitions Made between 1951 and 1962 by 200 Largest Manufacturing Corporations of 1962

Size of acquiring corporation[a]	Assets of group (millions)		Asset growth 1950–1962 (millions)	Number of acquisitions	Total assets acquired (millions)[b]	Acquired assets as percent of total		Asset growth
	1950	1962				1950	1962	
5 largest	$13,274.9	$ 36,447.3	$ 23,172.4	30	$ 651.1	4.9	1.8	2.8
6 to 10	7,403.3	17,905.8	10,502.5	35	782.5	10.6	4.4	7.5
11 to 20	8,237.0	19,471.6	11,234.1	47	278.3	3.4	1.4	2.5
21 to 50	12,389.0	31,597.0	19,208.0	232	2,905.8	23.5	9.2	15.1
51 to 100	11,910.7	30,625.9	18,715.0	709	4,888.9	41.0	16.0	26.1
101 to 150	6,833.3	17,654.8	10,821.4	434	2,223.0	32.5	12.6	20.5
151 to 200	4,305.4	11,625.1	7,319.6	382	2,052.8	47.7	17.7	28.0
Total 200	$64,353.6	$165,327.5	$100,973.1	1,869	$13,782.4	21.6	8.4	15.7

SOURCE: Bureau of Economics, Federal Trade Commission.

a Companies ranked by total assets in 1962.

b These figures include all acquisitions (including partial acquisitions) made by the acquiring company during the period 1951–1963 and are not limited to acquisitions of mining and manufacturing companies. In instances where asset data were unavailable, consideration paid has been used. Asset information was available for 1,016 of these acquisitions.

largest corporations' share of the total assets of manufacturing corporations increased by about 6.1 percentage points. Clearly, acquisitions played a central role in this increase in concentration. The $13,782,400,000 of assets acquired by these corporations were equal to 21.6 percent of their 1950 assets, 8.4 percent of their 1962 assets, and 15.7 percent of the growth in their assets between 1950 and 1962 (Table 9).

Only 16 of the 200 largest manufacturing corporations made no acquisitions during the period 1951–62 (Table 10); another 15 companies made acquisitions, but asset information was available for none of these (Table 10); and for 69 other companies the value of assets acquired was less than 10 percent of their total asset growth between 1950 and 1962. However, for 35 companies acquired assets exceeded 40 percent of the total growth in their assets between 1950 and 1962, and in the case of 23 companies acquired assets exceeded 50 percent of their asset growth during the period (Table 10).

Table 10. Acquired Assets as Percent of Asset Growth from 1950 to 1962 of the 200 Largest Manufacturing Corporations of 1962

Acquired assets as percent of total assets growth[a]	Number of acquiring corporations
0[b]	31
Less than 10	69
10 to 19.9	26
20 to 29.9	22
30 to 39.9	17
40 to 49.9	12
50 to 59.9	8
60 to 69.9	4
70 to 79.9	3
80 to 89.9	5
90 to 99	1
100 and over	2

SOURCE: Bureau of Economics, Federal Trade Commission.

[a] These figures include all acquisitions (including partial acquisitions) made by the acquiring companies during the period 1951–1963 and are not limited to acquisitions of mining and manufacturing companies. In instances where asset data were unavailable, consideration paid has been used.

[b] Includes 15 companies which made acquisitions but for which asset data were not available and 16 companies which made no acquisitions.

These facts indicate that although mergers played a significant role in the growth of most large corporations, their relative importance varied substantially among corporations.

Although we have not completed our analysis of the impact of mergers on the changing mobility of firms, I think it will show that in a good many cases . . . the reason for mobility among the largest corporations is that some firms are making very extensive use of mergers.

Acquisitions by 25 Corporations

A relatively few corporations accounted for a large share of the assets acquired by the 200 largest corporations; 10 companies accounted for 25.5 percent and 25 companies acquired 47.8 percent of all the assets acquired by the 200 largest corporations (Table 11). These leading 25 acquirers made at least 477 acquisitions. The 159 of their acquisitions for which asset data are available totaled $6,584 million. The 50 leading acquirers made 773 acquisitions;

Table 11. Twenty-five Leading Acquiring Manufacturing Corporations, 1951–1962

Rank by volume of acquisitions[a]	Number of acquisitions	Number for which assets available	Total assets acquired (millions)[b]	Percent of total assets acquired by 200 largest corporations
5 leaders	181	49	$ 2,216.4	16.1%
6 to 10	103	33	1,293.9	9.4
11 to 15	84	37	1,215.0	8.8
16 to 20	48	15	994.5	7.2
21 to 25	61	25	864.3	6.3
Total 25 companies	477	159	6,584.1	47.8
Total 50 companies	773	289	9,621.6	69.8
Total 200 companies	1,869	1,016	$13,782.4	100.0

SOURCE: Bureau of Economics, Federal Trade Commission.

[a] Acquiring corporations ranked by volume of assets acquired during 1951–1962.

[b] These figures include all acquisitions (including partial acquisitions) made by the acquiring companies during the period 1951–1962 and are not limited to acquisitions of mining and manufacturing companies. In instances where asset data were unavailable, consideration paid has been used. See Appendix A for source of merger data.

Table 12. Net Income after Taxes as Percent of
Net Worth for 165 Acquired Corporations[a]

Rate of return[b] (percent)	Number of companies
Negative	17
0.0 to 2.4	16
2.5 to 4.9	12
5.0 to 7.4	30
7.5 to 9.9	32
10.0 to 14.9	37
15.0 to 19.9	14
20.0 and over	7
Total	165

SOURCE: Bureau of Economics, Federal Trade Commission.

[a] Show rates of return for 165 of the 216 acquired corporations reported in Table 7.

[b] Computed from data contained in Moody's Industrial Manual.

they acquired about 70 percent of the total assets of all companies acquired by the top 200 corporations.

Financial Status of Large Acquired Concerns

One final aspect of recent mergers which may be of interest is the financial status of the large firms which were acquired.

We have found that very few large acquired corporations were failing concerns, or even losing money in the year prior to being acquired. In fact, a substantial percentage were very profitable enterprises. As shown in Table 12, only 17 of the 165 acquired corporations for which we have financial information were losing money in the year prior to being acquired.[20] These concerns represented only 10.3 percent of all corporations for which we obtained such financial information.

On the other hand, 58 of the acquired corporations enjoyed earnings on net worth of over 10 percent and 90 of over 7.5 percent in the year preceding acquisition. This suggests that many of the acquired concerns were very profitable enterprises, and had they

[20] The data in Table 12 are for the acquired corporations summarized in Table 7 for which we have developed financial information.

not been acquired they most likely would have continued as healthy economic enterprises capable of offering effective competition.

APPENDIX A: SOURCES OF ACQUISITION DATA

The merger data summarized in the accompanying tables were reported in company annual reports and prospectuses: *Moody's Industrial Manual, Standard Corporation Records*, and various newspapers, especially the *Wall Street Journal*.   Table 6 includes only those acquired companies for which it was possible to obtain information on assets, consideration paid, or which were among the 1,000 largest manufacturing companies in 1950, as reported in *Report of the Federal Trade Commission on Industrial Concentration and Product Diversification in the* 1,000 *Largest Manufacturing Companies: 1950*, January 1957, 650–56.   All companies in the latter group had assets of at least $11.5 million in 1950.   Frank J. Kottke, "Mergers of Large Manufacturing Companies, 1951–59," *The Review of Economics and Statistics*, November 1959, 430. Acquired companies which were among the 1,000 largest in 1950, but whose assets when acquired were unknown, were assumed to have assets equal to the assets of the smallest firm in their size class in 1950, i.e., $11.5 million for those companies ranking among the 501 to 1,000 largest and $40 million for those ranking among the 201 to 500 largest.   Where only the consideration paid was known, this figure was used as an estimate of the assets of the acquired concern.   Where only the sales of the acquired company were known, assets were estimated by applying an asset to sales ratio common to the industry in which the acquired concern operated.

Although the time series derived from the above sources do not include all "large" acquisitions, it is most accurate for the period 1959–1963. *News Front* (management's news magazine, New York City) directories of various years were consulted to obtain asset information beginning in 1959.

THE MOST RECENT DATA (1957) ANALYZED BY SHERMAN INDICATES *that the average American firm investing abroad had a profit rate considerably higher than the average of all U.S. corporations. The value of direct foreign investment by the average American firm operating abroad was also much greater than that of those firms operating only in the U.S. The average equity of firms investing abroad is well over twenty times that of all U.S. firms. Therefore, foreign profits are probably a major source of the higher profit rates of the large corporations. Investment abroad is extremely concentrated. Less than 2 percent of the American companies investing abroad in 1957 held 57 percent of all U.S. investments abroad. The U.S. ownership of foreign investments is far more concentrated than even the very concentrated ownership of domestic assets. Less than 1 percent of the companies received over 60 percent of the earnings whereas 65 percent of the companies received less than 1 percent of the earnings. Thus, it is evident that a few companies hold most U.S. investments abroad and receive most of the profits from these investments.*

3

CONCENTRATION OF
FOREIGN INVESTMENT

Howard J. Sherman

The latest complete and official study of profits on foreign investment by size of firm is a 1960 study for 1957 data.   Therefore,
these profit rates of firms abroad will be compared with rates for
all firms in the 1957 data.   In 1957, the profit rate (total profit
before tax, divided by total equity) of all American corporations
was 13 percent.[1]   The average equity (total equity divided by
total number of firms) of all American corporations was $391,705.[2]
American firms investing abroad had a considerably higher profit
rate (profit before tax from direct investment abroad divided by
value of direct investment abroad), namely, 15.4 percent.[3]   Moreover, the average American firm operating abroad had very high
average equity (value of direct investment abroad divided by
number of companies investing abroad), namely, $8,983,642.[4]   It

Reprinted from Howard J. Sherman, *Profits in the United States: An Introduction to a Study of Economic Concentration and Business Cycles* (Ithaca, N.Y.:
Cornell University Press, 1968), pp. 136–38.   Used by permission of Cornell
University Press.   Copyright © 1968 by Cornell University.   Footnotes have
been renumbered.
[1] Calculated from U.S. Treasury Department, Internal Revenue Service,
Statistics of Income, Corporation Income Tax Returns for 1957 (Washington, D.C.:
U.S.G.P.O., 1960).
[2] *Ibid.*
[3] U.S. Department of Commerce, Office of Business Economics, *United
States Investments in Foreign Countries* (Washington, D.C.: U.S.G.P.O., 1960),
pp. 144–45.
[4] *Ibid.*, p. 144.

would appear, therefore, that higher rates of foreign earnings are one source of the higher observed profit rates of the larger American firms.

As averages may be deceptive, it is useful to cite some of the more detailed data recently available on the characteristics and performance of American firms abroad.   There is pictured in the 1957 data mentioned above revealing extreme concentration in the holding by U.S. companies of investments abroad.[5]   Thus, the largest-sized class of companies is classified as those holding direct foreign investments of over $100 million dollars.   This class of companies included only 1.6 percent of all companies, but owned 57.2 percent of all U.S. investments abroad.   At the other end of the spectrum, 24.7 percent of the companies with foreign investments each invested less than $100 thousand dollars, and all together held only 0.1 percent of the U.S. foreign investment. Even the next 26.1 percent of companies, each investing $100 to $500 thousand abroad, held only 0.7 percent of all U.S. foreign investment.   In fact, in 1957 only 2,812 U.S. companies had any investment abroad.   Clearly, the U.S. ownership of foreign investments is far more concentrated than even the very concentrated ownership of domestic assets.

The same picture of extreme concentration may be seen in Table 1, which shows earnings from United States investments abroad.   It shows that less than 1 percent of the companies received 61.4 percent of the earnings, whereas 64.9 percent of the companies received less than 1 percent of the earnings.   Thus the data indicate that a few companies hold most of United States investment abroad, and that a few companies (presumably the same large companies for the most part) receive most of the earnings from United States investment abroad.

None of this, however, is sufficient proof that earnings abroad are a significant explanatory factor of the higher profit rates of large firms.   It may be accepted that profit rates earned abroad are higher than domestic profit rates.   It may also be accepted that earnings abroad are quite concentrated.   Two questions, nevertheless, remain unanswered.   Is the investment and profit concentration of United States corporations any higher abroad than domestically?   If so, does the greater profit rate earned abroad produce enough in quantitative terms to have a significant effect on average profit rates by asset size?   Comparisons with

[5] *Ibid.*, p. 145.

Table 1. Earnings on Foreign Investments
by Size of Earning in 1957

Net earnings of direct investments by size of earnings (lower limit)	Number of companies (all industries)	Amount of earnings	Companies	Earnings
$25,000,000	25	$2,464,000,000	0.9%	61.4%
10,000,000	30	443,000,000	1.1	11.0
5,000,000	58	411,000,000	2.1	10.2
2,500,000	72	242,000,000	2.6	6.0
1,000,000	139	209,000,000	4.9	5.2
500,000	138	91,000,000	4.9	2.3
100,000	524	123,000,000	18.6	3.1
1	944	28,000,000	33.6	0.7
0	335		11.9	0.0
Deficit firms	547	−133,000,000	19.4	losses
Total	2,812	$3,881,000,000	100.0	100.0*

SOURCE: U.S. Department of Commerce, Office of Business Economics, *United States Investments in Foreign Countries* (Washington, D.C.: U.S.G.P.O., 1960), adapted from Table 56, p. 145.

* Here 100.0% equals $4,014,000,000 which is $3,881,000,000 plus $133,000,000 deficit.

earlier data indicate that answers to these questions may help explain the facts, but a much more detailed study would be required to prove their importance.

THE FOUR FOLLOWING SELECTIONS ARE FROM A SERIES OF COMPRE-
*hensive studies of ownership and control of banking conducted by the
Staff of the Subcommittee on Domestic Finance, chaired by Congressman Wright Patman. The selections contain the following findings:*

*At the end of 1964, the 100 largest commercial banks in the U.S.
held 46 percent of all deposits in the 13,775 commercial banks in the
country. The 14 largest, or one tenth of 1 percent of all commercial
banks, held a quarter of all commercial bank deposits. A similar
pattern prevails in the 65 metropolitan areas studied; the three largest
banks held more than half the deposits in 59 of the 65 areas surveyed.
In the trust business, concentration is even greater. Less than 2
percent of the banks held 61 percent of all trust assets in national
banks.*

*A survey of the stockholding of the 210 largest banks holding
over 60 percent of the total deposits in the country shows that 94 percent
of the surveyed banks hold some of their own stock. Nearly one third
of the banks exercise influence over the voting of 5 percent or more
of their own shares. The Staff believes that control of even 1 or 2
percent of the stock in a "publicly held" corporation gives tremendous
influence over policies and operations. The diffusion of ownership
is such that the holder of even a small percentage of the stock is one of
the company's largest shareholders. Large shareholders are often
able to exert control far beyond their ownership because they can also
put representatives on the boards of directors of these companies.
Management, in turn, pays a great deal more attention to a large
shareholder who may own more than 100 times what the average
shareholder owns. Two hundred ten of the largest commercial banks
in the U.S., 258 insurance companies, and 189 mutual savings banks
were listed as shareholders "of record" (that is, others may be the
real owners) among the top 20 shareholders of record in the 300 largest
commercial banks. These "major financial institutions" were stockholders of record in 275 of the 300 largest banks as of March 1966.
In 72 percent of the 275 largest banks, at least 5 percent of the stock
is owned by these major financial institutions. Five percent or more
of the shares of nearly one half of the 275 commercial banks could be
voted exclusively by the major financial institutions reporting. In
two thirds of the 275 major banks, 5 percent or more of the shares
are held by other major commercial banks. Almost one half have
10 percent or more of their stock held by other major commercial
banks. Almost one third have 5 percent or more of their shares
voted exclusively by other major commercial banks. In New York,
for example, major banks hold and vote a significant percentage of*

46

shares in competing banks. Thus, supposedly competing financial institutions are tightly interlocked through common stock ownership, not to mention interlocking directorates. The presence of such significant common interests among the largest banks and insurance companies in the country raises some doubt as to whether or not they will compete vigorously and effectively.

There is, in fact, an emerging situation that might be referred to as bank minority control *of the largest nonfinancial corporations. Large blocks of stock in the largest* nonfinancial *corporations are controlled by the largest* financial *corporations (banks and insurance companies). Management control, when data collected by the Subcommittee are examined, is often apparently a fiction. At least 36 of the 200 largest nonfinancial corporations, usually regarded as "controlled by management," are revealed by the Subcommittee's investigation to be controlled by banks through minority holdings. Clearly, the bank ties revealed in this and other areas discussed in the Patman report demonstrate the need for substantial revision of the general view of who controls the largest corporations in the country.*

Analysis of investments and interlocks between major banks and corporations, based on data from the largest banks in ten major cities (49 banks in all), found that these 49 banks hold well over half the total trust assets in all banks in the country. Just 30 of these banks hold 52 percent of all trust assets. In seven of the ten cities, the banks studied hold more than 90 percent of all bank trust assets in the area.

One of the most significant gauges of the overall influence of the large banks on the economy of the U.S. is the formal interrelationships they have with the largest corporations. Analysis of the interlocking stock ownership between them shows that the 49 banks surveyed hold 5 percent or more of the common stock in 147 (29 percent) of the 500 largest industrial corporations. Seventeen of the 50 largest merchandising companies and transportation companies also have at least 5 percent of their common stock held by one or more of the 49 banks. These 49 banks are also represented on the boards of directors of 286 of the 500 largest corporations. The same pattern exists among the 50 largest merchandising, utilities, transportation and insurance companies.

4

CONCENTRATION OF BANKING

The Patman Committee

The latest figures on the concentration of banking in general (Table 1) shows that as of the end of 1964, the 100 largest commercial banks in the United States held 46.3 percent of all the deposits in the 13,775 commercial banks in the United States. Of these 100 giant banking institutions, the 14 largest, representing one-tenth of 1 percent of all commercial banks in the country, held 24 percent of all commercial bank deposits.   Looking at particular metropolitan areas (Table 2), FDIC figures indicate that in every one of 65 major metropolitan areas recently surveyed the 3 largest banks held more than 30 percent of all commercial bank deposits in the area; in 59 of these 65 areas the 3 largest banks held over 50 percent of all commercial bank deposits, and in 46 of these areas, almost 3 out of 4, the 3 largest banks held over 70 percent of all commercial bank deposits in the area.

In the trust business, as shown in Table 3, indications are that concentration is even greater than in banking in general. Taking trust assets of banks under Federal charter, i.e., national banks, as of the end of 1965, only 26 or 1.7 percent, accounted for

Reprinted from the Patman Committee Staff Report for the Domestic Finance Subcommittee of the House Committee on Banking and Currency, 90th Cong., 2nd. sess.   *Commercial Banks and Their Trust Activities: Emerging Influence on the American Economy* (Washington, D.C.: U.S. Government Printing Office, July 1968); Subcommittee Reprint of Staff Report on "Bank Stock Ownership and Control," December 29, 1966, pp. 804–8.   Footnotes and tables have been renumbered.

Table 1. Commercial Bank Deposits and Proportions of Total Held by the Largest Commercial Banks or Bank Groups, Dec. 31, 1964

Size group	Commercial banks			Commercial banks and bank groups*		
	Entire United States	50 States and District of Columbia	48 States and District of Columbia	Entire United States	50 States and District of Columbia	48 States and District of Columbia
All commercial banks:						
Number	13,775	13,760	13,736	13,395	13,380	13,356
Deposits (millions)	$308,427	$307,146	$306,426	$308,427	$307,146	$306,426
Largest 100 banks (or bank groups):						
Percent of number of all commercial banks	0.73	0.73	0.73	0.75	0.75	0.75
Deposits (millions)	$142,673	$142,199	$142,199	$147,834	$147,360	$147,360
Percent of deposits of all commercial banks	46.26	46.30	46.41	47.93	47.98	48.09
Largest 10 banks (or bank groups):						
Deposits (millions)	$63,645	$63,171	$63,171	$63,645	$63,171	$63,171
Percent of deposits of all commercial banks	20.64	20.57	20.62	20.64	20.57	20.62
Largest 5 banks (or bank groups):						
Deposits (millions)	$43,611	$43,137	$43,137	$43,611	$43,137	$43,137
Percent of deposits of all commercial banks	14.14	14.04	14.08	14.14	14.04	14.08
Largest 3 banks (or bank groups):						
Deposits (millions)	$32,664	$32,190	$32,190	$32,664	$32,190	$32,190
Percent of deposits of all commercial banks	10.59	10.48	10.50	10.59	10.48	10.50
Largest bank (or bank group):						
Deposits (millions)	$12,996	$12,970	$12,970	$12,996	$12,970	$12,970
Percent of deposits of all commercial banks	4.21	4.22	4.23	4.21	4.22	4.23
Largest 1 percent of the banks (or bank grops):						
Number	138	138	137	134	134	134
Deposits (millions)	$155,578	$155,104	$154,729	$160,129	$159,655	$159,606
Percent of deposits of all commercial banks	50.44	50.50	50.49	51.92	51.98	52.09
Largest $\frac{1}{2}$ of 1 percent of the banks (or bank groups):						
Number	69	69	69	67	67	67
Deposits (millions)	$127,860	$127,386	$127,386	$131,335	$130,816	$130,861
Percent of deposits of all commercial banks	41.46	41.47	41.57	42.58	42.61	42.71
Largest $\frac{1}{10}$ of 1 percent of the banks:						
Number	14	14	14	13	13	13
Deposits (millions)	$75,701	$75,227	$75,227	$73,325	$72,851	$72,851
Percent of deposits of all commercial banks	24.54	24.49	24.55	23.77	23.72	23.77

SOURCE: Federal Deposit Insurance Corporation Annual Report for 1964, p. 140.

* Figures for bank groups are the deposits of banks in each state controlled by a holding company registered under the Bank Holding Company Act of 1956, plus 1 group controlled through common stock ownership included for comparability with data for earlier years, treated for each case as though they were a bank and branches in the state.

Table 2. Relative Size of Largest Banks or Bank Groups in 65 Metropolitan Areas, June 30, 1964[a]

Principal county or counties in metropolitan area	Total deposits in all commercial banks (thousands)[b]	Percentage of deposits of all commercial banks in—[c]			Percentage of deposits of all commercial banks in—[d]		
		Largest bank	Largest 3 banks	Largest 5 banks	Largest bank or bank group	Largest 3 banks or bank groups	Largest 5 banks or bank groups
Metropolitan Areas in States with Statewide Branch Banking Prevalent							
Baltimore: Baltimore City and Baltimore County, Md.	$1,567,012	30.1	71.5	97.7	30.1	71.5	97.7
Hartford: Hartford County, Conn.	989,712	39.5	81.7	85.2	39.5	81.7	85.2
Honolulu: Honolulu County, Hawaii	750,563	38.8	79.6	90.7	38.8	79.6	90.7
Los Angeles: Los Angeles County, Calif.	12,015,392	33.4	71.2	86.3	33.4	71.2	86.3
Phoenix: Maricopa County, Ariz.	1,167,538	47.3	89.1	96.2	47.3	90.3	97.4
Portland: Clackamas and Multnomah Counties, Oreg.	1,222,631	41.9	89.3	94.1	41.9	89.3	94.1
Providence: Bristol, Kent, and Providence Counties, R.I.	976,234	52.4	93.0	98.9	52.4	93.0	98.9
Sacramento: Sacramento County, Calif.	955,632	47.8	85.6	91.5	47.8	85.6	91.5
San Bernardino: Riverside and San Bernardino Counties, Calif.	948,854	39.2	84.0	93.2	39.2	84.0	93.2
San Diego: San Diego County, Calif.	1,187,910	39.2	82.6	95.7	39.2	82.6	95.7
San Francisco: Alameda and San Francisco Counties, Calif.	8,204,851	39.5	76.9	87.4	39.5	76.9	87.4
San Jose: Santa Clara County, Calif.	1,202,335	42.3	76.8	92.1	42.3	76.8	92.1
Seattle: King County, Wash.	1,525,460	38.0	71.6	87.8	38.0	71.6	87.8
Metropolitan Areas in States with Limited-area Branch Banking Prevalent							
Akron: Summit County, Ohio	678,197	47.8	89.2	99.2	47.8	89.2	99.2
Albany: Albany, Rensselaer, and Schenectady Counties, N.Y.	1,088,463	34.5	67.1	80.8	34.5	67.1	80.8
Allentown: Lehigh and Northampton Counties, Pa.	699,250	20.5	45.6	64.2	20.5	45.6	64.2
Atlanta: Fulton and De Kalb Counties, Ga.	1,718,995	30.6	73.9	91.1	30.6	75.9	93.1
Birmingham: Jefferson County, Ala.	752,136	57.5	97.4	99.1	57.5	97.4	99.1
Boston: Suffolk County, Mass.	3,390,349	51.4	82.5	96.6	51.4	82.5	96.6
Buffalo: Erie and Niagara Counties, N.Y.	1,823,078	50.3	94.8	98.2	50.3	94.8	98.2
Cincinnati: Hamilton County, Ohio	1,333,644	32.1	84.0	97.9	32.1	84.0	97.9
Cleveland: Cuyahoga County, Ohio	4,211,452	36.2	75.9	97.7	36.2	75.9	97.7
Columbus: Franklin County, Ohio	991,549	46.0	92.8	97.4	50.6	97.4	99.2

Table 2 (continued)

Principal county or counties in metropolitan area	Total deposits in all commercial banks (thousands)[b]	Percentage of deposits of all commercial banks in—[c]			Percentage of deposits of all commercial banks in—[d]		
		Largest bank	Largest 3 banks	Largest 5 banks	Largest bank or bank group	Largest 3 banks or bank groups	Largest 5 banks or bank groups
Dayton: Montgomery County, Ohio	$530,498	50.6	89.9	94.7	50.6	89.9	94.7
Detroit: Wayne County Mich.	5,896,559	39.8	74.7	87.4	39.8	73.7	87.4
Gary: Lake County, Ind.	454,214	33.2	59.2	77.7	33.2	59.2	77.7
Indianapolis: Marion County, Ind.	1,381,328	39.1	96.1	99.7	39.1	96.1	99.7
Jersey City: Hudson County, N.J.	874,520	31.2	67.9	93.6	31.2	67.9	93.6
Knoxville: Knox County, Tenn.	346,934	43.6	85.5	100.0	43.6	85.5	100.0
Louisville: Jefferson County, Ky.	933,920	29.9	76.2	95.5	31.0	78.6	97.8
Memphis: Shelby County, Tenn.	1,173,302	43.5	93.0	97.2	43.5	93.0	97.2
Nashville: Davidson County, Tenn.	874,982	42.4	92.6	98.6	42.4	92.6	98.6
Newark: Essex and Union Counties, N.J.	2,540,343	21.0	55.6	67.7	21.0	55.6	67.7
New Orleans: Orleans County, La.	1,253,091	39.3	78.7	99.1	39.3	78.7	99.1
New York: Bronx, Kings, New York, Queens, and Richmond Counties, N.Y.	42,322,968	21.7	54.1	75.3	21.7	54.1	75.3
Norfolk: Norfolk City, Portsmouth City, and Norfolk County, Va.	393,068	48.6	77.8	91.9	48.6	77.8	91.9
Paterson: Bergen and Passaic Counties, N.J.	1,940,349	16.3	43.2	55.1	16.3	43.2	55.1
Philadelphia: Philadelphia County, Pa.	4,506,211	27.0	63.6	86.2	27.0	63.6	86.2
Pittsburgh: Allegheny County, Pa.	4,413,335	49.6	80.6	89.1	49.6	80.6	89.1
Richmond: Richmond City and Henrico County, Va.	883,962	29.9	73.4	90.0	29.9	73.4	90.0
Rochester: Monroe County, N.Y.	955,414	43.6	86.2	99.5	43.6	86.2	99.5
Springfield: Hampden County, Mass.	359,933	31.6	84.0	94.4	31.6	84.0	94.4
Syracuse: Onondaga County, N.Y.	576,712	33.1	78.2	99.8	33.1	78.2	99.8
Toledo: Lucas County, Ohio	608,541	50.8	88.1	98.5	50.8	88.1	98.5
Washington: District of Columbia	1,978,727	29.8	73.3	86.7	29.8	73.3	86.7
Wilkes-Barre: Luzerne County, Pa.	475,183	18.9	43.3	54.9	18.9	43.3	54.9
Youngstown: Mahoning and Trumbull Counties, Ohio	506,328	23.3	57.1	83.8	23.3	57.1	83.8
Metropolitan Areas in States with Unit Banking Prevalent							
Charleston: Kanawha County, W.Va.	297,475	29.5	68.1	81.6	29.5	68.1	81.6
Chicago: Cook County, Ill.	15,517,882	23.4	51.9	61.5	23.4	51.9	61.5

Table 2 (continued)

Principal county or counties in metropolitan area	Total deposits in all commercial banks (thousands)[b]	Percentage of deposits of all commercial banks in—[c]			Percentage of deposits of all commercial banks in—[d]		
		Largest bank	Largest 3 banks	Largest 5 banks	Largest bank or bank group	Largest 3 banks or bank groups	Largest 5 banks or bank groups
Dallas: Dallas County, Tex.	$3,487,140	33.9	76.2	81.6	33.9	76.2	81.6
Denver: Denver County, Colo.	1,394,161	27.7	67.6	83.7	27.7	67.6	83.7
Fort Worth: Tarrant County, Tex.	980,734	32.7	73.0	77.4	36.6	76.9	81.1
Houston: Harris County, Tex.	3,185,293	26.1	63.5	67.7	26.1	63.5	67.7
Jacksonville: Duval County, Fla.	733,730	27.9	71.6	80.6	33.7	81.5	90.4
Kansas City: Clay and Jackson Counties, Mo.	1,778,751	26.1	58.3	64.4	26.1	58.3	64.4
Miami: Dade County, Fla.	1,380,243	28.1	40.0	48.4	28.1	41.8	50.3
Milwaukee: Milwaukee County, Wis.	1,946,639	39.3	65.8	71.5	40.6	76.1	80.9
Minneapolis: Hennepin and Ramsey Counties, Minn.	2,637,232	22.5	59.6	67.9	44.9	83.5	90.9
Oklahoma City: Oklahoma County, Okla.	949,439	32.7	71.0	79.5	32.7	71.0	79.5
Omaha: Douglas County, Nebr.	623,683	41.5	78.7	85.6	41.5	84.5	89.5
San Antonio: Bexar County, Tex.	887,517	29.3	61.7	72.3	29.3	61.7	72.3
St. Louis: St. Louis City and St. Louis County, Mo.	3,293,581	21.6	47.8	55.4	21.6	48.2	58.6
Tampa: Hillsboro and Pinellas Counties, Fla.	1,111,623	11.8	34.2	49.1	11.8	34.2	49.1
Tulsa: Tulsa County, Okla.	753,537	38.0	75.8	83.6	38.0	75.8	83.6
Wheeling: Ohio County, W.Va.	107,662	40.9	81.6	96.0	40.9	81.6	96.0

SOURCE: Federal Deposit Insurance Corporation Annual Report for 1964, pp. 142–143.

NOTE: It is recognized that service areas for deposits vary with the type and size of account, and that a much greater proportion of the deposits in larger than in small banks is in large accounts. Ratios based on deposits without regard to these characteristics, therefore, may not be very accurate indicators of the shares of an area's deposits held by individual banks. Ratios that more nearly approximate these shares are currently being derived from the Corporation's most recent survey of deposits and will be released in a forthcoming publication.

[a] Principal counties in 60 standard metropolitan areas as defined by the Bureau of the Budget, with population of 400,000 or more on Apr. 1, 1960, and in 5 other areas included in tables 29 and 40 of the annual report for 1960, except that in Connecticut, Massachusetts, and Rhode Island (where standard metropolitan areas are defined in terms of cities and towns) they are counties with the majority of the population within standard metropolitan areas.

[b] Deposits in all commercial banks and branches located in county (or counties). These figures are as published by the Board of Governors of the Federal Reserve System in "Distribution of Bank Deposits by Counties in Standard Metropolitan Areas, June 30, 1964" (in the case of counties with mutual savings banks, deposits in all banks minus deposits in mutual savings banks).

[c] As tabulated deposits in a bank consist of those in head office and any branches within the area, or, if the head office is located elsewhere, of deposits in all branches within the area.

[d] A bank group includes banks that are members of a holding company registered under the Bank Holding Company Act of 1956, or (in 1 case) controlled through common stock ownership.

Table 3. Trust Department Assets
According to Trust Department Size

Trust department size	Number of banks	Per-cent of total	Assets of employee benefit accounts (millions)	Per-cent of total	Other trust assets (millions)	Per-cent of total	Total trust assets (millions)	Per-cent of total
Less than $10 million	1,110	70.5	$179	0.6	$2,067	3.4	$2,246	2.5
$10 to $99.9 million	350	22.2	1,418	5.0	10,310	16.9	11,728	13.1
$100 to $499.9 million	88	5.6	3,136	11.0	17,640	28.9	20,776	23.2
Over $500 million	26	1.7	23,835	83.4	30,935	50.8	54,770	61.2
Total	1,574	100.0	28,568	100.0	60,952	100.0	89,520	100.0

SOURCE: National Banking Review, June 1965, p. 489.

$54.7 billion, or 61.2 percent, of all trust assets in national banks. Only 114 national banks held more than $75 billion in trust assets or over 83 percent of the trust assets in all national banks. No comparable statistics are available for state-chartered banks.

In addition, it should be noted that a recent study by the Securities and Exchange Commission indicates that 20 large banks manage almost half of all noninsured private pension fund assets.[1]

[1] United States Congress, House of Representatives Committee on Interstate and Foreign Commerce, 89th Cong., 2nd sess., "Report of the Securities and Exchange Commission on the Public Policy Implications of Investment Company Growth" (Washington, D.C., December 2, 1966).

5

BANK STOCK OWNERSHIP AND CONTROL

The Patman Committee

While no survey of this kind could ever hope to be complete in the sense that every single share of every bank stock held can be accounted for, this survey has produced a substantial amount of useful and usable information on the ownership and control of a very high percentage of the shares of commercial bank stock outstanding.*

The first data available, which is included in this report, shows the bank stock holdings of 210 of the 300 largest commercial banks in the United States. This represents data now available from the 233 of the top 300 commercial banks that were listed as major bank stockholders in the study published in 1964 on the "Twenty Largest Stockholders of Record in Member Banks of the Federal Reserve System," as well as stockholdings in the 300 largest banks by the 258 insurance companies and 189 mutual savings banks listed in the same study as leading owners of commercial bank

Reprinted from the Patman Committee Staff Report for the Domestic Finance Subcommittee of the House Committee on Banking and Currency, 90th Cong., 2nd sess. *Commercial Banks and their Trust Activities: Emerging Influence on the American Economy* (Washington, D.C.: U.S. Government Printing Office, July 1968); Subcommittee Reprint of Staff Report on "Bank Stock Ownership and Control," December 29, 1966, pp. 815–16, 831–33, 877–79. Footnotes have been renumbered.

* *This information is based on a questionnaire survey of about 3,900 institutions drawn from names in the earlier study published by the Subcommittee on the "Twenty Largest Stockholders of Record in Member Banks of the Federal Reserve System."* — M.Z.

stock.[1]   This data shows that the above-mentioned major financial institutions were the stockholders of record in 275 of the 300 largest commercial banks in the United States as of March 1, 1966.

It should be pointed out that the total deposits in the 300 largest banks in the United States represent a very high percentage of the total deposits in all commercial banks in this country.   The most up-to-date figures available indicate that, as of December 31, 1965, the aggregate deposits of the 200 largest banks' deposits represented over 57 percent of the total deposits in all commercial banks.   Therefore, though this initial study deals with the bank stock holdings of only a small number of the almost 14,000 commercial banks in the United States, it deals with a very large percentage in terms of the total banking business of the nation.

In the case of insurance companies and mutual savings banks, all shares of bank stock reported on is beneficially owned by each insurance company and mutual savings bank, and is voted by the company or its authorized representative.   In the case of the bank stock held by commercial banks, it is in almost all cases held by the bank in its trust department or by a bank nominee for the benefit of others.   Because of this latter situation, the most significant information here is the extent to which the bank holding stock for others has voting power over the stock.   In other words, the extent to which the bank can exercise or influence the voting of shares determines the extent to which the bank actually controls the stock.   In a very real sense, as Professor Berle points out in his "Power Without Property," the ownership rights are often divided, the bank having the ownership right to vote the stock in many cases, and the beneficiary of the account obtaining the ownership right to money distributions only.

Commercial banks hold significant blocks of their own stock in various accounts.   Of the 210 banks of the top 300 reported on here, the data show that this practice of a bank holding its own stock ranges from holding none, up to a holding of over 46 percent of their own stock.   Out of the 210 of the top 300 banks for which data is now available 198, or 93.8 percent, hold some of their own shares; 120, or 56.9 percent, hold more than 5 percent of their own shares; and 62 banks, or 29.4 percent, hold more than 10 percent of their own shares; 17 banks have more than 20 percent of

[1] Throughout this survey, wherever commercial banks are stated as being stockholders, owners, or in control of commercial bank stock, the holdings of nominees of banks are included in all cases.

their own shares; and 7 banks hold more than one-third of the total number of shares outstanding in their own bank.

On the matter of voting rights, 31 of these 210 banks can vote alone over 5 percent of their own stock and 13 can vote over 10 percent.   If the percentage over which these banks have partial voting rights is added to those over which they have sole voting rights, 63 of these 210 banks, or 29.9 percent, exercise some (in many cases considerable) influence over the voting of 5 percent or more of their own shares.   Thirty-three banks have this power over 10 percent or more of their own shares, and seven banks have this power over more than 20 percent of their own shares. . . .

The question may be asked, What is a significant percentage of stock in terms of control of a widely held, publicly owned corporation?   This question cannot be answered with exact precision, but the general range of percentage that is significant to exercise control can be stated.

A recent study of chain banking[2] based on data presented in the subcommittee's earlier study, the "Twenty Largest Stockholders of Record in Member Banks of the Federal Reserve System," uses a 5 percent holding as significant in determining whether a chain banking situation exists.   Senator Couzins, many years ago, while inquiring into this question at a congressional hearing, stated, "I have sat on boards of directors where 2 and 3 percent of the stock dominated and controlled the policies of the companies, not because of their influence, and not necessarily their internal influence, but they have influence in the back and strings to pull which make it necessary, if you please, for the majority to do the wishes of the minority."[3]   And in a recent article in the *American Economic Review*,[4] examples are given whereby effective control of large nonfinancial corporations are said to be exercised with between 3.9 and 11 percent of the stock.   Earlier this year the management of TWA was said to believe that effective con-

[2] Jerome C. Darnell, "Chain Banking," *National Banking Review, 3*, 307, 308 (March 1966).

[3] U.S. Congress, Senate Committee on Banking and Currency, 73d Cong., 1st sess. (1933).   *Hearings on Stock Exchange Practices*, pt. 2, pp. 397–98.

[4] Robert J. Larner, "Ownership and Control in the 200 Largest Nonfinancial Corporations, 1929 and 1963," *American Economic Review, 56* (September 1966), 777, 779–80.   For further discussion on this point see Samuelson, *Economics* (New York: McGraw-Hill [4th ed., 1958]), p. 92, and Gordon, *Business Leadership in the Large Corporation* (Berkeley and Los Angeles: University of California Press, 1961), p. 23 ff.

trol could be accomplished with as little as 10 percent of TWA stock.[5]

The Securities and Exchange Commission, in a study several years ago, used the following breakdown in describing "control interests" in publicly owned corporations: (1) Majority control—over 50 percent interest; (2) working control—10 to 50 percent interest; and (3) working interest—1 to 10 percent interest.[6]

In practical terms, it is clear that control of a small percent, even 1 or 2 percent, of stock in a publicly held corporation can gain tremendous influence over a company's policies and operations. This is true for a number of reasons, among them the following: (1) When a corporation has thousands of shareholders almost all holding a small number of shares, a holder of even 1 percent of the shares may be by far one of the largest shareholders. (2) Many very small holdings are voted almost routinely and automatically for management for one reason or another. Therefore, management, who are "employees" of the shareowners, will be more apt to listen to and cater to the interests of the few larger more alert holders of shares than to very small shareowners, even though the former control only 1 or 2 percent each of the outstanding shares. (3) Many institutional shareholders, such as some pension funds, mutual funds and others, do not as a matter of policy vote shares held by them. This increases the voting power proportionately of those who do vote their shares, particularly those who have large blocks of stock. (4) Because the controllers of large blocks of stock representing a small percentage of the shares outstanding have influence and control over a corporation far beyond the proportion of shares held, they are often able to put representatives on the boards of directors of these companies. This is especially true where cumulative voting arrangements exist whereby the number of votes equals the number of shares held times the number of directors up for election. In such cases 1- or 2-percent stockholders have an excellent chance of electing one or more members to the board of the corporation in which they hold stock.

How, in practice, would this influence and control over a corporation by groups holding a small percentage of the shares work? First of all, most large banks are publicly owned with

[5] *Business Week* (April 16, 1966), p. 145.

[6] U.S. Congress, House of Representatives, Committee on Interstate and Foreign Commerce, *A Study of Mutual Funds* (Washington, D.C., Aug. 28, 1962), p. 399.

several thousand stockholders each. A recent list of the 36 largest commercial banks in the United States shows that the number of shareholders ranges from 2,400 to 200,000 shareholders. Twenty-five of these thirty-six commercial banks had more than 8,000 shareholders each.[7]

Looking at a specific example, the average number of shares held by each stockholder in a large midwestern bank is 367 shares. This represents only 0.009 percent of the number of shares outstanding in this bank. Therefore, an entity controlling only 1 percent of the shares in this bank has more than 100 times as many shares as the average stockholder. Obviously, management will pay a great deal more attention to someone who controls 100 times more stock than the average shareholder than he will to the average stockholder. The above example is not untypical of the pattern of stockownership among large commercial banks.

[A] very large percentage of the 300 largest commercial banks in the United States have other banks, as well as other competitor financial institutions, such as insurance companies and mutual savings banks, holding much more than 1 percent of their shares.

[T]he individual percentages of bank stock held by the 3 categories of financial institutions reported on in 275 of the 300 largest commercial banks in the United States . . . range from 0.01 to 71.92 percent. One hundred and ninety-nine of these 275 banks, or 72.4 percent, have 5 percent or more of their shares held by the financial institutions reporting; 149 banks, or 54.18 percent, have 10 percent or more of their shares held by the financial institutions reporting; and 65 banks, or 23.6 percent have 25 percent or more of their shares held by these financial institutions. Nine of these banks have over 50 percent of their shares held by the financial institutions reporting.

In the very important area of voting rights, the percentage of the total number of outstanding shares over which financial institutions have these voting rights is also quite significant. In the case of these 275 large banks, 130, or 47.3 percent, had 5 percent or more of their shares that could be voted exclusively by the financial institutions reporting. In the case of 83 banks, or 30.36 percent of the total, 10 percent or more of the shares outstanding could be voted exclusively by these financial institutions. And in the case of 23 banks, 20 percent or more of the shares outstanding could be voted exclusively by financial institutions.

[7] *News Front Magazine*, 10, p. 47, December 1966.

The holdings of commercial bank stock by commercial banks alone reveal a similarly heavy involvement.   The data reveal that 182 of the 275 major banks reported on, or 66.2 percent, have 5 percent or more of their shares held by commercial banks. Almost half (49.4 percent) of these 275 banks, 136 to be exact, have 10 percent or more of their shares held by commercial banks. And 44 of these banks, or 16 percent, have at least 25 percent of their shares held by commercial banks.

A significant number of these 275 major banks also appear to have large blocks of stock that can be voted exclusively by commercial banks.   Eighty-two banks, or 29.8 percent of the total, have 5 percent or more of their shares that can be voted solely by commercial banks, and 33 of these banks have at least 10 percent of their shares that can be voted exclusively by commercial banks. If the percentage over which commercial banks have partial voting control is considered along with that over which they have sole voting rights, the figures would be much larger still. . . .

To take one geographic area as an example, let us look at the situation in New York City.   No one could argue that these banks are not in the same market area and therefore are competing directly with each other.   And yet the percentage of shares that these banks hold and vote in their competitors' banks is very significant, especially when we consider that these stocks are widely held. . . .

Can these banks be expected to compete vigorously and effectively with this kind of stockholder interest in their competitor? And can we expect insurance companies to compete vigorously with these banks when insurance companies not only hold and vote large blocks of stock in these banks, such as the 213,335 shares, or 1.7 percent, that the Continental Insurance Co. of New York owns and votes in Manufacturers Hanover Trust Co., but also when the chairman of the board of the same insurance company sits on the board of directors of the Manufacturers Hanover Trust Co.?

Likewise, can we expect the Atlantic Mutual Insurance Co. of New York and the State Mutual Life Assurance Co. of America to compete vigorously with the Bank of New York for mortgage loans or savings when they own and vote 18,750 shares, or 2.5 percent, and 2,814 shares or 0.4 percent, respectively, of Bank of New York stock and they have high officials sitting on the board of directors of the Bank of New York?

These are but a few scattered examples of a very widespread

practice of stockownership and corporate interlock between supposedly competing financial institutions.   At some later point a
detailed breakdown by standard metropolitan area should be
carried out to determine in detail the extent of such ties in each
market area.   However, it can be said with certainty at this point
that such practices appear to be extremely widespread and present
serious problems concerning the true competitive situation among
financial institutions.

This initial look at the data collected in the subcommittee's
survey of commercial bank stockownership and control has been
designed to spotlight some of the highlights of the extremely
voluminous information obtained from financial institutions over
the last 8 months.   Because of the size and scope of the survey,
it was felt that the findings should be presented as they are developed rather than delay until all analysis is completed.

So far we have presented data and discussed the practice of
ownership and control by commercial banks of their own stock.
We have also examined at length the ownership and control of
commercial bank stock by financial institutions in general and
the problems attendant with such practices.

A preliminary examination of other information collected
indicates the serious need for future detailed examination of the
following areas:

(1) *The bank holding company problem.*   It appears that
there is a widespread practice of control of a large chain of
banks by one legal entity with stockholdings in each bank
amounting to something slightly under 25 percent of the
shares of each bank.   Under the Bank Holding Company
Act, a company is not required to register as a bank holding
company unless it owns 25 percent or more of the shares of
two or more banks.   In many situations it is relatively easy
to control a bank or any other corporation with far less than
a 25 percent stockholding.   Detailed data as to how widespread this practice is should be developed so that Congress
may consider the merits of amending the Bank Holding
Company Act.

(2) *The satellite bank problem.*   A large number of big banks
appear to have substantial stockholdings and voting authority
over stock of smaller banks in their general geographic area.
A detailed study of this situation done on the basis of a standard metropolitan area breakdown would yield important data,

hitherto unavailable, on the degree of indirect control large banks may exercise over smaller and perhaps competing banks. This may indicate far greater concentration in banking in a particular area than was previously thought to exist.

(3) *Use of employee profit-sharing plans to control bank stock.* Some banks appear to be using their employee profit-sharing plan funds to invest heavily in stock of their own bank and in stock of competitor banks. This could be used to further control the voting of the bank's own shares and to influence the operations of competitors through the ownership of stock in these banks. The exact extent to which this practice is used should be determined.

(4) *Relationship of interlocking stockholdings to interlocking corporate management.* There appears to be some relationship between the representation on the boards of directors of some commercial banks of officers and directors of insurance companies and mutual savings banks, and the size of the stockholdings in these same banks by the same mutual savings banks and insurance companies. Since these financial institutions are competing with one another, the extent of this practice would be significant in determining whether there is a relationship between these institutions which might significantly impede competition.

(5) *Financial institutions control of large blocks of nonfinancial corporation stock.* Since the holding of commercial bank stock seems to be so widespread and substantial among various types of financial institutions, [there should be an examination] of to what extent similarly large stockholdings in nonfinancial corporations are held by commercial banks and other financial institutions. It is a well-known fact that officers and directors of financial institutions are heavily represented on the boards of directors of hundreds of this country's leading industrial corporations. To what extent is this representation backed up by substantial voting power wielded by representatives of financial institutions on behalf of these institutions? In the case of commercial bank representatives, this would be done in almost all cases with stock in which the bank has no true investment. If the same financial institutions had substantial voting power and board representation in several competitors in the same industry, this situation could seriously affect the competitiveness of the industry. There is also the question of preferential loan

treatment for corporations on whose boards representatives of financial institutions sit. The prevalence of such a situation should be examined.

(6) *Interlocking stockholders by beneficial owners of bank stock.* From data received, there appear to be situations where the beneficial owners of large blocks of commercial bank stock are in fact holdings by a few families who have management connections with competitor banks in the same geographic area. Thus, the immediate family of an executive officer of one leading bank in a large community appears to control a substantial block of stock in its major competitor. Similarly, families of directors of one bank are large stockholders of major competitor banks. A detailed examination of the beneficial ownership of stock on a selective basis should be undertaken to uncover serious anticompetitive arrangements among the stockholders of competing commercial banks.

(7) *Continuing data on bank stock ownership and control by financial institutions.* The data presented in this study provides the first detailed information on the ownership and control of commercial bank stock ever compiled. Therefore, while this initial study cannot provide evidence of a trend over the years toward greater concentration of bank stockholdings in the hands of commercial banks, insurance companies, and mutual savings banks, this study can provide a benchmark for future studies. Serious consideration should be given to having such a survey done on a regular basis every few years to see if there is in fact a trend toward ever-increasing concentration of control among financial institutions of commercial bank stock.

The stockholding arrangements of commercial bank shares are extremely complex. The interlocking nature of these holdings is apparent. While this report is an effort to get at the heart of two major problems in this area, a serious effort should be made to examine in detail the data as they relate to the other questions raised above. Nevertheless, it can be stated at this point with some confidence that a serious examination into the need for a complete review and overhaul of existing laws and regulations in this area is in order.

6

BANKS AS THE DOMINANT INSTITUTIONAL INVESTOR

The Patman Committee

The trend of the last 30 to 40 years toward a separation of owner-ship from control because of the fragmentation of stock ownership has been radically changed toward a concentration of voting power in the hands of a relatively few financial institutions, while the fragmentation in the distribution of cash payments has been continued.

This new trend can be demonstrated statistically by examining the list of the 200 largest industrial companies in the United States studied initially by Berle and Means and up-dated by Robert J. Larner as of 1963 in a paper published in the *American Economic Review*.[1] Larner's conclusion, using criteria similar to Berle and Means, and data available from public documents such as corpo-ration proxy statements, and information filed with the various regulatory agencies such as the Interstate Commerce Commission, the Civil Aeronautics Board, Federal Power Commission and the Securities and Exchange Commission, was that the trend toward management control described by Berle and Means in 1932 had indeed continued unabated to the present day. Mr. Larner con-

Reprinted from the Patman Committee Staff Report for the Domestic Finance Subcommittee of the House Committee on Banking and Currency, 90th Cong., 2nd sess. *Commercial Banks and their Trust Activities: Emerging Influence on the American Economy* (Washington, D.C.: U.S. Government Printing Office, July 1968), pp. 13–16. Footnotes have been renumbered.

[1] Larner, "Ownership and Control in the 200 Largest Nonfinancial Corpora-tions, 1929 and 1963," *American Economic Review*, 56, 777 (September 1966).

cludes that over the 34-year period between 1929 and 1963, there
has been a significant movement toward management control of
the 200 largest nonfinancial corporations. Whereas Berle and
Means determined that in 1929, 44 percent of the 200 largest nonfinancial corporations were then management controlled, by 1963
the percentage had almost doubled to 84 percent.

When the Domestic Finance Subcommittee data are examined
in connection with the same group of companies, a different pattern
emerges. This emerging situation might be referred to as that
involving bank minority control. Thus, we see evidence of a
reversed pattern of control whereby large blocks of stock in the
largest nonfinancial corporations in the country are becoming
controlled by some of the largest financial corporations in the
country. This trend is shifting economic power back to a small
group, repeating in a somewhat different manner the pattern of
the trusts of the late nineteenth and early twentieth centuries.
Larner himself admits that lack of available data may have caused
mistaken classifications in his study.

Comparing Larner's list of the 200 largest nonfinancial corporations with the data collected by the Subcommittee, examples of
36 corporations which Larner has classified as management controlled but which could be considered as either bank minority
controlled or trending in that direction can be mentioned. These
36 major U.S. corporations are listed below with the names of
banks having the stated stock and director interlocks listed below
each company.[2]

American Airlines, Inc.
    Morgan Guaranty Trust Co.—7.5 percent common—1 direc-
        tor.
    Old Colony Trust—1 director.
    Cleveland Trust Co.—1 director.
    Continental Illinois National Bank & Trust—1 director.
    Detroit Bank & Trust—1 director.
American Smelting & Refining Co.
    Morgan Guaranty Trust Co.—15.5 percent common—1 direc-
        tor.
    Chase Manhattan Bank—1 director.
    Manufacturers Hanover Trust Co.—2 directors.
Boeing Co.

    [2] Where preferred issues are shown, they may be of different classes of pre-
ferred stock.

Chase Manhattan Bank—8.7 percent common.
First National City Bank—1 director.
Morgan Guaranty Trust Co.—1 director.
Burlington Industries, Inc.
Morgan Guaranty Trust Co.—14.5 percent common.
Chase Manhattan Bank—1 director.
Celanese Corp. of America.
Morgan Guaranty Trust Co.—7.5 percent common—5.9 percent preferred.
First National City Bank—5.6 percent preferred.
Chase Manhattan Bank—1 director.
Bankers Trust Co.—1 director.
Chicago & Northwestern Railway Co.
State Street Bank & Trust—13.8 percent common.
First National Bank of Chicago—2 directors.
Chicago, Rock Island & Pacific Railroad Co.
First National Bank of Chicago—69.7 percent common.
Continental Illinois National Bank & Trust—1 director.
Crown Zellerbach Corp.
Bankers Trust Co.—5.1 percent common—1 director.
Fidelity Bank—5.9 percent common.
Girard Trust Co.—7.4 percent preferred.
Duquesne Light Co.
Girard Trust Co.—11.3 percent preferred—7.9 percent preferred.
Mellon National Bank & Trust—2 directors.
Federated Department Stores, Inc.
First National Bank of Chicago—10.2 percent common.
Chase Manhattan Bank—1 director.
Central Trust Co., Cincinnati—2 directors.
Florida Power & Light Co.
Morgan Guaranty Trust Co.—10 percent preferred—5.3 percent preferred.
Manufacturers Hanover Trust—1 director.
General Dynamics Corp.
Bankers Trust Co.—6.2 percent common.
Morgan Guaranty Trust Co.—1 director.
Chemical Bank New York Co.—1 director.
Girard Trust Co.—1 director.
Honeywell, Inc.
Bankers Trust Co.—7.5 percent common—8.2 percent preferred.

State Street Bank & Trust—1 director.
Northern Trust Co., Chicago—1 director.
Illinois Central Railroad Co. (Illinois Central Industries, Inc.).
　　Continental Illinois National Bank & Trust—9.5 percent
　　　　common—1 director.
　　Harris Trust & Savings—1 director.
International Paper Co.
　　Girard Trust Co.—6.4 percent preferred.
　　Bankers Trust Co.—25.5 percent preferred—2 directors.
　　First National Bank, Boston—1 director.
　　State Street Bank & Trust—1 director.
　　Northern Trust Co., Chicago—1 director.
　　Chase Manhattan Bank—1 director.
International Telephone & Telegraph Corp.
　　National Bank of Detroit—5.9 percent preferred.
　　Chemical Bank New York Trust Co.—7 percent preferred.
　　National Shawmut Bank—1 director.
　　Chase Manhattan Bank—1 director.
　　First National City Bank—1 director.
Jones & Laughlin Steel Corp.
　　Mellon National Bank—6.9 percent common—2 directors.
　　Cleveland Trust Co.—1 director.
　　National City Bank, Cleveland—2 directors.
　　Pittsburgh National Bank—1 director.
Kennecott Copper Corp.
　　Morgan Guaranty Trust Co.—17.5 percent common.
　　First National City Bank—2 directors.
Kroger Co.
　　Central Trust Co., Cincinnati—6 percent common—1 director.
　　Fifth Third Union Trust Co.—1 director.
Long Island Lighting Co.
　　Morgan Guaranty Trust Co.—5.8 percent common.
　　First National City Bank—8.2 percent preferred—1 director.
　　Bankers Trust Co.—1 director.
National Distillers & Chemical Corp.
　　First National City Bank—12.4 percent preferred—16.4 per-
　　　　cent preferred—1 director.
　　Girard Trust Co.—8.2 percent preferred.
　　Chemical Bank New York Trust—2 directors.
National Steel Corp.
　　Pittsburgh National Bank—8.3 percent common—3 directors.
　　Chase Manhattan Bank—6.2 percent common.

Mellon National Bank—6.6 percent common.
National City Bank, Cleveland—1 director.
National Bank of Detroit—2 directors.
Manufacturers National Bank, Detroit—1 director.
Detroit Bank & Trust—1 director.
Chemical Bank New York Trust Co.—1 director.

Pacific Lighting Corp.
Mellon National Bank—5.2 percent preferred—5.6 percent preferred.

Pan American World Airways.
Chase Manhattan Bank—6.7 percent common.
First National Bank, Boston—1 director.
Cleveland Trust Co.—1 director.
First National City Bank—1 director.

Panhandle Eastern Pipeline Co.
Chase Manhattan Bank—5.6 percent common.
Morgan Guaranty Trust Co.—5.8 percent common.
First National City Bank—9.5 percent preferred.

J. C. Penney Co.
Chase Manhattan Bank—5.1 percent common.
First National City Bank—2 directors.

Pennsylvania Power & Light Co.
Girard Trust Co.—10.7 percent preferred—14.4 percent preferred—5.7 percent preferred.
Fidelity Bank, Philadelphia—8.8 percent preferred.
Mellon National Bank & Trust—1 director.

Philadelphia Electric Co.
Fidelity Bank, Philadelphia—5.6 percent common—10.9 percent preferred—12.2 percent preferred—1 director.
Provident National Bank, Philadelphia—5.6 percent common—1 director.
Girard Trust Co.—5.9 percent common—11.1 percent preferred—5.4 percent preferred—8.4 percent preferred—9.1 percent preferred—3 directors.
First Pennsylvania Bank & Trust—2 directors.
Philadelphia National Bank—2 directors.

R. J. Reynolds Tobacco Co.
Mercantile Safe Deposit, Baltimore—4.9 percent common—2 percent preferred.
Chase Manhattan Bank—1 director.

Southern California Edison Co.
National Shawmut Bank, Boston—6 percent preferred.

First National City Bank—8.2 percent preferred.
Sperry Rand Corp.
    Chase Manhattan Bank—5.1 percent common.
    First National Bank, Boston—1 director.
Standard Oil Co. of Ohio.
    National City Bank, Cleveland—6.1 percent common—31
       percent preferred—3 directors.
    Central National Bank, Cleveland—2 directors.
Trans World Airlines, Inc.
    State Street Bank & Trust—6.2 percent common.
    Chase Manhattan Bank—7.8 percent common.
    Morgan Guaranty Trust—7.4 percent common.
    Continental Illinois National Bank & Trust—1 director.
    First National Bank, Chicago—1 director.
    Manufacturers Hanover Trust Co.—1 director.
United Aircraft Corp.
    Chase Manhattan Bank—6.2 percent common—1 director.
    First National City Bank—2 directors.
    Hartford National Bank—4 directors.
    Connecticut Bank & Trust—1 director.
United Airlines, Inc.
    State Street Bank & Trust—6.8 percent common.
    Morgan Guaranty Trust Co.—8.2 percent common.
    First National City Bank—7.4 percent preferred.
    Continental Illinois National Bank & Trust—1 director.
    Society National Bank, Cleveland—1 director.
Westinghouse Electric Corp.
    First National City Bank—6.6 percent preferred—1 director.
    Union National Bank, Pittsburgh—6.6 percent preferred—
       1 director.
    Mellon National Bank—2 directors.
    Pittsburgh National Bank—1 director.
    First National Bank, Baltimore—1 director.
    Harris Trust & Savings—1 director.
    National City Bank, Cleveland—1 director.

In addition, a number of corporations within Larner's list of 200 largest nonfinancial corporations which he has classified as minority controlled by individuals or other nonfinancial corporations, may actually be controlled either by banks, through minority holdings, or jointly by bank and nonbanking interests. Such companies as the following 10 could fall in this category:

Aluminum Corp. of America.
    Mellon National Bank—25.3 percent common—15 percent
        preferred—3 directors.
    Union National Bank, Pittsburgh—7.7 percent preferred.
American Metal Climax, Inc.
    Morgan Guaranty Trust Co.—8.7 percent common.
    Manufacturers Hanover Trust Co.—1 director.
Atlantic Coast Line Co. (controlled Atlantic Coast Line RR. before
    recent merger with Seaboard Airline RR.)
    Mercantile-Safe Deposit & Trust, Baltimore—54.4 percent
        common—5 directors.
Deere & Co.
    Morgan Guaranty Trust Co.—8.0 percent common.
    Continental Illinois National Bank—1 director.
W. R. Grace Co.
    First National City Bank—3 directors.
    Manufacturers Hanover Trust—1 director.
Gulf Oil Corp.
    Mellon National Bank & Trust—17.1 percent common—
        4 directors.
Kaiser Aluminum & Chemical Corp.
    Morgan Guaranty Trust Co.—6.6 percent common—5.7
        percent preferred.
    First National City Bank—7.6 percent preferred.
Louisville & Nashville Railroad Co.
    Mercantile Safe Deposit, Baltimore—33.9 percent common—
        2 directors.
    Chemical Bank New York Trust—1 director.
Olin Mathieson Chemical Corp.
    Morgan Guaranty Trust Co.—6.8 percent common.
    Maryland National Bank—1 director.
Reynolds Metals Co.
    Chase Manhattan Bank—5.5 percent common.
    First National City Bank—7.5 percent preferred.
    Manufacturers Hanover Trust Co.—1 director.

The above lists of major industrial corporations with which
commercial banks have substantial connections total 46, just under
25 percent of the total in the Larner study.   The bank ties revealed
here and elsewhere in this study may require a substantial revision
of the discussion of control patterns among the leading nonfinancial
corporations in the United States.

7

INVESTMENTS AND INTERLOCKS BETWEEN MAJOR BANKS AND MAJOR CORPORATIONS

The Patman Committee

[N]ationwide, commercial banks are today the most important single institutional investor group and are likely to maintain this position indefinitely. Some of the consequences of this position in the economy have already been discussed in general terms. It is also clear from the previous discussion that concentration in the bank trust business is extremely high and far greater than in commercial banking in general. Having looked at the overall national picture, it is appropriate now to consider these and related problems in more detail as they relate to data obtained from the 49 banks in the 10 cities chosen for detailed study.[1] These 49 banks were asked to submit information on various aspects of

Reprinted from the Patman Committee Staff Report for the Domestic Finance Subcommittee of the House Committee on Banking and Currency, 90th Cong., 2nd sess. *Commercial Banks and their Trust Activities: Emerging Influence on the American Economy* (Washington, D.C.: U.S. Government Printing Office, July 1968), pp. 83, 88–92. Footnotes have been renumbered.

[1] The 10 cities are Baltimore, Boston, Cincinnati, Chicago, Cleveland, Detroit, Hartford, New York City, Philadelphia, and Pittsburgh. In seven cities the five largest banks by deposit size were chosen, while in New York the six largest banks were used. In Cincinnati and Detroit four banks were surveyed.

their trust department and other operations. The survey was conducted by having each bank compete four schedules. Schedule A requested information on trust department assets, both as to total amount and a breakdown by types of assets. Schedule B requested information on interlocks between banks and other types of businesses through the officers and directors of the banks. Schedule C requested information on the investments and administration of foundations, profit sharing plans and employee benefit plans managed by each bank, and Schedule D requested details on the overall stockholdings of trust departments, including voting rights, by corporation in which each trust department held 5 percent or more of a single class of stock.*

The Subcommittee obtained replies from all 49 banks surveyed. Two of the banks reported that they had no trust assets at all. The amount of total trust assets held by the remaining 47 banks range from $16.8 billion held by the Morgan Guaranty Trust Co. of New York City down to $10,175,000 in trust assets held by the Peoples Union Bank and Trust Co. of Pittsburgh, Pa.

In comparing the coverage in this detailed survey with the overall trust department survey of 2,890 banks, . . . we find that these 49 banks hold $135.2 billion in trust assets, or 54.03 percent of all the trust assets in the nationwide survey. Just 30 of the largest banks in the Subcommittee's 49-bank survey hold 51.73 percent of all trust assets in the nationwide survey. Therefore, the coverage obtained by studying in detail the submissions of 49 banks in 10 cities would seem adequate to develop a picture of bank trust department financial activities in general.

Table 1 lists the banks in the Subcommittee's 49-bank survey, in rank order, by amount of total trust department assets, with the percentage of all bank trust assets in the country held by each bank. Cumulative percentages for the banks as a percentage of the total bank trust assets nationally are also shown.

In terms of percentage of total trust assets in each of the 10 Standard Metropolitan Areas studied, the banks surveyed hold in the aggregate between 79.2 percent and 99.9 percent of the total bank trust assets in each respective metropolitan area. In 7 of the 10 cities, the banks studied hold over 90 percent of all bank trust assets in the area. . . .

One of the most significant gauges as to the overall influence of banks over the economy of the United States is their formal

* *Reproductions of these four schedules are printed in the original report, pp. 84–87.*—M.Z.

Table 1. Trust Department Assets of 49 Banks Surveyed, Listed in Order of Asset Holdings and Percent of Total Bank Trust Assets in FDIC Survey

Forty-nine bank survey rank	FDIC survey rank	Bank name	City	Amount (in thousands)	Percent of all bank trust assets	Cumulative percentage
1	1	Morgan Guaranty Trust Co.	New York	$16,824,731	6.73%	—
2	2	Chase Manhattan Bank	New York	13,644,056	5.45	12.18%
3	3	Bankers Trust Co.	New York	11,090,765	4.43	16.61
4	4	First National City Bank	New York	10,871,500	4.35	20.96
5	6	Mellon National Bank & Trust	Pittsburgh	7,629,595	3.05	24.01
6	7	Manufacturers Hanover Trust Co.	New York	7,337,657	2.93	26.94
7	9	First National Bank of Chicago	Chicago	5,430,293	2.17	29.11
8	10	Continental Illinois National Bank	Chicago	5,137,319	2.05	31.16
9	11	Chemical Bank New York Trust Co.	New York	4,593,253	1.84	33.00
10	12	Northern Trust Co.	Chicago	4,542,230	1.82	34.82
11	13	Old Colony Trust Co.	Boston	4,224,973	1.69	36.51
12	14	Harris Trust & Savings Bank	Chicago	3,669,072	1.55	38.06
13	16	Cleveland Trust Co.	Cleveland	3,605,442	1.44	39.50
14	17	National Bank of Detroit	Detroit	3,427,431	1.37	40.87
15	19	Girard Trust Bank	Philadelphia	2,930,613	1.17	42.04
16	20	First Pennsylvania Banking & Trust	Philadelphia	2,686,917	1.07	43.11
17	21	Mercantile-Safe Deposit & Trust	Baltimore	2,309,354	.92	44.03
18	24	Fidelity Bank	Philadelphia	2,014,975	.81	44.84
19	26	Pittsburgh National Bank	Pittsburgh	1,894,917	.76	45.60
20	27	Detroit Bank & Trust Co.	Detroit	1,752,773	.70	46.30
21	29	Provident National Bank	Philadelphia	1,676,209	.67	46.97
22	31	Connecticut Bank & Trust Co.	Hartford	1,622,488	.65	47.62
23	35	State Street Bank & Trust Co.	Boston	1,583,392	.63	48.25

24	39	New England Merchants National Bank	Boston	1,483,374	.59	48.84
25	41	National City Bank of Cleveland	Cleveland	1,463,474	.58	49.42
26	42	Hartford National Bank & Trust Co.	Hartford	1,435,339	.57	49.99
27	43	First National Bank of Boston	Boston	1,335,965	.53	50.52
28	45	Manufacturers National Bank of Detroit	Detroit	1,282,614	.51	51.03
29	51	Central Trust Co.	Cincinnati	923,994	.37	51.40
30	55	Union National Bank of Pittsburgh	Pittsburgh	830,954	.33	51.73
31	56	Fifth Third Union Trust Co.	Cincinnati	772,816	.31	52.04
32	58	Central National Bank of Cleveland	Cleveland	743,262	.30	52.34
33	65	First National Bank of Cincinnati	Cincinnati	645,327	.26	52.60
34	71	American National Bank & Trust Co.	Chicago	603,106	.24	52.84
35	75	Philadelphia National Bank	Philadelphia	574,108	.23	53.07
36	80	Equitable Trust Company	Baltimore	504,701	.20	53.27
37	82	Maryland National Bank	Baltimore	492,140	.20	53.47
38	89	National Shawmut Bank of Boston	Boston	446,914	.18	53.65
39	142	First National Bank of Maryland	Baltimore	192,483	.08	53.73
40	160	Union Commerce Bank	Cleveland	158,943	.06	53.79
41	178	United Bank & Trust Co.	Hartford	140,218	.06	53.85
42	188	Union Trust Co. of Maryland	Baltimore	133,361	.05	53.90
43	200	Provident Bank	Cincinnati	121,500	.05	53.95
44	207	Western Pennsylvania National Bank	Pittsburgh	116,018	.05	54.00
45	352	Society National Bank of Cleveland	Cleveland	47,927	.02	54.02
46	731	Simsbury Bank & Trust Co.	Hartford	12,612	.01	54.03
47	—	Peoples Union Bank & Trust Co.[b]	Pittsburgh	10,175[a]	.00	—
48	—	Northern Connecticut National Bank[b]	Windsor Locks.	—	—	—
49	—	Michigan Bank N. A.[b]	Detroit	—	—	—

[a] Figure as reported from schedule A of Subcommittee survey.
[b] Reported no trust assets to Subcommittee or FDIC.

interrelationships with the largest corporations in the country.   In order to determine the extent of these ties, this study compared the interlocking directorships and stockholdings of 5 percent or more of any one class of stock of a corporation provided by each bank with *The Fortune Directory* of 500 Largest U.S. Industrial Corporations.   The same was done for *Fortune's* list of 50 largest merchandising, transportation, life insurance and utility companies.[2]

To give some idea of the significance of these largest U.S. corporations, *Fortune's* list of 500 largest industrial corporations employed 12.3 million persons during 1966.   This figure represents 64.4 percent of all U.S. industrial employment during that year.   These 500 largest industrial corporations made 59.7 percent of the sales of all industrial companies in the United States during 1966 and accounted for 70.5 percent of all industrial profits during that year.   Therefore, it is clear that these major industrial companies represent a very significant portion, roughly two-thirds, of all American industrial business.   Although no comparable breakdown is available for the merchandising, life insurance, utilities and transportation groups, it is reasonable to assume that the 50 companies in each group on the *Fortune* list represent a very substantial portion of each industry.

MAJOR U.S. CORPORATIONS WITH 5 PERCENT OR MORE OF STOCK HELD BY BANKS SURVEYED

The number of industrial companies in the *Fortune* 500 largest industrial list having 5 percent or more of their common stock held by one or more of the 49 banks in the Subcommittee survey is 147. This represents 29.4 percent of the 500 companies in the list.   In addition, there are 17 merchandising companies and 17 transportation companies out of 50 largest in each category that also have one or more of the surveyed banks holding 5 percent or more of their common stock.

The number of separate cases where a survey bank holds 5 percent or more of the common stock of these major U.S. corporations is greater than the number of companies in which 5 percent or more is held.   This results from situations where more than one

[2] The Subcommittee decided to limit the survey to 5 percent or more holding of any class of stock, although effective control need not require control of a 5-percent holding, especially in very large corporations whose stock is widely held.

bank holds 5 percent or more of the stock of the same corporation. Among the 500 largest industrials there are 176 separate situations where the surveyed banks hold 5 percent or more of the common stock of a corporation.   There are 20 situations among the 50 largest merchandising companies and 23 situations among the 50 largest transportation companies in which the surveyed banks hold 5 percent or more of the common stock of a corporation.

INTERLOCKING DIRECTORSHIPS BETWEEN BANKS SURVEYED AND MAJOR U.S. CORPORATIONS

Interlocking directorships between the 49 banks surveyed and *Fortune's* list of 500 largest industrials, as well as between these banks and the 50 largest merchandising, life insurance, utilities and transportation companies is quite prevalent.   These 49 banks hold a total of 768 interlocking directorships with 286 of *Fortune's* 500 largest industrial corporations.   Thus, representation by these 49 banks on well over half of the list exists.   This is an average of almost 3 directorships for each corporation board on which representation is achieved.

Among the 50 largest transportation companies these banks hold 73 interlocking directorships with 27 companies, again almost 3 per company.   Within the 50 largest utilities group these banks hold 86 directorships in 22 companies, an average of almost 4 per company.   And, in the life insurance companies, which are in direct competition with commercial banks in several respects, these 49 banks hold 146 interlocking directorships with 29 of the 50 largest life insurance companies.   This is an average of 5 directorships per insurance company on whose boards these banks are represented.   A summary of this breakdown appears in Table 2.

It is interesting to note that 66 of the companies shown in the *Fortune* lists of 500 largest industrials and 50 largest merchandising, insurance, transportation and utilities have both more than 5 percent of their common stock held by one of the surveyed banks and one or more interlocking directorships with that same bank. This may be an indication that there is in many cases a direct relationship between a bank's holding a large block of stock and holding seats on the board of the corporation.

The above discussion includes only situations in which holdings of common stock are involved.   There are in addition a number of cases of large percentages of preferred stock being held

Table 2. Interlocking Directorships Between 49 Banks Surveyed and *Fortune* Directory of Largest U.S. Corporations

Fortune lists	Total number of company interlocks	Total number of director interlocks
500 largest industrials	286	768
50 largest merchandising	26	64
50 largest transportation	27	73
50 largest life insurance	29	146
50 largest utilities	22	86

by banks along with an interlocking directorship relationship with a single bank.*

* *The original report contains tables which "set forth in detail the stockholdings, interlocking directorate and pension fund management relationships between the 49 banks surveyed and those companies with the* Fortune *lists of 500 largest industrials and 50 largest merchandising, insurance, utilities and transportation companies in the United States. Also included are the voting rights that these banks have in the stock held."*—M.Z.

IT HAS BEEN WIDELY ACCEPTED THAT OWNERSHIP AND CONTROL OF *the large corporations have become separated, and that these corporations are now run by organization men beholden only to themselves. From Sheehan's investigation of data available to* Fortune Magazine, *however, he concludes that the evidence does not support this thesis. In 150 companies on the 1967* Fortune *list of the 500 largest industrial corporations, controlling ownership rests in the hands of an individual or the members of a single family—many of them new owners rather than descendants of nineteenth-century wealth. Sheehan uses the term "control" very conservatively to mean ownership of at least 10 percent of the company's voting stock—in contrast to the 5 percent criterion accepted by the Patman Committee.*

The list does not include companies in which coalitions assure working control nor does it include ones in which businessmen are known to wield great influence with holdings of less than 10 percent. For instance, Richard K. Mellon himself is the largest stockholder in Alcoa (2.98 percent) and in Gulf Oil (1.78 percent), owns .084 percent of GM, and is the second largest stockholder among the directors. But the only Mellon family company actually included on the list is Carborundum, in which Paul Mellon owns 11 percent of the shares.

Dispersion of stock tends to increase with company size. At least ten family-controlled companies rank among the top 100—the largest of which is Ford Motor, followed by E. I. Dupont de Nemours & Company. Twenty-three proprietary companies are in the 101 to 200 class; 39 in 201 to 300; 38 in 301 to 400; and 37 in the 401 to 500 class. There is a legitimate question concerning who has the power and what effect the alleged separation of ownership from control has on the conduct of the large corporations. However, the present evidence suggests that the demise of the traditional American proprietor has been exaggerated. Sheehan believes that the difference in actual business practice between so called management-controlled and proprietary companies is minor, a view supported by Larner's study in this volume.

8

PROPRIETORS IN THE WORLD OF BIG BUSINESS

Robert Sheehan

Who owns the 500 largest industrial corporations in the U.S., and—more to the point—who controls them? After more than two generations during which ownership has been increasingly divorced from control, it is frequently assumed that all large U.S. corporations are owned by everybody and nobody, and are run and ruled by bland organization men. The individual entrepreneur or family that holds onto the controlling interest and actively manages the affairs of a big company is regarded as a rare exception, as something of an anachronism. But a close look at the 500 largest industrial corporations does not substantiate such sweeping generalizations.

In approximately 150 companies on the current 500 list, controlling ownership rests in the hands of an individual or the members of a single family. Significantly, these owners are not just the remnants of the nineteenth-century dynasties that once ruled American business. Many of them are relatively fresh faces. In any event, the evidence that 30 percent of the 500 largest industrials are clearly controlled by identifiable individuals, or by family groups, is something to ponder. It suggests that the demise of the traditional American proprietor has been slightly exaggerated and that the much-advertised triumph of the organization is far from total.

Reprinted from Robert Sheehan, "Proprietors in the World of Big Business," *Fortune Magazine* (June 15, 1967), pp. 179–83, 242, by special permission of Fortune Magazine. ©1967 Time Inc.

It should be pointed out that, for the purposes of this report, the term "control" is used very conservatively. The list includes companies in which the largest individual stockholder owns 10 percent or more of the voting stock, or in which the largest block of shares—representing 10 percent or more of the total votes—is held by members of a single family. No attempt has been made to include in the group any of the various coalitions that may indeed assure working control for small groups of associates in many companies; nor does the figure include some businessmen known to wield great influence with holdings of less than 10 percent. For example, certain industrial companies in which the Mellons have a powerful influence are not included. Richard K. Mellon alone is the largest stockholder in Alcoa (2.98 percent) and in Gulf Oil (1.78 percent).   He also owns .084 percent of General Motors, and ranks as the second-largest stockholder on the G.M. board of directors. However, the only Mellon entry among the 150 corporations is Carborundum Co., in which Paul Mellon directly owns 11 percent of the shares.

Understandably, the incidence of controlling ownership is least prevalent among the very largest companies; dispersion of stock tends to increase with company size. Among the top 100 industrials there is only one in which a single individual holds over 10 percent of the stock—McDonnell Aircraft, sixty-sixth in size, where Chairman James S. McDonnell owns 13 percent of the shares.   (Donald Douglas Sr. and his son owned only 0.13 percent of troubled Douglas Aircraft, which McDonnell has just taken over.)

At least ten family-controlled companies rank among the top 100, and several of these are actively owner-managed. The largest is Ford Motor. Despite the wide dissemination of its stock since it went public in 1956, it can still be characterized as proprietary. Some 435,000 stockholders own the company's 109,236,159 shares, and the number of shares owned by Henry, Benson, and William Ford and their families is now down to a modest 11 percent of the total.   But the Ford family holdings are predominantly in Class B shares, which are entitled to 3,492 votes per share.   In terms of votes, the Ford family controls 39 percent of the company.

Next in size is E. I. duPont de Nemours & Co.   President Lammont du Pont Copeland and four other family members active in the company (Emil F., Henry B., Henry F., and Irénée du Pont Jr.) together own only 0.64 percent of the shares directly.   But together with individual and corporate associates, the du Ponts own 30 percent of Christiana Securities Co., which in turn owns 20 percent of E. I. du Pont de Nemours.

In Firestone Tire & Rubber Co., thirty-first on the 500 list, the four brothers—Harvey S. Jr., Raymond C., Leonard K., and Roger S. Firestone—all officers of the company, control 15 percent of the stock.   Other family owners with a similar strong managerial role include the O'Neils of General Tire (20 percent) and the Reynolds of Reynolds Metals (17 percent).   The Donald Danforth family controls 22 percent of Ralston Purina.   Trustees for the descendants of Charles H. Deere hold 14 percent of Deere & Co. The Pitcairn family owns 26 percent of Pittsburgh Plate Glass. The Pews and their family trusts maintain 44 percent of Sun Oil. And the E. H. Stuart family, directly and through a holding company, represents 51 percent of the ownership of Carnation Co.

Further down in the 500 rankings the proprietary companies are fairly evenly distributed.   Twenty-three are in the 101 to 200 category; 39 in 201 to 300; 38 in 301 to 400; and 37 in 401 to 500. The family companies are most numerous in the food and beverage industry, where a family name on the product is thought to have a particular appeal to the public.   Thirty-one family-held corporations in this field are on the 500 list.   They include H. J. Heinz, Geo. A. Hormel, Oscar Mayer, and Anheuser-Busch.   There are 18 family-controlled companies in textiles and apparel— M. Lowenstein & Sons, Cone Mills, Phillips-Van Heusen; 14 in appliances and electronics (but none in business machines and computers); 9 companies each in publishing and printing and in metal manufacturing; and 8 in chemicals.

Approximately 70 family-named companies among the 500 are still controlled by the founding family.   But many companies bearing family names are no longer controlled by that family. There are, to mention just a few, no Campbells involved in Campbell Soup, nor Peabodys in Peabody Coal, nor Wards in Ward Foods.

The progressive divorce of ownership from control, and all it implied, was pointed out 35 years ago by Adolf A. Berle Jr. and Gardiner C. Means in their influential book, *The Modern Corporation and Private Property*.   The authors noted that ownership of major U.S. corporations was becoming so widely diffused that the individual shareholder was becoming relatively powerless.   "Control," for all practical purposes, was passing into the hands of professional managers who often owned only a small fraction of their company's stock.   A major issue raised by Berle and Means was the question of power.   Where, in the absence of the pro-prietor, does ultimate accountability rest?   As Berle has empha-sized in subsequent books, the question has become more complex in recent years with the acquisition of vast holdings of common stocks by institutions—insurance companies, pension funds, and, above all, mutual funds.

But beyond these profound questions of power and politics, it was expected that the demise of the owner-manager would markedly affect the conduct and performance of business.   Some have predicted that the new managerial class, as essentially non-owners, would lack the self-interest in maximization of profits that inspired proprietors, would be inclined to curb dividends, and would be tempted to provide themselves with disproportionately large salaries and bonuses.   In contrast, others have argued that business has been stimulated by the rise of the managers to power. Owner-managers, the theory goes, are less dynamic, are sometimes inclined to nepotism and easy living, and are disinclined to risk the reinvestment of their surpluses in daring new opportunities.

Despite these theories, it is extremely doubtful that ownership or the lack of it motivates the conduct of executives in such a direct way.   At any rate, very few executives agree that the managers of a widely held company run their business any differently from the proprietors of a closely held company.   Competition is a great leveler, and both managers and proprietors respond to its pressures with equal spirit and objectivity.   Moreover, it is unrealistic to assume that because a manager holds only a small fraction of his company's stock he lacks the incentive to drive up its profits. Chairman Frederic G. Donner, for example, owns only 0.017 percent of G.M.'s outstanding stock; but it was worth about $3,917,000 recently.   Chairman Lynn A. Townsend owns 0.117 percent of Chrysler, worth about $2,380,000.   Their interest in the earnings of those investments is hardly an impersonal one.

Even some of the proprietors themselves admit that owning large blocks of stock in a company may not be an advantage at times.   Sherman Fairchild points out that "people can attack you for self-interest.   I like to be in a position with ownership where I can say I'm the same as the other shareholders."   But other owners are convinced that controlling ownership is a real advan-tage, that it gives their companies an edge over competitors, especially in situations where they have to act quickly and boldly. The owner-manager isn't subject to the restraints of an overly cautious board.   Thomas Mellon Evans, for example, played fast and rough building up H. K. Porter, and later, capturing control of and reorganizing Crane Co., the venerable Chicago plumbing manufacturer.   At both of these companies Evans slashed payrolls, removed many high-ranking officers, and closed down unprofitable branches.   These actions invited controversy and criticism of a kind that a slick professional management might not have risked.

To handle the actual operations of his companies, now that they are doing well, Evans hires the best professional managers he can find.   This reliance on outsiders is not unusual among the proprietors.   Fairchild, for example, stays out of routine operations and draws no salary from any of his companies.   (In addition to the two corporations on the 500 list that bear his name, Fairchild controls two smaller companies—Fairchild Recording Equipment and Front Projection.)   And one active owner-manager, J. Irwin Miller of Cummins Engine, leans heavily on his president, E. Don Tull, whom he pays $165,000 a year, $40,000 more than Miller pays himself as chairman.   Miller, of course, receives a tidy quarterly supplement in the form of dividends.

Recruiting professional managers for family companies, however, is not always easy.   Outsiders wonder whether the boss's son will decide to start his business career at the top.   Practically all family companies are hypersensitive on the subject of nepotism, and their comments on it often sould a bit defensive.   Says A. E. Staley, Jr., of A. E. Staley Manufacturing Co.; "I'm anxious to have any qualified man come into this business; if he happens to be my son, I won't deny him the opportunity."   And Jim Needham, of Needham Packing Co., says "If you can do a better job than the Needhams, you'll get a better job than the Needhams." Needham seems to mean what he says: the company has been aggressively hiring and promoting outsiders.

In the end, however, it would appear that the principal distinction that emerges between the proprietary and professionally managed companies is this: the family owners are intent on showing that they are just as aggressive, acquisitive, and dispassionately efficient as the tough-minded professionals.   The latter, with their chatty annual reports and cozy box-lunch shareholders' gatherings, are striving equally hard to cast their corporate images in the warmhearted family mold.

Part Two

WEALTH AND INCOME INEQUALITY

REAL PERSONAL WEALTH DISTRIBUTION MAY BE MASKED TO SOME *extent by wealth held through business and other organizations, financial intermediaries, and governments. Nonfunded retirement plans for corporate executives, for instance, keep wealth in the corporate sector while actually increasing lifetime income for the executives. Organizational sectors may function in many ways as holders of wealth on behalf of individuals, thereby making comparison of two personal wealth distributions unrealistic. This study is arbitrarily limited to the personal sector of the economy, and makes no adjustment for such hidden wealth holding.*

Using the "estate multiplier method," Lampman estimates the amount and composition of personal wealth held by the "top wealth-holders" in 1953. Corporate stock is the single most preferred asset, accounting for two fifths of 1953 gross estate. Real estate, with 22 percent, is next, and cash, with 9 percent, is third. Corporate stock increases as a share of wealth as the amount of wealth rises. Over 30 percent of the personal wealth in 1953 was held by the top wealth-holders, i.e., the 1.6 percent of the population with an estate of $60,000 or more. They owned at least 80 percent of the corporate stock, virtually all of the state and local government bonds, and between 10 and 33 percent of each of the other types of personal property. The wealthiest 1 percent of adults owned 24 percent of personal wealth in 1953, 31 percent in 1939, 36 percent in 1929, and 32 percent in 1922. If families are considered as the wealth-holding unit, this decline in inequality is more apparent than real, since married women increasingly are among the wealthiest individuals. Half the percentage decline among individuals between 1922 and 1953 disappears when wealth is analyzed by family. Not only has there been no decline in the concentration of stocks and bonds, but there has been a substantial increase in concentration: from 61.5 percent in the hands of the wealthiest 1 percent of adults in 1922 to 76 percent by 1953.

9

THE SHARE OF TOP WEALTH–HOLDERS IN NATIONAL WEALTH, 1922–1956

Robert J. Lampman

The Limits of Personal Wealth as Studied Here

Since there is a fractioning of the property rights attached to individual parcels of wealth, it is difficult to apportion or indicate the sharing of those rights by means of a wealth distribution. It is helpful to envision a distribution not only among individuals but also among sectors, including persons, financial intermediaries, business corporations, nonbusiness organizations, and governments. While it is possible to allocate the market value of assets held in full title to each sector and to allocate the market value of intersectoral promises, it is not possible thereby to indicate in all cases the power share of the persons in the several sectors. Power attaches to wealth in a complicated and shifting pattern and depends upon organizational position within one sector as much as or more than it does upon holding personal title to assets. Hence, the power or control aspects of wealth are not fully dis-

Reprinted from Robert J. Lampman, *The Share of Top Wealth-holders in National Wealth, 1922–1956* (Princeton, N.J.: Princeton University Press, 1962), pp. 3–8, 16–26, 208–10, by permission of the National Bureau of Economic Research. Footnotes and tables have been renumbered.

tributed in a personal wealth distribution.   Some residual power
stays with the nonpersonal sectors and attaches to persons only as
they are active within the individual sectors.   A changing relationship between persons and nonpersonal sectors can considerably
confound comparisons of personal wealth distributions over time.
Consider, for example, the introduction of nonfunded retirement
pay plans for corporate executives.   Such a plan would keep
wealth in the corporate sector while showing increased lifetime
income for the employees.   In other ways, the organizational
sectors may function as wealth-holders "on behalf of" individuals,
thereby making a comparison of two personal wealth distributions
quite unrealistic.   While personally-held wealth may not, in some
cases, connote any intersectoral power, it is still true, of course,
that such wealth is an important means to power within each
sector.

An interesting example of the intersectoral problem is trusteed
property which relates persons to financial intermediaries.   With
personal trust funds we are moving into the twilight zone where
classical property rights are shadowed.   Depending upon the
terms of the trust agreement, a beneficiary may have only a
contingent interest in only part of the income, he may have no
power of direction over the use of the property at any time, and he
may have no right to sell the property or even to dispose of it at
the time of his death.   The rights he does not have in the property
are exercised by the trustee under the supervision of the court and
subject to the limitations set forth by the creator of the trust.   On
the other hand, again depending upon the terms of the trust, a
beneficiary may enjoy full right to all income of the property, and
he may have power at some point to dispose of the principal or to
assign his rights to its income.

We proceed still further into the shadows if we consider the
assets of nonpersonal trust funds or foundations which have a
charitable purpose.   It should be recognized that these trust funds
are sometimes used as devices for control and magnification of the
control possible on other grounds.   The founder of such a trust
not only may direct the purposes for which income or principal
may be spent, but he may also settle on the trustees he names, who
in turn have the power to name their successors, the power to
manage (that is to say, to vote the stock of) the property in trust.
On the other hand, as in the case of the Ford family, the assignment
of nonvoting stock to a foundation may make possible continuation
of family control of the original corporation.   But in some cases

these control elements are of minor or no significance. A somewhat similar problem of intersectoral accounting arises about the assets of financial intermediaries. In the case of banks and insurance companies and trusteed pension funds, there is an element of control which attaches to the fiduciary responsibility of the officers who do not themselves own the property they are managing.

Quite arbitrarily, we have restricted the limits of inquiry in this study to what is defined as the personal sector of the economy, including households, farm and nonfarm unincorporated businesses, and personal trust funds.

Wealth-holding Decisions

In this study we are concerned with the behavior of wealth-holders in deciding how much and what kind of property they will hold. Each person makes decisions about borrowing, owning, and lending. More particularly, he decides whether to take direct title to consumer or producer capital goods or land; whether to hold representative capital, i.e., claims, in the form of cash or securities, upon the assets of other persons or corporations or governments; whether to participate in capital markets directly or through financial intermediaries such as banks, insurance companies, or trust funds. He must also make decisions about the ways in which he will transfer his assets or obligations to others. In making these decisions, people are guided by time preference, precautionary, speculative, and power motives to select investments which they believe best meet their needs.

The relative strength of these motives among various socioeconomic groupings may be assessed by a cross-sectional analysis of their asset holdings and debts at a moment in time. In some cases, such an analysis makes it possible to predict how decisions of persons will change as their age, income, size of estate, or other characteristics change.

The decisions made by individuals about wealth accumulation and wealth-holding are important, not only for the individual and his family, but for the whole economy. In the aggregate, these decisions have an important influence on the rate of capital accumulation, the price of capital, and the distribution of income, economic welfare, and power among persons. Finally, they determine which institutional arrangements will flourish and which will wither away from disuse.

From the point of view of the individual, wealth accumulation is a substitute for wages or salary or an additional income; it is a way to bridge the gaps in the lifetime flow of labor income due to illness, old age, unemployment, or the premature death of the family breadwinner.   It is, then, a way to security and independence.   Wealth is also a means of achieving power and influence over the chances of others in business, in government affairs, and in the expression and communication of ideas.   It is a way for one person to gain preferment for his heirs or otherwise to lengthen his shadow across generations to come.   Interestingly, wealth can be highly specialized to fulfill specific aims.   Thus, insurance and annuities will meet certain security aims, and corporate stock acts as a lever on the control of business affairs.   Trust agreements may be used to accomplish many specific purposes.

From the point of view of the individual firm, equity in the form of working capital is a practical necessity.   Although land and fixed capital could presumably be rented from others, again as a practical matter, money will not ordinarily be available for plant expansion except as it is "led" by equity.   From a national point of view, capital accumulation is necessary to raise living standards. If it is not done privately, it must be done socially.

Inequality of Wealth Distribution

Presumably, since wealth is a good thing to have, it would be good for all families to have some.   Also, it would seem that the wider the distribution of wealth, the broader the political base for capitalism.   There is doubtless a maximum degree of concentration of wealth which is tolerable in a democracy and compatible with an ideology of equality of economic opportunity.   However, inequality due to differences in wealth-holding by age and family responsibilities may have quite a different political meaning from a similar degree of inequality within either the young or the old age group.   Rigid class lines arise from great differences in inherited wealth as well as from different motivation, different opportunity for education, and different choice of occupation.   To some extent, the difference between "democratic" and "oligarchic" systems of wealth-holding will be drawn as the body politic considers the individual, on the one hand, or the family of several generations, on the other, as the appropriate wealth-holding unit.   To a considerable extent, American social policy has developed out of the belief that each generation of individuals should stand on its own with a minimum "handicapping" by previous generations.

In this connection, it should be emphasized that inequality of wealth-holding is not the only determinant of income inequality. Indeed, to the extent that wealth is held by low-ranking wage or salary earners, it tends to offset income inequality. While capital and land are basic factors in production, and while total wealth is over three times as large as total annual income, the owners of these factors do not receive in the form of property income the greater part of the product in this or any other country. Only about 25 percent of all income may be characterized as property income.[1]

The size distribution of income is determined by "(a) the rates of pay received by various agents of production and the extent of their utilization, and (b) the distribution among persons of the ownership of these productive agents. Two classes of productive agents must be distinguished: physical property or non-human capital, and human capital representing the productive capacity of individuals. In turn, the latter is divided into 'natural' endowment or 'abilities,' and productive capacity acquired by investment in training."[2] Thinking in these terms, this study is confined to the distribution of nonhuman capital.

There is no particular degree of concentration of wealth which is required for the working of a capitalist system. However, there may be a minimum degree of inequality consistent with a particular set of capitalist institutions, a particular technology, and a particular level of production. Composition of estate data generally show that nonproprietors place consumer capital and security objectives ahead of high yield at high-risk objectives. Only after the first set of objectives is achieved by accumulating property do most nonproprietors move on to the second. This suggests that, particularly as the proportion of the population who are proprietors falls, the availability of equity capital (at existing yields) is a function of the inequality of wealth distribution. If the inequality of wealth-holding were to be sharply reduced, maintenance of the present flow of equity capital could be accomplished only by raising equity yields or by new institutional

---

[1] The precise percentage which one selects depends upon what part of "proprietors' income" one assigns to property and what part to service income, how one treats undistributed corporate profits, and whether he imputes an income to consumer capital.

[2] Jacob Mincer, "A Study of Personal Income Distribution," unpublished Ph.D. dissertation, Columbia University, 1957, p. 136. See also Mincer, "Investment in Human Capital and Personal Income Distribution," *Journal of Political Economy*, August 1958, pp. 281–302.

Table 1. Different Estimates of Top Wealth-holders, 1953

Definition of wealth and mortality rates	Number of top wealth-holders	Aggregate gross estate (billion dollars)
Basic variant		
Adjusted mortality	1,659,000	309.2
White population mortality	1,417,000	257.2
Prime wealth variant		
Adjusted mortality	1,626,000	327.5
Total wealth variant		
Adjusted mortality	1,776,000	381.1

arrangements for transmuting security-motivated wealth-holding into high-yield-motivated holding.[3] This transmutation is accomplished by insurance company or pension fund purchase of corporate stock. It could also be accomplished by mutualization or provision of capital by patrons, as is indeed done in some cases of corporations' internal financing. . . .

Estimates of Top Wealth-holders

The first substantive problem [to be] attacked is the estimation of the number of top wealth-holders in 1953, that is, living persons with $60,000 or more. Starting with the number of decedents represented on estate tax returns (36,699), the estimate is made by "blowing up" that number of inverse mortality rates. Using adjusted mortality rates, which are selected to reflect the more favorable mortality rate of upper economic groups, an estimate of 1,569,000 top wealth-holders is derived (Table 1). Using the mortality rate of the white population without adjustment for class differences yields the considerably lower estimate of 1,417,000. The true number of top wealth-holders for that year probably lies

[3] It is worth noting here that there is an important distinction, as emphasized by Veblen, between the equity investor who seeks long-term profit out of self-managed business and the speculator who holds or sells on the basis of anticipated profits with no hope or intention of constructively influencing the policy of the business. Certainly the great majority of stockholders in large corporations belong in the latter category of equity investors and view the highly regulated stock market as an escape route from anticipated falls in value due to poor management. Hence, a wide equity market removes some of the "risk" while diluting control.

somewhere between these two estimates, but it is believed to be closer to the adjusted mortality estimate.   Hence, the greater part of th[is] discussion is in terms of the adjusted mortality estimates.

By the same blowing up process, the 1,659,000 top wealth-holders are estimated to have held $309.2 billion of gross estate. This amount, which is the basic variant estimate, refines the estate tax data in only one respect, namely, in multiplying life insurance amounts by different multipliers from those used for all other assets, so that insurance amounts are reduced from face value to estimates of owner's equity.   These basic variant estimates are then examined with some care to see how they compare with those which would be found by a census of living wealth-holders that used ideal definitions of personally-held wealth.   Our rough estimates lead to the conclusion that the basic variant aggregate estimates are not substantially different from an ideally arrived at estimate of "prime wealth," but are considerably lower than the aggregates of "total wealth."   That is, we found that about 1.66 million persons had $309.2 billion of basic variant wealth, 1.63 million persons had $327.5 billion of prime wealth, and 1.78 million persons had $381.1 billion of total wealth.

The adjustments of the basic variant made in estimating the prime wealth variant include subtraction for persons originally counted in the group by virtue of the excess of insurance face value over equity, addition for underreporting by taxpayers, additions for gifts and life insurance proceeds "in float" during the year, and subtractions for trust property, annuities, and pensions originally included in the basic variant.   The prime wealth variant is in turn modified to yield the total wealth variant estimates by making additions to the former for personal trust funds, annuities, and private and governmental pensions.

On the basis of the several estimates, it is concluded that for most purposes the basic variant estimates are close enough to prime wealth variant estimates to warrant their use in the discussion of top wealth-holder characteristics and the composition of their estates.   However, the difference between the basic variant and total wealth variant estimates is [quite] notable. . . .

Characteristics of Top Wealth-holders

The median age of the 1953 top living wealth-holders was 54 years (Table 2).   Over half of the number were between 40 and 60 years of age.   While top wealth-holders made up only 1.04 percent of

Table 2. Selected Characteristics of Top Wealth-holders, 1953

Characteristic	Both sexes	Men	Women
Number of persons	1,659,000	1,144,000	514,000
Median gross estate size ($)	112,800	116,800	105,200
Average gross estate size ($)	182,000	162,400	220,500
Share of top wealth (percent)	100	60	40
Median age (years)	54	52	57

the total population and only 1.6 percent of the adult population they accounted for 3.5 percent of the men over 50.

Approximately 1.4 million of the 1.7 million top wealth-holders are heads of households, the 0.3 million being (according to our estimate) the number of married women and dependent children in the group. We find that a minimum of 2.28 percent of households and 2.35 percent of married couples have at least one member owning $60,000 of gross estate (Table 3). This compares closely with the Survey of Consumer Finances finding that 3 percent of spending units in 1950 had $60,000 or more of total assets.

The association of age and size of estate is quite clear for men; that is, average estate rises with age and median age rises with estate size (Figure 1). (The latter association is remarkably slight, however. See Table 4.) For women, on the other hand, this relationship is much more irregular.

Women top wealth-holders have gradually increased, both in numbers and in wealth, relative to men so that they comprised one-third of all top wealth-holders in 1953 (while only one-fourth in 1922) and held 40 percent of the wealth of the group (Table 2). Women have a larger average estate size than men, although within most age groups there is no clear difference by sex, and although men have a higher median estate size than women.

Table 3. Percentage of Top Wealth-holders in Total Population and in Selected Groups, 1953

| | Top Wealth-holders | | |
	Both sexes	Men	Women
All persons	1.04	1.44	0.64
Adults (20 and over)	1.60	2.26	0.98
Persons (65 and over)	3.00	4.00	2.50
Married persons	1.40	2.30	0.70
Widowers and widows	2.69	3.10	2.60
Households with at least one top wealth-holder	2.28		

Figure 1. Average Gross Estate of Top Wealth-holders, by Sex and Age Group, 1953

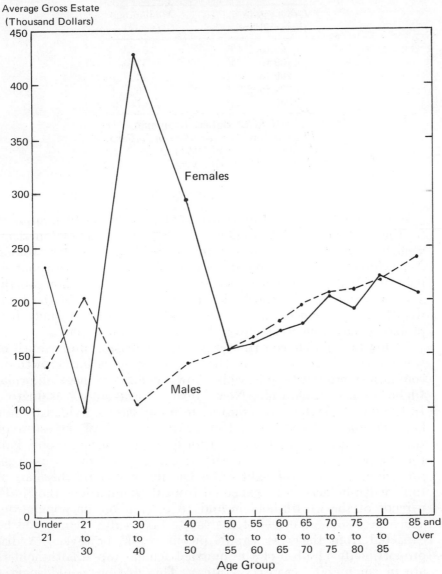

SOURCE: Lampman, *op. cit.*, Table 45.

Table 4. Median Age of Male Top Wealth-holders in Non-community Property States, by Gross Estate Size, 1953

Gross estate size (thousand dollars)	Median age (years)
60 to 100	54
100 to 200	53
200 to 500	53
500 to 2,000	56
2,000 and over	67

SOURCE: Robert Lampman, *The Share of Top Wealth-holders in National Wealth, 1922–1956* (Princeton, N.J.: Princeton University Press), Table 48.

The information on top wealth-holders furnishes little support for the popular idea that women own the greater part of American wealth.   The type of property in the holding of which women come closest to men is corporate stock.   While men, it is estimated, held $63 billion worth of stock, women held $54 billion worth. This was the case for the basic variant wealth, but in the total wealth variant, which takes into account personal trust funds, it is probable that women have over half the corporate stock.

One factor that contributes to the increasing importance of women as wealth-holders is the relative population growth in community property states, which now include Arizona, California, Idaho, Louisiana, Nevada, New Mexico, Texas and Washington. In these eight states ownership is, in many cases, divided by law between husband and wife.   Hence, the executor of the estate of the first spouse to die must report for estate tax purposes only half the property acquired after the marriage.   Despite this legal provision, this group of eight states has almost exactly the share of top wealth-holders to be expected from its population, that is 18 percent of the wealth-holders and 18 percent of the population. They have somewhat less of the estate tax wealth than would be expected from their per capita income rank, however.   A disproportionate number of the married female top wealth-holders are in community property states.   This finding would suggest that if the family were the wealth-holding unit rather than the individual, considerably more than 18 percent of the top wealth-holding families would be found in community property states.

Top wealth-holders are not evenly distributed according to

population among the states and regions. A good first approximation is that the higher the per capita income of a state or region is, the greater is the number of wealth-holders per thousand people and the higher is the average estate per wealth-holder. A second approximation, using past income ranks, would explain the fact that some states with a declining income rank, like the New England states, Kansas, and Nebraska, have more estate tax wealth than their current income rank would predict. The reverse situation may explain the relatively low share of Utah and Washington. Quite unexplained by this hypothesis is the failure of some central states—notably Michigan, Ohio, and Indiana—to turn up their share of estate tax wealth.

As would be expected, there is considerable overlap between top wealth-holder status and high income rank. Certain occupational groups, particularly the self-employed, professional, and managerial groups, are overrepresented among the top wealth-holders.

Composition of Estate

Among the top wealth-holders taken as a group, corporate stock is the single most preferred type of asset and accounted for 39 percent of gross estate in 1953. Real estate, with 22 percent, is second in importance, and cash (including deposits of all types in financial institutions) is third with 9 percent. While there have been cyclical swings, there has been remarkably little noncyclical change over the decades in the pattern of top wealth-holders' holdings of the various broad types of assets. The general pattern of investment in current dollars for top estates is virtually the same in the 1920's as in the 1950's even though there have been important changes in prices, incomes, and the structure of the economy. Top wealth-holders have a lower ratio of debt to gross estate in the postwar years than in the 1920's and a far lower ratio than in the depression decade of the 1930's.

Whether there has been any important change in "preference" of top wealth-holders for the several types of assets is a matter of judgment. Reducing each type of asset to constant dollars and comparing changes in constant dollar composition with changes in relative yields furnishes plausible evidence that cyclical changes in such composition are guided by yield changes and hence that there are not cyclical changes in preference. Over the long term it seems more sensible to think in terms of current dollar composition.

Changes in current dollar composition are compatible with changes in relative yields and it is, therefore, concluded that there have been no important changes in asset preferences.

The most important variable available to us in explaining differences in composition of estate is estate size, with larger estates having relatively more corporate stock and less real estate, more state and local bonds and less miscellaneous property (the largest component of which is unincorporated business). The percentage of estate held in stock tends to rise with age and the percentage held in miscellaneous property tends to fall. Liabilities decline gradually as a percentage of gross estate after age 40. Estates of women differ from men's estates of the same sizes principally in having a smaller share in insurance and in having smaller liabilities.

By first examining the estates of each sex by age groups within estate sizes and then looking at the estates by estate sizes within age groups (for a tabular version of the latter, in abridged form, see Table 5), we are able to identify real estate as predominantly a smaller-estate asset; U.S. bonds as a smaller-estate, older-age asset; state, local, and "other" bonds as larger-estate assets; stock as a larger-estate, older-age asset; cash as a smaller-estate, older-age asset; mortgages and notes as smaller-estate, older-age assets; life insurance as a lower- and middle-estate, middle-age asset; miscellaneous property as a lower- and middle-estate, younger-age asset; and debts and mortgages as younger-age liabilities.

From these and related facts of estate composition, this picture of changing preference emerges. As people get richer, they shift from purchase of consumer capital, including real estate and life insurance, to U.S. bonds and mortgages and notes. As they get still richer, they shift over to corporate stock and state, local, and "other" bonds. As people get older, they reduce their liabilities, "cash out" of miscellaneous property (which includes interest in unincorporated business) and life insurance, and convert to larger holdings of cash, U.S. bonds, corporate stock, and mortgages and notes. As wealth moves into the hands of women, liabilities are reduced, life insurance falls as a percentage of estate and, consequently, all other types of property rise in relative importance.

The differences in type of property held by the several estate sizes are associated with different degrees of inequality among top wealth-holders for each type of asset. The most unequally distributed type of property is state and local bonds and the least concentrated is real estate.

Table 5. Percentage of Gross Estate in Selected Assets and Liabilities for Three Gross Estate Sizes in Three Age Groups of Male Top Wealth-holders, 1953

Age group	Gross estate size (thousand dollars)		
	70 to 80	150 to 80	2,000 to 3,000
PERCENTAGE IN REAL ESTATE			
30 to 40	45	36	(10)[a]
55 to 60	35	29	16
75 to 80	37	28	4[b]
PERCENTAGE IN STOCK			
30 to 40	9	17	(67)[a]
55 to 60	20	28	40
75 to 80	22	33	68
PERCENTAGE IN CASH			
30 to 40	10	7	(3)[a]
55 to 60	13	11	2
75 to 80	17	12	6
PERCENTAGE IN MISCELLANEOUS PROPERTY			
30 to 40	30	27	(1)[a]
55 to 60	14	14	(9)[c]
75 to 80	6	7	4
PERCENTAGE IN DEBTS AND MORTGAGES (LIABILITIES)			
30 to 40	16	21	(1)[a]
55 to 60	6	10	28
75 to 80	3	5	3

SOURCE: Lampman, *op. cit.*, Table 82.

[a] No cases, age 40–50 substituted.

[b] Adjacent age groups have percentages of 17 and 11.

[c] 60–65 age group substituted as more representative.

Size Distribution

Over 30 percent of the assets and equities of the personal sector of the economy in 1953 are assignable to the top wealth-holders who were 1.6 percent of the total adult population that year (Figure 2). The top group owned at least 80 percent of the corporate stock, virtually all of the state and local government bonds, and between 10 and 33 percent of each other type of property in the personal sector in that year. These percentages are quite close to those found by the Survey of Consumer Finances for the same year.

Figure 2. Share of Personal Sector Equity* Held by Top Wealth-holders, 1953

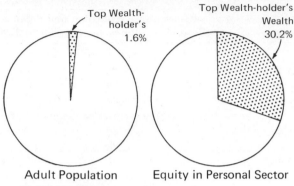

Adult Population   Equity in Personal Sector

SOURCE: Table 92, cols. 15 and 17.
* Prime wealth variant.

The top wealth-holder group has varied in number and percentage of the total population over the years. Also, its share of total wealth has varied. It appears, however, that the degree of inequality increased from 1922 to 1929, fell to below the pre-1929 level in the 1930's, fell still more during the war and up to 1949, and increased from 1949 to 1956. However, the degree of inequality was considerably lower in 1953 than in either 1929 or 1922.

To make a comparison of degrees of wealth concentration, it is convenient to consider a constant percentage of the total adult population. The top 1 percent of adults held 24 percent of personal sector equity in 1953, 31 percent in 1939, 36 percent in

Table 6. Share of Personal Sector Wealth (Equity) Held by Top Wealth-holders, Selected Years, 1922–1956

Year	Top 1 percent of adults	Top 0.5 percent of all persons	Top 2 percent of families[a]
1922	31.6	29.8	33.0
1929	36.3	32.4	
1933	28.3	25.2	
1939	30.6	28.0	
1945	23.3	20.9	
1949	20.8	19.3	
1953	24.2	22.7	28.5
1956	26.0	25.0	

[a] Families here defined as all adults less married females.

1929, and 32 percent in 1922.   It is probable that the decline thus
indicated in inequality among individual wealth-holders is greater
than would be found if families were considered as the wealth-
holding units, since it is apparent from the data that married
women are an increasing part of the top wealth-holder group.
Converting to a measure of "adults less married women" suggests
that half the percentage decline found for individuals between 1922
and 1953 would disappear on a family basis (Table 6 and Figure 3).

Two types of error in estimation are likely to offset each other
in some degree.   On the one hand, the selection of mortality rates
tends to understate the decline in inequality.   On the other hand,
the differences in completeness of reporting personal sector wealth

**Figure 3. Share of Personal Sector Wealth* Held by Top
Wealth-holders, Selected Years, 1922–1956**

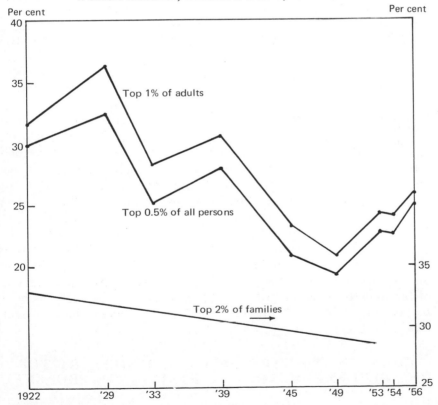

SOURCE: Lampman, *op. cit.*, Tables 6, 93, and 94.
* Equity, basic variant.

and estate tax wealth may tend to overstate the decline. It is difficult to imagine any combination of errors which would yield a result of increasing concentration over time.

Interestingly, the conclusions about changes in concentration of wealth over the years are not affected by selection of one or another variant of wealth.

The leading exception to the general picture of declining concentration is corporate stock. In the total wealth variant the top 1 percent of adults' share of each type of property declined between the 1920's and the 1950's, except for stock and state and local bonds. For stock, their share ranged from 60 to over 70 percent.

Inequality of wealth distribution is considerably greater in Great Britain than in the United States, but a pattern of similar decline in inequality is observable in the two countries.

Determinants of Changes in Inequality

. . . Three processes which may contribute to change [in the degree of inequality of wealth-holding] are . . . price change, accumulation of wealth out of income, and transfer of wealth. It is concluded that changes in the relative prices of assets held by rich and poor worked toward increasing the inequality of wealth-holding over the long period 1922–53, but that they contributed to lessening inequality during the intervening period of 1929–49. The fall in the share of wealth held by top families is ascribed largely to a failure to maintain a share of saving equal to their share of wealth. The decline of saving inequality is associated in turn with an observed decline in income inequality. The fact that the share of wealth of top individuals fell more than the share of top families is believed to be due to increasing splitting of wealth within families, principally between husbands and wives. One factor which encouraged such splitting was higher rates of income and estate taxation. The main wealth held by the top 2 percent of families from 33 percent in 1922 to 29 percent in 1953—is held to be compatible with observed price and income changes over this period. . . .

CHANGES IN SHARE OF WEALTH HELD BY TOP ONE PERCENT OF ADULTS, BY TYPE OF PROPERTY

Between 1922 and 1953 the top 1 percent of the adult population experienced a decline in the share of total equity in the personal sector and a decline in the share of most types of property (Table 7). Notable exceptions are "stock" and "other bonds," which appear to have changed little in degree of concentration. All studies of stock ownership indicate that this asset is highly concentrated.[4]

However, the unreasonable variation of some of these series plus the greater than 100 percent figures for state and local bonds yield a less than convincing picture. It would seem appropriate to review the possible sources of error in the whole process of estimating wealth distribution. The irregularities referred to above could have arisen out of random errors in the sampling process.[5] For example, the stock figure in one year could be too high because of an unrepresentative age distribution of decedents with large stock holdings. Another possible cause is the selection of mortality rates; we could have the wrong measure of the differential mortality enjoyed by the rich, or there could be errors in the way property is valued or classified on the estate tax returns. On the other hand, we could be confronted with difficulties in the national balance sheet aggregates for the several types of property.[6] It also is possible that we have double-counted some of the assets in personal trust funds in making adjustments to move from the basic to the prime to the total wealth variant for top wealth-holders.

[4] Butters, Thompson, and Bollinger give the following as their best estimate for 1949 (based on SRC data, tax return data, and their own field surveys): The upper 3 percent of spending units as ranked by income owned 75 percent of marketable stock; the top 1 percent, 65 percent; the top 0.5 percent, slightly over one-half; and the top 0.1 percent, about 35 percent of all the marketable stock owned by private investors. They indicate that these percentages would be higher if the stock held by personal trust funds were allocated to individuals. (*Effects of Taxation: Investments by Individuals*, Boston, 1953, p. 25, and also Chaps. XVI and XVII.) As to a ranking by size of stock holdings, the 1 percent of all spending units that owned $10,000 or more of stock accounted for at least two-thirds of the total value of stock reported to the 1952 Survey of Consumer Finances (*Federal Reserve Bulletin*, September 1952, p. 985). For one measure of concentration of stock ownership by use of a total wealth ranking, see Goldsmith, *Savings in U.S.*, III, Table W-53. He estimated that in 1950 those spending units with $60,000 or more of net worth held 76 percent of corporate stock. The reader is cautioned that rankings by income and wealth are not interchangeable.

[5] The top wealth-holder group held substantially more market value in stocks in 1953 than 1949. The aggregate gross estate of decedent top wealth-holders was 36.5 percent in stock in 1949, but 40.5 percent in stock in 1953.

[6] It seems probable, for example, that balance sheet difficulties are responsible for the high percentages for state and local bonds in 1929 and 1939.

Table 7. Share of Personal Sector Assets and Liabilities^a Held by Top One Percent of Adults, 1922, 1929, 1939, 1945, 1949, and 1953

Type of property	1922	1929	1939	1945	1949	1953
Real estate	18.0%	17.3%	13.7%	11.1%	10.5%	12.5%
U.S. govt. bonds	45.0	100.0	91.0	32.5	35.8	31.8
State and local bonds	88.0	b	b	b	77.0	b
Other bonds	69.2	82.0	75.5	78.5	78.0	77.5
Corporate stock	61.5	65.6	69.0	61.7	64.9	76.0
Cash	—	—	—	17.0	18.9	24.5
Mortgages and notes	—	—	—	34.7	32.0	30.5
Cash, mortgages, and notes	31.0	34.0	31.5	19.3	20.5	25.8
Pension and retirement funds	8.0	8.0	6.0	5.9	5.5	5.5
Insurance	35.3	27.0	17.4	17.3	15.0	11.5
Miscellaneous property	23.2	29.0	19.0	21.4	15.0	15.5
Gross estate	32.3	37.7	32.7	25.8	22.4	25.3
Liabilities	23.8	29.0	26.5	27.0	19.0	20.0
Economic estate	33.9	38.8	33.8	25.7	22.8	27.4

SOURCE: Lampman, *op. cit.*, Table 90 and Appendix Tables A-17 through A-21, col. 13.   National balance sheet data used for 1922, 1929, and 1939 are from Goldsmith, *Saving in U.S.*, III; for 1945, 1949, and 1953, from preliminary unpublished tables prepared by the National Bureau of Economic Research.

^a Total wealth variant.

^b In excess of 100 percent.   See text.

All of these considerations urge that the whole of Table 7 be used in evaluating any single figure in it, and that each individual item be treated with caution.*

* *Smith and Calvert (of the Statistics Division of the Internal Revenue Service), using techniques similar to those used by Lampman, concluded that in 1958, top wealth-holders made up 1.5 percent of the population and owned 32 percent of prime wealth owned by all individuals in the U.S.   Since 1953, the shares of real estate, notes and mortgages, and life insurance equity owned by top wealth-holders have increased, while federal bonds, corporate stock, and miscellaneous assets have remained about the same.   These data support Lampman's conclusion that the relative share of top wealth-holders has been increasing since 1949.   This increase is probably understated because of earlier arithmetical errors.   The top 1 percent of all wealth-holders, in different periods, continues to own about one-fourth of all wealth owned by individuals in the U.S.   See James D. Smith and Staunton K. Calvert, "Estimating the Wealth of Top Wealth-Holders from Estate Tax Returns," Proceedings of the* American Statistical Association, *September 1965, pp. 248–61.—M.Z.*

10

THE DISTRIBUTION OF WEALTH IN 1962

Dorothy Projector
Gertrude Weiss

EMPLOYMENT STATUS OF HEAD

Self-employed and Employed by Others

The self-employed as a group were in better circumstances than the units whose heads were employed by others. Their incomes were higher—with mean income for the self-employed group at $10,841 and for the group with heads employed by others, $6,990. The self-employed were also much wealthier; the midpoint in their wealth distribution, $21,958, compared with $4,895 for the units with heads employed by others. They were also somewhat older.

The employment classification is based on replies to questions about the head's employment rather than on the presence of business investment. Accordingly, units classified as in the employed-by-others group could, although they rarely did, have their own businesses arising from business activities of other members of the unit or from secondary activities of the head. And those in the

Reprinted from Dorothy Projector and Gertrude Weiss, *Survey of Financial Characteristics of Consumers* (Washington, D.C.: Federal Reserve System, August 1966), pp. 33–36, 98–99. Groups too small for separate analysis and too diverse to be combined have been omitted from this analysis. These are units headed by farm operators, farm laborers, persons under 65 years of age with no work experience during 1962, and those whose occupation was not reported. Tables have been renumbered.

self-employed group could, and occasionally did, report that they had no equity of any value connected with their self-employment.

The Survey showed that the greater wealth of the self-employed is not accounted for by their businesses alone. Their equities in owned homes were about twice and their holdings of liquid and investment assets about four times as much, on the average, as for the group employed by others. It is apparent, therefore, that the self-employed as a group are in very different financial circumstances from the group employed by others.

With so much disparity in the amount of their wealth, differences in the shape of the wealth distributions might be expected. The degree of inequality, however, as measured by the Gini coefficient is about the same for the two groups, with the coefficient for the self-employed only slightly higher. A different conclusion as to dispersion is drawn from comparing the quartile deviation, which is smaller for the self-employed than for employees, but this measure does not take account of the entire range of the distribution. When Lorenz curves are drawn for the two distributions, the curve for the self-employed is nearer to the line of equality below approximately the 7th decile, but at the upper end of the distribution the self-employed show greater inequality than the employees as to the distribution of wealth. In view of the great differences between them as to the size of their holdings, the significant conclusion is that the two groups differ relatively little as to the way wealth is distributed within the groups.

To determine whether differences exist in the kinds of investments held that can be attributed to occupation, the composition of portfolios of similar size was examined. Because the employment groups differed in their age composition—the self-employed being older on the average—and because there were differences in portfolio preferences among age groups, the comparison was confined to units headed by persons 35 to 64. A comparison of units similar as to amount of wealth was not made because the self-employed would obviously have smaller shares in homes. liquid assets, and the like, because their businesses are a substantial share of their total wealth. For example, at most wealth levels, business is at least one-third of the wealth of the self-employed.

Given the same total amount of liquid and investment assets, the self-employed generally have more of it invested in real estate and businesses not managed by the unit head than do the units with heads employed by others. Possibly both types of investment are related to active participation in their own businesses, either

Table 1. Share of Portfolio in Specified Form, Two Employment Status Groups, December 31, 1962

(Consumer units with head aged 35–64)

Group characteristic	Portfolio (mean in dollars)	Total	Liquid assets				Investment assets						
			All	Checking accounts	Savings accounts	U.S. savings bonds	All	Publicly traded stock	Mkt. sec. other than stock	Mortgage assets	Real estate	Business not managed by unit	Company savings plans
Head self-employed	$23,831	100	23	5	15	3	77	32	5	3	25	11	1
Size of portfolio:						Percentage distribution of dollar aggregate							
$1–499	170	100	99	46	42	11	1	−1	2	*	*	*	*
$500–1,999	882	100	80	28	39	13	20	*	*	5	9	5	*
$2,000–4,999	3,431	100	60	14	42	5	40	12	1	1	17	10	*
$5,000–9,999	7,302	100	42	13	27	2	58	27	*	1	28	1	*
$10,000–24,999	14,643	100	45	6	32	7	55	19	1	2	21	12	1
$25,000–49,999	32,825	100	31	6	19	6	69	16	*	3	49	1	1
$50,000–99,999	69,052	100	37	3	27	7	63	21	1	10	10	20	1
$100,000–499,999	186,875	100	13	4	7	2	87	28	3	3	35	17	1
$500,000 and over	1,233,720	100	9	2	6	*	91	58	14	2	10	7	*
Head employed by others	7,273	100	32	4	23	5	68	37	2	4	18	4	3
Size of portfolio:													
$1–499	178	100	97	43	39	15	3	1	1	*	*	*	2
$500–1,999	1,046	100	82	24	48	10	18	6	1	1	5	1	5
$2,000–4,999	3,252	100	70	12	49	9	30	9	1	6	8	*	6
$5,000–9,999	7,203	100	63	6	45	13	37	12	*	2	15	2	6
$10,000–24,999	15,033	100	42	4	32	6	58	19	1	5	26	3	4
$25,000–49,999	33,740	100	34	3	24	7	66	28	1	5	25	6	3
$50,000–99,999	72,226	100	22	2	15	5	78	43	1	5	23	4	3
$100,000–499,999	170,700	100	10	1	7	2	90	61	1	2	14	10	2
$500,000 and over	1,925,126	100	3	1	2	*	97	77	9	1	8	2	*

NOTE. Details may not add to totals because of rounding.

* Less than ½ of 1 percent.

Table 2. Percentage of Units Owning Specified Form of Portfolio, Two Employment Status Groups, December 31, 1962

(Consumer units with head aged 35–64)

Group characteristic	Total portfolio	Liquid assets All	Checking accounts	Savings accounts	U.S. savings bonds	Investment assets All	Publicly traded stock	Mkt. sec. other than stock	Mortgage assets	Real estate	Business not managed by unit	Company savings plans
Head self-employed	95	92	70	69	29	51	26	5	8	27	10	2
Size of portfolio:												
$1–499	100	100	63	54	11	4	1	3	*	*	*	*
$500–1,999	100	95	70	61	29	23	2	*	7	10	5	*
$2,000–4,999	100	96	58	88	31	61	28	3	5	20	12	*
$5,000–9,999	100	100	76	94	11	76	43	9	6	40	7	*
$10,000–24,999	100	92	81	83	32	86	51	3	6	45	23	*
$25,000–49,999	100	100	100	79	70	100	34	11	23	77	4	10
$50,000–99,999	100	100	91	77	43	100	86	15	34	34	39	2
$100,000–499,999	100	100	98	81	59	100	75	18	23	74	43	14
$500,000 and over	100	100	100	77	64	100	99	69	13	55	32	15
Head employed by others	82	81	63	66	32	34	18	2	5	12	3	7
Size of portfolio:												
$1–499	100	99	74	62	16	4	2	1	*	*	*	2
$500–1,999	100	99	76	77	36	28	11	1	1	7	2	9
$2,000–4,999	100	99	71	92	49	52	25	2	10	12	2	14
$5,000–9,999	100	99	80	96	66	68	43	3	4	25	4	10
$10,000–24,999	100	99	86	90	49	80	35	5	15	38	8	13
$25,000–49,999	100	100	93	90	46	88	54	8	15	42	6	7
$50,000–99,999	100	100	97	94	66	98	76	8	13	53	17	28
$100,000–499,999	100	100	100	91	41	100	97	17	33	39	42	10
$500,000 and over	100	100	100	82	49	100	100	70	7	50	17	19

* Less than ½ of 1 percent.

Table 3. Size of Wealth, December 31, 1962
(Percentage distribution of consumer units)

Group characteristic	All units	Nega-tive	Zero	$1–999	$1,000–4,999	$5,000–9,999	$10,000–24,999	$25,000–49,999	$50,000–99,999	$100,000–199,999	$200,000–499,999	$500,000–999,999	$1,000,000 and over
All units	100	2	8	16	19	16	23	11	4	1	1	*	*
1962 income:													
0–$2,999	100	1	23	19	18	15	17	7	1	*	*	*	*
$3,000–4,999	100	3	8	29	20	11	17	8	2	1	*	*	*
$5,000–7,499	100	2	1	15	25	21	22	8	5	1	*	*	*
$7,500–9,999	100	2	*	7	18	18	36	14	3	1	1	*	*
$10,000–14,999	100	1	*	2	13	16	35	20	10	3	1	*	*
$15,000–24,999	100	*	*	*	3	10	21	29	24	7	5	*	*
$25,000–49,999	100	*	*	*	*	*	5	8	22	27	27	7	4
$50,000–99,999	100	*	*	*	*	*	*	1	9	7	45	20	17
$100,000 and over	100	*	*	*	*	*	*	1	*	1	5	56	38
Age of head:													
Under 35	100	5	9	36	26	14	8	2	*	*	*	*	*
35–44	100	2	7	14	20	21	25	8	4	1	1	*	*
45–54	100	1	7	10	20	10	31	14	5	1	1	*	*
55–64	100	1	8	7	12	16	28	16	8	3	2	*	*
65 and over	100	*	11	8	13	18	25	15	5	1	2	1	*
Age groups													
Head under 35	100	5	9	36	26	14	8	2	*	*	*	*	*
1962 income:													
0–$2,999	100	5	33	45	9	4	*	4	*	*	*	*	*
$3,000–4,999	100	7	8	57	25	1	3	*	*	*	*	*	*
$5,000–7,499	100	3	1	30	35	22	7	1	1	*	*	*	*
$7,500–9,999	100	6	*	19	33	20	22	1	*	1	*	*	*
$10,000–14,999	100	*	*	10	27	36	18	8	*	1	*	*	*
$15,000–24,999	100	*	*	*	*	22	44	32	2	9	*	2	15
$25,000–49,999	100	*	*	*	*	9	29	*	*	5	36	90	5
$50,000–99,999	100	*	*	*	*	*	*	*	*	5	*		
Head 35–54	100	1	7	12	20	16	28	11	4	1	1	*	*
1962 income:													
0–$2,999	100	1	32	22	27	4	7	5	*	2	*	*	*
$3,000–4,999	100	2	10	28	22	13	19	5	1	5	*	*	*
$5,000–7,499	100	2	1	11	26	26	26	6	2	2	*	*	*
$7,500–9,999	100	*	1	4	17	18	46	13	2	2	3	*	*
$10,000–14,999	100	1	*	1	13	13	42	17	10	5	3	1	3
$15,000–24,999	100	1	*	*	5	12	23	35	18	8	25	30	15
$25,000–49,999	100	2	*	*	*	*	5	9	29	8	22	36	47
$50,000–99,999	100	*	*	*	*	*	2	2	23	5	12		
$100,000 and over	100												

Table 3 (continued)

Group characteristic	All units	Negative	Zero	$1–999	$1,000–4,999	$5,000–9,999	$10,000–24,999	$25,000–49,999	$50,000–99,999	$100,000–199,999	$200,000–499,999	$500,000–999,999	$1,000,000 and over
Head 55–64	100	1	8	7	12	16	28	16	8	3	2	*	*
1962 income:													
0–$2,999	100	*	18	14	15	16	27	7	4	*	*	*	*
$3,000–4,999	100	*	7	8	16	28	23	10	3	4	*	*	*
$5,000–7,499	100	2*	3	3	16	14	34	20	10	4	*	*	*
$7,500–9,999	100	*	*	1	3	19	35	27	9	4	2	*	*
$10,000–14,999	100	1	*	1	5	11	28	35	14	4	*	1	*
$15,000–24,999	100	*	*	*	*	6	17	19	36	15	8	1	*
$25,000–49,999	100	*	*	*	*	*	5	7	24	20	34	7	4
$50,000–99,999	100	*	*	*	*	*	*	*	2	7	62	15	15
$100,000 and over	100	*	*	*	*	*	*	*	2*	2	8	19	72
Head 65 and over	100	*	11	8	13	18	25	15	5	1	1	1	*
1962 income:													
0–$2,999	100	*	15	9	17	24	24	9	1	1	*	*	*
$3,000–4,999	100	*	6	8	14	10	32	22	5	*	2	*	*
$5,000–7,499	100	*	*	13	2	1	34	21	26	3	1	*	*
$7,500–9,999	100	*	*	*	1	17	22	38	7	7	8	*	*
$10,000–14,999	100	*	*	*	*	*	14	39	25	10	12	*	*
$15,000–24,999	100	4*	*	*	*	*	4	4	63	3	18	8	*
$25,000–49,999	100	*	*	*	*	*	*	7	1	35	19	30	8
$50,000–99,999	100	*	*	*	*	*	*	*	3	5	55	13	24
$100,000 and over	100	*	*	*	*	*	*	*	*	*	3	27	25
Employment status groups													
Head self-employed	100	1	*	3	8	14	29	19	16	5	4	1	1
1962 income													
0–$2,999	100	*	*	2	17	23	35	16	7	*	*	*	*
$3,000–4,999	100	4*	*	4	14	22	36	21	1	*	*	*	*
$5,000–7,499	100	4*	*	5	18	13	28	20	13	2	*	*	*
$7,500–9,999	100	*	*	4	2	18	49	21	*	5	1	*	*
$10,000–14,999	100	*	*	*	1	6	18	25	45	5	1	*	*
$15,000–24,999	100	*	*	*	*	5	12	18	36	14	13	1	1
$25,000–49,999	100	*	*	*	*	1	3	5	19	31	32	7	3
$50,000–99,999	100	*	*	*	*	*	*	2	8	10	18	37	24
$100,000 and over	100	*	*	*	*	*	*	*	*	2	4	69	25
Head employed by others	100	2	6	20	23	16	22	8	2	1	*	*	*
1962 income:													
0–$2,999	100	2	26	33	22	8	5	2	*	*	*	*	*
$3,000–4,999	100	4	8	38	25	10	12	2	*	1	*	*	*
$5,000–7,499	100	2	1	18	28	24	21	4	2	1	*	*	*
$7,500–9,999	100	2*	*	8	22	20	33	12	3	2	1	*	*
$10,000–14,999	100	1	*	2	16	19	38	19	4	5	1	*	*
$15,000–24,999	100	1	*	*	4	12	25	34	18	*	2	*	*
$25,000–49,999	100	*	*	*	*	*	9	14	32	23	19	2	2
$50,000–99,999	100	*	*	*	*	*	*	*	29	9	31	14	16
$100,000 and over	100	*	*	*	*	*	*	*	*	*	7	19	73

Table 3 (continued)

Group characteristic	All units	Negative	Zero	$1–999	$1,000–4,999	$5,000–9,999	$10,000–24,999	$25,000–49,999	$50,000–99,999	$100,000–199,999	$200,000–499,999	$500,000–999,999	$1,000,000 and over
Head retired	100	*	13	9	12	20	24	15	4	1	2	*	*
1962 income:													
0–$2,999	100	*	16	10	14	26	24	9	1	1	*	*	*
$3,000–4,999	100	*	7	10	8	11	30	26	6	7	3	*	*
$5,000–7,499	100	*	*	*	*	2	22	44	25	7	*	*	*
$7,500–9,999	100	*	*	1	*	*	39	48	11	*	1	*	*
$10,000–14,999	100	*	*	*	*	*	8	21	14	27	33	3	*
$15,000–24,999	100	*	*	*	*	8	8	*	74	*	15	3	*
$25,000–49,999	100	*	*	*	*	*	*	*	2	*	2	62	34
$50,000–99,999	100	*	*	*	*	*	*	*	*	*	85	3	12
$100,000 and over	100	*	*	*	*	*	*	*	*	*	13	*	87

[NOTE: Examples of how to read the table: The first line of the table shows that among all consumer units of the 1962 population, 10 percent had a total wealth of less than one dollar, and another 16 percent more than one dollar but less than $1,000. Twenty-six percent, in other words, had less than $1,000 of "wealth," including liquid assets, checking and savings accounts, and "investments," including real estate, stocks, and bonds.

If we look at the category of consumer units labelled "Head Employed by Others," and within that category at those in the $3,000–$4,999 income group, we see that 50 percent had wealth totalling less than $1,000. It is worth noting that this income group includes workers above the "poverty line" but—for the most part—below the median income for units whose heads were employed by others ($4,895). Put simply, this means that workers' families that earned enough to keep themselves from being "poor" by official standards but who were still in the bottom half of the income ladder, had a total amount of "wealth" to fall back on of less than $1,000.—M.Z.]

* Less than 1/2 of 1 percent.

currently or in the past.   For example, an interest may be retained in a business in which a unit member was formerly active, or property owned by a member of the unit may be rented to a business conducted by a member.   Those employed by others, and especially those with substantial portfolios, tend to have larger shares invested in publicly traded stock than do the self-employed (Table 1).

Even though there is no systematic difference between the two groups as to the share of portfolios of similar size held in liquid assets, holders of the various types of liquid assets are relatively more numerous in the group employed by others.   Owners of checking accounts, of savings accounts, and of U.S. savings bonds are more frequent in the group employed by others than among the self-employed with portfolios of similar size (Table 2).

The smaller incidence of checking accounts among the self-employed may reflect the reporting method rather than a true difference between the groups in the extent to which they use checking accounts.   In measuring wealth, it is especially difficult to distinguish between business and personal holdings for the self-employed.   Respondents were asked to report as checking accounts only those used wholly for personal purposes, and to report business accounts and those used for both business and personal transactions as part of investment in business.   As a result, the self-employed are shown to be less likely to have checking accounts, especially when compared with employees having portfolios of similar size.   This classification problem cannot be readily solved, however, because results from the opposite procedure would have been equally difficult to interpret.

Miss Goldsmith summarizes and re-analyzes findings from many different studies of income distribution in the U.S. over the quarter century from the Great Depression (1929) to 1955. There has been a rise in the real mean family income from 1929 to 1955 at an average yearly rate of about 1.5 percent before taxes and 1 percent after taxes. What is debatable, however, is how distribution of income has shifted, i.e., how the share of total personal and national income received by individuals and families ranked by amount of income has changed.

Kuznets' study of the relative income shares of the top 5 percent of individuals, based on income tax returns, and Goldsmith's study of relative family income, covering the full range of incomes, are the two major studies. Kuznets concluded that there has been a drastic reduction of about 40 percent in the share of income received by the top 5 percent of individuals between 1929 and 1948. Goldsmith's family data indicate a similar, though somewhat dampened decline. This decline is imputed to an increase in the relative importance of wages and salaries as income sources and to changes in the relative distribution of various types of income. The greatest narrowing of income apparently came during the Great Depression and during the Second World War.

There are, however, several limitations to using personal income data: variations from year to year; inadequate differential cost of living indexes for rich and poor; inability to identify and compare shifts of specific individuals or families; and inadequate data on the number and composition of the lower income strata. A more important limitation results from the failure to take into account income, such as "expense accounts" and fringe benefits of many kinds, which the higher income strata receive from corporations. In addition, specific tax allowances, such as depletion allowances, also increase the actual income received but not noted by the wealthy. Kuznets' reliance on income tax data also results in a failure to take under-reporting into account. The exclusion of capital gains from the income measure also results in an underestimate of the income of the higher brackets.

Perlo, in the next article, discusses many of these inadequacies in Kuznets' analysis. However, Goldsmith concludes that, although measurements of these types of incomes are not available, and although these measurements doubtlessly would show the decline in income shares to be smaller, their impact would not be sufficient to change the general pattern.

Most important, however, is the failure to distinguish between the *relative distribution of income* emerging from production *compared to the distribution of* personal *income.   National income* includes *and* personal income excludes *elements of production not paid out to persons.   Some of these elements are undistributed corporate profits, corporate inventory valuations, taxes on corporate profits, and contributions for social insurance.   Undistributed corporate earnings, which go predominantly to the top income strata, account for a larger relative share of the national income in the postwar than in the prewar period.   When such factors are taken into account, the alleged increase in income equality is seen very differently.   Converting to national income measurements reduces the percentage decline in the income of the top 5 percent from 1929 to 1950–55 by about one third (from 30 to 20 percent).   From 1939 to 1950–55, the corresponding reduction is about three fourths (from 20 to only 5 percent).   And this 5 percent decline is probably a statistical rather than a real one.   Therefore, Goldsmith concludes that if income is measured in terms of* national income rather than personal income flows, there probably has been *no* reduction between 1939 and 1950–55 in the relative share of income received by the top 5 percent.*

11

CHANGES IN THE SIZE
DISTRIBUTION OF INCOME

Selma F. Goldsmith

This paper attempts to summarize some recent findings concerning changes that have taken place in income distribution in the United States during the past twenty-five years. The discussion is directed primarily at the question of whether or not there has been a reduction over this period in relative income differences among families and individuals. If so, how large has it been, and to what extent are the available figures influenced by particular concepts and definitions?

To those who are working in this field it will be apparent that the materials presented here are not essentially new but merely summarize some of the statistical findings and analyses that have recently appeared or will shortly appear in a number of journal articles, government publications and other sources. However, these materials are sufficiently scattered and the subject important enough so that a summary should prove useful. It must be obvious that the limitations of this paper make it impossible to cover many important aspects of this broad subject.

Although there is some argument as to its exact magnitude, partly as a result of problems of appropriate deflation procedures, there is general agreement that there has been a very substantial increase in total and average real income over the past quarter century. In terms of the personal income series of the Office of

Reprinted from the *American Economic Review*, Vol. 47, No. 2 (May 1957), 504–18, by permission of the publisher. Footnotes have been renumbered.

Business Economics, total real income flowing to families and unattached individuals increased between 1929 and 1955 at an average annual rate of approximately 3 or 2.5 percent a year, depending on whether income is measured before or after federal individual income taxes. The number of families and unattached individuals sharing in the income total has increased at an average rate of about 1.4 percent per year. Thus, real mean family income has risen at an average yearly rate of about 1.5 percent on a before-tax basis or slightly over 1 percent on an after-tax basis, from 1929 to 1955.

The increase in average real income has been reflected in a very substantial upward shift in the income-size distribution of consumer units (families and unattached individuals). For example, with family incomes expressed in terms of 1950 prices—and ignoring for the moment certain important problems of comparability of data—we find that the proportion of consumer units with before-tax incomes over $3,000 increased from one-third in 1929 to two-thirds in 1954. The proportion above $4,000 rose from one-fifth to one-half and the proportion above $5,000 from about 13 to 35 percent.[1]

The income-size distributions available for selected intermediate years within the 1929–54 period indicate that a very large part of the upward shift in real incomes occurred between 1941 and 1944. For example, about one-half of the 1929–54 increase of 33 percentage points in the proportion of consumer units with real (1950 dollar) incomes over $3,000 took place between 1941 and 1944. However, the available price indexes do not reflect certain hidden price increases that occurred during the war so that the deflated figures overstate somewhat the wartime rise in real incomes and understate the increase in the early postwar years.

Of equal significance with the absolute income figures are estimates of the changes in relative income distribution over the past twenty-five years. I propose first to summarize what the available figures show and then to appraise as best we can the validity of these findings.

The two statistical series on income-size distribution to which we can turn, present essentially the same pattern for the post-1929 period; namely, a marked decline in the percentage share of total income accruing to the top income group.

[1] Selma F. Goldsmith, "Relation of Census Income Distribution Statistics to Other Income Data," to be published in Vol. 23 of *Studies in Income and Wealth* (National Bureau of Economic Research).

The first of these series, developed by Professor Kuznets, presents annual data on relative income shares received by successive top percentiles of the population; e.g., by the 5 percent of men, women, and children covered on those individual income tax returns reporting the largest per capita incomes in each year.[2] The second series, developed by my colleagues and myself, is on a family rather than a population basis and covers the full range of family incomes for selected years.[3] The top 5 percent in this series refers to families and unattached individuals having the largest family personal incomes in each year.

Starting with Kuznets' series, in 1929 the incomes received by the top 5 percent of the population amounted to about 32 percent of the total income receipts of all individuals (measured before income taxes and excluding net capital gains). In 1939, this relative share had dropped to 28 percent, reflecting mainly a loss in relative share by the topmost percentile of the population. After 1939 declines were registered by all bands within the top 5 percent. By 1946, the relative share of this top group had fallen to 20 percent and in 1948 it is estimated at somewhat over 19 percent (Table 1). For the 1929–48 period as a whole, this represented a decline of 40 percent in the relative share of before-tax income received by the top 5 percent of the population. Kuznets has recently conjectured that this narrowing of relative income differences is part of a long-time secular swing that followed a period of widening income inequality during the second half of the last century.[4]

The family income distributions show a similar though somewhat dampened post-1929 decline for the top income group. The relative share of the top 5 percent of consumer units is estimated at 30 percent in 1929 and at under 21 percent in 1944 and in the postwar period.

Both the Kuznets' and family income series represent before-

[2] Simon Kuznets, *Shares of Upper Income Groups in Income and Savings* (National Bureau of Economic Research, 1953).

[3] Office of Business Economics, "Income Distribution in the United States by Size, 1944–50," a Supplement to the *Survey of Current Business* (U.S. Department of Commerce, 1953); "Income Distribution in the United States, 1950–53," and "1952–55," *Survey of Current Business*, March, 1955, and June, 1956; Selma Goldsmith, George Jaszi, Hyman Kaitz, and Maurice Liebenberg, "Size Distribution of Income since the Mid-thirties," *Review of Economics and Statistics*, February, 1954.

[4] Simon Kuznets, "Economic Growth and Income Inequality," *American Economic Review*, March, 1955.

Table 1. Percentage Shares of Income Received by Top 5 Percent, Selected Years

Year	Top 5 percent of population (Kuznets)			Top 5 percent of Consumer units	
	Economic income variant (1)	Disposable income variant (2)	Economic income variant plus realized net capital gains (3)	Family personal income (4)	Income after federal individual income tax liability (5)
1929	32.2	33.8	34.8	30.0	29.5
1935–36	28.8	27.9		26.5	
1939	27.8	26.8	27.8	25.8	24.8
1941	25.7	23.0		24.0	21.5
1944	18.7	15.8		20.7	
1946	20.0	17.7	21.4	21.3	
1947	19.1			20.9	
1948	19.4				
1952				20.5	18.2
Percent decrease:					
1929 to 1946	38	48	38	29	
1939 to 1946	28	34	23	17	
1929 to 1948	40				
1929 to 1952				32	38
1939 to 1952				21	27

SOURCES: Columns 1 and 2, which represent, respectively, before-tax income exclusive of capital gains, and income after federal individual income taxes but inclusive of realized net capital gains, from Simon Kuznets, *Shares of Upper Income Groups In Income and Savings* (National Bureau of Economic Research, 1953), pages 453, 635, 637 (with 1948 extrapolated by Kuznets' "basic variant" series, page 599).   For column 1, an estimate of 17.4 is obtained for the year 1953 by applying to data from *Statistics of Income, Part 1, 1953* (U.S. Treasury Department) and from July, 1956, issue of *Survey of Current Business* (U.S. Department of Commerce) the various adjustments used by Kuznets to derive his economic income variant series.   (Shares, pages 280, 302, 360–361, 366–367, 387, 412–413, 423–424, 571, 577, and 579.)   Comparability between 1953 and the earlier years in column 1 is impaired, however, by the introduction of the split-income provision in 1948.   Column 3 derived by adding to column 1 Kuznets' adjustment to include net capital gains (page 599, column 5 minus column 1) and subtracting his adjustment for unwarranted inclusions (page 622, column 4 minus column 1).   Column 4, which represents personal income before income taxes flowing to families and unattached individuals and excludes capital gains and losses, for 1952 from "Income Distribution in the United States, by Size, 1952–55," *Survey of Current Business*, June, 1956; 1946 and 1947 from "Income Distribution in the United States, by Size, 1944–50," a supplement to the *Survey of Current Business* (1953); 1941, 1935–36 and 1929 from Selma Goldsmith, George Jaszi, Hyman Kaitz and Maurice Liebenberg, "Size Distribution of Income since the Mid-thirties," *Review of Economics and Statistics*, February, 1954; 1939 derived by interpolation between 1935–36 and 1941 using column 1 as a basis.   Column 5, which represents column 4 minus federal individual income tax liabilities other than those on net capital gains, for 1952 and 1941 derived from sources listed for column 4 for those years; 1929 and 1939 obtained by subtracting from amounts underlying column 4 federal individual income tax liabilities excluding liabilities on net capital gains, estimated from data in *Statistics of Income, Part 1, 1929 and 1939* (U.S. Treasury Department).

tax incomes and in deriving both of them data from federal individual income tax returns represented the primary source material.   The difference between them reflects a number of factors, such as differences in the basic unit of measurement (the family versus the person), in the concept of income, and in the adjustments that were made in the basic tax-return statistics by Kuznets, on the one hand, and by the various sets of persons who initially developed the family distributions for selected prewar and postwar years, on the other.

The family income distributions also tell us how the decrease in relative income share of the top 5 percent of the consumer units was spread among other income groups. Between 1929 and 1947, for example, the 9 percentage points of decline in the share of the top 5 percent were offset by the following gains: 3½ percentage points by the lowest 40 percent of families and unattached individuals, 2¼ points by the middle quintile, 2¾ points by the fourth quintile, and ¾ points by the 15 percent of consumer units directly below the top 5.[5]

A salient point is that for the lowest 40 percent of consumer units, the period of greatest relative gains was between 1941 and 1944. Since 1944, there has been little change in the relative distribution of family income according to the available figures.

Kuznets has also developed a series in terms of disposable income (i.e., income after federal individual income taxes and inclusive of capital gains). For the top 5 percent of the population, the relative share in total disposable income dropped from almost 34 percent in 1929 to well under 18 percent in 1946, the last year for which this series is available. This represented a decrease of 48 percent, 10 points more than the 38 percent drop in the before-tax income share from 1929 to 1946 (Table 1).

These decreases in relative income shares are reflected strikingly in the average income figures for the top income sector. Kuznets' per capita disposable income of the top 5 percent is about one-eighth lower in 1946 than in 1929, even in current dollars; i.e., before allowance for the higher prices prevailing in the latter year (Table 2). On a before-tax basis the current-dollar per capita income of the top 5 percent just about kept up with the rise in the consumer price index for the period 1929–46 but fell behind by 1948.[6] However, attention must be called to the limited applicability of the consumer price index in this context. Not until we are able to develop differential cost-of-living indexes appropriate for the various income groups and can solve the problem of how to

[5] Goldsmith, *op. cit.*

[6] Geoffrey Moore showed that this fall took place within the top 1 percent of the population. See "Secular Changes in the Distribution of Income," AEA *Papers and Proceedings*, May, 1952.

**Table 2. Average Income of Entire Population and of
Top 5 Per Cent, Selected Years**

| | Average income per capita (Kuznets) | | | | |
| | Economic income variant | | Disposable income variant | | |
Year	Total population	Top 5 per cent	Total population	Top 5 percent	Consumer price index 1947–49 = 100
1929	$ 674	$4,339	$ 690	$4,666	73.3
1939	537	2,982	528	2,831	59.4
1941	700	3,594	664	3,052	62.9
1946	1,234	4,926	1,166	4,118	83.4
1948	1,400	5,421			102.8
Percent increase:					
1929 to 1946	83	14	69	−12	14
1939 to 1946	130	65	121	45	40
1929 to 1948	108	25			40

SOURCES: Averages (see Table 1 for definitions) derived from Simon Kuznets, *Shares*, pp. 635, 637, 641, 644 (with 1948 extrapolated from 1947 by Kuznet's "basic variant" series). Consumer price index from Bureau of Labor Statistics.

deflate the portions of income used for income taxes and saving, will we be in a position to measure with precision changes in the distribution of real income.

Several related statistical series lend support to the finding that there has been a reduction in relative income differences in the post-1929 and particularly in the post-1939 period. The before-tax income measures include:

1. Changes in the Relative Importance of the Various Types of Income in the Personal Income Total. Since 1929 there has been a striking increase in the percentage that wages and salaries and transfer payments constitute of the personal income total flowing to families and unattached individuals. These payments together accounted for 61 percent of total personal income in 1929, 67 percent in 1939, and 73 percent in 1950–55 (Table 3). In contrast, there was a marked reduction in the shares of dividends and interest—types of income that are heavily concentrated in the upper end of the family income scale.[7]

[7] For a discussion of the relative importance of wages and salaries and other income shares in national income, see Edward F. Denison, "Income Types and the Size Distribution," AEA *Papers and Proceedings*, May, 1954, and "Distribution of National Income; Pattern of Income Shares since 1929," *Survey of Current Business*, June, 1952. Also, Jesse Burkhead, "Changes in the Functional Distribution of Income," *Journal of the American Statistical Association*, June, 1953, and George J. Schuller, "The Secular Trend in Income Distribution by Type," *Review of Economics and Statistics*, November, 1953.

Table 3. Percent Distribution of Family Personal Income by Major Types of Income and Relative Importance of Compensation of Employees in National Income, Selected Years

	1929	1939	1949	1950–55 average
Family personal income:				
Wages and salaries and other labor income	59.6	63.3	64.8	67.5
Transfer payments	1.7	4.0	5.9	5.4
Subtotal	61.3	67.3	70.7	72.9
Business and professional income:				
Farm	7.1	6.1	6.4	5.2
Nonfarm	10.5	10.2	10.7	9.8
Dividends and interest	14.7	12.6	8.2	8.3
Rental income	6.4	3.8	4.0	3.8
Total	100.0	100.0	100.0	100.0
Compensation of employees as a percent of national income originating in:				
Economy as a whole	58.2	66.1	65.2	67.3
Ordinary business sector (corporations, partnerships, and proprietorships)	61.2	65.8	64.0	66.4
All other sectors	46.9	67.2	69.8	70.7
All nonfarm corporations	74.5	80.9	75.8	76.6
Manufacturing corporations	75	81	74	75

SOURCES: Upper bank derived by adjusting U.S. Department of Commerce personal income series from *Survey of Current Business*, July, 1956, as described on pages 17–18 and 67 of "Income Distribution in the United States, by Size 1944–1950," U.S. Department of Commerce, 1953. Lower bank, except last line, derived from Table 12 (and underlying data) of 1954 *National Income* supplement and July, 1956, issue of *Survey of Current Business*. Last line derived from *Survey of Current Business*, November, 1956, page 20.

2. Changes in the Relative Distribution of the Various Types of Income. By examining the shares of the top 5 per cent in separate types of income, Kuznets found that the relative shares of this top group, based on data from tax returns, declined from 1929 to 1948 for wages and salaries, dividends, interest, and—to a lesser extent—for rental income. More recently, Herman Miller compared the wage and salary data reported in the last two Decennial Censuses of Population for detailed occupation and industry groups and found three factors making for a narrowing of income differentials within the wage and salary sector between

1939 and 1949: (*a*) decreases in relative income dispersion for men within practically all of the 118 occupations and 117 industries he studied; (*b*) relatively greater gains in median wage and salary income for low-paid than for high-paid occupations and industries; and (*c*) an increase in the proportion of workers classified in occupations with comparatively little income dispersion.[8]   Unfortunately similar data are not available from the Census for 1929.

Of particular interest to those in the teaching profession is Miller's finding that when the industries are ranked by size of median wage or salary and grouped into deciles, the educational services industry dropped from the third highest decile in 1939 to the fourth from the bottom in 1949.

3. *A Narrowing of Relative Income Differences, as Measured by Mean Incomes, between the Farm and Non-farm Population.*   Because average incomes are lower for farm than for nonfarm consumer units—even with allowance for income received in kind—a narrowing in this differential, barring other changes, will work in the direction of reducing relative income differences in the over-all income distribution.   Per capita income of persons on farms was three times as large in 1949 as in 1939— reflecting in part the relatively low level of farm income in the earlier year—whereas the corresponding ratio was two and one-half for persons not living on farms.[9]   Despite the fall in farm incomes in the past few years, the ratio of per capita income in 1952–55 to that in 1939 is still substantially higher for farm residents than for nonfarm.

Another recent study that has bearing on the subject under discussion is the analysis of changes since 1929 in income distribution by states that has been made by members of the staff of the Office of Business Economics.[10]   As part of this study, per capita incomes in the various states for selected years are expressed as percentages of the national average, and these percentages are compared over time.   Two major conclusions emerge.

First, "there has been a significant narrowing over the past

---

[8] Herman P. Miller, *Income of the American People* (New York, 1955), and "Changes in the Industrial Distribution of Wages in the United States: 1939–49," to be published in Vol. 23 of *Studies in Income and Wealth* (National Bureau of Economic Research).

[9] *Farm Income Situation* (No. 159, Agricultural Marketing Service, U.S. Department of Agriculture), July 17, 1956.

[10] *Personal Income by States Since 1929*, a Supplement to the *Survey of Current Business*, 1957.

quarter of a century in the relative differences in average-income levels among states and regions. . . .   As shown by the coefficient of variation, relative dispersion in the state per capita income array was reduced by nearly 40 percent from 1927–29 to 1953–55."

Second, the period of greatest narrowing of state per capita incomes was that of the war years, 1942–44.   Only a small part of the reduction in dispersion occurred in the prewar period, and "the regional differentials obtaining in 1944 were carried over with only moderate alteration into the postwar period and since then have tended to remain relatively stable in most regions."

These findings are remarkably consistent with those for the relative distribution of family income by size.   As was noted earlier, the period of greatest gain in relative income share for the two lowest quintiles in the family income size distributions was between 1941 and 1944, and after 1944 the available data show little change in the relative distribution of family personal income by size.   Of course, the narrowing of state differentials in average income does not of itself prove that there was a reduction in the relative dispersion of income by size, but it does lend credence to the finding that such a reduction took place.

We turn now to certain limitations in the income statistics. To save time I shall simply list four of the general ones: (*a*) Income for a single year is not a satisfactory measure of income inequality. (*b*) We do not have differential cost-of-living indexes appropriate for various income groups; so that we cannot measure with precision changes in the distribution of real income.   (*c*) The available statistics on the number and composition of families at the lower end of the income scale are particularly unsatisfactory.   (*d*) When we compare income shares of a given quintile or the top 5 percent in two periods, we are not comparing what has happened to an identical group of families, because the families comprising the quintile may be quite different in the two periods.   For certain purposes, as, for example, in interpreting the change in the income share of the top quintile or top 5 percent of families over, say, a five- to ten-year time span, it would be extremely helpful to know the extent to which the families comprising the top sector differed in the terminal periods.   Unfortunately, such family income data do not exist.

Next are several more specific limitations in the concept or coverage of the income measure that is used in determining relative income shares.   Included in what follows are several points raised by George Garvy at the meeting of the American Economics

Association three years ago and by Joseph Pechman at the latest Conference on Research in Income and Wealth of the Association.[11]

It is argued, in the first place, that various types of deferred compensation and a sizable amount of income in kind charged to business expense escape measurement in all of the income-size distribution series. Since these types of income presumably have grown in relative as well as absolute importance in the postwar period and since they accrue to a greater extent to upper than to middle or lower income groups, their exclusion from the basic statistics has the effect of exaggerating the decline in the relative share of total income received by the top income sector. Liberal expense accounts, free vacations, deferred compensation contracts, stock options given to corporate executives, and employer contributions to private pension, health, and welfare funds (these contributions are excluded from the family income-size distribution statistics though not from the monthly and annual personal income series) are the main items that have been listed.

Second, special tax allowances introduced in recent years, such as liberalized depreciation and depletion allowances, operate in the direction of understating the real income shares of top income groups in the postwar period. The splitting of dividend income among the children in the family for the purpose of reducing income tax liabilities would work in the same direction to the extent that the practice has grown in recent years, and full allowance for this factor cannot be made on the basis of the available statistics.

Aside from their effect on upper income shares, the items listed thus far, with one exception, have an important element in common: in the present state of our knowledge, reliable statistical magnitudes cannot be assigned to them. The exception relates to employer contributions to private pension funds for which reasonably good annual totals can be derived. However, this item is

[11] George Garvy, "Functional and Size Distributions of Income and Their Meaning," AEA *Papers and Proceedings*, May, 1954, and Joseph A. Pechman, "Comments on Mrs. Goldsmith's Paper," to be published in Vol. 23 of *Studies in Income and Wealth*. Also see, J. Keith Butters, Lawrence Thompson, and Lynn Bollinger, *Effects of Taxation: Investments by Individuals* (1953), pp. 104–9; reviews of Kuznets' *Shares* etc., by Dudley Seers, *Economic Journal*, June 1955, and Victor Perlo, *Science and Society*, Spring, 1954; Robert J. Lampman, "Recent Changes in Income Inequality Reconsidered," *American Economic Review*, June, 1954; and George Garvy, "A Report on Research on Income Size Distribution in the United States" (National Bureau of Economic Research, 1955, mimeographed).

probably much more widely distributed than the others on the list and its inclusion would presumably have only a minor effect on the relative income share of the top 5 percent.   (It may be noted that contributions to private pension funds are excluded from the family income measure in order to treat these funds in the same manner as public funds; i.e., benefits from them rather than contributions to them are included in family income.)

Third, another limitation of the statistics which, in this case, has been addressed only to the Kuznets' series relates to understatement of reportable amounts of income by top-sector taxpayers.   Kuznets measured top-sector incomes as the amounts reported by taxpayers on unaudited income tax returns (except for adjustments to add tax-exempt interest and imputed rent). It is argued that the percentage of understatement in reportable amounts of income for upper bracket taxpayers may be larger in recent than in prewar years and that the introduction of an allowance for this factor into the Kuznets' series would dampen the post-1929 or post-1939 decline in the relative income share of the top percentiles of the population.

Unlike Kuznets' series, the family income distributions have been adjusted to allow for income understatement on tax returns in all years and, with the possible exception of 1929, this adjustment included at least some of the income brackets in which the top 5 percent of consumer units resided.   However, mainly because a sufficiently detailed description of methodology is not available in the case of the family distribution for 1929, it is not possible to determine the magnitude of the adjustment for understatement of income that was applied in the top sector of tax returns in that year and compare it with the corresponding adjustment for the postwar period.   As was noted earlier, the post-1929 decline in the relative income share of the top 5 percent is smaller in the family distributions than in the Kuznets' series where no adjustment for this factor is made.   This suggests that the statistical adjustment for income understatement in the family distributions has been relatively larger in postwar years than in 1929, but until a complete reworking of the 1929 distribution is attempted this cannot be definitely asserted.   (It may be noted that the 1929 distribution included in the family income series represents the Brookings Institution's set of estimates for that year [*America's Capacity to Consume*, 1934] adjusted to remove capital gains and losses, which are excluded from the income definition used in family distributions for later years, and to reduce the Brookings' allowance for understatement of business income on tax returns for closer comparability with the figures for later years. Thus the resulting 1929 distribution incorporates a smaller allowance for income understatement in the upper income sector than the original Brookings Institution estimates but the magnitude of the allowance that remains could not be determined.)

Fourth, an important point that has been raised frequently by all of those concerned with the statistics on relative income distribution is the effect of the exclusion of capital gains from the income measure. The tax incentive to convert property and even other types of income into capital gains is of course well known, and it is argued that the practice has become increasingly widespread in recent years, particularly within the upper income sector.

By limiting capital gains and losses to the realized amounts reported on individual income tax returns (i.e., before statutory percentage reductions and limitations on losses) and by attributing these amounts to the year in which they were realized—both of these are, of course, debatable procedures—Kuznets measured the effect on upper income shares of adding net capital gains to ordinary income. On the basis of his figures, the percentage decline in the relative before-tax income share of the top 5 percent is the same for the period 1929 to 1946 whether or not capital gains are included (38 percent; see Table 1). For 1939–46, the percentage decline is reduced by the inclusion of realized capital gains by about one-sixth (from 28 to 23 percent), and it appears likely that the reduction for the post-1939 period would be more significant if the series were brought up through 1955.

We cannot assign reliable measures to the other factors that have been listed but there is little doubt that taken together they would serve to reduce the post-1929 decline in upper income shares. How large must they be if they were to eliminate the decline entirely? Using Kuznets' series, rough estimates of these amounts can be derived.

In 1946 the aggregate income of the top 5 percent of the population was 35 billion dollars exclusive of capital gains and 39 billion with realized net capital gains included—20.0 and 21.4 percent of the respective income totals for that year (Table 1). In order for the relative share of the top 5 percent to have been as large as in 1929—32.2 percent exclusive of capital gains or 34.8 percent with net capital gains included—a minimum of some 30 to 35 billion dollars would have to be added to the 1946 amounts. It is difficult to imagine that the factors listed above can account for magnitudes of anything like this size.

To reach 1939 rather than 1929 levels, the amount which would have to be added to the income of the top 5 percent in 1946 is in the neighborhood of 18 billion dollars if income is measured exclusive of capital gains, or 15 billion if realized capital gains are included. Again, it seems highly unlikely that the adjustments could be this large.

When we consider the postwar period by itself, the relative magnitudes involved are smaller but nevertheless substantial. The personal income flow to families and unattached individuals in 1955 was at an annual rate of somewhat under 300 billion dollars. Thus if the factors listed above accounted for 3 to 4 billion and accrued entirely to the top 5 percent of consumer units, the relative income share of this top group would be increased by 1 percentage point; i.e., from the presently estimated 21 percent to 22 percent; if they totaled 6 to 8 billion, the increase would be 2 percentage points, etc. In the present state of our statistical knowledge we cannot say which figure would be closest to the actual situation.

Intriguing in this connection is the decrease that has taken place between 1950 and 1953 in the number of federal individual income tax returns reporting high incomes. The number of tax returns decreased in practically all income brackets (before income taxes) above $200,000 between 1950 and 1951, in all brackets above $50,000 between 1951 and 1952, and in all brackets above $30,000 between 1952 and 1953, the last year for which these statistics are available.[12]   These decreases are in marked contrast to the general upward shift that took place lower on the income scale. For example, the number of returns reporting incomes between $10,000 and $30,000 was 50 percent larger in 1953 than in 1950, whereas the number above $200,000 was one-third smaller.

The decreases may well be connected with the stability in dividend payments to individuals in the years 1950–53 and the decline in statutory amounts of net capital gains reported on tax returns in 1952 and 1953. Both of these represent important components of total income for top income tax returns. Total dividends to persons remained close to nine billion dollars in each of these years and the excess of statutory capital gains over losses

[12] *Statistics of Income, Part 1, 1950, 1951* and *1952*, and *Preliminary Report for 1953* (Internal Revenue Service, U.S. Treasury Department).

reported on individual income tax returns declined from about three billion in 1950–51 to two and one-half billion in 1952 and to slightly over two billion in 1953.

Nevertheless, in view of the general increase in incomes and in particular the almost certain increase in upper bracket salaries in this period, the decrease is puzzling and merits close investigation, particularly if it should not be reversed in 1954 and 1955—years in which dividends increased sharply and realized capital gains almost certainly did. Such an investigation would require a more detailed tabulation of high-income returns than has been customary—in particular an exhaustive tabulation of all deductions and of all items relevant to the tax shelters that have been noted.

Fifth, the points noted thus far lie within the framework of personal income as the basic measure of the income flow to consumers. Of concern to many of us has been the fact that the relative distribution of income as it emerged from production may have changed over time in a different way from the distribution of personal income.[13]

The major differences between the production measure of the income flow—national income—and the personal income measure are that national income includes and personal income excludes elements of production not paid out to persons—undistributed corporate profits, the corporate inventory valuation adjustment, taxes on corporate profits, and contributions for social insurance—whereas the reverse is the case for elements of income received by persons but not accruing in production—transfer payments and government interest.

In particular, the fact that the undistributed earnings of corporations have accounted for a larger relative share of national income in the postwar period than before the war, coupled with the fact that they accrue to a relatively large extent to top-income groups, suggests that the post-1929 or post-1939 decline in the income share of the top sector would be smaller when such earnings are taken into account than when they are excluded from the income base.

Using Kuznets' data, Allan Cartter recently demonstrated that by including undistributed corporate profits and corporate income taxes in the income measure—allocating them between the

---

[13] The effects on relative income distribution of other modifications in income definition such as adding to family personal income the value of free government services and subtracting excise, sales, property, and other taxes in addition to individual income taxes cannot be covered within the confines of this paper.

top 5 percent and all other income groups combined on the basis of Kuznets' distribution of dividends—the decline in the relative income share of the top 5 percent of the population from 1937 to 1948 was reduced from the one-fourth shown by Kuznets to only 5 percent (if corporate income taxes are not shifted; to 13 percent if part of these taxes are assumed to be shifted).[14]   This appears at first glance to be in striking contrast to Kuznets' own calculations which showed that for the period 1939–46 the inclusion of undistributed corporate profits had only a moderate effect on the decline in the relative income share of the top 5 percent.   (The decline shown by Kuznets was 34 percent for disposable income and 27 percent for disposable income plus these profits.   Kuznets assumed no shifting.)

The difference in these results reflects in part differences in the time period studied.   Cartter's take-off point, 1937, was a year with very much smaller undistributed corporate profits than 1939; and in 1948 these retained earnings represented a larger share of the national income total than in 1946.   Thus Cartter's choice of the time period 1937–48 would be expected to produce more striking results than 1939–46.

But the main difference is due to the definition of undistributed corporate profits.   Kuznets included only undistributed profits *per se*, whereas Cartter distributed corporate income taxes as well.   Since factor incomes measured before rather than after income taxes are more useful for many types of economic analysis, it is preferable to impute these taxes along with undistributed profits to obtain a measure of the share of the upper income group in total national product measured at factor costs.

On the basis of rough allocations between the top 5 percent and the other 95 percent of consumer units of undistributed corporate profits, the corporate inventory valuation adjustment, corporate income taxes, and the other items of definitional difference between personal and national income, the following conclusions are reached: From 1929 to the average of 1950–55, converting from a personal income to a national income basis reduces the percentage decline in the relative income share of the top 5 percent of the population by about one-third (i.e., the decline is reduced from about 30 to about 20 percent).   The exclusion of transfer payments accounts for only a small part of

[14] Allan M. Cartter, "Income Shares of Upper Income Groups in Great Britain and the United States," *American Economic Review*, December, 1954.

Table 4. Percentage Shares of Top 5 Percent of Consumer Units in Family Personal Income and Rough Estimates of Corresponding Shares Using Various Other Definitions of Income, Selected Years

	1929	1939	1950–55 average	Percent decrease* 1929 to 1950–55	1939 to 1950–55
1. Family personal income (before income taxes)	30.0	25.8	20.7	31	20
2. Family personal income after federal individual income tax liability	29.5	24.8	18.5	37	25
Family personal income plus:					
3. Undistributed corporate profits	31	27	22	29	16
4. Undistributed corporate profits and corporate income taxes	32	28	26	20	7
5. Undistributed corporate profits, corporate income taxes, and inventory valuation adjustment	33	27	25	22	6
6. Family personal income minus transfer payments	31	27	22	28	19
7. National income (= line 5 minus transfer payments and government interest, plus contributions for social insurance)	33	27	26	21	5
8. National income minus corporate and individual income taxes	31	25	20	36	20

SOURCES: Lines 1 and 2 from sources cited in Table 1, columns 4 and 5. Lines 3–5 estimated by distributing each of the 3 corporate profits items (*Survey of Current Business*, July, 1956, Table 1) between the top 5 and the other 95 percent of consumer units in proportion to Kuznets' estimates of the distribution of dividend receipts (*Shares*, p. 649). For lines 6 and 7, rough estimates of the corresponding distribution of the other income items listed were derived as explained in *Review of Economics and Statistics*, February, 1954, page 20. Line 8 obtained by subtracting corporate income taxes (see line 4) and federal individual income tax liabilities (see line 2) from amounts underlying line 7.

* Based on unrounded figures.

the reduction; the major part is due to adding corporate income taxes along with retained corporate earnings (Table 4).

From 1939 to 1950–55 the corresponding reduction is about three-fourths. In place of a 20 percent decline in the relative share of the top 5 percent in personal income, there is a decline of only about 5 percent on a national income basis (i.e., the relative share of the top 5 percent in national income is estimated at about 27 percent in 1939 and about 26 percent in 1950–55). Again, the major reason for the dampening of the decline is the inclusion of retained corporate earnings and particularly corporate income taxes. The 5 percent decline is too small to be regarded as statistically significant and in fact may be due entirely to limitations of the statistics such as those listed under the first three points above. In other words, if income is measured in terms of the value of national production at factor costs rather than in terms of personal income flows, there appears to have been no reduction in the relative share of the top 5 percent of consumer units for the period 1939 to 1950–1955. On the other hand, if income is measured after income taxes, the decline since 1939 is sizable (Table 4) but as is true also for the post-1929 period as a whole, the reduction is overstated to an unknown extent by limitations in our income-share measures.

IN HIS EARLIER CRITIQUE OF KUZNETS' STUDIES, PERLO COMES *to conclusions similar to those of Goldsmith. His major point is that studies such as that of Kuznets focus on the distribution of income among individuals or families rather than among social and economic classes. Using this approach, Kuznets ignores the vast increase in corporate profits since 1929. Trends in the distribution of income from production have been the opposite of what Kuznets claimed for personal income, with the greatest increase occurring in the share going to corporate capitalists.*

Perlo argues that mere shifting of income among individuals and families within the same capitalist class, as income is split among descendants, would show up as decreased income concentration by Kuznets' method. Perlo also criticizes studies which use income tax statements without taking into account underreporting by those in the higher brackets—underreporting which is done to the greatest extent on income from dividends, interest, and rent and to the least extent on income from wages and salaries. Moreover, Kuznets estimates the income of those in the lower brackets by subtracting the income-tax-reported incomes of the top 5 percent from Commerce Department total income figures, thus exaggerating the incomes of the poor by the same amount that incomes of the wealthy are underestimated. The declining trend results, according to Perlo, largely from the increasingly important systematic tax evasion and avoidance which began as a "big business" in the 1930s with the introduction of ostensibly progressive income taxes. (The real relative tax burden on rich and poor is discussed by Budd in the next article.) Perlo also discusses the role of undistributed profits, coming to conclusions similar to Goldsmith's. A third weakness is Kuznets' failure to adjust for the tendency of the wealthy to split incomes.

Perlo claims that his studies reveal that, taken together, these three main errors in Kuznets' approach wholly eliminate the evidence for a downtrend in income inequality. In fact, in the years of Kuznets' study (1929 and 1948) the share of the top 1 percent of income receivers was about one-sixth of total personal income; that of the top 5 percent was 30 percent of the total.

12

A REVIEW OF "SHARES OF UPPER INCOME GROUPS IN INCOME AND SAVINGS"

Victor Perlo

Dr. Simon Kuznets [in his book, *Shares of Upper Income Groups in Income and Savings*] concludes that the shares of the upper income groups in total income have declined sharply since 1929, and especially since 1939. The share of the top 1 percent of the population in his "basic variant" of income falls from 14.65 percent in 1929 to 8.38 percent in 1948. The share of the top 5 percent falls from 26.36 percent to 17.63 percent over the same period. After-tax income shares drop still more rapidly.

These conclusions have received an unusual amount of publicity, probably more than any other piece of economic research in the United States in a long time. They have become part of official folklore, with references in government publications and presidential speeches. Arthur F. Burns, chief economic adviser to the President, speaks of a "social revolution" involved in Kuznets' results, and newspaper commentators have shown still less restraint in their panegyrics.

Most of the publicity preceded publication of the volume. It was based on a preliminary pamphlet which gave the main results, but only a sketch of the methods used, and on newspaper interviews and speeches. Since the appearance of the lengthy volume

Reprinted from *Science and Society*, Vol. 18, No. 2 (Spring 1954), 168–73 by permission of the publisher. The selection originally appeared as a book review.

itself in the spring of 1953, there has not been serious discussion or criticism in formal economic circles.   However, scattered comment has criticized particular aspects of the work.

The Kuznets work reflects years of painstaking labor by a skilled staff.   Different statistical series were reconciled with care and accuracy.   Technical pitfalls were avoided, in such matters as the handling of tax-exempt interest and fiduciary income.   To an extent unusual for a work of this type, the raw material is given which enables the student to retrace the steps taken.   Many of the tables can prove invaluable to research workers.

But technical virtuosity is not the main requirement.   Most vital are the assumptions and definitions which underlie the calculations.   Here Kuznets adopts a series of major premises which are wholly invalid.   Even more fundamentally, he concentrates attention on a secondary problem.   The main question in the field is the distribution of income among different classes in society, rather than among individuals.   Commerce Department figures show that between 1929 and 1948 corporate profits increased 244 percent, farm income 212 percent, income of unincorporated non-farm enterprises 177 percent, and private wages and salaries 156 percent (all before taxes).   Thus trends in the distribution of income from production have been the opposite of Kuznets' conclusions, with the share of the most powerful economic group, the large corporate interests, increasing the most.

In terms of social policy, it makes little difference—within certain limits—how many capitalists share in the distribution of corporate profits.   Suppose, for example, the Rockefeller and du Pont fortunes are divided among an increasing number of family members, so that the shares of the leading Rockefeller and du Pont are less than formerly; while the total Rockefeller and du Pont incomes are rising relative to the national income.   Then, according to Kuznets' approach, there is less concentration of income.   But in reality, in terms of class groupings, there is more concentration.   It is difficult to believe that a sufficient broadening of the top capitalist groups occurred to result in markedly different trends as between the class distribution of income and the distribution of individual incomes.   Therefore, the undeniable trend towards greater class concentration of private income provides a test and a check which should be applied to evaluate any study of the shares of top-bracket individuals.

It is within this narrower framework that Kuznets adopts biased premises.   He assumes—except for minor technical adjustments—that wealthy individuals report on income tax returns all of their incomes, not only as required by law, but as required to show their true income status. He assumes that wealthy stock-holders have no stake in undistributed corporate profits. He assumes that wealthy people make no efforts to pad their numbers of dependents or split incomes for tax purposes. These assumptions are stated in Kuznets' text only in qualified form. But his calculations are premised on their absolute validity.

1. TAX-RETURN INCOME VERSUS ACTUAL INCOME

Kuznets measures upper-bracket incomes as equal to that reported on tax returns, save for technical adjustments. Upper-income individuals have a powerful incentive to report as little net taxable income as possible, either by plain hiding of income, or by "inter-pretations" which reduce income and increase deductions. It is common knowledge that the "art" of keeping income low for tax purposes has become a big business today. It has become the main occupation of accountants, and is a service widely advertised by business advisory concerns.

The general amount and character of income unreported for tax purposes has been studied. Selma F. Goldsmith, also of the National Bureau of Economic Research, estimated that in the period 1944–46, 14 percent of all personal income was not reported. While only 5 percent of wages and salaries were unreported, 29 percent of entrepreneurial income, 24 percent of dividends, 63 percent of interest, and 55 percent of rent income went unreported. In short, non-reporting reaches huge dimensions exactly in the types of property income characteristic of the higher income groups. The wage earners, whose main earnings are taxed at the source, have little or no opportunity to get out of their tax payments.

However, even if the poor could and did evade taxes as much as the rich, this would not be reflected in Kuznets' method. He uses tax returns only for the top income groups. He does not use the tax returns of the poor. He uses the Commerce Department estimates of total income receipts. These are compiled mainly from reports of outpayments by government and business. There is generally no motive for biased reporting, and reasonable accuracy in the total results. Kuznets' estimates of lower-bracket incomes are the residuals obtained by subtracting the income-tax returns of the wealthy from the Commerce Department totals. Thus the incomes of the poor are exaggerated, by the same amount that those of the wealthy are underreported.

This shows that Kuznets attributes too low a share in total income to the top brackets. It doesn't yet touch the declining trend in that share. Here, the answer is equally simple. It is common knowledge, as explained by the New Deal tax expert Randolph Paul in his *Taxation for Prosperity*, that systematic tax evasion and avoidance began during the 1930s, and were raised to the level of a big business during World War II. This business has been continually "perfected" since.

Thus the bias in Dr. Kuznets' figures is least in 1929, greater by 1939, and really huge in post-World War II years. The "declining shares" of the upper income groups are largely statistical measures of the declining extent to which they report their income for tax purposes.

One would think that Kuznets would give serious consideration to non-reporting of income. Indeed, a chapter is devoted largely to the reliability of tax return data. It includes impressive facts, such as a summary of the Internal Revenue Bureau audits of 1948 upper-income tax returns. Two-thirds of the audited returns had errors, and 88 percent of the main errors consisted of underreporting of income. The Bureau assessed net additional taxes of 7.2 percent on all audited returns, and over 10 percent on those with errors. Such audits are necessarily superficial. Legal loopholes take care of much unreported income. Tax agents are concerned only with the residual, and on this, the normal practice is for tax agents and tax accountants to "compromise." Thus the assessments reflect only a small part of actual unreported income.

In a series of tables, Kuznets shows the reduction *ad absurdum* of his own method. For recent years, when most people filed income tax returns, he shows the incomes of the lowest 20 percent of the population as a residual, by subtracting tax-return income from total income. For 1948 the per capita income of this lowest 20 percent comes out to 108 percent of the average for all people; their dividend and interest receipts to 128 percent of the average, and their rent receipts to 270 percent of the average. This lowest group is shown as receiving more property income, of all kinds, per capita, than the group comprising the second layer from the top in income (the 6–10 percent bracket).

How does Kuznets get around such impressive pieces of evidence? He claims they provide ground for "assuming" that underreporting is largely in the lower income brackets, and for the "inference" that in the upper income brackets underreporting is trivial. At the crucial point, really by ignoring his own evidence and a mountain of additional evidence not considered, Kuznets saves his calculations by assumption and inference. Here is the "scientific" method of apologetics—129 long tables of statistics, checked well for precision and internal consistency, combined with refusal to apply data, and substitution of absurd general assumptions when faced with the vital question—are the correct figures put into the calculating machines?

2. UNDISTRIBUTED CORPORATE PROFITS

Kuznets omits undistributed corporate profits from his estimate of upper-bracket income (and total income as well). Incomes derived from corporate enterprise are the main forms of income of the highest brackets. Traditionally, and in 1929, most corporate profits were paid out in dividends. The wealthy individual spent part on consumption, reinvested the remainder to increase his profit base and power position. Today, in large part because of higher tax rates, most corporate profits are not paid out in dividends, but reinvested directly. To the wealthy individual, it doesn't make too much difference, except for the tax saving. Lawrence Seltzer, in his *The Nature and Tax Treatment of Capital Gains and Losses*, another recent National Bureau publication, shows that, by and large, the reinvested profits are reflected in the market prices of the stocks. The individual investor can take out his profit, if he wishes, by selling part of his stock, and paying the lower rate of tax on capital gains. Securities companies stress the value of so-called "growth stocks" to investors for this reason (e.g. the *United Investment Report* of the United Business Service, January 11, 1954).

Undistributed corporate profits (also incompletely reported) jumped from $2.5 billion in 1929 to $13.5 billion in 1948, and four-fifths of this amount accrued to the credit of the top 5 percent of income receivers. By omitting undistributed profits, Kuznets converts a formal shift in the method of recording profits, a shift to the advantage of the wealthy, into a purely fictitious reduction in their income shares.

3. INCOME SPLITTING AND DEPENDENTS

A third source of error is in Kuznets' identification of the top 1 percent and 5 percent of income receivers. He makes no adjustments for the tendency of wealthy persons to split incomes, to increase their exemption claims as tax rates rise, and in particular, no adjustments for changes in the law in 1944 and 1948, which permitted additional exemptions.   The effects of these law changes are identifiable and roughly measurable from income tax statistics. Thus, Kuznets' top 1 percent in 1948 represents a smaller proportion of the population than his top 1 percent in 1929.   To a certain extent, therefore, the "decline" shown in the share of the upper income groups simply reflects a narrowing of Kuznets' count of these groups.

The above discussion points out three errors in Kuznets' premises, all working in the same direction.   Each time, the assumption is biased to show a declining trend in top-bracket shares.

Do these errors account for all or only part of the decline in the share of the upper income groups shown by Kuznets?   Butters, Thompson, and Bollinger, in their excellent book *Effects of Taxation, Investment by Individuals* (Cambridge, Mass., 1953), note that Kuznets overstates the decline in upper income shares by failing to take account of unreported income.   They consider it unlikely that this factor is sufficient to account of all of the decline shown.   Geoffrey H. Moore, of the National Bureau of Economic Research, made alternative calculations including the allocation of a pro-rata share of undistributed corporate profits to wealthy individuals.   This substantially reduced, but did not eliminate, the downward trend in the share of the top brackets.

It is true that no one bias, by itself, accounts for all of Kuznets' results.   The present writer, in conjunction with the Labor Research Association, has assayed corrections for all three of the main errors in Kuznets' work.   In our opinion, these are minimal corrections.   But in their combined effect, they wholly eliminate the downtrend.   These calculations, roughly, show the upper 5 percent with one-third of the national income in both 1929 and 1948, and the upper 1 percent with about one-sixth of the national income in each of these years.

The Kuznets work, regardless of intentions, provides valuable propaganda backing for current attempts to reduce taxes on the wealthy, and to increase them on the poor as well as for reactionary steps in other economic fields.   Refutation of Dr. Kuznets' conclusions is important for those who consider that economic concessions to ordinary people, and not to wealthy, are needed to help people cope with the difficult times ahead.

BUDD PRESENTS DATA ON THE DISTRIBUTION OF PERSONAL INCOME
*from 1929 to 1962, by fifths, and by the top 5 percent of consumer units.
He points out that the income concept in his distributions is not that
arising directly from productive activity or the operation of the
market—points stressed by Goldsmith and Perlo in their articles.
Using the Gini concentration ratio as a measure of departure from
income equality, Budd shows that the relative distribution of income
has remained stable since 1944.   He is able to do this, even though he
uses the personal income concept.   The importance of the income tax
as a way of redistributing income more equitably is shown by comparing before- and after-tax personal incomes.   The income tax
pushes the distribution in the direction of greater equality, though the
effect is rather modest.   However, if the total tax burden is analyzed,
including sales, excise, property, and payroll taxes, the effect is the
opposite.   The percentage of income paid in taxes of all kinds is
actually smaller at higher incomes, according to studies by Musgrave.
Families with incomes at the bottom of the distribution, earning under
$2,000, paid out one-third of their income in taxes, compared to the
slightly higher amount of 36 percent paid out by those in the top income
bracket of $15,000 and over.*

13

INEQUALITY IN INCOME AND TAXES

Edward C. Budd

Much of our knowledge of the extent of inequality in the distribution of income and of changes in inequality over time is based on the work of the Office of Business Economics (OBE). . . .

[Data on] the full range of years covered by the series may be found in Table 1. This table gives the shares in total income of consumer units (families and unattached individuals), when ranked from lowest to highest by income and grouped into fifths or quintiles, and the share of the top 5 percent of all income recipients. Thus, in 1962 the poorest fifth of consumer units obtained less than 5 percent of total income, and the richest fifth, nearly half (46 percent). Had income been equally distributed, each group would, of course, have had 20 percent of the total.

Alternatively, the data in Table 1 could be cumulated from lowest to highest; on this basis, the lowest two fifths received 15.5 percent of total income in 1962; the lowest four fifths, 54 percent; the lowest 95 percent, 80 percent of total income. When shown graphically, the resulting curve is called a Lorenz curve. Were income distributed equally, this curve would correspond with the 45° line or diagonal; the latter may therefore be appropriately termed the line of equality. A widely used measure of inequality—

Reprinted from Edward C. Budd, ed., "An Introduction to a Current Issue of Public Policy," *Inequality and Poverty*, pp. x–xix, by permission of W. W. Norton & Company, Inc. Copyright © 1967 by W. W. Norton & Company, Inc.

Table 1. Percent Distribution of Family Personal Income[a] by Quintiles and Top 5 Percent of Consumer Units,[b] Selected Years, 1929–1962

Quintiles	1929	1935–1936	1941	1944	1947	1950	1951	1954	1956	1959	1962
Lowest	3.5	4.1	4.1	4.9	5.0	4.8	5.0	4.8	4.8	4.6	4.6
Second	9.0	9.2	9.5	10.9	11.0	10.9	11.3	11.1	11.3	10.9	10.9
Third	13.8	14.1	15.3	16.2	16.0	16.1	16.5	16.4	16.3	16.3	16.3
Fourth	19.3	20.9	22.3	22.2	22.0	22.1	22.3	22.5	22.3	22.6	22.7
Highest	54.4	51.7	48.8	45.8	46.0	46.1	44.9	45.2	45.3	45.6	45.5
Total	100	100	100	100	100	100	100	100	100	100	100
Top 5 percent	30.0	26.5	24.0	20.7	29.9	21.4	20.7	20.3	20.2	20.2	19.6
Gini concentration ratio	.49	.47	.44	.39	.40	.40		.39	.39		.40

SOURCE: For 1944–1962: Office of Business Economics, U.S. Department of Commerce; figures from *Survey of Current Business*, March 1955, p. 20; April 1958, p. 17; and April 1964, p. 8. Comparable estimates for years following 1962 are not available at this time. For 1935–36 and 1941: S. Goldsmith, *et al.*, "Size Distribution of Income Since the Mid-Thirties," *Review of Economics and Statistics*, Vol. 36 (February 1954), p. 9. For 1929: S. Goldsmith, "The Relation of Census Income Distribution Statistics to Other Income Data," *Studies in Income and Wealth*, Vol. 23, p. 92. For this year Mrs. Goldsmith gives a figure (12.5 percent) for only the two lowest quintiles combined; this percentage was allocated between the two percentiles by using the reversal of a Gini curve, as described by M. J. Bowman in *Readings in the Theory of Income Distribution*, Blakiston (1951). I am indebted to Alan MacFadyen for suggesting and carrying out this allocation, and for computing the Gini concentration ratios from the underlying OBE distributions by a method described by J. N. Morgan, "The Anatomy of Income Distribution," *Review of Economics and Statistics*, Vol. 44 (August 1962), p. 281.

[a] Family personal income includes wage and salary receipts (net of social insurance contributions), other labor income, proprietors' and rental income, dividends, personal interest income, and transfer payments. In addition to monetary income flows, it includes certain nonmonetary or imputed income such as wages in kind, the value of food and fuel produced and consumed on farms, net imputed rental value of owner-occupied homes, and imputed interest. Personal income differs from national income in that it excludes corporate profits taxes, corporate saving (inclusive of inventory valuation adjustment), and social security contributions of employers and employees, and includes transfer payments (mostly governmental) and interest on consumer and government debt.

[b] Consumer units include farm operator and nonfarm families and unattached individuals. A family is defined as a group of two or more persons related by blood, marriage, or adoption, and residing together.

Figure 1. Lorenz Curves for the Distribution
of Family Personal Income*

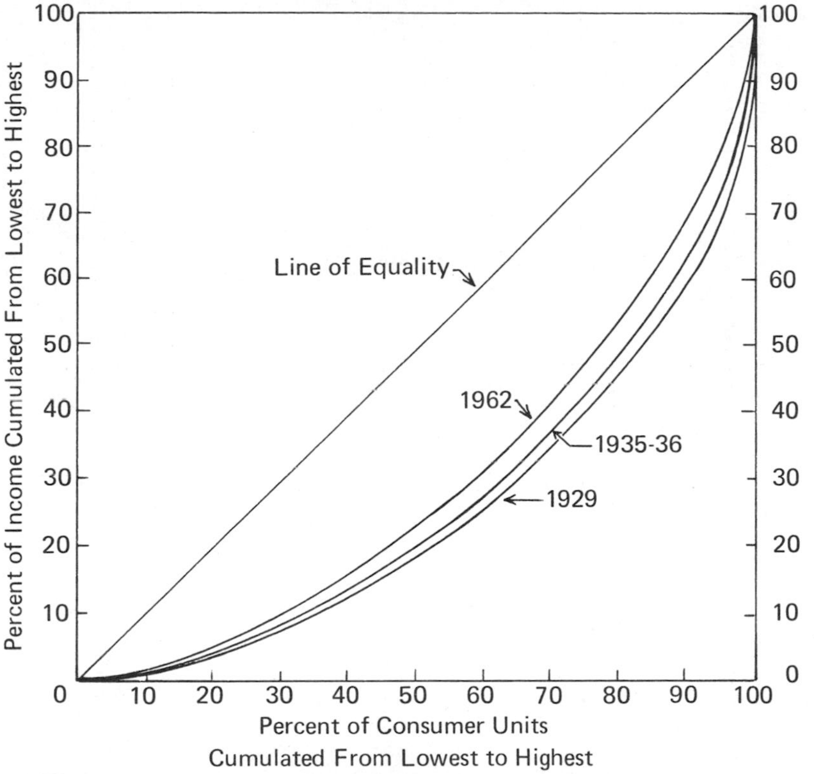

* The Lorenz curve for 1941 lies between those for 1935–36 and for 1962;
Lorenz curves for years from 1944 on are virtually identical with the 1962
curve.

the Gini concentration ratio, or coefficient of inequality—is the
ratio of the area between the Lorenz curve and the line of equality,
to the entire area lying under this line. Lorenz curves for the
1929, 1935–36, and 1962 distributions are shown in Figure 1;
concentration ratios for these and other years are given in Table 1.

A somewhat different way of presenting the underlying distributions, in terms of the average (mean) income of one group
relative to the average for all groups taken together, is shown in
Table 2. The mean income of all consumer units in 1962, when
measured in dollars of 1965 purchasing power, was $7,640. The
poorest quintile, however, had incomes which averaged only 23
percent of this figure, or $1,760; the mean income of the richest
quintile, on the other hand, was close to 2.3 times the mean for all

Table 2. Mean Family Personal Income per Consumer Unit, and Mean Income of Each Quintile and Top 5 Percent of Consumer Units, Expressed as a Percentage of the Mean Income for All Consumer Units, Selected Years 1929–1962

	1929	1935–1936	1941	1947	1950	1954	1959	1962
	Mean income per consumer unit							
Current dollars	$2,340	$1,630	$2,210	$4,130	$4,440	$5,360	$6,620	$7,260
Constant (1965) dollars	4,460	3,940	4,900	5,740	5,820	6,190	7,160	7,640
	Mean income of quintile expressed as a percent of mean income of all consumer units							
Lowest	18%	21%	21%	25%	24%	24%	23%	23%
Second	45	46	48	55	55	56	55	55
Third	69	71	77	80	81	82	82	82
Fourth	97	105	112	110	111	113	113	114
Highest	272	259	244	230	231	226	228	228
All quintiles	100	100	100	100	100	100	100	100
Top 5 percent	600	530	480	414	428	406	400	392
Highest quintile minus top 5 percent	163	168	165	167	165	166	171	173

SOURCE: First part: *Survey of Current Business*, April 1964, p. 5.   Converted to constant (1965) dollars by use of the OBE implicit price deflator for personal consumption expenditure.   Second part: Computed from Table 1, by dividing the income share of each quintile by 20 percent (or .20), the share of the top 5 percent by .05, and the share of the highest quintile minus the top 5 percent by .15.

units (and hence about 10 times that of the lowest quintile), or about $17,400. The top 5 percent enjoyed incomes which averaged 392 percent of the average income for all, or close to $30,000.

These figures are averages, of course, not the incomes making one eligible for membership in the class. In 1962, anyone with an income below $3,100 (again in dollars of 1965 purchasing power) would have found himself in the lowest quintile; on the other hand, it would have taken an income of over $10,400 to have placed him in the richest quintile, and over $18,000 to have put him in the top 5 percent. The range between $3,200 and $10,400 included the remaining three fifths of consumer units in 1962.

The income concept underlying the distributions in Table 1 and Table 2 is not that arising directly from productive activity, or so-called national income, but already reflects some of the redistributive effects of governmental and private institutions. For example, it excludes from labor earnings social security taxes paid to government and includes only a portion of corporate income—that part paid directly to stockholders in dividends, not the portion paid to the government in taxes or retained by corporations themselves in undistributed profits. Included are other items of a nonproductive character: interest payments on consumer and government debt and transfer payments (largely social insurance benefits and veterans' payments). While size distributions of national income would undoubtedly be useful in analyzing sources of inequality resulting directly from the operation of the market, empirical estimates are not at present available. As Mrs. Goldsmith's article suggests, the share of the top 5 percent is no doubt greater in national income than in personal income.

The importance of the personal income tax as a redistributive device can be determined by comparing distributions of personal income (Table 1 and Table 2) and disposable income (Table 3 and Table 4). As might be expected, the income tax pushes the after-tax distribution in the direction of more equality, although the effect is rather modest. In 1962, for example, the share of the top 5 percent was reduced by about 2 percentage points, with this increase spread over the four lowest quintiles. On a before-tax basis, the mean income of the richest quintile was 10 times that of the poorest quintile; on an after-tax basis, 9 times. The top 5 percent had before-tax incomes which averaged 17 times those of the bottom quintile, and after-tax incomes averaging 14 times those of the bottom.

Other taxes, such as sales, excise, property, and payroll taxes,

Table 3. Percent Distribution of Family Personal Income after Federal Individual Income Tax Liability by Quintiles and the Top 5 Percent of Consumer Units Ranked by Size of After-tax Income, Selected Years, 1929–1962

Quintiles	1929	1941	1950	1951	1954	1956	1959	1962
Lowest	12.6 {	4.3	5.1	5.4	5.3	5.2	4.9	4.9
Second		9.9	11.4	11.9	12.1	11.9	11.5	11.5
Third	13.9	15.9	16.8	17.2	17.4	16.9	16.8	16.8
Fourth	19.5	23.1	22.7	22.8	22.8	22.6	23.0	23.1
Highest	54.0	46.9	44.0	42.7	42.8	43.4	43.8	43.7
Total	100	100	100	100	100	100	100	100
Top 5 per cent	29.5	21.5	19.2	18.4	18.2	18.1	18.0	17.7

SOURCE: Same as for Table 1. Estimates for 1929 from S. Goldsmith, "Impact of the Income Tax on Socio-Economic Groups of Families in the U.S.," *Income and Wealth*, Series X (Bowes and Bowes), 1964, p. 268.

Table 4. Mean Family After-tax Income per Consumer Unit, and Mean After-tax Income of Each Quintile and Top 5 Percent of Consumer Units, Expressed as a Percentage of the Mean After-tax Income for All Consumer Units, Selected Years, 1929–1962

	Mean income per consumer unit					
	1929	1941	1950	1954	1959	1962
Current dollars	$2,320	$2,110	$4,070	$4,840	$5,940	$6,220
Constant (1965) dollars	4,430	4,680	5,330	5,700	6,440	6,840
	Mean income of quintile expressed as a percent of mean income of all consumer units					
Lowest	n.a.	22%	26%	25%	25%	25%
Second	n.a.	50	57	59	58	58
Third	70	80	84	86	84	84
Fourth	98	116	114	114	115	116
Highest	270	235	220	216	219	219
All quintiles	100	100	100	100	100	100
Top 5 percent	590	430	384	363	360	354
Highest quintile minus top 5 percent	163	159	165	166	172	173

n.a.—Not available

SOURCE: First part: *Survey of Current Business*, April 1964, and S. Goldsmith, *Income and Wealth*, Series X, p. 268. Second part: Computed from Table 3 by the method described in Table 2.

Table 5. Taxes As a Percent of Income for 1958

Tax source	Under $2,000	$2,000–3,999	$4,000–5,999	Family Personal Income Class $6,000–7,999	$8,000–9,999	$10,000–14,999	$15,000 and over	Total
Broadly-defined income concept[a]								
1. *Total taxes*	33.1%	29.6%	28.6%	27.7%	25.4%	25.2%	36.3%	29.5%
Federal taxes								
2. Individual income	2.1	5.0	6.6	8.8	8.3	9.6	15.8	9.4
3. Corporation income	3.5	2.9	2.6	2.7	2.8	3.6	10.5	4.6
4. Excises and customs	4.6	3.6	3.5	3.3	3.2	2.9	1.7	2.9
5. Estate and gift							1.6	.3
6. Social security	8.3	6.5	5.4	3.6	2.6	1.7	.8	3.3
7. Total	18.6	18.0	18.1	18.4	16.9	17.8	30.4	20.8
State and local taxes								
8. Individual income	.6	.9	.6	.3	.2	.3	.6	.5
9. Corporation income	.1	.2	.1	.1	.1	.2	.5	.2
10. Property	6.8	5.	4.6	4.1	3.8	3.0	2.1	3.7
11. Excises and customs	5.5	4.3	4.2	4.0	3.8	3.4	2.1	3.5
12. Estate and gift							.4	.1
13. Social security	1.5	1.1	1.0	.8	.6	.5	.2	.7
14. Total	14.5	11.6	10.5	9.3	8.5	7.4	5.9	8.7
Money-income concept[b]								
15. *Federal*, Total	19.5	19.3	19.2	19.3	17.8	18.9	31.8	21.9
16. *State and local*, Total	15.2	12.3	11.1	9.9	9.1	7.8	6.2	9.3
17. *Total*, all levels	34.7	31.6	30.3	29.2	26.9	26.7	38.0	31.2

SOURCE: R. A. Musgrave, "Estimating the Distribution of the Tax Burden," *Income and Wealth*, Series X, 1964, Table II, p. 192. The estimates are based on the following assumptions with respect to tax incidence: all sales and excise taxes, one third of corporate income taxes, and one half of employers' social security contributions are shifted to consumers in the form of higher prices.

[a] Family personal income (as defined in note 2 to Table 1) plus social security contributions, corporate retained earnings and profits taxes, and realized capital gains. (Including both, the latter may involve some double counting.)
[b] "Broadly defined income" minus nonmonetary or imputed income as described in footnote 2 to Table 1.

Table 6. Differential Incidence, 1958

Tax source	Under $2,000	$2,000– 3,999	$4,000– 5,999	$6,000– 7,999	$8,000– 9,999	$10,000– 14,999	$15,000 and over
			Family personal income class				
Broadly defined income concept							
Federal, Total	+2.2	+2.8	+2.7	+2.4	+3.9	+3.0	−9.4
State and local, Total	−5.8	−2.9	−1.8	−0.6	−0.2	+1.3	+2.8
Total, all levels	−3.6	−0.1	−0.9	+1.8	+4.1	+4.3	−6.6
Money-income concept							
Federal, Total	+2.4	+2.6	+2.7	+2.6	+4.1	+3.0	−10.1
State and local, Total	−5.9	−3.0	−1.8	−0.6	+0.2	+1.5	+3.1
Total, all levels	−3.5	−0.4	+0.9	+2.0	+4.3	+4.5	−7.0

SOURCE: Musgrave. *op. cit.*, Table III, p. 194. "Table III repeats the overall results of Table II in the form of differential incidence. The figures show the loss (−) or gain (+), expressed as a percent of income, which results as the actual tax structure is substituted for a general proportional income tax" (pp. 193, 195).

appear to have an opposite effect on income distribution. A study by Professor Musgrave for 1958, the results of which are summarized in Table 5 and Table 6, indicates that the percentage of income paid in taxes of all kinds was actually smaller at higher incomes. Only for the top 5 percent of consumer units with incomes above $15,000 did taxes take a larger proportion of income than at lower levels; the bottom group paid almost as large a percentage as the top one. While some of Musgrave's assumptions with respect to the shifting and incidence of certain taxes might be questioned, modifying them would not materially alter the results. In contrast to transfer payments, the evidence suggests that tax policy has not had a broadly redistributive effect.

Part Three

POVERTY: EXTENT, CAUSES, AND CONSEQUENCES

WILCOX DISCUSSES A VARIETY OF WAYS TO "MEASURE" POVERTY, *the types of budgets involved, and their relative merits for ascertaining the conditions under which the poor live. Usually, poverty is measured using budgets which supposedly cover the costs of goods and services needed to satisfy what are considered to be basic requirements. Though the composition of the group living in poverty changes somewhat, the size remains the same: about one-fifth of the population. This number can be determined by using either the standards of the Social Security Administration or those of the Council of Economic Advisers. These standards tend to understate the numbers of the poor, because the budgets are built on the basis of a diet designed for temporary emergency situations.*

The best known budget used by the U.S. Government is the "modest but adequate" City Worker's Family Budget, of the Department of Labor. The average amount of this budget stood at $9,191 in 1966. It was not intended nor used to measure poverty. The incomes of more than two-thirds of the country's families fell below it in 1966. Yet it contains nothing but goods and services necessary for a healthful, self-respecting mode of life, care of children, and participation in community life. Detailed examination reveals no luxuries. If a $9,000 budget is "modest," the meaning of the $3,000 poverty line ought to be clear.

14

THE MEASUREMENT OF POVERTY

Clair Wilcox

THE EXTENT OF POVERTY

How extensive is poverty in the United States? The answer will depend upon the standard that is used for its measurement. Poverty may be defined either in relative or in absolute terms. It has been proposed, for instance, that families in the bottom quintile of the income scale or families getting less than half of the median family income be defined as poor. Poverty, it is said, is a matter of social status. If one man gets less than another, he feels that he is poor; and if he feels poor, he *is* poor.

The phenomenon that would be measured by such a definition would be inequality, not poverty. But it is to the problems that are peculiar to poverty that the attention of society should be turned. These are the problems that are created by serious deprivation and by the misery that it entails. With a relative standard, there would be no measure of those who were really in need. In a prosperous country, a family might be counted as poor even though it was well housed, well clothed, well fed, and otherwise well cared for. Nor would there be a measure of the progress that might be made in lifting people out of poverty. The same percentage of the population would always be defined as poor, no matter how much their condition might have been improved.

Reprinted from Clair Wilcox, *Toward Social Welfare* (Homewood, Ill.: Richard D. Irwin, Inc., 1967), pp. 25–30, with permission of the publisher.

153

The standards by which poverty is usually judged are stated as absolutes. Such standards are established by preparing family budgets that cover the costs of goods and services that are found to be needed to satisfy basic requirements. The cost of food is estimated by determining the calories and nutrients needed for an adequate diet for persons of different sexes and ages, translating them into the types and quantities of foods customarily consumed, and pricing these foods at the markets where the families in question customarily buy. Rents are based on standards of structural safety, sanitation, ventilation, and cubic feet of space per person. Clothing rations for each member of the family are designed to assure cleanliness, dryness, warmth, and presentability. On similar bases, allowances are made for household equipment, toilet articles, medical and dental care, school supplies, streetcar fares, and so on. All these goods and services are priced, and the cost of the total budget is thus obtained. Such budgets are set at different levels, depending upon the character and the quantity of the goods and services that they include. Most of them allow for something more than bare subsistence; some of them for much more than others. Even though stated as absolutes, these standards are not rigid; they are adjusted from time to time, not automatically but through the exercise of judgment as conditions change.

Measures of Poverty

The most widely publicized estimate of the extent of poverty in the United States was that made by the Council of Economic Advisers in 1964.[1] The Council's estimate was based upon a study by the Social Security Administration of the income needed to support a nonfarm family of four. The SSA had established two standards for such a family, both based on estimates of dietary costs prepared by the Department of Agriculture. One provided for a "low-cost" budget, permitting the minimum diet consistent with the food preferences of the lowest third of the population and adequate to avoid basic nutritional deficiencies. This budget allowed 28 cents per person per meal, or $3.36 per family per day. On the basis of an Agriculture study made in 1955 showing that 35 percent of the expenditures of low-income families went for food, the size of the total budget was calculated by multiplying the food allowance by

[1] *Economic Report of the President, 1964*, Chap. 2.

three.   The resulting budget stood at $3,955.   This called for a far higher level of expenditure than welfare agencies were allowing for families receiving public assistance.   To meet the administrative need of these bodies, the SSA prepared a second budget. This was an "economy budget" based on a deficiency diet designed for temporary or emergency use.   It allowed 23 cents per person per meal for food or $2.74 per family per day.   Multiplied by three, this allowance set the total budget for a nonfarm family of four in 1962 at $3,165.[2]   On the basis of this figure, the CEA adopted $3,000 as its family poverty line.   In the same way, it arrived at $1,500 as the line for a single individual.   It thus found more than 9,000,000 families and 5,000,000 unrelated individuals, altogether some 35,000,000 people, a fifth of the nation, to be in poverty in 1962.

The Council's estimate was criticized on many grounds.   By taking as its basis a budget for a family of four not living on a farm, it set its figure for income needed by smaller families and by families living on farms too high.   By confining its figure for income received to money income, it disregarded such real income as the rental value of owners' homes and the value of food produced by families in their own gardens.   By confining this figure to income received during a single year, it disregarded the ability of many families to draw upon savings from earlier years or to borrow and repay in later years.   In all of these ways, it tended to overstate the extent of poverty.

In response to these criticisms, the Social Security Administration reworked its budget estimate to make allowance for differences in the size and composition of families and in their location.   As a result, it counted fewer aged people and fewer residents of farms among the poor, but more families with many children and more families living in urban areas.   Though the composition of the group in poverty differed, its size remained the same: about one fifth of the population.[3]   The SSA did not attempt to correct the Council's estimate to allow for income in kind, for past savings, or for possible borrowing.   In this respect, the tendency toward overstatement of the amount of poverty remained.

There are other respects, however, in which the estimates of the SSA and the CEA tended to understate rather than overstate

[2] Mollie Orshansky, "Counting the Poor: Another Look at the Poverty Profile," *Social Security Bulletin*, Vol. 27 (1965), pp. 3–29.

[3] Mollie Orshansky, "Recounting the Poor: A Five-Year Review," *Social Security Bulletin*, Vol. 29 (1966), pp. 20–37.

the numbers of the poor.   The budget used was built on the foundation of a diet that was deemed appropriate only for temporary use in an emergency.   It assumed that foods would be bought more economically, handled less wastefully, and prepared more skillfully than would in fact be the case.   It was to be doubted that families could be adequately fed for as little as 23 cents per person per meal.   If the budget had been built on the foundation of the low cost rather than the emergency allowance for food, it would have stood closer to $4,000 than to $3,000.   To get the total budget, moreover, the food allowance was multiplied by three, a ratio held to be appropriate in 1955.   But according to a study made in 1961, the fraction of total expenditures then going for food was not a third but a quarter.   Accordingly, unless allowances for items other than food were to be held below their customary share, the multiplier should have been not three but four.   On this basis, the total economy budget would have stood at more than $5,000 a year.   When these considerations are weighed against the Council's failure to allow for income in kind, for savings, and for ability to borrow, it does not appear that its estimate of the extent of poverty can have been too high.

Family Budget Studies

It was the purpose of the Council's estimate to establish a rough index by which to mark the overall dimensions of the problem of poverty.   Budget studies made for more than 60 years have had a number of other purposes.   They have been used in fixing the amount of money paid to persons on relief, in measuring changes in the cost of living, and in setting wage rates in union contracts. Most of these studies not only specify the family's need for food but spell out its requirements for other goods and services.   Here, the budget maker must decide what items are to be included and what quantities and qualities are to be allowed.   He will begin by prescribing the way in which the family's income ought to be spent, basing his prescriptions on standards of adequacy established by experts in the various fields.   He will then seek to determine how these standards are to be met by resorting to sample studies to discover how expenditures are actually made.   There is thus a large element of subjective judgment in the figure at which he finally arrives.

Budgetary requirements may be set at lower or higher levels, depending upon the budget maker's purposes.   The fraction of families whose incomes will not permit them to satisfy these requirements will vary accordingly. In 1960, the Social Security Administration found 22 percent of the people living in households that fell below its economy budget described above. It prepared another budget costing a third more, basing it on a more adequate dietary provision; and it found another 8 percent of the people whom it characterized as "near poor," altogether 30 percent of the population, falling below this line.[4] Oscar Ornati prepared budgets at three levels for a family of four in New York City in 1960. The first was a "minimum subsistence" budget, appropriate for a family living on relief; its cost was $2,660, and the incomes of one tenth of the city's families fell below this level. The second was a "minimum adequacy" budget, appropriate for families receiving other welfare services; its cost was $4,348, and the incomes of one fourth of the families fell below this level. The third was a "minimum comfort" budget, appropriate for civil service employees; its cost was $5,600, and the incomes of two fifths of the families fell below this level.[5]

The best known of the budgets is the "modest but adequate" City Worker's Family Budget prepared by the Department of Labor. This budget is designed for a standard family consisting of a man aged 35, his wife, a son aged 13, and a daughter aged 8. It can be adjusted, however, for differences in the size and composition of different families. The budget, originally based on living standards prevailing around the time of World War II, was priced in each of the major cities of the United States in 1946–47.[6] It was revised to conform to standards prevailing in the 1950s and priced in 1959[7] and again revised to embody the standards of the 1960s and priced in 1966.[8] The average cost of the budget stood at $3,118 in 1947, at $6,148 in 1959, and at $9,191 in 1966.

The costs of all such budgets have risen sharply over the years, and so, in consequence, have the figures taken as representing the poverty line. In part, this increase is to be attributed to a rise in the level of prices. In part, it reflects an increase in the standard

[4] *Ibid.*, p. 25.

[5] Oscar Ornati, *Poverty Amid Affluence* (New York: Twentieth Century Fund, 1966), Chap. 2.

[6] Lester S. Kellogg and Dorothy S. Brady, "The City Worker's Family Budget," *Monthly Labor Review*, Vol. 66 (1948), pp. 135–70.

[7] Helen H. Lamale and Margaret S. Strotz, "The Interim City Worker's Family Budget," *Monthly Labor Review*, Vol. 83 (1960), pp. 785–808.

[8] Phyllis Groom, "A New City Worker's Family Budget," *Monthly Labor Review*, Vol. 90 (1967), pp. 1–8.

of living.   Robert Hunter[9] set the cost of supporting a family of
five in New York City in 1904 at $460, a figure that would run to
$1,500 at the prices prevailing in 1964, or only half of that used as
a poverty line by the CEA.   Ruth Mack records a poverty line
based on current welfare budgets as rising by 40 percent, at constant prices, between 1935 and 1960.[10]   The Department of
Labor attributes a minor part of the 50 percent increase in its
budget from 1959 to 1966 to a rise in prices; a major part to the
fact that it provided for the purchase rather than the rental of
housing, for more general ownership of automobiles, for better
dental care, and for other improvements in the standard of living.

The City Worker's Family Budget was not intended, nor has
it been used, to serve as a basis for a poverty line.   The incomes of
more than half of the country's families fell below the level at
which it stood in 1959; the incomes of nearly two thirds fell below
its level in 1966.   Yet, according to the Department, it provides
nothing more than the goods and services needed for a healthful,
self-respecting mode of living, for the nurture of children, and for
normal participation in the life of the community.   Detailed
examination of the items it contains reveals none that appears to
be luxurious or extravagant.[11]   If a $9,000 budget is indeed
"modest," the $3,000 poverty line adopted by the CEA was even
more so.

[9] Robert Hunter, *Poverty* (New York: Macmillan Co., 1907), p. 52.

[10] Margaret S. Gordon (ed.), *Poverty in America* (San Francisco: Chandler
Publishing Co., 1965), p. 98.

[11] "The City Worker's Family Budget," *Bureau of Labor Statistics Bulletin*,
No. 1570–1, 1967.

ACCORDING TO BIXBY, OVER ONE QUARTER OF THE NATION'S *children are in families with incomes below the taxable limit. A quarter of these children have no father in the home. Low-income children suffer from poor nutrition and overcrowded housing in rundown neighborhoods. The ones from broken homes are twelve times as likely to have to live with relatives as are other children. Even crude data dividing children into only two income groups, above and below $4,000, indicate that children from ages five to fourteen in homes with incomes of over $4,000 visited the dentist three times as often as those from homes with incomes below that amount. There is a similar relationship with doctor's care. Yet these differences certainly do not reflect the need for care.*

Low-income children are much less likely to go to college, and less likely, if they do go, to stay and graduate. The smaller the husband's earnings, the more likely the wife is to work. In 1959, in families in which the father earned less than $3,000, mothers of preschool children were three times as likely to work outside the home as were those whose husbands were earning more than $10,000. The lower the family income, the worse the arrangements to care for the children of working mothers. Of children under twelve whose mothers worked full time and received public assistance, one in nine was left on his own. Even those cared for are often left with a relative under eighteen years old. "Moonlighting" is probably much more frequent among low-income families, the result being that children in low-income families have less contact with their fathers, also. Combined divorce and separation rates show family disruption to be greater in low-income families.

15

SOME EFFECTS OF LOW INCOME ON CHILDREN AND THEIR FAMILIES

Lenore E. Bixby

To be a child in a family with inadequate income often means to be a child deprived of the kinds of food he needs to grow to healthy adulthood. It often means living in overcrowded quarters, with no decent place to play; going without preventive health care; and having little chance for more than a high school education. For about one in four it means that there is no father in the home; the mother is likely to work while the child is still very young.

INCIDENCE OF LOW INCOMES

A discussion of the effects of inadequate income implies the existence of a standard of adequacy. There is, however, no single accepted standard of adequate family income, although on certain cutoff points there is little or no argument.

How Many Children Are in Low-income Families?

Robert Lampman, in a study paper prepared in 1959 for the Joint Economic Committee, estimated that in 1957 about one-fifth of

Reprinted from the *Social Security Bulletin*, Vol. 24 (1961), 12–17, by permission of the publisher. The article is adapted from a talk given by Mrs. Bixby at the November 1961 meeting of the Interdepartmental Committee on Children and Youth. Footnotes and tables have been renumbered.

the children in the United States were in families that had low incomes. Lampman defined a "low-income person" as "one with an income equivalent to that of a member of a four-person family with total money income of not more than $2,500 in 1957 dollars."[1] In 1957 purchasing power this is the same as the $2,000 in 1947 that a congressional subcommittee on low-income families adopted as a minimum income figure for study purposes in 1949.

By another criterion, it is estimated that in 1959 almost one-fifth of the families, with nearly one-fourth of the nation's children, had low incomes. These are families with incomes below the taxable limit under present Federal income tax laws—that is, less than $1,325 for a mother and child and less than $2,675 for a married couple with two children and $4,000 for a family of six.

That this is a conservative gauge of low income is evident from the fact that an income below the taxable limit is generally not much more than twice the amount needed for an adequate diet at low cost, according to the food plan issued by the U.S. Department of Agriculture.[2] The average family actually spends about one-third of its income for food.[3] Moreover, the food plan makes no allowances for "snacks," for meals eaten out, or for serving guests. It assumes that the housewife is a skillful cook, a good manager, and a careful shopper who will choose the most nutritionally economical foods from those in season.

The estimate that about 16 million children under age 18, or one-fourth of the total, are in families with incomes below the taxable limit was developed from the Bureau of the Census income distributions for families classified by number of related children, which are summarized in Table 1. For the purposes of these estimates it was assumed that each family contained two adults in addition to the number of children specified. In fact, 20–25 percent of the families with children under age 18 contained at least three adults, and about 5 percent contained only one adult. Cutoff points for the taxable incomes assume the standard 10-percent deduction, although many families have larger deductions.

[1] Robert J. Lampman, "The Low Income Population and Economic Growth," prepared for the Joint Economic Committee in connection with its *Study of Employment, Growth, and Price Levels* (Study Paper No. 12, Joint Committee Print, 86th Congress, 1st session), December 16, 1959.

[2] *Family Economics Review*, published quarterly by the Department's Institute of Home Economics.

[3] See Department of Agriculture, *Food Consumption and Dietary Levels of Households in the United States* (ARS 62-6, August 1957).

**Table 1. Distribution of Families by Total Money Income
in 1959, by Number of Children under Age 18**
(Noninstitutional population of the United States)

Total money income	Families with specified number of children					
	1	2	3	4	5	6 or more
Number (in thousands)	8,858	8,432	5,182	2,389	1,103	1,030
Percent	100.0	100.0	100.0	100.0	100.0	100.0
Less than $1,000	4.6 %	3.6 %	4.1 %	4.7 %	4.1 %	8.4 %
$1,000–1,999	6.4	4.9	4.7	7.4	9.8	13.6
$2,000–2,999	9.1	6.3	7.1	8.3	9.1	13.7
$3,000–3,999	11.4	9.3	8.9	10.5	12.8	12.3
$4,000–4,999	11.3	13.2	12.7	13.7	13.4	13.3
$5,000–5,999	13.4	15.5	15.7	14.7	14.0	12.2
$6,000–7,999	20.2	23.4	22.2	21.1	17.5	17.0
$8,000–9,999	11.1	12.3	11.5	9.4	9.5	5.5
$10,000 or more	12.5	11.7	13.0	10.0	9.7	4.1
Median income	$5,534	$5,833	$5,792	$5,367	$5,048	$4,136

SOURCE: Bureau of the Census, *Current Population Reports*, P-60, *Consumer Income*, No. 35.

As a result of these assumptions the number with incomes below the taxable limits is probably underestimated. Any overstatement of the number of families with small incomes that results from the tendency of respondents in field surveys to forget small or irregular receipts is thus probably more than offset.

Who Are the Families With Low Incomes?

Incomes vary both from family to family and for the same family at different stages in its life cycle, but year after year certain groups of families tend to have lower incomes than the population as a whole. Prominent among these groups are nonwhite families generally, families where the head does not work full time throughout the year, and broken families—especially those headed by women. Subfamilies—that is, families that do not maintain their own household but make their home with a relative—are also likely to be found in the low-income group.

The differences in income between families in which both parents are present and those with only the mother present are particularly striking. At the latest count, about 1 in every 12 children (more than some 5 million in all), were living in homes with only the mother present. Special tabulations of Census Bureau data for 1956 indicate, however, that about one-fourth of the children in families with incomes below the taxable limit had no father in the home. These data show also that the average income of families consisting only of a mother and children was about one-third the average received when there were two parents and children but no other persons in the family.

EFFECTS ON LIVING CONDITIONS

Low income characteristically means poor nutrition, poor housing, little or no preventive medical care. The facts hardly need documentation, but the extent of deprivation suffered by low-income families has been made clear in various studies.

Nutrition

A clear relationship between family income and the quantities of nutrients provided by the diet of nonfarm families was found by the Department of Agriculture in its 1955 Household Food Consumption Survey.[4] For the 8 million or more children on farms, where income typically is lower than it is in cities, adequacy of diet is less closely related to income. In seasons of the year when homegrown and homepreserved fruits and vegetables have generally been used up, however, farm diets provide less vitamin A and vitamin C—important nutrients for children—than do city diets.

Housing

There are many examples of the inverse relationship between income and overcrowding and the direct correlation between income and the physical qualities of housing, the extent of conveniences, the quality of the neighborhood, and so on. Moreover, broken families whose incomes tend to be low are likely to share the home of relatives. In 1959, almost a fourth of the one-parent families but only 2 percent of the married couples with children lived in a relative's home.[5]

[4] Report No. 6, March 1957.
[5] Derived from Bureau of the Census, *Current Population Reports*, Series P–20, *Population Characteristics*, No. 100.

The fact that overcrowded housing in rundown neighborhoods—with lack of privacy at home and lack of proper play space—may have unfortunate effects on children needs no underlining.

Medical Care

The National Health Survey,[6] like previous surveys, found that the amount of medical care received by a family was related to the family income. The frequency of visits to the dentist provides not only a measure of the amount of dental care received but an index of ability to obtain preventive health care in general. It is therefore significant that there are substantial variations with family income in the number of dental visits by children. Among children aged 5–14, for example, those in families with incomes of $4,000 or more visited a dentist three times as often as did the children in families with incomes of less than $4,000. The variations would be more apparent if data were available for finer income intervals.

Children in families with incomes of $4,000 or more also visited physicians more frequently than those in lower-income families. The differences are most striking at the younger ages— 0–4 and 5–14—where children in the higher-income families saw a doctor one and one-half times as often as children in lower-income families.

It is clear from the Survey that the difference does not reflect variations in need for medical care. The amount of family income—using the same broad income classification—was not related to the number of days missed from school because of illness or the number of days of restricted activity or days spent in bed because of disability.

EFFECTS ON EDUCATION

Children in homes with inadequate income are less likely to go to college than those whose families are better off. When they do go, they are less likely to stay to graduate.

An Office of Education study, published in 1958, reported lack of financial resources as a major cause of transfer or of dropping

[6] Public Health Service, *Health Statistics from the U.S. National Health Survey: C–1, Children and Youth: Selected Health Characteristics, United States July 1957–June 1958* (October 1959).

Table 2

1959 income of family	Percent
Less than $3,000	12
3,000–4,999	25
5,000–7,499	28
7,500–9,999	55
10,000 and over	65

SOURCE: John B. Lansing, Thomas Lorimer, and Chikashi Moriguchi, *How People Pay for College*, September 1960, p. 108, Table 41.

out of college completely. For students who stayed to graduate, the median income of the families was $1,000 higher than for students who dropped out by the end of the first term, and it was almost $500 higher than for all nongraduates. Students' ability, however, as measured by placement tests, bore almost no relationship to family income.[7]

A sample survey just completed for the Office of Education by the Michigan Survey Research Center shows a sharp correlation between family income and actual or expected college attendance. Of the children aged 20–29 in 1960, for example, the proportion that had attended or were attending college was about five times as large when family income exceeded $7,500 as when it was less than $3,000, as shown in Table 2.

It is interesting that for younger children there is a similar relationship between parents' income and plans for the child to attend college. The younger the child, however, the more likely his family is to be planning for his college education.

A recent report by the Bureau of Labor Statistics compares the experience of high school graduates in seven communities with that of students who dropped out of high school or who graduated but did not go on to college.[8] It shows that economic need was not a major reason for dropping out of high school, if the phrase is interpreted to mean that the family could not supply the child with the necessities for school attendance. A study of two Louisiana parishes (counties), where information was obtained on

[7] Robert E. Iffert, *Retention and Withdrawal of College Students*, Bulletin 1958, No. 1.
[8] *School and Early Employment Experience of Youth: A Report on Seven Communities, 1952–57*, BLS Bulletin No. 1277, August 1960.

the occupation of the father, suggests, however, that dropouts are much less common among the upper socio-economic groups.[9] The parents' interest in education seemed to be related to their socio-economic status.

The study by the Bureau of Labor Statistics provides telling evidence of lower earning power and higher unemployment rates among dropouts. Undoubtedly, further evidence exists that young people who drop out of school early have only a limited choice of jobs and lower earnings potential and that, as a result, the unfavorable economic situation in which they grow up tends to be perpetuated for them and for their children.

EFFECTS ON EMPLOYMENT OF FAMILY MEMBERS

Working Mothers

Despite the large number of married women who now work—many from choice—it is still true that the smaller the husband's earnings the more likely the mother is to work. Among mothers with preschool children (under age 6) the proportion in the labor force in 1959 was more than three times as large when the husband earned less than $3,000 than when his earnings exceeded $10,000.[10]

Mothers are also much more likely to work when there is no father in the home to share family responsibilities than when he is present. In March 1959, the proportion of mothers in the labor force varied with the age of the children and the presence of the father, as shown in Table 3.

The Children's Bureau has just released a report summarizing what is known and what is not known about the effects of a mother's employment on the development and adjustment of the individual child and also on family structure and functioning.[11] The evidence, though incomplete and inconclusive, suggests "that the quality of the family life influences the effects of a mother's outside employment more than her employment influences the quality of the family life."

[9] Alvin L. Bertrand and Marion B. Smith, *Environmental Factors & School Attendance: A Study in Rural Louisiana*, Louisiana Agricultural Experiment Station, Bulletin No. 533, May 1960.

[10] Jacob Schiffman, "Family Characteristics of Workers, 1959," Reprint No. 2348, from the *Monthly Labor Review*, August 1960, Table 5.

[11] Elizabeth Herzog, *Children of Working Mothers*, Children's Bureau Publication No. 382, 1960.

Table 3

Age of children in years	Percent Married, husband present	Widowed, divorced, or separated
6–17, none younger	40	66
Under 6	19	45
None under 3	25	53
Some under 3	16	40
Total under 18	28	57

SOURCE: Jacob Schiffman, "Family Characteristics of Workers, 1959," Reprint No. 2348, From the *Monthly Labor Review*, August 1960, Table 5.

Woefully little is known about the quality of substitute care, which can be crucial for a child's development and adjustment if the mother does work. There is no doubt, however, that total lack of care is hazardous. A national survey undertaken in 1958 by the Bureau of the Census for the Children's Bureau showed that 1 in 13 of the children under age 12 whose mothers worked full time were left to take care of themselves.[12] A study made by the Bureau of Public Assistance of families receiving aid to dependent children in late 1958 shows that 1 in 9 of the children under age 12 whose mothers worked full time were left on their own.[13] The difference suggests that lower incomes are associated with less adequate arrangements for care. Moreover, about one-third of the relatives taking care of the child, when arrangements for care were reported, were under age 18. Because of their age, it seems likely that they were older siblings who might be out of school for the purpose.

Teenagers Helping Out

There is some evidence that teenagers are brought into the labor force when the father loses his job. A special survey of unemployment in Utica, New York, shows that when men aged 45–54 become unemployed the number of family members (other than

[12] See Henry C. Lajewski, "Working Mothers and Their Arrangements for Care of Their Children," *Social Security Bulletin*, August 1959.

[13] Bureau of Public Assistance, *Characteristics and Financial Circumstances of Families Receiving Aid to Dependent Children*, Bureau Report No. 42, 1960, Table 28.

the wife) in the labor force increases from 4 out of every 10 to 7 out of 10.[14]

"Moonlighting" Fathers

Low earnings may cause a man with heavy family responsibilities to "moonlight"—to take on a second job—a course that surely has an effect on family life and the children's relationship to the father. A recent report by the Bureau of Labor Statistics shows that in December 1959, for example, 6.5 percent of the married men held two or more jobs simultaneously.[15] This was about twice as high a proportion of multiple jobholders as for other men and three times as high as for women.

Information is lacking on the extent to which need or opportunity leads a worker to take a second job. It is noteworthy, however, that 40 percent of the men with more than one job reported the occupation in their primary jobs as farmer, laborer, service worker, or factory operative—typically low paid. On the other hand, professional and technical men led all others in the rate of dual jobholding—presumably because their experience and skill open opportunities for extra work, and some, such as teachers, strive for a level of living higher than their salaries provide.

Migratory Workers

It is impossible even to outline in this summary report the hazards for child life when a family follows the migratory stream. The evidence is clear that it is a very low earning potential that creates our migratory labor force, and that the children of migrant workers have the least opportunities for proper development. In many cases they themselves work at a very young age, and many of them do not have the advantage of even an elementary school education or minimal health protection.

EFFECTS ON FAMILY STABILITY

As already suggested, poor and overcrowded housing and pressure for earnings to supplement or substitute for those of the father may affect family life unfavorably.

[14] A. J. Jaffe and J. R. Milavsky, *Unemployment, Retirement and Pensions*, paper presented at the Fifth Congress of the International Association of Gerontology, San Francisco, August 1960.

[15] Gertrude Bancroft, "Multiple Jobholders in December 1959," *Monthly Labor Review*, October 1960.

Table 4

Years of school completed	Divorce and separation rates per 1,000 women (standardized for age)		
	Combined	Divorce	Separation
Elementary:			
0–8	10.7	3.8	6.9
High School:			
1–3	9.9	4.9	5.0
4	7.0	4.0	3.0
College:			
1–3	7.1	4.7	2.4
4 or more	5.4	3.4	2.0
Total	8.7	4.1	4.6

There is relatively little direct evidence on the relationship between income level and divorce and separation rates. Paul Glick's analysis of Census data for 1950, however, shows the rates of separation for women (standardized for age) varying inversely with years of school completed,[16] which is one of the best indicators of socio-economic status. Divorce rates were found lowest for women with four or more years of college and highest for those with one to three years of high school (the problem dropout group), but the rate for those who had no secondary schooling was also relatively low. When divorce and separation rates for women aged 15–54 are combined, it seems clear that family disruption is associated with low economic status, as shown in Table 4.

A special study of 1950 data for Philadelphia shows that divorce as well as desertion tends to be inversely correlated with occupational levels.[17] These findings raise a question on the validity of the cliché that desertion is the poor man's divorce—one that is supported, however, by Dr. Glick's finding that divorced men had higher incomes than men separated from their families. In any case, much more research is needed on the relationship between family stability and economic status.

The impact that family breakdown has on children may be inferred more directly from the way the proportion of families with children under age 18 that include only one parent—usually the mother—varies according to the education of the family head.

[16] Paul G. Glick, *American Families*, a volume in the Census Monograph Series, New York, 1957, Chap. 8, especially Table 102.
[17] William M. Kephart, "Occupational Level and Marital Disruption," *American Sociological Review*, August 1955.

Table 5

Years of school completed	Percent
Elementary:	
0–8	11.7
High school:	
1–3	9.5
4	8.2
College:	
1–3	6.3
4 or more	2.9

SOURCE: Bureau of the Census, *Current Population Reports*, Series P-20, *Population Characteristics*, No. 100, Table 6. Comparable data on the education of the head are not available for subfamilies.

In March 1959 the 2.2 million one-parent families (including those with a widowed parent) represented 9 percent of the nation's 25 million families with children. The percentage of families that contained only one parent varied according to the education of the family head, as shown in Table 5.

These data suggest that when the family head has a college degree the child has four times as good a chance of living in a home with two parents as when the head never went beyond elementary school. Some but certainly not all of the difference reflects the fact that widows are older and therefore tend to have less education.

No evidence is available on the relationship of illegitimate first conceptions and economic status. Certainly it is clear that the well-to-do have a better chance than the poor of avoiding and of concealing an illegitimate birth. Moreover, it probably would not be disputed—though factual evidence is sparse—that multiple illegitimate births generally occur to women in the lowest socio-economic groups.

16

NEGROES' HEALTH IS FOUND LAGGING

Robert B. Semple, Jr.

The health gap between Negroes and whites is widening despite increased Federal aid and steady advances in medical science, two New York public health officers [have] reported. . . .

In papers prepared for a conference on the conditions of Negroes' health sponsored by Howard University, Dr. James G. Haughton and Paul M. Demsen presented detailed statistical evidence suggesting that the health of Negroes, judged by mortality tables, had improved much more slowly than the health of whites in recent years.

Mr. Densen is deputy administrator of the Health Services Administration in New York City, and Dr. Haughton is the first deputy administrator. They are among several hundred physicians, scholars and Government officers who are participating in the two-day conference, one of a series of meetings being held by the university in conjunction with its 100th anniversary.

"There is a great tragedy in all this," Dr. Haughton declared, "and the tragedy is that in this great health revolution some segments of the population have been left behind." He gave the following examples:

In 1930, pregnant Negro mothers were twice as likely to die in childbirth as pregnant white women. In 1964, the mortality rate was 22.3 per 100,000 live births among white mothers but 89.9 for nonwhites.

In 1940, 14 times as many nonwhite mothers [as white mothers] were delivered by midwives. . . .   In 1960, the figure was 23 times as many.

Between 1960 and 1964, the number of newly reported cases of tuberculosis in New York City increased by 1 percent among Negroes but decreased by 12 percent among Puerto Ricans and 28 percent among whites.

Mr. Densen, who co-authored his paper with Dr. Alfred Haynes, associate professor of internal health at Johns Hopkins University in Baltimore, asserts that the Negro American was at a serious disadvantage almost from the time of conception.   In 1963, he said, the death rate per 1,000 live births was 13.7 for the white population and 26.7 for the nonwhite.

"What is even more discouraging," the authors declared, "is that the gap in infant mortality is also widening.   In 1950, the infant mortality rate for the nonwhite was 66 percent higher than the rate of the white, but in 1964 the rate for the nonwhite was 90 percent higher."

Both papers argued that the differences in the health of the white and Negro populations were not racially determined.   The basic problem, they suggested was that modern medicine simply had failed to reach the poor Negro.

INACCESSIBILITY CRITICIZED

"The most important factor may be the limited accessibility of services," Dr. Haughton said.   "Many of our services are available but inaccessible because there are built-in deterrents.   Our clinic schedules are arranged for the convenience of the medical staff, not the patient.   Even the location of the services may serve as a deterrent."

17

A NOTE ON DEATH IN VIETNAM

Maurice Zeitlin

Men from poor families are overrepresented among troops killed in Vietnam, according to the findings to be reported in a forthcoming article by myself and Kenneth Lutterman, with James W. Russell.

The alleged universalistic standards of the armed forces are affected by the class origins of the enlisted men and officers. Based on individual data on all 380 servicemen from Wisconsin who died in Vietnam through 1967, we found that 27.6 percent came from families classified as "poor" by official standards, in contrast to the comparable cohort figure of 12.4 percent in the population. That is, about twice as many sons of poor families die in Vietnam as would if their share of the dead were equitable or proportional. The disproportionate representation of the poor is even greater among nonofficers.

Most striking is the finding that *within each economic class*—farmers, workers, and middle class—the poor are also overrepresented by about twice their equitable share of the dead. Taking poverty level into account does not eliminate differential class mortality in Vietnam. Among the poor and nonpoor, farmers' and middle-class sons are underrepresented; in contrast, manual workers are overrepresented among the "nonpoor."

The poor are probably overrepresented among the dead in Vietnam because they are least likely to qualify for—or know of—specific types of draft deferments, especially college deferments;

the same may apply, although less so, to manual workers who are not poor compared to the nonpoor in nonmanual occupations.

Deaths in Vietnam also occur from accidents and personal illness. Separating deaths from hostile action and deaths from other causes, we found that there is a general tendency for servicemen from poor families—in all ranks combined and in all branches of the service—to be more likely to die in hostile action than their counterparts from families that are not poor. Among workers' and farmers' (though not middle-class) sons—again, with all branches and ranks combined—the servicemen from poor families are more likely than nonpoor to be killed in hostile action. When poverty level is taken into account, the differences between economic classes are not systematic. However, of all strata, poor workers have the highest proportion of deaths from hostile action. The differences in death from hostile action may occur because jobs in the armed forces carry different amounts of risk with them, and job allocation probably falls along stratification lines, the poor (and poor workers in particular) are least likely to be assigned to administrative, supply, or other less risky positions, and more likely to be exposed to hostile action and the risk of death.

INCREASED OUTPUT HAS REDUCED POVERTY FROM THE PROBLEM OF *a majority to that of a minority. According to Galbraith, two major types of poverty persist in the U.S.: case and insular poverty. In the first, some quality peculiar to the individual or family involved—from mental deficiency to excessive procreation—prevents him from participating in the general well-being. Insular poverty characterizes communities whose members' "homing instinct" causes them to stay in an island of poverty rather than to migrate to areas of higher income. Escape may not be possible in some circumstances, however: in an urban slum, race or poverty may confine individuals to an area of limited opportunity and the environment may perpetuate the handicaps of the young.*

A tolerably well-distributed advance in income, argues Galbraith, will not remedy modern poverty, though it may have some effect. Required are measures to break the self-perpetuation of poverty: investment in adequate education and care of poor children, and the provision of other necessary services by the government; and slum clearance and expansion of low and middle-income housing. Personal, educational, mental, and physical handicaps can also be remedied if we use the knowledge we already have and invest in people. Preoccupation with production and material investment diverts our attention from the more urgent question of how we employ our resources.

18

THE NEW POSITION
OF POVERTY

John Kenneth Galbraith

"The study of the causes of poverty," Alfred Marshall observed at the turn of the century, "is the study of the causes of the degradation of a large part of mankind." He spoke of contemporary England as well as of the world beyond. A vast number of people both in town and country, he noted, had insufficient food, clothing, and houseroom; they were: "Overworked and undertaught, weary and careworn, without quiet and without leisure." The chance of their succor, he concluded, gave to economic studies "their chief and their highest interest."[1]

No contemporary economist would be likely to make such an observation about the United States. Conventional economic discourse does make occasional obeisance to the continued existence of some poverty. "We must remember that we still have a great many poor people." This usefully allays uneasiness about the relevance of conventional economic goals and especially of economic efficiency. For some people, wants must be synthesized. Hence the importance of the goods is not *per se* very high. But others are far closer to need. And hence we must not be cavalier about the urgency of providing them with the most for the least. The sales tax may have merit for the opulent, but it still bears

Reprinted from John Kenneth Galbraith, *The Affluent Society* (New York: New American Library, A Mentor Book, 1958), pp. 250–58. Reprinted by permission of the publisher, Houghton Mifflin Company and the author. Copyright © 1958 by John Kenneth Galbraith.

[1] *Principles of Economics* (8th ed.), pp. 2–4.

heavily on the poor. Thus poverty survives in economic discourse partly as a buttress to the conventional economic wisdom. Still, in a world of a weekly industrial wage of eighty dollars and a $3960 median family income, it can no longer be presented as a universal or massive affliction. It is more nearly an afterthought.

The privation of which Marshall spoke was, a half century ago, the common lot at least of all who worked without special skill. As a general affliction, it was ended by increased output which, however imperfectly it may have been distributed, nevertheless accrued in substantial amount to those who worked for a living. The result was to reduce poverty from the problem of a majority to that of a minority. It ceased to be a general case and became a special case. It is this which has put the problem of poverty into its peculiar modern form.

II

For poverty does survive. There is no firm definition of this phenomenon and again, save as a tactic for countering the intellectual obstructionist, no precise definition is needed. In part it is a physical matter; those afflicted have such limited and insufficient food, such poor clothing, such crowded, cold and dirty shelter that life is painful as well as comparatively brief. But just as it is far too tempting to say that, in matters of living standards, everything is relative, so it is wrong to rest everything on absolutes. People are poverty-stricken when their income, even if adequate for survival, falls markedly behind that of the community. Then they cannot have what the larger community regards as the minimum necessary for decency; and they cannot wholly escape, therefore, the judgment of the larger community that they are indecent. They are degraded for, in the literal sense, they live outside the grades or categories which the community regards as acceptable. In the mid-fifties, by acceptable estimate, one family in thirteen in the United States had a cash income from all sources of less than a thousand dollars. In addition a very large number of individuals, not members of families, were in this income class. To some extent family life is itself a luxury of an adequate income. The hard core of the very poor was declining but not with great rapidity.[2]

[2] *Statistical Abstract, 1957*, p. 312. In 1955, 7.7 percent of families were estimated to have had incomes of less than $1000 as compared with 8.8 in 1954, 8.6 in 1953 and 8.5 in 1952. These figures reflected a reduction from 11.5 percent in 1950 when, however, prices were considerably lower.

A substantial share of these low incomes are in agriculture—in 1964, 27.4 percent of all farm families had cash incomes of less than a thousand dollars as compared with 4.9 percent of urban families who were below this level. These rural families had further incomes in the form of shelter and farm-grown food which causes the estimate of cash income to understate their position. However, there is probably more danger of exaggerating than of minimizing the contribution of the unpainted shacks, the reluctant animals, and the barren garden patches by which the rural poor eke out their income.

This agricultural poverty has a tendency to be concentrated in specific areas. The Appalachian plateau and its valleys, parts of the southern coastal plain and the Piedmont plateau, the country of low hills between the Appalachians and the Mississippi, the cutover lands of the Lake States, the Ozark plateau, all provide examples. In 1950 in such areas nearly a million farm families had *gross* receipts of less than $1200 and about a quarter of a million had less than $250. In the southern Appalachians the average net income of *all* full-time farmers in 1949 was less than $500. In the southern Piedmont the average was only slightly higher. In 1950 a million and a half farm families, principally in the above-mentioned areas, had net cash incomes from all sources of less than a thousand dollars.[3] The modern locus of poverty is even more the rural than the urban slum.

III

One can think of modern poverty as falling into two broad categories. First there is what may be called *case* poverty. This, one encounters in every community, rural or urban, however prosperous that community or the times. Case poverty is the poor farm family with the junk-filled yard and the dirty children playing in the bare dirt. Or it is the grey-black hovel beside the railroad tracks. Or it is the basement dwelling in the alley.

Case poverty is commonly and properly related to some characteristic of the individuals so afflicted. Nearly everyone else has mastered his environment; this proves that it is not intractable. But some quality peculiar to the individual or family involved—mental deficiency, bad health, inability to adapt to the discipline of modern economic life, excessive procreation,

[3] *Development of Agriculture's Human Resources*, A Report on Problems of Low Income Farmers (United States Department of Agriculture, 1955). Figures showing gross receipts exclude farmers over sixty-five years of age.

alcohol, insufficient education, or perhaps a combination of several of these handicaps—have kept these individuals from participating in the general well-being.

Second, there is what may be called *insular* poverty—that which manifests itself as an "island" of poverty. In the island everyone or nearly everyone is poor. Here, evidently, it is not so easy to explain matters by individual inadequacy. We may mark individuals down as intrinsically deficient; it is not proper or even wise to so characterize an entire community. For some reason the people of the island have been frustrated by their environment.

This is not the place to explore in detail the causes of insular poverty. They are complex and many of the commonly assigned causes are either excessively simple or wrong. The resource endowment or the fertility of the land, the commonplace explanations, have little to do with it. Connecticut, a state of high incomes, has few resources and a remarkably stony soil. West Virginia is richly endowed. Connecticut has long been rich and West Virginia poor.

Insular poverty has something to do with the desire of a comparatively large number of people to spend their lives at or near the place of their birth. This homing instinct causes them to bar the solution, always open as an individual remedy in a country without barriers to emigration, to escape the island of poverty in which they were born. And so long as they remain they are committed to a pattern of agricultural land use or of mining, industrial, or other employment which is unproductive, episodic, or otherwise unremunerative.[4] Meanwhile the poverty of the community insures that educational opportunities will be limited, that health services will be poor, and that subsequent generations will be ill-prepared either for mastering the environment into which they are born or for migration to areas of higher income outside. It is a reasonable presumption, too, that the homing instinct operates most powerfully among the poorly educated.

[4] Thus in the Appalachian plateau, settlement occurred along the valleys on farms which were of the small scale appropriate to a largely self-sufficient agriculture. Time has rendered such agriculture obsolete. Other areas produce the same crops far more efficiently; changing standards have made what once seemed a tolerable standard of living exceedingly primitive. Yet the massive reorganization of land use that would be required—far larger farms or conceivably highly capitalized forest enterprises—are far beyond the capacities, both educational and financial, of the people involved. Meanwhile the homing instinct causes them—or at least a large number—to persist in the area.

In some circumstances escape may not be possible.   Especially in the urban slum, race or poverty may confine individuals
to an area of intrinsically limited opportunity.   And once again
the environment perpetuates its handicaps through poor schools,
evil neighborhood influences, and bad preparation for life.

The most certain thing about modern poverty is that it is
not efficiently remedied by a general and tolerably well-distributed
advance in income.   Case poverty is not remedied because the
specific individual inadequacy precludes employment and participation in the general advance.   Insular poverty is not directly
alleviated because the advance does not necessarily remove the
specific frustrations of environment to which the people of these
islands are subject.   This it not to say that it has no effect.
Secure job opportunities elsewhere, a concomitant of industrial
advance, work against the homing instinct.   And so even more
directly does the spread of industrialization.   The appearance of
industry in parts of the Tennessee Valley area has had a strong
remedial effect on the insular poverty of those areas.   But it
remains that advance cannot improve the position of those who,
by virtue of self or environment, cannot participate or are not
reached.

IV

These circumstances have caused a profoundly interesting although
little recognized change in what may be termed the political
economy of poverty.   With the transition of the very poor from
a majority to a comparative minority position, they ceased to be
automatically an object of interest to the politician.   Political
identification with those of the lowest estate has anciently brought
the reproaches of the well-to-do, but it has had the compensating
advantage of alignment with a large majority.   Now any politician who speaks for the very poor is speaking for a small and also
inarticulate minority.   As a result the modern liberal politician
aligns himself not with the poverty-ridden members of the community but with the far more numerous people who enjoy the far
more affluent income of (say) the modern trade union member.
Ambrose Bierce, in *The Devil's Dictionary*, called poverty "a file
provided for the teeth of the rats of reform."   It is so no longer.
Reform now concerns itself with people who are relatively well-to-
do—whether the comparison be with their own past or with those
who are really at the bottom of the income ladder.

The poverty-stricken are further forgotten because it is assumed that with increasing output poverty must disappear. Increased output eliminated the general poverty of all who worked. Accordingly it must, sooner or later, eliminate the special poverty that still remains. As we have just seen, this is not to be expected or, in any case, it will be an infinitely time-consuming and unreliable remedy. Yet just as the arithmetic of modern politics makes it tempting to overlook the very poor, so the supposition that increasing output will remedy their case has made it easy to do so too.

To put the matter another way, the concern for inequality had vitality only so long as the many suffered privation while a few had much. It did not survive as a burning issue in a time when the many had much even though others had much more. It is our misfortune that when inequality declined as an issue, the slate was not left clean. A residual and in some ways rather more hopeless problem remained.

V

An affluent society, that is also both compassionate and rational, would, no doubt, secure to all who needed it the minimum income essential for decency and comfort. The corrupting effect on the human spirit of a small amount of unearned revenue has unquestionably been exaggerated as, indeed, have the character-building values of hunger and privation. To secure to each family a minimum standard, as a normal function of the society, would help insure that the misfortunes of parents, deserved or otherwise, were not visited on their children. It would help insure that poverty was not self-perpetuating. Most of the reaction, which no doubt would be almost universally adverse, is based on obsolete attitudes. When poverty was a majority phenomenon, such action could not be afforded. A poor society, as this essay has previously shown, had to enforce the rule that the person who did not work could not eat. And possibly it was justified in the added cruelty of applying the rule to those who could not work or whose efficiency was far below par. An affluent society has no similar excuse for such rigor. It can use the forthright remedy of providing for those in want. Nothing requires it to be compassionate. But it has no high philosophical justification for callousness.

Nonetheless any such forthright remedy for poverty is beyond reasonable hope. Also, as in the limiting case of the alcoholic or the mental incompetent, it involves difficulties. To spend income requires a minimum of character and intelligence even as to produce it. By far the best hope for the elimination, or in any case the minimization, of poverty lies in less direct but, conceivably, almost equally effective means.

The first and strategic step in an attack on poverty is to see that it is no longer self-perpetuating. This means insuring that the investment in children from families presently afflicted be as little below normal as possible. If the children of poor families have first-rate schools and school attendance is properly enforced; if the children, though badly fed at home, are well nourished at school; if the community has sound health services, and the physical well-being of the children is vigilantly watched; if there is opportunity for advanced education for those who qualify regardless of means; and if, especially in the case of urban communities, law and order are well enforced and recreation is adequate—then there is a very good chance that the children of the very poor will come to maturity without grave disadvantage. In the case of insular poverty this remedy requires that the services of the community be assisted from outside. Poverty is self-perpetuating because the poorest communities are poorest in the services which would eliminate it. To eliminate poverty efficiently we should invest more than proportionately in the children of the poor community. It is there that high-quality schools, strong health services, special provision for nutrition and recreation are most needed to compensate for the very low investment which families are able to make in their own offspring.

The effect of education and related investment in individuals is to enable them either to contend more effectively with their environment, or to escape it and take up life elsewhere on more or less equal terms with others. The role of education as an antidote to the homing instinct which crowds people into the areas of inadequate opportunity and frustration is also clear. However, in the strategy of the attack on insular poverty a place remains for an attack on the frustrations of the environment itself. This is particularly clear in the case of the slum. Slum clearance and expansion of low and middle-income housing removes a comprehensive set of frustrations and greatly widens opportunity. There is a roughly parallel opportunity in the rural slum. By identifying a land use which is consistent with a satisfactory standard of living, and by assisting with the necessary reorganization of land and capital, public authority can help individuals to surmount frustrations to which they are now subject. The process promises to be expensive and also time-consuming. But the question is less one of feasibility than of will.[5]

Nor is case poverty in the contemporary generation wholly intransigent. Much can be done to treat those characteristics which cause people to reject or be rejected by the modern industrial society. Educational deficiencies can be overcome. Mental deficiencies can be treated. Physical handicaps can be remedied. The limiting factor is not knowledge of what can be done. Overwhelmingly it is our failure to invest in people.

VI

It will be clear that to a remarkable extent the requirements for the elimination of poverty are the same as for social balance. (Indeed a good deal of case poverty can be attributed to the failure to maintain social balance.) The myopic preoccupation with production and material investment has diverted our attention from the more urgent questions of how we are employing our resources and, in particular, from the greater need and opportunity for investing in persons.

Here is a paradox. When we begin to consider the needs of those who are now excluded from the economic system by accident, inadequacy, or misfortune—we find that the normal remedy is to make them or their children productive citizens. This means that they add to the total output of goods. We see once again that even by its *own terms* the present preoccupation with material as opposed to human investment is inefficient. . . .

But increased output of goods is not the main point. Even to the most intellectually reluctant reader it will now be evident that enhanced productive efficiency is not the *motif* of this volume. The very fact that increased output offers itself as a by-product of the effort to eliminate poverty is one of the reasons. No one would be called upon to write at such length on a problem so easily solved as that of increasing production. The main point lies elsewhere. Poverty—grim, degrading, and ineluctable—is not remarkable in India. For few the fate is otherwise. But in the

[5] The problem of the rural slum, and its reorganization, is one on which one must say either very little or very much. I have had to follow the first course here. I have treated the problem at more length in "Inequality in Agriculture—Problem and Program," J. J. Morrison Memorial Lecture, Ontario Agricultural College, Guelph, Canada, 1956.

United States the survival of poverty is remarkable. We ignore it because we share with all societies at all times the capacity for not seeing what we do not wish to see. Anciently this has enabled the nobleman to enjoy his dinner while remaining oblivious to the beggars around his door. In our own day it enables us to travel in comfort through south Chicago and the South. But while our failure to notice can be explained, it cannot be excused. "Poverty," Pitt exclaimed, "is no disgrace but it is damned annoying." In the contemporary United States it is not annoying but it is a disgrace.

CAUDILL, WHOSE ROOTS IN APPALACHIA DATE BACK TO THE 1790s, *has practiced law in the mountain courthouses for twenty years, as well as serving in the Kentucky legislature. He analyzes the combination of political economic forces which have turned Appalachia into a "depressed" area.*

For six decades, absentee corporations held the region's mineral wealth in their control, with the result that the region's booms and busts depended on the profit-rates of the corporations. The courts upheld and enlarged corporate control and privileges gained in the nineteenth century, so that with the advent of new technology, the region was despoiled. Thousands of acres of timber were cut by the companies without compensating the owners; waters were diverted and polluted; livestock died of hunger and thirst; roads were run through fertile gardens; poisonous waters were sluiced onto crop land; and coal grit was hurled onto fields of corn—all with the aid and approval of the courts.

The companies were granted rights they had never paid for and gained control over the present estate and future heritage of the land. New methods of surface or strip mining replaced or supplemented tunneling. Huge sheets of coal half a mile long, eight feet thick and fifty wide were bared in a few days. Because it was cheaper to the companies, the region's men were put out of work and its streams and land ruined. Auger mining accentuated and perhaps finalized the region's desolation. Yet the companies prevented even minimal attempts by the state to reclaim and stabilize the land, and state governors fail to enforce even moderate legislation to restrain the mine owners.

The essential element in all this, according to Caudill, is that the region has constituted a colonial appendage of corporations centered in the industrial East and Middle West. Timber, coal, crops and workers were exploited for the profits of the corporations; the corporations corrupted or intimidated public officials. The result was that little money remained to maintain decent schools, libraries, hospitals and other institutions necessary for a decent life.

The only organized resistance came from the United Mineworkers Union which, after violent struggles, was able to improve the working and living conditions of the miners and to build health facilities for the miners. However, the union accepted the domination of the big companies and tried to protect the miners in the big mines at the expense of those in the small ones. As a result, low wages and dangerous working conditions came to predominate once more. In an attempt to change these conditions, the UMW called a major strike in 1959. The strike failed, however, at the cost of several months of violence, during which miners were killed and the National Guard was called in.

The Federal Government, meanwhile, acts as if in collusion with the mineowners, failing to make even token enforcement of minimum wage requirements of the Fair Labor Standards Act. Fewer and fewer remain at work. And now the coal industry, faced with competition from petroleum and natural gas, is itself in rapid decline, taking with it what remains of the region and its people.

19

THE RAPE OF THE APPALACHIANS: THE 1950s

Harry Caudill

Strip mining, a branch of the industry which had previously been practiced in such flat coalfields as western Kentucky and southern Illinois, invaded the Cumberlands on a vast scale [in the 1950s].

For nearly sixty years the greater part of the region's mineral wealth had lain in the iron clutch of absentee corporations. They had prospered and bankrupted and prospered again. But through their triumphs and tragedies, their successes and failures, the corporations had clung to all the old rights, privileges, immunities, powers and interests vested in them by their nineteenth-century

Reprinted from Harry M. Caudill, *Night Comes to the Cumberlands* (Boston: Little, Brown, an Atlantic Monthly Press Book, 1963), pp. 305–16, 325–32, by permission of Atlantic-Little, Brown and Co. Copyright © 1962, 1963 by Harry M. Caudill.

land and mineral deeds.   These relics from a laissez-faire century were construed to authorize the physical destruction of the land and the abject improverishment of its inhabitants.   With strip mining and its companion, the auger-mining process, the shades of darkness moved close indeed to the Cumberlands.

The courts have written strings of decisions which not only uphold the convenants and privileges enumerated in the ancient deeds and contracts but which, in the opinion of many lawyers, greatly enlarge them as well.   We have seen that when the mountaineer's ancestor (for the seller is, in most instances, long since dead) sold his land he lived in an isolated backwater.   Coal mining was a primitive industry whose methods had changed little in a hundred years and which still depended entirely on picks and shovels.   To the mountaineer "mining" meant tunneling into a hillside and digging the coal for removal through the opening thus made.   That the right to mine could authorize shaving off and destroying the surface of the land in order to arrive at the underlying minerals was undreamed of by buyers and sellers alike.

But technology advanced.   The steam shovel grew into a mighty mechanism and was replaced by gasoline and diesel-powered successors.   "Dozers" and other efficient excavators were perfected.   Ever cheaper and safer explosives came from the laboratories.   These marvelous new tools enabled men to change the earth, abolishing its natural features and reshaping them as whim or necessity might require.   And as these developments made possible a radically new application of the privileges granted in the yellowed mineral deeds, the courts kept pace.   Year by year they subjected the mountaineer to each innovation in tools and techniques the technologists were able to dream up.   First, it was decided that the purchase of coal automatically granted the "usual and ordinary" mining rights; and then that the usual mining rights included authority to cut down enough of the trees on the surface to supply props for the underground workings.   This subjected thousands of acres to cutting for which the owners were uncompensated.   It gave the companies an immensely valuable property right for which they had neither bargained nor paid.

Next came rulings which gave the companies the power to "divert and pollute" all water "in or on" the lands.   With impunity they could kill the fish in the streams, render the water in the farmer's well unpotable and, by corrupting the stream from which his livestock drank, compel him to get rid of his milk cows and other beasts.   They were authorized to pile mining refuse wherever they desired, even if the chosen sites destroyed the homes of farmers and bestowed no substantial advantage on the corporations.   The companies which held "long-form" mineral deeds were empowered to withdraw subjacent supports, thereby causing the surface to subside and fracture.   They could build roads wherever they desired, even through lawns and fertile vegetable gardens. They could sluice poisonous water from the pits onto crop lands. With impunity they could hurl out from their washeries clouds of coal grit which settled on fields of corn, alfalfa and clover and rendered them worthless as fodder.   Fumes from burning slate dumps peeled paint from houses, but the companies were absolved from damages.

The state's highest court held in substance that a majority of the people had "dedicated" the region to the mining industry, and that the inhabitants were estopped to complain of the depredations of the coal corporations, so long as they were not motivated by malice.   Since malice seldom existed and could never be proved, this afforded no safeguard at all.   The companies, which had bought their coal rights at prices ranging from fifty cents to a few dollars per acre, were, in effect, left free to do as they saw fit, restrained only by the shallow consciences of their officials.   When the bulldozer and power shovel made contour strip-mining feasible and profitable in mountainous terrain, the court promptly enforced the companies' right to remove the coal by this unusual and wholly unforeseen method.

The court spurned as unimportant the fact that competent engineers swore only 20 percent of the coal in a virgin boundary could be recovered even when both strip and auger mining were employed in unison.   It brushed aside proof that strip mining destroys the land and eradicates the economic base on which continued residence within the region is predicated.   It substantially adjudicated away the rights of thousands of mountaineers to house and home.   It bestowed upon the owner of a seam of coal the right to destroy totally the surface insofar as any known system of reclamation is concerned.   It delivered into the hands of the coal corporations the present estate and future heritage in the land—in effect an option to preserve or ruin present and future generations.   These fateful decisions of the state's highest court, decisions medieval in outlook and philosophy, are now buttressed by the hoary doctrine of *stare decisis* and can be dislodged only by social and political dynamite.   And while there is strong reason to suppose that the court as presently constituted views these

decisions with uneasiness and dismay, its relatively enlightened
judges feel duty-bound to apply them in new appeals.   This long
line of judicial opinions opened the way for what may prove to be
the final obliteration of the plateau's future as a vital part of the
nation and its history.

It is probable that this process of judicially straitjacketing the
mountaineers for the benefit of the coal companies reached its
apogee in a decision handed down by the Court of Appeals on
November 15, 1949.   The appeal came up from the Circuit Court
of Pike County.   It involved one of the earliest stripping operations to be undertaken in eastern Kentucky.   The Russell Fork
Coal Company had cut the top off a mountain on Weddington
Fork of Ferrells Creek, leaving ten acres of loose earth, mixed to
a great depth with stones and fragments of trees.   This vast mass
of unstable rubble lay on the upper reaches of a narrow valley, on
the floor of which several families made their homes.   It was
created in an area which had been battered by flash floods throughout its history, so that even the feeblest of minds could have
anticipated their recurrence at almost any time.   On the night of
August 2, 1945, the calamity came in the form of a cloudburst and,
foreseeably, thousands of tons of dirt, rocks and shattered tree
trunks from the devastated mountain were flung down the hillside
into the raging creek.   Like a titanic scythe the rolling rubble
swept downstream, working havoc among the houses, stores and
farms.   When the dazed inhabitants recovered sufficiently they
sued the coal company for damages on the reasonable assumption
that its digging had triggered a misfortune which nature, left
undisturbed, would not have visited upon them.   The appellate
bench reversed the verdict of the jury and the judgment of the
trial court.   It ruled, in effect, that the rain was an Act of God
which the coal operator could not have foreseen and that, had the
rain not fallen, the rubble would have remained safely in place.
Besides, the stripping had been done in the "same manner as was
customary at all strip mines."   Usurping the fact-finding prerogative of the jury, the judges, sitting as a self-appointed superjury,
found the stripper innocent of wrongdoing and negligence.

In another case several years later, a mountaineer claimed
that a company had plowed up his mountainsides, covered his
bottomland with rubble, caused his well to go dry and, in his words,
had "plumb broke" him.   After he had heard all the evidence and
arguments of counsel the trial judge dismissed the case.   In doing
so he told the mountaineer, "I deeply sympathize with you and

sincerely wish I could rule for you. My hands are tied by the rulings of the Court of Appeals and under the law I must follow its decisions. The truth is that about the only rights you have on your land is to breathe on it and pay the taxes. For all practical purposes the company that owns the minerals in your land owns all the other rights pertaining to it."

By 1950 there were hundreds of "worked-out" ridges along whose edges ran slender banks of outcrop coal. It was of high quality but only extended into the hill a hundred feet or so. Tunnel and pillar mining had long since withdrawn most of the coal, leaving only a few supporting pillars and barrier walls. In order to remove the mineral by conventional methods, a thick barrier pillar must be left intact on the outer fringes of the seam. It comprises the principal support for the overlying mountain, affording stability and tending to prevent "squeezes"—those uncontrollable shiftings of the mountain which occur when too much coal is taken out. Then, too, as a practical matter all the mineral cannot be removed from the inside. As the miners approach the outside the roof of stone becomes increasingly "rotten" so that on the outer edges it is extremely difficult to shore up, no matter how thickly timbers and roof-bolts are applied. Hence the bands of outcrop coal were a loss in so far as the owners were concerned and were written off as such.

Nor had all the coal in the interior of the mountains been removed. In the earlier years of the industry some 50 to 60 per-cent was recovered and the rest was required for supports. As techniques and tools improved, the percentage of recovery steadily rose. Finally in the most thoroughly mechanized mines—those employing roof bolts, conveyors, shuttle cars and coal moles— recovery soared to 85 or 90 percent and some operators boasted that they "brought it clean," removing all except the outcrop. This permitted colossal "general falls" to bring the roof crashing down behind them as the machines rapidly chewed their way through the pillars in the pullback to the entries. But in all the mines the outcrop remained. In some places where the Big Bosses had first driven their headings nearly forty years before the seams had been of extraordinarily high quality and very thick. For example, Consolidation Coal Company began its operations in 1912 in seams more than eight feet thick but by 1948 it had developed especially designed machines to work in veins only thirty-six inches thick. Engineers were tantalized by the old workings where thick bands of mineral lay temptingly near the outside of the mountains.   Truck roads could be "dozed" to them at little cost and the rural highway program had already brought roads near countless such hollowed ridges.

But the engineers could devise no means of recovering the coal from the inside.   The problem of roof supports was insoluble. Heartened by the powerful new earth-moving machines they resorted to "surface mining."   If the coal could not be tunneled out from the interior it could be gouged out from the exterior. Dynamite and bulldozer could remove the "overburden."   The coal could be "pop shot" with light charges of explosives, and loaded by giant shovels directly into trucks.

The recovery of coal by the "open-cut" method had previously never been feasible in the mountains, though it had occasionally been practiced in the low hills on the fringes of the plateau.   But by 1950, strip mining was not only feasible but was increasingly profitable.

Typically a strip-mine operator needed only a tiny crew of men.   He required two bulldozers, one of which could be substantially smaller than the other.   He required an air compressor and drill for the boring of holes into the rock overlying the coal. He also required a power shovel for use in loading the coal from the seam into the trucks.   These four machines could be operated by as many men.   To their wages were added those of a night watchman and two or three laborers, and the crew was complete.   With these men and machines the operator first built a road from the nearest highway up the hillside to the coal seam.   The bulldozers pursued the seam around the hillside, uprooting the timber and removing all the soil until the coal was reached.   Then the dirt was scraped from the sloping mountainside above to expose the crumbling rock.   This cut proceeded along the contours of the ridge for half a mile.   Then rows of holes were drilled in the rock strata and were tamped with explosives.   When the explosives were set off, most of the dirt and rock was blown violently down the mountainside.   The remainder lay, soft and crumbly, on top of the coal.   The "dozers" then bestrode the shattered "overburden," and with their steel snouts shoved it down the steep slopes.   This process left the outer edge of the outcrop exposed. A sheet of coal eight feet thick, fifty feet wide and half a mile long could thus be bared within a few days.

Next, holes were drilled in the glittering black seam of coal. Small charges of dynamite loosened thousands of tons of the mineral, leaving it easily available to the shovel's big dipper.   A

number of truckers were hired to haul it away, at a cost of perhaps
seventy-five cents a ton.   It was carried to the nearest ramp or
tipple where it was cleaned, sized and loaded into gondolas.

It is instantly apparent that this method of recovery is vastly
cheaper than shaft or drift mining.   Six or eight men can thus dig
more coal from the outcrop than five or six times their number can
mine underground.   The bulldozers, shovels and drills are expensive, but not more so than their subterranean counterparts.   They
can produce a ton of coal for little more than half the cost imposed
on a competitor in a deep pit.   Where the strip mine lies close to
the loading ramp so that the haul bill can be minimized the price
differential is even more striking.

In the flat country of western Kentucky, where thousands of
acres had already been devastated by strip mining, the coal seams
lie only thirty to sixty feet beneath the surface.   The overburden
is scraped off and the coal is scooped out.   Inevitably such topsoil
as the land affords is buried under towering heaps of subsoil.
When the strippers move on, once level meadows and cornfields
have been converted to jumbled heaps of hardpan, barren clay
from deep in the earth.   This hellish landscape is slow to support
vegetation and years elapse before the yellow waste turns green
again.   In the meantime immense quantities of dirt have crept
into the sluggish streams, have choked them, and brackish ponds
have formed to breed millions of mosquitoes.

The evil effects of open-cut mining are fantastically magnified
when practiced in the mountains.   Masses of shattered stone,
shale, slate and dirt are cast pell-mell down the hillside.   The
first to go are the thin remaining layer of fertile topsoil and such
trees as still find sustenance in it.   The uprooted trees are flung
down the slopes by the first cut.   Then follows the sterile subsoil,
shattered stone and slate.   As the cut extends deeper into the
hillside the process is repeated again and again.   Sometimes the
"highwall," the perpendicular bank resulting from the cut, rises
ninety feet; but a height of forty to sixty feet is more often found.
In a single mile, hundreds of thousands of tons are displaced.

Each mountain is laced with coal seams.   Sometimes a single
ridge contains three to five veins varying in thickness from two-
and-a-half to fourteen feet.   Since each seam can be stripped, a
sloping surface can be converted to a steplike one.

After the coal has been carried away, vast quantities of the
shattered mineral are left uncovered.   Many seams contain
substantial quantities of sulphur, which when wet produces toxic

sulphuric acid.   This poison bleeds into the creeks, killing minute vegetation and destroying fish, frogs and other stream-dwellers.

Strip mining occurs largely in dry weather.   In late spring, in summer, and in early fall the bulldozers and shovels tear tirelessly at the vitals of the mountains while trucks rumble away with their glittering cargoes.   Above the operations and their haul roads lie mantles of tawny dust.   In the hot sunshine the churned earth turns powder dry and the jumbled spoil-banks lie soft almost to fluffiness.

The seam seldom lies less than a hundred feet above the base of the mountain.   Sometimes it is near the top.   Again it may lie midway between base and crest.   But wherever the seam is situated the spoil bank extends downward like a monstrous apron. Stones as large as army tanks are sent bounding and crashing through trees and undergrowth.   Lesser stones find lodgment against trees and other obstacles, and behind them countless tons of soil accumulate.

During the hot season the nearby creek takes on a sallow hue after even the slightest shower.   People living along its bank watch apprehensively as the rising highwall deepens the loose earth on the dead and blasted slopes.   They remember the horror of other years when flash floods pounded hillsides scratched by hoes and bull-tongue plows.   They guess what will ensue if a similar downpour falls upon the ravaged slopes which overlook their farms and homes.

Then come the rains of autumn and the freezes and thaws of winter.   The descending water flays the loose rubble, carrying thousands of tons of it into the streams and onto the bottoms. The watery scalpel shaves inches from the surface in almost instantaneous sheet erosion.   At the same time it carves gullies which deepen until the streams reach the undisturbed soil far beneath.   The rain has a kindlier effect, however, and eventually lessens its ravages by compacting the surface.   Gradually the beating drops create a hard shell which affords considerable protection to the underlying dirt.   Then in late November the saturated spoil-banks freeze.   In the icy grip of winter they lie hard as ice and perfectly stable.   The freezing water pushes the dirt outward, leaving deep fissures extending far underground. When warmer weather melts the ice the earth crumbles and subsides downhill in tremendous landslides.   Snows and rains then saturate the loosened masses again and the process is repeated until the displaced soil reaches the stream beds.

Within a few years after the "strip operator" has slashed his way into the hillside the unresting elements have carried away most of his discarded overburden.   The dirt has vanished, leaving immense expanses of sere brown sandstone and slabs of sickening gray slate.   A few straggly clusters of broom sage and an occasional spindly sycamore take root and struggle to survive.

Initially the strippers worked only in the outcrop of exhausted mines but as their machines and techniques improved, they pushed into virgin seams.   The great cuts appeared on the sides of ridges from which no coal had yet been withdrawn.   They scalped away only a thin filament on the outer edges of the hill, leaving the body of the coal bed undisturbed.   The coal auger made its appearance as a device for removing that portion of the outcrop which could not be reached by stripping.   As a rule of thumb ten feet of overburden can profitably be removed for each foot of coal in the seam. When the highwall rose straight up so far it could not be advantageously increased, much of the outcrop remained.   The auger allowed the recovery of a large part of the remaining mineral.   It is a gigantic drill which bores straight back into the coal seam, spewing out huge quantities of the mineral with each revolution of the screw.   The drills range from seventeen inches to six feet in diameter.   When the point has penetrated the entire length of the bit a new section is attached and the drilling continues.   Eventually it extends some seventy yards under the hill, piercing the entire barrier pillar.

The bore holes must be somewhat smaller in diameter than the seam is thick, and a few inches are left between the insertions. Consequently, the auger can bring out little more than half the coal.   Initially its use was justified on the ground that it prevented the loss of the otherwise unrecoverable barrier pillars, but after the already disemboweled hills were stripped and augered the big bits moved into virgin ridges and began to rend seams which had never felt a pick.   Usually stripping preceded the augers but after a time some auger men dispensed with strip mining altogether. They simply made cuts sufficient to face up the seams, then the monstrous screws were set to work while the lines of trucks labored to carry away their product.

Where augering is done in a previously unmined ridge the crumbly "bloom" and a few yards of weathered roofstone is shoved over the hillside.   Then the bore holes follow each other in interminable procession around the meandering ridge.   They proceed along the edges of sharp spurs, around the "turn of the point," and back to the main ridge again. When the end of the ridge is passed, the cutting and boring continues on its reverse side. Thus the bore holes from one side of the mountain extend toward the ends of those drilled from the other side. Under these circumstances coal production is fantastically cheap. A well-financed operation augering in a four- to six-foot seam can realize a net profit of close to a dollar on the ton even in the depressed coal market prevailing as this is written in 1962. A six-foot auger turning uninterruptedly can load fifteen tons in less than one minute. If the fleet of trucks can keep pace with the bulldozers and augers, the profit can be fabulous, amounting to millions of dollars in a few years. Quite naturally the possibility of such quick and easy enrichment has excited many coal companies and the politicians through whom they dominate the state and county governments.

Strip and auger mining have one very real advantage over conventional methods: they eliminate the need for men to go under the hill. In augering, only the revolving steel bits pierce the mountainside, and their human attendants need never follow them. The peril of fire and slate-fall which dogs the underground miners in even the safest pits does not pursue the surface workman. But when this is said, nothing more in defense of the process can be forthcoming.

Augering in virgin ridges is fantastically wasteful. Rarely do the bits extend into the mountain more than a quarter of its width. Hence, even if the boring proceeds from both sides, a solid block is often left in the center of the ridge which contains at least 50 percent of the seam's original tonnage. When allowance is made for the huge quantities left between the holes and over and under them, another 25 percent of the seam's content is unretrieved. Competent mining engineers have testified that such an augering project is highly successful if 20 percent of the total coal is removed. Nor can the remainder be mined at a future time without totally destroying the terrain.

It will at first appear that shafts could be driven into the hill for mining the remaining coal by conventional methods, but unfortunately when the ridge has been augered on both sides this is no longer possible. The bore holes are so close together they leave no pillars of sufficient thickness to support the roof. Within a few years after air is admitted into the seam a chemical reaction causes the remaining coal to crumble. The weight of the overlying rock and soil crushes down through the thin walls remaining between

the holes.   The coal marooned in the center of the mountain is
thus sealed against the outside world.   Moreover, tunnel and
pillar mining requires ventilation as well as roof supports, and if a
reliable air supply is to be maintained at the working faces this
exterior wall cannot be reduced under forty feet in thickness without running the risk that the mountain's weight will crack and
shatter it, allowing the precious oxygen to leak out.   Thus, even
if an entry is managed it must operate within the confining limits
of a forty-foot barrier pillar following the furthermost penetrations
of the auger bits.   Generally, when this indispensable safeguard
is deducted, too little coal is left to justify the expense of mining it.
Thus the auger skims off a thin layer of cream and leaves the
balance of a rich and vitally important coal bed in such a state
that mining engineers can presently offer no hope for its ultimate
recovery.   Prudence cannot permit the continued gross wastage
of so vital a resource.

Open-cut strip mining does not always follow the meandering
borders of the ridge.   A different procedure is used when the vein
lies near the top of the hill.   Then the strippers blast and carve
away the stone and soil overlying the coal, shoving it over the
brink of the mountain until at last the entire seam lies black and
glistening in the sunlight.   Such an operation can transform a
razorback spur into a flat mesa.   Sometimes the hill's altitude is
decreased by 20 per cent while its thickness is much increased.
When the strippers have departed and the rains and freezes have
flayed such a decapitated mountain for a season or two, it takes
on an appearance not unlike the desolate, shattered tablelands of
Colorado.   But these man-made mesas lie in a rainy area and
the layers of loose soil cloaking the slopes will not stay *in situ*.
Wraithlike, the rubble melts away, only to reappear at countless
places downstream.

Stripping and augering spread at an accelerating rate through
the 1950s.   For a long time they were viewed as a tentative and
minor industry, one that could deface splotches of land but was
unlikely to ever afford serious competition for conventional mines
or to constitute a real threat to the region's soil, water and natural
beauty.   But this casual viewpoint has been dispelled.   In 1954
Kentucky's Governor Lawrence Wetherby advocated a mild bill
designed to restrain the operators from the worst of their abuses.
Immediately the holding companies and the industry reacted as if
they had been stung by a huge bee.   Lobbyists dragged out all
the timeworn arguments again and the lawmakers were solemnly

assured that strip and auger mining are good for the region's economy, creating jobs and bringing prosperity to Main Street. A diluted version of an initially weak bill was passed but successive governors have failed to enforce even its mild strictures.   For all practical purposes the operators are permitted to conduct their affairs in complete absence of supervision or control.   Little effort is made to reclaim or stabilize the land, and indeed, reclamation is rarely possible once the surface has been so violently disturbed. . . .

THE SCENE TODAY

The present crisis is compounded of many elements, human and material.   They have produced what is probably the most seriously depressed region in the nation—and the adjective applies in much more than an economic sense.   They have brought economic depression, to be sure, and it lies like a gray pall over the whole land.   But a deeper tragedy lies in the depression of the spirit which has fallen upon so many of the people, making them, for the moment at least, listless, hopeless and without ambition.

The essential element of the plateau's economic malaise lies in the fact that for a hundred and thirty years it has exported its resources, all of which—timber, coal, and even crops—have had to be wrested violently from the earth.   The nation has siphoned off hundreds of millions of dollars' worth of its resources while returning little of lasting value.   For all practical purposes the plateau has long constituted a colonial appendage of the industrial East and Middle West, rather than an integral part of the nation generally.   The decades of exploitation have in large measure drained the region.   Its timber wealth is exhausted and if its hillsides ever again produce arrow-straight white oaks, tulip poplars and hemlocks, new crops of trees will first have to be planted and allowed to mature.   Hundreds of ridges which once bulged with thick seams of high-quality coal have been emptied of all that lay in their vitals and their surfaces have been fragmented for the pitiful remnants in the outcrop.   While billions of tons still remain undisturbed they lie in inferior seams and are of poorer quality.   The magnificent veins through which Percheron horses once hauled strings of bank cars have been worked out.

Even more ruinous than the loss of its physical resources is the disappearance of the plateau's best human material.   Most of the thousands who left were people who recognized the towering

importance of education in the lives of their children, and craved
for them better schools than Kentucky afforded.   Too many of
those who remained behind were without interest in real education
as distinguished from its trappings.   If their children attended the
neighborhood schools the parents had done their duty.   Too often
they were far less ambitious and such ambition as they possessed
was to evaporate in the arms of Welfarism and in the face of
repeated failures.

From the beginning, the coal and timber companies insisted
on keeping all, or nearly all, the wealth they produced.   They were
unwilling to plow more than a tiny part of the money they earned
back into schools, libraries, health facilities and other institutions
essential to a balanced, pleasant, productive and civilized society.
The knowledge and guile of their managers enabled them to
corrupt and cozen all too many of the region's elected public
officials and to thwart the legitimate aspirations of the people.
The greed and cunning of the coal magnates left behind an agglom-
eration of misery for a people who can boast of few of the facilities
deemed indispensable to life in more sophisticated areas, and even
these few are inadequate and of inferior quality.

Only one facet of the industry ever sought to return to the
region any substantial part of the wealth it produced.   The
United Mine Workers' program of health, welfare and retirement
benefits funneled back to the coal counties millions of dollars
otherwise destined for the pockets of distant shareholders.   To
compound the tragedy of the plateau, even this program is today
showing unmistakable signs of breakdown and failure.   The union
and the trustees of its fund were headed for inevitable trouble after
the end of the second boom in 1948.   Its seeds germinated in the
same soil that sprouted the difficulties of the late 1920s: the industry was grossly overexpanded and was prepared to produce twice
as much coal as its markets could consume.   In 1948 the tremendous new truck-mining industry was overgrown and, hard though
they struggled to mechanize their mines with the cast-off relics of
their big competitors, the little operators were never really able to
compete.   A widespread double standard blanketed the coalfields.
The big rail mines were sternly forced to comply with the wage
and hour contracts negotiated year after year with the United
Mine Workers, but John L. Lewis and his associates looked the
other way where the truck mines were concerned.   Fearing that
if these small pits were shut down the resulting labor surplus might
break the contracts in the big mines, they tolerated clandestine

wage cuts.   It became customary for the truck-mine operator to sign the contract and then ignore it.   He paid his workmen five or ten dollars per day less than the scale wage and sent only a token contribution to the Health and Welfare Fund.   Thus the truck mines existed for a decade, by sufferance of the union.

Then in the spring of 1959 the United Mine Workers undertook to change all this.   Wages in many of the truck mines had sunk to ridiculous levels and in others the miners were "gang working" as partners and dividing the meager profits equally. But however they managed and toiled, many were earning no more than eight dollars a day and some as little as four dollars. Despite the pious provisions of the Federal Wage and Hour Law most operators paid as little as the miners could be persuaded to accept.   But for a man with a wife and "a gang of young'-uns," with no money, no property and nowhere to go, any income is better than none.   Thus when the union suddenly attempted to force the small pits to comply fully and faithfully with the contract their efforts ended in ignominious defeat.   The miners in the little "dog-holes" had lost faith in the "organization."   It had let them work at ever-lessening wages for ten years, preaching automation and higher pay to men who grew increasingly desperate with each passing year.   In their cynical eyes John L. Lewis, once their hero and idol, had become a traitor to their interests.

When the 1959 strike was called, the response was far from uniform.   Some of the workmen quit and picketed those who attempted to work.   The strike dragged on for months amid recurrences of violence reminiscent of the 1930s.   Men were slain, ramps and tipples were blasted and burned, and eventually the state's National Guard was sent into the troubled counties to preserve order.   But the strike failed.   In the long run practically all the truck miners deserted the union and went back to work. Today they mine many trainloads of coal daily but pay nothing into the Welfare Fund.   Their miners no longer pay union dues. Their locals have folded up and disappeared.   In retaliation against them the U.M.W.   Fund trustees canceled their hospital cards and Welfare benefits and thousands of truck-mine laborers are now stranded at the mercy of their employers and the customers who buy their coal.   It is a harsh world for everyone, but in all America there is no worker—not even the imported Mexican "wetback"—who occupies a position more exposed and helpless than the men who dig coal in these little pits.

The Federal Government makes only a token effort to enforce

the minimum wage requirements of the Fair Labor Standards Act. Almost always when complaints are called to the attention of the United States Attorneys they are too busy to deal with them and the miner in question receives a form letter advising him to bring suit for back-wages in "a court of competent jurisdiction." But lawsuits cost money and the miner has none, so the suit is not brought, the delinquency is not collected and the low wages continue. His union has ostracized him as a yellow dog and a scab. Some of the magnificent union hospitals stand half-empty while their skilled physicians resign in disgust because there are so few patients to attend.[1] The truck-mine operator is earning little on the coal he sells and competition from the increasing numbers of strip and auger companies constantly deflates the price of his product. While other Americans are enjoying prosperity, planning expensive vacations in new automobiles and buying corporate stocks in unprecedented numbers, the truck miner who is fortunate enough to have a job works for minuscule wages and wonders from payday to payday whether his employer will be able to pay even the pittances for which he has contracted.

Even worse, the Federal Government treats him as a second-class citizen when it comes to safety. Of all the things John L. Lewis can boast of having accomplished for his followers, the Federal Mine Safety Code is the most important. But Congress gave Lewis only half a loaf, specifically restricting the act's application to mines employing fifteen or more men. Small pits were left to the tender mercies of their bosses and of state inspectors; the carnage continued in them unabated. Most of the plateau's coal counties now go two or three years at a time without a fatal accident in a railroad mine, but the dreary reports of dead and mangled bodies continue to filter with chilling frequency from the little operations. Truck mines produce approximately 12 percent of the plateau's coal output and $33\frac{1}{3}$ percent of its killed and injured miners. Strangely enough the state's senior senator, himself an eastern Kentuckian, is an outspoken defender of this industrial mayhem, and for several years has almost single-handedly staved off Federal safety enforcement in the smaller coal mines.

So the miners, the employed workmen who by hundreds make a skimpy living in the truck mines of the plateau, live on a downward spiral which for several years has appeared to be nearing

[1] In October of 1962, the trustees of the Fund announced that four of its hospitals in the plateau would be permanently closed on June 30, 1963.

rock bottom. With low wages, lack of union membership and protection, and in most instances without even Workmen's Compensation coverage, such a miner is fortunate to keep corn bread and beans on the dinner table in the poor shack he so often calls home.

So trifling were his wages that in many instances the "dog-hole miner" could not survive without the free food doled out to him monthly from the great stores of the United States Department of Agriculture. Though his situation was unusually severe, a miner recently remarked to me that for eleven eight-hour shifts of work he collected twenty-nine dollars in wages. It is apparent that he, his wife and three children would starve to death if his labor afforded their only support. It is true that some truck mines are so efficiently organized and have grown so large that they are able to pay decent wages, though few attempt the union scale. The largest ones, however, mine as much as a thousand tons a day and their owners pay twenty dollars for an eight-hour shift. Their miners live reasonably well but it should not be inferred that they set the standards for the industry. In most areas truck mining has degenerated into a ghastly economic mire which holds miner and operator alike enchained. Often the employer is fortunate if he can earn twenty dollars a day for himself, and his employees are lucky if they take home eight or ten dollars. In those pits in which the miners work as partners they are practically unsupervised by safety bosses. Each co-worker thinks of himself as his own boss and of equal voice in the management of the mine and, in consequence, none can enforce safety discipline. Yet they continue to dig coal from the thinning seams, producing it for incredibly low prices and adding to a coal glut which can only depress prices, earnings and wages still further.

Here and there a few rail mines still operate. During the last fifteen years there has been a relentless consolidation as the bigger companies steadily bought up the smaller ones. With roaring machines and shrunken crews, these corporate giants continue to pour coal from the black veins into the clattering tipples. But where nearly eight thousand men once toiled for United States Coal and Coke Company in the Big Black Mountain, fewer than seventeen hundred are now at work. Where five thousand miners once went under the hill for Consolidation Coal Company at Jenkins and McRoberts, nine hundred survivors are still on the payroll. But at neither place has coal production lessened. To

the contrary, with advancing mechanization it has steadily
swollen.

These fortunate hundreds earn a basic union wage in excess of
twenty-four dollars a day and enjoy all the benefits the union contract bestows.   They present a sharp contrast to the pauperized
dog-hole miners.   The two, and frequently they are blood brothers,
are prince and pauper.   The workman for Inland Steel, Bethlehem
Mines, International Harvester, and United States Steel owns his
home in a camp or in one of the rural areas.   He has improved the
house and installed a furnace and plumbing.   His home is neat
and well-painted.   He drives and owns a late-model automobile
and his children attend school regularly.   He hopes to send
at least some of them to college, perhaps to the University of
Kentucky.   He has a thousand dollars or so on deposit in a local
bank.   The magnificent facilities at the Miner's Memorial
Hospitals exist primarily for his care.   When he or any member
of his family is ill or injured, doctors, surgeons and hospitalization
cost him nothing.   The trustees have lowered the retirement age
and when he reaches his sixtieth birthday he can leave the mines
and draw from the Fund a monthly retirement check of seventy-
five dollars.   The mine in which he works is well ventilated and
under the orders of Federal Safety Inspectors has been made as
safe as human ingenuity can vouchsafe.   If, despite the precau-
tions, he is injured, compensation benefits up to a total of $15,300
await him.   His union shelters him from coercion by company
officials and has long since forced the closing of the scrip office.
In most camps the company store is little more than a memory.

But there are portents of trouble for these union miners and
their organization.   The United Mine Workers has shrunk its
membership and raised the living standards of those who remain.
In so doing it has kept abreast of progress because progress is bigness, efficiency, technological advancement and organization.   At
the same time, it has created a favored class, a sort of blue-collar
royalty amid a populace of industrial serfs.   The combination of
giant companies and giant union is driving the truck mines from
the scene.   Each spring the beginning of the lake trade finds
fewer truck mines in operation.   Within a few more seasons, the
rail-mine operators can confidently expect the last of their small
competitors to have been relegated to the scrap heap of history.
But they are confronted with competition from other quarters—
savage rivalry they cannot dispose of in so cavalier a fashion.

The rising crescendo of strip and auger mining is pouring growing quantities of extremely low-priced coal onto the market. So long as unspoiled ridges invite the bulldozers and big screws, the Big Bosses will face a gruesome dilemma. At great cost to their stockholders they have made ready to market clean and high quality coal. Ironically, this product is now becoming old-fashioned. The trend is toward lower prices and quality, and therefore the huge complex washeries may be little more than outmoded symbols of a departed time. In consequence, the union and its members are losing their economic and political importance. When coal was dug by simple tools and machines the many men who operated them could give fiscal chilblains to industrialists and government officials across the land. The nation was dependent upon coal, and hence on the miner's skills, but this dependence is seeping fast away. In coal production the cornerstone is still the dust-blackened, blue-collar miner, but he is surrendering his primacy to the white-collar expert whose skill and cunning has worked a far-reaching revolution in so short a time. The growing petroleum glut and the network of natural gas pipelines lessen coal's importance with each passing season. Within a few years tireless atomic reactors will provide much of the electric power now made from coal. Though the nation will surely grow steadily, coal is unlikely ever again to be a prime industry. Its path is downward, and the men and communities who are dependent upon it are tied to a descending star. Since coal is, for all practical purposes, the plateau's only industry, the region and its people are tied to an industrial albatross.

THE VICTIMS OF POVERTY ARE NOT THE CAUSE OF POVERTY, ARGUES *Lumer. Taking issue with Galbraith and others, he argues that the causes of poverty are not individual, but social; its existence and extent are ultimately rooted in the capitalist system of production and distribution in the U.S. Lumer presents evidence on the prevalence of low wage industries, and on the failure of the minimum wage legislation to cover 15 million of 44 million people in the labor force. Lack of labor organization and lack of coverage by minimum wage legislation have nothing to do with individual failings or low productivity. Besides the underpaid, there are the unemployed and underemployed, many of whom are hidden by official methods of measurement and reporting of unemployment.*

In this so-called "welfare state," says Lumer, even the inadequate legislation in existence was won through hard struggle against the opposition of big business. Social security and unemployment benefits are insufficient even for minimal needs, and public assistance ("welfare") usually subjects its recipients to humiliation and indignity. Even the inadequate unemployment benefits are not extended to between 30 and 40 percent of the unemployed; and one-fourth of the aged are excluded from social security benefits. Farm subsidies go to the rich; practically nothing gets to small farmers. Seven percent of the federal budget goes for alleged welfare purposes compared to at least 60 percent (in 1965) for military expenditures. The basic source of poverty today is the large corporations' drive for maximum profits, which entails suppressing wages, exploiting consumers, and using the economic resources of government for the corporations' benefit while the people pay the bill. Poverty will not decline by any "natural" process, nor are the poor and the mass of workers distinct and separable groups. The distribution of national income has remained stable since World War II; the rise in real wages is exaggerated.

Layoffs, dislocation of workers, plant relocations or closing down, "depressed areas," discrimination, and technological advance all hit the workers disproportionately. Workers as a class face the constant threat of unemployment and the pressure of economic insecurity. The poor are merely the sector of the working class who are in the worst position. The new labor-displacing technologies, such as automation, are appearing at a time when the exceptional circumstance of relatively full-employment during and after the Second World War are coming to an end. The ebb and flow of poverty, concludes Lumer, is inherent in our capitalist economy.

206

20

WHY PEOPLE ARE POOR

Hyman Lumer

Blaming Poverty on Its Victims

The notion has been widely propagated in this country that if anyone is poor or unemployed it is because there is something wrong with him. The great depression of the thirties did much to dispel this fallacy, but it persists nevertheless as the stock-in-trade of reaction.

In its crudest version it takes the form of the slanderous allegation that the poor and the jobless are the lazy and the shiftless. This version is today part of the arsenal of the ultra-Right and its standard-bearer Barry Goldwater. Typical of his views are such pronouncements as these:

"I'm tired of professional chiselers walking up and down the streets who don't work and have no intention of working." (*New York Times*, July 19, 1961.)

"The fact is that most people who have no skills have no education for the same reason—low intelligence or low ambition." (*New York Times*, January 16, 1964.)

Similar views are expressed editorially by the *Wall Street Journal* (March 11, 1964), which regards poverty as an individual problem and its relief as the responsibility of the poor themselves. The editorial asserts that "almost all of us are up from poverty and almost none of our forebears considered it anybody's responsibility but his own to get up." Johnson's anti-poverty policy is

Reprinted from Hyman Lumer, *Poverty: Its Roots and Its Future* (New York: International Publishers, 1965), pp. 13–32. Reprinted by permission of International Publishers Co., Inc. Copyright © 1965.

condemned on the grounds that its logic "demands that the shiftless as well as the deserving have equal right to the fruits of the productive. Since there are those only too willing to live at the expense of others, that approach may only swell the ranks of the shiftless and help perpetuate poverty." To be sure, there *are* those who are "only too willing to live at the expense of others," but the successful practitioners of this philosophy are far more likely to be found within the clientele of the *Wall Street Journal* than among the poor.

There are others who would reject any such openly slanderous characterization of the poor, but who nevertheless ascribe poverty to individual peculiarities or shortcomings. Among these is Galbraith, who maintains that the general poverty of the working class has been abolished, leaving only individually-produced forms. He reduces present-day poverty, therefore, to what he calls "case poverty" and "insular poverty."

The former he defines as poverty related to "some quality peculiar to the individual or family involved—mental deficiency, bad health, inability to adapt to the discipline of modern economic life, excessive procreation, alcohol, insufficient education, or perhaps a combination of several of these handicaps. . . ." The latter he defines as a geographical "island" of poverty most of whose inhabitants do not wish to leave it, thus rejecting the solution to their poverty offered by emigration. (*The Affluent Society*, pp. 252–53.)

Herman P. Miller similarly argues that modern poverty reflects the shortcomings of the poor. In his book *Rich Man, Poor Man* (1964) he states (p. 81): "If a distribution has a top and a middle, it must also have a bottom and somebody must be there. The important question is why they are there and how much they get. People are not all equally endowed with good health, intelligence, creativity, drive, etc. In any society a premium will be paid to those who are most productive."

"There are," he says, "millions of fine, respectable, honest men whose native intelligence is quite low and who lack training to do any but the most menial work. They are poor because their productivity is low" (p. 69). On the other hand, "by and large, the wealthy in the United States contain some of the best and most essential talents—doctors, lawyers, engineers, entertainers, artists, plant managers, etc. While the association between ability and income is far from perfect, ordinary observation shows

that many of the most talented are among the highest paid"
(p. 125).

In short, the lazy and incompetent are generally poor; the
talented and industrious are generaly well off.   One may help
the poor by means of social welfare measures or private charity,
but the divergence in status is inherent in the nature of things.
A statistical distribution must have a lower range as well as an
upper—in ability as in income.   Again, the poor are reduced to
a "statistical segment," and as such the category is eternal.

Such an explanation will not stand up.   The basic causes of
poverty are not individual but social.   Individual differences can
at most determine who is most apt to be poor, given the existence
of poverty.   But they cannot explain either its existence or its
extent.   The reasons for these must be sought in economic and
social factors beyond the individual's control, ultimately in the
character of the processes of production and distribution.   True,
there are people who suffer poverty because of personal handicaps
or just plain misfortune.   Such people need special consideration
and help.   But to take such a social work approach to the overall
problem of poverty in our society is only to cover up the real
causes.

First of all, the bulk of those in the lowest-paying jobs are
not there because of lack of intelligence or other personal deficiencies but for quite other reasons.   A large part of them, for
example, are Negroes, Puerto Ricans or Mexican-Americans who
are victims of discrimination.   Others may be workers—particularly older workers—displaced from jobs by automation or the
closing down of plants and unable to find anything better.

Secondly, the unemployed Appalachian coal miner or Pittsburgh steelworker is not out of a job because of his "low productivity."   On the contrary, it is the multiplication of his productivity by means of new machinery and its utilization by his former
employer to reduce the number of workers on his payroll that are
responsible.   If workers are victims of technological change in our
society, this has nothing to do with their personal characteristics.
"It was no sloth on the part of the coal miner," writes Bagdikian
(*In the Midst of Plenty*, p. 182), "that caused petroleum to emerge
as the more versatile fuel.   It was no weakness in the railroad
engineer that made the car and truck dominate transportation.
Not was it because farmers worked less hard that expensive
machinery became more profitable than the simple plow. . . . Yet,

the politics and social values of the commercial community, which depend on this versatility and change, assume that poverty and unemployment are casual, self-imposed and self-liquidating."

The Low-wage Industries

It is noteworthy that half of all families below the $3,000-a-year mark are headed by an employed person earning less than that amount. Some of these are individuals working part time, but in large part they are individuals whose hourly rates are so low that even a full year's work pays them only a poverty-level income. Thus, a worker paid less than $1.50 an hour would earn less than $3,000 even if he worked as many as 50 weeks out of the year. And there are more than 12 million workers in this country whose hourly pay falls below $1.50. These are found in farm, domestic, retail trade, restaurant, laundry, hospital and some factory jobs. About one million earn less than 50 cents an hour.

The present federal minimum wage provision of $1.25 an hour covers only 29 million of a total of 44 million (this total excludes some 25 million self-employed, government workers, executives, professionals and outside salesmen). Among the 15 million not covered, many earn well under $1.25 an hour. As of June 1963, more than 1.5 million non-supervisory restaurant workers averaged $1.14 an hour. Average earnings of nearly half a million hotel workers were $1.17. Some 2 million farm workers averaged 89 cents an hour. ("The Wage-Hour Law—A Lift Out of Poverty," *American Federationist*, August 1964.)

The main reasons for these shamefully low wages are lack of coverage by the minimum wage law and lack of organization. They are not the result of low productivity. Thus, where the law applies in a section of an industry (as it does in the largest retail units), wages are considerably higher than in the rest of the industry. Moreover, while a janitor in a retail store is no less "productive" than one, say, in an auto plant, the latter is better paid thanks to union organization.

In other words, a large proportion of the poor are in that category simply because they are grossly underpaid. Their poverty is a product of capitalist exploitation; indeed, their condition is the measure of what would be the lot of most workers were it not for union organization and protective legislation.

A minimum wage of $2.00 an hour covering all workers, though it would make no one rich, would eliminate much of what is now classed as poverty. And such a minimum is not at all infeasible. Yet it is bitterly resisted not only by employers in the low-wage industries but by big business as a whole. And this is only natural in a capitalist economy, in which the drive for profits dictates that wages, as a cost of production, be held to a minimum. Here, in fact, lies the ultimate root of poverty; [we shall say more on this in the section, "The Nature and Roots of Poverty."]

To this mass of grossly underpaid workers must be added the unemployed and underemployed. At first glance their numbers among the poor may seem insignificant: in addition to the one-half of the poor classified as employed, the Administration figures list only 6 percent as jobless and the remaining 44 percent as unemployable (the aged, the incapacitated, women with children, etc.)

These figures are misleading. For one thing, not all those classified as "unemployable" are necessarily so. The official figures notoriously understate unemployment by omitting those not working but not actively looking for work at the moment. Among the poor this number is especially large, for they experience the greatest difficulty in finding work and are most likely to give up the search as hopeless. There are also the many women with children who do not work simply because no suitable child care facilities are available. And certainly many of the elderly struggling to survive on social security pensions would take work if suitable jobs existed. In short, with greater availability of jobs and child care facilities the number of "unemployables" would dwindle greatly. We need only recall, in this connection, how drastically it shrank during the World War II years.

Further, the official statistics list as employed those working part time, even when this is involuntary. The number of such individuals, who should be considered as at least partially unemployed, is likewise especially high among the poor.

The "Welfare State" Myth

Finally, there is the poverty of those unable to work. In a society which is habitually plagued with unsalcable surpluses of goods and which is capable of producing enough of life's necessities for all, there is no valid reason why these should be poor. Indeed, few things speak so eloquently of the exploitative character of our society as its failure to maintain its aged and incapacitated at a level of ordinary decency.

The fact is that the widely acclaimed "welfare state" in our country is but a myth. The patchwork of social welfare measures which now exists has been won only in hard struggle against the opposition of big business, and the victories wrested from it have been meager indeed. Present standards are woefully lacking and are considerably behind even those of other capitalist countries. Often they are little advanced beyond the levels of the thirties and more often, in view of the great rise in living costs, they have fallen behind those levels.

The myth is effectively exposed in an article by Andrew Hacker ("Again the Issue of the 'Welfare State,'" *New York Times Magazine*, March 22, 1964). He points out that "a welfare state is one that guarantees a broad series of economic protections that any citizen can claim when he is no longer able to provide for himself. In the welfare state, the benefits an individual receives are political rights, not charity, and there should be no occasion for apology or embarrassment in applying for them. Moreover, the services made available by a welfare state will parallel in quality and coverage those open to individuals who are able to draw on private resources."

Obviously, says Hacker, no such condition exists in the United States. Unemployment benefits, he notes, average about $35 a week, scarcely enough to begin to live on, and even in the best states the average is only a dollar or two higher. The average social security pension is $17.70 a week for a single person and $29.72 a week for a couple. And only a small fraction of the elderly have private pensions, savings or other resources of any size. The average payment under the aid to dependent children (ADC) program is about $21 a week for a fatherless family of three. Public assistance allowances are notoriously low and insecure, and the humiliations and indignities to which welfare clients are subjected are equally notorious.[1]

In addition, large numbers are excluded from even such benefits as these. We have already noted the 15 million or more who are not covered by the federal minimum wage law. Exclusion from unemployment benefits is equally great. "Currently," wrote the *American Federationist* in July 1963, with reference to the unemployed, ". . . only half of these are drawing benefits. Between 30 and 40 percent of the unemployed are denied benefits because of where they work and because of restrictions in state eligibility requirements. Ten to twenty percent have been out

[1] For a detailed picture, see Edgar May, *The Wasted Americans* (1964).

of work so long that they have exhausted their benefit rights."
Similarly, one-fourth of the aged are excluded from social security
benefits.

Ironically, it is the poor who are benefited least. The agricultural workers are excluded as a group from virtually all social
welfare benefits. Others are ineligible for social security or unemployment benefits because their earnings are too low to qualify.
Farm legislation is designed to give huge subsidies to the big
farmers but practically nothing to the struggling small farmers.
And not infrequently benefits due are not claimed because of
ignorance of the procedures involved or because of their formidable
character.

Finally, the limitations of our social welfare program are
indicated by the fact that only 7 percent of the federal budget is
allotted for these purposes while 60 percent goes for military
expenditures. If we include state and local outlays, total social
welfare expenditures average some $33 billion a year as against
federal expenditures of more than $50 billion for military purposes.

Limited and inadequate as they are, these social welfare outlays are a target of unremitting attack. A Goldwater crusades
for an end to compulsory social security as an invasion of personal
freedom, and attacks the poor as lazy and shiftless parasites on
society, deserving of nothing. Others conduct an unending fight
to cut relief appropriations and trim relief roles of "chiselers." In
state legislatures, unemployment compensation levels, far from
being increased, are under constant assault. During the past year
two states—Wyoming and Pennsylvania—have lowered them,
and it is not out of the question that others may follow suit.

As for further steps in fighting poverty, widespread resistance
can be expected to carrying out even the minimal program of the
Johnson administration. This resistance (to whose strength the
fate of medicare and other social welfare legislation up to this
date testifies) emanates from the spokesmen of big business generally, which does not take kindly to any moves in behalf of the
poor that threaten to eat into its profits. Basically, poverty
today stems from the drive of the giant corporations for maximum
profits, which means not only holding wages down and not only
sweating extra profits out of the small farmers, the small businessmen, the Negro people and other groups, but also holding government welfare expenditures to a minimum. As against being
taxed for such expenditures, monopoly capital strives rather to
use the economic resources of the government for its own benefit,

with the working people footing the tax bill. The poverty of those without work or unable to work is thus no less a product of capitalist exploitation than that of the masses of underpaid workers. . . .

THE NATURE AND ROOTS OF POVERTY

The "Underclass" Theory

It has become customary to speak of poverty in the United States today as "poverty in affluence." That is, where once the great majority of working people were poor and poverty was the "normal" condition, now most workers are at least reasonably well off and the poor constitute a minority which, for one reason or another, has been bypassed by affluence. As Harrington puts it (*The Other America*, pp. 9–10): "Today's poor, in short, missed the political and social gains of the thirties. They are, as Galbraith rightly points out, the first minority poor in history. . . .

"The first step toward the new poverty was taken when millions of people proved immune to progress."

From this it is but a step to the idea that the poor of today, in contrast to those of the past, constitute a new, distinct class in our society. This is implied in Harrington's phrase "the other America." It is more explicitly stated by others.

Gunnar Myrdal, in his book, *Challenge to Affluence* (1962), speaks of "a vicious circle tending to create in America an underprivileged class of unemployed, unemployables, and underemployed who are more and more hopelessly set apart from the nation at large and do not share in its life, its ambitions, and its achievements" (p. 10). Elsewhere he refers to a tendency to "trap an 'underclass' of unemployed and, gradually, unemployable and underemployed persons and families at the bottom of a society, while for the majority of people above that layer the increasingly democratic structure of the educational system creates even more real liberty and equality of opportunity . . ." (p. 34).

The *New Republic* (February 15, 1964) editorially carries the idea a step further: "The Marxist theory of an army of the poor swelling into a revolutionary majority has proved wholly false, but instead the poor have become in our affluent society a sealed-off community with its own crippled values, liable to erupt into crime and psychopathic violence. . . . But the way to get rid of them is for the poor who form a sub-class and who think of themselves as such to be absorbed back into human society as human beings; and for this the Peace Corps approach is required."

Another variant of the "two Americas" theme is presented by S. M. Miller in an article entitled "The Politics of Poverty" (*Dissent*, Spring, 1964), in which he says that while the "urban poor is composed of many strata . . . the poor in the largest urban centers are rapidly evolving into a 'colored' poor of Negroes and Spanish-name persons." He continues: "This group might be described as a 'new' working class. The 'old' working class, who still comprise the bulk of skilled and semi-skilled union members as well as the majority of blue collar workers, is made up of 'old-settler' Protestant recruits largely from farm and rural areas and the second and third generation of the predominantly Catholic Eastern and Southern European nations. The 'new' working class is more likely to be 'colored,' unskilled, in low-wage service and non-unionized industries, e.g., hospitals."

He concludes: "The United States today is increasingly moving into a dual economy in which the main sector is characterized by the provision of high standards of living, somewhat stable employment, and other rewards for those who are able to stay in it. On the other hand, the marginal sector centers around low-level service trades and occupations, filled by individuals of low skill who are from minority groups or left-over immigrant populations, receiving relatively little of what the economy produces."

The essence of these views, in sum, is that the problem of poverty is no longer that of the working class as a whole but is now the special problem of a minority—an "underclass"—left behind in the accession of the great majority of workers to affluence, and separated from that majority by a widening gap. The task of fighting poverty, therefore, is that of bringing this remnant into the mainstream of a society advancing toward ever greater affluence, meanwhile giving its members every possible form of assistance in their unfortunate plight. In the words of the 1964 *Economic Report of the President*, the task is one of attacking "the poverty that remains" after the achievements of the New Deal and speeding its diminution (p. 73).

We have presented this conception of the problem at some length because it is so widely prevalent. We submit, however, that it is also essentially erroneous, no less so than the idea that poverty is the product of individual characteristics. Indeed, the two are not unrelated. To make clear both our objections to this conception and the true status of poverty as we see it, we propose to deal with two of its corollaries.   One is that the rise of affluence and the corresponding decline of poverty constitute a natural development in our society.   The second is that today poverty and unemployment are distinct and separate problems.

On the Decline of Poverty

The 1964 *Economic Report of the President* asserts that "steadily rising productivity, together with an improving network of private and social insurance and assistance, has been eroding mass poverty in America" and that "the sources of poverty have been eroded as a by-product of a general advance in economic well-being and of measures designed to achieve other social goals" (pp. 55, 73). This process, it is maintained, is leading to the eventual elimination of poverty.   The purpose of a "war on poverty" is to supplement it and speed it up.

This is directly related to the thesis that, thanks to a pronounced rise in the real earnings of workers, an equalization of incomes has been taking place and a narrowing of the "income gap"—in the eyes of some, to such a degree as to constitute a virtual "income revolution."

Unequestionably, real wages have risen greatly since the thirties.   But both the magnitude and the significance of the rise have been considerably exaggerated.   The figures employed do not sufficiently take into account the effect of unemployment and the fact that in large measure the improvement reflects the sharp decline in joblessness since the depression years of the thirties. Furthermore, the figures show that the increase was principally a wartime phenomenon.   They demonstrate, writes Gabriel Kolko, "that most of the increase was due to the rapid rise in weekly hours and employment during wartime 1939–44, and that growth in real income since 1944 has been minor.   The gross, after-tax, average weekly real income of production workers in manufacturing, who accounted for one-quarter of the non-agricultural wage and salary workers, increased 53 percent from 1939 through 1944, but only 17 percent from 1944 through 1960."   (*Wealth and Power in America*, 1962, p. 77.)

The same is true of family income.   And here, Kolko points out, the increase is also due in part to such factors as a sharp rise in the number of working wives and a growth of moonlighting.

As for the distribution of income, this has remained virtually unchanged throughout the postwar period.   The 1964 *Economic*

Report of the President states (p. 60): "The one-fifth of families with the highest incomes received an estimated 43 percent of total income in 1947 and 42 percent in 1962. The one-fifth of families with the lowest incomes received 5 percent of the total in 1947 and 5 percent in 1963." Clearly, whatever improvement may have taken place during the war years, there has been none since then. Though all incomes have risen substantially, the income gap remains as wide as ever.

The Administration figures show a marked decrease in poverty during the postwar period. But here, too, there has been a sharp slowing down of the decrease in recent years. The proportion of families with annual incomes below $3,000 fell from 32 percent in 1950 to 23 percent in 1956, but by 1962 it had fallen only to 20 percent. (1964 *Economic Report of the President*, p. 59.)

Furthermore, this method of measuring changes in the incidence of poverty is itself open to question. Oscar Ornati, in a paper prepared for the National Policy Committee on Pockets of Poverty, points out that the Administration figures exaggerate the decline because they use the 1947 yardstick of substandard income as the basis for estimating poverty both in 1947 and today. "By taking past standards that go back far enough," he argues, "we are bound to find that there are *no* poor today, which is a patent absurdity." Hence, poverty must be measured in relation to *contemporary* yardsticks, a procedure which yields much less encouraging results. Ornati writes: "What should be compared is the number who lived 'below adequacy' in 1947 by 1947 standards of adequacy with those who lived 'below adequacy' in 1960 by 1960 standards. When this is done, we find that the numbers of abject poor, the numbers of those living 'below adequacy' and below minimum comfort levels have not changed very much. In 1947, by 1947 standards, 27 percent of all people lived below levels of minimum adequacy and in 1960, by 1960 standards, they amounted to 26 percent. In 1947 the proportion living below minimum comfort was 39 percent while in 1960 it was 40 percent.

"The story is different when abject poverty is considered. Here, when the number of poor, living at or below subsistence levels in 1947 and 1960 are compared, the proportion decreased from 15 percent to 11 percent although their actual number only decreased from 21 to 20 million."[2] (*Poverty in America*, 1964.)

To sum up, it is clear that the gains made by the American

[2] By current standards, minimum subsistence is defined as $2,500 a year, minimum adequacy as $3,500 and minimum comfort as $5,500, in each case for a family of four.

working people since the thirties have been considerably more modest than we are generally led to believe. Moreover, these gains have occurred chiefly during the war years; in the postwar period they have been greatly reduced or have ceased altogether. Even the much-heralded decline of poverty, which persisted for some time after the war, has for a number of years been reduced to almost negligible proportions. The relative status of the poor has shown little or no improvement, whether in their share of the national income or in their advance toward an adequate living standard.

The gains achieved, therefore, have been principally a product of the special conditions created by World War II, which did away with the levels of mass unemployment and poverty of the depression thirties. With the passage of these conditions, however, there is no basis for assuming that poverty will of necessity continue to decline as in the past—that we are in the course of a long-term trend leading to the extinction of poverty. Certainly the experiences of recent years offer no guarantee of this. Moreover, the sustained economic upswing of the past four years cannot be expected to last indefinitely, and with the onset of a new recession the decline may well come to a complete halt or be reversed. In the event of a serious depression—a possibility which should by no means be ruled out—poverty could climb sharply from its present level.

Unemployment and Poverty

Historically, poverty and unemployment have always gone hand in hand. Layoffs, short work weeks and chronic lack of work have been intertwined with low wages as causes of mass poverty in the ranks of the working class, and in periods of depression the upsurge of unemployment has meant an upsurge of poverty.

Today, however, there is a tendency to separate the two—a tendency growing out of the concept of the "new" poor described above. In support of this view, it is argued that on the one hand only a small part of the poor are unemployed (as distinct from "unemployable"), and that on the other hand the unemployed are not usually poor—that their spells of joblessness are not sufficient to reduce their yearly incomes to the poverty level.

More basically, however, the separation is made on the grounds that poverty today is not primarily economic in origin but is very largely the poverty of those by-passed by affluence because of personal characteristics or misfortune. Hence the remedy lies not so much in the economic sphere as in that of social welfare and public assistance. Unemployment, on the other hand, *is* economic in origin and the remedy accordingly lies in the sphere of economic reform.

This point of view is most clearly delineated by Henry S. Reuss, Democratic congressman from Wisconsin, in his book *The Critical Decade* (1964). "Much of the problem of poverty," he writes, "arises from causes outside the operation of our economic system. But the problem of unemployment derives directly from the system itself." He continues: "We can alleviate this kind of poverty [due to personal disabilities] through compassionate social measures, but we cannot entirely eliminate its causes." On the other hand: "In the case of unemployment, concern for its victims would be an inadequate response—the causes for most of it can be eradicated" (p. 130).

Furthermore, the exponents of this view maintain, since poverty is static or decreasing whereas unemployment is growing alarmingly, the latter is the more serious problem, as well as one demanding more fundamental solutions. It is therefore the fight against joblessness, not poverty, which is the more basic task today.

With the emphasis placed on the fight for jobs one can fully agree. But the separation of this from the fight against poverty is unwarranted. As already pointed out the coincidence of poverty and unemployment is much greater than the official statistics indicate. Also, as suggested above, the ultimate roots of *all* present-day poverty are economic. The intimate relationship of the two is shown, moreover, by the fact that the slowdown in the decline of poverty largely coincides with the rise of joblessness. Indeed, this rise is one of the main reasons for the renewed concern over poverty today.

Most important, however, is the *nature* of the rise. For it is no transient occurrence, but is associated with an accelerating technological revolution among whose effects is the displacement of workers from their jobs in ever greater numbers. It is this displacement which threatens to swell the ranks of the poor anew, and at a growing pace. It is noted by A. H. Raskin ("The New Poor," *New Leader*, March 30, 1964), who says: "Automation is creating a new class of poor, a class whose members may prove much less docile in their poverty than those who were born into the slums and never left them. This new class is made up of workers dispossessed by the machine: their skills, security and status all washed into nothingness by the course of technology."

Added to those fired as a consequence of automation are the growing numbers of young people never hired. Then there are those workers whose jobs are wiped out by the closing down of plants and the shifting of production to other areas—a process which occurs with growing frequency as automation spreads. What happens to these workers is described as follows in a document issued by the Senate Subcommittee on Poverty (*The War on Poverty: The Economic Opportunity Act of 1964*):

"Following a plant closing in Trenton in October 1961, 1,900 employees—almost two-thirds of the work force—were still unemployed and looking for work 9 months later. In Sioux City, Iowa, 40 percent of the former employees remained unemployed 6 months after the June 1963 closing of their plant. In Iron City, Wis., a mine closed in August of 1962, leaving about 40 percent of the miners still looking for work 9 months later. In Fargo, N. Dak., a third of the former employees were still unemployed a year after their plant closed.

"Some of these workers, who have non-transferable skills or are 'too old' at 40 or 50 to be reabsorbed, are unable to get regular jobs or, in many cases, any work at all. . . . Still others, somewhat luckier, are able to find steady work, but in low-pay occupations and industries, at wage rates which are insufficient to keep the family out of the grip of poverty" (p. 37).

These workers are described as inhabiting an "economic underworld of the bypassed." But such a fate is not confined to some special group; it is one which menaces the great mass of American working people. From the threat of displacement by automation and related developments no worker in our capitalist economy is fully immune, whatever his seniority, skill or competence. The great bulk of the working people face a mounting degree of economic insecurity which renders their installment-plan affluence increasingly unstable and uncertain.

The displaced workers are not mere isolated victims of circumstance; they are a harbinger of what the continued advance of automation holds in store for growing numbers. They constitute a bridge between the working class as a whole and the poor—a bridge built of insecurity, displacement, unemployment and low-wage jobs. The poor, therefore, are not a separate class or an "underclass" but are part of the working class and the working people as a whole, the end product of a process of impoverishment in which every worker is in danger of being engulfed. Hence the war on poverty and the war on unemployment are not separate struggles but are parts of one single war.

In the comparative prosperity of the war and postwar years the tide of poverty has receded. But with the passing of these exceptional circumstances, together with the growing impact of the new technological revolution, it threatens to rise anew. What this indicates is that we are by no means on the highway to universal affluence with the poor constituting a dwindling remnant of the by-passed. Rather, poverty in its ebb and flow is a condition inherent in our capitalist economy.

Part Four

CONTEMPORARY CAPITALISM

THE REQUIREMENTS OF TECHNOLOGY AND SIZE HAVE INCREASED *the corporation's need for specialized talent and the organization of this talent. Organized intelligence is, in fact, says Galbraith, a new factor of production. A shift matching the earlier one from land to capital is presently occurring. Power has passed to the association of men with the diverse technical knowledge and experience required by modern technology and planning. This, the technostructure, is the new locus of power in the business enterprise and American society, according to Galbraith. It is the result of processes Berle has also focussed on—processes such as separation of ownership and control in the large corporations; increasing size; dispersion of stockholding; the ability of the corporations to finance from internal savings; and their dominant economic position.*

Control of capital and control of markets are indispensable to planning. Control of supply and demand, economics of scale, and monopoly will serve the corporations' planning function. Decisions within the technostructure are now rooted in the organization, where technology and planning are uninfluenced by outsiders, rather than in the individuals. The security of profits which the large corporations have—contrary to popular myth, Galbraith says the large corporations simply do not lose money—removes them from the influence of the market. They control rather than are controlled by the market. Thus, Galbraith says that, with the technostructure as controlling intelligence, the giant corporations—whose economic dominance cannot be doubted, but whose widespread benefits cannot be doubted either—are now the basic planning units of our society.

21

THE TECHNOSTRUCTURE AND THE CORPORATION IN THE NEW INDUSTRIAL STATE

John Kenneth Galbraith

The tendency to an excess of savings, and the need for an offsetting strategy by the state, is an established and well-recognized feature of the Keynesian economy. And savings, we have seen, are supplied by the industrial enterprise to itself as part of its planning. There is high certainty as to their availability, for this is the purpose of the planning.

At the same time the requirements of technology and planning have greatly increased the need of the industrial enterprise for specialized talent and for its organization. The industrial system must rely, in the main, on external sources for this talent. Unlike capital it is not something that the firm can supply to itself. To be effective this talent must also be brought into effective association with itself. It must be in an organization. Given a competent business organization, capital is now ordinarily available. But the mere possession of capital is now no guarantee that the requisite talent can be obtained and organized. One should

Reprinted from John Kenneth Galbraith, *The New Industrial State* (New York: New American Library, A Signet Book, 1968), pp. 68–70, 81–95. Reprinted by permission of the publisher, Houghton Mifflin Company. Copyright © 1967 by John Kenneth Galbraith. Footnotes have been renumbered.

expect, from past experience, to find a new shift of power in the industrial enterprise, this one from capital to organized intelligence. And one would expect that this shift would be reflected in the deployment of power in the society at large.

This has, indeed, occurred.   It is a shift of power as between the factors of production which matches that which occurred from land to capital in the advanced countries beginning two centuries ago.   It is an occurrence of the last fifty years and is still going on. A dozen matters of commonplace observation—the loss of power by stockholders in the modern corporation, the impregnable position of the successful corporate management, the dwindling social magnetism of the banker, the air of quaintness that attaches to the suggestion that the United States is run from Wall Street, the increasingly energetic search for industrial talent, the new prestige of education and educators—all attest the point.

This shift of power has been disguised because, as was once true of land, the position of capital is imagined to be immutable. That power should be elsewhere seems unnatural and those who so argue seem to be in search of frivolous novelty.   And it has been disguised because power has not gone to another of the established factors as they are celebrated in conventional economic pedagogy. It has not passed to labor.   Labor has won limited authority over its pay and working conditions but none over the enterprise. And it still tends to abundance.   If overly abundant savings are not used, the first effect is unemployment; if savings are used one consequence is a substitution of machine processes for unskilled labor and standard skills.   Thus unskilled labor and workers with conventional skills suffer, along with the capitalist, from an abundance of capital.

Nor has power passed to the classical entrepreneur—the individual who once used his access to capital to bring it into combination with the other factors of production.   He is a diminishing figure in the industrial system.   Apart from access to capital, his principal qualifications were imagination, capacity for decision and courage in risking money including, not infrequently, his own.   None of these qualifications are especially important for organizing intelligence or effective in competing with it.

Power has, in fact, passed to what anyone in search of novelty might be justified in calling a new factor of production.   This is the association of men of diverse technical knowledge, experience or other talent which modern industrial technology and planning require.   It extends from the leadership of the modern industrial enterprise down to just short of the labor force and embraces a large number of people and a large variety of talent. It is on the effectiveness of this organization, as most business doctrine now implicitly agrees, that the success of the modern business enterprise now depends. Were this organization dismembered or otherwise lost, there is no certainty that it could be put together again. To enlarge it to undertake new tasks is an expensive and sometimes uncertain undertaking. Here one now finds the problem of an uncertainly high supply price at the margin. And here one finds the accompanying power. Our next task is to examine in some depth this new locus of power in the business enterprise and in the society. . . .

In the past, leadership in business organization was identified with the entrepreneur—the individual who united ownership [and] control of capital with capacity for organizing the other factors of production and, in most contexts, with a further capacity for innovation.[1] With the rise of the modern corporation, the emergence of the organization required by modern technology and planning and the divorce of the owner of the capital from control of the enterprise, the entrepreneur no longer exists as an individual person in the mature industrial enterprise.[2] Everyday discourse, except in the economics textbooks, recognizes this change. It replaces the entrepreneur, as the directing force of the enterprise, with management. This is a collective and imperfectly defined entity; in the large corporation it embraces chairman, president, those vice presidents with important staff or departmental responsibility, occupants of other major staff positions and, perhaps, division or department heads not included above. It includes, however, only a small proportion of those who, as participants, contribute information to group decisions. This latter group is very large; it extends from the most senior officials of the corporation to where it meets, at the outer perimeter, the white and blue collar workers whose function is to conform more or less mechanically to instruction or routine. It embraces all who bring specialized knowledge, talent or experience to group decision-making.

[1] "To act with confidence beyond the range of familiar beacons and to overcome that resistance requires aptitudes that are present in only a small fraction of the population and [they] define the entrepreneurial type as well as the entrepreneurial function." Joseph A. Schumpeter, *Capitalism, Socialism and Democracy*, Second Edition (New York: Harper, 1947), p. 132.

[2] He is still, of course, to be found in smaller firms and in larger ones that have yet to reach full maturity of organization. I deal with this evolution in the next [section].

This, not the management, is the guiding intelligence—the brain— of the enterprise.   There is no name for all who participate in group decision-making or the organization which they form.   I propose to call this organization the Technostructure.

THE CORPORATION

Few subjects of earnest inquiry have been more unproductive than study of the modern large corporation.   The reasons are clear. A vivid image of what *should* exist acts as a surrogate for reality. Pursuit of the image then prevents pursuit of the reality.

For purposes of scholarly inquiry, the corporation has a sharp legal image.   Its purpose is to do business as an individual would but with the added ability to assemble and use the capital of several or numerous persons.   In consequence, it can undertake tasks beyond the reach of any single person.   And it protects those who supply capital by limiting their liability to the amount of their original investment, insuring them a vote on the significant affairs of the enterprise, defining the powers and the responsibilities of directors and officers, and giving them access to the courts to redress grievance.   Apart from its ability to mobilize capital and its lessened association with the active life of any individual, the corporation is not deemed to differ functionally from the individual proprietorship or partnership.   Its purpose, like theirs, is to conduct business on equitable terms with other businesses and make money for the owners.

Such corporations do exist and in large numbers.   But one wonders if the natural interest of the student of economics is the local paving firm or body repair shop.   Or is it General Motors and Standard Oil of New Jersey and General Electric?

But these firms depart sharply from the legal image.   In none of these firms is the capital pooled by original investors appreciable; in each it could be paid off by a few hours' or a few days' earnings. In none does the individual stockholder pretend to power.   In all three cases, the corporation is far more influential in the markets in which it buys materials, components and labor and in which it sells its finished products than is commonly imagined to be the case with the individual proprietorship.

In consequence, nearly all study of the corporation has been concerned with its deviation from its legal or formal image.   This image—that of "an association of persons into an autonomous legal unit with a distinct legal personality that enable it to carry on business, own property and contract debts"[3]—is highly normative. It is what a corporation should be. When the modern corporation disenfranchises its stockholders, grows to gargantuan size, expands into wholly unrelated activities, is a monopoly where it buys and a monopoly where it sells, something is wrong.

That the largest and most famous corporations, those whose names are household words and whose heads are accorded the most distinguished honors by their fellow businessmen, should be considered abnormal must seem a little dubious.

Additionally, it must be evident that General Motors does not have much in common with the Massachusetts Institute of Technology professors who pool their personal funds and what they can borrow from the banks and their friends to supply some erudite item to the Department of Defense and thus, in their modest way, help to defend the country and participate in capital gains. Their enterprise, created, owned and directed by themselves and exploiting the advantages of the corporate form, approaches the established image. General Motors as clearly does not.

The answer is that there is no such thing as *a* corporation. Rather there are several kinds of corporations all deriving from a common but very loose framework. Some are subject to the market; others reflect varying degrees of adaptation to the requirements of planning and the needs of the technostructure. The person who sets out to study buildings on Manhattan on the assumption that all are alike will have difficulty in passing from the surviving brownstones to the skyscrapers. And he will handicap himself even more if he imagines that all buildings should be like brownstones and have load-carrying walls and that others are abnormal. So with corporations.

2

The most obvious requirement of effective planning is large size. This, we have seen, allows the firm to accept market uncertainty where it cannot be eliminated; to eliminate markets on which otherwise it would be excessively dependent; to control other markets in which it buys and sells; and it is very nearly indispensable for participation in that part of the economy, characterized by exacting technology and comprehensive planning, where the only buyer is the Federal Government.

[3] Harry G. Guthmann and Herbert E. Dougall, *Corporation Financial Policy*, Second Edition (New York: Prentice-Hall, Inc., 1948), p. 9.

That corporations accommodate well to this need for size has scarcely to be stressed. They can, and have, become very large. But because of the odor of abnormality, this adaptation is not stressed. The head of the largest corporation is automatically accorded precedence at all business conventions, meetings and other business rites and festivals. He is complimented for his intelligence, vision, courage, progressiveness and for the remarkable rate of growth of his firm under his direction. But the great size of his firm—the value of its assets or the number of its employees—is not praised although this is its most striking feature.

Nothing so characterizes the industrial system as the scale of the modern corporate enterprise. In 1962 the five largest industrial corporations in the United States, with combined assets in excess of $36 billion, possessed over 12 percent of all assets used in manufacturing. The 50 largest corporations had over a third of all manufacturing assets. The 500 largest had well over two-thirds. Corporations with assets in excess of $10,000,000, some 2000 in all, accounted for about 80 percent of all the resources used in manufacturing in the United States.[4] In the mid nineteen-fifties, 28 corporations provided approximately 10 percent of all employment in manufacturing, mining and retail and wholesale trade. Twenty-three corporations provided 15 percent of all the employment in manufacturing. In the first half of the decade (June 1950–June 1956) a hundred firms received two-thirds by value of all defense contracts; ten firms received one-third.[5] In 1960 four corporations accounted for an estimated 22 percent of all industrial research and development expenditure. Three hundred and eighty-four corporations employing 7,000 or more workers accounted for 87 percent of these expenditures; 260,000

[4] Hearings before the Subcommittee on Antitrust and Monopoly of the Committee of the Judiciary, United States Senate, Eighty-Eighth Congress, Second Session, Pursuant to S. Res. 262. Part I. *Economic Concentration. Overall and Conglomerate Aspects* (1964), p. 113. Data on the concentration of industrial activity in the hands of large firms, and especially any that seem to show an increase in concentration, sustain a controversy in the United States that, at times, reaches mildly pathological proportions. The reason is that much of the argument between those who see the market as a viable institution and those who feel that it is succumbing to monopolistic influences has long turned on these figures. These figures are thus defended or attacked according to predilection. However, the general orders of magnitude given here are not subject to serious question.

[5] Carl Kaysen, "The Corporation: How Much Power? What Scope?" in *The Corporation in Modern Society*, Edward S. Mason, ed. (Cambridge: Harvard University Press, 1959), pp. 86–87.

firms employing fewer than 1,000 accounted for only 7 percent.[6]

Planning is a function that is associated in most minds with the state. If the corporation is the basic planning unit, it is appropriate that the scale of operations of the largest should approximate those of government. This they do. In 1965, three industrial corporations, General Motors, Standard Oil of New Jersey and Ford Motor Company, had more gross income than all of the farms in the country. The income of General Motors, of $20.7 billion, about equaled that of the three million smallest farms in the country—around 90 percent of all farms. The gross revenues of each of the three corporations just mentioned far exceed those of any single state. The revenues of General Motors in 1963 were fifty times those of Nevada, eight times those of New York and slightly less than one-fifth those of the Federal Government.[7]

Economists have anciently quarreled over the reasons for the great size of the modern corporation. Is it because size is essential in order to reap the economies of modern large scale production?[8] Is it, more insidiously, because the big firm wishes to exercise monopoly power in its markets? The present analysis allows both parties to the dispute to be partly right. The firm must be large enough to carry the large capital commitments of modern technology. It must also be large enough to control its markets. But the present view also explains what the older explanations don't explain. That is, why General Motors is not only large enough to afford the best size of automobile plant but is large enough to afford a dozen or more of the best size; and why it is large enough to produce things as diverse as aircraft engines and refrigerators, which cannot be explained by the economies of scale; and why, though it is large enough to have the market power associated with monopoly, consumers do not seriously complain of exploitation. The size of General Motors is in the service not of monopoly or the economies of scale but of planning. And for this planning— control of supply, control of demand, provision of capital, min-

[6] M. A. Adelman, Hearings before the Subcommittee on Antitrust and Monopoly of the Committee on the Judiciary, United States Senate, Eighty-Ninth Congress, First Session, Pursuant to S. Res. 70, Part III. *Economic Concentration. Concentration, Invention and Innovation* (1965), pp. 1139–40.

[7] Data from *Fortune*, U.S. Department of Agriculture and *Statistical Abstract of the United States.*

[8] Cf. Joe S. Bain, "Economics of Scale, Concentration and the Condition of Entry in Twenty Manufacturing Industries," *The American Economic Review,* Vol. XLIV, No. 1 (March 1954).

imization of risk—there is no clear upper limit to the desirable size. It could be that the bigger the better. The corporate form accommodates to this need. Quite clearly it allows the firm to be very, very large.

3

The corporation also accommodates itself admirably to the needs of the technostructure. This, we have seen, is an apparatus for group decision—for pooling and testing the information provided by numerous individuals to reach decisions that are beyond the knowledge of any one. It requires . . . a high measure of autonomy. It is vulnerable to any intervention by external authority for, given the nature of the group decision-making and the problems being solved, such external authority will always be incompletely informed and hence arbitrary. If problems were susceptible to decision by individuals, no group would be involved.

One possible source of such intervention is the state. The corporate charter, however, accords the corporation a large area of independent action in the conduct of its affairs. And this freedom is defended as a sacred right. Nothing in American business attitudes is so iniquitous as government interference in the *internal* affairs of the corporation. The safeguards here, both in law and custom, are great. There is equally vehement resistance to any invasion by trade unions of the prerogatives of management.

There is also, however, the danger of intervention by the owners—by the stockholders. Their exclusion is not secured by law or sanctified by custom. On the contrary, either directly or through the agency of the Board of Directors, their power is guaranteed. But being legal does not make it benign. Exercise of such power on substantive questions requiring group decision would be as damaging as any other. So the stockholder too must be excluded.

In part this has been accomplished by the simple attrition of the stockholder's power as death and the distribution of estates, the diversifying instincts of trusts and foundations, the distributional effects of property settlements and alimony, and the artistic, philanthropic and social enjoyments of non-functional heirs all distribute the stock of any corporation to more and more hands. This process works rapidly and the distribution need by no means be complete to separate the stockholder from all effective power. In the mid nineteen-twenties, in the first case to draw wide public attention to this tendency, it became known that Colonel Robert W. Stewart, the Chairman of the Board of Directors of the Standard Oil Company of Indiana, had, in concert with some of the men who later won immortality as the architects of the Teapot Dome and Elk Hills transactions, organized a highly specialized enterprise in Canada called the Continental Trading Company. This company had the sole function of buying crude oil from Colonel E. A. Humphreys, owner of the rich Mexica field in east central Texas, and reselling it to companies controlled by the same individuals, including Standard Oil of Indiana, at a markup of twenty-five cents a barrel. It was an excellent business. No costs were involved, other than a small percentage to the Canadian lawyer who served as a figurehead and went hunting in Africa whenever wanted for questioning, and for mailing back the proceeds after they had been converted into Liberty Bonds. (If some of these had not been used, carelessly, to bribe Secretary of the Interior Albert B. Fall and others to pay the deficit of the Republican National Committee, Continental might have forever remained unknown as was unquestionably intended.) It was Colonel Stewart's later contention that he had always intended to turn over the profit to Standard Oil of Indiana. But, absentmindedly, he had allowed the bonds to remain in his own possession for many years and had cashed some of the coupons. In 1929 Standard of Indiana was only 18 years distant from the decree which had broken up the Standard Oil empire of John D. Rockefeller of which it had been an important part. The Rockefellers still owned 14.9 percent of the voting stock of the Indiana Company and were deemed to have the controlling interest. They reacted sternly to the outrage; the elder Rockefeller had, on notable occasions, imposed a somewhat similar levy on his competitors, but never on his own company. With the aid of the publicity generated by the Teapot Dome scandal, his own high standing in the financial community, his brother-in-law Winthrop W. Aldrich (who solicited proxies), and a very large expenditure of money, John D. Rockefeller, Jr., was able to oust the Colonel, although not by a wide margin.[9] (The latter had the

[9] Cf. Adolf A. Berle, Jr. and Gardiner C. Means, *The Modern Corporation and Private Property* (New York: Macmillan, 1934), pp. 82–83. Of the 8,465,299 shares represented, Rockefeller got the votes of 5,510,313. Stewart retired on a pension of $75,000 a year. M. R. Werner and John Starr, *Teapot Dome* (New York: The Viking Press, Inc., 1959), pp. 274–75.

full support of his Board of Directors.). In the absence of the scandal and his ample resources, Rockefeller, it was realized with some shock, would have had little hope.

In most other large corporations, the chance for exerting such power would have been less and it has become increasingly less with the passage of time. Professor Gordon's prewar study of the 176 largest corporations showed that at least half of their stock was held in blocks of less than 1 percent of the total outstanding. In less than a third of the companies was there a stockholder interest large enough to allow of potential control, i.e., the election of a Board of Directors, and "the number of companies in which any large degree of *active* leadership is associated with considerable ownership is certainly even smaller."[10]   That was a quarter of a century ago; the dispersion of stock ownership, which was then much greater for the older railroad corporations than for newer industrial corporations, has almost certainly continued.[11]   It means that to change control more stockholders must be persuaded, against the advice of management, to vote their stock for someone whom, in the nature of the case, they do not know and will not be disposed to trust.   The effort must also contend with the tendency of the indifferent to give proxies to management.   It is also in face of the requirement that the loser of a proxy battle, if he is an outsider, must pay the cost.   And it must contend finally with the alternative, always available to the dissatisfied stockholder, of simply selling his stock.   Corporate size, the passage of time and the dispersion of stock ownership do not disenfranchise the stockholder.   Rather, he can vote but his vote is valueless.

4

To be secure in its autonomy, the technostructure also needs to have a source of new capital to which it can turn without having,

[10] R. A. Gordon, *Business Leadership in the Large Corporation* (Washington: Brookings, 1945), Chap. II.   The median holdings of management were 2.1 percent of the stock.   In 56 percent of the companies, management owned less than one percent; in only 16 of the companies did it own as much as 20 percent of the stock outstanding.   A more recent study by Mabel Newcomer, *The Big Business Executive* (New York: Columbia University Press, 1955), showed that by 1952 there had been a further reduction in management holdings.

[11] This is explicitly confirmed by a study by R. J. Larner, "The 200 Largest Nonfinancial Corporations," *The American Economic Review*, Vol. LVI, No. 4, Part 1 (September 1966), pp. 777–87, which appeared just as [*The New Industrial State*] was going to press.

as a *quid pro quo*, to surrender any authority over its own decisions. Here capital abundance enters as a factor. A bank, insurance company or investment banker cannot make control of decision, actual or potential, a condition of a loan or security underwriting if funds are readily available from another and more permissive source and if there is vigorous competition for the business.

The complexity of modern technological and planning decisions also protects the technostructure from outside interference. The country banker, out of his experience and knowledge of the business, can readily interpose his judgment, as against that of a farmer, on the prospects for feeder cattle—and does. Not even the most self-confident financier would wish to question the judgment of General Electric engineers, product planners, stylists, market researchers and sales executives on the culturally advanced toaster taken up in the last chapter. By taking decisions away from individuals and locating them deeply within the technostructure, technology and planning thus remove them from the influence of outsiders.

But the corporation accords a much more specific protection to the technostructure. That is by providing it with a source of capital, derived from its own earnings, that is wholly under its own control. No banker can attach conditions as to how retained earnings are to be used. Nor can any other outsider. No one, the normally innocuous stockholder apart, has the right to ask about an investment from retained earnings that turns out badly. It is hard to overestimate the importance of the shift in power that is associated with availability of such a source of capital. Few other developments can have more fundamentally altered the character of capitalism. It is hardly surprising that retained earnings of corporations have become such an overwhelmingly important source of capital.

5

There remains one final source of danger to the autonomy of the technostructure. That arises with a failure of earnings. Then there are no retained earnings. If new plant is needed or working capital must be replenished, there will have to be appeal to bankers or other outsiders. This will be under circumstances, i.e., the fact that the firm is showing losses, when the right of such outsiders to inquire and to intervene will have to be conceded. They cannot be told to mind their own business. Thus does a shortage of capital, though limited in time and place, promptly revive the power of the capitalist. And it is in times of such failure of earnings, and then only, that the stockholder of the large corporation can be aroused. In large corporations, battles for control have been rare in recent times. And in all notable cases involving large corporations—the New York Central, Loew's, TWA, the New England railroads, Wheeling Steel, Curtis Publishing—the firm in contention was doing badly at the time. If revenues are above some minimum—they need not be at their maximum for no one will know what that is—creditors cannot intervene and stockholders cannot be aroused.

Here, too, the corporation, and the industrial system generally, have adapted effectively to the needs of the technostructure, though, surprisingly, the nature of the adaptation has been little noticed. The adaptation is, simply, that big corporations do not lose money. In 1957, a year of mild recession in the United States, not one of the 100 largest industrial corporations failed to return a profit. Only one of the largest 200 finished the year in the red. Seven years later in 1964, a prosperous year by general agreement, all of the first 100 again made money; only 2 among the first 200 had losses and only 7 among the first 500. None of the 50 largest merchandising firms—Sears, Roebuck, A & P, Safeway, *et al.*— failed to return a profit. Nor, predictably, did any of the 50 largest utilities. And among the 50 largest transportation companies only 3 railroads and the momentarily unfortunate Eastern Airlines, failed to make money.[12]

The American business liturgy has long intoned that this is a profit and loss economy. "The American competitive enterprise system is an acknowledged profit and loss system, the hope of profits being the incentive and the fear of loss being the spur,"[13] This may be so. But it is not true of that organized part of the economy in which a developed technostructure is able to protect its profits by planning. Nor is it true of the United States Steel Corporation, author of the sentence just cited, which has not had losses for a quarter of a century.

6

As always, no strong case is improved by overstatement. Among the 200 largest corporations in the United States—those that form

[12] *The Fortune Directory*, August 1958, August 1965.
[13] United States Steel Corporation. *Annual Report, 1958.*

the heart of the industrial system—there are few in which owners
exercise any important influence on decisions. And this influence decreases year by year. But there are exceptions. Some
owners—the du Pont, and in lesser measure the Firestone and
Ford, families are examples—participate, or have participated,
actively in management. Thus they earn influence by being part
of the technostructure and their influence is unquestionably
increased by their ownership. Others, through position on the
Board of Directors, have power in the selection of management—in decision on those who make decisions. And yet others
may inform themselves and intervene substantively on individual
decisions—a merger, a plant acquisition or the launching of a new
line.

In the last case, however, there must always be question as to
how much the individual is deciding and how much has been
decided for him by the group which has provided the relevant
information; the danger of confusing ratification with decision
must again be emphasized. And in all circumstances it is important to realize that corporate ceremony more or less deliberately
disguises the reality. This deserves a final word.

Corporate liturgy strongly emphasizes the power of the Board
of Directors and ultimately, thus, of the stockholders they are
assumed to represent. The rites which attest this point are
conducted with much solemnity; no one allows himself to be
cynical as to their substance. Heavy dockets, replete with data,
are submitted to the Board. Time is allowed for study. Recom-
mendations are appended. Given the extent and group character
of the preparation, rejection would be unthinkable. The Board,
nonetheless, is left with the impression that it has made a decision.

Corporate procedure also allows the Board to act on financial
transactions—changes in capital structure, declaration of dividends, authorization of lines of credit. These, given the control
by the technostructure of its sources of savings and capital supply,
are frequently the most routine and derivative of decisions. But
as elsewhere noted, any association with large sums of money
conveys an impression of power. It brings it to mind for the
same traditional reasons as does a detachment of soldiers.

With even greater unction although with less plausibility,
corporate ceremony seeks also to give the stockholders an impression of power. When stockholders are (or were) in control of a
company, stockholders' meetings are an occasion of scant ceremony The majority is voted in and the minority is voted out,

with such concessions as may seem strategic, and all understand the process involved. As stockholders cease to have influence, however, efforts are made to disguise this nullity. Their convenience is considered in selecting the place of meeting. They are presented with handsomely printed reports, the preparation of which is now a specialized business. Products and even plants are inspected. During the proceedings, as in the report, there are repetitive references to *your* company. Officers listen, with every evidence of attention, to highly irrelevant suggestions of wholly uninformed participants and assure them that these will be considered with the greatest care. Votes of thanks from women stockholders in print dresses owning ten shares "for the excellent skill with which you run *our* company" are received by the management with well-simulated gratitude. All present show stern disapproval of critics. No important stockholders are present. No decisions are taken. The annual meeting of the large American corporation is, perhaps, our most elaborate exercise in popular illusion.

ADAMS TAKES ISSUE WITH GALBRAITH'S VIEWS. THAT THE *corporations dominate the economy, he says, is clear. This is not the result of technological imperatives, however, but rather of the acceptance of rationalizations for monopoly and government policies based on those rationalizations. Technological size and administrative size differ. Technological efficiency may require smaller rather than larger plants. In fact, of the 60 most important inventions in recent years, most came from research not done by large corporations. Most research is now done by the federal government, paid for by the people, and used for the private benefit of the corporations. It is the socialization of risk and the privatization of profit and power, says Adams.*

Innovations are taken over and used by the larger corporations, once they have been proved successful by smaller domestic companies and/or foreign competitors. The large corporations themselves are not the innovators. The competitive market, not the self-serving, self-perpetuating industrial oligarchy, is the best instrument to serve society, Adams believes. The electric power industry's competition with TVA; the airline oligopoly's competition from nonscheduled airlines; and the effects of foreign competition on the steel giants— all illustrate that "monopoloid" planning is done in the interests of monopoly power, not society at large. Competition, along with government policies designed to promote competition rather than monopoly, are necessary for progress, innovation, and the general welfare.

22

COMPETITION, MONOPOLY, AND PLANNING

Walter Adams

In "The New Industrial State," Galbraith once again examines the reality of corporate giantism and corporate power, and outlines the implications for public policy. He finds that the giant corporation has achieved such dominance of American industry, that it can control its environment and immunize itself from the discipline of all exogenous control mechanisms—especially the competitive market. Through separation of ownership from management it has emancipated itself from the control of stockholders. By reinvestment of profits (internal financing), it has eliminated the influence of the financier and the capital market. By brainwashing its clientele, it has insulated itself from consumer sovereignty. By possession of market power, it has come to dominate both suppliers and customers. By judicious identification with, and manipulation of the state, it has achieved autonomy from government control. Whatever it cannot do for itself to assure survival and growth, a compliant government does on its behalf—assuring the maintenance of full employment; eliminating the risk of, and subsidizing the investment in, research and development; and assuring the supply of scientific and technical skills required by the modern technostructure.

In return for this privileged autonomy, the industrial giant

Reprinted from Walter Adams, *Planning, Regulation, and Competition* in *Hearing before Subcommittees of the Select Committee on Small Business*, United States Senate, 90th Cong., 1st sess. (Washington, D.C.: U.S. Government Printing Office, June 29, 1967), pp. 11–16, 34.

performs society's planning function. And this, according to Galbraith, is not only inevitable (because technological imperatives dictate it); it is also good. The market is dead, we are told; and there is no need to regret its passing. The only remaining task, it seems, is to recognize the trend, to accept it as inexorable necessity, and, presumably, not to stand in its way. . . .

[H]ere is a blueprint for technocracy, private socialism, and the corporate state. The keystone of the new power structure is the giant corporation, freed from all traditional checks and balances, and subject only to the countervailing power of the intellectual in politics—those Platonic philosopher-kings who stand guard over the interests of the Republic. Happily, this blueprint need not cause undue alarm: first, because Galbraith's analysis rests on an empirically unsubstantiated premise; and second, because even if this analysis were correct, there would be more attractive public policy alternatives than Galbraith suggests.

Galbraith's contention that corporate giantism dominates American industry requires no adumbration. On that there is consensus. But Galbraith fails to prove that this dominance is the inevitable response to technological imperatives, and hence beyond our control. Specifically, he offers little evidence to demonstrate that Brobdingnagian size is the prerequisite for, and the guarantor of:

(1) operational efficiency;
(2) invention, innovation, and technological progress; and
(3) effective planning in the public interest.

Let me comment briefly on each of these points, and in so doing indicate that the competitive market need not be condemned to the euthanasia which Galbraith thinks is inexorable, and perhaps even desirable.

EFFICIENCY

In the mass-production industries, firms must undoubtedly be large, but do they need to assume the dinosaur proportions of some present-day giants? The unit of technological efficiency is the plant, not the firm. This means that there are undisputed advantages to large-scale integrated operations at a single steel plant, for example, but there is little technological justification for combining these functionally separate plants into a single adminis- trative unit. United States Steel is nothing more than several Inland Steels strewn about the country, and no one has yet suggested that Inland is not big enough to be efficient. A firm producing such divergent lines as rubber boots, chain saws, motorboats, and chicken feed may be seeking conglomerate size and power; it is certainly not responding to technological necessity. In short, one can favor technological bigness and oppose administrative bigness without inconsistency.

Two major empirical studies document this generalization. The first, by Dr. John M. Blair, indicates a significant divergence between plant and company concentration in major industries dominated by oligopoly. It indicates, moreover, that between 1947 and 1958, there was a general tendency for plant concentration to decline, which means that in many industries technology may actually militate toward optimal efficiency in plants of "smaller" size.[1]

The second study, by Prof. Joe Bain, presents engineering estimates of scale economies and capital requirements in 20 industries of above-average concentration. Bain finds that "[C]oncentration by firms is in every case but one greater than required by single-plant economies, and in more than half of the cases very substantially greater."

In less precise language, many multiplant industrial giants have gone beyond the optimal size required for efficiency. Galbraith acknowledges the validity of Bain's findings, but dismisses them by saying, "The size of General Motors is in the service not of monopoly or the economies of scale, but of planning. And for this planning . . . there is no clear upper limit to the desirable size. It could be that the bigger the better."[2]

If size is to be justified, then, this must be done on grounds other than efficiency. I shall return to this point.

TECHNOLOGICAL PROGRESS

As in the case of efficiency, there is no strict correlation between giantism and progressiveness. In a study of the 60 most important inventions of recent years, it was found that more than half came from independent inventors, less than half from corporate research, and even less from the research done by large concerns.[3] Moreover, while some highly concentrated industries spend a large share

[1] U.S. Senate Antitrust and Monopoly Subcommittee, Economic Concentration, pp. 1541–51.

[2] *Ibid.*, p. 76.

[3] Jewkes, Sawers, and Stillerman, "The Sources of Invention," Chap. IV.

of their income on research, others do not; within the same industry, some smaller firms spend as high a *percentage* as their larger rivals.   As Wilcox points out, "The big concern has the ability to finance innovation; it does not necessarily do so.   There is no clear relationship between size and investment in research."[4]

Finally, roughly two-thirds of the research done in the United States is financed by the federal government, and in many cases the research contractor gets the patent rights on inventions paid for with public funds.   The inventive genius which ostensibly goes with size would seem to involve socialization of risk and privatization of profit and power.

The U.S. steel industry, which ranks among the largest, most basic, and most concentrated of American industries—certainly part of the industrial state that Professor Galbraith speaks of— affords a dramatic case in point.   It spends only 0.7 percent of its revenues on research and, in technological progressiveness, the giants which dominate this industry lag behind their smaller domestic rivals as well as their smaller foreign competitors.   Thus, the basic oxygen furnace—considered the "only major break- through at the ingot level since before the turn of the century" was invented in 1950 by a miniscule Austrian *firm* which was less than one-third the size of a single *plant* of the United States Steel Corp. The innovation was introduced in the United States in 1954 by McLouth Steel which at the time had about 1 percent of domestic steel capacity—to be followed some 10 years later by the steel giants: United States Steel in December 1963, Bethlehem in 1964, and Republic in 1965.   Despite the fact that this revolutionary invention involved an average operating cost saving of $5 per ton and an investment cost saving of $20 per ton of installed capacity, the steel giants during the 1950s, according to *Business Week*, "bought 40 million tons of the wrong capacity—the open-hearth furnace" which was obsolete almost the moment it was put in place.[5]

Only after they were subjected to actual and threatened com- petition from domestic and foreign steelmakers in the 1960s did the steel giants decide to accommodate themselves to the oxygen revolution.   Thus, it was the cold wind of competition, and not the catatonia induced by industrial concentration, which proved conducive to innovation and technological progress.[6]

[4] "Public Policies Toward Business," 3d ed., p. 258.

[5] *Business Week* (Nov. 16, 1963), pp. 144–46.

[6] Adams and Dirlam, "Big Steel, Invention, and Innovation," *Quarterly Journal of Economics* (May 1966).

PLANNING IN THE PUBLIC INTEREST

Modern technology, says Galbraith, makes planning essential, and the giant corporation is its chosen instrument. This planning, in turn, requires the corporation to eliminate risk and uncertainty, to create for itself an environment of stability and security, and to free itself from all outside interference with its planning function. Thus, it must have enough size and power not only to produce a "mauve and cerise, air-conditioned, power-steered, and power-braked automobile"[7]—unsafe at any speed—but also enough power to brainwash customers to buy it. In the interest of planning, producers must be able to sell what they make—be it automobiles or missiles—and at prices which the technostructure deems remunerative.

Aside from the unproved premise—technological necessity— on which this argument rests, it raises crucial questions of responsibility and accountability. By what standards do the industrial giants plan, and is there an automatic convergence between private and public advantage? Must we, as a matter of inexorable inevitability, accept the proposition that what is good for General Motors is good for the country? What are the safeguards—other than the intellectual in politics—against arbitrary abuse of power, capricious or faulty decisionmaking? Must society legitimatize a self-sustaining, self-serving, self-justifying, and self-perpetuating industrial oligarchy as the price for industrial efficiency and progress?

This high price need not and should not be paid. The competitive market is a far more efficacious instrument for serving society—and far more viable—than Galbraith would have us believe. Let me illustrate:

(1) In the electric power industry a network of local monopolies, under Government regulation and protection, was long addicted to the belief that the demand for electric power was inelastic—that rates had little to do with the quantity of electricity used. It was not industrial planning, carried on by private monopolists under public supervision, but the yardstick competition of TVA which demonstrated the financial feasibility of aggressive rate reductions. It was this competitive experiment which proved that lower electric rates were not only possible but also profitable—both to the private monopolists and to the customers they served.

[7] "The Affluent Society," p. 253.

(2) In the airline oligopoly, also operating under the umbrella of government protectionism, the dominant firms long suffered from the same addiction.   They refused to institute coach service on the grounds that it would eliminate first-class service and— through a reduction in the rate structure—bring financial ruin to the industry.   Again it was the force and discipline of competition—from the small, nonscheduled carriers, operating at the margin of the industry—which proved that the giants and their overprotective public regulators were wrong.   As this committee observed, it was the pioneering and competition of the nonskeds which "shattered the concept of the fixed, limited market for civil aviation.   As a result, the question is no longer what portion of a fixed pie any company will get, but rather how much the entire pie can grow."[8]

Again, a bureaucracy-ridden, conservative, overcautious, over-protected industry was shown to have engaged in defective planning—to its own detriment as well as the public's.

(3) In the steel industry, after World War II, oligopoly planning resulted in truly shabby performance.   There was an almost unbroken climb in steel prices, in good times and bad, in the face of rising or falling demand, increasing or declining unit costs.   Prices rose even when only 50 percent of the industry's capacity was utilized.   Technological change was resisted and obsolete capacity installed.   Domestic markets were eroded by substitute materials and burgeoning imports.   Steel's export-import balance deteriorated both in absolute and relative terms; whereas the industry once exported about five times as much as it imported, the ratio today is almost exactly reversed, and steel exports are confined almost exclusively to AID-financed sales guaranteed by "Buy American" provisos.   We may be confident that if this deplorable performance is to be improved, it will come about through the disciplining force of domestic and foreign competition, and not through additional planning or an escalation of giant size.   It will come about through an accommodation to the exigencies of the world market, and not by insensitive monopolistic pricing, practiced under the protectionist shelter of the tariffs which the industry now seeks.

Without multiplying such examples, it is safe to say that monopoloid planning is done in the interest of monopoly power. Seldom, if ever, is society the beneficiary.

[8] Senate Report No. 540, 82d Cong., first sess., 1951.

In conclusion, I would note that industrial giantism in America is not the product of spontaneous generation, natural selection, or technological inevitability. In this era of "Big Government," it is often the end result of unwise, manmade, discriminatory, privilege-creating governmental action. Defense contracts, R. & D. support, patent policy, tax privileges, stock-piling arrangements, tariffs, subsidies, etc., have far from a neutral effect on our industrial structure. Especially in the regulated industries—in air and surface transportation, in broadcasting and communications—the writ of the State is decisive. In controlling these variables the policymaker has greater freedom and flexibility than is commonly supposed; the potential for promoting competition and dispersing industrial power is both real and practicable.[9]

It seems to me that Professor Galbraith keeps coming back to the charade of antitrust, but a competitive society is the product not simply of negative enforcement of the antitrust laws; it is the product of a total integrated approach on all levels of government—legislative, administrative, and regulatory. An integrated national policy of promoting competition—and this means more than mere enforcement of the antitrust laws—is not only feasible but desirable. No economy can function without built-in checks and balances which tend to break down the bureaucratic preference for letting well enough alone—forces which erode, subvert, or render obsolete the conservative bias inherent in any organization devoid of competition. Be it the dictates of the competitive market, the pressure from imports or substitutes, or the discipline of yardstick competition, it is these forces which the policymaker must try to reinforce where they exist and to *build into* the economic system where they are lacking or moribund. The policy objective throughout must be to promote market *structures* which will *compel* the conduct and performance which is in the public interest.

The disciplining force of competition is superior to industrial planning—by the private or public monopolist, the benevolent or authoritarian bureaucrat. It alone provides the incentives and compulsions to pioneer untried trails, to explore paths which may lead to dead ends, to take risks which may not pay off, and to try to make tomorrow better than the best. . . .

If, indeed, as Professor Galbraith tells us . . . the new industrial state is not the product of operational efficiency, if, indeed, it is

[9] Adams and Gray, "Monopoly in America," Macmillan, 1955.

not the virtuosity of technological progressiveness that explains giantism in American industry, then what is the justification for this giantism? Why do we have to tolerate it?

Professor Galbraith claims that the great virtue of the giant corporation is that it has the ability to plan. And he said giantism gives these corporations, and I am quoting his statement now, "gives *them* advantages in planning *their* own future and assuring *their* own survival."

Well, that is just the point. The planning that is done by these giants is motivated by private advantage, not public benefit. Is this a happy social instrument to be used? Are we going to tolerate it or are we going to do something about it?

LARNER INVESTIGATES THE CONSEQUENCES OF THE ALLEGED *separation of ownership and control as reflected in the conduct of large corporations. These empirical questions, central to the theories formulated by Berle, Galbraith, and others, have scarcely been investigated. Larner's is the most recent and comprehensive study. Adams argues that operational efficiency, innovation, and the public interest do not gain from the dominance of the large corporations; Larner's study indicates that the separation of ownership and control in the large corporations does not have the consequences for profits that it is widely alleged to have.*

He separates 128 management-controlled corporations from 59 owner-controlled ones, all of which are in the top 500, and finds the following: Taking into account assets, industrial concentration, Federal Reserve Board indices of economy-wide growth and fluctuations of profit rates, and equity-asset ratios as an index of one kind of risk, the rate of profit earned by management firms was only one-half of a percentage point lower than the rate for owner-controlled firms—a phenomenon of minor importance. Both types of corporations are approximately equally profit-oriented.

A subsidiary hypothesis, that the owner-controlled firms are greater risk-takers than management-controlled firms, is not supported either. Larner also raises the question of the direct financial stake held by managers in the firms they control. His evidence indicates that, of the 93 chief executives of large corporations which he studied, 41 owned stock with a market value exceeding one million dollars. His study of the relationship between profitability, size and growth of firms, and the compensation of the 93 chief executives found that the corporation's dollar profit and rate of return on equity are the major variables determining the level of executive compensation. Thus, compensation of executives has been effectively harnessed to the stockholders' interests in profits. Larner's conclusion is that much ado has been made about nothing in the writings on the alleged separation of ownership and control in large corporations.

23

THE EFFECT OF MANAGEMENT-CONTROL ON THE PROFITS OF LARGE CORPORATIONS

Robert J. Larner

INTRODUCTION

A major thesis of *The Modern Corporation and Private Property*, the classic study of Adolf Berle and Gardiner Means, is that "Ownership of wealth without appreciable control and control of wealth without appreciable ownership appear to be the logical outcome of corporate development."[1] Since the publication of the Berle and Means book in 1932, social scientists have devoted considerable analytical and research efforts to the twofold question of whether separation of ownership and control exists in America's largest corporations, and if it does exist, what its implications are for the goals and behavior of these corporations. A recent empirical study concludes that control by management rather

This original article is printed by permission of Robert J. Larner. It is drawn from material in the author's doctoral dissertation, "Separation of Ownership and Control and Its Implications for the Behavior of the Firm" (University of Wisconsin, 1968). The dissertation was written under the supervision of Professor Leonard Weiss, whose guidance is gratefully acknowledged.
    [1] Adolf A. Berle and Gardiner C. Means, *The Modern Corporation and Private Property* (New York: The Macmillan Co., 1932), p. 69.

than by stockholders existed in more than 80 percent of the 200 largest nonfinancial corporations in 1963,[2] but some observers hold that ownership control still characterizes the largest American corporations.[3]

The greater part of the scholarly activity, however, has been focused on the possible behavioral consequences of separation of ownership and control, and it is here that controversy and conflicting hypotheses abound. Berle and Means argue—and a substantial number of economists concur—that separation of ownership and control has made the concepts and analytical tools of traditional economic theory irrelevant to the study of large management-controlled corporations operating in the highly concentrated markets denoted by the terms oligopoly and monopoly; and that economic theory requires a new set of concepts and tools if it is to explain the behavior of the modern corporation.[4] Looking to the broader social implications of separation of ownership and control, Berle and Means contend that, since managers now perform the entrepreneurial function and stockholders are simply suppliers of capital (yet the stockholders receive *all* of the corporation's profits), the traditional logic and justification of profits have been invalidated. This development, they argue, lays the foundation for making the large corporation and its market power responsible to the entire society rather than to the stockholders alone.[5]

To understand the debate over the implications of separation of ownership and control for the behavior of the modern corporation, it is first necessary to understand the conception of the business enterprise in traditional (neo-classical) economy theory. Neo-classical economic theory views the business enterprise, or

[2] Robert J. Larner, "Ownership and Control in the 200 Largest Nonfinancial Corporations, 1929 and 1963," *American Economic Review*, LVI (September, 1966), 777–87.

[3] See, for example, Ferdinand Lundberg, *The Rich and the Super-Rich* (New York: Bantam Books, 1969), particularly Chapter Six, where Lundberg argues that business enterprises in the United States are typically owned and controlled by a family or small group of business associates. See also the two-volume Staff Report for the Subcommittee on Domestic Finance, Committee on Banking and Currency, U.S. House of Representatives, 90th Congress, entitled *Commercial Banks and Their Trust Activities: Emerging Influence on the American Economy*, where a trend toward bank minority control is suggested (Vol. I, pp. 12–13). The conflicting conclusions stem from disagreement over the size of stockholding necessary for ownership control and over the completeness of the corporate reports filed with the Securities and Exchange Commission.

[4] Berle and Means, *op. cit.*, pp. 345–51.

[5] *Ibid.*, pp. 352–57.

firm, in terms of an individual proprietorship in which a single owner-entrepreneur, as a function of ownership, combines and commands the other factors of production and exercises control. The origin of this view can be explained in part by the importance of small proprietorships and partnerships in the early history of capitalist manufacturing in England, Europe and the United States, and in part by the fact that in a competitive market the firm is merely a passive reactor to events. In a competitive market the firm faces a given price, determined by the forces of supply and demand, and in the long run must produce at the profit-maximizing level of output if it is to earn the normal rate of return necessary for its survival. Since economic theory seeks to explain and predict the behavior of firms, to the degree that forces external to the firm determine this behavior, the organizational structure and internal characteristics of the firm become irrelevant. Specifically, locating the true decision-makers or control group within a firm makes no contribution to explaining the firm's behavior if the enterprise is operating in an environment where, simply to survive, it must adhere strictly to the dictates of market forces.

But the large corporation that confronted Berle and Means— and which is even more characteristic of American industry today—typically operates in an oligopolistic industry, therefore enjoying some degree of freedom from deterministic market constraints. Market forces still limit, to a greater or lesser degree, the behavior of the large corporation, but they no longer determine it within narrow limits. Those in control of the large corporation have some measure of discretion in determining policy, but with the traditional assumption that every economic agent strives to maximize his self-interest, there is no longer an *a priori* reason to believe that managers who exercise control will necessarily direct this discretionary power toward the same ends as would the owners if they had control. Where the corporation has some degree of market power, the decision-making group—whether managers or stockholders—can have a definite and significant effect on the decisions made.

The traditional owner-entrepreneur is assumed to strive to maximize his firm's profits because these profits accrue directly to him as personal income. Today's corporate executives, how-ever, in their function as managers, have no legal claim to the corporation's profits, which accrue to stockholders as dividends and capital gains; yet these executives are responsible for the decisions which play a major role in determining the size of the corporation's profits.   Can we legitimately assume that managers, uniquely among all economic agents, forsake their own self-interest and seek instead to maximize the welfare of another group, the stockholders?   John Kenneth Galbraith in *The New Industrial State* labels this assumption the "Approved Contradiction" and argues that profit maximization is no longer a relevant assumption in studying the behavior of the mature corporation.   Instead, Galbraith claims, the management of large corporations aims to maximize the rate of growth of the corporation's sales, subject to a minimum profit constraint, as a means of enhancing its own compensation, prestige and technical virtuosity.[6]

Galbraith's hypothesis concerning the goal of the large corporation is closely related to an older argument put forward by William Baumol that "the typical oligopolist's objectives can usefully be characterized, approximately, as sales maximization subject to a minimum profit constraint."[7]   Thus, as long as profits are large enough to keep stockholders content with sufficient dividends and capital gains and to provide adequately for financing the company's growth, management will devote its energies to increasing total revenue rather than to obtaining larger profits.   Managers attempt to increase the size of their companies because "executive salaries appear to be far more closely correlated with the scale of operations of the firm than with its profitability."[8]

Baumol also believes that managers are less inclined to risk-taking than are owners because "gambling or risk-taking for managers comes close to a heads you win, tails I lose affair."[9] If the gamble is successful, the executive is not likely to receive much permanent addition to his income because executive compensation shows a weak response to increases in the firm's profits. In fact, Baumol claims, brilliant but nonrepeatable accomplishments have the negative effect of raising expectations for future conduct to an unrealistically high level.   And if the gamble fails,

[6] John Kenneth Galbraith, *The New Industrial State* (Boston: Houghton Mifflin Co., 1967), Chap. XV.

[7] William J. Baumol, *Business Behavior, Value and Growth* (New York: Macmillan Co., 1959), p. 49.   Baumol later modified his theory by replacing the current level of sales with the rate of growth of total revenue as the variable to be maximized in the managerial objective function.   Galbraith's theory, then, is virtually identical to Baumol's modified formulation of the goals of management-controlled firms in an oligopolistic industry.

[8] *Ibid.*, p. 46.

[9] *Ibid.*, p. 90.

the managers suffer embarrassment and may even be turned out of office.

Two testable hypotheses emerge from the Baumol–Galbraith analysis: (1) profit rates of management-controlled corporations are smaller than those of owner-controlled corporations and (2) the fluctuations of profit rates are smaller for management-controlled corporations than for owner-controlled corporations. We shall return to these hypotheses in the next section.

Not all observers who admit to separation of ownership and control, however, concede the behavioral implications suggested by Baumol and Galbraith. Paul Baran and Paul Sweezy in *Monopoly Capital*, for instance, while acknowledging that owner-ship and control have been separated in the large corporation, argue that managers can still be expected to seek maximum profits because their incomes and status are directly related to their company's profitability.[10] Moreover, managers, constituting the leading echelon of the property-owning class, are motivated by the drive to accumulate. Baran and Sweezy claim that accumulation has always been the prime mover of the capitalist system and that under modern capitalism the function of accumulation has simply been transferred from the individual capitalist to the corporation, which regularly uses retained earnings (profits minus dividends) to finance its growth.

Arguments within the traditional neo-classical framework have also been used to deny that any significant behavioral implications stem from separation of ownership and control. Henry Manne, for example, has suggested that, regardless of what managers may like to do, any significant deviation from profit-maximizing behavior would cause the corporation's stock to be undervalued in the market (relative to its value under more efficient management), and the prospect of substantial capital gains would make the company an attractive target for a takeover effort. Fear of displacement, then, compels managers to act in the interest of stockholders.[11]

In a similar vein, Armen Alchian has argued that the job market for corporate executives functions to enforce profit-maximizing behavior on managers. Competition among executives for advancement within the same company and the desire of

[10] Paul A. Baran and Paul M. Sweezy, *Monopoly Capital* (New York: Monthly Review Press, 1966), pp. 33–44.

[11] Henry Manne, "Mergers and the Market for Corporate Control," *Journal of Political Economy*, LXXII (April, 1965), 110–20.

executives to offer the greatest appeal to potential employers insure that managers will be sufficiently concerned with profits.[12] Alchian's analysis, of course, assumes that executives evaluate one another primarily according to success in producing past profits and implies a much larger degree of inter-firm executive mobility than seems to exist.[13]

In the first section of this paper I have suggested why the issue of separation of ownership and control is important to a consideration of the goals and behavior of the large corporation. I shall turn now to an examination of the empirical evidence.

MANAGEMENT–CONTROL AND PROFITS

In order to test the Baumol-Galbraith hypotheses relating the level and stability of profits to type of corporate control, I used the model developed by Professors Marshall Hall and Leonard Weiss to measure the relation between profit rates and firm size.[14] In the Hall-Weiss study, firms which were among the 500 largest nonfinancial corporations of 1963 were separated into a group of management-controlled corporations and a group of owner-controlled corporations. Those corporations in which no individual, family, or group of business associates owned 10 percent or more of the outstanding voting stock were classified as management-controlled, while an individual or group stockholding of 10 percent or more put the corporation in the owner-control category.[15]

Of the 330 corporations in the Hall-Weiss study, 187 were used in my study—128 management-controlled firms and 59 owner-controlled firms. In all but eight cases, data were available for each of the years from 1956 through 1962. In the eight cases, data from two to six years were available.

I wanted to measure the relation of the level and stability of

[12] Armen Alchian, "Corporate Management and Property Rights," in *Economic Policy and the Regulation of Securities* (Washington: American Enterprise Institute, 1968), p. 186.

[13] See David Roberts, *Executive Compensation* (Glencoe, Ill.: The Free Press, 1959), Chap. 4.

[14] Marshall Hall and Leonard Weiss, "Firm Size and Profitability," *Review of Economics and Statistics*, XLIX (August, 1967), 319–31. The permission of Professors Hall and Weiss to use their model and the data in their study is gratefully acknowledged.

[15] The principal source used to determine type of corporate control was the definitive proxy statement for 1964 filed with the Securities and Exchange Commission by each of the 187 corporations used in this study.

firm profits to type of control; but many other variables, of course, also influence firm profits.   Accordingly, the technique of multiple regression analysis was used to measure the separate influence of each of a number of variables on firm profits.   I took the following independent variables from the Hall-Weiss study: the assets of the firm; the four-firm concentration ratio for the principal industry in which the firm operates;[16] changes in the Federal Reserve Board's industry indexes of industrial production, which reflect changes in demand and cost conditions and control for industry-wide growth and instability; variables for each of the seven years in order to control for the effect of economy-wide growth and fluctuations on firm profit rates; and the equity-asset ratio for each firm to adjust for one kind of risk, the amount of leverage.[17] In addition, I used a "dummy" variable with a value of one for management-controlled firms and a value of zero for owner-controlled firms.   The Baumol-Galbraith hypothesis predicts that the coefficient of this "dummy" variable will be negative and statistically significant, indicating that management-controlled companies are less profitable than owner-controlled companies.

The regression results do show a negative coefficient for the "dummy" variable indicating management-control, and the coefficient is statistically significant at the 95 percent level of confidence, indicating that the coefficient could not differ in value from zero, by chance, more than one time in twenty.

The magnitude of the coefficient, however, is small—one-half of one percent—when compared with the average rate of profit of 11 percent for all 187 firms over all years.   Thus, the rate of profit

[16] The four-firm concentration ratio for an industry is the proportion of total industry output accounted for by the four largest producers.   The reader is referred to Chapter 3 of my doctoral dissertation for a more complete explanation of the reasons for including each of the independent variables in the regression.

[17] The equity-asset ratio is the proportion of total assets financed by equity capital (common stock and accumulated retained earnings).   The debt-asset ratio, which measures the firms leverage, is the proportion of total assets financed by debt capital (long-term corporate bonds).   Where the firm has no preferred stock, the equity-asset and debt-asset ratios sum to 1.0.   Since interest payments to bondholders are a fixed cost which the firm must meet each year, the greater the debt-asset ratio or the greater the leverage the greater will be the fluctuation in the rate of return to common stockholders from a given stream of yearly earnings.   Hence, where the debt-asset ratio is high (the equity-asset ratio is low), stockholders require a larger return to compensate for the greater risk.   For a more complete discussion of leverage, see Pearson Hunt, Charles M. Williams, and Gordon Donaldson, *Basic Business Finance* (Third ed.; Homewood, Ill: Richard D. Irwin, Inc., 1966), pp. 378–82.

earned by management-controlled firms was only one-half of a percentage point lower (about 4½ percent less) than the rate of profit earned by owner-controlled firms. This evidence, though by no means conclusive, does provide some support for the hypothesis of managerial discretion, but suggests that the degree of this discretion is not nearly as large as is often implied. It would appear that the proponents of theories of managerial discretion have expended considerable time and effort in describing a phenomenon of relatively minor importance. The large management-controlled corporations seem to be just about as profit-oriented as as the large owner-controlled corporations.[18]

The hypothesis that management-controlled firms are more conservative and less prone to risk-taking than owner-controlled firms was tested in another multiple regression calculation in which the dependent variable is the variance[19] in the profit-equity ratio for each firm over the seven-year period, 1956–1962. The independent variables are: average assets for 1956 to 1962, the four firm concentration ratio, the variances of the change in the indexes of industrial production used in the first regression, the average equity-asset ratio, and the "dummy" variable for management-control. Again, the Baumol-Galbraith hypothesis predicts a negative and statistically significant coefficient for the dummy management-control variable. The actual coefficient, however, is positive but not statistically significant. Although the evidence from this regression is only suggestive, it does *not* support the hypothesis that managers are more inclined to avoid risk than are owners.

---

[18] Two other studies of the relation between management-control and firm profits were done about the same time: David R. Kamerschen, "The Influence of Ownership and Control on Profit Rates," *American Economic Review*, LVIII (June, 1968), 432–47; and R. J. Monsen, John S. Chiu, and David E. Cooley, "The Effect of Separation of Ownership and Control on the Performance of the Large Firm," *Quarterly Journal of Economics*, LXXXII (August, 1968), 435–51.

Kamerschen finds that management-control exerts no important influence on the rate of profit, while Monsen, *et al.* find that the management-controlled corporations in their sample group earned a significantly lower rate of profit than did the owner-controlled corporations.

[19] Variance is a statistical measure of dispersion around the mean or average value. The year-to-year profit rate of a risk-avoiding firm should be stable around its average value for some period, while the profit rate of a firm more inclined to taking risks should show relatively large year-to-year fluctuations and, thus, a larger variance.

EXECUTIVE COMPENSATION

If managers rather than stockholders are able effectively to control the policies of large corporations, why have they not pursued goals other than large profits? One explanation that has been offered is that corporate executives are motivated by altruism and a sense of stewardship—they view themselves primarily as trustees of the stockholders' wealth—morally and legally obliged to preserve this wealth and to increase it as much as possible. Some corporate executives may well be so motivated, but a more general and realistic explanation may be simply that managers have a substantial financial stake in the prosperity and profitability of the corporations which employ them.

In measuring an executive's financial stake in his corporation, the absolute rather than relative size of his stockholding is important. A 1 percent stockholding in a corporation whose net worth is 100 million dollars will not give the executive ownership control of the company, but it will give him a million dollar financial stake in the company and provide him with the opportunity to receive huge capital gains if the company is well-managed (and to suffer huge capital losses if the company is poorly managed).[20] In addition, executive compensation—salary, bonuses, and particularly stock options—may depend upon the profit performance of the corporations they manage.

To measure the financial stake of executives in their companies and to investigate the determinants of executive compensation, data were collected on the compensation and stockholdings in 1962 and 1963 of 94 chief executive officers[21] of unregulated industrial firms that were among the 300 largest nonfinancial corporations of 1963. A summary of the findings is presented in Table 1.

The yearly median value of the common stock held by the chief executive officers in their respective corporations was found to be $658,359. Forty-one of the 93 executives held stock whose

[20] Berle and Means themselves note, "It may well be that the prospect of receiving 1 or 2 per cent of the total added profit which could be produced by their own more vigorous activity would be sufficient inducement to produce the most efficient operation of which the [managerial] controlling group are capable," (p. 302).

[21] Only firms with the same chief executive officer (typically, the president or chairman of the board) for all of 1962 and 1963 were included. Originally, data were collected for 100 chief executives, but six were dropped because of incomplete information on compensation, stock options or stockholdings.

Table 1. Compensation and Stock Ownership of Chief Executive Officers in Large Corporations, 1962 and 1963

Form of income	Median value (per year)
Salary and bonuses	$158,221
Dividends from common stock in employing corporation	23,605
Market value of common stock in employing corporation	658,359

SOURCE: Data on salary, bonuses, and stockholdings were taken from the definitive proxy statements filed by each of the 94 corporations with the Securities and Exchange Commission.   I was able to obtain the shares of common stock in his own corporation held by each executive on a given day (usually during the first quarter of the year) shortly before his company filed its annual proxy statement with the SEC.   The market value of the stockholdings was calculated by multiplying these shares by the closing price of the company's stock on the New York Stock Exchange for the same day.   In calculating the executive's dividend income, I assumed that he held the same amount of stock throughout the entire year.

market value exceeded one million dollars in at least one of the two years.   Lawrence Fisher's findings[22] show that the median before-tax rate of return (including dividends, capital gains and adjustment for transactions costs), compounded annually, from random investment in common stocks listed on the New York Stock Exchange was 9.8 percent during the years 1926 to 1960. On this basis we can estimate the median expected annual income for these executives (from ownership of their corporation's stock) to be $64,519—a large part of which would be in the form of lower-taxed capital gains.   This expected income from stock ownership is 41 percent as large as the median income the executives received in the form of salary and bonuses, and would be even larger if after-tax figures could be compared.

In a recently published study of executive compensation in 50 of the nation's largest manufacturing corporations, Wilbur Lewellen finds that, for the period 1955–1963, nearly half of the total after-tax remuneration realized by the top executives of these companies consisted of "ownership-oriented" rewards such as stock options, profit-sharing bonuses, and deferred compen-

[22] Lawrence Fisher, "Outcomes for 'Random' Investments in Common Stocks Listed on the New York Stock Exchange," *Journal of Business*, XXXVIII (April, 1965), p. 153.

sation.[23]   Stock options alone accounted for 36 percent of the total after-tax remuneration, and were as important as salary and bonuses, which accounted for 38 percent of the total.[24]   Since the value of stock options is directly related to the market price of the corporation's stock, which in turn is dependent upon the expected future profit performance of the firm, the use of stock options as a major part of the executive compensation package—together with the executive's sizable holdings of his corporation's stock—has produced a substantial degree of identity between managerial and stockholder interests.

I conclude by reporting the findings of my own research, which, with the use of multiple regression analysis, sought to relate the compensation and income of the 94 chief executive officers in 1962 and 1963 to the profitability, size and growth of their companies.   I use *compensation* to refer only to payments by corporations to executives for their managerial services and *income* to refer to the sum of compensation and the dividends and capital gains which executives receive in their role as stockholder. *Compensation* has four components: (1) salary, (2) cash and stock bonuses, (3) corporate contributions to savings and stock purchase plans, and (4) the realized value of stock options.[25]

[23] Wilbur G. Lewellen, *Executive Compensation in Large Corporations* (New York: National Bureau of Economic Research, 1968), p. 141.

[24] *Ibid.*, p. 142.

[25] The realized value of stock options was calculated in the following manner. If the option was exercised, the option price was subtracted from the closing price of the stock on the New York Stock Exchange for the day six months after the exercise of the option or two years after its issuance, whichever was later, to obtain the undiscounted value of the option.   Under the provisions of the Internal Revenue Tax Code in effect in 1962 and 1963, executives could not dispose of stock purchased through options for at least two years from the date the option was granted, including at least six months from the date the option was exercised, if they wanted their gain taxed at the lower capital gains rate rather than at personal income tax rates.   This value was then discounted at a 10 percent rate to the year in which the option was issued, and the entire discounted value of the option was regarded as part of that year's compensation.

If the option was still outstanding on December 31, 1966, and the stock's closing price on that day was greater than the option price, it was assumed that the option had been exercised on June 30, 1966, held for six months to qualify for capital gains taxation, and sold on December 31.   Its value was then computed as described above.   Where the closing price was less than or equal to the option price, the option was given a value of zero.

The reader is referred to Section 3, Chapter 4 of my dissertation for a more detailed explanation of the variables and procedures used in the multiple regression analysis of executive compensation.

Profitability is measured by: (1) the net income—stockholders' equity ratio—which is the rate of return on what the stockholders themselves have invested, and by (2) the level of dollar profits, because the productivity of executives is measured in terms of the dollar amount by which they increase firm earnings—and because neither profit rate nor firm size adequately reflects executive productivity.

Assets and sales revenue are used as alternate measures of the firm's size. Growth is measured by year-to-year changes in the level of assets and sales revenue.

The results of the regression analysis indicate that the corporation's dollar profit and rate of return on equity are the major variables determining the level of executive compensation, and are more important as explanatory variables than are either size or growth. The findings concerning executive income are not as clear-cut as the ones concerning executive compensation, but part of the reason for this seems to lie with the difficulty of finding the appropriate time period in which to measure capital gains. Moreover, it seems to be an accepted tenet of economic theory that dividends and capital gains depend closely on the firm's profit or profit-making potential. The point of contention has been executive compensation; it is here that this evidence may prove useful.[26]

In summary, it would appear that the nature of financial incentives and rewards in management-controlled corporations is such that executive compensation and income have been effectively harnessed to the diligence with which managers pursue the interest of stockholders. While the phenomenon labelled separation of ownership and control appears to exist in most of America's largest nonfinancial corporations, the effects on the profit orientation of these corporations have been minor—certainly too small to justify the considerable attention they have received in the literature for the past 37 years.

[26] Lewellen, in his study, also finds that company profits are a somewhat better predictor of executive remuneration, particularly of salary and bonus levels, than are sales (p. 247).

ACCORDING TO PERLO, LARGE CORPORATIONS DOMINATE INDUSTRY, *and groups of these giants, in turn, are controlled by giant banks. Banks are usually the core of the control of nonfinancial corporations. They achieve this control not merely through stockholding, but through representation on the boards of directors and through informal and/or legal arrangements which result from their control of financing, their links with other firms, their strategic position in mergers, and their access to vital business information. Perlo stresses that maximum secrecy prevents access to accurate information on who owns the banks. Recent investigations by the Patman Committee (see Chapters 4–7, this volume) have added some information, although the Committee also stresses that critical information is withheld and inaccessible.*

A community of interest unites given groups of bankers and industrialists, resulting in the fusion of banking and industrial capital. The corporations are owned and controlled by the wealthiest families in America. While the link between given families and/or individuals and specific firms becomes more vague, their interests become more widespread and more integrated throughout the top financial and nonfinancial levels. This does not mean the "capitalist" has "vanished," as Berle and other managerial apologists maintain, but only that he is less visible. Perlo claims to identify centers of control in ownership groups for most large corporations analyzed. He also presents evidence on the predominance of outside directors on the boards of directors of the ten largest corporations.

Managers are not merely hired hands, however, but have lifetime tenure in powerful positions—often international in scope of responsibility. Their tenure is based on serving the controlling outside interests. Most important to understand, says Perlo, is that the managers and controlling owners have the same class interests. Similar social origins, experiences, and associations unite them. In their common class, it is the largest banker-industrialists who take the special "profits of control," having nothing to do with the defense of capitalist profits as a reward for risk-taking. Because of their great wealth, which is usually inherited to begin with, these men are able to accelerate the movement toward monopoly throughout the economy and to earn excessive profits at the expense of the working people.

264

24

OWNERSHIP AND CONTROL OF CORPORATIONS: THE FUSION OF FINANCIAL AND INDUSTRIAL CAPITAL

Victor Perlo

[In the present century the size of the individual corporation typically reaches] the point where one or a few companies dominate a given industry. Still more significant is the exercise of simultaneous control over the affairs of a whole series of these giants by a single power center.

Super-corporate empires running into the tens of billions of dollars have arisen in this way, their spheres covering a wide range of finance, industry and trade within the country and overseas. The giant banks are the centers of these empires. Their position arises along two related lines. One line, and the original source of banking power, is the virtually limitless need for financing of the great corporations, both in their organization and in their subsequent expansion.

The banks which can supply this financing obtain a great, and sometimes paramount, influence in the affairs of the corpora-

Reprinted from Victor Perlo, *The Empire of High Finance* (New York: International Publishers, 1957), pp. 40–55. Reprinted by permission of International Publishers Co., Inc. Copyright © 1957. Footnotes have been renumbered.

265

tion. They often become the very core of the control group;
they obtain representation on the board of directors; they exercise
a veto power on all major policy questions; they can direct orders
for materials to allied firms and transport to allied railroads.   This
influence may exceed by a wide margin that indicated by the
actual stockholdings of the banks.

Most outside funds for expansion supplied through the banking houses and insurance companies are raised through bonds,
which in theory have no votes but in fact involve an important
degree of power, expressed formally in various financial and operating restrictions on the borrower.

In the minority of cases the lending bankers are granted
decisive legal control over operations.   Thus, a small group of
Texas families owns almost all the stock of Anderson, Clayton &
Co., the largest cotton merchandising company. But its capital
for postwar expansion was supplied through the Morgan banking
interests.   As one condition, 90 percent of the controlling shares
in the subsidiaries which compress and warehouse the cotton are
held in a voting trust agreement by a committee controlled by
the Guaranty Trust and the Morgan law firm, Davis, Polk, Ward-
well, Sunderland & Kiendl.[1]

More typically, however, the power position of the lending
bank is based less on formal agreements than on its role as the
supplier of funds, connecting link with other industrial firms,
negotiator of mergers, source of all kinds of economic information,
and contact point for all-important political influence.

The second line of banking power is the ownership of control
blocks of stock by and through the big banks.   This is often overlooked, and the illusion created thereby that banking power in
industry is quite divorced from stock ownership.

Goldsmith estimated that the share of financial institutions in
corporation stock increased from 7.9 percent in 1900 to 14.2 percent in 1929 and 23.6 percent in 1949.[2]   Our estimate for 1954,
which may not wholly be comparable with Goldsmith's, is one-
third.   The government study of large stockholdings in the 200
giants of industry showed that in 1938 financial institutions held
about one-half of these controlling blocks.[3]   By 1954 this pro-

[1] Moody's *Industrials*, 1953.

[2] Raymond W. Goldsmith, *The Share of Financial Intermediaries in National
Wealth and National Assets, 1900–1949* (New York, 1954), Table 16, p. 69.

[3] TNEC, *Monograph No. 29, The Distribution of Ownership in the 200
Largest Nonfinancial Corporations* (Washington, D.C., 1940), pp. 601–2.

portion reached about two-thirds. Indicative of the accelerated concentration of corporation stock in financial hands during the "Eisenhower boom," 77 percent of the net purchases of stock during 1954 went to these institutional investors.[4]

Bank stockholdings arose historically and continue to grow through a variety of ways: banker-promoters receive large blocks of shares as part of their price for organizing mergers and new corporations; they receive "proxies" for the voting of blocks of shares they place with certain customers, especially foreign stockholders; they handle the estates of wealthy clients, voting their stock in the big corporations.

For example, a number of families of the steel barons whose properties were put together into United States Steel by the House of Morgan became clients and associates of the Morgan banking interests, not only in steel, but in other industries as well.

The large banking houses control additional blocks of shares accumulated by affiliated financial institutions, such as insurance companies, investment trusts, and brokerage houses.

Stockholding by financial institutions is impersonal in form, but not in substance. The essence of the power of the leading bankers is their ownership of the most vital control blocks of all, the shares of the great banks. These stocks are very closely held. They are not traded on the stock exchanges. The "floating supply," that anybody with the funds may buy, is small. Maximum secrecy surrounds the identity of the owners.

As the greatest monopolies expand through wars and mergers, control is increasingly exercised through a combination of these two lines of power—use of the financial resources of the banks, and of the largest blocks of stocks, also carried by the financial institutions.

The report of the Pujo Committee in 1913 recognized the importance of both of these as means for establishment of banker control over industry.[5] But subsequent literature has largely lost sight of the second, which resulted in a seeming narrowing of the basis of finance capital, and opened the door to the apologists who "abolished" finance capital.

Both lines of power are still vital, and banker stockholdings are in fact larger than ever.

[4] Senate Committee on Banking and Currency, *Factors Affecting the Stock Market* (Washington, D.C., 1955), Tables 4, 5, p. 95.
[5] House Report No. 1593, *Pujo Committee Report*, 62nd Cong., 3rd sess. (Washington, D.C., 1913).

THE OLIGARCHY

Anna Rochester cites the Morgan interests as the best known example of the power derived from the complex financial resources of the banks, and refers to it as: "the most advanced stage of capitalist development. . . . Industrial companies drawn in originally through Morgan investment banking are held in line through Morgan dominance in the banking world, but at the same time the Morgan banking power is now supported by the great Morgan industrial corporations."[6]

This most advanced form of control does not reflect an antagonism between banking and industry, nor the taking over of industry by the banks in any crude sense. Its general basis is characterized by the "community of interest" principle advocated by the leading banker in the early decades of the monopolies, J. Pierpont Morgan. Under this principle a group of the wealthiest moguls in industry and in finance combine their holdings to establish control over a whole series of corporations. The banks are key to this structure, but the erstwhile industrial magnates become part of the banking group.

The upshot, then, is not the conquest of one by the other, but the *merging* of industrial and financial magnates into an all-powerful *financial oligarchy*. This oligarchy is not, by any means, wholly unified. It is divided into groups, with different spheres of control, although various of these join their interests in particular corporations. The development of the financial oligarchy with its ramified controls increases many times the effective concentration of economic power. *For while 200 large corporations dominate the economic life of the country, 8 centers of high finance control most of these 200 corporations.*

The individuals exercising control are mainly the multimillionaires descended from the tycoons involved in the original formation of the trusts over 50 years ago. Some new interests have risen to the ranks of the mighty; some old families have become bankrupt or have died out. Outstanding is the entrenched aristocracy of American wealth, the so-called "60 families" who pile up added billions of dollars each year. The classic book about the rich American families is Gustavus Myers' *History of the Great American Fortunes*. Most of the fortunes described by Myers, some stretching back over 150 years, are still prominently represented in the circles of the financial oligarchy today—Astor,

---

[6] Anna Rochester, *Rulers of America* (New York, 1936), p. 105.

Figure 1. Growth of Great Family Fortunes

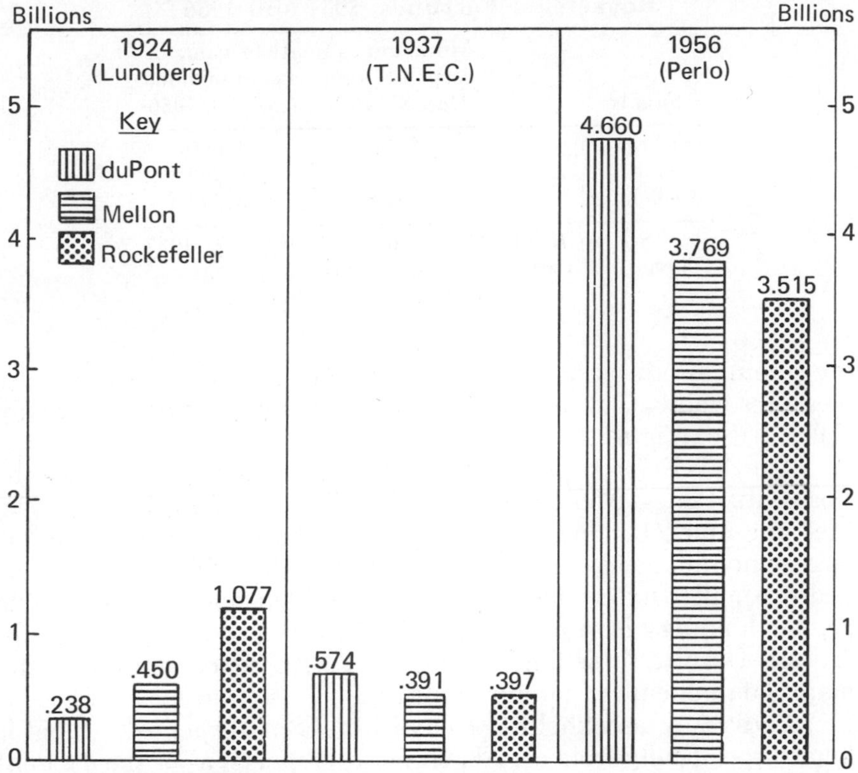

Billions   Billions

1924 (Lundberg)	1937 (T.N.E.C.)	1956 (Perlo)

Key
- duPont
- Mellon
- Rockefeller

duPont: .238 (1924), .574 (1937), 4.660 (1956)
Mellon: .450 (1924), .391 (1937), 3.769 (1956)
Rockefeller: 1.077 (1924), .397 (1937), 3.515 (1956)

NOTES: The 1924 estimates are on a more liberal basis than those for later years; the 1937 and 1956 figures are minimum, incomplete estimates.

Goelet, Field, Vanderbilt, du Pont, Gould, Crocker, Morgan, Rockefeller, Havemeyer, Duke, Guggenheim, Mellon, and Ford are examples.

The public is told by press and television, by learned professors and skilled advertisers, that these great fortunes have been shrunken or dissipated through charities, high taxes, and egalitarian legislation. This is another leading theme in the People's Capitalism lullaby. C. Wright Mills, in *The Power Elite*, shatters it, and concludes: "The fabulously rich, as well as the mere millionaires, are still very much among us . . . the corporate rich of America, whose wealth and power is today comparable with those of any stratum, anywhere or anytime in world history."[7]

Mills, relying on income tax data, shows that these fortunes

[7] C. Wright Mills, *The Power Elite* (New York, 1956), p. 94.

Table 1. The du Pont, Mellon and
Rockefeller Fortunes, 1937 and 1956

Family	Minimum estimate of value of corporate property, in millions	
	Dec. 31, 1937	April 30, 1956
Du Pont	$574	$4,660
Mellon	391	3,769
Rockefeller	397	3,515

SOURCE: TNEC Monograph No. 29, 1937, Table 6, p. 116; 1956 (see Appendix 1).

are unimpaired as compared with the 1920s. More precise measures show that actually they have been multiplied many times. (See Figure 1.)

The TNEC computed the fortunes of such families as the Fords, du Ponts, Mellons, and Rockefellers as of 1937. It measured the market value of their reported shareholdings in the 200 largest nonfinancial corporations. It excluded holdings in banks and in smaller industrial corporations, hidden holdings in the 200 giants, holdings in unincorporated ventures, and personal properties. Despite these limitations, the TNEC report embraced the major components of family wealth.

These key stockholdings have not been dispersed. This is known specifically from certain corporate reports, as of the du Pont holdings in E. I. du Pont de Nemours; and from semi-official biographical accounts, as in the case of the Rockefeller Standard Oil holdings. Indeed, the fact of multiplied stock prices since 1937 would make any major sale of stock by one of these families too costly taxwise, even with the mere 25 percent capital gains tax, to be considered except in an emergency.

Combining TNEC data with other sources, it is possible to estimate the 1956 du Pont, Mellon, and Rockefeller fortunes, on a basis roughly comparable with that of the TNEC study (see Table 1).

Each of these family fortunes has multiplied between 8 and 10 times during the past two decades. This multiplication factor may be exaggerated for statistical reasons,[8] but the actual amounts

[8] The vagaries of the stock market—at a low point in December 1937 and at a high point in April 1956—and the inclusion of some additional corporate holdings in 1956.

shown for 1956, though not precise, are incomplete and certainly minimum estimates of these families' fortunes.

Thus today, for the first time, it is possible to speak of a number of *multi-billionaire* families in America.

These statistics of personal wealth, impressive as they are, do not adequately convey either the full power of these families, nor their comparative standings. The power of each of these major families arises from the vast corporate empires controlled through their shareholdings. In the case of the Rockefellers this embraces assets of over 60 billion dollars, 17 times the family fortune, and several times larger than the empires controlled by the du Ponts or Mellons.

Moreover, there are propertied men, no one of them in the family wealth class of the du Ponts, Mellons, or Rockefellers, who, by their historically developed functioning as a unified group, are comparable in total wealth and power. In this way, the Morgans and the various families associated with them compare with the Rockefellers; the Chicago or Cleveland groups with the du Ponts or Mellons.

To present the real picture, therefore, our concern here will not be mainly with tracing the particular holdings and degree of activity in financial affairs of individuals or families, no matter how wealthy. We will concentrate instead on the financial institutions through which their holdings and activities are centralized. At the same time, it must be remembered that the great banks, like other corporations, are not really anonymous institutions, but are controlled by a narrow clique of the very wealthy, the "Power Elite"[9] who exert enormous power and derive great profits from the whole range of American economy by virtue of that control.

With the development of monopoly capitalism, this most advanced and complex form of industrial control becomes more general. At the same time the distinction between the banker and the industrialist becomes more vague—as the banker and the industrialist merge into the unified banker-industrialist. The identity of the individual with a particular company or line of industry also becomes more vague, as he joins with a group of tycoons, and spreads his interests over a wider and wider range.

To illustrate this molding of economic power into a common basic form, consider the evolution of the Rockefeller and Morgan

[9] The term is that of C. Wright Mills, who brilliantly analyzes the relationship between the individuals of the Elite and their institutions of Power.

power. The Rockefellers began as oil magnates, with no interest in financial institutions, doing their own banking through the Standard Oil Co. The Standard Oil companies have grown hundreds of times and still provide the largest part of the Rockefeller *profits*. But the *power* of the Rockefeller empire is no longer centered in the Standard Oil Corp., but rather in the Chase Manhattan Bank, and its associated insurance companies and investment banking agencies. Moreover, the industrial interests of the Rockefellers, largely through their banking connections, now extend to aircraft, utilities, and a wide range of other industries besides oil. The Morgans began as bankers, and until as recently as 1940 remained a closed partnership. But today J. P. Morgan & Co., the key bank of the Morgan group, is a "public" corporation like the other banks, with "outside" directors from the industrial corporations in which the Morgans have an interest as well as "inside" directors consisting of full-time bankers.

Until recently one giant of industry retained a semblance of isolation from bankers and the network of interlocking directorates and mixed stock ownership. However, in 1956 Ford Motors authorized sale of stock to the "public" through a Wall Street investment banking syndicate, and hereafter will be increasingly associated with the financial oligarchy. In 1954 Campbell Soup, the largest "private" food company, made a similar stock distribution. Large private industrial companies are now limited mainly to the textile industry.

THE "MANAGERIAL REVOLUTION"

As the control of industry has grown more complex in character, and increasingly centered in a network of financial institutions, it has become easier to conceal. When the giant corporations were first organized, the controlling banking interests openly laid out their empires and flaunted their power. But as opposition to this power increased, as its harmful effects on the people were exposed, the tendency grew to obscure and disguise its very existence.

The dominant financial interests hide behind the legal fiction of the anonymous "corporate person"[10] as a law unto itself. As the great majority of industrial property-owners, the small shareholders, lost all influence over corporate activity, the corporation appeared to them to become something apart from private property rights.

[10] In some countries a corporation is known as a "*Société Anonyme.*"

Encouraging this illusion, Berle writes: "The capital is there; and so is capitalism.   The waning factor is the capitalist.   He has somehow vanished in great measure from the picture, and with him has vanished much of the controlling force of his market-place judgment."[11]

The concept arose of the separation of ownership from control in the large corporation.   Its essential falsity was expressed very clearly by Sweezy:

> In recent years we have read much about separation of ownership from control in the large corporation.   This is a correct description of actual trends if it is taken to mean that concentration of control over capital is not limited by the concentration of ownership.   If, however, it is interpreted as implying that control passes out of the hands of the owners altogether and becomes the prerogative of some other group in society, it is completely erroneous.   What actually happens is that the great majority of owners are stripped of control in favor of a small minority of owners.   The large corporation means, thus, neither the democratization nor the abrogation of the control functions of property, but rather their concentration in a small group of large property owners.[12]

Sweezy refers to "some other group in society" to which control supposedly passes.   What is this other group?   It is the hired managers and executives of large corporations.   As the financial overlords became involved in larger networks, they increasingly separated themselves from active management of particular enterprises.   They concentrated their personal economic activity within the financial houses or family holding companies from which the manifold investments were handled. The daily supervision of affairs in the industrial corporations, and even in many banking corporations, was more and more turned over to hired executives.

Formal responsibility was shifted from those actually in control to the hired managers and "front men."   This tendency became particularly prominent with the outbreak of the great

[11] Adolf A. Berle, Jr., *The 20th Century Capitalist Revolution* (New York, 1954), p. 39.
[12] Paul M. Sweezy, *The Theory of Capitalist Development* (New York, 1956; originally published in 1942), pp. 261–62.

economic crisis of the 1930s, the utter failure of the tycoons of Wall Street to ward off its calamitous effects on the people, and the development of popular struggle against big business.   When Republic Steel gunmen shot down striking steel workers in 1937, the responsibility was assigned to the executive, Tom Girdler, and not to the Cleveland financiers who completely controlled the corporation, and who had hired Girdler and made the major policy decisions.

Various professors and writers, from outright apologists for big business to well-meaning liberals, accepted at face value the facade of hired managers concealing the true character of control. They developed the theory that the managers now controlled the large corporations, and that these managers were a new and distinct class in society.

The concept of "management control" first appeared prominently in a book by Berle and Means, published in 1933, *The Modern Corporation and Private Property*.   These authors failed to trace the connections of large corporations with financial institutions.   Instead, where there was not an obvious basis for control in well-publicized centers of stock ownership, they usually classified a company as under "management control."   They found that as of 1930, 44 percent of the largest companies, with 58 percent of the assets, were "management-controlled."[13]

The later studies of the 1930s, based on more adequate information, largely overcame the weaknesses of the work by Berle and Means, and established outside centers of control for most of the corporations that these authors had classified as "management-controlled."   The TNEC study found that concentrated stockholdings constituted an adequate basis for control of most giant corporations: "About 60, or less than one-third of the 200 corporations, were without a visible center of ownership control.   This does not mean, however, that an actual center of control was lacking, but only indicates that a study of the 20 largest record holdings failed to disclose such a center."[14]

The National Resources Committee study, depending mainly on financial connections and interlocking directorates, filled in many of the gaps.   [I have combined] information on stockholdings with analysis of financial connections and interlocking direc-

[13] Adolf A. Berle, Jr. and Gardiner C. Means, *The Modern Corporation and Private Property* (New York, 1932), p. 94.
[14] TNEC, *Monograph No. 29*, p. 103

torates, thereby establishing definite centers of control for almost all large corporations analyzed.[15]

At any rate, even the prewar studies disposed factually of the "management-control" theory.   But shortly after they appeared, the theory was formalized and built into a system by the writer James Burnham in his book *The Managerial Revolution*.   He claimed that capitalism was being supplanted by a new "managerial" society, whereby a bureaucracy of industrial managers would run the country.   According to Burnham, the "managerial revolution" had been substituted for the socialist revolution, and Marxism was thoroughly discredited.   Moreover, he argued that the "managerial revolution" was a world-wide phenomenon common to various social formations, of which the fascist type in Germany was most efficient.   In the United States also, he argued, "managerial society" must ultimately develop along the political lines of Hitler Germany.

Thus Burnham supplied a rationale for the continuation (in disguised form) of capitalism.   He endeavored to win acquiescence in fascist-type rule by big business as an "inevitable" outgrowth of the supposed trend towards control by the "managers."

Burnham was in no sense an economist, nor did he present any supporting data.   But his theory was so valuable for big business that it could not be permitted to die a natural death.   Instead it was widely popularized, made into part of the economic folklore of our times, presented as dogma to college students and the general public.

The "managers" are depicted as men risen from the ranks— "workers" who made good.   Their supposed rule is projected as proof of the democratic or at least benevolent character of American capitalism.

Professor Samuelson of M.I.T. writes in his best-seller textbook:

> If not the stockholders, who do make corporate decisions?   Primarily, the increasingly important class of *professional managers. . . .*

---

[15] Berle and Means classified 36 large industrial corporations as "management controlled" (besides several not included in later lists of large corporations). The TNEC study found definite centers of control for 15 of these.   The National Resources Committee study established control centers for 11 of the 21 remaining. [I have found] definite control centers for 7 of the 10 corporations unclassified before World War II.   That leaves just 3 of the Berle and Means list of 36 as possible candidates for "management control."

This suggests that the future problem may not be one of choosing between large monopolistic corporations and small-scale competitors, but rather that of devising ways to improve the social and economic performance of large corporate aggregates.[16]

No longer is monopoly to be feared, for it is not run by capitalists, but by managers, who may be converted into public servants! The most extravagant version is that of Berle, who claims that management control has imbued big business with a "corporate soul," which he hopes will harness capitalism to the advance of social welfare.   Berle's view is roundly denounced by the anti-monopoly economists, Adams and Gray, who write of his doctrine of the "corporate soul": "This is the ultimate rationalization of monopoly, the prelude to final legitimization, which is the goal of all aspirants for monopoly power."[17]

While most of the business and academic world accept the validity of the "managerial revolution" theory, they are not wholly agreed as to its desirability.   As against its advocate Samuelson, Professors Purdy, Lindahl and Carter charge that the managers set themselves up as a "perpetual totalitarian business elite . . . rather than a group of stewards working for the interests of stockholders, employees, and the general public. . . . Only a Rockefeller can wage a successful struggle against an arbitrary management fortified with a strong corporate treasury."[18]

Of course, some of these arguments are sheer nonsense.   As if any big capitalist is after anybody's welfare except his own, or acts as "steward" for somebody else if he does not see a profit in it! Obviously, this discussion must be divorced from that twisted morality, which in the case of these authors glorifies the Rockefellers and other vested families, and attacks the "greedy" Girdlers, Wilsons, and other hired executives—and in the case of other authors glorifies the hired strike-breakers, speed-up artists, and government contract-getters, as against the "coupon-clippers" behind the scenes.

Despite the propagandist purpose of the "managerial revolution" theory, it is necessary to examine some of the evidence cited by its advocates.

[16] Paul A. Samuelson, *Economics* (second ed.; New York, 1951), pp. 128–30.

[17] Walter Adams and Horace M. Gray, *Monopoly in America* (New York, 1955), p. 22.

[18] Purdy, Lindahl, and Carter, *Corporate Concentration and Public Policy* (New York, 1950), pp. 26, 108.

Table 2. "Outside" and "Inside" Directors of Ten Largest Non-Financial Corporations, 1955

Corporation	Number of directors "Outside"[a]	"Inside"[b]
American Telephone & Telegraph Co.	18	2
Standard Oil Co. (New Jersey)	0	16
General Motors Corp.	20	13
United States Steel Corp.	13	5
Pennsylvania Railroad	14	4
New York Central Railroad	14	1
Socony-Mobil Oil Co.	2	10
Standard Oil Co. (Indiana)	3	13
Southern Pacific Railroad	14	2
Gulf Oil Corp.	6	3

SOURCE: Poor's *Register of Directors and Executives*, 1955.

[a] "Outside" directors are those whose principal business attachment is not with the listed company. Usually they represent large stockholders, affiliated financial institutions, or corporations in related industries.

[b] "Inside" directors are paid executives of the listed company, usually without substantial stock ownership.

Prominent is the argument that salaried officials, or "inside" directors, constitute a majority on the boards of most large corporations, and "outside" directors, primarily representing financial interests, are a minority. This argument simply disregards or distorts the facts.

In seven of the ten largest non-financial corporations, as of early 1955, so-called "outside" directors were a majority, usually an overwhelming majority.[19]

The three exceptions, with a majority of "inside" directors, are all Standard Oil companies. [F]ar from exhibiting "managerial" control, this merely reflects the tightness of the Rockefeller grip on the oil companies, which permits them to put the affairs of their largest industrial corporation formally in the hands of hired managers without risking loss of actual control.

[19] Among academic studies of this subject, the best documented, by Professor Mabel Newcomer, shows that of over 5,000 directors of large corporations in 1949, only 37.3 percent were officers, or "inside" directors. This was an increase from 25.7 percent in 1900, but of course the development of a responsible corporate bureaucracy was still in its early stages at the turn of the century. (Mabel Newcomer, *The Big Business Executive* [New York, 1955], Table 5, p. 28). Professor Stanley Vance claimed to show a majority of "inside" directors, but by means of dubious statistical methods and a confused classification which lumped together members of owning families with hired executives.

In smaller companies, there is often a majority of "inside directors." But this is usually because here the large stockholding families more often appear *personally*, rather than through trusted employees, among the salaried managers. And in some companies outside directors are limited for legal reasons, as with the electric power holding systems. . . .

The largest giant of them all, American Telephone & Telegraph, heads the list of the so-called "management-controlled" corporations. But what is the actual situation? Of the 18 directors, only 2 are salaried officials! The outside bankers not only dominate the board, but constitute the majority of the executive committee.

The statement that "only a Rockefeller" can challenge a group of managers is also not in accord with the evidence. Recent years have seen numerous examples of dominant shareholdings or financial groups firing the top executives of large corporations. Lever Brothers, the British-controlled soap manufacturers, fired the well-known Charles Luckman as chief executive. The Merrill Lynch interests controlling Safeway Stores fired Lingan A. Warren, despite the fact that he had acquired a prominent position in the retail world. Finally, the epitome of the dictatorial manager, Sewell Avery, was dropped by the Chicago financiers who really dominate the "management-controlled" Montgomery Ward. When Robert R. Young and his associates defeated the Morgan interests for control of New York Central, they replaced the president, William White, and a number of other top executives. The Wall Street forces "took care of" their loyal servant, White, however, and promptly made him president of another railroad under their control, the Delaware & Hudson.

This is not to say that corporate managers are mere "hired hands." The executives of Standard Oil, somewhat like the permanent Civil Servants of the British Foreign Office, have lifetime tenure in positions of great responsibility, often international in scope. But the tenure is secure, and the responsibility exercised, only so long as it conforms with the general policy lines laid down by the controlling outside interests.

Of course, conflicts arise. Corporation officials and executives "bargain" with the controlling stockholders over the division of the spoils, and sometimes fairly sharp differences arise. Moreover, occasionally hired executives rise to positions of considerable influence, and may participate in control, by virtue of exceptional ability or where an uneasy balance of power exists among owning groups. For example, Charles E. Mitchell became a dominant figure in the National City Bank during the 1920s because of his skill in the aggressive sale of stock, and because of personal difficulties which impeded active exercise of control by the largest stockowning family. In the case of Bethlehem Steel, the managing group, consisting of large stockholders from the time of establishment of the corporation, probably exert effective control, although in close concert with leading Wall Street financial interests. Frequently business managers become prominent in politics, as representatives of dominant financial interests, rather than as controllers of corporate policies.

Regardless of the exact distribution of power in any given case, the most vital point is the identity of class interests as between managers and controlling stockholders. Burnham's attempt to draw a class distinction is in complete disregard of the facts.

Contrary to the Horatio Alger mythology of "People's Capitalism," corporate executives are drawn overwhelmingly from the propertied classes. Nepotism is normal in filling top jobs throughout the network of industry and finance. When a man of lesser property rises to a high place, often as not he gets there by "marrying the boss's daughter." Even in the absence of such personal ties, the poor man rises to the corporate top only by dint of the most strenuous, unscrupulous efforts to serve his masters at the expense of the company's workers, customers, and rivals.

These conclusions may be gleaned from recent academic studies, such as that of professors Warner and Abegglen. They found that two-thirds of all top business executives were the sons of owners or executives of business firms or of professional men, and concluded: "Whatever our national hopes, the business leaders of America are a select group, drawn for the most part from the upper ranks. Only to a limited extent may it be said that every man's chances are as good as the next man's, for birth in the higher occupational levels improves these life chances considerably."[20]

Mabel Newcomer, in a more elaborate study, found that the chances of a son of a business executive attaining a top corporate post were 139 times the chances of a semiskilled or unskilled worker's son,[21] and that corporate chairmen and presidents were overwhelmingly from moneyed families of Anglo-Saxon Protestant origin.

The corporate bureaucracy, like the government bureaucracy,

[20] Lloyd Warner and James Abegglen, *Big Business Leaders in America* (New York, 1955), p. 14.

[21] Newcomer, *op. cit.*, Table 18, p. 55.

has increased in size with the growth of giant corporations.   But even more than government bureaucrats, the corporate managers are part of, as well as agents of, a ruling group, the financial oligarchy.

THE FRUITS OF CONTROL

Capitalism has grown far more complex than it was in the days when the capitalist peronally supervised the labor of workers and derived his profits directly from the exploitation of that labor. The essence of that relationship remains as the amount of profits derived from exploitation of labor has multiplied.   The particular characteristic of monopoly capitalism, in this respect, is the monopolization of profits, going far beyond the centralization of capital in a few strong hands.

The control group in a corporation, which, as has been shown, may supply a small proportion of the total capital invested, appropriates a much larger share of the total profits, often amounting to the lion's share.

Traditional economic theory recognizes that the rate of return on "risk capital" is normally several times as large as the rate of interest, paid for the mere use of money "without risk" on the part of the lender.   Now, to be realistic, economists must define an additional category, the *profits of control*.   These profits are realized in a variety of forms.   Their existence is often hidden, appearing neither in the books of corporations nor in the tax returns of individuals.   In my earlier work, *The Income "Revolution,"* it is estimated that the top 1 percent of the population had effective income of more than 16 billion dollars in 1948, over and above the 19 billion dollars reported on their tax returns.[22]   A major portion of the 16 billion dollars, in addition to a small part of the 19 billion, consisted of the profits of control.

Because of the lack of precise statistics on the subject, Table 3 is presented only as a rough approximation of what the actual situation may be in the United States today.

Here the whole concept of profits as the "reward for risk-taking," as taught in the schools of the land, is turned upside down.

A small savings bank depositor can obtain interest of 2 or 3 percent with little *formal* risk.   However, because of the tendency to inflation which has persisted over most of the half century of

[22] Victor Perlo, *The Income "Revolution"* (New York, 1954), Table 7, p. 45.

Table 3. Return on Different Capitals

Kind of capital	Possible range of rate of annual return
Control capital	25%–50%
Risk capital (ordinary share capital)	4%–12%
Personal savings at interest	2%– 3%

monopoly capitalism, the entire interest return often merely compensates for the decline in the purchasing power of the saver's capital, and sometimes falls short of the loss in real values.

A small investor may purchase stocks and receive 4 to 6 percent annually in dividends. If he is reasonably lucky in his selection of securities and timing, he will average as much again in the appreciation in the value of his shares, for a total return of 8 to 12 percent. But he risks losing out altogether through the vagaries of the stock market and his unavoidable ignorance of the full situation in particular corporations. The cards are stacked against his buying and selling the "right" stocks at the "right" times. Often, he will be urged by promoters to buy particular securities *after* they have been marked up in price through advance purchases by "insiders" who knew that profits would increase. As he is buying, the "insiders" may well be unloading, to anticipate the next downturn in profits. The small investor is apt to have money for investment only in good times, when stock prices are high, and is often forced to sell in bad times, when stock prices are low.

The men with the really big money, participants in or closely connected with the highest financial and political circles, are able to reap fabulous rates of profit from the actual control of corporate affairs, and *without substantial risk*. They avoid risk because they themselves can arrange to acquire their profits of control, they know before the event those happenings which dictate the advisability of purchases of sales, and have money when the best opportunities arise.

We are told, for example, that Laurance Rockefeller multiplied a portion of his capital five times in as many years through investments in a series of corporations in which he took control.[23] That is the equivalent of 38 percent compounded annually. The eight to ten times rise in the values of the "blue chip" investments of the Rockefellers, Mellons, and du Ponts, is partly traceable to control on a higher level—the ability to establish federal govern-

[23] *Fortune* (March, 1955).

ment policies designed to enhance the profits of these families' controlled corporations.

This difference between an ordinary return beset with risks, and a riskless king-sized rate of profit, is what inspires the numerous battles for corporate control in America. It explains why a corporate directorship, even in a company without book profits, is a valued prize.

Some will say: if a man can make 38 percent each year, that is the American way, that is the reward for competitive enterprise, and more credit to the winner. One may have whatever moral judgment he wishes, but he should be aware of the circumstances and consequences of the 38 percent profit. Usually it is possible not because of any particular ability on the part of the beneficiaries, but because of the wealth already in their possession, mainly through inheritance. The acquisition of the profits of control, although in rivalry with other groups of powerful men, furthers the process of monopolization of the entire economy. It is realized mainly as extra-large profits, at the expense of the labor of the working population, in a variety of ways which are none the less costly for their frequent invisibility. Finally, control profits are often accomplished through business and government policies which reach new depths of irresponsibility to the general welfare.

THE MAJOR ECONOMIC PROBLEM OF THE U.S. IN THE NEXT DECADES, *Gillman argues, is to channel increasing investment funds into socially beneficial rather than destructive outlets. Large corporations tend, in combination, to produce investment funds or "savings" in excess of private investment outlets. The disparity between potential investment funds and available investment outlets is a chronic threat of crisis in the American capitalist economy—a threat that is accentuated by the new capital-saving technologies.*

A major economic crisis has been prevented only because of the increasing absorption of excess investment funds in expenditures for the military. Only war and expenditures for war have so far provided relatively full employment. Federal expenditures alone come to within 90 percent of private investment, with much of the latter being conditioned by those federal expenditures. Government spending now seems necessary to achieve full employment, not, as the Keynsians argued, to maintain it after private investment has achieved it. Siphoning off private investment funds for government military expenditures does not add to the nation's productive capacity, Gillman claims, but merely absorbs those funds. In this way, although an economic crisis is prevented, the danger of such a crisis is concealed. Capital exports, which once absorbed excess investment funds, are now limited by the growth of the Communist sector and by colonial revolutions.

To effectively absorb "savings," the "welfare state" would have to be built from taxes on wealth rather than from those on popular consumption. This would also entail overcoming the opposition of the wealthy. They prefer expenditures on war and preparation for war because, Gillman argues, it gives them profits, protects their investments, and expands domestic and foreign markets. Expenditures for public welfare, however, may accustom the people to such prerogatives as employment and well-being, thereby increasingly restricting the sphere of private capitalism.

The other alternative is even less palatable to capitalists: The government might correlate wages, productivity, prices and profits, and the growth of the labor force so that savings at full employment will not exceed potential investment outlets. This, however, would require socialist planning and public ownership and control of the economy.

25

DISPOSITION OF EXCESS SAVINGS

Joseph M. Gillman

A. THE PROBLEM

Assuming a Third World War unthinkable, then the most important economic problem to be faced by the United States in the next
20 years is the creation of socially useful outlets to substitute for
the present-day military expenditures in the maintenance of full
employment.

B. THE THESES

Present-day industrial technology is to an ever-increasing degree
capital-saving as well as labor-saving. At the same time, under
large-scale business organization and management, it is highly
productive of investment funds, or savings. Savings, thereby,
tend to exceed private investment outlets and fail to get invested.
When savings are not invested, production and employment fall
to the lower investment levels. It was the growing disparity
between potential savings and potential investment in the 1920s
that was the principal cause of the crisis and depression of 1929–
1939. And it is the potentially still greater disparity between the
two which the newer technologies are generating today that hangs

Reprinted from Joseph M. Gillman, *Problems of United States Economic
Development* (New York: Committee for Economic Development, 1958), Vol.
2, pp. 22–24, by permission of the publisher. Tables have been renumbered.

over the American economy as a threat of a still more serious crisis and a still more severe depression. What, in the main, has so far prevented this threat from becoming a reality, has been the increasing absorption of this excess saving in expenditures for the military.

C. HISTORICAL BACKGROUND

For a hundred years and more before World War I the savings of the nation were used to build its productive plant and pay up the capital borrowed abroad. These were the years when the capital ratio—the ratio of the value of the material capital in use to wages of production workers—was almost continuously rising.

By the end of World War I, and in large measure as a consequence of that war, we had paid up our foreign debt. In the decade following, the rate of capital formation was minimized by the increased use of controller instruments in the production processes, by the application of scientific management, and by the growing vertical integration of industry. Investment possibilities declined. The capital ratio ceased to rise.

To be sure, we used much capital that decade in the electrification of factories, homes and household equipment; in a housing boom; in building the automobile and subsidiary industries.

But with all that, our savings grew faster than these and other existing investment outlets would absorb. Large amounts then found their way into speculative stock markets, into pyramiding holding companies, and into purchase of foreign bonds of doubtful value. When the speculative bubble burst, the Great Depression became inevitable.

During the Depression all net new investment virtually stopped. Replacements from depreciation reserves were so productive that they sufficed to carry the economy through the ten years of depression demand and into the first two years of war production. Beyond depreciation allowances those ten years, savings had no place to go and income, production and employment remained low. Replacements alone cannot much advance employment; only net new investment can do that.

It was not until war production took over fully that these excess savings were siphoned off the market, relieving their downward pressure on the economy. The war raised investment to the full level of the nation's saving potentials. The war "solved" the unemployment problem.

D. THE NEW CRISIS

1. Dependence on Military Expenditures

At first, when the war was over, a number of temporary, war-induced stimuli kept the economy operating at the high wartime production levels. Principal among these were financing reconversion and the making up of shortages in housing, in household durables, in automobiles; equipping the large additions to the labor force; providing accommodations for the rapid rise in the rate of family formation and for the new high rate of population growth; the migration of industry to new geographic areas in the South and West. When these stimuli waned, the war in Korea gave the economy a fillip. Like all wars, this war, too, absorbed savings which were becoming a depressant on the economy.

Today, despite large new investments in the technologies of electronics and automation, we again seem to depend on the military to spend us out of a possible depression. Since the end of the Korean war, gross private domestic investment has on the whole equalled recorded gross private saving, and, as a percent of the GNP, has equalled that of the pre-Depression full-employment levels. Still, large amounts of government spending seem to have been necessary to prop up production and employment. Federal expenditures alone have come to within 90 percent of private investment. And the point should be made that a goodly portion of this private investment has been conditioned by the large expenditures of government.

2. If Peace Comes

We seem to have come down to the fact that in the second half of the twentieth century we face a new relationship in the saving-investment equation as it affects business fluctuations between booms and depressions. Before the development of the new technologies it may well have been true, as Keynesians have argued, that government spending above receipts would be required to maintain full employment in the event private investment failed to absorb all the savings which emerge at full employment. Now it appears that private investment, even to the full extent of emerging savings, cannot alone guarantee full employment. Government spending, and in ever-increasing amounts, federal government spending, seem now required, *in addition*, to achieve that goal. And since some 80 percent of the federal spending is for the purchase of goods and services for the national security, it is to the increased spending for past and future wars, apparently, that we must now look to provide a full-employment economy.

What we see is that the savings which present-day technology serves to produce are so great relative to the investment requirements for the new efficient capital that, unless they are absorbed in part outside the private investment sector, the economy will fall into a chronic depression. The gross private saving, against which we have just matched gross private domestic investment, does not measure *all* the savings available for investment. Large and increasing amounts are siphoned off by the government in taxes and spent on military and similar unproductive services. *This use of saving does not add to the productive capacity of the nation, as private investment does. Instead, it absorbs increasing portions thereof. These expenditures thus conceal the conditions which constitute an economic crisis.* It is in this context that the most important economic problem confronting America the next 20 years must be evaluated.

The question is: Suppose peace comes—what other means, besides military expenditures, are available for absorbing the uninvestable savings of the country?

E. POSSIBLE ANSWERS

1. Capital Exports

One answer could be to increase capital exports. In the nineteenth century capital exports helped England, for example, to dispose of her excess savings and so to expand her economy. Today, however, capital export potentials are quite limited. They are limited by the growth of the Communist sector of the world and by the revolt of former colonies against domination by foreign investors. And they are limited by our own choosing—by our policy of "containment." We limit our economic dealings with the Communist bloc for fear of aiding its growth. We must now cultivate our own garden.

2. The "Welfare State"

Another answer to our question, in addition to the above, could be an increase in *social consumption*—building the welfare state as Keynesians and liberal economists generally conceive it. But this answer requires considerable amplification. It is easy enough to specify substitutes for the military. It is not so easy to implement them.   It is not enough to "spend more," say, for education, public health, the cultural arts.   This would not be enough to offset the military expenditures which since 1952 have averaged about 45 billion dollars a year.   Similarly, mere "slum clearance" will not much help provide such offsets.   The offsets, to be effective, must be projected on a total, national scale of magnitude.

Further, two primary requirements must be met in spending for the social welfare.   These requirements involve going against some of our most deep-seated traditions.   One is that the cost of the public welfare must be met from taxes on wealth—from taxes on savings.   Otherwise the objective of absorbing excess savings will not be realized.

The second is that these costs must *not* be financed from taxes on consumption.   Consumption taxes are *sui generis* a depressant on the economy.   Today all these costs are met from just such taxes.   The cost of our public schools, for example, is borne almost entirely by taxes on real estate—as much a consumption tax as any avowed sales tax.   To be effective in the sense of the present context, education would become a charge on the general funds of the Treasury, the same as aircraft carriers and hydrogen bombs.

But here is the rub.   Whereas wealth will permit itself to be taxed for purposes of the military, it will not readily tolerate taxation of the same magnitude for the public welfare.   In the first it may see compensating benefits, in that expenditures for the military help expand foreign as well as domestic markets.   In the second it may see sheer extravagance—as an unrewarding consumption of profits.   Public housing for the ill-housed millions is deemed a threat to private real estate interests.

Further, expenses for the military can be revoked with relative ease.   Expenses for the public welfare, once embarked upon, cannot so readily be revoked.   The people will not easily relinquish a prerogative which at once gives them protection against unemployment and advances their well-being.

A federalized system of education, federally financed from taxes on wealth, by the way, offers an ideal substitute for present-day military expenditures.   Such a system would not only absorb a major portion of these expenditures, but would also satisfy a most pressing need of the times.   In the next 20 years America will increasingly call for a citizenry that will be able not only to design and operate automated factories, but also to accommodate to a culturally complex world.   Without the new technological training, millions will fall by the wayside as unemployed misfits, adding to the unemployment problem which automation, in any case, will tend to create. Without a broad knowledge of the humanities, we shall fail to know how to relate to the diverse cultures of a changing world. This new education must begin in our elementary schools and carry through into the colleges and universities. The problem will be how at the same time to preserve local responsibility.

Our fragmented educational system of today cannot meet these needs of tomorrow; nor does it command the resources to finance them. The same holds true for the public health, housing, recreation, the cultural arts. The new leisure which the new technologies will effect will call for vastly increased recreational and cultural facilities. Not every municipality can afford an art gallery, an opera house, a symphony orchestra. Yet all these are at hand if projected on a national basis, financed from taxes on unusable wealth.

F. AN ALTERNATIVE

Should absorption of the nation's excess saving by the above means prove unfeasible, the government might have to contrive to *prevent its emergence* by setting limits to profits. Government might so correlate wages, productivity, prices and profits with one another and with the rate of growth of the labor force that savings at full employment shall not exceed the rate of potential investment. That, of course, would entail the transfer of the power to make major business decisions from private enterprise to a government agency. It would mean socialist planning. But socialist planning is not now the order of the day of capitalist America. It *might* become that, if in the next 20 years we permit our economy, through the pressure of uninvestable savings, to slide back into a new round of devastating depressions.*

* *Gillman's thesis is elaborated and documented in his* Prosperity in Crisis *(New York: Marzani and Munzell, 1965). A similar thesis is argued by Paul Baran and Paul Sweezy, utilizing the concept of "economic surplus" and focussing on the tendency of a system dominated by a few hundred large corporations to produce an increasingly large absolute and relative surplus that is redistributed among them. This would be a chronic source of depression, they argue, since neither capitalist consumption nor investment could absorb the rising surplus, were there not counter-tendencies. Among the central counter-tendencies are: the growth of advertising, product differentiation, the general growth of the unproductive sector and the multiplication of waste. Most important, they also argue, is the role of military spending by government. Only war and its aftermath prevent the excess potential from resulting in the underemployment of men and productive capacity—and depression. See their* Monopoly Capital: As Essay on the American Economic and Social Order *(New York: Monthly Review Press, 1966).—M.Z.*

Much of the thinking about the so-called new capitalism is based neither on critical study nor on empirical findings, according to Magdoff. A realistic appraisal of American capitalism must include analysis of the following: (1) an economy that has not achieved reasonably full employment since 1953; (2) an economy that would have 20 to 24 million unemployed if not for military expenditures; (3) an economy increasingly dependent on credit financing; and (4) an economy in which, despite 20 years of "prosperity," one-fifth of the population is poor by official standards, and one-third of the men of military age are below health and educational standards required for armed service.

Military spending and its multiplier effects show that in addition to about 7.4 million employed in "national defense," another 6 to 9 million are employed as a result of the economic stimulation of these projects. This is a major determinant of the "success pattern" of our economy. Magdoff points out that military spending is especially important in the business cycle because it is concentrated in capital goods industries (which are most vulnerable to booms and bursts) and thus helps raise profits and prevent recession.

The civilian economy is adding little new net investment in plant and equipment, in part because of inadequate investment outlets, in part because monopoly can safely slow down new investment to protect old capital equipment. Although foreign investment provides a major outlet for new investment, there is increasing competition for these outlets from the other capitalist countries.

Another problem is that the profits of foreign investment are so great as to be in excess of domestic outlets. Private and public debt have been increasing, yet the economy is not growing at a rate sufficient to guarantee further new production and investment. This makes the entire economy more vulnerable to weaknesses in the banking system. Moreover, to sustain even larger debt, business must obtain larger profits to repay the debt and interest charges. If the economy is stagnating, profits must come from reducing the share of wages and salaries—which means that wage and salary earners sustaining the economy by credit spending will be unable to meet their obligations. Greater proportions of consumer income are now going to pay amortization and interest charges than in the past.

Withal, military spending, foreign investment, and the spread of credit have not been able to reduce persistent unemployment. In fact, there has been an upward trend in unemployment since 1953. Magdoff argues that the problem of unemployment is bound to be aggravated in the 1970s because the rapid increase in the size of the labor *force (resulting from the post-war baby boom) is coinciding with a slow-down in net investment and new jobs generated.   This constant dilemma is inseparable from the existence of poverty, the reduction of which has markedly slowed down in the post-World War II era. Poverty grows with economic decline and slowdown, and with technological labor-displacing change.   Negroes—at the lowest level of the working class—are hit hardest by these changes.   Low wages, unemployment and underemployment will not be eliminated by ending discrimination, nor by job training and skill improvements, because the causes of poverty lie in the behavior of the capitalist market system itself: the structure and location of industry, methods of distribution, the price structure, and the way profits are made and used.   Magdoff shows that, even if special privileges are given to Negroes, the income distribution among whites must be radically changed in a more equitable direction.   Otherwise, neither is Negro income distribution likely to change much in the foreseeable future, nor is poverty among blacks (or whites) likely to be significantly reduced.*

26

PROBLEMS OF UNITED STATES CAPITALISM

Harry Magdoff

Wave upon wave of prosperity, accompanied by ever higher levels of production and consumption, nourish the belief that the U.S. economy has found new sources of strength and that remaining weaknesses can be fairly easily overcome. The main reasons for this renewed faith are advanced in varying degrees by both radical and conservative commentators: (1) the new technology is in effect a second industrial revolution and is performing a role similar to the first industrial revolution in fostering long-range economic growth; (2) the new competition between socialism and capitalism induces extensive aid and investment in the Third World, which in turn creates new markets for advanced capitalist countries; (3) the political acceptance of the Welfare State as a necessary approach to social development; and (4) the availability of an economic "tool box" which can be used to manœuvre a capitalist economy so as to avoid serious crises.

Since the U.S. is the leading and dominant member of the capitalist world, the set of ideas that are used to explain its success are easily extended to actual or potential developments in other capitalist countries. As these ideas spread and become entrenched

Reprinted from Harry Magdoff, *Socialist Register* (New York: Monthly Review Press, 1965), pp. 62–79, by permission of the publisher. First published in the United States by Monthly Review Press, 116 West 14th St., New York, N.Y. 10011. Made and printed in Great Britain by the Garden City Press Ltd., Letchworth, Hertfordshire. © Monthly Review Press 1965.

they often become implicit assumptions—almost axioms—for further thinking and action.   In one fashion or another they have entered into the programmes and practices of socialist parties and trade unions in the capitalist world, into the economic and political planning of governments in the Third World, and even into some of the brave new thinking and planning of some sectors of the socialist world.

It is of course important that political programmes and policies are adapted to new circumstances with the help of theory which adequately explains the changed circumstances.   But the difficulty with a good deal of the thinking about the new capitalism is that it seems to be influenced not so much by critical study as by an eagerness to discover the "new" as distinct from the "old" or by the usefulness of the new ideas in serving particular political goals.

Support for this inference arises from an examination of some of the key features of recent U.S. economic developments.   Among the facts of U.S. economic life which call for a more realistic appraisal of the new capitalism are the following: (1) an economy that has not been able to achieve reasonably full employment in any year since 1953; (2) an economy that but for the military effort might have from 20 to 24 million unemployed; (3) an economy which in addition to the reliance on military spending is growing increasingly dependent on injections of credit; and (4) an economy in which after 20 years of prosperity, fully a third of the young men of military age do not meet required standards of health and education.

FAILURE IN PERFORMANCE

The outstanding aspect of U.S. economic performance is that over 8 percent of the labour force is unemployed and almost 10 percent engaged in the armed forces or employed to meet military requirements.   In other words, at the peak of its prosperity the civilian economy—private capital, government and non-profit institutions—is able to utilize only 82 percent of the labour force.[1]

[1] The government data on unemployment show 4 million unemployed during the first half of 1964.   But these are only the full-time unemployed.   If one takes into account the part-time unemployed, that is, those working involuntarily part-time, the full measure of unemployment reaches 5.4 million.   Added to this are 1.4 million concealed unemployed, resulting in an estimate of 6.4 million unemployed (See *The Toll of Rising Interest Rates*, Conference on Economic Progress [Washington, D.C.: August 1964].)   The concept of "concealed unemployment" is used because the government measures as unemployed only

One might argue that this is not a fair evaluation since the very existence of such a large military undertaking might inhibit the expansion of the civilian economy.   Such an argument would be significant if there were full employment and a shortage of industrial capacity and raw materials.   But this is not the case.   Not only is there idle labour, but idle machinery, capacity to make more machinery, and a good supply of raw materials—enough to attain full employment if the economic and political institutions were able to do so.

But this is far from the whole story.   The more than 55 billion dollars spent annually on what the government agencies classify as "national defence" has a chain-reaction effect on the rest of the economy, just as other forms of investment and spending have a "multiplier" effect.   It is estimated that for every one dollar spent on "national defence" another one dollar to one dollar and forty cents of economic product is stimulated.   A crude, but conservative, calculation shows that in addition to the approximately 7.4 million people engaged in some phase of "national defence," another 6 to 9 million are employed due to the economic stimulus of defence spending.[2]

All this adds up to the rather striking conclusion noted above: 20 to 24 million persons, out of a labour force of 78 million, are either unemployed, engaged directly or indirectly by "national defence" projects, or employed because of the economic stimulation of these projects.   While the non-utilization of such magnitudes by a civilian economy would be of crisis proportions, we are not at this point engaging in the popular game of "what might have

---

those able to work and seeking work.   Those who, due to the lack of jobs, do not actively seek jobs are thus excluded from the labour force.   Thus, in the official labour force data for 1963, 98 percent of white men, ages 35 to 44, are counted in the civilian labour force, but only 95 percent of Negro men in these age groups are included.   In the 45 to 54 age group, the comparable percentages are 96 percent and 91 percent; in the 55 to 64 age group, 87 percent and 83 percent.   (See *Manpower Report of the President*, U.S. Government Printing Office [Washington, D.C.: March 1964].)

The estimate of 7.4 million employed directly and indirectly due to military spending is made by the U.S. Arms Control and Disarmament Agency in *Economic Impacts of Disarmament* (Washington, D.C.: 1962).

[2] The estimate of the multiplier effect of military spending was given in the report of the U.S. Arms Control and Disarmament Agency referred to in footnote 1.   The translation of the multiplier from dollar terms to employment was made by using the ratio of gross private product (gross national product less government expenditures for employment) to non-government employment.

been if . . ." or "what may be if. . . ." The estimates are presented here merely to get a more realistic evaluation of the success pattern of the U.S. economy.

One observation though is needed, in this context, about the special bearing of military spending on the business cycle. Without discussing causes, the mechanics of the cycle are such that the capital goods industries are the major elements of up-and-down business swings. The post-war recessions followed this traditional pattern. Thus, in the 1957–1958 recession the production of consumer goods declined 5 percent while the production of equipment goods went down 20 percent. The special relevance of military spending in the business cycle is not so much its size as its concentration in the industries that do most of the swinging. For example, federal government spending generated the following percentages of total demand in capital goods industries: engines and turbines, 20 percent; metal-working machinery and equipment, 21 percent; electric industrial equipment and apparatus, 17 percent; machine-shop products, 39 percent.[3]

Thus, military spending acts as a very convenient backstop at the strategic weak spots of the business cycle. It also acts as a special defence arm of business profits. The volatility of business profits is related to the basic overhead costs of running a business. Once sales are large enough to meet overhead costs (the break-even point), profits rise much more rapidly than further advances in sales. Conversely, if sales drop sufficiently below the break-even point, losses accumulate at an increasing momentum. Mild recessions can thus turn into severe depressions if losses in key capital goods industries force complete shut-down of many plants. However, the orders for military goods in the otherwise vulnerable industries help to pay for overhead costs, build resistance to depression losses, and inhibit the cumulative effects of recessions. In similar fashion, the strategic concentration of military procurement in metals and machinery can keep prices high and thus raise the general profit level of capital goods industries.[4]

[3] "Interindustry Structure of the United States, a Report on the 1958 Input-Output Study" in *Survey of Current Business* (November 1964).

[4] In 1958, for example, federal government spending accounted for the following percentages of total demand in metal mining and manufacture: iron and ferro-alloy mining, 12.8 percent; non-ferrous metal ores mining, 35.6 percent; primary iron and steel manufacturing, 12.5 percent; primary non-ferrous metal manufacturing, 22.3 percent. "Interindustry Structure of the United States," *op. cit.*

DECLINING IMPORTANCE OF CAPITAL INVESTMENT

The failure of the civilian economy to fully utilize the economic resource of the country is reflected in the declining role of capital investment.   Thus, total investment in fixed capital (producers' durable equipment and non-residential construction) represented 10.3 percent of the gross national product (the total ouput of goods and services) during the years 1947–1957.   This percentage declined to 8.6 percent during the years 1958–1964.[5]

This is hardly the behaviour of an economy that is spurred ahead by major technological changes, let alone by an industrial revolution, whether first or second.   Note that the above percentages are based on total investment in plant and equipment: capital goods needed to replace worn-out equipment as well as net additions to the stock of capital.   Since the replacement needs are increasing, the relative decline in net new capital (over and above replacement needs) would be larger than indicated above.

Note also that in recent years a larger percentage of the total investment has been going into office buildings, shopping centres, banks, etc., rather than in the kind of productive equipment used to make new or more products.   In 1957 only 28 percent of the total expenditures for plant and equipment went into commercial enterprises (as distinguished from manufacturing, mining, transportation and public utilities).   In 1964 the proportion rose to 34 percent.[6]

Nor is this the whole story.   The capital that was invested for the purpose of expanding the production of goods, after the initial post-war boom, was used in large measure to meet military needs.   The evidence for this is seen in the specially large role of military demand in most of the growth industries—in those industries with an expansion rate that could only be achieved by investment in new plant and equipment.   In 1958, for example, purchases by the federal government accounted for the following percentages of total demand in important growth industries: radio, television and communication equipment, 41 percent; electronic components and accessories, 39 percent; scientific and control instruments, 30 percent; aircraft, 87 percent.[7]

[5] Percentages calculated from data in *Economic Report of the President*, U.S. Government Printing Office (Washington, D.C.: 1964).   The 1964 data were obtained from *Economic Indicators* (November 1964), U.S. Government Printing Office.

[6] *Economic Indicators* (November 1964).

[7] "Interindustry Structure of the United States," *op.cit.*

The declining relative importance of capital investment, even in the face of substantial military needs, should come as no surprise if one takes into account the tendency in a capitalist economy for productive capacity to outpace effective consumer demand. Nor should the relative weakness of capital investment in the midst of significant technical changes be especially unexpected considering the decisive way the large corporations can, if they have enough power, protect their "old" capital investment when it is in their interest to do so. Evidence presented before the Subcommittee on Antitrust and Monopoly of the U.S. Senate confirmed the potential power of the large corporations and the post-war increase in such power. The 100 largest manufacturing corporations, it was shown, held close to 57 percent of the net capital assets of all manufacturing companies in 1962, as compared with close to 46 percent in 1947.[8]

One area of capital investment, on the other hand, did show a striking move forward: foreign investments by U.S. capital. The total flow of capital out of the U.S. in the form of direct investments added up to $6.3 billion for the combined years 1947–1955. This jumped to $15.8 billion for the years 1956–1964.[9]

The analysis of this change in relation to U.S. foreign policy and imperialist involvement is beyond the scope of this article. What is significant for the present discussion is that this upsurge in investment, along with U.S. Government loans and grants to other countries, helped to support demand for U.S. production of equipment and metals.[10] These, as noted above, are the industries which are most vulnerable to cyclical decline.

Important as the high level of exports of machinery and other manufactures may be to the proper functioning of the U.S. economy, the increase of such exports—or even their maintenance

---

[8] Testimony of Dr. John Blair before Senate Subcommittee on Antitrust and Monopoly, November 1964.

[9] The data for 1947–1960 appear in *Balance of Payments, Statistical Supplement*, revised edition, U.S. Government Printing office (Washington, D.C.: 1963) Data for years after 1960 from different issues of *Survey of Current Business*.

[10] In 1958, exports accounted for the following percentages of total demand: construction, mining, and oil field machinery, 26.9 percent; metalworking machinery and equipment, 14 percent; engines and turbines, 14.8 percent; general industrial machinery and equipment, 13.4 percent. Note that exports and military procurement accounted for between 33 and 46 percent of the total demand in the following industries: engines and turbines; construction, mining and oil field machinery; metalworking machinery and equipment; machine shop products; radio, TV and communication equipment; electronic components and accessories; scientific and control instruments.

—may become increasingly difficult. The trouble is not only the competition of other industrialized nations; it is concerned with the persistent negative balance of payments the U.S. has been experiencing in recent years.

The popular explanation of the negative balance of payments usually points to the excess of U.S. exports over imports of goods, and then pinpoints the balance-of-payments illness on military spending abroad, aid to other countries, and private foreign investments. What is usually ignored is the interrelation between U.S. foreign policy, its economic and political activity in the rest of the world and its export markets. (Note, for example, that in 1963 alone, foreign affiliates of U.S. industrial companies bought at least $5 billion of U.S. goods. This represented about 23 percent of all U.S. exports of merchandise in 1963.)

Obviously the adverse balance of payments cannot go on forever within the present political and economic arrangements among nations. However, the U.S. may not be able to reduce its financial contributions and also maintain its export volume. Nor can the solution be sought via foreign investments. For the facts are that the U.S. takes in more than it sends out as a result of foreign investment: from 1956–1964, U.S. corporations sent out $16 billion for direct foreign investments; in the same years the rest of the world returned to the U.S. about $23 billion as dividends, interests and branch profits resulting from direct investments.[11]

Neither the reduction of the flow of foreign investments nor an increase in foreign investments (except in the unlikely event that foreign investments continue to grow at an increasing rate) will remedy the situation. For the excess of what U.S. corporations draw out of foreign countries over what they send in is a direct result of the mathematics of such investment. In fact, this behaviour is the reason corporations make foreign investments. But inevitable as this imbalance may be, it also creates other problems. When other countries reach difficulties in repaying their loans to the U.S. or paying out the continuous profits on U.S. investments, their recourse is to try to increase their exports to the U.S. and to reduce their imports from the U.S. This can be a difficult pill for the U.S. to swallow so long as it is unable to sustain enough effective demand internally to keep its own labour force fully employed.

[11] *Balance of Payments, op. cit.* Data for years after 1960 from different issues of *Survey of Current Business.*

THE ECONOMY GROWS ON CREDIT

The initial post-war boom—say, the first eight to ten years—had real roots in the private market economy: on the one hand, the need to build up stocks of capital investment goods, housing, and consumer durable goods (cars, household equipment) which had been neglected and had deteriorated during many years of depression and war; on the other hand, the ability of the private market to finance the purchase of these goods due to the large accumulations of savings under the New Deal's wartime economic controls. The post-war boom was strengthened at first by the U.S. dominant world trade position (arising from the war devastation of other industrialized nations) and then intensified and given new life by government spending for the Korean War.

The boom fed itself for a period, bringing with it new peaks in housing, construction, capital investment, and a multitude of consumer goods. But even this boom was inadequate to provide full employment. Moreover, the capital investment stimulus began to peter out after 1957, as suggested by the data given above.

Since 1957, in the absence of a private-economy based boom, military spending stepped in as a revitalizing force. "National defence" expenditures rose continuously from $44.4 billion in 1957 to $56.8 billion a year in 1963 and in 1964. Whether this action was in response to economic need or for a "higher" political purpose is not germane to the present argument. What is important though is that this type of dynamic prop, together with foreign investment and government military and economic activity abroad, gave a significant boost to the economy and also helped to shore up the more vulnerable, the more unstable, economic sectors.

Such strong stimulation was still not enough to keep the economy at prosperity levels; what was needed, it turned out, was heavier and heavier doses of debt. Even the state and local government could not keep up their governmental obligations and thus make their economic contribution as well without an increasing reliance on debt. During the ten years prior to 1957, state and local governments added on the average a little over $3 billion a year to their total debt load. Since 1957 these government units have been adding close to $6 billion a year.[12] The debt-creating ability of lower government organizations is quite different from that of the federal government because the states and local units

[12] *Economic Report of the President*, 1964.

Table 1

Year	Gross private product (in billions)	Net private debt after repayments (in billions)	Debt as a percentage of gross private product
1945	$178.4	$139.9	78%
1950	263.8	250.9	95
1955	363.5	402.5	111
1960	455.3	588.4	129
1963	526.7	752.9	143

do not have the power to create and regulate the supply of money and credit.   Their debt-carrying capacity is ultimately limited by their revenue-raising ability, which is quite inferior to that of the federal government.   To the extent that a rise in state and local government spending depends, as in recent years, increasingly on a greater proportion of debt, the inner limitations on debt expansion will inhibit expansion of this type of government activity.

While it is conceivable that the possible difficulties of lower governments' finances could be resolved by a drastic overhaul of the U.S. public finance and government structure, the same solution is not available for the private economy operating within a capitalist framework.   The issue should become more apparent if we examine a few key facts.   The net debt owed by private individuals and institutions (corporations, farms and individuals) increased on the average of $32 billion a year during the ten years prior to 1957.   Since 1957 the average annual increase has been 50 percent higher—close to $48 billion a year.[13]   Part of this rise is attributable to a higher price level.   But this is a minor element; the noteworthy change is the relative increase in debt compared with the total private (non-government) gross product, the latter also reflecting higher prices (see Table 1).[14]

The danger here is not the debt itself.   Credit is a useful financial instrument to help a complex economy function smoothly; it is especially useful to lubricate the mechanism of an expanding economy.   Credit can serve as a handmaiden to a society in which productive wealth is accumulating, on the basis of which the economy can keep on increasing its production and investment. But it is quite another matter when a semi-stagnant economy

[13] *Ibid.*
[14] *Ibid.*

keeps on increasing its debt burden. For this is an economy which can continue to maintain itself on a fairly steady keel only with ever-increasing dosages of credit.

The dangers of such an eventuality are twofold. First, a weakness in the banking system that creates the credit can more readily result in a cumulative downturn of the economy. Second, to sustain an ever larger debt, business eventually has to obtain larger profits to repay the debt, plus interest charges. In a semi-stagnant economy, larger profits cannot come from greater accumulation of capital but by reducing the share going to wages and salaries.

The potential dilemma in this event is that wage and salary earners need to increase their income steadily since they too are spending and sustaining the economy by increased use of credit. From 1960–1963 new mortgage debt on privately owned homes increased 40 percent, from $20 to $28 billion. In the same period, there was no increase in the value of new housing construction of one- to four-family units. Another way of looking at these figures is that during these four years $95 billion of new mortgages were added as compared with less than $72 billion of construction activity on new private homes.[15] The reasons behind this strange discrepancy are no doubt: (1) the willingness of financial institutions to lend on easier terms, which also reflect inflated, speculative values, and (2) the desire or need by consumers to keep up the feverish pace of buying, which can only be maintained by stretching debt obligations.

A similar pattern is seen in the greater dependence of the consumer durable goods market on increasing injections of consumer credit. From 1960–1963 the annual average instalment credit extended to consumers amounted to 88 percent of all consumer durable goods purchased. This compares with 69 percent in 1947–1950.[16]

The net effect of all this borrowing is obviously a greater drain on consumer income. In 1951, 14 percent of consumer income went to carry their debts (amortization and interest). In 1963

[15] "The New Dimension in Mortgage Debt," Technical Paper No. 15, National Industrial Conference Board (New York: 1964).

[16] *Economic Report of the President*, 1964. Not all of consumer instalment credit is used for the purchase of consumer durable goods. About two-thirds of instalment credit is backed specifically by paper on consumer durable goods. However, a substantial portion of the remaining credit is also used for the purchase of consumer durable as is part of the non-instalment credit which was not included in these figures.

Table 2. Changes in Labour Force and Employment

Years	Increase in total labour force (in millions)	Increase in employment
1930–1940	6.1	2.0
1940–1950	8.5	12.2
1950–1960	8.4	7.0
1960–1970 (projection)	12.6	—
1970–1975 (projection)	7.3	—

SOURCE: *Economic Report of the President* transmitted to Congress, January 1964, and *Manpower Report of the President* transmitted to Congress, March 1964.

the figure was 21 percent.[17]   No arbitrary limit can be set on a safe maximum percentage of income for debt service. But a maximum there must be. And to the extent that there is such a maximum, there is an eventual restraint on an economy which requires ever larger doses of credit to keep moving ahead.

ROOTS OF PERSISTENT UNEMPLOYMENT

All of the special stimuli of recent U.S. economic development— military spending, foreign investment, and the spread of debt— working together have been unable to make any headway in resolving the problem of persistent unemployment. Quite the opposite: the trend of unemployment has been upward since 1953. Nor is there any evidence in sight that this trend will be reversed in the years ahead. As will be seen from the data, the problem of achieving full employment must become increasingly difficult.

The background information which can be used to appreciate the dimensions of the problem are presented in Table 2.   The first line of this table gives a bird's-eye view of the net effect of the depression years on unemployment. In contrast with future decades, the rise of over 6 million in the labour force was relatively small.   The labour force is measured by government agencies to determine the number of people of working age who are looking for jobs. Because of the technique used in measuring the labour force, the 6 million increase may be understated since the absence of job opportunities discouraged many from looking for work. Be that as it may, the outline of the picture is clear for the 1930–

[17] *Wall Street Journal*, 17 June 1964.

1940 decade.   The 2 million net increase in jobs fell short by 4 million to meet even a conservative estimate of the number of new jobs required.   This means that in 1940 there were 4 million more unemployed than in 1930.

The direction was completely reversed in the next decade as a result of war and immediate post-war needs.   The growth of employment was large enough not only to provide jobs for all new workers but even to eliminate the unemployment created in the preceding decade.   Hence, in 1950 unemployment was back to approximately the level in 1930.

The labour force continued to grow in the following decade by about the same amount as from 1940–1950.   But in those years the growth in employment slowed down.   For part of the decade, as described above, there was a strong upward lift to the economy, resulting in a drop in the official unemployment rate below 3 percent in 1953.   Even this, it should be noted, was achieved with the assistance of a close to 2 million rise in the size of the armed forces. (Government estimates are based on the concept of the "civilian labour force."   In this fashion the armed forces are excluded from data on labour force and unemployment.)   The low "civilian" unemployment rate was short-lived, due to the subsequent slowing down in the general rate of economic growth.   The net effect over the decade as a whole was the generation of more employment.

We now come to the nub of the present and future unemployment pressures.   The labour force is bound to increase by more than 12.5 million from 1960–1970—an increase that is 50 percent more than in the two preceding decades.   The explanation for the enlarged increase in the labour force is quite simple.   Earlier growth of the labour force was influenced by the declining birthrate of the 1920s and 1930s.   Birthrates were especially low during the depression years.   Consequently the increase in the labour force was relatively low in the 1950s, and especially so in the mid 1950s, when the babies born during the depth of the depression reached working age.

Today we are beginning to get the effect of the rise in birthrates that accompanied improved economic conditions in the 1940s. But more important, the expansion of the labour force in the next five years will be even larger as a result of the so-called birth-rate explosion during the early post-war years.   Nor does this unusually large increase in the labour force come to an end in 1970.   As can be seen from the last line of Table 2, projecting from the present population it is reasonable to expect that the labour force will grow by about 7.3 million from 1970–1975.   This five-year increase is almost as large as the ten-year increase between 1950 and 1960. In other words, the labour force will grow from 1970–1975 at double the rate experienced from 1940–1960.

Some simple arithmetic can provide us with the dimensions of the problem.   To attain relatively full employment by 1970, close to 15 million new jobs would have to be added by 1970 as compared with 1960: 12.6 million jobs for the net additions to the labour force (see Table 2) and about 2.2 million full-time jobs to reduce the unemployment rate to 3 percent.[18]   Neither the experience of the early 1960s or of the past decade justify the expectation of employment increases of such a magnitude.   Only during the period of massive intervention by the government during World War II, and while benefiting from the immediate aftermath of such government intervention, did the U.S. economy prove capable of creating anything near 15 million new jobs in a decade.   And even that performance of 12 million jobs would, if duplicated, leave 5.5 million unemployed at the end of 1970.   In terms of current developments, it is more realistic to expect 10 million unemployed—even if the economy can avoid a major economic downturn in the interim.

This analysis highlights a special feature of the post-war U.S. economy.   The period of rapid capital accumulation coincided with a period of relatively slow growth of the labour force.   This has shifted—and apparently will continue for some time ahead—to the opposite: a rapid rise in the labour force accompanied by a slow-down in capital accumulation.   A key phase of the latter development is clearly illustrated in Table 3.

Starting with 1957—the year we have selected as in the nature of a turning point—and ending in 1963, 4.3 million non-farm jobs were added.   Though not large enough to prevent a rise in unemployment, this increase was nevertheless significant in size.   Now where did these jobs come from?   Almost two-thirds of the additional jobs (2.8 million) arose directly or indirectly by government activity.   If the jobs created by non-profit institutions (hospitals, universities, etc.) are eliminated, it turns out that only 900,000 jobs were generated by private market activity.   And even that is not the full story.   Many of these jobs were part-time.   If an adjustment is made for the latter, then only 300,000 jobs were

[18] This calculation assumes no reduction in the size of the armed forces. The unemployment figures were adjusted to take into account part-time unemployment, but not the concealed unemployed.

Table 3. Job–Growth Generated by Public and Private Demand

Item	1957	1963	Increase from 1957–1963
		Millions	
Total non-farm employment	52.9	57.2	4.3
Less government employees	7.6	9.6	2.0
Equals: Private non-farm employment	45.3	47.7	2.4
Less jobs owing to government purchases from business	5.9	6.7	.8
Equals: Jobs generated independent of government spending	39.4	41.0	1.6
Less employment by non-profit institutions	2.6	3.3	.7
Equals: Jobs generated by private demand	36.8	37.7	.9
Less adjustment for voluntary part-time employment	1.7	2.3	.6
Equals: Full-time jobs generated by private demand	35.1	35.4	.3

SOURCE: Manpower Report of the President transmitted to Congress, March 1964.

NOTE: Detail may not add up to totals because of rounding off decimals. Government refers to federal, state and local. Above data do not include the self-employed.

created by the private economy after six years—most of which were years of economic upswing.[19]

The insufficiency of jobs created by private industry is only in part due to increased productivity and automation. The effect of increasing productivity is shown in Table 4. As noted there, manufacturing output almost doubled between 1957 and 1964, but the number of production workers in manufacturing remained the same. Still it is not productivity that creates the problem; it is the fact that production does not keep pace with and overtake the rise in productivity. The failure of the private economy as a job-producer is a failure—despite valiant "pump-priming" efforts—to invest enough capital and grow sufficiently to keep pace with

[19] The 1964 data classified in this fashion were not available at the time of this writing. Preliminary data indicate that employment on the private market account improved in 1964, but hardly enough to alter the main argument. If 1962 were taken as the terminal year, employment on private market account would show an absolute decline from 1957.

Table 4. Productivity of Production Workers in Manufactures

Selected years	Production index of manufactures (1947 = 100)	Production workers employed in manufactures		Output per productive worker (1947 = 100)
		Number (in thousands)	Index (1947 = 100)	
1947	100	12,990	100	100
1953	124	14,055	108	115
1957	144	13,189	102	141
1964 (10 month average)	196	12,813	99	198

SOURCE: Production indexes computed from data in *Economic Report of the President* transmitted to Congress, January 1964, and *Economic Indicators* (November 1964), U.S. Government Printing Office. Employment data—*Manpower Report of the President* transmitted to Congress, March 1964, and *Monthly Report on the Labour Force* (October 1964), U.S. Department of Labour.

growing productivity and a growing labour force. Nor has government activity shown the ability to cope with a growing labour force and increasing productivity except at the time of World War II.

THE DISEASE OF POVERTY

The nature of the long economic boom, and its pattern of change, is well reflected in the continuous existence of large-scale poverty. For despite the important reforms introduced by the New Deal in the 1930s, the political acceptance of the Welfare State, the tremendous advance in productive capacity, and the very sizeable expansion of inner markets, no less than two-fifths of the nation, still live in poverty or in a state of economic deprivation in the U.S.[20]

Naturally the huge growth in the economy also brought about a drastic reduction in poverty. But what needs to be noted in terms of this analysis is the marked slow-down in recent years in the reduction of poverty. It should not be surprising to find that the pattern of change in poverty resembles the pattern of change

[20] This statement and the subsequent details on poverty are from *Poverty and Deprivation in the U.S.*, Conference on Economic Progress (Washington, D.C.: April 1962). The national committee of the conference includes industrialists and leaders of national trade unions and farm organizations. The research and analysis of the conference is under the direction of Leon H. Keyserling, former chairman of the President's Council of Economic Advisers.

in capital investment.   The great reduction in poverty took place during the World War II era—the years of war and immediate aftermath.   From the extreme of the depression (1935–36) to 1947 there was an average annual reduction of 4.8 percent in the total number of people living in poverty.   From 1947–53—when unemployment was relatively low, capital accumulation still relatively high, and the economy restimulated by the Korean War—the average annual rate of reduction in the number of people living in poverty dropped to 2.7 percent.   And from 1953–1960—when unemployment began to mount and the maintenance of prosperity required further artificial stimulation—the rate of annual decline in poverty fell to 1.1 percent.   At the latter rate of change it would take another ninety years to eliminate poverty in the U.S.—this in a country that has right now the resources and the capacity to do so if the society were organized for such a purpose.

The determination of what constitutes poverty in the wealthy U.S. necessarily involves certain arbitrary definitions.   A discussion of these definitions would require too much space here. Suffice it to say that though the several studies on this subject made by different authorities in recent years do differ in detail, there is substantial agreement on the extent of poverty.   We are using here the study made by the Conference on Economic Progress, *Poverty and Deprivation in the U.S.* (see footnote 20), which used U.S. Department of Labour investigation of budgets of city workers' families to determine the standards of poverty.   In addition, the Conference report introduced the concept of "economic deprivation" which includes people living about the stark poverty level but below what the Labour Department investigation found to be a "modest but adequate" worker's family budget.

The simple summary of the Conference report on the 1960 income situation in the U.S. is as follows: 34 million people in families and 4 million unattached individuals (that is, unattached economically to a family unit) lived in poverty; 37 million people in families and 2 million unattached individuals lived in deprivation.   The total of 77 million comprised two-fifths of the U.S. population in 1960.

Without dwelling on the sociology of this poverty, one resultant of the persistent poverty is worth reporting on at this point.   Faced with the fact that one-half of the draft registrants are rejected as unfit for military service, President Kennedy appointed a task force to study the health and education of U.S. youth.   This task force found that one-third of all young men in the nation turning 18 years of age would be found unqualified if they were to be examined for induction into the armed forces. Of these, one-half would be rejected for medical reasons. The remainder would fail through inability to meet the educational standards of at least an eighth-grade level of educational attainment, and a large part of this category could not meet the educational standards of a fifth-grade level.

The President's Task Force concluded on the basis of its study: "Although many persons are disqualified for defects that probably could not be avoided in the present state of knowledge, the majority appear to be victims of inadequate education and insufficient health services."[21]   The Task Force, however, did not point out that they were referring to the young men who were born and brought up during the years of their country's great wave of prosperity and historic economic achievements.

Those who believe that poverty can be eliminated within the economic and social institutions of a capitalist society see the issue of poverty as primarily a matter of social welfare.   Better schooling, housing, medical attention, and more government spending to create jobs will, they maintain, break the back of poverty. What is not understood, even by the most energetic reformers, is that poverty is itself a product of prosperity.   The economic system, as it operates, creates a reserve of the poor benefits from it.   In periods of rapid expansion and in periods of war, the marginal group in society is available for work and fighting. During such times the reserve of the poor may diminish, to be eventually built up again as the economy slows down, as technological change displaces workers, and when there are economic declines.   Moreover, the roots of poverty are intertwined with the very functioning of the economy: the structure of industry, the methods of distribution, and the way prices and profits are formed.

THE NEGRO RESERVES

While the majority of the poor are white, the concentration of poverty among Negroes and the unique way they are used in the advanced U.S. civilization offers a valuable laboratory illustration of the operating mechanics of poverty.

Living at the lowest economic levels of the society, the Negroes are available as the ultimate reserve in times of labour shortage.

[21] *Ibid.*

In recent history the most important breakthrough in economic advance of the Negro occurred in World War I and World War II. But as soon as the labour shortage eases, the Negroes' advance slows down or declines.   The mechanics of the operation even during prosperous times are presented as one of the conclusions of a recent study: "White workers capture the newly growing fields in which labour resources are scarce, pay levels are good, prospects for advancement are bright, the technology is most advanced, and working conditions the most modern.   These fields seem relatively less and less attractive to white workers, however, as the economy continues to expand and newer fields appear.   Finally, the once new fields stagnate, and white workers are reluctant to enter them. Even though wages in these fields may increase rapidly, they now are low by the standards of the newer, more highly skilled occupations associated with newer technologies in rapidly expanding fields.   At this point Negroes secure these jobs, which are quite attractive in comparison to what had formerly been available to them.   Although working conditions and wages in the now older fields may have improved over time, they are conditioned by an older technology and customs.   Moreover, newer technology is likely to result in reduced manpower needs.   Thus the Negroes' newest and best opportunities often turn out to be quite vulnerable. Their gains in the operative occupations during the 1940s and 1950s are now increasingly susceptible to recent technological and market changes."[22]

The role of the Negro as a shock-absorber of economic and technological dislocations shows up in agriculture as well as industry.   The growth of technology on the farm, the upsurge of large industrialized farms associated with war needs and the type of government subsidies, resulted in a sharp decline in the farm population.   While this meant, among other things, the removal of large numbers of tenant farmers and farm labourers, the impact fell primarily on the Negroes.   Thus, the percentage of white farmers and farm labourers increased from 81 percent in 1940 to 85 percent in 1960, while the percentage of Negroes declined in the same period from 19 percent to 15 percent.[23]

In like fashion, when unemployment increases, the extent of unemployment among Negroes rises more rapidly than among whites.   The official government figures on unemployment indi-

[22] Dale L. Hiestand, *Economic Growth and Employment Opportunities for Minorities* (New York and London, 1964), p. 114.
[23] Calculated from data in Hiestand, *op. cit.*

Table 5. 1963 Income Distribution
of Whites and Non-whites[a]

Annual money income	Percentage of families	
	White	Non-white[b]
Under $2,000	9.0%	25.1%
$2,000 to $3,999	15.1	31.1
$4,000 to $5,999	20.1	19.6
$6,000 to $9,999	34.3	18.1
$10,000 and over	21.5	5.7
	100.0	100.0

SOURCE: *Consumer Income*, Consumer Population Report, Series P–60, No. 43, 20 September 1964.   U.S. Department of Commerce.

[a] These data represent only money income and do not include nonmonetary income such as consumption of food raised on one's farm or the value of room and board supplied to farm and service workers.

[b] Over 90 percent of non-whites are Negro.

cate a rate of unemployment among Negroes in 1963 of close to 11 percent as compared with 5 percent for whites—more than double.   The spread itself has been widening as the economy slowed down—the Negro unemployment rate in 1948 was only 63 percent higher than the white rate.   The same applies to unemployment among youth.   In 1963 the teenage unemployment was 25.4 percent for male Negroes and 14 percent for whites, as compared with 7.1 percent and 6.3 percent in 1953.[24]   Although employment opportunities increased in 1964, a special government study issued in August 1964 estimated that one-third of the Negro young people, including those who have given up looking for jobs, were without work.

The net result of the two different worlds is seen in Table 5. . . . The sharply contrasting patterns are suggestive of the differences between a centre of empire and a colonial dependency. The analogy can be extended in many different directions.   The main point is that the elimination of discrimination, even if it be more than token, would be but a minor element in any radical alteration of the income distribution of the Negro population. For it is not discrimination that causes this difference.   Institutionalized discrimination contributes to particular forms of poverty

[24] *Manpower Report of the President*, U.S. Government Printing Office (Washington, D.C.: March 1964).

among Negroes and enhances the privileges of many whites.   But in the main, discrimination is the medium—in the context of U.S. economics and social history—by which a special kind of poverty and a special kind of labour reserve is maintained.

As in the case of white poverty, Negro poverty—more clearly seen because of its extreme character—is a function of the industrial and economic structure.   Elimination of discrimination will not eliminate such major sources of poverty as unemployment, casual and intermittent jobs and low-paid occupations.   More education, more job training and equal opportunity may only result in having better-educated, better-trained and more "equal" unemployed and low-paid workers.   For the sources of poverty result from the behaviour of the market system itself: the structure and location of industry, methods of distribution, the price structure, and the way profits from industry and land ownership are accumulated and used.   The economy functions in such a manner that it produces and reproduces poverty and economic deprivation.

The significance of this proposition is not yet well understood even by advanced groups leading the social and political struggle for freedom and equality of Negroes.   This lack of understanding is no doubt due in part to the acceptance of the myths about the new capitalism and the consequent faith in what a good and wise government could accomplish.

A more careful examination of Table 5 may help to see this question in better perspective.   A casual inspection of the two columns shows that from a purely statistical point of view, equality between the two groups could be achieved only if a large number of whites would be pushed down the economic ladder in order to make room for non-whites.   While a society based on social justice might make a significant advance along this line, it is clear that very little, if any, progress can be made towards such an end in a society that rewards its citizens according to property ownership and work skills (where education and long training are of key importance).

Let us assume for the sake of this argument a society that is bent on reform, but reform in a practical fashion.   The present distribution of incomes of whites will not be disturbed.   This necessarily means that the distribution of income of the close to 5 million Negro families will not be changed.   But as the economy grows and the number of Negro families increases (say, at 2 percent per year), special privileges will be given Negroes so that they get an advantage over whites for the better jobs. Hence, we will assume that new jobs and new income opportunities for Negroes will be such that 24 percent of them will result in incomes of $10,000 a year and over, instead of the 5.7 percent shown in Table 5.   Only a little over 6 percent of the new jobs will result in annual income of less than $2,000, as compared with the 25.5 percent shown in Table 5.   Similar drastic changes will be effected, in our assumed world, for the in-between job opportunities.   The net result of all these assumptions is that it would still take a hundred years for the income distribution of Negroes to equal that of the whites.

Of course, we have merely been playing a mathematical game in the preceding paragraph in order to illuminate the severity of the problem.   The historical facts are quite clear.   The same Census Bureau study which produced the data shown in Table 5 also presented comparative income information for the entire post-war period.   An examination of these data reveals that despite the turmoil of recent years and the talk of progress, the relative position of Negro income compared to white income has not changed.   In 1948 the median income of non-white families was 53 percent of the median income of white families.   In 1963 the percentage was still 53 percent.   Any significant break-through in this kind of inequality and the achievement of results in the ne[ar] future, and not a hundred years from now, places on the agenda the need for a new type of industrialization and a reconstruction of the physical wealth of the society.   Such changes would be in direct conflict with the operations of a private market economy that creates and continuously refreshes the sources of poverty.   If the goal of the society is Negro-white equality and the elimination of poverty, then the solution cannot be found in a new capitalism or through the adaptation of the Negro to the new capitalism.   If the history of colonialism and the development of national independence can serve as a teacher, then we need to recognize that to achieve equality the Negro must become equal by becoming the master of his own destiny.   Seen in the light of issues of this magnitude, the various proposals for even radical tinkering with the existing economic set-up are akin to the romantic and utopian socialist ideas of an earlier era.

Part Five

THE STRUCTURE OF POWER

THE ESSENTIAL ELEMENTS OF THE POLITICAL PROCESS IN THE *United States, according to Truman, are: organized interest groups; widely held but unorganized interests ("potential groups"); and multiple or overlapping group memberships. The total pattern of government over time represents a protean complex of criss-crossing relationships that change in strength and direction with alterations in the power and standing of interests, both organized and unorganized.*

Organized interest groups, although cohesive, are never solid and monolithic, because they contain competing claims within them as the result of overlapping memberships that link individuals of disparate interests. Such overlapping, however, is insufficient to obviate the possibility of irreconcilable conflict between groups with little over- lapping, such as the NAM and the United Steelworkers. Such obviation of conflict, according to Truman, depends on the existence of potential interest groups which may crystallize as the result of a disturbance in established relationships and expectations.

Widely held but unorganized interests, or "rules of the game," such as the emphasis on fair play and individual dignity, are essential to the democratic process. These "rules" are acquired through early socialization. If they are violated for a prolonged period by public officials, then either existing or potential interest groups, or other officials, will act to reassert the enforcement of the "rules." It is therefore, Truman says, multiple memberships in potential groups based on widely held and accepted interests that serve as a balance wheel in the political system. In this way, government activity is the resultant of interest group activity.

This equilibrium can, however, be upset by "morbific politics." Violation of democratic norms by men of power, may undermine faith in rules of the game, and precipitate organization and forms of struggle outside the prevailing rules, in the interest of "justice." The under- privileged may rate egalitarian demands above the claims of peaceful change; the privileged may rate "law and order" above the claims of social justice. Thus, if groups with overlapping memberships operate essentially within sharply defined social strata or classes with specialized priorities and meanings, the stability of the system is endangered. Different interpretations of the "rules" might become sources of conflict between strata; caste and class interpretations of reality may differ so substantially as to lead to social conflict. Con- flict can also occur as a result of the recognition of the fact that only certain class interpretations of the broad interest are expressed by government institutions, and that other social claims are frustrated; under such conditions, the claims of organized and unorganized interests may become explosive.

316

27

INTEREST GROUPS AND THE NATURE OF THE STATE

David B. Truman

Men, wherever they are observed, are creatures participating in those established patterns of interaction that we call groups. Excepting perhaps the most casual and transitory, these continuing interactions, like all such interpersonal relationships, involve power. This power is exhibited in two closely interdependent ways. In the first place, the group exerts power over its members; an individual's group affiliations largely determine his attitudes, values, and the frames of reference in terms of which he interprets his experiences. For a measure of conformity to the norms of the group is the price of acceptance within it. Such power is exerted not only by an individual's present group relationships; it also may derive from past affiliations such as the childhood family as well as from groups to which the individual aspires to belong and whose characteristic shared attitudes he also holds. In the second place, the group, if it is or becomes an interest group, which any group in a society may be, exerts power over other groups in the society when it successfully imposes claims upon them.

Many interest groups, probably an increasing proportion in the United States, are politicized. That is, either from the outset or from time to time in the course of their development they make their claims through or upon the institutions of government. Both

Reprinted from David B. Truman, *The Governmental Process: Political Interests and Public Opinion* (New York: Alfred A. Knopf, 1951), pp. 505–24, by permission of the publisher. Copyright 1951 by Alfred A. Knopf, Inc. Footnotes have been renumbered.

the forms and functions of government in turn are a reflection of the activities and claims of such groups. The constitution-writing proclivities of Americans clearly reveal the influence of demands from such sources, and the statutory creation of new functions reflects their continuing operation. Many of these forms and functions have received such widespread acceptance from the start or in the course of time that they appear to be independent of the overt activities of organized interest groups. The judiciary is such a form.   The building of city streets and the control of vehicular traffic are examples of such a function.   However, if the judiciary or a segment of it operates in a fashion sharply contrary to the expectations of an appreciable portion of the community or if its role is strongly attacked, the group basis of its structure and powers is likely to become apparent. Similarly, if street construction greatly increases tax rates or if the control of traffic unnecessarily inconveniences either pedestrians or motorists, the exposure of these functions to the demands of competing interests will not be obscure.   Interests that are widely held in the society may be reflected in government without their being organized in groups.   They are what we have called potential groups. If the claims implied by the interests of these potential groups are quickly and adequately represented, interaction among those people who share the underlying interests or attitudes is unnecessary.   But the interest base of accepted governmental forms and functions and their potential involvement in overt group activities are ever present even when not patently operative.

The institutions of government are centers of interest-based power; their connections with interest groups may be latent or overt and their activities range in political character from the routinized and widely accepted to the unstable and highly controversial.   In order to make claims, political interest groups will seek access to the key points of decision within these institutions. Such points are scattered throughout the structure, including not only the formally established branches of government but also the political parties in their various forms and the relationships between governmental units and other interest groups.

The extent to which a group achieves effective access to the institutions of government is the resultant of a complex of interdependent factors. For the sake of simplicity these may be classified in three somewhat overlapping categories: (1) factors relating to a group's strategic position in the society; (2) factors associated with the internal characteristics of the group; and

(3) factors peculiar to the governmental institutions themselves. In the first category are: the group's status or prestige in the society, affecting the ease with which it commands deference from those outside its bounds; the standing it and its activities have when measured against the widely held but largely unorganized interests or "rules of the game"; the extent to which government officials are formally or informally "members" of the group; and the usefulness of the group as a source of technical and political knowledge. The second category includes: the degree and appropriateness of the group's organization; the degree of cohesion it can achieve in a given situation, especially in the light of competing group demands upon its membership; the skills of the leadership; and the group's resources in numbers and money.   In the third category are: the operating structure of the government institutions, since such established features involve relatively fixed advantages and handicaps; and the effects of the group life of particular units or branches of the government.

The product of effective access, of the claims of organized and unorganized interests that achieve access with varying degrees of effectiveness, is a governmental decision. Note that these interests that achieve effective access and guide decisions need not be "selfish," are not necessarily solidly unified, and may not be represented by organized groups. Governmental decisions are the resultant of effective access by various interests, of which organized groups may be only a segment.   These decisions may be more or less stable depending on the strength of supporting interests and on the severity of disturbances in the society which affect that strength.

A characteristic feature of the governmental system in the United States is that it contains a multiplicity of points of access. The federal system establishes decentralized and more or less independent centers of power, vantage points from which to secure privileged access to the national government.   Both a sign and a cause of the strength of the constituent units in the federal scheme is the peculiar character of our party system, which has strengthened parochial relationships, especially those of national legislators.   National parties, and to a lesser degree those in the states, tend to be poorly cohesive leagues of locally based organizations rather than unified and inclusive structures. Staggered terms for executive officials and various types of legislators accentuate differences in the effective electorates that participate in choosing these officers.   Each of these different, often opposite, localized patterns (constituencies) is a channel of independent access to the larger party aggregation and to the formal government. Thus, especially at the national level, the party is an electing-device and only in limited measure an integrated means of policy determination. Within the Congress, furthermore, controls are diffused among committee chairmen and other leaders in both chambers. The variety of these points of access is further supported by relationships stemming from the constitutional doctrine of the separation of powers, from related checks and balances, and at the state and local level from the common practice of choosing an array of executive officials by popular election. At the federal level the formal simplicity of the executive branch has been complicated by a Supreme Court decision that has placed a number of administrative agencies beyond the removal power of the president. The position of these units, however, differs only in degree from that of many that are constitutionally within the executive branch. In consequence of alternative lines of access available through the legislature and the executive and of divided channels for the control of administrative policy, many nominally executive agencies are at various times virtually independent of the chief executive.

Although some of these lines of access may operate in series, they are not arranged in a stable and integrated hierarchy. Depending upon the whole political context in a given period and upon the relative strength of contending interests, one or another of the centers of power in the formal government or in the parties may become the apex of a hierarchy of controls. Only the highly routinized governmental activities show any stability in this respect, and these may as easily be subordinated to elements in the legislature as to the chief executive. Within limits, therefore, organized interest groups, gravitating toward responsive points of decision, may play one segment of the structure against another as circumstances and strategic considerations permit. The total pattern of government over a period of time thus presents a protean complex of crisscrossing relationships that change in strength and direction with alterations in the power and standing of interests, organized and unorganized.

There are two elements in this conception of the political process in the United States that are of crucial significance and that require special emphasis. These are, first, the notion of multiple or overlapping membership and, second, the function of unorganized interests, or potential interest groups.

The idea of overlapping membership stems from the conception of a group as a standardized pattern of interactions rather than as a collection of human units. Although the former may appear to be a rather misty abstraction, it is actually far closer to complex reality than the latter notion. The view of a group as an aggregation of individuals abstracts from the observable fact that in any society, and especially a complex one, no single group affiliation accounts for all of the attitudes or interests of any individual except a fanatic or a compulsive neurotic. No tolerably normal person is totally absorbed in any group in which he participates. The diversity of an individual's activities and his attendant interests involve him in a variety of actual and potential groups. Moreover, the fact that the genetic experiences of no two individuals are identical and the consequent fact that the spectra of their attitudes are in varying degrees dissimilar means that the members of a single group will perceive the group's claims in terms of a diversity of frames of reference. Such heterogeneity may be of little significance until such time as these multiple memberships conflict. Then the cohesion and influence of the affected group depend upon the incorporation or accommodation of the conflicting loyalties of any significant segment of the group, an accommodation that may result in altering the original claims. Thus the leaders of a Parent-Teacher Association must take some account of the fact that their proposals must be acceptable to members who also belong to the local taxpayers' league, to the local chamber of commerce, and to the Catholic Church.

The notion of overlapping membership bears directly upon the problems allegedly created by the appearance of a multiplicity of interest groups. Yet the fact of such overlapping is frequently overlooked or neglected in discussions of the political role of groups. James Madison, whose brilliant analysis in the tenth essay in *The Federalist* we have frequently quoted, relied primarily upon diversity of groups and difficulty of communication to protect the new government from the tyranny of a factious majority. He barely touched on the notion of multiple membership when he observed, almost parenthetically: "Besides other impediments, it may be remarked that, where there is a consciousness of unjust or dishonorable purposes, communication is always checked by distrust in proportion to the number whose concurrence is necessary." John C. Calhoun's idea of the concurrent majority, developed in his posthumously published work, *A Disquisition on Government* (1851), assumed the unified, monolithic character of the groups whose liberties he was so anxious to protect.   When his present-day followers unearth his doctrines, moreover, they usually make the same assumption, although implicitly.[1]   Others, seeking a satisfactory means of accounting for the continued existence of the political system, sometimes assume that it is the nonparticipant citizens, aroused to unwonted activity, who act as a kind of counterbalance to the solid masses that constitute organized interest groups.[2]   Although this phenomenon may occur in times of crisis, reliance upon it reckons insufficiently with the established observation that citizens who are nonparticipant in one aspect of the governmental process, such as voting, rarely show much concern for any phase of political activity.   Multiple membership is more important as a restraint upon the activities of organized groups than the rarely aroused protests of chronic nonparticipants.

Organized interest groups are never solid and monolithic, though the consequences of their overlapping memberships may be handled with sufficient skill to give the organizations a maximum of cohesion.   It is the competing claims of other groups *within* a given interest group that threaten its cohesion and force it to reconcile its claims with those of other groups active on the political scene   The claims within the American Medical Association of specialists and teaching doctors who support group practice, compulsory health insurance, and preventive medicine offer an illustration.   The presence within the American Legion of public-housing enthusiasts and labor unionists as well as private home-builders and labor opponents provides another example   Potential conflicts within the Farm Bureau between farmers who must buy supplementary feed and those who produce excess feed grains for the market, between soybean growers and dairymen, even between traditional Republicans and loyal Democrats, create serious political problems for the interest group.   Instances of the way in which such cleavages impose restraints upon an organized group's activities are infinitely numerous, almost as numerous as cases of multiple membership.   Given the problems of cohesion and internal group politics that result from overlapping membership, the emergence of a multiplicity of interest groups in itself contains no dangers for the political system, especially since such

[1] Cf. John Fischer: "Unwritten Rules of American Politics," *Harper's Magazine* (November, 1948), pp. 27–36.

[2] Cf. Herring: *The Politics of Democracy*, p. 32.

overlapping affects not only private but also governmental "members" of the organized group.

But multiple membership in organized groups is not sufficiently extensive to obviate the possibility of irreconcilable conflict. There is little overlapping in the memberships of the National Association of Manufacturers and the United Steelworkers of America, or of the American Farm Bureau Federation and the United Automobile Workers. Overlapping membership among relatively cohesive organized interest groups provides an insufficient basis upon which to account for the relative stability of an operating political system. That system is a fact. An adequate conception of the group process must reckon with it. To paraphrase the famous words of John Marshall, we must never forget that it is a going polity we are explaining.

We cannot account for an established American political system without the second crucial element in our conception of the political process, the concept of the unorganized interest, or potential interest group. Despite the tremendous number of interest groups existing in the United States, not all interests are organized. If we recall the definition of an interest as a shared attitude, it becomes obvious that continuing interaction resulting in claims upon other groups does not take place on the basis of all such attitudes. One of the commonest interest group forms, the association, emerges out of severe or prolonged disturbances in the expected relationships of individuals in similar institutionalized groups. An association continues to function as long as it succeeds in ordering these disturbed relationships, as a labor union orders the relationships between management and workers. Not all such expected relationships are simultaneously or in a given short period sufficiently disturbed to produce organization. Therefore only a portion of the interests or attitudes involved in such expectations are represented by organized groups. Similarly, many organized groups—families, businesses, or churches, for example—do not operate continuously as interest groups or as political interest groups.

Any mutual interest, however, any shared attitude, is a potential group. A disturbance in established relationships and expectations anywhere in the society may produce new patterns of interaction aimed at restricting or eliminating the disturbance. Sometimes it may be this possibility of organization that alone gives the potential group a minimum of influence in the political process.   Thus Key notes that the Delta planters in Mississippi "must speak for their Negroes in such programs as health and education," although the latter are virtually unorganized and are denied the means of active political participation.[3]   It is in this sense that Bentley speaks of a difference in degree between the politics of despotism and that of other "forms" of government. He notes that there is "a process of representation in despotisms which is inevitable in all democracies, and which may be distinguished by quantities and by elaboration of technique, but not in any deeper 'qualititative' [sic] way."   He speaks of the despot as "representative of his own class, and to a smaller, but none the less real, extent of the ruled class as well."[4]   Obstacles to the development of organized groups from potential ones may be presented by inertia or by the activities of opposed groups, but the possibility that severe disturbances will be created if these submerged, potential interests should organize necessitates some recognition of the existence of these interests and gives them at least a minimum of influence.

More important for present purposes than the potential groups representing separate minority elements are those interests or expectations that are so widely held in the society and are so reflected in the behavior of almost all citizens that they are, so to speak, taken for granted.   Such "majority" interests are significant not only because they may become the basis for organized interest groups but also because the "membership" of such potential groups overlaps extensively the memberships of the various organized interest groups.[5]   The resolution of conflicts between the claims of such unorganized interests and those of organized interest groups must grant recognition to the former not only because affected individuals may feel strongly attached to them but even more certainly because these interests are widely shared and are a part of many established patterns of behavior the disturbance of which would be difficult and painful.   They are likely to be highly valued.

These widely held but unorganized interests are what we have previously called the "rules of the game."   Others have described

[3] Key: *Southern Politics*, pp. 235 and *passim*.
[4] Bentley: *The Process of Government*, pp. 314–15.   Copyright 1908 by and used with the permission of Arthur F. Bentley.
[5] See the suggestive discussion of this general subject in Robert Bierstedt: "The Sociology of Majorities," *American Sociological Review*, Vol. 13, No. 6 (December, 1948), pp. 700–10.

these attitudes in such terms as "systems of belief," as a "general ideological consensus," and as "a broad body of attitudes and understandings regarding the nature and limits of authority."[6] Each of these interests (attitudes) may be wide or narrow, general or detailed. For the mass of the population they may be loose and ambiguous, though more precise and articulated at the leadership level. In any case the "rules of the game" are interests the serious disturbance of which will result in organized interaction and the assertion of fairly explicit claims for conformity. In the American system the "rules" would include the value generally attached to the dignity of the individual human being, loosely expressed in terms of "fair dealing" or more explicitly verbalized in formulations such as the Bill of Rights. They would embrace what . . . we called "the democratic mold," that is, the approval of forms for broad mass participation in the designation of leaders and in the selection of policies in all social groups and institutions. They would also comprehend certain semi-egalitarian notions of material welfare. This is an illustrative, not an exhaustive, list of such interests.

The widely held, unorganized interests are reflected in the major institutions of the society, including the political. The political structure of the United States, as we have seen, has adopted characteristic legislative, executive, and judicial forms through the efforts of organized interest groups. Once these forms have been accepted and have been largely routinized, the supporting organized interest groups cease to operate as such and revert to the potential stage. As embodied in these institutional forms and in accepted verbal formulations, such as those of legal and constitutional theory, the interests of these potential groups are established expectations concerning not only *what* the governmental institutions shall do, but more particularly *how* they shall operate. To the extent that these established processes remain noncontroversial, they may appear to have no foundation in interests. Nevertheless, the widespread expectations will receive tacit or explicit deference from most organized interest groups in consequence of the overlapping of their memberships with these

[6] Kluckhohn: *Mirror for Man*, pp. 248 and *passim;* Sebastian de Grazia: *The Political Community: A Study of Anomie* (Chicago: University of Chicago Press, 1948), pp. ix, 80, and *passim;* Almond: *The American People and Foreign Policy*, p. 158; Charles E. Merriam: *Systematic Politics* (Chicago: University of Chicago Press, 1945), p. 213.

potential groups.[7]   Violation of the "rules of the game" normally will weaken a group's cohesion, reduce its status in the community, and expose it to the claims of other groups.   The latter may be competing organized groups that more adequately incorporate the "rules," or they may be groups organized on the basis of these broad interests and in response to the violations.

The pervasive and generally accepted character of these unorganized interests, or "rules," is such that they are acquired by most individuals in their early experiences in the family, in the public schools (probably less effectively in the private and paro- chial schools), and in similar institutionalized groups that are also expected to conform in some measure to the "democratic mold." The "rules" are likely to be reinforced by later events.   Persons who aspire to, or occupy, public office of whatever sort are par- ticularly likely to identify with these expected behaviors as part of their desired or existing roles.   With varying degrees of effec- tiveness the group life of government agencies—legislative, execu- tive, and judicial—reinforces the claims of these unorganized interests, which overlap those of the official group itself and those of "outside" political interest groups.   Marked and prolonged deviation from these expected behaviors by public officials, who are expected to represent what Bentley calls the " 'absent' or quiescent group interests," will normally produce restrictive action by other governmental functionaries, by existing organized interest groups, by ones newly organized in consequence of the deviations, or by all three.

It is thus multiple memberships in potential groups based on widely held and accepted interests that serve as a balance wheel in a going political system like that of the United States.   To some people this observation may appear to be a truism and to others a somewhat mystical notion.   It is neither.   In the first place, neglect of this function of multiple memberships in most discussions of organized interest groups indicates that the observa- tion is not altogether commonplace.   Secondly, the statement has no mystical quality; the effective operation of these widely held interests is to be inferred directly from verbal and other behavior in the political sphere.   Without the notion of multiple member- ships in potential groups it is literally impossible to account for the existence of a viable polity such as that in the United States or

[7] Cf. Bentley: *The Process of Government*, p. 397, and MacIver: *The Web of Government*, p. 79.

to develop a coherent conception of the political process. The strength of these widely held but largely unorganized interests explains the vigor with which propagandists for organized groups attempt to change other attitudes by invoking such interests.[8] Their importance is further evidenced in the recognized function of the means of mass communication, notably the press, in reinforcing widely accepted norms of "public morality."[9]

The role of the widespread unorganized interests and potential groups does not imply that such interests are always and everywhere dominant. Nor does it mean that the slightest action in violation of any of them inevitably and instantly produces a restrictive response from another source. These interests are not unambiguous, as the long history of litigation concerning freedom of speech will demonstrate. Subjectively they are not all equally fundamental. Thus since the "rules" are interests competing with those of various organized groups, they are in any given set of circumstances more or less subject to attenuation through such psychological mechanisms as rationalization. Moreover, the means of communication, whether by word of mouth or through the mass media, may not adequately make known particular deviations from the behavior indicated by these broad interests.

In a relatively vigorous political system, however, these unorganized interests are dominant with sufficient frequency in the behavior of enough important segments of the society so that, despite ambiguity and other restrictions, both the activity and the methods of organized interest groups are kept within broad limits. This interpretation is not far from Lasswell's view of the state as a relational system defined by a certain frequency of subjective events.[10] According to his definition, "the state . . . is a time-space manifold of similar subjective events. . . . That subjective event which is the unique mark of the state is the recognition that one belongs to a community with a system of paramount claims and expectations."[11] All citizens of the state as thus conceived need not experience this "event" continuously or with equal intensity. Nor need the attitudes of all citizens be favorable

---

[8] Cf. Lazarsfeld, *et al.: The People's Choice*, preface to 2d edition, pp. xxi–xxii.

[9] Cf. Paul F. Lazarsfeld and Robert K. Merton: "Mass Communication. Popular Taste and Organized Social Act," in Lyman Bryson (ed.): *The Communication of Ideas* (New York: Harper and Brothers, 1948), pp. 102ff.

[10] Lasswell: *Psychopathology and Politics*, pp. 240–61.

[11] *Ibid.*, p. 245.

toward these "claims and expectations."   But the existence of the state, of the polity, depends on widespread, frequent recognition of and conformity to the claims of these unorganized interests and on activity condemning marked deviations from them.   "All this," says Lasswell, "is frequently expressed as the 'sense of justice'. . . ."[12]

Thus it is only as the effects of overlapping memberships and the functions of unorganized interests and potential groups are included in the equation that it is accurate to speak of governmental activity as the product or resultant of interest group activity.   As Bentley has put it:

> There are limits to the technique of the struggle, this involving also limits to the group demands, all of which is solely a matter of empirical observation. . . . Or, in other words, when the struggle proceeds too harshly at any point there will become insistent in the society a group more powerful than either of those involved which tends to suppress the extreme and annoying methods of the groups in the primary struggle.   It is within the embrace of these great lines of activity that the smaller struggles proceed, and the very word struggle has meaning only with reference to its limitations.[13]

To assert that the organization and activity of powerful interest groups constitutes a threat to representative government without measuring their relation to and effects upon the widespread potential groups is to generalize from insufficient data and upon an incomplete conception of the political process.   Such an analysis would be as faulty as one that, ignoring differences in national systems, predicted identical responses to a given technological change in the United States, Japan, and the Soviet Union.

INTEREST GROUPS AND MORBIFIC POLITICS

No conception of the political process is adequate that does not take into account the possibilities of revolution and decay.   There is some danger that recognition of the censoring and restraining functions of the widespread but unorganized interests in a viable polity will lead to the comforting but unwarranted assumption of

[12] *Ibid.*, p. 246.
[13] Bentley: *The Process of Government,* p. 372.   Copyright 1908 by and used with the permission of Arthur F. Bentley.

some immanent harmony in the body politic.   The existence of a going polity testifies to the present effectiveness of these functions, but it does not justify the projection of a present equilibrium into the indefinite future.   Predictions concerning future stability, if they can be made at all, must be based upon an accumulation of research and measurement, even the barest outlines of which we cannot undertake in these pages.   We can indicate, however, some of the factors that might contribute to the growth of a morbific politics and that might justify the predictions of those who view with alarm the development of organized political interest groups.

Because the unorganized interests may not be a central concern of most individuals and because those interests may have to be activated in the face of insistent violations, there is no guarantee that they will become operative in time to avoid profound disturbance or collapse.   In a domestic crisis the continued latency of these unorganized interests may prevent the development of a viable compromise and encourage resort to less orderly means of adjustment.[14]   In an international crisis the ineffectiveness of these interests may permit diplomatic or military decisions to be so warped and may allow shifts in prevailing policy to be so delayed that the governmental system will not survive the supreme test of war.   These are typical possibilities.   The conflict between more restricted organized interests may at any time be carried beyond safe limits before the struggle is seen as one affecting the interests of extensive potential groups.

Group conflict and a certain inconsistency of governmental policy are not in themselves signs of the weakening of the widespread potential groups.   A measure of conflict is an unavoidable consequence of the multiplication of groups and of specialized individual activities.[15]   The process of accommodating group claims, moreover, does not necessarily produce a nice symmetry of public policy.   As in the feverish activity of the early New Deal, the adoption of superficially contradictory policies may in a larger view be a means of assuring the strength of the system rather than a sign of its decomposition.[16]   Nor is dollar economy an indication of the health of the process.   Fiscal neatness may or may not be a symptom of political stability.   There is evidence,

[14] Cf. Williams: *The Reduction of Intergroup Tensions*, p. 75.

[15] See *ibid.*, p. 56 and *passim*.

[16] See O. H. Taylor: "Economics Versus Politics", in Douglass Brown, *et al.: The Economics of the Recovery Program* (New York: McGraw-Hill Book Company, 1934), pp. 160–88.

moreover, that the American political system is inherently productive of fiscal confusion and is "not highly suited to a straightforward business-like management of finance." As Herring has
further observed: "Government has matters other than finances to
manage. Our present form of government is not to be judged
simply in terms of its ineptness for fiscal control."[17]   Except as
fiscal confusion may frustrate the expressed objectives of political
policy, matters of financial efficiency are not close to the foundations of the governmental system.

The effective activation of widespread unorganized interests
depends upon the character of the society's means of communication, broadly conceived. We have previously seen that one of the
elements in a president's ability to lead these interests is the ease
with which he can gain for his statements ample space in the media
of mass communication. Research evidence indicates that individuals who hold a broad interest of the type we are here concerned
with may or may not see a given set of events as bearing upon that
interest. How they will perceive such occurrences depends not
only upon the importance they attach to the interest but also upon
the adequacy of the information available to them concerning the
events.[18]   The quality and character of the mass media, therefore,
and of the various means of interpersonal communication—rumors,
letters, and conversations—are of fundamental importance in
assuring the influence of unorganized interests. Not only censor-
ship and distortion in the channels of communication but inadequate coverage may prevent the assertion of claims based upon the
interests of potential groups. There are indications, for example,
that one reason for the improvements in recent years in the treatment of Negroes in the United States is that most of them are
likely to know when one of their number is dealt with in a manner
seriously violating the "rules of the game" and that many will act
on the basis of such information.[19]   Successive claims of this sort
in defense of the "rules of the game" not only may check the
specific violations but also may strengthen the affected interests
throughout the society. In the absence of adequate communication, restraints upon governmental acts that violate widespread

[17] Pendleton Herring: "The Politics of Fiscal Policy," *Yale Law Journal*,
Vol. 47, No. 5 (March, 1938), pp. 737–38.
[18] M. Brewster Smith: "Personal Values as Determinants of a Political
Attitude," *The Journal of Psychology*, Vol. 28 (1949), pp. 477–86.
[19] See Arnold and Caroline Rose: *America Divided: Minority Group Relations in the United States* (New York: Alfred A. Knopf, Inc., 1948), p. 192.

unorganized interests must rely upon officials' "memberships" in the potential groups. While these "memberships" are not to be discounted, without the likelihood of additional support they may be too weak to effect significant restraints.

Broadly speaking, the communications channels include not only the media but also group organizations to facilitate the expression of claims. Not only freedom of speech and of the press, but also the third in the classic triumvirate, freedom of assembly, is essential to the activation of unorganized interests. These freedoms are parts of the "rules of the game" in a representative democracy and at the same time are essential elements in the continued vitality of the unorganized interests. Obstacles to organization not only may obstruct communication but, by frustrating expectations based on the "rules of the game," may even weaken attachment to segments of the governmental institution. One of the most serious consequences of the courts' restrictive interpretations of the law in cases dealing with the organization of labor, especially between the 1890s and the 1930s, was workers' loss of confidence in the judiciary, reflected in a very general and not wholly unwarranted assumption that judges would not deal "fairly" with workers' attempts to organize.[20]

Since the major target for the claims of extensive potential groups is the institution of government, the established governmental patterns may operate to weaken the effect of widespread interests. Peculiarities of structure may so restrict and dam up the channels of adjustment that the "justice" interest may conflict with the claim for nonviolent change. Such a situation in the society as a whole is not materially different from those we have discussed in connection with particular organized interest groups. Just as the structure of the American Federation of Labor in the 1920s and early 1930s was poorly representative of the dynamic elements within the group and among workers generally, so conventional patterns within the institution of government may be so rigid that they undermine the acceptance of representative methods of peaceful change. Established patterns of access, defended and rationalized in terms of the ambiguous "rules of the game," may block the assertion of claims based on alternative interpretations of widely held interests.

Adequate research has never been done on the incidence of widespread unorganized interests and on the extent to which they

[20] Millis and Montgomery: *Organized Labor*, pp. 669–70.

are central in the attitude hierarchies of various segments of the population.   Such research needs to be carried on not only in terms of demographic aggregates, but also on the basis of classifications that reflect the relative power of individuals and organized groups.[21]   The methods for such research are not fully developed, but existing techniques could provide far more information than is presently available.   Though adequate evidence of this sort is not at hand, however, it seems probable that the widespread unorganized interests are adequately strong within power centers in and outside the government in the United States.   If this assumption is valid, dangers to the continuance of representative government derive less from lack of basic support for these interests than from other features of the political system.

Perhaps the outstanding characteristic of American politics, as we have noted earlier, is that it involved a multiplicity of co-ordinate or nearly co-ordinate points of access to governmental decisions.   The significance of these many points of access and of the complicated texture of relationships among them is great. This diversity assures a variety of modes for the participation of interest groups in the formation of policy, a variety that is a flexible, stabilizing element.   On the other hand, multiple and generally co-ordinate lines of access mean that the locus of initiative in the making of policy is not sharply defined and that the necessity for maintaining a certain comity among many of these points of control—especially in the legislature, the executive, and the political parties—may promote delay and inaction.[22]   In times of undramatized crisis, as in the diplomatic maneuvers in the months prior to a war or in the early phases of a severe inflation, delay or stalemate may have consequences that will threaten the stability of the system.   The peculiarities of American government have not prevented it from dealing with admitted crises of war and depression, but they may keep it from preventing or avoiding such severe tests of its capacity to survive.

Overlapping membership among organized interest groups and among these and potential groups is, as we have seen, the principal balancing force in the politics of a multigroup society such as the United States.   We have further observed that these unifying

[21] See Almond: *The American People and Foreign Policy*, Chap. 6; Avery Leiserson: "Opinion Research and the Political Process," *Public Opinion Quarterly*, Vol. 13, No. I (Spring, 1949), pp. 31–38; Truman: "Political Behavior and Voting."

[22] Cf. Almond: *The American People and Foreign Policy*, pp. 144–45.

widespread interests are not always mutually consistent and unambiguous. Variations in group experiences and, consequently, in frames of reference invite differences in the importance attached to these partially inconsistent interests, and their ambiguity permits divergent rationalizations in terms of these diversified frames of reference. Thus if the society has developed great differences in personal wealth, egalitarian demands may be rated above the claims of peaceful change by those in less privileged positions; and orderly adjustment may be regarded as more important than freedom of speech or assembly by those whose economic status is high. Each segment, moreover, can rationalize its preferences in terms of its own view of "fairness" and "individual dignity."

It follows that the stabilizing effects of overlapping memberships may be limited or eliminated if they operate primarily or exclusively within sharply defined social strata or classes that are characterized in part by the specialized priorities and meanings they give the widespread and ambiguous interests. An extreme hypothetical example may clarify this point. Assume a situation in which virtually all interaction takes place within social strata and in which there are few or no organized groups whose membership is drawn from more than one class. Overlapping memberships then would tend to reconcile differences within rather than between social levels. Since individuals group experiences would largely be confined to a single stratum of the society, definitions of potential group interests, such as the proper limits to freedom of speech, would vary sharply from one social level to another. Moreover, if experiences were confined within class lines in this fashion, freedom of speech, for example, might be valued highly in one class but be regarded as dispensable in another. In such a case overlapping memberships in a potential "free speech" group might not effectively moderate conflicts between organized interest groups whose members were drawn exclusively from different social classes.

Reference to such a state of affairs is often implied in banal political phrases about "human rights versus property rights." The appearance of such statements in political discourse does not necessarily mark the demise of effective overlapping and may signify the reverse. But genuine stratification of memberships and of the limiting "rules," combined with restricted movement from one stratum to another, might weaken a system like that in America long before, or even without, the emergence of class warfare in the crude Marxist sense. Widespread interests might then fail to restrict the activities of antagonistic organized groups belonging to different classes, and differing interpretations of these "rules" might instead become sources of conflict *between* strata of the society.

The problems presented by rigid stratification are somewhat akin to those implied in the frequently expressed concern over any weakening of civilian control over our growing military establishment. A group of professional military officers, recruited at an early age, trained outside of civilian institutions, and practising the profession of arms in comparative isolation from other segments of the society, easily may develop the characteristics of a caste. Such a group not only will generate its own peculiar interests but also may arrive at interpretations of the "rules of the game" that are at great variance with those held by most of the civilian population. In such a case multiple membership in other organized groups is slight and that in potential widespread groups is unlikely.

The dynamics and power implications of class stratification in the United States are largely unexplored territory.[23]   Vagueness of class lines, however, and a concomitant mobility from class to class have been marked characteristics of American society almost from its beginnings. There is some evidence that ease of mobility may be less great now than in times past, and occasionally it is asserted that the society shows a trend toward division into two sharply separate classes. The criteria of social class are not sufficiently established to justify such assertions, and adequate data on such supposed trends have never been collected.[24]

The expectations implied by the widespread unorganized interests characteristic of the United States would seem to require the existence of a great many patterns of interaction that cut across, or are independent of, class lines. If this be true, then any tendency for organized interest groups of the association type to operate within class lines or to be much more numerous in some classes of the population than in others may be a source of political instability. Evidence on this score is not altogether satisfactory, partly owing to the wide variety of senses in which the word "class" is used. Several bodies of data, however, indicate: (1) that the frequency of membership in formal organizations of the association type increases from the lower to the upper reaches of the

[23] Edward Shils: *The Present State of American Sociology* (Glencoe, Ill.: The Free Press, 1948), pp. 15–25.

[24] See, for example, the statement in Centers: *The Psychology of Social Classes*, p. 74.

class structure, and (2) that the members of many, if not most, such groups are drawn from the same or closely similar status levels.[25] At the same time, the findings of Warner and his associates in Newburyport led them to conclude that the number of formal organizations that cut across several classes and that facilitated social mobility served as an important unifying influence in the community.[26]

The specialization of organized interest groups along class lines and the atrophy or deficiency of such groups in the less privileged classes may be a source of political instability for at least two reasons. In the first place, organized interest groups normally provide standardized procedures for asserting group claims and for settling conflicts. Established interest organizations, moreover, may be presumed to have conformed in some measure to the interests of potential groups in the community. Segments of the population that lack such organized means of participation in the political process may none the less experience drastic changes in expected relationships, changes that may result in their making increased demands upon the political institutions. In the absence of standardized means of participation they may more readily identify with movements that poorly reflect widespread unorganized interests or that explicitly repudiate portions of them. Extensive unemployment and severe inflation bring such drastic changes, and the history of movements of the fascist type illustrates the destructive forms that such situations can produce. In the second place, even where the widespread unorganized interests are strong enough to prevent the emergence of a movement of the sort just mentioned, specialization of organized groups in certain classes of the population may provide a pattern of governmental access in which only those groups reflecting a particular class interpretation of the broad interests can gain expression through the governmental institutions. The emergence in the disadvantaged classes of groups that reflect materially different interpretations of the widespread interests may encourage conflict and at the same time provide an inadequate basis for peaceful settlement. The

[25] Warner and Lunt: *The Social Life of a Modern Community*, Chap. 16; Lazarsfeld, *et al.: The People's Choice*, pp. 145–47. For some suggestions on the reasons for less working-class participation in formal organizations see Seymour Bellin and Frank Riessman, Jr.: "Education, Culture and the Anarchic Worker," *Journal of Social Issues*, Vol. 5, No. 1 (Winter, 1949), pp. 24–32.

[26] Warner and Lunt: *The Social Life of a Modern Community*, pp. 114ff., 301ff.

appearance of groups representing Negroes, especially in the South, groups whose interpretations of the "rules of the game" are divergent from those of the previously organized and privileged segments of the community, are a case in point.[27] Caste and class interpretations of widespread unorganized interests may be at least as ready a source of instability as conflicts between more restricted organized groups.

This rather cursory examination suggests that a pathogenic politics in the United States is possible, though not necessarily imminent. The processes through which unorganized interests restrain the activities of organized groups may not become operative in time to avert serious crises. Potential groups may remain latent as a result of deficiencies in the means of communication. The claims of both organized and unorganized interests may assume an explosive character as a result of restraints upon the ability to organize, in consequence of rigidity in the established patterns of access, and as an outgrowth of delay and inaction made possible by the diffusion of lines of access to governmental decisions. The frustration of group claims may be dangerously prolonged and the bitterness of group conflict may be intensified through class interpretations of the "rules of the game." Similarly, the expectations of groups emerging out of the less privileged segments of the society may be poorly represented or dangerously frustrated in consequence of the concentration of, and privileged access of, organized groups among persons of higher status.

These factors are obviously not the only ones that might lead to a disruption of representative government in the United States. Others might be mentioned, but it is not the purpose of these pages to develop a complete theory of the process of revolution as it might operate in America.[28] We are here merely interested in pointing out that no political system is proof against such upheaval and concerned with noting what kinds of connections may exist between the development of a revolutionary crisis and the presence of a multiplicity of highly organized interest groups. None of the

---

[27] Cf. Myrdal: *An American Dilemma* (New York: Harper, Row, 1944), Chap. 1 and *passim;* Williams: *The Reduction of Intergroup Tensions*, pp. 62–63.

[28] Among the most suggestive treatments of this subject are Crane Brinton: *The Anatomy of Revolution* (New York: W. W. Norton & Company, Inc., 1938); Lyford P. Edwards: *The Natural History of Revolution* (Chicago: University of Chicago Press, 1927); George S. Pettee: *The Process of Revolution* (New York: Harper and Brothers, 1938); and Pitrim Sorokin: *The Sociology of Revolution* (Philadelphia: J. B. Lippincott Company, 1925).

factors of instability discussed in the preceding paragraphs is inherently a consequence of the existence of such groups. The crucial element in all of them is the relationship of these groups and of the established patterns of access to the widespread potential groups in the society. This relationship in each instance may become morbid either because the unorganized interests are inadequately activated or because recurrent and prolonged frustration of more restricted claims leads to the rejection of a large segment of the "rules of the game." In a healthy political system there is a connection between some minimum recognition of the claims of organized groups and the vitality of widespread unorganized interests. Without such recognition, the latter cease to be accepted as "rules of the game." As Hartz has observed in somewhat different terms: "Norms of policy that recognize nothing but the interplay of [organized] interest pressures are inadequate; but norms that scarcely recognize them at all lead directly to a disillusionment with the political process."[29] The continued strength of civil liberties, representative techniques, and other widespread interests requires that support of these "rules" not become identified with the prolonged frustration of organized group demands.[30]

The strength of the unorganized "rules of the game" in the United States has been remarked by foreign observers from De Tocqueville to Myrdal. The latter, for example, speaks of them as being more "explicitly expressed" and "more widely understood and appreciated" in America than in other Western nations.[31] The great political task now as in the past is to perpetuate a viable system by maintaining the conditions under which such widespread understanding and appreciation can exist. These conditions are not threatened by the existence of a multiplicity of organized groups so long as the "rules of the game" remain meaningful guides to action, meaningful in the sense that acceptance of them is associated with some minimal recognition of group claims. In the loss of such meanings lie the seeds of the whirlwind.

[29] Louis Hartz: *Economic Policy and Democratic Thought* (Cambridge, Mass.: Harvard University Press, 1948), p. 310.

[30] There is a resemblence between the position taken in these pages and the concept of *anomie*. For an acute analysis of the political implication of Durkheim's theory, see Sebastian de Grazia: *The Political Community, op. cit.*

[31] Gunnar Myrdal: *An American Dilemma, op. cit.*, p. 3. For similar comments, see Alexis de Tocqueville: *Democracy in America* (New York: Alfred Knopf, 1945), Vol. 1, pp. 196–98.

BECAUSE OF THE ABSENCE OF GENUINE "PUBLICS," CLASHING *political parties, civil servants of independence and integrity, and organized opposition movements bearing their own vision of things as they ought to be, misplaced images of the past serve to justify a prevailing order in which a power elite has risen to ascendance. Mills, one of America's few independent and original social theorists in recent times, argues that the United States, since the Second World War, has become a militarized capitalist country with a permanent-war economy. The means of power—economic production, violence, and political administration—have become enlarged, centralized, and increasingly coordinated and inseparable in the new political economy.*

The three institutional orders—economic, political, and military—are joined in numerous ways into a triangle of power: the corporation executives, the political directorate, and the high military. As their domains increasingly coincide, as their decisions take on historical significance, and as the traffic between the three becomes frequent, they emerge as the power elite.

As a result of the country's economy being internally dominated by a few hundred corporations that are administratively and politically interrelated, the country's economic decisions are made by corporation men who moved into the area of political direction during World War II. The apparently permanent military threat has fostered the ascendance of the higher military to a firm position of power among the power elite. This threat has also made it possible for military definitions of reality to become the standard of judgment for virtually all political and economic actions.

The unity of the elite rests on their psychological similarity and social intermingling; their common backgrounds, interests, and perceptions; upon the intertwining of the institutional orders over which they preside; and upon "explicit coordination." The elite have taken advantage of the fact that their several interests can be realized through informal and formal arrangements. The so-called "veto groups" and "countervailing powers" have been relegated to the realm of the middle levels of power. The expanding hierarchies of the power elite replaced the old balance that included these groups.

Responsible parties representing and clarifying policies do not exist; major decisions of war and peace are made in secret, with citizens knowing little about them and affecting them even less. The independent organizations which exist are either ineffective or irrelevant; the mass organizations, to the extent that they have become effective (and, therefore, larger), have become inaccessible to indi-

338

vidual influence.   These mass organizations are controlled from the top and integrated in many ways into the prevailing order dominated by the power elite.

The decline of the old middle class of independent proprietors; the ascendance of the dependent new middle class (atomized and unorganized even on an economic level); the end of labor insurgence; and the decline of politics in mid-twentieth century America are among the factors involved in creating the situation in which the power elite has established itself.   The ideal of democracy, Mills believes, has become a legitimation of its opposite.   Unified at the top, drifting and stalemated in the middle, and politically fragmented at the bottom, American society has become a mass society.

28

THE STRUCTURE OF POWER IN AMERICAN SOCIETY

C. Wright Mills

I

Power has to do with whatever decisions men make about the arrangements under which they live, and about the events which make up the history of their times.   Events that are beyond

Reprinted from Irving Louis Horowitz, ed., *Power, Politics and People: The Collected Essays of C. Wright Mills* (New York: Oxford University Press, Ballantine Books, 1963), pp. 23–38.   Reprinted by permission of Oxford University Press, Inc.   Copyright © 1963 by the Estate of C. Wright Mills.

human decision do happen; social arrangements do change without benefit of explicit decision.   But in so far as such decisions are made, the problem of who is involved in making them is the basic problem of power.   In so far as they could be made but are not, the problem becomes who fails to make them?

We cannot today merely assume that in the last resort men must always be governed by their own consent.   For among the means of power which now prevail is the power to manage and to manipulate the consent of men.   That we do not know the limits of such power, and that we hope it does have limits, does not remove the fact that much power today is successfully employed without the sanction of the reason or the conscience of the obedient.

Surely nowadays we need not argue that, in the last resort, coercion is the "final" form of power.   But then, we are by no means constantly at the last resort.   Authority (power that is justified by the beliefs of the voluntarily obedient) and manipulation (power that is wielded unbeknown to the powerless)—must also be considered, along with coercion.   In fact, the three types must be sorted out whenever we think about power.

In the modern world, we must bear in mind, power is often not so authoritative as it seemed to be in the medieval epoch: ideas which justify rulers no longer seem so necessary to their exercise of power.   At least for many of the great decisions of our time—especially those of an international sort—mass "persuasion" has not been "necessary"; the fact is simply accomplished.   Furthermore, such ideas as are available to the powerful are often neither taken up nor used by them.   Such ideologies usually arise as a response to an effective debunking of power; in the United States such opposition has not been effective enough recently to create the felt need for new ideologies of rule.

There has, in fact, come about a situation in which many who have lost faith in prevailing loyalties have not acquired new ones, and so pay no attention to politics of any kind.   They are not radical, not liberal, not conservative, not reactionary.   They are inactionary.   They are out of it.   If we accept the Greek's definition of the idiot as an altogether private man, then we must conclude that many American citizens are now idiots.   And I should not be surprised, although I do not know, if there were not some such idiots even in Germany.   This—and I use the word with care—this spiritual condition seems to me the key to many modern troubles of political intellectuals, as well as the key to much political bewilderment in modern society. Intellectual "conviction" and moral "belief" are not necessary, in either the rulers or the ruled, for a ruling power to persist and even to flourish. So far as the role of ideologies is concerned, their frequent absences and the prevalence of mass indifference are surely two of the major political facts about the western societies today.

How large a role any explicit decisions do play in the making of history is itself an historical problem. For how large that role may be depends very much upon the means of power that are available at any given time in any given society. In some societies, the innumerable actions of innumerable men modify their milieux, and so gradually modify the structure itself. These modifications—the course of history—go on behind the backs of men. History is drift, although in total "men make it." Thus innumerable entrepreneurs and innumerable consumers by ten-thousand decisions per minute may shape and re-shape the free-market economy. Perhaps this was the chief kind of limitation Marx had in mind when he wrote, in *The 18th Brumaire* that: "Men make their own history, but they do not make it just as they please; they do not make it under circumstances chosen by themselves. . . ."

But in other societies—certainly in the United States and in the Soviet Union today—a few men may be so placed within the structure that by their decisions they modify the milieux of many other men, and in fact nowadays the structural conditions under which most men live. Such elites of power also make history under circumstances not chosen altogether by themselves, yet compared with other men, and compared with other periods of world history, these circumstances do indeed seem less limiting.

I should contend that "men are free to make history," but that some men are indeed much freer than others. For such freedom requires access to the means of decision and of power by which history can now be made. It has not always been so made; but in the later phases of the modern epoch it is. It is with reference to this epoch that I am contending that if men do not make history, they tend increasingly to become the utensils of history-makers as well as the mere objects of history.

The history of modern society may readily be understood as the story of the enlargement and the centralization of the means of power—in economic, in political, and in military institutions. The rise of industrial society has involved these developments in the means of economic production. The rise of the nation-state has involved similar developments in the means of violence and in those of political administration.

In the western societies, such transformations have generally occurred gradually, and many cultural traditions have restrained and shaped them. In most of the Soviet societies, they are happening very rapidly indeed and without the great discourse of western civilization, without the Renaissance and without the Reformation, which so greatly strengthened and gave political focus to the idea of freedom. In those societies, the enlargement and the co-ordination of all the means of power has occurred more brutally, and from the beginning under tightly centralized authority. But in both types, the means of power have now become international in scope and similar in form. To be sure, each of them has its own ups and downs; neither is as yet absolute; how they are run differs quite sharply.

Yet so great is the reach of the means of violence, and so great the economy required to produce and support them, that we have in the immediate past witnessed the consolidation of these two world centers, either of which dwarfs the power of Ancient Rome. As we pay attention to the awesome means of power now available to quite small groups of men we come to realize that Caesar could do less with Rome than Napoleon with France; Napoleon less with France then Lenin with Russia. But what was Caesar's power at its height compared with the power of the changing inner circles of Soviet Russia and the temporary administrations of the United States? We come to realize—indeed they continually remind us—how a few men have access to the means by which in a few days continents can be turned into thermonuclear wastelands. That the facilities of power are so enormously enlarged and so decisively centralized surely means that the powers of quite small groups of men, which we may call elites, are now of literally inhuman consequence.

My concern here is not with the international scene but with the United States in the middle of the twentieth century. I must emphasize "in the middle of the twentieth century" because in our attempt to understand any society we come upon images which have been drawn from its past and which often confuse our attempt to confront its present reality. That is one minor reason why history is the shank of any social science: we must study it if only to rid ourselves of it. In the United States, there are indeed many such images and usually they have to do with the first half of the nineteenth century. At that time the economic facilities of the United States were very widely dispersed and subject to little or to no central authority. The state watched in the night but was without decisive voice in the day. One man meant one rifle and the militia were without centralized orders.

Any American, as old-fashioned as I, can only agree with R. H. Tawney that "Whatever the future may contain, the past has shown no more excellent social order than that in which the mass of the people were the masters of the holdings which they ploughed and the tools with which they worked, and could boast . . . 'It is a quietness to a man's mind to live upon his own and to know his heir certain.'"

But then we must immediately add: all that is of the past and of little relevance to our understanding of the United States today. Within this society three broad levels of power may now be distinguished. I shall begin at the top and move downward.

II

The power to make decisions of national and international consequence is now so clearly seated in political, military, and economic institutions that other areas of society seem off to the side and, on occasion, readily subordinated to these. The scattered institutions of religion, education and family are increasingly shaped by the big three, in which history-making decisions now regularly occur. Behind this fact there is all the push and drive of a fabulous technology; for these three institutional orders have incorporated this technology and now guide it, even as it shapes and paces their development.

As each has assumed its modern shape, its effects upon the other two have become greater, and the traffic between the three has increased. There is no longer, on the one hand, an economy, and, on the other, a political order, containing a military establishment unimportant to politics and to money-making. There is a political economy numerously linked with military order and decision. This triangle of power is now a structural fact, and it is the key to any understanding of the higher circles in America today. For as each of these domains has coincided with the others, as decisions in each have become broader, the leading men of each—the high military, the corporation executives, the political directorate—have tended to come together to form the power elite of America.

The political order, once composed of several dozen states with a weak federal center, has become an executive apparatus which has taken up into itself many powers previously scattered, legislative as well as administrative, and which now reaches into all parts of the social structure. The long-time tendency of business and government to become more closely connected has, since World War II, reached a new point of explicitness. Neither can now be seen clearly as a distinct world. The growth of executive government does not mean merely the "enlargement of government" as some kind of autonomous bureaucracy; under American conditions, it has meant the ascendancy of the corporation man into political eminence. Already during the New Deal, such men had joined the political directorate; as of World War II they came to dominate it. Long involved with government, now they have moved into quite full direction of the economy of the war effort and of the post-war era.

The economy, once a great scatter of small productive units in somewhat automatic balance, has become internally dominated by a few hundred corporations, administratively and politically interrelated, which together hold the keys to economic decision. This economy is at once a permanent-war economy and a private-corporation economy. The most important relations of the corporation to the state now rest on the coincidence between military and corporate interests, as defined by the military and the corporate rich, and accepted by politicians and public. Within the elite as a whole, this coincidence of military domain and corporate realm strengthens both of them and further subordinates the merely political man. Not the party politician, but the corporation executive, is now more likely to sit with the military to answer the question: what is to be done?

The military order, once a slim establishment in a context of civilian distrust, has become the largest and most expensive feature of government; behind smiling public relations, it has all the grim and clumsy efficiency of a great and sprawling bureaucracy. The high military have gained decisive political and economic relevance. The seemingly permanent military threat places a premium upon them and virtually all political and economic actions are now judged in terms of military definitions of reality; the higher military have ascended to a firm position within the power elite of our time.

In part, at least, this is a result of an historical fact, pivotal for the years since 1939: the attention of the elite has shifted from domestic problems—centered in the thirties around slump—to international problems—centered in the forties and fifties around war. By long historical usage, the government of the United States has been shaped by domestic clash and balance; it does not have suitable agencies and traditions for the democratic handling of international affairs. In considerable part, it is in this vacuum that the power elite has grown.

1. To understand the unity of this power elite, we must pay attention to the psychology of its several members in their respective milieux. In so far as the power elite is composed of men of similar origin and education, of similar career and style of life, their unity may be said to rest upon the fact that they are of similar social type, and to lead to the fact of their easy intermingling. This kind of unity reaches its frothier apex in the sharing of that prestige which is to be had in the world of the celebrity. It achieves a more solid culmination in the fact of the interchangeability of positions between the three dominant institutional orders. It is revealed by considerable traffic of personnel within and between these three, as well as by the rise of specialized go-betweens as in the new style high-level lobbying.

2. Behind such psychological and social unity are the structure and the mechanics of those institutional hierarchies over which the political directorate, the corporate rich, and the high military now preside. How each of these hierarchies is shaped and what relations it has with the others determine in large part the relations of their rulers. Were these hierarchies scattered and disjointed, then their respective elites might tend to be scattered and disjointed; but if they have many interconnections and points of coinciding interest, then their elites tend to form a coherent kind of grouping. The unity of the elite is not a simple reflection of the unity of institutions, but men and institutions are always related; that is why we must understand the elite today in connection with such institutional trends as the development of a permanent-war establishment, alongside a privately incorporated economy, inside a virtual political vacuum. For the men at the top have been selected and formed by such institutional trends.

3. Their unity, however, does not rest solely upon psychological similarity and social intermingling, nor entirely upon the structural blending of commanding positions and common interests. At times it is the unity of a more explicit co-ordination.

To say that these higher circles are increasingly co-ordinated, that this is *one* basis of their unity, and that at times—as during open war—such co-ordination is quite wilful, is not to say that the co-ordination is total or continuous, or even that it is very sure-footed.   Much less is it to say that the power elite has emerged as the realization of a plot.   Its rise cannot be adequately explained in any psychological terms.

Yet we must remember that institutional trends may be defined as opportunities by those who occupy the command posts. Once such opportunities are recognized, men may avail themselves of them.   Certain types of men from each of these three areas, more far-sighted than others, have actively promoted the liaison even before it took its truly modern shape.   Now more have come to see that their several interests can more easily be realized if they work together, in informal as well as in formal ways, and accordingly they have done so.

The idea of the power elite is of course an interpretation.   It rests upon and it enables us to make sense of major institutional trends, the social similarities and psychological affinities of the men at the top.   But the idea is also based upon what has been happening on the middle and lower levels of power, to which I now turn.

III

There are of course other interpretations of the American system of power.   The most usual is that it is a moving balance of many competing interests.   The image of balance, at least in America, is derived from the idea of the economic market: in the nineteenth century, the balance was thought to occur between a great scatter of individuals and enterprises; in the twentieth century, it is thought to occur between great interest blocs.   In both views, the politician is the key man of power because he is the broker of many conflicting powers.

I believe that the balance and the compromise in American society—the "countervailing powers" and the "veto groups," of parties and associations, of strata and unions—must now be seen as having mainly to do with the middle levels of power.   It is these middle levels that the political journalist and the scholar of politics are most likely to understand and to write about—if only because, being mainly middle class themselves, they are closer to them. Moreover these levels provide the noisy content of most "political" news and gossip; the images of these levels are more or less in accord with the folklore of how democracy works; and, if the master-image of balance is accepted, many intellectuals, especially in their current patrioteering, are readily able to satisfy such political optimism as they wish to feel.   Accordingly, liberal inter-pretations of what is happening in the United States are now virtually the only interpretations that are widely distributed.

But to believe that the power system reflects a balancing society is, I think, to confuse the present era with earlier times, and to confuse its top and bottom with its middle levels.

By the top levels, as distinguished from the middle, I intend to refer, first of all, to the scope of the decisions that are made. At the top today, these decisions have to do with all the issues of war and peace.   They have also to do with slump and poverty which are now so very much problems of international scope.   I intend also to refer to whether or not the groups that struggle politically have a chance to gain the positions from which such top decisions are made, and indeed whether their members do usually hope for such top national command.   Most of the com-peting interests which make up the clang and clash of American politics are strictly concerned with their slice of the existing pie. Labor unions, for example, certainly have no policies of an inter-national sort other than those which given unions adopt for the strict economic protection of their members; neither do farm organizations.   The actions of such middle-level powers may indeed have consequence for top-level policy; certainly at times they hamper these policies.   But they are not truly concerned with them, which means of course that their influence tends to be quite irresponsible.

The facts of the middle levels may in part be understood in terms of the rise of the power elite.   The expanded and centralized and interlocked hierarchies over which the power elite preside have encroached upon the old balance and relegated it to the middle level.   But there are also independent developments of the middle levels.   These, it seems to me, are better understood as an affair of entrenched and provincial demands than as a center of national decision.   As such, the middle level often seems much more of a stalemate than a moving balance.

1. The middle level of politics is not a forum in which there are debated the big decisions of national and international life. Such debate is not carried on by nationally responsible parties representing and clarifying alternative policies.   There are no such parties in the United States.   More and more, fundamental issues never come to any point or decision before the Congress,

much less before the electorate in party campaigns. In the case of Formosa, in the spring of 1955 the Congress abdicated all debate concerning events and decisions which surely bordered on war. The same is largely true of the 1957 crisis in the Middle East. Such decisions now regularly by-pass the Congress, and are never clearly focused issues for public decision.

The American political campaign distracts attention from national and international issues, but that is not to say that there are no issues in these campaigns. In each district and state, issues are set up and watched by organized interests of sovereign local importance. The professional politician is of course a party politician, and the two parties are semifeudal organizations: they trade patronage and other favors for votes and for protection. The differences between them, so far as national issues are concerned, are very narrow and very mixed up. Often each seems to be fifty parties, one to each state; and accordingly, the politician as campaigner and as Congressman is not concerned with national party lines, if any are discernible. Often he is not subject to any effective national party discipline. He speaks for the interests of his own constituency, and he is concerned with national issues only in so far as they affect the interests effectively organized there, and hence his chances of re-election. That is why, when he does speak of national matters, the result is so often such an empty rhetoric. Seated in his sovereign locality, the politician is not at the national summit. He is on and of the middle levels of power.

2. Politics is not an arena in which free and independent organizations truly connect the lower and middle levels of society with the top levels of decision. Such organizations are not an effective and major part of American life today. As more people are drawn into the political arena, their associations become mass in scale, and the power of the individual becomes dependent upon them; to the extent that they are effective, they have become larger, and to that extent they have become less accessible to the influence of the individual. This is a central fact about associations in any mass society; it is of most consequence for political parties and for trade unions.

In the thirties, it often seemed that labor would become an insurgent power independent of corporation and state. Organized labor was then emerging for the first time on an American scale, and the only political sense of direction it needed was the slogan, "organize the unorganized." Now without the mandate of the slump, labor remains without political direction. Instead of economic and political struggles it has become deeply entangled in administrative routines with both corporation and state. One of its major functions, as a vested interest of the new society, is the regulation of such irregular tendencies as may occur among the rank and file.

There is nothing, it seems to me, in the make-up of the current labor leadership to allow us to expect that it can or that it will lead, rather than merely react. In so far as it fights at all, it fights over a share of the goods of a single way of life and not over that way of life itself. The typical labor leader in the U.S.A. today is better understood as an adaptive creature of the main business drift than as an independent actor in a truly national context.

3. The idea that this society is a balance of powers requires us to assume that the units in balance are of more or less equal power and that they are truly independent of one another. These assumptions have rested, it seems clear, upon the historical importance of a large and independent middle class. In the latter nineteenth century and during the Progressive Era, such a class of farmers and small businessmen fought politically—and lost— their last struggle for a paramount role in national decision. Even then, their aspirations seemed bound to their own imagined past.

This old, independent middle class has of course declined. On the most generous count, it is now 40 percent of the total middle class (at most 20 percent of the total labor force). Moreover, it has become politically as well as economically dependent upon the state, most notably in the case of the subsidized farmer.

The *new* middle class of white-collar employees is certainly not the political pivot of any balancing society. It is in no way politically unified. Its unions, such as they are, often serve merely to incorporate it as hanger-on of the labor interest. For a considerable period, the old middle class *was* an independent base of power; the new middle class cannot be. Political freedom and economic security *were* anchored in small and independent properties; they are not anchored in the worlds of the white-collar job. Scattered property holders were economically united by more or less free markets; the jobs of the new middle class are integrated by corporate authority. Economically, the white-collar classes are in the same condition as wage workers; politically, they are in a worse condition, for they are not organized. They are no vanguard of historic change; they are at best a rear-guard of the welfare state.

The agrarian revolt of the nineties, the small-business revolt that has been more or less continuous since the eighties, the labor revolt of the thirties—each of these has failed as an independent movement which could countervail against the powers that be; they have failed as politically autonomous third parties. But they have succeeded, in varying degree, as interests vested in the expanded corporation and state; they have succeeded as parochial interests seated in particular districts, in local divisions of the two parties, and in the Congress. What they would become, in short, are well-established features of the *middle* levels of balancing power, on which we may now observe all those strata and interests which in the course of American history have been defeated in their bids for top power or which have never made such bids.

Fifty years ago many observers thought of the American state as a mask behind which an invisible government operated. But nowadays, much of what was called the old lobby, visible or invisible, is part of the quite visible government. The "governmentalization of the lobby" has proceeded in both the legislative and the executive domain, as well as between them. The executive bureaucracy becomes not only the center of decision but also the arena within which major conflicts of power are resolved or denied resolution. "Administration" replaces electoral politics; the maneuvering of cliques (which include leading Senators as well as civil servants) replaces the open clash of parties.

The shift of corporation men into the political directorate has accelerated the decline of the politicians in the Congress to the middle levels of power; the formation of the power elite rests in part upon this relegation. It rests also upon the semiorganized stalemate of the interests of sovereign localities, into which the legislative function has so largely fallen; upon the virtually complete absence of a civil service that is a politically neutral but politically relevant, depository of brain-power and executive skill; and it rests upon the increased official secrecy behind which great decisions are made without benefit of public or even of Congressional debate.

IV

There is one last belief upon which liberal observers everywhere base their interpretations and rest their hopes. That is the idea of the public and the associated idea of public opinion. Conservative thinkers, since the French Revolution, have of course Viewed With Alarm the rise of the public, which they have usually called the masses, or something to that effect. "The populace is sovereign," wrote Gustave LeBon, "and the tide of barbarism mounts." But surely those who have supposed the masses to be well on their way to triumph are mistaken. In our time, the influence of publics or of masses within political life is in fact decreasing, and such influence as on occasion they do have tends, to an unknown but increasing degree, to be guided by the means of mass communication.

In a society of publics, discussion is the ascendant means of communication, and the mass media, if they exist, simply enlarge and animate this discussion, linking one face-to-face public with the discussions of another. In a mass society, the dominant type of communication is the formal media, and publics become mere markets for these media: the "public" of a radio program consists of all those exposed to it. When we try to look upon the United States today as a society of publics, we realize that it has moved a considerable distance along the road to the mass society.

In official circles, the very term, "the public," has come to have a phantom meaning, which dramatically reveals its eclipse. The deciding elite can identify some of those who clamor publicly as "Labor," others as "Business," still others as "Farmer." But these are not the public. "The public" consists of the unidentified and the nonpartisan in a world of defined and partisan interests. In this faint echo of the classic notion, the public is composed of these remnants of the old and new middle classes whose interests are not explicitly defined, organized, or clamorous. In a curious adaptation, "the public" often becomes, in administrative fact, "the disengaged expert," who, although never so well informed, has never taken a clear-cut and public stand on controversial issues. He is the "public" member of the board, the commission, the committee. What "the public" stands for, accordingly, is often a vagueness of policy (called "open-mindedness"), a lack of involvement in public affairs (known as "reasonableness"), and a professional disinterest (known as "tolerance").

All this is indeed far removed from the eighteenth century idea of the public of public opinion. The idea parallels the economic idea of the magical market. Here is the market composed for freely competing entrepreneurs; there is the public composed of circles of people in discussion. As price is the result of anonymous, equally weighted, bargaining individuals, so public opinion is the result of each man's having thought things out for himself and then contributing his voice to the great chorus. To be sure, some may have more influence on the state of opinion than others, but no one group monopolizes the discussion, or by itself determines the opinions that prevail.

In this classic image, the people are presented with problems. They discuss them. They formulate viewpoints. These viewpoints are organized, and they compete. One viewpoint "wins out." Then the people act on this view, or their representatives are instructed to act it out, and this they promptly do.

Such are the images of democracy which are still used as working justifications of power in America. We must now recognize this description as more a fairy tale than a useful approximation. The issues that now shape man's fate are neither raised nor decided by any public at large. The idea of a society that is at bottom composed of publics is not a matter of fact; it is the proclamation of an ideal, and as well the assertion of a legitimation masquerading as fact.

I cannot here describe the several great forces within American society as well as elsewhere which have been at work in the debilitation of the public. I want only to remind you that publics, like free associations, can be deliberately and suddenly smashed, or they can more slowly wither away. But whether smashed in a week or withered in a generation, the demise of the public must be seen in connection with the rise of centralized organizations, with all their new means of power, including those of the mass media of distraction. These, we now know, often seem to expropriate the rationality and the will of the terrorized or—as the case may be— the voluntarily indifferent society of masses. In the more democratic process of indifference, the remnants of such publics as remain may only occasionally be intimidated by fanatics in search of "disloyalty." But regardless of that, they lose their will for decision because they do not possess the instruments for decision; they lose their sense of political belonging because they do not belong; they lose their political will because they see no way to realize it.

The political structure of a modern democratic state requires that such a public as is projected by democratic theorists not only exist but that it be the very forum within which a politics of real issues is enacted.

It requires a civil service that is firmly linked with the world of knowledge and sensibility, and which is composed of skilled men who, in their careers and in their aspirations, are truly independent of any private, which is to say, corporation, interests.

It requires nationally responsible parties which debate openly and clearly the issues which the nation, and indeed the world, now so rigidly confronts.

It requires an intelligentsia, inside as well as outside the universities, who carry on the big discourse of the Western world, and whose work is relevant to and influential among parties and movements and publics.

And it certainly requires, as a fact of power, that there be free associations standing between families and smaller communities and publics, on the one hand, and the state, the military, the corporation, on the other. For unless these do exist, there are no vehicles for reasoned opinion, no instruments for the rational exertion of public will.

Such democratic formations are not now ascendant in the power structure of the United States, and accordingly the men of decision are not men selected and formed by careers within such associations and by their performance before such publics. The top of modern American society is increasingly unified, and often seems wilfully co-ordinated: at the top there has emerged an elite whose power probably exceeds that of any small group of men in world history. The middle levels are often a drifting set of stalemated forces: the middle does not link the bottom with the top. The bottom of this society is politically fragmented, and even as a passive fact, increasingly powerless: at the bottom there is emerging a mass society.

These developments, I believe, can be correctly understood neither in terms of the liberal nor the Marxian interpretation of politics and history. Both these ways of thought arose as guidelines to reflection about a type of society which does not now exist in the United States. We confront there a new kind of social structure, which embodies elements and tendencies of all modern society, but in which they have assumed a more naked and flamboyant prominence.

That does not mean that we must give up the ideals of these classic political expectations. I believe that both have been concerned with the problem of rationality and of freedom: liberalism, with freedom and rationality as supreme facts about the individual; Marxism, as supreme facts about man's role in the political making of history. What I have said here, I suppose, may be taken as an attempt to make evident why the ideas of freedom and of rationality now so often seem so ambiguous in the new society of the United States of America.

SWEEZY, ONE OF THE WORLD'S LEADING MARXIAN ECONOMISTS, *attempts to sketch the essential outlines of a theory of the "American ruling class." His concern is to lay bare the structure of that class, its internal sources of differentiation and integration, its international role, and its domestic methods of rule. Studies of the national class structure, especially of the upper economic strata, were virtually non-existent when this article was written 18 years ago (a situation in social science which has scarcely changed since, with the exceptions of the fundamental contribution of C. Wright Mills—especially in* The Power Elite—*and the valuable work recently done on the structure of the national upper class, by G. William Domhoff and Ferdinand Lundberg). Sweezy, therefore, is compelled to offer what is essentially a set of interlocking hypotheses concerning the structure and function of the ruling class in the United States, while the studies concerning many of the most important hypotheses are yet to be done.*

Social classes exist in the real world—not merely as categories in the heads of social scientists. They are made up, says Sweezy, of freely intermarrying families, the lines between them (however shady they may be) drawn on the basis of their position in the economic structure or property system. Classes vary historically in the extent of their cohesion, consciousness, organization, and autonomy; their memberships are relatively stable, but new members are always being added and old ones cast out. In the United States, the two fundamental classes are: the owners of the means of production (the large capitalists) and the wage workers directly engaged in production. Between them are ranged the so-called middle classes: the historically new and important strata of the "new middle class" of workers in administrative, professional, clerical and sales positions as employees of the large capitalist enterprises and the old middle class, or petite bourgeoisie, *of self employed owners of their tools and businesses.*

These economic *classes form the core of the* social *classes (the latter being modifications of the former) since intermarriage tends to integrate strata in the same general economic situation—strata that, nonetheless, differ in their technical relations to the system of production and distribution. The core of the ruling class is made up of big capitalists (and other big property owners, although capital is the decisive form of productive property). Within this class there is a national hierarchy of upper strata having their own local or regional economic bases, the most important ones being located in the largest and most important industrial and financial cities. They are integrated by personal and familial bonds, informal and formal associations, and by a network of institutional relations of which the largest corporations form the foundation. These corporations unify the ruling class, direct its activities, and shape its lines of authority throughout the country.*

The content of the ideology of this class is basically determined by its "class situation," but its ideas are standardized, articulated, and transmitted by newspapers and journals designed primarily for use by its members. The family and educational system perpetuates this structure from generation to generation. The capitalist class rules through its members in the economy's key positions—members who either (1) do the job themselves, (2) hire and fire those who do, or (3) pay for the upkeep of political machines to do the job for them. Divided by a myriad of financial, regional, and ideological differences, the members of the American ruling class are, nonetheless, integrated by their overriding common class interests in the preservation of the capitalist system and their ruling position in it.

29

THE AMERICAN RULING CLASS

Paul M. Sweezy

I

One *Monthly Review* reader, a graduate student of sociology at one of our larger universities, writes to the editors that "in the December and January issues your editorials used the term 'ruling class' no less than eighteen times." He thinks that "by using this term so repetitiously you lay yourselves open to the serious accusation of surface-scratching analysis only." Don't we, he asks, owe MR readers "a probing analysis of a concept that is so complex and crucial"?

It would be easy to answer that the concept of the ruling class is well established in Marxian theory and that we are merely trying to apply the ideas and methods of Marxism to the analysis of the current American scene. But our correspondent would probably not be satisfied. He would hardly deny the relevance of Marxian theory, but he might say that, after all, Marx wrote a century ago, that he never made a special study of the American ruling class even of his own day, and that in any case the free and easy use of theoretical abstractions can be very dangerous. Wouldn't it be better to drop the appeal to authority and tell MR readers what we mean

Reprinted from Paul M. Sweezy, *The Present As History: Essays and Reviews on Capitalism and Socialism* (New York: Monthly Review Press, 1962), pp. 120–38. Reprinted by permission of Monthly Review Press. Copyright 1953 by Paul M. Sweezy, Monthly Review Press. The selection was originally published as a two-part article in the May and June 1951 issues of *Monthly Review*.

by the "ruling class" in terms that will permit them to judge for themselves whether our usage is justified?

The challenge seems an eminently fair one, and in this article I shall attempt to meet it.

First, however, let me enter a disclaimer. I couldn't give complete answers even if I wanted to. "The American ruling class" is a big subject. An exhaustive study of it would involve a full-dress analysis of the past and present of American society as a whole. That is a job not for an individual or even a small group of individuals; it is a job for all American social scientists working together and over a long period of time. But unfortunately American social scientists, with but few exceptions, are not interested in studying the ruling class; on the contrary, this is a "sensitive" subject which they avoid like the plague. The result is that relatively little valuable work has been done on the ruling class. Some day the American Left will no doubt make good this deficiency, but in the meanwhile there's no use pretending it doesn't exist. In the course of writing this article, I have become even more acutely conscious of it than I was at the outset.

This doesn't mean that American social scientists have done no work at all on the subject of class. The founders of American sociology—men like Lester Ward and William Graham Sumner— were very much interested in classes and their role in American society and wrote a surprisingly large amount on the subject. And in recent years, sociologists and social anthropologists have made a considerable number of field studies of American communities, studies in which problems of social stratification have played a prominent part.

These field studies (of which the Lynds' *Middletown* was one of the first and also one of the best examples) contain a great deal of useful information, but they all suffer from one fatal defect from our present point of view: they are confined to single communities and have almost nothing to say about social classes on a nation-wide scale. Contemporary sociologists and social anthropologists seem, almost as if by common agreement, to have decided that national social classes are not a proper subject of investigation.

The American Left, of course, does not share this view; in fact, it has long been very much alive to the existence and importance of a national ruling class. And left-wing writers have contributed many studies which throw valuable light on the subject— such works as Harvey O'Connor's *Mellon's Millions* and *The Guggenheims*, Anna Rochester's *Rulers of America*, and Ferdinand

Lundberg's *America's Sixty Families*. But these left-wing works have been for the most part factual studies of particular aspects or elements of the ruling class. Generalizations about the ruling class as a whole have tended to run in terms of an oversimplified theory of Wall Street control of the country. This theory has many merits, especially for mass propaganda purposes, but it can hardly be considered an adequate substitute for a scientific analysis of the structure of the American ruling class.

General Characteristics of Social Classes

As an initial step it will be valuable to review the general characteristics of social classes, or in other words to establish the main outlines of a usable theory of social class.

The first thing to be stressed is that social classes are real living social entities; they are not artificial creations of the social scientist. This can best be explained by an illustration. Suppose a social scientist is analyzing a given population. He can divide it into "classes" by dozens of different criteria: for example, by height, by weight, and by color of hair. Each system of classification will yield different results. One person in the six-foot class will be in the 200-pound class and in the brown-hair class; another will be in the 150-pound class and the blond-hair class. By choosing his criteria appropriately the social scientist can thus divide the population up in all sorts of different ways, and any given division is his own artificial creation which may not matter at all to the people themselves. It is not so with social classes. The members of the population are keenly aware of the existence of social classes, of their belonging to one, of their desires to belong (or to avoid belonging) to another. If the social scientist wants to investigate social classes he has to take these facts as his starting point, and any attempt to impose artificial criteria of class membership will result only in confusion and failure. In others words, social classes are obstinate facts and not mere logical categories.

Recognition of this is the beginning of any attempt to deal seriously with social classes. In the past, American social scientists have been all too ready to deny the reality of social classes, to assume that they exist only in the mind of the observer. Fortunately, however, this is becoming less and less frequent. One great merit of recent sociological field work is that it has shown conclusively that America is a class society and that the American people know it is a class society. In this connection, the best-known work is that of Lloyd Warner and his various associates.   It is conveniently summarized in Warner, Meeker, and Eells, *Social Class in America* (1949), Chapter 1.   (The reader should be warned, however, that this book does not live up to its title: it is about social classes in individual communities and has only a limited usefulness from the point of view of the problems analyzed in this article.)

The fundamental unit of class membership is the family and not the individual.   The proof of this is simply that everyone is born into a certain class, the class to which his family belongs. The basic test of whether two families belong to the same class or not is the freedom with which they intermarry (either actually or potentially).

Families and their mutual relations are thus the stuff of a class system.   But this does not exclude individuals from a crucially important role in the functioning of the system.   Generally speaking, it is the activity (or lack of activity) of an individual which is responsible for the rise or fall of a family in the class pyramid.   The familiar American success story illustrates the process: the lower-class lad who marries at his own social level, then achieves wealth and by so doing establishes his children in the upper reaches of the social hierarchy.   But the process works both ways; there is also the man who loses his fortune and thereby plunges his family to the bottom of the social ladder. It should be noted that in nearly all cases the individual himself does not succeed in making a complete shift from one class to the other.   The *nouveau riche* is never fully accepted in his new social environment; and the man who loses his position never fully accepts his new environment.   It is only the families that in each case, and in the course of time, make the adjustment.

A social class, then, is made up of freely intermarrying families. But what is it that determines how many classes there are and where the dividing lines are drawn?   Generally speaking, the answer is obvious (and is borne out by all empirical investigations): the property system plays this key role.   The upper classes are the property-owning classes; the lower classes are the property-less classes.   This statement is purposely general in its formulation.   The number of classes and their relations to each other differ in different systems.   For example, there may be several upper classes based on different kinds as well as on different amounts of property.   We shall have to examine the American case more specifically.   But before we do this, we must note other things which hold pretty generally for all classes and class systems.

It would be a mistake to think of a class as perfectly homogeneous internally and sharply marked off from other classes. Actually, there is variety within the class; one class sometimes shades off very gradually and almost imperceptibly into another. We must therefore think of a class as being made up of a core surrounded by fringes which are in varying degrees attached to the core. A fringe may be more or less stable and have a well-defined function in relation to the class as a whole, or it may be temporary and accidental. Moreover, we must not think of all the class members (in either the family or the individual sense) as playing the same role in the class. Some are active, some passive; some leaders, some followers; and so on. Here we touch upon all the complex questions of class organization, cohesion, effectiveness, and the like. And finally, we must not imagine that all members of a class think and behave exactly alike. There are differences here too, though clearly the values and behavior norms of the class set fairly definite limits to the extent of these differences. A person who deviates too far from what the class considers acceptable is, so to speak, expelled from the class and is thenceforth treated as a renegade or deserter (the common use of the expression "traitor to his class" is symptomatic—and significant—in this connection).

In all these respects, of course, there is wide variation between different classes and class systems. Some classes are relatively homogeneous, well-defined, effectively organized, and to a high degree class-conscious. Others are loosely-knit, amorphous, lacking in organization, and hardly at all class-conscious. Further, some classes in the course of their life histories pass through different stages, in the course of which all these variables undergo more or less thorough changes. These are all problems to be investigated in the particular case; there are no general answers valid for all times and places.

One more point has to be noted before we turn to the American case. There is no such thing as a completely closed class system. All systems of which we have historical record display interclass mobility, both upwards and downwards. In some systems, however, mobility is difficult and slow; in others it is easy and rapid. A social class can be compared to a hotel which always has guests, some of whom are permanent residents and some transients. In a relatively static system, the average sojourn is long; arrivals and departures are infrequent, and the proportion of permanent residents is high. In a dynamic system, guests come and go all the time; the hotel is always full but always with new people who have only recently arrived and, except in a few cases, will soon depart.

The American Class System

The United States is a capitalist society, the purest capitalist society that [has] ever existed. It has no feudal hangovers to complicate the class system. Independent producers (working with their own means of production but without hired labor) there are, but both economically and socially they constitute a relatively unimportant feature of the American system. What do we expect the class structure of such a pure capitalist society to be?

Clearly, the two decisive classes are defined by the very nature of capitalism: the owners of the means of production (the capitalist class), and the wage laborers who set the means of production in motion (the working class). There is no doubt about the existence or importance of these two classes in America. Taken together they can be said to constitute the foundation of the American class system.

The foundation of a building, however, is not the whole building; nor does the American economic system contain only capitalists and workers. For one thing, as we have already noted, there are independent producers (artisans and small farmers), and to these we should add small shopkeepers and providers of services (for example, the proprietors of local gas stations). These people make up the lower middle class, or *petite bourgeoisie*, in the original sense of the term. For another thing, there are a variety of types which stand somewhere between the capitalists and the workers and cannot easily be classified with either: government and business bureaucrats, professionals, teachers, journalists, advertising men, and so on. These are often, and not inappropriately, called the new middle classes—"new" because of their spectacular growth, both absolutely and relatively to other classes, in the last 75 years or so. Finally, there are what are usually called declassed elements—bums, gamblers, thugs, prostitutes, and the like—who are not recognized in the official statistics but who nevertheless play an important role in capitalist society, especially in its political life.

Viewing the matter from a primarily economic angle, then, we could say that the American class structure consists of capitalists, lower middle class in the classical sense, new middle classes, workers, and declassed elements.   There is no doubt, however, that this is not a strictly accurate description of the actual living social classes which we observe about us.   If we apply the criterion of intermarriageability as a test of social class membership, we shall often find that people who from an economic standpoint belong to the new middle classes are actually on the same social level as the larger capitalists; that smaller capitalists are socially indistinguishable from a large proportion of the new middle classes; and that the working class includes without very much social distinction those who perform certain generally comparable kinds of labor, whether it be with their own means of production or with means of production belonging to others.

These considerations lead us to the following conclusion: the social classes which we observe about us are not *identical* with the economic classes of capitalist society.   They are rather *modifications* of the latter.   This is, I believe, an important point.   If we keep it firmly in mind we shall be able to appreciate the decisive role of the economic factor in the structure and behavior of social classes while at the same time avoiding an overmechanical (and hence false) economic determinism.

How shall we describe the actual social-class structure of America?   This is partly a matter of fact and partly a matter of convention, and on neither score is there anything that could be called general agreement among students of American society. Warner and his associates, for example, say that in a typical American community there are exactly six classes, to which they give the names upper-upper, lower-upper, upper-middle, lower-middle, upper-lower, and lower-lower.   There are a number of objections to this scheme, however.   It is based on studies of small cities; the dividing lines are largely arbitrary; and the labels suggest that the only important thing about classes is their position in relation to other classes.   Warner and his associates admit that there are some communities which lack one or more of the six classes they believe they found in "Jonesville" and "Yankee City"; and one hesitates to speculate on how many classes they might plausibly claim to find, by using essentially the same methods, in a really big city.   Their scheme, in other words, while representing a serious attempt to cope with the problem, is unsatisfactory.   Its inadequacy is particularly obvious when we attempt to pass beyond the individual community and deal with social classes on a national scale.

What we need is a scheme which both highlights the fundamental economic conditioning of the social-class system and at the same time is flexible enough to encompass the anomalies and irregularities which actually characterize it.

The starting point must surely be the recognition that two social classes, at bottom shaped by the very nature of capitalism, determine the form and content of the system as a whole. I prefer to call these classes the ruling class and the working class. The core of the ruling class is made up of big capitalists (or, more generally, big property owners, though the distinction is not very important since most large aggregates of property have the form of capital in this country today). There are numerous fringes to the ruling class, including smaller property owners, government and business executives (in so far as they are not big owners in their own right), professionals, and so on; we shall have more to say on this subject later. The core of the working class is made up of wage laborers who have no productive property of their own. Here again there are fringes, including, especially, independent craftsmen and petty traders.

The fringes of the ruling class do not reach to the fringes of the working class. Between the two there is a wide social space which is occupied by what we can hardly avoid calling the middle class. We should not forget, however, that the middle class is much more heterogeneous than either the ruling class or the working class. It has no solid core, and it shades off irregularly (and differently in different localities) into the fringes of the class above it and the class below it. Indeed we might say that the middle class consists of a collection of fringes, and that its social cohesion is largely due to the existence in all of its elements of a desire to be in the ruling class above it and to avoid being in the working class below it.

This generalized description of the social-class structure seems to me to have many merits and no fatal defects. The terminology calls attention to the chief functions of the basic classes and indicates clearly enough the relative positions of the three classes in the social hierarchy. More important, the use of the fringe concept enables us to face frankly the *fact* that the dividing lines in American society are not sharply drawn, and that even the borderlands are irregular and unstable. This fact is often seized upon to "prove" that there are *no* classes in America. It cannot be banished or hidden by the use of an elaborate multiclass scheme like that of Warner and his associates, for the simple reason that such a scheme, however well it may seem to apply to some situations, breaks down when applied to others.   What we must have is a scheme which takes full account of the fact in question without at the same time obscuring the fundamental outlines and character of the class system itself.

I shall next try to show that, at least as concerns the ruling class, the scheme proposed above does satisfy these requirements.

II

Every community study shows clearly the existence of an upper social crust which is based on wealth.   The nucleus is always the "old families" which have transmitted and usually augmented their fortunes from one generation to the next.   Around this nucleus are grouped the *nouveaux riches*, the solidly established lawyers and doctors, the more successful of the social climbers and sycophants, and people whose family connections are better than their bank accounts.   Taken all together, these are the people who comprise what is called "society."   Except in very large cities, the whole community is aware of their existence and knows that they constitute a more or less well-defined "upper class."

So much is obvious.   Certain other things, however, are not so obvious.   It is not obvious, for example, that these local "upper classes" are in fact merely sections of a national upper class, nor that this national upper class is in fact the national ruling class. What we shall have to concentrate on therefore are two points: first, the structure of the national ruling class; and second, how the ruling class rules.

The Structure of the National Ruling Class

That the local upper crusts are merely sections of a national class (also of an international class, but that is beyond the scope of the present article) follows from the way they freely mix and inter-marry.   The facts in this regard are well known to any reasonably attentive observer of American life, and no attempt at documenta-tion is called for here.   I merely suggest that those sociologists who believe that only field work can yield reliable data could provide valuable light on the mixing of the local upper crusts by a careful field study of a typical summer or winter resort.

The national ruling class, however, is not merely a collection of interrelated local upper crusts, all on a par with each other.   It is rather a hierarchy of upper crusts which has a fairly definite organizational structure, including lines of authority from leaders to followers. It is here that serious study of the ruling class is most obviously lacking, and also most urgently needed. I shall confine myself to a few hints and suggestions, some of which may turn out on closer investigation to be mistaken or at any rate out of proportion.

Generally speaking, the sections of the national ruling class are hierarchically organized with hundreds of towns at the bottom of the pyramid and a handful of very large cities at the top. Very small communities can be counted out: normally the wealth and standing of their leading citizens is no more than enough to gain them entry into the middle class when they go to the city. Even towns as large as five or ten thousand may have only a few representatives in good standing in the national ruling class. You can always tell such a representative. Typically, he is a man "of independent means"; he went to a good college; he has connections and spends considerable time in the state capital and/or the nearest big city; he takes his family for part of the year to a resort where it can enjoy the company of its social equals. And, most important of all, he is a person of unquestioned prestige and authority in his own community: he is, so to speak, a local lieutenant of the ruling class.

Cities, of course, have more—I should also judge proportionately more—national ruling-class members. And, as a rule, those who live in smaller cities look up to and seek guidance from and actually follow those who live in larger cities. Certain of these larger cities have in turn acquired the position of what we might call regional capitals (San Francisco, Chicago, Cleveland, Boston, and so on): the lines of authority in the given region run to and end in the capital. The relation which exists among these regional capitals is a very important subject which deserves careful study. There was a time in our national history when it would probably have been true to say that the sections of the ruling class in the regional capitals looked up to and sought guidance from and actually followed the New York section, and to a considerable extent this may still be the case. At any rate this is the kernel of truth in the Wall Street theory. My own guess, for what it is worth, is that economic and political changes in the last thirty years (especially changes in the structure and functions of the banking system and the expansion of the economic role of the state) have reduced the relative importance of New York to a marked degree, and that today it is more accurate to describe

New York as *primus inter pares* rather than as the undisputed leader of all the rest.

The ruling-class hierarchy is not based solely on personal or family relations among the members of the ruling class. On the contrary, it is bulwarked and buttressed by a massive network of institutional relations. Of paramount importance in this connection are the corporate giants with divisions, branches, and subsidiaries reaching out to all corners of the country. The American Telephone and Telegraph Company, with headquarters in New York and regional subsidiaries covering forty-eight states, is in itself a powerful force welding the unity of the American ruling class; and it is merely the best-developed example of its kind. Formerly, a very large proportion of these business empires were centered in New York, and it was this more than anything else that gave that city a unique position. Today that proportion is much reduced, and cities like Pittsburgh, Cleveland, Detroit, Chicago, and San Francisco play a relatively more prominent part than they used to. In addition to corporations, an integrating role in the ruling class is performed by businessmen's organizations like the National Association of Manufacturers, the Chambers of Commerce, the Rotary and other so-called service clubs; by colleges and their alumni associations; by churches and women's clubs; by scores of fashionable winter and summer resorts (not all located in this country); and by a myriad of other institutions too numerous even to attempt to list. (It will be noted that I have not mentioned the two great political parties in this connection. The reason is not that they don't to some extent play the part of an integrator of the ruling class: they do, and in a variety of ways. But their main function is quite different, namely, to provide the channels through which the ruling class manipulates and controls the lower classes. Compared to this function, their role *within* the ruling class is of quite secondary significance.)

Finally, we should note the key part played by the press in unifying and organizing the ruling class. To be sure, not all organs of the press figure here; the great majority, like the political parties, are instruments for controlling the lower classes. But the more solid kind of newspaper (of which the *New York Times* is, of course, the prototype), the so-called quality magazines, the business and technical journals, the high-priced newsletters and dopesheets—all of these are designed primarily for the ruling class and are tremendously important in guiding and shaping its thinking. This does not mean that they in some way make up or determine the *content* of ruling-class ideas—this content is basically determined by what I may call the class situation (about which more will be said presently)—but it does mean that they stand-ardize and propagate the ideas in such a way that the entire ruling class lives on a nearly uniform intellectual diet.

All of the formal and informal, the personal and institutional, ties that bind the ruling class together have a twofold character: on the one hand they are transmission belts and channels of com-munication; and on the other hand they are themselves molders of ideas and values and behavior norms—let us say for short, of ruling-class ideology. And here we have to note another mech-anism of the greatest importance, the mechanism by which the class passes its ideology on from one generation to the next. The key parts of this mechanism are the family and the educational system. Ruling-class families are jealous protectors and indoc-trinators of ruling-class ideology; the public school system faith-fully reflects it and even, contrary to popular beliefs, fosters class distinctions; and private preparatory schools and colleges finish the job of dividing the ruling-class young from their compatriots. (In this connection, we must not be confused by the fact that a considerable number of lower-class families succeed in getting their sons and daughters into the private preparatory schools and col-leges. This is merely a method by which the ruling class recruits the most capable elements of the lower classes into its service and often into its ranks. It is probably the most important such method in the United States today, having replaced the older method by which the abler lower-class young people worked their way directly up in the business world.)

How the Ruling Class Rules

Let us now turn, very briefly, to the question of how or in what sense the ruling class can be said to rule. This is a question which can easily lead to much mystification, but I think it can also be dealt with in a perfectly simple, straightforward way.

The question has two aspects: economic and political. The ruling class rules the economy in the sense that its members either directly occupy the positions in the economy where the key decisions are made or, if they don't occupy these positions them-selves, they hire and fire those who do. The ruling class rules the government (using the term as a shorthand expression for all levels of government) in the sense that its members either directly occupy the key positions (largely true in the higher judiciary and the more honorific legislative jobs, increasingly true in the higher administrative jobs), or they finance and thus indirectly control the political parties which are responsible for staffing and managing the routine business of government.   In short, the ruling class rules through its members who (1) do the job themselves, (2) hire and fire those who do, or (3) pay for the upkeep of political machines to do the job for them.   That this rule through the members of the class is in fact *class rule* does not require to be separately demonstrated; it follows from the nature and structure of the class as we have already analyzed them.

This analysis of the way the ruling class rules is, of course, sketchy and oversimplified.   I think nevertheless that it will stand up provided we can meet one objection, namely, that if the ruling class really ruled it would not put up with New Deals and Fair Deals and trade unions and John L. Lewises and Sidney Hillmans and all sorts of other outrages—*you* may not think them outrages, but the important thing from our present point of view is that the upper class *does* think them outrages.   I have found in lectures and conversations about the ruling class that this is by far the most important and frequent objection to this analysis.

A full answer, I think, would require a careful examination of the nature and limits of political power, something which obviously cannot be undertaken here.   But the main point is clearly indicated in the following passage from Lincoln Steffens's *Autobiography*.   The passage concludes a chapter entitled "Wall Street Again":

> It is a very common error to think of sovereignty as absolute.   Rasputin, a sovereign in Russia, made that mistake; many kings have made it and so lost their power to premiers and ministers who represented the "vested interests" of powerful classes, groups, and individuals. A dictator is never absolute.   Nothing is absolute.   A political boss concentrates in himself and personifies a very "wise" adjustment of the grafts upon which his throne is established.   He must know these, reckon their power, and bring them all to the support of his power, which is, therefore, representative and limited.   Mussolini, in our day, had to "deal with" the Church of Rome. A business boss has to yield to the powerful men who support him.   The Southern Pacific Railroad had to "let the

city grafters get theirs." The big bankers had to let the life insurance officers and employees get theirs. J. P. Morgan should have known what he soon found out, that he could not lick Diamond Jim Brady. Under a dictatorship nobody is free, not even the dictator; sovereign power is as representative as a democracy. It's all a matter of what is represented by His Majesty on the throne. In short, what I got out of my second period in Wall Street was this perception that everything I looked into in organized society was really a dictatorship, in this sense, that it was an organization of the privileged for the control of privileges, of the sources of privilege and of the thoughts and acts of the unprivileged; and that neither the privileged nor the unprivileged, neither the bosses nor the bossed, understood this or meant it.

There is, I think, more sound political science packed into that one paragraph than you will find in the whole of an average textbook. And it clearly contains the fundamental answer to the contention that the upper class doesn't rule because it has to put up with many things it doesn't like. Obviously the ruling class has to make concessions and compromises to keep the people, and especially the working class, in a condition of sufficient ignorance and contentment to accept the system as a whole. In other words, the ruling class operates within a definite framework, more or less restricted according to circumstances, which it can ignore only at the peril of losing its power altogether—and, along with its power, its wealth and privileges.

We must next consider the problem of "class position," which determines the basic content of ruling-class ideology. Here I can do no more than indicate what is meant by the expression. This, however, is not so serious a deficiency as at first sight it might appear to be; for once the nature of class position is understood it will be seen to be the very stuff of contemporary history, the constant preoccupation of anyone who attempts to interpret the world from a socialist standpoint.

Class position has two aspects: the relation of the class to its own national social system, and the relation of the national social system to the world at large. For purposes of analyzing the position of the American ruling class we can identify it with the body of American capitalists; in respect to basic ideology, the fringes of the ruling class have no independence whatever. The problem therefore can be reduced to the state of American capitalism on the one hand, and the place of American capitalism in the world on the other.   American capitalism has now reached the stage in which it is dominated by a strong tendency to chronic depression; while world capitalism, of which America is by far the most important component, is faced by a young, vigorous, and rapidly expanding international socialist system.   These are the conditions and trends which determine the basic content of ruling-class ideology.

One final problem remains, that of divisions and conflicts within the ruling class.   We are now in a position to see this problem in its proper setting and proportions.   Aside from more or less accidental rivalries and feuds, the divisions within the ruling class are of several kinds: regional (based on economic differences and buttressed by historical traditions and memories—the North-South division is the clearest example of this kind); industrial (for example, coal capitalists vs. oil capitalists); corporate (for example, General Motors vs. Ford); dynastic (for example Du Ponts vs. Mellons); political (Republicans vs. Democrats); and ideological (reactionaries vs. liberals).   These divisions cut across and mutually condition one another, and the dividing lines are irregular and shifting.   These factors introduce elements of indeterminacy and instability into the behavior of the ruling class and make of capitalist politics something more than a mere puppet show staged for the benefit (and obfuscation) of the man in the street.   But we must not exaggerate the depth of the divisions inside the ruling class: capitalists can and do fight among themselves to further individual or group interests, and they differ over the best way of coping with the problems which arise from the class position; but overshadowing all these divisions is their common interest in preserving and strengthening a system which guarantees their wealth and privileges.   In the event of a real threat to the system, there are no longer class differences—only class traitors, and they are few and far between.

In conclusion, let me say that I have tried to cover a great deal of ground in this essay on the American ruling class.   I recognize that this procedure necessarily results in many gaps and omissions, but I hope that it also has compensating advantages.   In particular, I hope that a bare outline of the whole subject may serve most effectively to bring into sharp relief the essential problems.   I hope also that it will convince the reader not only that *Monthly Review* is justified in talking about the ruling class but that it would be impossible to discuss intelligently the current situation in this country and in the world at large without doing so.*

* *A recent attempt to utilize quantitative sociological methods to demonstrate the existence of a "governing class" in the United States—following Sweezy, E. Digby Baltzell, and C. Wright Mills—is G. William Demhoff's* Who Rules America? *(Englewood Cliffs, N.J.: Prentice-Hall, 1967). In his most recent work, Gabriel Kolko has applied the theory of the ruling class to understanding the role of the United States as a world power, including its intervention in Vietnam. See his* The Roots of American Foreign Policy *(Boston: Beacon Press, 1969).*—M.Z.

MARCUSE FOCUSES ON THE FORMATION AND DETERMINATION OF THE *deepest layers of consciousness in what he terms "advanced industrial civilization." He therefore implicitly rejects the distinction between "capitalist" and "socialist" industrial societies. Once-critical ideas and the liberties necessary to defend them—freedom of speech, thought, and conscience—have lost their former content and function in a society like our own which, Marcuse believes, increasingly satisfies the needs of individuals through the existing system of production. Contemporary industrial society thus tends, by the way it organizes its technological base, to be totalitarian; it operates through the manipulation of needs by vested interests, mobilizing society as a whole, above and beyond any particular individual or group interests.*

The machine process itself is the most effective instrument of political coordination, superseding the terroristic political coordination of society under past forms of totalitarianism. Our own totalitarianism, Marcuse argues, exists despite the "pluralism" of parties, newspapers, and countervailing powers. Intellectual and material needs that perpetuate obsolete forms of the struggle for existence are implanted by this system. Freedom, under such conditions, requires the negation of the present modes of existence. The individual's innermost needs are no longer his own but are the products of a society whose dominant interests demand repression. Individuals—indoctrinated and manipulated, no longer autonomous, no longer capable of distinguishing true from false needs—must free themselves—but how? This becomes more unimaginable, the more rational, productive, technical, and total the repressive administration of society becomes. The consciousness of servitude has itself been repressed. The distinguishing feature of advanced industrial society is, Marcuse claims, its effective suffocation of those needs that demand liberation. Liberty itself is made into an instrument of domination; the content of what can be chosen and is chosen is determined by the repressive whole, rather than by the rational, critical individual.

Marcuse claims that the given and the possible can no longer be distinguished in a society like our own in which needs that serve to preserve the ruling system are also needs of the underlying population. Social control is anchored in these new needs. Thus, the prevailing forms of social control are technological in a new sense, since they appear as the embodiment of Reason for the benefit of all social groups and interests, making contradiction seem irrational and opposition impossible. In fact, this is the expression, on a psychological level, of the passing of historical forces once representing potentially new forms of existence.

372

Today, introjection *is no longer possible;* mimesis *is the result.*
The critical dimension of consciousness—negative thought—has
disappeared, and individuals identify themselves with and find
satisfaction in their own repression. False consciousness replaces
real consciousness. Ideas or actions that reach beyond the present
order are repressed and manipulated. A pattern of one-dimensional
thought and behavior reigns.

30

THE NEW FORMS OF CONTROL

Herbert Marcuse

A comfortable, smooth, reasonable, democratic unfreedom prevails
in advanced industrial civilization, a token of technical progress.
Indeed, what could be more rational than the suppression of
individuality in the mechanization of socially necessary but painful performances; the concentration of individual enterprises in
more effective, more productive corporations; the regulation of
free competition among unequally equipped economic subjects;
the curtailment of prerogatives and national sovereignties which
impede the international organization of resources. That this
technological order also involves a political and intellectual
coordination may be a regrettable and yet promising development.

The rights and liberties which were such vital factors in the origins and earlier stages of industrial society yield to a higher stage of this society: they are losing their traditional rationale and content.   Freedom of thought, speech, and conscience were—just as free enterprise, which they served to promote and protect— essentially *critical* ideas, designed to replace an obsolescent material and intellectual culture by a more productive and rational one.   Once institutionalized, these rights and liberties shared the fate of the society of which they had become an integral part.   The achievement cancels the premises.

To the degree to which freedom from want, the concrete substance of all freedom, is becoming a real possibility, the liberties which pertain to a state of lower productivity are losing their former content.   Independence of thought, autonomy, and the right to political opposition are being deprived of their basic critical function in a society which seems increasingly capable of satisfying the needs of the individuals through the way in which it is organized.   Such a society may justly demand acceptance of its principles and institutions, and reduce the opposition to the discussion and promotion of alternative policies *within* the status quo. In this respect, it seems to make little difference whether the increasing satisfaction of needs is accomplished by an authoritarian or a non-authoritarian system.   Under the conditions of a rising standard of living, non-conformity with the system itself appears to be socially useless, and the more so when it entails tangible economic and political disadvantages and threatens the smooth operation of the whole.   Indeed, at least in so far as the necessities of life are involved, there seems to be no reason why the production and distribution of goods and services should proceed through the competitive concurrence of individual liberties.

Freedom of enterprise was from the beginning not altogether a blessing.   As the liberty to work or to starve, it spelled toil, insecurity, and fear for the vast majority of the population.   If the individual were no longer compelled to prove himself on the market, as a free economic subject, the disappearance of this kind of freedom would be one of the greatest achievements of civilization.   The technological processes of mechanization and standardization might release individual energy into a yet uncharted realm of freedom beyond necessity.   The very structure of human existence would be altered; the individual would be liberated from the work world's imposing upon him alien needs and alien possibilities.   The individual would be free to exert autonomy over a life that would be his own. If the productive apparatus could be organized and directed toward the satisfaction of the vital needs, its control might well be centralized; such control would not prevent individual autonomy, but render it possible.

This is a goal within the capabilities of advanced industrial civilization, the "end" of technological rationality. In actual fact, however, the contrary trend operates: the apparatus imposes its economic and political requirements for defense and expansion on labor time and free time, on the material and intellectual culture. By virtue of the way it has organized its technological base, contemporary industrial society tends to be totalitarian. For "totalitarian" is not only a terroristic political coordination of society, but also a non-terroristic economic-technical coordination which operates through the manipulation of needs by vested interests. It thus precludes the emergence of an effective opposition against the whole. Not only a specific form of government or party rule makes for totalitarianism, but also a specific system of production and distribution which may well be compatible with a "pluralism" of parties, newspapers, "countervailing powers," etc.

Today political power asserts itself through its power over the machine process and over the technical organization of the apparatus. The government of advanced and advancing industrial societies can maintain and secure itself only when it succeeds in mobilizing, organizing, and exploiting the technical, scientific, and mechanical productivity available to industrial civilization. And this productivity mobilizes society as a whole, above and beyond any particular individual or group interests. The brute fact that the machine's physical (only physical?) power surpasses that of the individual, and of any particular group of individuals, makes the machine the most effective political instrument in any society whose basic organization is that of the machine process. But the political trend may be reversed; essentially the power of the machine is only the stored-up and projected power of man. To the extent to which the work world is conceived of as a machine and mechanized accordingly, it becomes the *potential* basis of a new freedom for man.

Contemporary industrial civilization demonstrates that it has reached the stage at which "the free society" can no longer be adequately defined in the traditional terms of economic, political, and intellectual liberties, not because these liberties have become insignificant, but because they are too significant to be confined within the traditional forms. New modes of realization are needed, corresponding to the new capabilities of society.

Such new modes can be indicated only in negative terms because they would amount to the negation of the prevailing modes. Thus economic freedom would mean freedom *from* the economy—from being controlled by economic forces and relationships; freedom from the daily struggle for existence, from earning a living. Political freedom would mean liberation of the individuals *from* politics over which they have no effective control. Similarly, intellectual freedom would mean the restoration of individual thought now absorbed by mass communication and indoctrination, abolition of "public opinion" together with its makers. The unrealistic sound of these propositions is indicative, not of their utopian character, but of the strength of the forces which prevent their realization. The most effective and enduring form of warfare against liberation is the implanting of material and intellectual needs that perpetuate obsolete forms of the struggle for existence.

The intensity, the satisfaction and even the character of human needs, beyond the biological level, have always been preconditioned. Whether or not the possibility of doing or leaving, enjoying or destroying, possessing or rejecting something is seized as a *need* depends on whether or not it can be seen as desirable and necessary for the prevailing societal institutions and interests. In this sense, human needs are historical needs and, to the extent to which the society demands the repressive development of the individual, his needs themselves and their claim for satisfaction are subject to overriding critical standards.

We may distinguish both true and false needs. "False" are those which are superimposed upon the individual by particular social interests in his repression: the needs which perpetuate toil, aggressiveness, misery, and injustice. Their satisfaction might be most gratifying to the individual, but this happiness is not a condition which has to be maintained and protected if it serves to arrest the development of the ability (his own and others) to recognize the disease of the whole and grasp the chances of curing the disease. The result then is euphoria in unhappiness. Most of the prevailing needs to relax, to have fun, to behave and consume in accordance with the advertisements, to love and hate what others love and hate, belong to this category of false needs.

Such needs have a societal content and function which are determined by external powers over which the individual has no control; the development and satisfaction of these needs is heter-onomous. No matter how much such needs may have become the individual's own, reproduced and fortified by the conditions of his existence; no matter how much he identifies himself with them and finds himself in their satisfaction, they continue to be what they were from the beginning—products of a society whose dominant interest demands repression.

The prevalence of repressive needs is an accomplished fact, accepted in ignorance and defeat, but a fact that must be undone in the interest of the happy individual as well as all those whose misery is the price of his satisfaction. The only needs that have an unqualified claim for satisfaction are the vital ones—nourishment, clothing, lodging at the attainable level of culture. The satisfaction of these needs is the prerequisite for the realization of *all* needs, of the unsublimated as well as the sublimated ones.

For any consciousness and conscience, for any experience which does not accept the prevailing societal interest as the supreme law of thought and behavior, the established universe of needs and satisfactions is a fact to be questioned—questioned in terms of truth and falsehood. These terms are historical throughout, and their objectivity is historical. The judgment of needs and their satisfaction, under the given conditions, involves standards of *priority*—standards which refer to the optimal development of the individual, of all individuals, under the optimal utilization of the material and intellectual resources available to man. The resources are calculable. "Truth" and "falsehood" of needs designate objective conditions to the extent to which the universal satisfaction of vital needs and, beyond it, the progressive alleviation of toil and poverty, are universally valid standards. But as historical standards, they do not only vary according to area and stage of development, they also can be defined only in (greater or lesser) *contradiction* to the prevailing ones. What tribunal can possibly claim the authority of decision?

In the last analysis, the question of what are true and false needs must be answered by the individuals themselves, but only in the last analysis; that is, if and when they are free to give their own answer. As long as they are kept incapable of being autonomous, as long as they are indoctrinated and manipulated (down to their very instincts), their answer to this question cannot be taken as their own. By the same token, however, no tribunal can justly arrogate to itself the right to decide which needs should be developed and satisfied. Any such tribunal is reprehensible, although our revulsion does not do away with the question: how can the people who have been the object of effective and productive domination by themselves create the conditions of freedom?

The more rational, productive, technical, and total the repressive administration of society becomes, the more unimaginable the means and ways by which the administered individuals might break their servitude and seize their own liberation. To be sure, to impose Reason upon an entire society is a paradoxical and scandalous idea—although one might dispute the righteousness of a society which ridicules this idea while making its own population into objects of total administration. All liberation depends on the consciousness of servitude, and the emergence of this consciousness is always hampered by the predominance of needs and satisfactions which, to a great extent, have become the individual's own. The process always replaces one system of preconditioning by another; the optimal goal is the replacement of false needs by true ones, the abandonment of repressive satisfaction.

The distinguishing feature of advanced industrial society is its effective suffocation of those needs which demand liberation— liberation also from that which is tolerable and rewarding and comfortable—while it sustains and absolves the destructive power and repressive function of the affluent society. Here, the social controls exact the overwhelming need for the production and consumption of waste; the need for stupefying work where it is no longer a real necessity; the need for modes of relaxation which soothe and prolong this stupefication; the need for maintaining such deceptive liberties as free competition at administered prices, a free press which censors itself, free choice between brands and gadgets.

Under the rule of a repressive whole, liberty can be made into a powerful instrument of domination. The range of choice open to the individual is not the decisive factor in determining the degree of human freedom, but *what* can be chosen and what *is* chosen by the individual. The criterion for free choice can never be an absolute one, but neither is it entirely relative. Free election of masters does not abolish the masters or the slaves. Free choice among a wide variety of goods and services does not signify freedom if these goods and services sustain social controls over a life of toil and fear—that is, if they sustain alienation. And the spontaneous reproduction of superimposed needs by the individual does not establish autonomy; it only testifies to the efficacy of the controls.

Our insistence on the depth and efficacy of these controls is open to the objection that we overrate greatly the indoctrinating power of the "media," and that by themselves the people would feel and satisfy the needs which are now imposed upon them. The objection misses the point. The preconditioning does not start with the mass production of radio and television and with the centralization of their control. The people enter this stage as preconditioned receptacles of long standing; the decisive difference is in the flattening out of the contrast (or conflict) between the given and the possible, between the satisfied and the unsatisfied needs. Here, the so-called equalization of class distinctions reveals its ideological function. If the worker and his boss enjoy the same television program and visit the same resort places, if the typist is as attractively made up as the daughter of her employer, if the Negro owns a Cadillac, if they all read the same newspaper, then this assimilation indicates not the disappearance of classes, but the extent to which the needs and satisfactions that serve the preservation of the Establishment are shared by the underlying population.

Indeed, in the most highly developed areas of contemporary society, the transplantation of social into individual needs is so effective that the difference between them seems to be purely theoretical. Can one really distinguish between the mass media as instruments of information and entertainment, and as agents of manipulation and indoctrination? Between the automobile as nuisance and as convenience? Between the horrors and the comforts of functional architecture? Between the work for national defense and the work for corporate gain? Between the private pleasure and the commercial and political utility involved in increasing the birth rate?

We are again confronted with one of the most vexing aspects of advanced industrial civilization: the rational character of its irrationality. Its productivity and efficiency, its capacity to increase and spread comforts, to turn waste into need, and destruction into construction, the extent to which this civilization transforms the object world into an extension of man's mind and body makes the very notion of alienation questionable. The people recognize themselves in their commodities; they find their soul in their automobile, hi-fi set, split-level home, kitchen equipment.

The very mechanism which ties the individual to his society has changed, and social control is anchored in the new needs which it has produced.

The prevailing forms of social control are technological in a new sense.   To be sure, the technical structure and efficacy of the productive and destructive apparatus has been a major instrumentality for subjecting the population to the established social division of labor throughout the modern period.   Moreover, such integration has always been accompanied by more obvious forms of compulsion: loss of livelihood, the administration of justice, the police, the armed forces.   It still is.   But in the contemporary period, the technological controls appear to be the very embodiment of Reason for the benefit of all social groups and interests— to such an extent that all contradiction seems irrational and all counteraction impossible.

No wonder then that, in the most advanced areas of this civilization, the social controls have been introjected to the point where even individual protest is affected at its roots.   The intellectual and emotional refusal "to go along" appears neurotic and impotent.   This is the socio-psychological aspect of the political event that marks the contemporary period: the passing of the historical forces which, at the preceding stage of industrial society, seemed to represent the possibility of new forms of existence.

But the term "introjection" perhaps no longer describes the way in which the individual by himself reproduces and perpetuates the external controls exercised by his society.   Introjection suggests a variety of relatively spontaneous processes by which a Self (Ego) transposes the "outer" into the "inner."   Thus introjection implies the existence of an inner dimension distinguished from and even antagonistic to the external exigencies—an individual consciousness and an individual unconscious *apart from* public opinion and behavior.[1]   The idea of "inner freedom" here has its reality: it designates the private space in which man may become and remain "himself."

Today this private space has been invaded and whittled down by technological reality.   Mass production and mass distribution claim the *entire* individual, and industrial psychology has long since ceased to be confined to the factory.   The manifold processes of introjection seem to be ossified in almost mechanical reactions.

[1] The change in the function of the family here plays a decisive role: its "socializing" functions are increasingly taken over by outside groups and media. See my *Eros and Civilization* (Boston: Beacon Press, 1955), p. 96ff.

The result is, not adjustment but *mimesis:* an immediate identification of the individual with *his* society and, through it, with the society as a whole.

This immediate, automatic identification (which may have been characteristic of primitive forms of association) reappears in high industrial civilization; its new "immediacy," however, is the product of a sophisticated, scientific management and organization. In this process, the "inner" dimension of the mind in which opposition to the status quo can take root is whittled down.   The loss of this dimension, in which the power of negative thinking—the critical power of Reason—is at home, is the ideological counterpart to the very material process in which advanced industrial society silences and reconciles the opposition.   The impact of progress turns Reason into submission to the facts of life, and to the dynamic capability of producing more and bigger facts of the same sort of life.   The efficiency of the system blunts the individuals' recognition that it contains no facts which do not communicate the repressive power of the whole.   If the individuals find themselves in the things which shape their life, they do so, not by giving, but by accepting the law of things—not the law of physics but the law of their society.

I have just suggested that the concept of alienation seems to become questionable when the individuals identify themselves with the existence which is imposed upon them and have in it their own development and satisfaction.   This identification is not illusion but reality.   However, the reality constitutes a more progressive stage of alienation.   The latter has become entirely objective; the subject which is alienated is swallowed up by its alienated existence.   There is only one dimension, and it is everywhere and in all forms.   The achievements of progress defy ideological indictment as well as justification; before their tribunal, the "false consciousness" of their rationality becomes the true consciousness.

This absorption of ideology into reality does not, however, signify the "end of ideology."   On the contrary, in a specific sense advanced industrial culture is *more* ideological than its predecessor, inasmuch as today the ideology is in the process of production itself.[2]   In a provocative form, this proposition reveals the political aspects of the prevailing technological rationality.   The productive apparatus and the goods and services which it produces

[2] Theodor W. Adorno, *Prismen: Kulturkritik und Gesellschaft* (Frankfurt: Suhrkamp, 1955), p. 24ff.

"sell" or impose the social system as a whole.   The means of mass transportation and communication, the commodities of lodging, food, and clothing, the irresistible output of the entertainment and information industry carry with them prescribed attitudes and habits, certain intellectual and emotional reactions which bind the consumers more or less pleasantly to the producers and, through the latter, to the whole.   The products indoctrinate and manipulate; they promote a false consciousness which is immune against its falsehood.   And as these beneficial products become available to more individuals in more social classes, the indoctrination they carry ceases to be publicity; it becomes a way of life.   It is a good way of life—much better than before—and as a good way of life, it militates against qualitative change.   Thus emerges a pattern of *one-dimensional thought and behavior* in which ideas, aspirations, and objectives that, by their content, transcend the established universe of discourse and action are either repelled or reduced to terms of this universe.   They are redefined by the rationality of the given system and of its quantitative extension.

The trend may be related to a development in scientific method: operationalism in the physical, behaviorism in the social sciences.   The common feature is a total empiricism in the treatment of concepts; their meaning is restricted to the representation of particular operations and behavior.   The operational point of view is well illustrated by P. W. Bridgman's analysis of the concept of length:[3]

> We evidently know what we mean by length if we can tell what the length of any and every object is, and for the physicist nothing more is required.   To find the length of an object, we have to perform certain physical operations. The concept of length is therefore fixed when the operations by which length is measured are fixed: that is, the concept of length involves as much and nothing more than the set of operations by which length is determined.   In general, we mean by any concept nothing more than a set of operations; *the concept is synonymous with the corresponding set of operations.*

[3] P. W. Bridgman, *The Logic of Modern Physics* (New York: Macmillan, 1928), p. 5.   The operational doctrine has since been refined and qualified. Bridgman himself has extended the concept of "operation" to include the "paper-and-pencil" operations of the theorist (in Philipp J. Frank, *The Validation of Scientific Theories* [Boston: Beacon Press, 1954], Chap. 2).   The main impetus remains the same: it is "desirable" that the paper-and-pencil operations "be capable of eventual contact, although perhaps indirectly, with instrumental operations."

Bridgman has seen the wide implications of this mode of thought for the society at large:[4]

> To adopt the operational point of view involves much more than a mere restriction of the sense in which we understand "concept," but means a far-reaching change in all our habits of thought, in that we shall no longer permit ourselves to use as tools in our thinking concepts of which we cannot give an adequate account in terms of operations.

Bridgman's prediction has come true. The new mode of thought is today the predominant tendency in philosophy, psychology, sociology, and other fields. Many of the most seriously troublesome concepts are being "eliminated" by showing that no adequate account of them in terms of operations or behavior can be given. The radical empiricist onslaught . . . thus provides the methodological justification for the debunking of the mind by the intellectuals—a positivism which, in its denial of the transcending elements of Reason, forms the academic counterpart of the socially required behavior.

Outside the academic establishment, the "far-reaching change in all our habits of thought" is more serious. It serves to coordinate ideas and goals with those exacted by the prevailing system, to enclose them in the system, and to repel those which are irreconcilable with the system. The reign of such a one-dimensional reality does not mean that materialism rules, and that the spiritual, metaphysical, and bohemian occupations are petering out. On the contrary, there is a great deal of "Worship together this week," "Why not try God," Zen, existentialism, and beat ways of life, etc. But such modes of protest and transcendence are no longer contradictory to the status quo and no longer negative. They are rather the ceremonial part of practical behaviorism, its harmless negation, and are quickly digested by the status quo as part of its healthy diet.

One-dimensional thought is systematically promoted by the makers of politics and their purveyors of mass information. Their universe of discourse is populated by self-validating hypotheses which, incessantly and monopolistically repeated, become hypnotic definitions or dictations. For example, "free" are the institutions which operate (and are operated on) in the countries of the Free World; other transcending modes of freedom are by definition

[4] P. W. Bridgman, *The Logic of Modern Physics, op. cit.*, p. 31.

either anarchism, communism, or propaganda. "Socialistic" are all encroachments on private enterprises not undertaken by private enterprise itself (or by government contracts), such as universal and comprehensive health insurance, or the protection of nature from all too sweeping commercialization, or the establishment of public services which may hurt private profit. This totalitarian logic of accomplished facts has its Eastern counterpart. There, freedom is the way of life instituted by a communist regime, and all other transcending modes of freedom are either capitalistic, or revisionist, or leftist sectarianism. In both camps, non-operational ideas are non-behavioral and subversive. The movement of thought is stopped at barriers which appear as the limits of Reason itself.

Such limitation of thought is certainly not new. Ascending modern rationalism, in its speculative as well as empirical form, shows a striking contrast between extreme critical radicalism in scientific and philosophic method on the one hand, and an uncritical quietism in the attitude toward established and functioning social institutions. Thus Descartes' *ego cogitans* was to leave the "great public bodies" untouched, and Hobbes held that "the present ought always to be preferred, maintained, and accounted best." Kant agreed with Locke in justifying revolution *if and when* it has succeeded in organizing the whole and in preventing subversion.

However, these accommodating concepts of Reason were always contradicted by the evident misery and injustice of the "great public bodies" and the effective, more or less conscious rebellion against them. Societal conditions existed which provoked and permitted real dissociation from the established state of affairs; a private as well as political dimension was present in which dissociation could develop into effective opposition, testing its strength and the validity of its objectives.

With the gradual closing of this dimension by the society, the self-limitation of thought assumes a larger significance. The interrelation between scientific-philosophical and societal processes, between theoretical and practical Reason, asserts itself "behind the back" of the scientists and philosophers. The society bars a whole type of oppositional operations and behavior; consequently, the concepts pertaining to them are rendered illusory or meaningless. Historical transcendence appears as metaphysical transcendence, not acceptable to science and scientific thought. The operational and behavioral point of view, practiced as a "habit of thought" at large, becomes the view of the established universe of discourse and action, needs and aspirations. The "cunning of Reason" works, as it so often did, in the interest of the powers that be. The insistence on operational and behavioral concepts turns against the efforts to free thought and behavior *from* the given reality and *for* the suppressed alternatives. Theoretical and practical Reason, academic and social behaviorism meet on common ground: that of an advanced society which makes scientific and technical progress into an instrument of domination.

"Progress" is not a neutral term; it moves toward specific ends, and these ends are defined by the possibilities of ameliorating the human condition. Advanced industrial society is approaching the stage where continued progress would demand the radical subversion of the prevailing direction and organization of progress. This stage would be reached when material production (including the necessary services) becomes automated to the extent that all vital needs can be satisfied while necessary labor time is reduced to marginal time. From this point on, technical progress would transcend the realm of necessity, where it served as the instrument of domination and exploitation which thereby limited its rationality; technology would become subject to the free play of faculties in the struggle for the pacification of nature and of society.

Such a state is envisioned in Marx's notion of the "abolition of labor." The term "pacification of existence" seems better suited to designate the historical alternative of a world which—through an international conflict which transforms and suspends the contradictions within the established societies—advances on the brink of a global war. "Pacification of existence" means the development of man's struggle with man and with nature, under conditions where the competing needs, desires, and aspirations are no longer organized by vested interests in domination and scarcity—an organization which perpetuates the destructive forms of this struggle.

Today's fight against this historical alternative finds a firm mass basis in the underlying population, and finds its ideology in the rigid orientation of thought and behavior to the given universe of facts. Validated by the accomplishments of science and technology, justified by its growing productivity, the status quo defies all transcendence. Faced with the possibility of pacification on the grounds of its technical and intellectual achievements, the mature industrial society closes itself against this alternative. Operationalism, in theory and practice, becomes the theory and practice of *containment*.   Underneath its obvious dynamics, this society is a thoroughly static system of life: self-propelling in its oppressive productivity and in its beneficial coordination.   Containment of technical progress goes hand in hand with its growth in the established direction.   In spite of the political fetters imposed by the status quo, the more technology appears capable of creating the conditions for pacification, the more are the minds and bodies of man organized against this alternative.

The most advanced areas of industrial society exhibit throughout these two features: a trend toward consummation of technological rationality, and intensive efforts to contain this trend within the established institutions.   Here is the internal contradiction of this civilization: the irrational element in its rationality.   It is the token of its achievements.   The industrial society which makes technology and science its own is organized for the ever-more-effective domination of man and nature, for the ever-more-effective utilization of its resources.   It becomes irrational when the success of these efforts opens new dimensions of human realization.   Organization for peace is different from organization for war; the institutions which served the struggle for existence cannot serve the pacification of existence.   Life as an end is qualitatively different from life as a means.

Such a qualitatively new mode of existence can never be envisaged as the mere by-product of economic and political changes, as the more or less spontaneous effect of the new institutions which constitute the necessary prerequisite.   Qualitative change also involves a change in the *technical* basis on which this society rests—one which sustains the economic and political institutions through which the "second nature" of man as an aggressive object of administration is stabilized.   The techniques of industrialization are political techniques; as such, they prejudge the possibilities of Reason and Freedom.

To be sure, labor must precede the reduction of labor, and industrialization must precede the development of human needs and satisfactions.   But as all freedom depends on the conquest of alien necessity, the realization of freedom depends on the *techniques* of this conquest.   The highest productivity of labor can be used for the perpetuation of labor, and the most efficient industrialization can serve the restriction and manipulation of needs.

When this point is reached, domination—in the guise of affluence and liberty—extends to all spheres of private and public existence, integrates all authentic opposition, absorbs all alternatives. Technological rationality reveals its political character as it becomes the great vehicle of better domination, creating a truly totalitarian universe in which society and nature, mind and body are kept in a state of permanent mobilization for the defense of this universe.

Part Six

SOCIAL CONFLICT AND THE STRUGGLE FOR POWER

COL. RIGG IS THE AUTHOR OF *War: 1974*, PUBLISHED IN 1958, *which predicted much of what has occurred since in Vietnam. In the following article he argues that America's cities may become our own Vietnam: sporadic urban "riots"—given leadership, organization, and political direction—may become urban insurrection. In the concrete jungles of the great metropolises, organization can translate poverty, racial issues, and unrest among minorities into an urban guerrilla movement of serious potential. A national paralysis of very serious proportions might arise under such conditions.*

Today, he says, you need not point to the "red flag of communism" to appreciate the fact that violence, dissidence and disaffection can threaten the United States from within. National Guard units may end up being on permanent active duty in many of our cities, as activists of the left who now protest against the war in Vietnam energize and organize violence by whites and blacks alike to protest against poverty and their environment. Militancy has replaced defeatism and complacency in the slums.

From a military standpoint, Rigg claims, successful warfare against urban-based guerrillas in American cities could be as difficult and prolonged as the fighting in Vietnam if the insurrection is well organized. Thus, there are several problems to confront: political and intelligence penetration of the insurrectionary forces; provision of accurate information on the facilities used by the urban guerrillas; development of a whole new manual of military operations for such urban warfare; coordination of the police, FBI, Army, National Guard, and local political authority; and the establishment of vital communications networks. "Limited wars" are likely right here in our own country; therefore, Rigg urges, U.S. Army units must be trained to know every American city intimately. American troops must be fully prepared to go to war against their fellow Americans.

390

31

MADE IN U.S.A.

Col. Robert B. Rigg

During the next few years organized urban insurrection could explode to the extent that portions of large American cities could become scenes of destruction approaching those of Stalingrad in World War II. This could result from two main causes:
• Man has constructed out of steel and concrete a much better "jungle" than Nature has created in Vietnam.
• There is the danger and the promise that urban guerrillas of the future can be organized to such a degree that their defeat would require the direct application of military power by the National Guard and the active Army.

This degree of destruction can easily come about because of these two circumstances. After all, we have seen many square blocks totally ruined in Watts, Detroit and elsewhere, where there was no organized resistance. Were organized insurrection to break out and military power needed to suppress it, destruction in city square miles could mount tremendously over what we have seen.

However, while application of pure military firepower would be a poor solution, political efforts might prove not much better. There are measures that offer a better solution if we are to keep our cities from becoming battlegrounds: penetration by police intelligence, application of military intelligence, and reliance on traditional FBI methods. Such efforts must begin now so as to prevent organized urban guerrilla violence from gaining momentum.

To prevent and to curb urban violence of any order we must establish an effective system of intelligence in the ghettos of urban America. If penetration were professionally effective, such a system could warn of any plans for organized violence by subversive elements. Further, should organized violence break out, such an espionage system would be able to keep riot control and counter-violence forces informed during a disturbance.

The real prevention of urban violence and insurrection begins with social, economic and political efforts. But alongside these measures and efforts there must be the "peripheral insurance policy" of an inside intelligence system that can warn of serious outbreaks and help curb them.

Furthermore, there will also be needed among the well established political-tactical-military informants those who can help guide troops and police through the maze of buildings, stair-wells, streets, alleyways, tunnels and sewers that may be the key to tactical success.   In the countryside we would call this elementary or "grass roots" intelligence; in the city there will be a similar need.

Just as China was plagued with rural guerrilla warfare from the 1920s to the late 1940s, so too, if present trends persist, could the United States experience similar strife and violence. The singular difference is that the fighting would be urban in nature. Furthermore, it is likely to be of such a special brand that can bear only the unique label, "Made in the USA." Thus, the United States may inadvertently provide the world with a new brand of internal warfare that could haunt and harass large metropolitan areas for decades to come.

This possibility is alarming in light of the population explosion and the urban growth which by the 1980s may result in strip cities extending from Miami to Boston, from Chicago to Detroit, from San Francisco to San Diego—not to mention similar areas abroad.   Of further import for the near future is the fact that the older "core cities"—such as Chicago, New York, Detroit, Newark, Oakland, Los Angeles and others—could become concrete jungles where poverty could spread with their growth. Additionally, such cement-and-brick "jungles" can offer better security to snipers and city guerrillas than the Viet Cong enjoy in their jungles, elephant grass and marshes. This suggests protracted warfare of a very new kind if city guerrilla forces become well organized by dissident and determined leaders.

City warfare is not new. What would make this type of conflict new, different, and more terrifying would be two elements. One would be the very geographical extent of the concrete jungles that are now simply called ghettos: such slum areas can expand rapidly as suburbia grows and absorbs the more affluent. The other would be lawless forces intoxicated by the ease and security with which they might successfully defy police, National Guardsmen, and Army regulars. The concrete blocks of our great ghettos have vertical acreage and horizontal mileage that offer such tactical protection and vantage points as to make future snipers much "braver" and city guerrillas much bolder than unorganized rioting mobs have been so far.

These are only a few of the trends in the United States which flash warning that our nation could be in for such violent street disorders that to suppress them would ultimately require the civil use of military power on a scale never heretofore visualized.

Racial issues, poverty, political unrest among minorities, the population explosion, and the rapid growth of strip cities that absorb the decaying old core cities—all these represent a combination of future factors and trends that could plague metropolitan areas and breed more violent and better organized disorder. That urban violence has spread significantly makes the outlook grim, because street violence has found acceptance among minorities.

Today's riots bring more than temporary disorder. They instill a new frame of mind among minorities—an outlook that visualizes rebellion against society and authority as a successful venture for the future. So far the unruly elements, with no real organization, have demonstrated that they can do unusual damage wantonly and indiscriminately. But the sick seed can grow into a menacing weed if in the future the potentials of organization are exploited.

So far the causes of urban violence have been emotional and social. Organization, however, can translate these grievances into political ones of serious potential, and result in violence or even prolonged warfare. Thus, we may find that the danger to a free America is greater from within than from without.

If present trends persist, it is possible that in the next decade at least one major metropolitan area in the United States could be faced with guerrilla warfare of such intensity as to require sizable U.S. Army elements in action and National Guard units on active duty for years. No doubt such an urban conflict could be contained, subdued and defeated, but the effort could possibly require years of concerted military action before even effective social improvements could have impact.   This is what the war in South Vietnam has demonstrated.   Further, if organized guerrilla resistance spreads to several cities and requires the use of many military units, a national paralysis of very serious proportions might ensue.

The strange thing about this ominous prospect is that such warfare in alleys, streets, cellars, sewers and rooftops could erupt and be carried out initially by organized guerrillas with no prodding by communists or other political movements.   It could erupt simply from poverty or racial or local issues, and expand into more blood-spilling violence during which a more overriding political issue—communist or other—could be conveniently inserted by subversive leaders.

Today you need not point to the red flag of communism to appreciate that violence, dissidence and disaffection of other sorts can threaten the United States from within.   A future political brand of internal guerrilla threat may now be so faceless as to not appear on the attorney general's black list for some time to come.   Yet the potential threat could be so ominous as to rank alongside communism.   Nevertheless, the threat of future communist exploitation of American urban unrest remains potent.

Communist China and Cuba represent potential grave internal threats to the United States.   They can covertly subsidize insurgent elements within our urban areas although so far, according to the FBI, they have not done so.   However, in some intelligence circles of our government it is known that the more dangerous conspirators in ghettos are being prompted by members of the pro-Chinese wing of the American Communist party.

The riots in Newark and Detroit have opened new opportunities for these communist nations which have a well-known record of exporting revolution.   Suddenly they learn that there are ill-disciplined elements in the continental United States which can engage in violence without even a political cause.   Snipers who will fire from roof-tops and high-rise windows out of nothing more than the urge to violence and vengeance against society are certainly ripe for political coercion by Red China's and communist Cuba's secret agents who seek men of this type the world over.

Some advocates of Black Power regard outbreaks of violence as a necessary part of what Adam Clayton Powell called "the black revolution that is going to purge American democracy." Powell pronounced this on 26 July 1967, just as the Detroit riot began to subside. On the same day, Black Power leader Stokely Carmichael issued a similar manifesto from Cuba, at the very time when the Organization of American States was announcing that Castro was continuing his support of communist terrorists and guerrillas in Venezuela. In its report, the OAS special committee made the main point that Cuba's activities include training, arming and transporting guerrillas for operations in other countries.

Extremely bitter since the Bay of Pigs invasion, Castro has become a would-be exporter of revolution. With Carmichael at his elbow, Castro gave his "blessing" to riots in U.S. cities and called for guerrilla warfare there.

On 3 August, while still in Cuba, Carmichael repeated his prediction of "urban guerrilla warfare" against the U.S. government: "Our only answer is to destroy that government or to be destroyed while trying to destroy the government." At any rate, "we are going to start with guns to get our liberation."

A few days later in New York another advocate of violence, H. Rap Brown, called on Negroes to arm themselves against a white "conspiracy of genocide," while labeling riots in Newark, Detroit and Plainfield as "dress rehearsals for revolution."

These are straws in the wind, but nevertheless many hundreds applaud locally, and millions listen nationally, while would-be Nazis and members of the American Communist party draw much smaller crowds, generate only token enthusiasm, and represent a weak threat, internally. But these groups can exploit advocates of Black Power and violence. Responsible Negro leaders work elsewhere with real power and purpose for more meaningful progress, but they may end up as "Uncle Toms" if the advocates of violence persist.

In the future, forceful leaders—or even careless ones—could easily evoke and provoke protracted violence so as to cause National Guard units to be on almost permanent active duty in many of our cities.

Every nation at times has its would-be Hitlers. So far the United States has been able to survive the extreme rantings of such radicals who have never been able to muster political forces of consequence, much less military forces. But the appeal, and sometime success, of guerrillaism is an intoxicant that could "inspire" urban minority leaders or future would-be Hitlers—men of ruthless purpose and gnawing ambition.

Time, and the crowding circumstances of the population explosion, can breed wholesale urban violence. Social and economic progress promise to be of help here, but we cannot be too certain that such efforts will always succeed. For example, not long ago, modern housing in Anacostia, D.C., was vandalized by youthful gangs of the community. With no unified leadership, they smashed and destroyed property wholesale and so intimidated store-owners and passers-by that one of Washington's major newspapers wrote a series of articles on this modern-day phenomenon which portends problems in future communities. Why? Because here was a state of mind that manifested itself very boldly. Its overtones for the future are obvious.

Urban riot has been established as an instrument of racial rebellion. But the riots have not been strictly one of Negroes clashing with whites; often the rioters were relieving their frustrations at their ghetto surroundings and relative poverty, and upon authorities. It is important to remember this, especially where it pertains to slums. Violence in the future may even be by whites protesting against poverty and their environment. White or black, here is where the political aspect looms large because communist elements can penetrate urban America and foment serious trouble.

The future brand of trouble may not necessarily be communist-inspired. Activists of the left who now expend their energies in protesting against the Vietnam war could become a growing source of urban unrest and trouble. The future problem of city violence bears no particular political label at the moment but it does indicate that trouble can arise from the left or right, or from black or white. Poverty and social problems exist in rural areas, but they can reach explosive and serious proportions only in our cities.

The personal right to own firearms is being seriously debated in Washington today. The argument will linger, and probably with no conclusive results, for a long time. The stark fact remains that from Chicago to the Congo, anyone who wants to shoot can buy small arms and even mortars. World War II, the many limited wars since, and all the military aid programs have flooded the world with arms and ammunition. If a subversive force or organization wants arms, they are available. If their leaders want them on a wholesale scale, arms for the urban guerrillas of the United States will not be hard to obtain.

Today, one trend is self-evident: metropolitan police cannot cope with even disorganized violence where it reaches high proportions. Tomorrow, police and National Guard units may not be able to cope with urban violence that is well organized.

Another trend is toward organization for violence. Over the past two decades organization has spread in the ghettos of America. It began with street gangs who boldly formed semi-uniformed clubs and deliberately engaged in "rumbles" for "sport" or diversion. Now the overtones of racialism and the more public recognition of poverty-area-contrast with other communities have brought movements designed to "fight their way up and out." In short, the trend is toward organization designed for aggression in behalf of racial and poverty issues. Militancy prevails in slums where heretofore there was only the defeatism of complacency. For the future, militancy can be expected to prevail. Elements of American poverty have discovered the ally of aggression. Added, however, will be organization behind the militancy, and the second ingredient of arms in place of rocks and bottles. A disorganized mob throws rocks, bricks, and bottles. An organized mob of the future will be armed, and will not be content to gather its armament from street rubble.

"Fight for something" is an old American tradition. Any time hence, people in a large slum in a congested metropolitan area could fight in guerrilla fashion for their own local aims. They might not be fighting the federal government, but merely the city or the state. As in Vietnam today, the fighters by night could be workers by day. Roof-tops, windows, rooms high up, streets low down, and back alleys nearby, could become a virtual jungle for patrolling police or military forces at night when hidden snipers could abound, as they often do against U.S. and allied forces in Vietnam in daylight. Could local police or National Guard units carry out search-and-destroy campaigns in the cement-block jungles of high-rise buildings?

Even in the face of large-caliber artillery, the battle of Stalingrad demonstrated that a city of steel, concrete and brick offers unusual protection to its defenders and great obstacles to its assailants. Consider a creeping guerrilla war by night in a typical portion of the old core of an American city. Police patrols and National Guardsmen could be sniped at by night for months and suffer heavy casualties from determined but hidden foes. Such warfare would not need to be fought by lone guerrillas in the lower streets. Vietnam's jungles have no elevators and stairwells in their tree-tops, but city buildings do—and a multitude of vacant

rooms to which to flee.   No jungle's tree branches are as secure.
The degree of security for city guerrillas is almost too imposing to
suggest.   Mao Tse-tung's concept of prolonged war could be
applied—by city guerrilla forces so determined—to the same
extent that he waged it about China's countryside.

Police, National Guard, and active Army units could hardly
carry out successful clear-and-hold operations in the steel-and-
concrete jungle of high-rise buildings without resorting to a campaign that would almost reach the destruction experienced by
Stalingrad.   The problem is difficult enough in the sometimes
peaceful countryside of Vietnam today, but what tank or bulldozer is going to flatten an old 20-story apartment or office building
that is sniper-ridden by night and vacant by day?   Here, urban
guerrillas could shoot down into the streets, drop fire bombs, and
not even need mortars.   Plainly, the finest "jungle" for insurrection was not created by Nature; it has been built by man.

From a military standpoint, successful warfare against urban-
based guerrillas in American cities could be as difficult and
prolonged as the fighting in Vietnam if the insurrection is well
organized.

Unless the decay of core cities can be cured by social, economic and political means, Detroit's relatively small square
mileage of violence of 1967 could look insignificant in military and
damage terms, compared to what could be a virtual Stalingrad in
an American city by 1970 or 1980.

While the patterns of future urban insurrection may vary,
there will be certain problems to confront, if the violence is
organized.

Problem No. 1 would be organization itself.   To combat this
would require political and intelligence penetration of high order
and expertise.   Here, penetration must be deep enough so as to
warn of secret subversive plans, to pinpoint leaders, and to dis-
rupt organization itself.

Problem No. 2 would concern the identification of hideouts,
areas where weapons are stored, sources of arms, guerrilla means
of transportation, access and escape routes, and probable resistance spots.   In other words, we must have intimate and accurate
information on the facilities used by urban guerrillas before and
during trouble.

Problem No. 3 relates to tactical military action against
organized resistance once conflict begins.   Hopefully, this assumes
that at least fair intelligence and espionage would continue to meet

the problems mentioned. But no intelligence report has ever been prepared that included complete information on the enemy *after* the fighting started. Tactical action has always had to rely on what little was known and what could be learned through intelligence gathered by scouting and combat. Imagine a building or a block of buildings that houses innocent people but is used at night by snipers and insurrectionists with fire bombs. Tactical action here would take on the proportions of search-and-plant operations by day, and retaliation, maneuver, and fighting by night. Night fighting will call for a very delicate decision as to which darkened window to shoot at and which roof-top to blast by mortar fire or to assault by helicopter. A whole new manual of military operations, tactics and techniques needs to be written in respect to urban warfare of this nature. There are none on the subject today.

Problem No. 4 includes police-Guard-Army and local authority (particularly political), coordination, communications and control. Here also is a very big problem that can be greatly aggravated by chaos and street fighting. For every city, for every emergency, this one requires much planning in depth. Planning is vital, particularly in terms of political and military control and coordination of all efforts. Once chaos and conflict ensue, command and coordination become even more crucial and necessary. Communications in terms of standing operating procedure, integrated radio networks, liaison, procedures, and the like, are big problems that must be solved before conflict, and modified to meet the demands of the situation.

Problem No. 5 can be termed "Mixture X." It includes everything from control and safety of a few dozen (or hundreds) of refugees fleeing from buildings to hostages being held by seasoned guerrillas or being used by them as escape shields. It includes the sick and wounded among the innocent. It includes the supply of food and medicine—and medical treatment—to trapped people. It includes evacuation by helicopters and by fire fighters, of people trapped in burning buildings. It includes the protection of firemen from sniper fire, the need of which last summer's Detroit riot demonstrated in very grim and dramatic fashion. Plainly, firemen need the Red Cross badge of safety to protect them in their valor and work. They didn't have even this in Detroit. They may suffer heavy casualties during organized urban insurrection of the future unless they are somehow more respected by some agreement or other measure.

Success in coping with organized urban warfare will not rest on agreements, but rather depend on tactics and techniques yet to be formulated. The overall problem, and success in meeting it, depend heavily on a new measure of organization, coordination and study among officials of the city, state, National Guard, police, active Army and FBI. While these organizations understand the problem and are alert to it, much work lies ahead.

The implications are clear. American military and political plans must now, more than ever before, be based upon meeting a new kind of internal violence.

The most delicate type of so-called "limited war" lies ahead. Military force and military restraint of a new order call for new types of training and discipline. Traditionally, and normally, soldiers are taught to fire back, to gain the objective, and to seize the high ground. These tactical principles can no longer be applied unless we want to see street blocks become battlegrounds of utter destruction. Greater firepower and more troops have already raised the ante of escalation in Vietnam.

There is one lesson we must learn from even this type of limited war. When urban guerrilla warfare strikes, meeting it will require the highest degree of calmness ever demanded of the American soldier since the traditional "Don't one of you fire until you see the white of their eyes." This means that the active Army, National Guard, and police must use the pressure of their presence, the force of probing, and the expertise of military intelligence, without resorting to serious outbreaks of firepower, much less wanton shooting. The implications here are serious in respect to military training and operations. Each unit and each soldier must be expected to endure the highest incidence of sniping, apply the utmost of maneuvering and—at times—resort to the least firing. This is a large order for any force, but only through such disciplines and techniques can urban guerrilla warfare be contained within bounds, limited in destructive powers, held within limits, and destroyed by the most singular means—and that is through seizure rather than through destruction by firepower. Military intelligence, police and detective efforts and FBI penetration can make greater progress toward defeating future urban guerrillas than any military firepower.

Such planning must include training troops for urban insurrection. For the National Guard this means a complete change of direction in training as something of first priority. For the active Army, such training has serious overtones to the extent that it must train for the concrete jungle as well as for the other kind. Further, it means that Army units must be oriented and trained to know the cement-and-asphalt jungle of *every* American city. It means that maneuvers and exercises, heretofore carried out about the countryside, in the future can be conducted in large cities. Possibly the sight of such maneuvers in several cities could prove a deterrent to urban insurrection. Today's trend implies that very soon American troops will be maneuvering in metropolitan areas to an extent more than ever before imagined. Here they will be required to learn about and memorize details of many metropolitan communities, their buildings, streets, alley-ways, roof-tops, and sewers, just as once they learned the use of terrain features of open country. This is the only way to solve the intelligence, social, economic and political problems associated with serious Third Front warfare which could bear the unfortunate label of "Made in the USA."

32

PATTERNS OF DISORDER

National Advisory Commission on Civil Disorders

Disorders are often discussed as if there were a single type. The "typical" riot of recent years is sometimes seen as a massive uprising against white people, involving widespread burning, looting, and sniping, either by all ghetto Negroes or by an uneducated, Southern-born Negro underclass of habitual criminals or "riffraff." An agitator at a protest demonstration, the coverage of events by the news media, or an isolated "triggering" or "precipitating" incident, is often identified as the primary spark of violence. A uniform set of stages is sometimes posited, with a succession of confrontations and withdrawals by two cohesive groups, the police on one side and a riotous mob on the other. Often it is assumed that there was no effort within the Negro community to reduce the violence. Sometimes the only remedy prescribed is application of the largest possible police or control force, as early as possible.

What we have found does not validate these conceptions. We have been unable to identify constant patterns in all aspects of civil disorders. We have found that they are unusual, irregular, complex, and, in the present state of knowledge, unpredictable social processes. Like many human events, they do not unfold in orderly sequences.

Moreover, we have examined the 1967 disorders within a few

Reprinted from National Advisory Commission, *Report of the National Advisory Commission on Civil Disorders* (Washington, D.C.: U. S. Government Printing Office, 1968), pp. 63–65.

months after their occurrence and under pressing time limitations. While we have collected information of considerable immediacy, analysis will undoubtedly improve with the passage and perspective of time and with the further accumulation and refinement of data. To facilitate further analysis we have appended much of our data to this report.

We have categorized the information now available about the 1967 disorders as follows:

• The pattern of violence over the nation: severity, location, timing, and numbers of people involved;
• The riot process in a sample of 24 disorders we have surveyed:* prior events, the development of violence, the various control efforts on the part of officials and the community, and the relationship between violence and control efforts;
• The riot participants: a comparison of rioters with those who sought to limit the disorder and with those who remained uninvolved;
• The setting in which the disorders occurred: social and economic conditions, local governmental structure, the scale of federal programs, and the grievance reservoir in the Negro community;
• The aftermath of disorder: the ways in which communities responded after order was restored in the streets.

Based upon information derived from our surveys, we offer the following generalizations:

1. No civil disorder was "typical" in all respects. Viewed in a national framework, the disorders of 1967 varied greatly in terms of violence and damage: while a relatively small number were major under our criteria and a somewhat larger number were serious, most of the disorders would have received little or no national attention as "riots" had the nation not been sensitized by the more serious outbreaks.

2. While the civil disorders of 1967 were racial in character, they were not *inter*racial. The 1967 disorders, as well as earlier disorders of the recent period, involved action within Negro neighborhoods against symbols of white American society— authority and property—rather than against white persons.

3. Despite extremist rhetoric, there was no attempt to subvert the social order of the United States. Instead, most of those

---

* *The Statement on Methodology in the Appendix of the* Report *describes the survey procedures.*—M.Z.

who attacked white authority and property seemed to be demanding fuller participation in the social order and the material benefits enjoyed by the vast majority of American citizens.

4. Disorder did not typically erupt without preexisting causes as a result of a single "triggering" or "precipitating" incident. Instead, it developed out of an increasingly disturbed social atmosphere, in which typically a series of tension-heightening incidents over a period of weeks or months became linked in the minds of many in the Negro community with a shared reservoir of underlying grievances.

5. There was, typically, a complex relationship between the series of incidents and the underlying grievances. For example, grievances about allegedly abusive police practices, unemployment and underemployment, housing, and other conditions in the ghetto, were often aggravated in the minds of many Negroes by incidents involving the police, or the inaction of municipal authorities on Negro complaints about police action, unemployment, inadequate housing or other conditions. When grievance-related incidents recurred and rising tensions were not satisfactorily resolved, a cumulative process took place in which prior incidents were readily recalled and grievances reinforced. At some point in the mounting tension, a further incident—in itself often routine or even trivial—became the breaking point, and the tension spilled over into violence.

6. Many grievances in the Negro community result from the discrimination, prejudice and powerlessness which Negroes often experience. They also result from the severely disadvantaged social and economic conditions of many Negroes as compared with those of whites in the same city and, more particularly, in the predominantly white suburbs.

7. Characteristically, the typical rioter was not a hoodlum, habitual criminal or riffraff; nor was he a recent migrant, a member of an uneducated underclass or a person lacking broad social and political concerns. Instead, he was a teenager or young adult, a lifelong resident of the city in which he rioted, a high school dropout—but somewhat better educated than his Negro neighbor —and almost invariably underemployed or employed in a menial job. He was proud of his race, extremely hostile to both whites and middle-class Negroes and, though informed about politics, highly distrustful of the political system and of political leaders.

8. Numerous Negro counterrioters walked the streets urging rioters to "cool it." The typical counterrioter resembled in

many respects the majority of Negroes, who neither rioted nor took action against the rioters, that is, the noninvolved. But certain differences are crucial: the counterrioter was better educated and had higher income than either the rioter or the noninvolved.

9. Negotiations between Negroes and white officials occurred during virtually all the disorders surveyed. The negotiations often involved young, militant Negroes as well as older, established leaders. Despite a setting of chaos and disorder, negotiations in many cases involved discussion of underlying grievances as well as the handling of the disorder by control authorities.

10. The chain we have identified—discrimination, prejudice, disadvantaged conditions, intense and pervasive grievances, a series of tension-heightening incidents, all culminating in the eruption of disorder at the hands of youthful, politically-aware activists—must be understood as describing the central trend in the disorders, not as an explanation of all aspects of the riots or of all rioters. Some rioters, for example, may have shared neither the conditions nor the grievances of their Negro neighbors; some may have coolly and deliberately exploited the chaos created by others; some may have been drawn into the melee merely because they identified with, or wished to emulate, others. Nor do we intend to suggest that the majority of the rioters, who shared the adverse conditions and grievances, necessarily articulated in their own minds the connection between that background and their actions.

11. The background of disorder in the riot cities was typically characterized by severely disadvantaged conditions for Negroes, especially as compared with those for whites; a local government often unresponsive to these conditions; federal programs which had not yet reached a significantly large proportion of those in need; and the resulting reservoir of pervasive and deep grievance and frustration in the ghetto.

12. In the immediate aftermath of disorder, the status quo of daily life before the disorder generally was quickly restored. Yet, despite some notable public and private efforts, little basic change took place in the conditions underlying the disorder. In some cases, the result was increased distrust between blacks and whites, diminished interracial communication, and growth of Negro and white extremist groups. . . .

O'DELL, AN ACTIVE MEMBER OF WHAT HE CALLS THE RESISTANCE TO *the militarization of American life, argues that the so-called Negro riots are, in fact, rebellions against the exploited colonial situation in which the black residents of the ghettos of America's cities are compelled to live. These revolts were the spontaneous expression of the same drive for freedom manifested in the anti-slave rebellions of Negro slaves, and the anti-British rebellions of white colonial settlers before them. The ghetto, like the slave plantation, is an institutionalized form of racism whose special function is to facilitate the exploitation of the black population confined within it.*

Growing numbers of black men and women are transforming the ghettos from centers of exploitation into battlegrounds. In what the press and officials call "looting," the black community is merely reclaiming and confiscating property which is rightfully theirs. Anti-colonial wars abroad and black rebellion at home are part of the same struggle, and racism justifies the repression of Vietnamese peasants and "niggers" alike. Non-violent protest has passed to violent revolt because conditions have worsened in the very course of the so-called civil rights movement. These revolts are centered among young black workers, distinguished from other workers only by their color and their especially exploited condition.

Contrary to Rustin and others, O'Dell argues (and is supported by evidence presented in the preceding study by the National Advisory Commission), that these young blacks are neither declassed anti-social elements nor a distinct lower class, but an integral part of the national working class of men and women who must sell their labor power to live. "Riots" and "anti-social elements" are the language of repression—terminology which justifies "whatever force is necessary" to crush the black revolts. If there were real "riots," they were among the police and National Guard troops who destroyed black-owned businesses, indiscriminately shot into apartment buildings, forcibly entered black residences, took thousands of political prisoners, and murdered unarmed men and women.

State power is being organized to wage the colonial war in the United States, and special training and arsenals are being provided to police and armed forces, accompanied by increasingly open political activity and racist ideology among police associations. Militarism and the military presence are rapidly becoming the main features of governmental power in American life. Militarism and racism are inseparable, and embodied in the special presence of southerners among the key congressional, military, and executive militarists. An unyielding and growing movement of resistance to these regressive forces, O'Dell concludes, will be the bearer of a new morality in America which will assert the primacy of human life.

406

33

THE JULY REBELLIONS AND THE "MILITARY STATE"

J. H. O'Dell

There is a[n] . . . American folksong whose lyrics speak philo-sophically concerning time and the turn of the seasons.

What was earlier in this decade described as our summers of dis-content, now turns into seasons of growing popular revolt against the conditions of life in America. The war in Vietnam continues as does the determined popular resistance to the war by large sections of the American people. The Military Establishment grows more brutal and arrogant, at home and abroad. The freedom-consciousness of the black ghettos becomes more articu-late in act as well as in word, as one of the major institutions of racism (the ghetto condition) comes under assault. This is part of the cutting edge of an emerging new Resistance Movement. The month of July proved to be the premier month as 37 cities, stretching across the continent from East Harlem to San Bernar-dino, California, and as far South as Riviera Beach, Florida, were shaken by revolts of varying magnitude, large and small.

These events call attention, in a dramatic way, to the fact that, in the midst of its much-boasted affluence, the self styled "Great Society" like its predecessors, Rome and the Third Reich, has fallen upon bad times.

The defenders of the *ancien regime* respond with characteristic venom. "Get those niggers . . . get those niggers" is the police

Reprinted from *Freedomways*, Vol. 7, No. 4 (1967), published at 799 Broad-way, New York, N.Y. Reprinted by permission of the publisher.

yell in Newark and Plainfield, New Jersey as they fan out to occupy the ghetto. "The gooks are still in there . . . burn down as much as possible," echo similar voices on television, coming from Lien Ho and Bon Son, Vietnam, on the other side of the world, an area also being "pacified," U.S. style. The language of insult even comes from the lips of the Texan who has been called America's accidental President, as he describes the leaders of the ghetto revolts. His audience is a convention of chiefs of police and he is asking for support for his "safe streets" legislation.

The language of insult is accompanied by the language of confusion as the American people are given a definition of these events in the ghetto as "riots." This is the term repeated over and over again by the news media and the most prominent leaders of white American opinion.

For all practical purposes, to understand these events and what they mean it is necessary to clear up the problem of definitions. This is particularly necessary because language is used by the oppressor, often very effectively, to keep freedom fighters on the defensive. American society has a long history of charging its black victims with "guilt" by cleverly using the language as a weapon. In this, as in so many other ways, the U.S. shows how very much it is a part of the "Western World."

When one reads the history of the Negro people in the U.S. especially the long slavery period, one reads of Nat Turner's *rebellion*, or of Denmark Vesey's *revolt* and of the more than 200 other slave *revolts*. These were violent efforts by men, individually or collectively, to throw off the chains of slavery exploitation. And if, in the course of events, they set fire to a plantation or took some food from the slaveholders' warehouse, freedom-loving mankind the world over hailed this as quite naturally in the spirit of liberty. Only the slavemasters and their allies regarded such events as "riots" and the men struggling to throw off the yoke of slavery as "hoodlums."

More than a century before these freedom revolts by African slaves under the rule of the American Republic, a series of similar events had shaken British rule in the colony of Virginia. In 1676 the Governor's plantation was stripped of its crops and domestic animals, and a militia was organized among the planters, farmers and white indentured servants to back up their demands for lower taxes, and an end to corruption and favoritism in the government. This was known as "Bacon's Rebellion" named after Nathaniel Bacon, its leader, who died in jail, while 29 of his compatriots were hanged by the British authorities, and dozens of others jailed and fined.

The Royal Commission appointed by the Crown to "investigate these disturbances" was sharply divided in its opinion between those who argued that "the unrest is just the work of a few rabble who could be put down by a [military] force of 200 men" and the more conciliatory commissioners who contended "the unrest is widespread because of real grievances . . . which should be investigated."

Each of these events, in its own time-setting, was a landmark in the development of greater political consciousness among the aggrieved population

THE NATURE OF THE CURRENT REVOLTS

In the slavery period of our American experience, the main institution of confinement [wa]s the plantation. In the post-slavery period, especially since the First World War, the main institution of confinement for the black population in the United States [has been] the ghetto.

The Negro ghetto has been described often and elaborately. It is an enclave within the larger American urban setting, whose inhabitants pay high rents for slum houses or buy second-hand houses at inflated real estate prices; an area of run-down schools, over-crowded and poorly staffed, with a curriculum which is designed to give the child an inferior education, and consequently handicap him in the competition for college or a good job later in life. The ghetto family pays marked-up prices for poor quality food and other merchandise—with the weighted scale in the meat market and the padded credit accounts in the furniture store everyday forms of robbery. It is a population preyed upon by petty hustlers and charlatans and a variety of other social parasites who wouldn't be allowed to "operate" in other communities. It is a population occupied by a police force acting as overseers on this urban plantation.

By way of definition, the functional role of the ghetto, as an institutionalized form of racism, is to facilitate the special exploitation of the black population, through the mechanisms we have described. As such, the ghetto is merely an up-dated, modified version of the nineteenth century slave quarters, in the American system of exploitation. And the revolts against the conditions in the ghetto today are linked by history to the revolts against slavery in the past.   Such terms as "riots" and "hoodlums" have no place in any honest, objective appraisal of these events.

The central continuing fact of American economic and social history over the past three and a half centuries is the special exploitation and robbery of the Negro community.   As a corollary to this reality, the central theme in the life and history of the Afro-American population is one continuous struggle to free itself from this agonizing situation.   The recent rebellions in Newark, Detroit, and revolts elsewhere over the past four years are but the latest examples highlighting this truth.

No useful purpose is served by Negro civil rights leaders straining to disassociate themselves from the forces of the ghetto rebellion.   Whitney Young's cautious statement that "the vast majority of Negroes are exercising patience, restraint and loyalty" is as irrelevant to understanding the Freedom Movement today, as it is reassuring to the "white power-structure" for whom such statements are obviously intended.

What is new, and therefore very relevant, is the fact of a growing number of youthful black men and women who are no longer patient but fed up; no longer restrained but ready to "go for broke"; and are indeed loyal, to *themselves* and their people because they are convinced the country is not loyal to them.

Disappointed in the Civil Rights Movement and its leaders, to whom they looked for *their* emancipation too; disillusioned, they have begun to act on their own.   They didn't create the ghetto slums, but as the victims they are making the ghettos of America the New Battleground.   They are confronting the whole fabric of exploitation in the ghetto, at the level that they see it functioning: the absentee-owned stores, and the property of the absentee-slumlords, and the police occupation force representing the State power of the colonial regime.

If as some people say, these revolts "have nothing to do with civil rights," it is only because the very concept "civil rights" is too narrow to deal with the basic economic and political problems facing the black population today.   If the method of resistance is no longer exclusively non-violent, it is because violence is the language of America and they, the colonized, wish to be heard.   If they are not making their appeal by way of moral argumentation, it is because they have concluded, *from the record*, that the leadership of this nation is basically immoral in its dealing with non-white people, the world over.   So their Manifesto is in the deed rather than the rhetoric and in this course of action they are making the title of James Baldwin's famous essay "The Fire Next Time" a prophetic reality.

Unlike the violence which has characterized American life and history, the violence of the ghetto rebellion is not motivated by greed and inhumanity. It is a form of resistance to deprivation and a protest against being ignored by the Affluent Society.

In their confiscation of food and useful merchandise from stores whose owners have been looting their pockets for years, they are showing their contempt for the "property rights" of all the petty exploiters and regard this as a way of "getting even."

In their combative defiance of the armed forces of the regime, and risking life and limb in the contest, they are giving their answer to current popular notions among "sociologists" concerning the "emasculation of the Negro male."

Like millions of their countrymen, Negro Americans increasingly understand that a government which is currently spending $75 billion a year on war and outerspace efforts to put a man on the moon has no intention of providing adequate funds to end joblessness, slum conditions and correct educational deprivation in the ghettos. In spite of the official deceptive propaganda to the contrary, racist wars abroad are not in the least likely to serve the cause of multi-racial democracy at home. If anything, racist wars abroad make the forces of domestic racism more arrogant and the colonized nationalities in America (Afro-American, Spanish-speaking and Indian), all of whom are the victims of facism, have an instinctive understanding of this.

So, certain of the colonized are acting upon their own definitions for they are convinced ours is a struggle for survival in a hostile racist society. One does not have to be a die-hard advocate of violence or anarchy to recognize the validity of a social rebellion by the oppressed which takes a violent form. Riots have little to do with freedom; revolts or rebellions against oppression have everything to do with freedom.

All reasonable people prefer to see social change and social emancipation effected in as peaceful and constructive a manner as possible. We are reminded that Detroit had the largest non-violent civil rights march in the history of any one city in America. In June (1963), 125,000 people—including thousands from the ghetto—marched for Freedom Now! led by Martin Luther King and Walter Reuther. This was two months before the March on Washington. I remember in 1959 how hundreds of people came from the Newark ghetto to the nation's capital for the national

"March for Integrated Schools" which brought 25,000 people to Washington, led by Jackie Robinson, A. Philip Randolph and others.   Today, Newark has thousands of black children on split-shifts in overcrowded, rundown schools, as do most ghettos across the country.   As is well known there are more completely segregated schools in the Northern urban centers today than there were when the Supreme Court's decision on public education was declared in 1954, while the South has desegregated only about 25 percent of its school districts during this period.

Through law suits and a variety of non-violent direct actions against segregation, for more than a decade, the many organizations of the Freedom Movement forced the nation to look at segregation and the daily humiliations that institution imposed upon Negro Americans.[1]   Since 1964, in flash-seasons of violent direct action, the dispossessed in the ghettos are forcing the country to look at their condition as a particular class (the most painfully exploited), among Negro Americans.   This is the same struggle for human dignity appearing in different forms.

The revolts against the ghetto condition are centered among the youth and the poorest sections of the working class; those whose economic circumstances today are very similar to the condition of the majority of the American working class during the Great Depression.

In a lengthy article in the *New York Times Magazine*, Bayard Rustin makes a quite different appraisal, in the following:

> Daniel Patrick Moynihan is correct in locating the riots in the "lower class" or in the words of another controversial man, Karl Marx, in the "lumpenproletariat" or "slum proletariat."   Lower class does not mean working class; the distinction is often overlooked in a middle-class culture that tends to lump the two together.
>
> The distinction is important.   The working class is employed.   It has a relation to the production of goods and services; much of it is organized in unions.   It enjoys a measure of cohesion, discipline and stability lacking in the lower class.   The latter is unemployed or marginally employed.   It is relatively unorganized, incohesive,

[1] It is not true, as Eric Hoffer suggests, that the non-violent movement for civil rights was (or is) a movement of "middle class Negroes."   It embraced all social classes in Negro life because all classes are affected, in varying degrees, by the reality of segregation and racial discrimination.

unstable.   It contains the petty criminal and antisocial elements.[2]

Further on in the article, Rustin coins the phrase "black slum proletariat" to describe his "lower class," or lumpenproletariat.

Of course one does not have to be an especially keen observer of society to recognize that the working class has many gradations within it—ranging from the poorest paid, unskilled and semi-skilled workers to the higher paid skilled workers, who are usually able to secure more steady employment than the unskilled for rather obvious reasons.   In an industrial society of rapidly advancing technology the job experience of the unskilled is likely to include more part-time work ("marginal employment") and longer periods of unemployment than the skilled worker.

However, they are all part of the working class because their class position is not determined by which one has a job and which is unemployed.

The auto worker in Detroit who operates a tool and die machine and the farm laborer in Arkansas or Texas who picks vegetables are both part of the working class because neither owns the means of production (land, factory and machines) and each sells his labor power for wages.   The Rustin-Moynihan thesis is mistaken because it sets up a quite artificial division between employed and unemployed workers by suggesting that only the employed are part of the working class, the rest being "lower class" or "lumpenproletariat."

Unemployment and marginal employment (part-time employment) make up a big part of the job experience of millions of black workers in America.   This reality is linked to the whole history of institutionalized racism in America.   The sharecropper or tenant farmer who is pushed off the land by the rapid changes in technology in agriculture may settle with his family in Charleston, Savannah, or New York.   He will live in the ghetto slums because that is the only kind of social environment a racist society has designed for him and his family.   He will begin to look for work as a common laborer on a construction gang, or down on the waterfront or he may join a group of migrant workers headed for the truck farms of New Jersey, upstate New York or Florida.

In any of these, as longshoreman, construction worker or migrant worker his employment is likely to be "marginal" at best, due to many factors, including the seasonal character of some

[2] "The Way Out of the Ghetto," August 13, 1967.

work, or lack of seniority required for steady employment, in such industries as maritime.   However as (part-time) longshoreman, construction worker or farm laborer, that he is part of the working class of America should be obvious.

The working class within the ghetto, which is predominantly Negro, and the working class which lives outside the ghetto and is multi-ethnic, are component parts of the same class.   Marx used the phrase *lumpenproletariat* to describe what he called "declassed elements"; rejects from the working class; parasites who live on the lower depths of society and who are basically not concerned with employment because they have found other ways to live. Marx's emphasis was on the *parasitism* of this group, as distinct from the working class.

There are such anti-social elements in the ghettos, and in the course of a revolt they may "get into the act," because they *are* petty parasites.   The liquor store is often their target, on such occasions.   However, to attribute the ghetto revolts to the activity of this group, "locating the riots in the lumpenproletariat" as Rustin proposes, is to be grossly out of touch with everyday life in the ghetto.

Joblessness, police brutality, and the lack of recreational facilities are among the things deeply resented by the youth, the middle-aged, the unemployed and the employed alike.   The revolt is to be "located" in their resentment.

One wonders whether or not there is a relationship between Bayard Rustin's analysis of what he calls "the riots" and his call for the police to "stop the riots by whatever force is necessary," a sentiment which fortunately did not find its way into the text of the statement[3] issued by the four national civil rights leaders on the same day.

WHO RIOTED?

In taking into account the significance of these events one would be remiss not to recognize there was an element of rioting in this whole picture.   The trigger-happy, panicky, ruthless conduct of many police and National Guardsmen was on the scale of a riot. Apartment buildings "suspected of hiding snipers" were sprayed with machine-gun bullets.   In some areas a point was made of systematically damaging Negro-owned businesses which had been

[3] *New York Times*, July 27, 1967, p. 19.

left untouched by the uprising. In Plainfield, the occupation troops conducted Nazi-type, house-to-house raids upon the ghetto neighborhoods, under the pretense of "looking for guns." This was in clear violation of the Constitutional protection against illegal search and seizure. They also sprayed a kind of nerve gas on the streets of the ghetto which temporarily paralyzes whomever it contacts. In Detroit more than six thousand political prisoners were taken and there are reports that part of Belle Isle recreation park was converted into a temporary concentration camp. This was a grim replay of similar scenes occurring in the South a few years ago when State Fair Grounds were converted into concentration camps and public school buses were used to transport children to jail. We must add to these examples the wanton assassination by policemen of three unarmed black men in the Algiers Motel in Detroit, during the week of the revolt.

The police, State Troopers and National Guardsmen literally rioted as they occupied the ghettos last summer, just as they had done in Watts, San Francisco, and elsewhere since 1964. The long list of civilian dead and injured in the ghetto is testimony to this fact.

This riotous conduct by the Armed Forces of the State, directed against the local civilian population, is in the classic style of colonial rule and is, today, the most overt expression of the growing fascist pattern developing in the United States.

THE COLONIAL WAR AT HOME

The arrogant display of military force at the local level is supplemented by a court system whose decisions regarding bail are often merely a convenient way of making the colonized hostage of the State. When a court sets bail at from $10,000 to $200,000 for an everyday wage earner, or a youth whose family is on welfare, or an unemployed worker, that amounts to a declaration by the State that these "citizens" are really hostages of the State (see Table 1).

The State power at the local level is expanding its arsenal of weapons and troop reserves all in the name of "riot control." In New York City a Tactical Patrol Force (TPF), organized in 1959 with 75 troops, now reportedly has 650. This is an elite corps, sent into combat against the youth in the Puerto Rican ghetto (El Barrio) in East Harlem for four nights last summer. A similar type TP unit had been used to keep the Negro ghetto on East Side Detroit under surveillance during the previous summer

Table 1

Place	Number of political prisoners taken	Date
Albany, Georgia	700	December 1961
Birmingham, Alabama	3,200	June 1963
Selma and Central Alabama	3,000	January–March 1965
Watts	3,952	August 1965
Detroit	6,670	July 1967

(1966) even though there had been no violent eruptions in that city.

The City Councils in both Newark and Tampa (Florida) have given approval to spend tens of thousands of dollars for "emergency shipments" of new weapons. These, and other examples which could be cited, are a further extension of the pattern of domestic military build-up for which Jackson, Mississippi received some attention when its City Council bought an armored tank for use against non-violent Civil Rights demonstrations a few years ago.

The general enlargement of the arsenal of weapons is accompanied by an active build-up in the size of the police forces, often way out of proportion to any civilian public-safety requirements. Why, for instance, does liberal New York City, with a population two and a half times larger than Los Angeles, have a police force six times larger than Los Angeles?[4]   There is also the matter of the kind of conservative ideology cultivated among the police, especially in the cities with large Negro or Spanish-speaking populations. This is not a monolithic picture. There are undoubtedly many decent men on the various police forces—men who have a good relationship with the people in the communities and are a credit to their profession. We are concerned here with general patterns of governmental power which are developing in our country. The kind of racist campaign conducted by the Police Benevolent Association to defeat the Civilian Review Board in New York, and the brutal beatings given peace marchers by the Los Angeles police (June 23) during demonstrations against the war in Vietnam, while President Johnson was speaking at a fund-raising banquet there, are significant cases in point.

Despite certain concessions to civil rights and a number of important court decisions favorable to the defense of civil liberties, militarism and the military presence are rapidly becoming the main

[4] See *New York Times*, July 20, 1967.

features of governmental power in American life. Whether expressed in the form of armed Tactical Units occupying the ghettos, a police mobilization to brutalize peace marchers, or a massive military build-up in Southeast Asia, the economic, political and psychological ascendancy of militarism is a primary factor shaping the character of national life in our country today.   In its ultimate expression, this development represents a serious, totalitarian threat to Constitutional liberties.

There are times when the contemporary spirit of a nation's institutions creeps through in the most unexpected places.   At the World's Fair in Montreal, "Expo 67," the male guides at the U.S. Pavilion were dressed in the uniform of various branches of the Armed Forces.   The spirit of militarism is abroad in the land, stretching its corpse-like influence over the fabric of the Republic. This, at once, reflects and contributes to the fact that governmental conduct has sunk to the lowest level of barbarity, public deception and dehumanization of any period since the blood-bath which overthrew Reconstruction, in the last century.

Frederick Douglass, in commenting on the passage of the Fugitive Slave Act and its impact, once said: ". . . the Mason and Dixon's line has been obliterated; New York has become as Virginia and the power [of slavery] . . . remains no longer a mere state institution but is now an institution of the whole U.S. . . . coextensive with the Star Spangled Banner. . . ."

As in 1852, once again, it is true today.   The line between Mississippi and Michigan, between Birmingham and Newark is rapidly being obliterated as the rise of the Military Establishment takes on a special meaning.   Policemanship as a style of government is no longer confined to the Southern-way-of-life but is now becoming institutionalized on a national level.   And the line between foreign and domestic policy is fading out as well, as militarism and the military presence become "coextensive with the Star Spangled Banner."

The escalation of the war in Vietnam and the escalation of the military budget (which is one of the hidden purposes behind all such military adventures), quiet aside from the senseless death toll and dishonor it has brought the nation, have had as a net result the *escalation of the economic and political power of the Military Establishment*.   This escalation, like the war itself, has taken place at a geometric rate of acceleration during the four years of the Johnson presidency.

The economic power of the military is in that lion's share of the National Budget, earmarked under the euphemism "defense." This military budget has been increased from $35 billion in 1963 to $70.3 billion in the current fiscal year 1967–68. This does not include appropriations for the space program. As a point of reference and comparison, the military budget of the U.S. is 20 percent larger than the military budget of Britain, the Soviet Union, France and China *combined*, even though the total population of these four countries adds up to five times the population of our country.[5]

The political power of the military resides in the neo-confederate chairmen of key committees in Congress, as well as in key personalities in the executive branch of the government. In addition to Secretary of State Dean Rusk of Georgia and General William Westmoreland of South Carolina, the Commander of the U.S. forces in Vietnam, the following are included:

Name	State	Chairman
Richard Russell	Georgia	Senate Armed Services Committee
L. Mendel Rivers	South Carolina	House Armed Services Committee
John Stennis	Mississippi	Senate Preparedness Sub-Committee
F. Edward Hébert (From Leander Perez's Dixiecrat machine)	Louisiana	House Preparedness Sub-Committee
John McClellan	Arkansas	{ Senate Committees
James Eastland	Mississippi	Investigating the
		"Riots" }
Russell Long	Louisiana	Senate Democratic "Whip"

These are the king-pins of the new Confederacy through whom the hawks in the Pentagon exercise their influence.   Since his days as Senate Majority Leader, Lyndon Johnson has been the high priest among them.

The manpower resources of the Military Establishment rest directly in the draft system, but also indirectly in the labor of the three and a half million workers,[6] whose paychecks derive from employment in the factories and offices of those companies contracted to engage in the production, transportation and stock-

[5] See "The Military Balance, 1966–67," published by the Institute for Strategic Studies, London, pp. 8–27.

[6] Estimated by economist Victor Perlo in his book, *Militarism and Industry* (New York: International Publishers, 1963).

piling of military hardware, napalm and other weapons of mass destruction.

It is the combination of manpower, recruited in the labor market at relatively high wages to manufacture military weapons, and the manpower guaranteed by the "forced-labor" of the draft system which constitutes the manpower pool made available to the Military Establishment.   Serious defections in either of these areas of manpower resource, by large numbers of people refusing as a matter of conscience to cooperate with militarism, would be a major contribution toward keeping alive the tradition of civilian-controlled government in our country.

Sensitive to this, the draft has been hurriedly renewed for four years by Congress.   The railroad workers strike, the first in 20 years, has been broken by the government, with the public rationale that "one thousand box cars of ammunition must be sent to Vietnam each week."   Such is the atmosphere created that auto workers, on strike against the Ford Motor Company (Secretary of Defense McNamara's home-base), are told by their leaders to cross their own picket lines in order to guarantee shipments of truck parts needed by the military for Vietnam.

We are reminded that Mussolini and Italian fascism came to power under the slogan of "getting the trains running on time."

In his important book, *The Accidental President*, the political analyst Robert Sherrill makes the following observation:

> It was during his [Johnson's] years as the most powerful man in Congress that the permanent diplomatic and military establishment . . . were given the funds and the freedom by Congress to gain the overwhelming influence that they still have today and *which it is not likely will be taken from them in normal fashion.*[7]

THE NEW "RESISTANCE MOVEMENT"

The road which leads from the "Indian massacres" of the last century to the Pentagon and another from the oppressive slave plantation to the ghetto are major conjunctive highways running through the very center of U.S. life and history.   In turn, they shape the mainstream contours of American national development. The idea that there is no warlike tradition of militarism in America,

[7] *The Accidental President* (New York: Grossman Publishers), p. 16.   Italics added.

is, of course, one of the most cherished of national myths.   Popular belief in this mythology serves as an opiate and a blinder for U.S. colonialism, past and present.   There is, indeed, no goosestepping tradition of the Hitler Germany kind in America but that is a matter of national style.

In the present period in the evolution of the American social system, the structured Military Establishment with its staggering financial resources in the public treasury, its ideology of barbarism and its manipulative control over the lives of millions, especially the youth, represents the main social cancer in the body politic of the nation.   It is an historically-evolved deformity which, at once, aggravates and brings into visible focus all the other social contradictions underlying the American Way of Life.   The contradiction between squandered wealth and dehumanizing poverty; the contradiction between a congenital racism and feeble efforts at becoming a Democracy; the contradiction between a tradition of civilian-controlled government, academic and other institutions, on the one hand, and the institutional power-requirements of the military-industrial complex on the other—all of these are exacerbated by the escalation of the power of the military in the affairs of the nation today.   Any leadership—whether in civil rights, peace, labor, church or the academic community—which ignores this reality and the dangers inherent in it is a leadership which is already obsolete.

The most hopeful development on the national scene in this period is the fact that this reality is being confronted by a growing mood of *resistance* among large sections of American people.   The revolts against the ghetto condition are but one form of this.   The peace coalition represented by the National Mobilization to End the War in Vietnam, with its new emphasis on direct action, expressed in the movement slogan "Confront the Warmakers," is another form, as are the college and university campus demonstrations against military recruitment and military research.   In addition there is the growing subculture which has been called "Hippies."   Despite certain hang-ups which limit the effectiveness of their example, the "Hippies" are engaged in a creative, irreverent assault upon all of the hypocritical, moribund, anti-human values and mores of the present social order.   Therefore, they too are an important component of the emerging new Resistance Movement.

This Movement, for an end to the tyranny of racism-militarism, and for a revolution in American values, is a vital stream of humanist consciousness in American life.   It also marks a nodal point, a qualitative change, in the deepening sense of "alienation" felt by a cross-section of the American people. Cutting across racial, class and ethnic lines, this sense of alienation from the present governmental structure is a rapidly growing phenomenon embracing a few millions. The Resistance Movement is the *organized* expression of this much larger phenomenon, and is just in the beginning stages of its development. Yet the nationwide visibility it is getting as a result of its varied activities is also beginning to awaken the ranks of organized labor: that decisive social force still tragically handicapped by a conservative bureaucracy in the AFL-CIO.

The basic objective of the Resistance Movement is to mobilize and build a massive organized grassroots opposition among the American people, capable of bringing to a halt and reversing the current trend towards a Military State in our country. The style is confrontation—on many levels—with the military machinery, its economy and its ideology. The program is to rescue human life from this juggernaut and redirect the nation to a course of genuine social progress. The immediate focus is upon ending the military intervention in Vietnam. Vietnam, more than any other issue in this century, symbolizes the dangerous shift of decision-making, institutional power into the hands of the military. It also epitomizes (in such acts as the burning of villages, the bombings of schools and hospitals, the mutilation of bodies for "souvenirs," etc.) the continued erosion and dehumanization of the American national character.

For all Freedom Fighters, therefore, the watchword is RESISTANCE! Unyielding resistance, and the building of a movement for all seasons. Whether in the streets of the ghettos, on the college campuses, at the Pentagon or elsewhere, the movement of confrontation-resistance is the vehicle for asserting a new social morality in America; a civilized morality which asserts the primary value of *human life* and its right to survive as the basis for liberty and the pursuit of happiness.

WILENSKY ARGUES THAT THE CONCEPTS OF CLASS AND CLASS CON-*sciousness are misleading in the quest for an understanding of the social reality in the United States. His question is: where do the ideas of class and class consciousness fit the situation of American labor well, and where do they fit badly? His theses are that in the United States, as in other rich countries, class consciousness among manual workers is a transitional phenomenon characterizing workers not yet accustomed to the modern metropolis and work place; that a clearly defined working class no longer exists, if, indeed, it ever did; and that much behavior and many attitudes said to be rooted in class are instead a matter of race, religion, ethnic origin, education, age, and stage in the family life cycle. Members of any one of these groups, Wilensky claims, display more homogeneity of behavior and belief than all manual workers or even union members. Insofar as class categories remain useful, it is the line which divides stably-employed, well-educated, well-paid workers from the lower class that is becoming more important than the split between upper working class and lower middle class.*

Wilensky views class in functionalist terms as a system of distribution of so-called "rewards" in society—who gets whatever is valued and why. The idea of class consciousness in Marxian theory—which refers to an awareness in the members of a class of their common interests and of the opposing interests of another class (or classes) and the readiness to act collectively to realize their class interests—is not applicable to American labor, except sporadically and in brief periods of its early history, especially during rapid industrialization. Such consciousness is fading into memory.

Depending on how you ask the question, Americans will tell you there are no classes, many classes, that they belong to the middle class, that they belong to the working class. There is considerable cross-class identification and little class allegiance, except in the upper strata, where identification and allegiance are considerable. Political identification, however, tends along class lines: workers (especially union workers) are likely to vote Democratic. Labor unions do much to mobilize the committed vote, activate class disposition, and reinforce party appeals. This happens, suggests Wilensky, through inter-related steps in which the development of pro-labor orientations leads to the acceptance of union discipline, development and transfer of political skills, and increased political interest.

Not only are American workers rarely class-conscious, they are becoming less so, especially compared to European labor. Wilensky argues that union leaders and rank-and-file have become integrated into the system essentially as the result of the impact of continued economic growth on the structure of opportunity.

34

CLASS, CLASS CONSCIOUSNESS, AND AMERICAN WORKERS

Harold L. Wilensky

For centuries, social critics and social scientists have given us the images with which we construct our picture of the world. Among the concepts that have done the most to mislead us in our search for an understanding of social reality are "class" and "class consciousness." European students of labor—*théoricien et militant* alike—take for granted the utility of such ideas. In America, academic journals and the press are filled with references to the "middle class" or "working class"; discussions of the affluent worker becoming "middle class" are commonplace. And the constitutions of many American unions only yesterday contained the ringing slogans of class warfare.

This rhetoric—whether it is tolerated by nostalgic exsocialists who head a few modern labor unions or whether it is taken more seriously, as in popular discussions of the affluent worker—obscures more than it reveals of the shape of American society. I should like to ask, "Where do the ideas of class and class consciousness fit the situation of American labor well, and where do such ideas fit badly?" I shall argue that, in the United States and in other rich countries, class consciousness among manual workers is a transitional phenomenon—characterizing workers not yet accus-

Reprinted from Harold L. Wilensky, "Class, Class Consciousness, and American Workers," Chapter 2 in William Haber, ed., *Labor in a Changing America* (New York: Basic Books, 1966), pp. 12–28, by permission of the publisher. © 1966 by Basic Books, Inc., Publishers, New York.

tomed to the modern metropolis and the modern work place; that a clearly defined working class no longer exists, if it ever did; that much behavior and many attitudes said to be rooted in class are instead a matter of race, religion, ethnic origin, education, age, and stage in the family life cycle. Indeed, almost any of these traditional groupings of the population display more homogeneity of behavior and belief than "labor," if by the latter term we mean all manual workers or even all union members.

Finally, if we want to use economic classifications that yield uniformity in ideology or mentality, we must turn to such categories as "small entrepreneur" (a small part of the lower middle class) or to particular crafts (a small part of the upper working class) and to the established professions (a minority of the upper middle class). Insofar as class categories remain at all useful, the line that divides stably-employed, well-educated, well-paid workers from the lower class is becoming more important than the split between upper working class and lower middle class. Whether we are witnessing the *embourgeoisement* of the workers or the sinking of the middle class into the proletariat, the top of one and the bottom of the other seem to form a new middle mass, a population that increasingly shares common values, beliefs, and tastes. And the process goes on in every rich country.

In general, I hope that all this will add up to a more realistic picture of the position, prospects, and mentality of that minority of the urban labor force that we customarily label "manual worker" or "working class" and its relation to other classes.

THE IDEA OF SOCIAL CLASS

All students of stratification are concerned with the distribution of rewards in society—who gets whatever is valued and why. They are also interested in the effect of the distribution of rewards on human behavior.[1] But there is no agreement about what

[1] The necessity of specialization—universal differences in role based on sex, age, work, and authority—leads everywhere to social stratification. People classify one another in categories and place these categories above or below one another on a scale of superiority and inferiority. The criteria of ranking vary; anything valued and unequally distributed may suffice: wealth, power, magic, women, and so on. Despite the recurrent dream of absolute equality— for example, the "classless society"—every society past or present has had some system of stratification. Distinctions are made. Some positions are honored, others not. Some are accorded more authority than others. Who is and who is not honored—the priest, the workman, the scholar, or the warrior—the dis-

rewards shared by what strata and what positions held by what groups are significant in explaining social structure and change; for instance, how we decide whether a man is a member of the working class or whether the working class is becoming middle class.

Karl Marx's definition of class, although imprecise, tends to emphasize, not sources of income (wages, profit, rent), not amount of income, not type of occupation, but what he called "the relations of production"—that is, *authority relations rooted in the distribution of property rights*, political power anchored in economic power.[2] Individuals form a class only insofar as they are locked in political combat with another class. Marxist discussion of "class consciousness" has since followed this line, emphasizing three criteria. In the Marxian view, a man is said to be class conscious when he is (1) rationally aware of his own class interests and identifies with them; (2) aware of other class interests and rejects them as illegitimate; and (3) aware of and ready to use collective political means to realize his class interests.[3]

In this Marxian sense, is American labor class conscious?

---

tance between top and bottom positions; the difference between rich and poor, leader and rank-and-file; these and other features of stratification systems vary from place to place, time to time. But power and prestige differences do appear everywhere. Among the reasons are these: (1) Any society has to distribute people among its different positions and induce them to perform essential duties. (2) Every society has a hierarchy of values based on the fact of scarcity. (3) Differences in the distribution of these values (for example, income, power) move people to go after positions and to perform once they are in them. (4) As long as the family has anything to do with bringing up children and as long as some of the behavior and possessions unequally valued and unequally distributed are learned or acquired in the family, then some inequality will be perpetuated. (5) The various criteria of stratification are related—power differences among men are universal; those with power can use it to obtain for themselves and their kin those things which are valued (a man of power can use connections to get his son a good job; a man of wealth can buy his son a good education). Cf. K. Davis and Wilburt E. Moore, "Some Principles of Stratification," *American Sociological Review*, X (1945), 242–49.

[2] For the best recent discussion of Marx's theory of class, see Ralf Dahrendorf, *Class and Class Conflict in Industrial Society* (Stanford: Stanford University Press, 1959), Chap. 1. The task of evaluating Marx is beyond the scope of the present essay. Note, however, that by Marx's own definition of class, the abolition of private ownership of the means of production cannot lead to the "classless society" because authority is obviously neither tied to the legal title of property nor confined to the industrial sphere. For a balanced summary of sociological critiques of Marx, see *ibid.*, Chap. 4.

[3] C. Wright Mills, *White Collar* (New York: Oxford University Press, 1951), Chap. 15.

MARXIAN CLASS CONSCIOUSNESS
IN AMERICAN LABOR HISTORY

Surely, for brief episodes, during our most rapid industrialization, American labor displayed a militancy that fits the Marxian model and that has its contemporary counterpart in the labor movements of less developed countries.   In the last quarter of the nineteenth century, American labor protest was intermittently tame and violent, economic and political; labor organizations were unsteady, easily diverted to elaborate political programs (from greenbackism to the single tax, from revolutionary anarchism to Marxian socialism, from Owen's "estate guardianship" to producers' and consumers' cooperation).   Obstinate employers used private armies; the courts declared unions to be criminal conspiracies (until use of the injunction in the late nineteenth century gave them a better weapon); and the government broke strikes by use of local, state, and federal troops.   In the 1880s, especially during and just after the depression of 1884–1885, labor protest began to sweep the land.   Skilled and unskilled, women and men, native and foreign-born—never before (and not again until the 1930s) had American labor displayed such a drive to organize.

The peak of immigration was reached that decade, and streams of newcomers caught the enthusiasm.   "Labor organizations assumed the nature of a real class movement. . . . General strikes, sympathetic strikes . . . nationwide political movements became the order of the day."[4]   Employer associations quickly counteracted with lockouts, blacklists, armed guards, and detectives.   When the wave of strikes failed, a consumer-boycott movement of epidemic proportions got under way.   This was a time of great upheaval, when the Knights of Labor, an inclusive labor organization espousing the ideal of producers' cooperation, spearheaded a mid-eighties mass movement culminating in an unsuccessful nationwide strike for the eight-hour day.   It was the time, too, of the famous bomb explosion on Haymarket Square, which touched off a period of hysteria and police terror in Chicago and resulted in the unjust conviction and execution of innocent men.[5]   The strength of employer opposition and the unwieldiness of the Knights' own organization threw the labor movement into decline.

[4] Selig Perlman, *A History of Trade Unionism in the United States* (New York: Macmillan, 1928), p. 84.

[5] *Ibid.*, pp. 68–105; and Charles A. Beard and Mary R. Beard, *The Rise of American Civilization* (New York: Macmillan, 1933), II, 73, 220ff.

As the movement broke up, the American Federation of Labor (AFL) was established to organize workers on straight trade-union lines, for better wages, hours, and working conditions through collective bargaining—foreshadowing the form in which labor protest was to be cast during the next century. The last gasp of nineteenth-century working-class militancy came in the form of the Homestead strike of 1892 (which involved a violent battle between an army of 300 Pinkerton detectives hired by Andrew Carnegie and armed strikers, including women and boys, who were finally overcome by the militia) and the great Pullman strike of 1894, which was broken with the aid of federal troops, a federal injunction, and the imprisonment of its leaders.

This enormous thrust upward from the people of poverty and low status was again repeated in the early days of Franklin Roosevelt's New Deal and provoked much the same militant fear on the part of the wealthy and well-born. In the 1930s, with almost revolutionary fervor, autoworkers in Flint, Michigan, seized control of corporate property in the famous sit-down strikes.

Marxian class consciousness? Yes, sporadic, loosely organized, and, as America has grown richer, fading into memory. Today, some of those sit-down strikers—or their sons—peacefully negotiate contracts with employers, serve on community welfare council boards, run for municipal office (and occasionally win), and live the modestly comfortable middle-class life of trade-union officials. The spontaneous protest movements of yesterday have become the "business unions" of today—large stable organizations sanctioned by contracts and the law. American labor today has limited goals: better wages, shorter hours, and improved conditions of employment. Its means are mainly economic: the establishment of collective-bargaining agreements enforced in part by arbitration of grievances. Occasional legal strikes over the terms of the agreement occur, but these have become the accepted alternative to massive state control of labor relations. A decreasing proportion of union members and of the total labor force is now drawn into strikes. The strike weapon, though not obsolete, has been blunted.

Similarly, in politics, the period of early industrialization saw many efforts to base political parties on distinctive working-class interests and membership. But, in recent decades, American labor has taken its place in the coalition of interest groups that dominates the Democratic party nationally and in the machinery of both major parties at local levels.

ATTITUDES TOWARD CLASS TODAY

The theme that class consciousness in American labor has dwindled is consistent with what we know of the attitudes of the American population toward social class and class conflict.   Keeping in view the Marxian sense of class consciousness, what can we say about awareness of classes?   Surveys using a variety of questions, leading and neutral, fixed and open-ended, indicate that most Americans think that classes exist, but there is little agreement about their nature and number, and there is great variation in how people on the same income and occupational level identify themselves.

In such research, the pitfalls are many and the results not very gratifying.   There is the well-known problem that phrasing affects response: the researcher gets what he asks for.   Thus, if you suggest that "Some people say that there are social classes in the U.S.A.   They call them lower, middle, and upper social classes," and then ask, "Which would you put yourself in?" the vast majority will choose the comfortable "middle."   Add "working class" as one of your alternatives and a third to half of these "middle class" identifiers will switch to "working class."   Leave the matter open—"What social classes do you think there are [in this city]" and "which one of them are you in?"—and as many as half the population will either deny the existence of classes or in some way indicate that the idea is meaningless.[6]

If you now confine yourself to those who think that classes exist and ask them for the number and characteristics of the classes, you will tap a great range of rather vague ideas.   Few Americans see labor and capital as the classes; few see them at war.   Various groups and strata emphasize various criteria of ranking—the value of material possessions (house, furniture, cars, clothing), type of job or job opportunities, amount of education, income or economic security (the lower strata emphasize this more), refinement of taste and manners (college people sometimes emphasize this), "morals" (the thrift-spendthrift theme is strong here among some members of the lower middle class), or social origins.   The number of classes named is similarly variable.

Finally, the context of questioning and the area of life covered by the questions affect criteria for the definition of the classes.   If

[6] Cf. Richard Centers, *The Psychology of Social Class* (Princeton: Princeton University Press, 1949), and Joseph A. Kahl, *The American Class Structure* (New York: Rinehart, 1957), Chap. 6.   Using four census tracts in Minneapolis representing four rental levels, Gross asked 935 subjects all three questions

you go to a man in the evening and ask about the neighbors, he will think about status symbols and styles of life—consumption, house, car, leisure uses; if you talk to him on the job and ask about the people there, he will think of authority—the authority of bosses, of skill and expertise.[7] The average American is a Veblenian at home, a modified Marxist at work.

In assessing class consciousness in American labor, it is perhaps more important to examine the types of people who label themselves upper, middle, or working class. By any objective measure, there is considerable cross-class identification. About a fifth of all manual workers call themselves middle class; more than a fifth of all professional, business, and white-collar people identify as working class.[8] The clearest and most consistent awareness of class is at the top; a hard core of business, profes-

---

described above. Here is a comparison of percentages using one or another label by form of question, along with results from other studies using roughly comparable questions:

			Form of question and sample				
Percentage saying:	UML Minneapolis[a]	UMWL Minneapolis[a]	UMWL U.S.A.[b]	UMWL U.S.A.[c]	Open Minneapolis[a]	Open U.S.A.[d]	Open Tallahassee[e]
Upper	5	2	3	4	1	3	2
Middle	76	42	43	36	31	47	43
White-collar	—	—	—	—	—	—	3
Working	—	45	51	52	11	11	6
Lower	10	3	1	5	3	4	2
No classes	2	1	1	—	14	—	25
Don't know	4	2	1	3	20	28	—
Other classes	3	5	—	—	15	8	9
No response	—	—	—	—	5	—	10
Total	100	100	100	100	100	100	100
	(935)	(935)	(1,097)	(1,337)	(935)	(5,217)[f]	(320)

[a] Neal Gross, "Social Class Identification in the Urban Community," *American Sociological Review*, XVIII (1953), 398–404. Four census tracts chosen to represent four rental levels.

[b] Richard Centers, *op. cit.*, p. 77. Centers reports on two national samples. These samples were cross sections of white males. These are the results which Centers obtained in his sample of July 1945.

[c] *Ibid.*, p. 77. This is Centers' cross section of February 1946.

[d] "The People of the U.S.—A Self Portrait," *Fortune*, XXI (1940), 14. A national cross-section quota sample.

[e] John L. Haer, "An Empirical Study of Social Class Awareness," *Social Forces*, XXXVI (1957), 117–21. Area probability sample.

[f] Total, not reported in the *Fortune* article, is cited in Haer, *op. cit.*, p. 119.

[7] Cf. Kahl, *op. cit.*, p. 86.

[8] *Ibid.*, pp. 161–62. In my study of the Detroit area, about two in five of the white men in the upper working class (defined by income and occupation) aged 21–55 identify as middle class given the four choices; even one in four of the men on relief say that they are middle class.

sional, and technical people plus some of the clerical and sales people call themselves middle class no matter how you ask the question. Among workers, the more skilled are the most class conscious—consistent with the fact that labor organization emerged first among employees in a strategic market or technical position (printers, locomotive engineers, cutters in the garment industry).

What about the rejection of other class interests as illegitimate and the willingness to act out such sentiments politically? The few recent American studies that have looked for this evidence of class consciousness have turned up precious little of it. For instance, a sample of white men in Philadelphia, half Protestant, half Catholic, was asked in 1953: "To which one of these groups do you feel you owe your allegiance—business or labor?" They were also asked whether they agreed or disagreed with six policy statements, three taken from the CIO, three from the NAM. To be scored class conscious, a man had to choose sides, agree with all his side's policy statements, and disagree with the others. By this measure, only minorities of every group were class conscious: 40 percent of the big businessmen in the sample, 25 percent of the small businessmen, 28 percent of unionized workers, and only 13 percent of nonunionized workers. On the allegiance question, more union workers were neutral than were pro-labor.[9]

A similar study of unionized textile workers in Paterson, New Jersey, a highly industrialized city with a long history of industrial conflict, showed similar results. "How do classes get along?" these workers were asked. "In general are they like enemies, or like equal partners, or like leaders and followers?" As Table 1 suggests, the most common responses to this and similar questions reflect more a pattern of paternalism than one of class warfare. One worker said, "If the bosses would treat the working people right, they would get along all the time. It's like a dog with a bone. If you give him food, he will be all right. Just treat us right and we'll follow right along." Another expressed his general approval of the class system in this most un-Marxian way: "The people who have money own businesses, and the rest of the people work for them. If there were no rich people, who would the poor

---

[9] Oscar Glantz, "Class Consciousness and Political Solidarity," *American Sociological Review*, XXIII (1958), 375–83. The sample of 201 Protestants and 199 Catholics was a multistage sample of households, stratified and purposive at the first stage (precincts of varying occupational and religious composition), and random, with different probabilities, at the second stage.

**Table 1. Attitudes about Class Relations
among Ninety-five Textile Workers
in Paterson, New Jersey
(Including Multiple Answers)**

Paternalism	27
Enemies	21
Partnership	19
Snobbish or jealous	12
Vague	8
Don't know	14

people work for?" Twenty-eight percent expressed such pater-
nalistic views. One in five saw classes as partners; about one in
five, as enemies. Over one in three held some other view, mostly
vague. Most of these unionists felt that the class system was
both inevitable and desirable. And although one in three thought
that the system was becoming more rigid, half thought that it was
becoming more open, especially for the next generation.[10]

The most intensive recent survey of the political expression of
working-class consciousness was carried out among 375 blue-
collar men in Detroit. If we are to uncover Marxian class consciousness anywhere, it would be in this study.[11] The sample was
chosen from seven ethnically homogeneous neighborhoods: one
of them northwest European, three mainly Negro, three Polish—
generally overrepresenting the economically deprived and uprooted. They were interviewed when severe unemployment was
a fresh memory—down from a recession peak of 20 percent of the
labor force in 1957–1958 to 6 percent at the time of the interview
in 1960. All but 10 percent used class imagery in response to at
least one of eight unstructured questions designed to elicit spontaneous expressions of class symbolism (who was his favorite
president and why, etc.). The closer one pushed these men to a
Marxian model, however, the smaller the fraction that one could

[10] Jerome Manis and Bernard Meltzer, "Attitudes of Textile Workers to
Class Structure," *American Journal of Sociology*, LX (1954), 30–35. The
sample: 200 randomly-selected members of the TWUA-CIO in Paterson, New
Jersey. Ninety-five men were interviewed, including sixty-seven operatives,
nineteen craftsmen, and nine laborers. Median age: fifty. Median residence
in Paterson: forty years.

[11] John C. Leggett, "Uprootedness and Working-Class Consciousness,"
American Journal of Sociology, LXVIII (1963), 682–92. Cf. Alfred W. Jones,
Life, Liberty, and Property (New York: J. B. Lippincott, 1941), a sophisticated
study of attitudes among Akron residents on such issues as the sit-down strikes
of 1936.

call class-conscious. From mere class verbalization, characterizing 26 percent of the sample, the measure moved toward militancy
as follows: (1) "When business booms in Detroit, who gets the
profits?" Answers such as "rich people" or "big business" were
considered indicators of moderate "skepticism" and covered 30
percent. (2) Favoring a statement about picketing a landlord
was scored "militant radicalism"; 23 percent went this far. (3)
Agreeing with the statement that the wealth of our country should
be divided up equally so that people would have an equal chance
to get ahead counted as militant egalitarianism. Only 10 percent
would go all the way, the same tiny fraction that failed to verbalize
in class terms at all.

Do class attitudes affect a man's politics? Do class-conscious
union members, however few, act out their militancy?

THE LABOR VOTE

During the presidential campaign of 1948, when President Truman
was running for office, I had an opportunity to study political
action in a local union of the autoworkers in southeast Chicago.
A local officer recounted an incident in a plant across the street
that was discussed during the campaign by members of his local.
He was telling me about the union shop, not politics, and he said
he would give me an example of how important it was "from the
standpoint of discipline" that workers be pro-union:

> There was a guy over there who was bitterly against
> Roosevelt. . . . Then Roosevelt died and the boys in
> the shop felt pretty bad. They decided that they would
> have three minutes' silence on the day Roosevelt was
> buried. Well, this old guy had it all figured out ahead
> of time. When the bell rang all the fellows stood up at
> their machines in absolute quiet. . . . And then this
> old geezer began to . . . make as much noise as he
> could. . . . The funny thing is that [the workers] didn't
> do a thing. They just turned away from him and
> wouldn't even speak to him afterwards. . . . They came
> over to the union and the first thing was they insisted that
> he be thrown out of the union or at least suspended for a
> couple of months. We had a big meeting about that and
> I told the boys that that wasn't a real punishment, that
> the agony of having to work with the men would be a lot
> worse than having a leave of absence. I told them that
> they should fine him and make him keep on working. So

that's what they did. They fined him $100 and the money went for a fund to build a statue of Franklin Roosevelt . . . [When he came to the local meeting to pay the fine, he] stood right up there in front of all his fellow workers and he said that he had been wrong and that he was sorry. . . . It took a lot of courage to admit that he was wrong. That made a terrific difference. You have no idea. He's made a good union man.

The Democratic New Deal tradition was still strong among the union activists in 1948 and—as in the case of the story—they slid easily from problems of discipline on strictly union matters to problems of discipline on strictly political matters. The president of Local 166, one member commented, "can't get it through his head that a guy can be Republican and still be for the union."[12]

For a quarter of a century, studies of voting and political orientation have shown that American labor unions have, with their emphasis on issues rather than man or party, solidified the political direction of those exposed to their influence, helping to keep their active members in the old New Deal–Fair Deal coalition, revived in President Johnson's "Great Society." The years 1944–1952 saw the emergence of a new postwar, post-Roosevelt political generation—a loosening of the ties that bind ethnic Catholics to the urban Democratic machines[13] and a breakup of the lower-middle-class–working-class coalition that formed the basis of Democratic strength for two decades. There is some evidence that, nationally, the lower half of the working class, including the Negro minority, had politically significant elements that were becoming alienated from both the Democratic party and the political process.[14] For the minority involved directly

[12] Harold L. Wilensky, "The Labor Vote: A Local Union's Impact on the Political Conduct of Its Members," *Social Forces*, XXXV (1956), 114. The following discussion of the labor vote is drawn from this article, which also assesses evidence on political behavior of union members and activists up to 1956.

[13] Samuel Lubell, *The Future of American Politics* (New York: Harper, 1951) and Seymour M. Lipset, *et al.*, "The Psychology of Voting," in *Handbook of Social Psychology*, ed. Gardner Lindzey (Cambridge, Mass.: Addison-Wesley, 1954), II.

[14] An analysis by Morris Janowitz and Dwaine Marvick of the Survey Research Center data on the 1952 election campaign shows that nonvoting among lower-lowers (defined by income and occupation) reached 45 percent, and those who voted gave Stevenson only a 5 percent plurality. Catholics as a whole gave Stevenson a similarly small plurality. Like the farmers, the lower middle class made major shifts to Eisenhower. *Competitive Pressure and Democratic*

with unions, however, the old ties to the liberal-labor wing of the Democratic party remained strong.   From 1936 to 1952, comparisons between the candidate and/or party preferences and participation of union and nonunion voters on roughly the same socioeconomic level consistently show that the union voters are less apathetic and are more inclined to vote Democratic.[15]   For example, Louis Harris, analyzing poll results for 1952, concludes that: (1) while the rest of the nation was going 3:2 for Eisenhower, union members were voting over 3:2 for Stevenson ("the labor vote held remarkably well"); (2) fewer than one in ten Catholic union members bolted the Democrats, compared to three in ten of the nonunion Catholics; (3) labor and economic issues were a bit more salient for union members and their families than for the rest of the population; (4) union members were solidly convinced that their economic welfare was tied to continued Democratic rule; but (5) the families of union members voted 9:8 for Eisenhower, slipping from their normal 2:1 Democratic inclination.   (Two out of every ten members of union families bolted from the voting pattern of their household breadwinner.)[16]   These

Consent (University of Michigan, Institute of Public Administration, 1956). President Johnson's even more overwhelming victory over Barry Goldwater in 1964 similarly cut across class lines; every bloc of voters moved to the Democrats because of fear of extremism in domestic affairs and recklessness in foreign affairs.

[15] See Gallup poll results reported for 1936, 1940, and 1944, in V. O. Key, Jr., _Politics, Parties, and Pressure Groups_ (3rd ed.; New York: Crowell Co., 1952), p. 79.   On 1948, see David Truman in F. Mosteller, _et al._, "The Pre-Election Polls of 1948," _Social Science Research Council Bulletin_, LX (1949), 229–230; and Angus Campbell and Robert L. Kahn, _The People Elect a President_ (Ann Arbor: Survey Research Center, 1952), pp. 27–28.   On 1952, see Angus Campbell, G. Gurin, and Warren E. Miller, _The Voter Decides_ (Evanston: Row, Peterson, 1954), pp. 72–73.

[16] Labor Was Not an Issue in the Election," in _Labor and Nation Timely Papers_, Vol. I, No. 1 (1953), 15–25, and Louis Harris, _Is There a Republican Majority?_   (New York: Harper, 1954), pp. 148–49.   R. W. Dodge, using interviews with an area probability sample of the adult population in Detroit in 1951–1952, found that about 80 percent of the people in union families who indicated a political preference favored the Democratic party, while the nonunion segment had only a slight Democratic majority.   The contrast held for the labor-backed mayoralty candidate in 1951, whose main support, however weak, came from persons in union (especially CIO) families.   "Some Aspects of the Political Behavior of Labor Union Members in the Detroit Metropolitan Area" (unpublished doctoral dissertation, University of Michigan, 1953).   Only two of these studies—Harris, _op. cit._, and Bernard R. Berelson, Paul F. Lazarsfeld and W. H. McPhee, _Voting_ (Chicago: University of Chicago Press, 1954)—use controls for such politically-relevant social categories as race, ethnicity, and religion.

studies suggest that although labor unions change few votes (the John L. Lewis endorsement of Willkie is often cited),[17] they do much to mobilize the committed vote, to activate class disposition, and to reinforce party appeals.[18]

That class consciousness can combine with union activity to yield uniform voting is shown in an analysis of the hard-core supporters of G. Mennen Williams, the liberal Democratic governor of Michigan from 1948 to 1960, now Assistant Secretary of State in charge of African affairs. Recognizing Governor Williams' strong commitment to civil rights, almost all of the Negroes, union and nonunion, militant and tame, voted for him in 1958. But when we look at the Williams vote among whites, we find: (1) militant unionists, 81 percent; (2) moderate unionists, 72 percent; (3) nonmilitant unionists (the ones who merely mention class in discussing issues or avoid class symbolism entirely), 52 percent; (4) militant nonunionists (only 5 cases); (5) moderate nonunionists, 50 percent; (6) nonmilitant nonunionists, 38 percent.[19] Clearly, that minority of workers who are highly class-conscious and are exposed to a lively union act out their ideology in the political arena.

We can see the process by which this takes place. Comparison of the political orientation of members and nonmembers or of union actives and inactives suggests that: (1) routine experience in union social and economic affairs leads to a generalized pro-labor orientation; (2) this orientation leads to acceptance of union discipline in strikes and collective bargaining; (3) the younger, more ambitious, better educated and sometimes more skilled workers who become involved in local union activity and take charge of union affairs develop transferable political skills in the union office and come to see political action as a necessary exten-

[17] E.g., see Irving Bernstein, "John L. Lewis and the Voting Behavior of the CIO," *Public Opinion Quarterly*, V (1941), 233–249.

[18] Cf. Key, *op. cit.*, pp. 79–80. Berelson, *et al.*, *op. cit.*, pp. 37–53, report that in Republican Elmira, in 1948, not only did union members vote more Democratic than nonmembers of the same occupation, class, education, age, or religion, but also that the more pro-union workers were more Democratic, and, in an IAM-AFL local studied, the more interaction the members had with other union members, the more Democratic the vote. Also, those FDR voters who were identified working class remained most loyal to Democrats in 1948, *ibid.*, pp. 253–73.

[19] John C. Leggett, "Working-Class Consciousness, Race, and Political Choice," *American Journal of Sociology*, LXIX (1963), 171–76. Three in four of the sample belonged to a union; eight in ten of these were members of a CIO union.

sion of the collective-bargaining process; (4) locally, they cultivate political influence to protect their institutional privileges—gain police support in the maintenance of picket lines; (5) in national campaigns, they articulate the national union line at a local level in informal ways, and, less often through precinct organization, see discipline in the political sphere as a normal part of trade-union loyalty; (6) all this adds up to increased political interest and activity both in and out of the union, and, when the available "friends of labor" are mainly liberal Democrats, it gives the political focus of the activists a broader "labor-liberal" flavor.[20]

STRUCTURAL ROOTS OF IDEOLOGICAL DIVERSITY: THE LIMITS OF CLASS ANALYSIS

That we find some workers who are class conscious even in a Marxian sense, that we can point to a labor vote which pro-labor politicians count on should not obscure equally important and perhaps increasingly important facts about American society. The membership of American labor organizations is only about a third of all nonagricultural employees, compared with more than half in England and more than two-thirds in Sweden. American labor is conservative. Compared to European labor, it shows a low degree of class consciousness. Its leaders have become integrated into the power and status structure of a private-enterprise

---

[20] Harold L. Wilensky, "The Labor Vote," *op. cit.*, p. 120. Cf. two sample surveys of the Detroit area—Dodge, *op. cit.*, and Arthur Kornhauser, A. J. Mayer, and H. L. Sheppard, *When Labor Votes* (New York: University Books, 1956). The latter found, for a general UAW population, what appeared in the Chicago local that I examined. Cf. two case studies which showed a positive relation between activity and acceptance of labor political effort. Arnold Rose, *Union Solidarity* (Minneapolis: University of Minnesota Press, 1952), pp. 79, 165 and J. Seidman, J. London, and B. Karsh, "Political Consciousness in a Local Union," *Public Opinion Quarterly*, XV (1951–1952), 692–702. Though popular speculation is abundant, systematic analysis of the character of labor as a political force is rare. In addition to Seidman, *et al.*, Kornhauser, *et al.*, and Wilensky, see F. Calkins, *The CIO and the Democratic Party* (Chicago: The University of Chicago Press, 1952); and H. E. Freeman and M. Showel, "Differential Political Influence of Voluntary Associations," *Public Opinion Quarterly*, XV (1951–1952), 703–14. The latter, on the basis of a pre-election survey in 1950 in the state of Washington using an area probability sample, concludes that business, political, and veterans' associations exert *widest* positive influence; labor and church organizations, *narrowest*. Unions, like the Catholic Church, apparently achieved high saturation of a small target; positive influence was confined to their own membership; in fact, labor's hypothetical endorsement had a negative effect on candidate preference among nonmembers.

economy and a pressure-group polity. The mass of unorganized wage and salaried workers is similarly integrated into the mainstream of community life.

These characteristics of American labor can be explained in large part by the impact of continued economic growth on the structure of opportunity. If, on the whole, the rich were getting richer, and the poor, poorer; if occupations were becoming more manual and less skilled; if depressions were frequent and severe; if, in short, the opportunity to rise in the social and economic scale was declining while mass aspirations were rising, we might expect American labor to swing in a politically class-conscious direction. The evidence suggests just the opposite.

Occupational and income changes have brought a vast heterogeneity to the labor force. This heterogeneity is epitomized by the growing middle layers of American society—the new middle class of white-collar and professional people, the increasingly skilled upper crust of manual workers. Advanced specialization has made for finer distinctions of status and a multiplication of occupational worlds. Instead of two armies massed on an industrial battlefield—"labor" on one side, "capital" on the other —we have immense variation in interest and attitude within the ranks of each, and a consequent decline in the solidarity of each.[21] On the management side, the complexity of internal cleavages follows the increased complexity of organization—with increased bargaining over power and budget between staff advisors of specialized knowledge and power-conscious executives, between levels of authority, or on the same level of authority between rival advisors and rival supervisors. Although it is still useful to distinguish between the managers and the managed, the lines are becoming a bit blurred. On the labor side, even unionized workers divide on age, sex, seniority, and skill lines, not to mention the division by religion, nationality, and race. Union or nonunion American workers display much diversity in values, beliefs, and ways of life.

[21] Wilbert E. Moore, "Occupational Structure and Industrial Conflict," in *Industrial Conflict*, edited by Arthur Kornhauser and others (New York: McGraw-Hill, 1954), pp. 221 ff.

CYNICISM, ARGUES HODGES, IS A CONSTANT FEATURE OF THE LABOR *movement, an informal philosophy of labor which results from the workers' awareness that they are exploited and used for the benefit of the bosses. It is a reflection of their disillusionment with the labor movement and collective struggle; their resignation to getting what they can for themselves and their families; and their contempt for all movements, parties, and principles. Cynicism is the conception of the political world as essentially hostile to the interests of manual workers. Young workers are especially likely to be cynics, having been least affected by labor's earlier struggles and most affected by the ethos of individual gain.*

Cynicism is essentially the worker's response to his alienation, from his work and from a society that exploits him. In the United States, Henry Miller has embodied this cynicism in his novels, as summarized in his statement "I don't want it when I'm dead. I want it now." This form of cynicism fortifies demands for higher wages and better working conditions by undermining the authority of the boss and the "system." Yet it is not akin to the Marxian concept of class consciousness, says Hodges, because the latter glosses over the fundamental opposition between manual and intellectual workers. Manual workers are a group, cynics say, whose interests defy constant and faithful representation. The philosophy of working class cynicism is hostile to both capitalism and socialism, because it embodies the workers' experience of betrayal by their leaders, exploitation by the system, and resentment of their social status. Cynicism is a variant of the philosophy of anarcho-syndicalism, but without the ideals or ultimate illusions.

35

CYNICISM IN THE LABOR MOVEMENT

Donald Clark Hodges

There is an increasing tendency among the working classes to become politically indifferent. In the face of the bureaucratization of public life, the average laborer has tended to give up struggling for collectively improved conditions of work in favor of improving his individual circumstances and those of his family. His interest in the public has waned in proportion to belief in his own political impotence. All classes show the effects of increased bureaucratization, but in different degrees. Despite labor's increased gains, anyone who has worked on the assembly line or as a shop steward knows that political apathy is more prevalent in the ranks of labor than anywhere else.[1] Moreover, this indifference of the worker to politics is an expression not merely of apathy but of downright cynicism.[2] White collar workers tend to be

Reprinted from *The American Journal of Economics and Sociology*, Vol. 21, No. 1 (January 1962), pp. 29–36, by permission of the publisher and the author. Footnotes have been renumbered.

[1] The author is an ex-industrial worker and a former shop steward of Local 201, United Electrical, Radio and Machine Workers of America (C.I.O.),Bridgeport, Conn.

[2] The most recent studies in the sociology of cynicism include: Ely Chinoy, *Automobile Workers and the American Dream* (Garden City: Doubleday, 1955, pp. 83–86), on the laborer's "alienation from his work" and resentment at taking orders; C. Wright Mills, *The New Men of Power* (New York: Harcourt, Brace, 1948, pp. 266–74) on the developed habits of submission, low level of aspiration, and apathy of unskilled laborers—the underdogs of American labor; Hadley Cantril, *The Politics of Despair* (New York: Basic Books, 1958, pp. 35–46, 68–76); Karl Bednarik, *The Young Worker of Today: A New Type*, ed. J. P. Mayer, tr. R. Tupholme (Glencoe: Free Press, 1955, pp. 28–73, 128–30).

merely indifferent to politics; denim workers are irreverent, bitter, and scornful.   The white collar worker does not have a long tradition behind him of criticism and social protest, so that his political indifference is comparatively mild.   The bitter struggles of manual workers against capital, management, and the State have fostered disillusionment of an altogether different stamp.

The manual laborer is still the best authority on where the shoe of management pinches and the heel of capital treads.   The most bitter cynics are manual laborers imbued with anachist and syndicalist ideas.   Some are revolutionary romanticists; others, realists disillusioned with the lofty hopes and vain promises of militant trade unionism.   The cynicism of labor intellectuals tends to be abstract and impersonal because it seldom arises directly from a life of manual labor.   Although it helps to clarify the workers' sense of futility, it is not the source of cynicism in the labor movement.   That source is the degradation of the laborer to an appendage of the machine and to an instrument of another's gain.   To fully appreciate the philosophy of cynicism it helps to have been a laborer oneself, to have worked for lower wages in proportion to the unskilled character, monotony, and drudgery of labor, to have paid for wage boosts, health and social insurance plans by speed-ups and by rises in the cost of living, to have suffered from the comparison between manual and intellectual work, and to have lost faith in the leadership of labor bureaucrats and ex-workers, who have made a career out of trade unionism.

I

Unlike radical and conservative philosophies of labor, which follow the ebb and flow of economic prosperity and depression, cynicism is a constant feature of the labor movement.   It is tied neither to the fortunes of revolutionary trade unionism nor to the ups and downs of business unionism, but is an informal philosophy of labor that is endemic to the working classes.   As a philosophy of unorganized as well as organized labor, it is common to strike-breakers and scabs as well as to militant trade unionists.   Unorganized workers, who constitute the poorest and most demoralized stratum of the proletariat, cannot afford to turn down jobs and to assist in the struggles of organized workers who offer them no assistance.   (Their sympathies may be with the strikers, but their stomachs favor their employers.)   Cynicism is common not only to free trade unionism, but also to the labor movements in fascist and communist countries. Since the experience of industrial workers is similar everywhere, resentment against the bosses becomes articulate as a philosophy of labor that is independent of all political parties.

"There are two wings to every bird of prey" (Eugene Debs). In American public life the right wing corresponds to the Republican party, and the left wing, to the Democratic party. Unlike Republicans and Democrats, cynics have no faith in political creeds, which to civic minded and public spirited citizens is even worse than atheism. On the one hand, left-wingers are impatient with reality in insisting that workers should preserve a spirit of militancy under all circumstances. On the other hand, right-wingers are uncritical of social conditions even when they have the power to change them. In contrast to both, and to liberals who hew to the middle of the road, cynics are distinguished by their contempt for all movements, parties, and principles, which is another way of saying that they are politically unprincipled.

Cynicism is a conception of the political world and everything it represents as essentially hostile to the interests of manual labor. As an inseparable feature of the labor movement, it comes closest to expressing the informal philosophy of the workers. It shows up in the observations of American workers "in the sad comment, 'The only reason a man works is to make a living'; in the occasional overflow of resentment, 'Sometimes you feel like jamming things up in the machine and saying good-bye to it'; in the cynical observation, 'The things I like best about my job are quitting time, pay day, days off, and vacations. . . .'"[3]

The term "cynicism" is used by Bednarik to describe the psychological condition of the young worker in a Welfare State.[4] The young worker's withdrawal from public life, his escape into privacy and into pleasure hunting is attributed partly to the higher standard of living made possible by the Welfare State and partly to his disillusionment with it for not having provided an even higher standard. The young worker, writes Bednarik, constitutes a new type that is more cynical and more independent than the old: "he disregards all the artificial higher social systems and aims at a group system on anarchic lines . . . the new type feels himself to be largely independent of and superior to society, even though he may acknowledge and take into account the real

[3] Chinoy, *op. cit.*, p. 85.
[4] Bednarik, *op. cit.*, pp. 109, 111–12.

power of that society and of the State."[5]   The young worker is
cynical of social norms and draws his personal ideal from the
distractions of the age, i.e., from the artificial wealth of films and
advertising.[6]   Unreserved egoism is believed necessary in order to
combat the selfishness of the world.   "The one idea of the modern
worker is to 'grab all you can get hold of.'"[7] This personal ideal is
the expression of what Bednarik calls "socialized father hate":
"The young worker of today, in his detached attitude towards the
State and its social institutions, is like a son who is always demanding and taking; and the only reason why he has not become totally
estranged from his father is that he is obliged at least to listen to
his orders and admonitions, if only the better to circumvent them.
The same goes for his attitude towards industrial society in general,
the factory where he is employed and the party and trade-union
organizations which form part of his working world.   For him
they all represent a sort of father-world . . . the advantages of
which he uses without feeling himself deeply committed."[8]

The philosophical equivalent of this type of cynicism among
young workers is perhaps best exemplified by Max Stirner's *The
Ego and His Own*.   Unlike Proudhon, who equated property with
theft (the belief of anarchists who are moral idealists), Stirner
does him one better by calling alien property a "present": "Why
so sentimentally call for compassion as a poor victim of robbery,
when one is just a foolish, cowardly giver of presents?   Why . . .
put the fault on others as if they were robbing us, while we ourselves bear the fault in leaving the others unrobbed.   The poor
are to blame for there being rich men.[9]   This is not necessarily a
call to robbery, but it is a plea that the workers should liberate
themselves from any reverence for the rights of property and the
State, and that they should take advantage of any and every
opportunity to reimburse themselves for losses.   This type of
cynicism has become increasingly popular among young workers.

II

Much of modern cynicism is suggestive of ancient Cynicism, which
has also been called by historians "a philosophy of the proletariat."

[5] *Ibid.*, pp. 33–34.
[6] *Ibid.*, p. 34.
[7] *Ibid.*, p. 56.
[8] *Ibid.*, p. 52.
[9] Max Stirner (pseud. for Caspar Schmidt), *The Ego and His Own*, tr. S. T.
Byington (New York: Boni and Liveright, n.d.), pp. 331–32.

The Cynics were irreverent toward culture, disloyal to the State, resentful toward authority, anti-intellectual, and scornful of conventional morality.   Like the Hebrew Prophets, they regarded the love of money as the root of all evil.[10]   Like the Prophets, they championed the interests of the underdog.   To its critics, Cynicism has been equated with a philosophy of degeneracy: "The Cynic differed from the modern hobo in having a vocation; but, like the hobo, was sometimes a robber, sometimes a thief, sometimes a beggar and had no inhibitions except against useful labor. . . . Greek Cynicism was chiefly a relaxation of the ordinary restraints of civilized man and freeing of the natural impulses; among these impulses are indolence, selfishness, envy and ill-nature."[11] This is decidedly an unsympathetic account.   It fails to consider that Cynicism was also a response to the alienation of the worker from his work and from a society that exploited the laborer for all he was worth.   Manual labor, according to Lucian, is an evil not because it is intrinsically contemptible (the Platonic and Aristotelian view), but because it implies an injustice to the laborer.   To the upper classes, he says: "All that costly array of means of enjoyment which you so gloat over is obtained . . . through how many men's blood and death and ruin.   To bring these things to you many seamen must perish; to find and fashion them many laborers must endure misery. . . . "[12]   Dudley, the historian of Cynicism, also notes the similarities between ancient and modern cynicism: "In modern times the movement most akin to Cynicism is Anarchism. . . . It is especially interesting to find Kropotkin recognizing the 'best exposition from the Ancient World of the principles of Anarchism' is the *Republic* of Zeno, which was of course composed when Zeno was under the influence of Cynicism."[13]

Henry Miller is one of the few Americans to have given expression to the informal philosophy of cynicism of the workers.   He stands almost alone among self-conscious and philosophically articulate cynics in this country.   He has been acknowledged as the "minnesinger of the lumpenproletariat" because his outraged sympathies are for the oppressed stratum of unorganized unskilled laborers and because his books and essays idealize the values of

[10] Farrand Sayre, *Diogenes of Sinope* (Baltimore: J. H. Furst, 1938), p. 25.

[11] *Ibid.*, p. 47.

[12] Quoted by Sayre, *ibid.*, p. 8.

[13] Donald R. Dudley, *A History of Cynicism* (London: Methuen, 1937), pp. 211–12.

the unemployed vagrant, "hobo" or "bum." Yet his cynicism is an attack upon the social system for taking advantage of all "producers," skilled as well as unskilled, whom he identifies with the "little" or "common" man, i.e., "the man who does the dirty work."[14]   Miller's cynicism is directed against the joy-killers of the western world and is summarized in the statement: "I don't want it when I'm dead.   I want it now."[15]   In part, his message is sex instead of sacrifice.   Miller is already widely known for his apotheosis of sexual freedom.   However, just as important to an understanding of his writings is his constant note of cynicism: "To be sure, it is the general expectation among those who believe in a new order that the common man will eventually inherit the fruit of all the inventions and discoveries now being made.   But over whose dead body, I'd like to ask? . . .   The great bugaboo here in America is the 'dictatorship of the proletariat.'   Looking at the rank and file . . . does any one honestly believe that these men and women will dictate the future of America?   Can slaves become rulers overnight?   These poor devils are begging to be led, and they are being led, but it's up a blind alley."[16]

The cynicism of manual workers is constructive in serving the purpose of higher wages and better conditions of work.   However, it is even more fundamentally destructive in undermining the authority of the boss and the "system."   The cynic's dominant sentiment is that of resentment. . . .   Class Hostility of this kind is founded upon the sense of inferiority in being a worker, in having to take orders, in being treated like a machine instead of a human being of the same value and importance as the employer.   The worker's psychology is based upon a comparison: "I get the smallest part of the money which my employer makes. . . ."

By this comparison the worker is a "sucker," a "fall guy." " 'What they call honest toil is a mug's game. . . . You know that as well as I do.' "[17]   By the same comparison the employer is on top of the ant-heap because he has a "racket."   Although he operates within the law, his mentality is fundamentally criminal, i.e., aimed at taking advantage.   If the boss accedes to the demands of the workers for higher wages, it is only because he has

[14] Henry Miller, *To Remember to Remember* (New York: New Directions, 1947), p. xxxvi.

[15] *Ibid.*, p. xxxv.

[16] *Ibid.*, p. xviii.

[17] Celine (pseud.), *Journey to the End of the Night*, tr. J. H. P. Marks (Boston: Little, Brown, 1934), p. 308.

something sinister up his sleeve, such as higher prices or speed-ups. Writes Celine: " 'Commiseration of the fate and the condition of the down-at-heel? I tell you, worthy little people, life's riffraff, forever beaten, fleeced, and sweating, I warn you that when the great people of this world start loving you, it means that they are going to make sausage meat of you.' "[18]

III

Cynicism is not a philosophy of the proletariat in Marx's meaning of the term. For the proletariat, in the Marxian sense, includes engineers and technicians besides manual laborers. The Marxian concept of the working class glosses over the fundamental opposition between manual and intellectual workers, so that it is consistent for a Marxist to argue that the leadership of the proletariat is the prerogative of its intellectuals. On the contrary, the cynic holds that manual laborers are a group whose interests defy constant and faithful representation. It is possible to represent faithfully and constantly the interests of professional workers because their interests, like those of their representatives, are the interests of white collar workers generally. But it is impossible, the cynic argues, to do the same for the class of manual laborers because their representatives, whether political officials or trade union bureaucrats, are white collar workers imbued with white collar values.

Cynics are critical not only of capitalism but also of socialism. Cynicism is neither a movement nor a school, in the strict sense, but the inchoate philosophy of labor of the unknown and unsung manual laborer. "A plague on all your houses" is the attitude of cynics toward political movements which place the welfare of the business and professional classes above the interests of the plodders and grubbers. The tendency is for manual laborers to become increasingly cynical about the pretensions of labor leaders to lead them toward a better future. Socialists of every hue and variety, whether democratic or authoritarian, utopian or scientific, are regarded with suspicion; so also are trade-union bureaucrats who believe in the principles of business unionism. Cynicism is the expression of the attitude of manual laborers disillusioned with the claims of anyone to better their conditions without profiting in the meantime at their expense. It is a symptom of resentment

[18] *Ibid.*, p. 64.

against the entire world of white collar workers, against higher education as well as higher salaries.

Industry cannot survive without a class of manual laborers. Yet this class is becoming progressively disaffected with the world of white collars and white hands, so that it serves it with increasing reluctance. With greater mechanization, the unskilled laborer shows less respect for drudge labor. With the increasing tendency to cynicism, businessmen and politicians are regarded as worse than ordinary criminals, and techniques of illegitimately earning a living are regarded with tolerance and even approbation. For the cynic, the world owes him a living, so that he feels justified in violating the law as long as there is no injury to his fellow workers. It is noteworthy that the modern tradition that helped to justify this attitude overtly championed industrial sabotage and assassination of key political figures, while idealizing such epic but criminal heroes as the Russian bandit, Pugachev, and the English legendary figure of Robin Hood.[19] That tradition is generally known as anarcho-syndicalism or revolutionary trade unionism, and is the tradition that inspired the Industrial Workers of the World (I.W.W.) in this country.

Cynicism is a variant of anarchism—anarchism without ideals or ultimate illusions, apathetic, easy-going instead of strenuous, non-sectarian, hence, more broadly appealing and far more suitable to the conditions and mentality of contemporary workers than the older tradition of militant idealism and self-sacrifice. In this country cynicism is a realistic acquiescence in the fact that social idealism has already received its funeral rites. It is a sad commentary upon the promise of American politics that the dream of a classless society has reality only as a museum-piece, and that few Americans in public life pay anything but lip-service to the ideal of social justice. Indeed, there has been only one eminent American in recent years who was capable of declaring publicly: "While there is a lower class I am in it; while there is a criminal element I am in it; while there is a soul in prison, I am not free."[20]

[19] Robert Hunter, *Violence and the Labor Movement* (New York: Macmillan, 1914), p. 278; Eugene Pyziur, *The Doctrine of Anarchism of Michael A. Bakunin* (Milwaukee: Marquette University, 1955), pp. 101–9.

[20] Miller, *op. cit.*, pp. 170, 196, quoted from Eugene V. Debs. [*Debs was the leader of the early twentieth century mass socialist movement in the U.S., and its candidate for President before World War I.—M.Z.*]

STUDIES OF CLASS CONSCIOUSNESS AMONG AMERICAN WORKERS *have relied almost entirely on survey techniques. In contrast, Peck based this study of workers' consciousness on his own work in several plants in Milwaukee over a period of four years, his own role as a shop steward, and on his use of the group discussion interview technique. Further, his focus is on what grass roots leaders think, rather than on the ideas of workers selected at random without regard for their position in the leadership structure of the working class.*

He finds that while the stewards articulate their ideas in the slogans of Gomperism, the content of their political philosophy is class-oriented: political friends and enemies are differentiated in terms of their class allegiances. Their question is what the candidate or party will do for the working man and whether he will represent the interests of laboring people as a whole. This class outlook is central to understanding the way the rank-and-file leaders view the two-party system. The Republican party is viewed as the organ of Big Business, the Democratic party as that of the working class. The dominant view of the stewards is that the workers belong in the Democratic party, since it generally favors their interests, and because there is no viable political alternative—especially given the ordinary workers' predominant loyalty to the Democrats. A minor but influential point of view sees both parties as hostile to the interests of the workers and controlled by the wealthy and propertied classes. The rank-and-file leaders hope for a realignment of class interests within the framework of the two-party system, so that the parties would genuinely reflect basic class divisions in America.

Few stewards openly advocated a labor party, and when they did it was essentially because they believed in making the political arena more competitive and in allowing greater choice. Most stewards think that a labor party would absorb independent trade unionism, and that it might lead to communism. Moreover, they think the two-party system still provides sufficient political alternatives and that labor is too weak to launch its own party anyway. Most important is the fact that even those who are "class conscious" are not convinced that the workers and the capitalists are irreconcilable enemies. Therefore, the major problem is knowing who labor's "friends" and "enemies" are within the existing parties.

448

36

THE RANK–AND–FILE UNION LEADER'S CONSCIOUSNESS

Sidney M. Peck

The shop steward is the rank-and-file union representative in the department or division of the industrial plant. . . . The steward constitutes the closest union link to the rank-and-file worker. He is often referred to as the "key man in the union movement." . . . This is a descriptive social-psychological study of the social and political ideology which informs the industrial union steward. . . . Two primary research techniques are used in this study. The first instrument is technically known as *participation-observation*. This refers to research observations based upon nearly four years of work experience in several Milwaukee industrial settings. . . . The second research tool may be termed the *group discussion interview process*. This technique was used to survey the patterned ideology of union stewards. . . .*

Stewards typically contend that organized labor, in the past, has not devoted enough effort to organized political activity. They point with pride to the fruits of victory which labor can reach when proper organizational forms are developed. Stewards believe that the most urgent task facing labor leadership in this area is to awaken the political potential of the general membership. They attribute the lack of political concern to the low level of political

Reprinted from Sidney M. Peck, *The Rank-and-File Leader* (New Haven, Conn.: College and University Press, 1963), pp. 32–33, 40–41, 283–96, by permission of the publisher. Footnotes are not included.

* *This method is designed to stimulate a genuine informal group discussion. See Peck's discussion of this method on pp. 70ff. of his book.*—M.Z.

information available to the average worker. Therefore, most stewards advocate a more comprehensive political education program to reach the rank-and-file member in order to heighten political awareness and expand political action. In suggesting this outlook, union stewards also reveal a defensive concern about "political bossism." They emphasize the traditional hostility with which American workers greet political dictation and deny the existence of "bossism" in labor's ranks. At the same time, stewards recognized the need for leadership guidance in the selection of political candidates. Thus, they agree that organized labor bodies have a right (and need) to recommend (endorse) candidates for political office. As the 34 year-old inspector (UAW 438) stated in her forthright manner:

> There are many people who go to the polls and don't know who they are voting for. But if they do know that the labor party [group] is in back of a person and they are part of labor themselves, they definitely have faith in the incumbents.

2. LABOR AND THE TWO PARTIES

Although stewards agreed to the need for labor endorsement, they did not subscribe to a straight party-line approach. Even though it will become apparent that union stewards are definitely committed to the Democratic party, they strongly resist endorsement of the Democratic ticket per se; they believe that political candidates should be supported according to their "individual merits" rather than party affiliation.

Samual Gompers' time-honored slogan "Reward our friends and punish our enemies" is adhered to by rank-and-file leaders. It is apparent that many stewards "make up their minds" about a candidate in terms of this approach. Thus, a 42-year-old Teamster griever crudely underlined the *business* of politics when he confided, "You know, there's an old saying, 'one hand washes the other,' you know. Simple as down to that . . . you take care of me and I take care of you." But, the general understanding of Gompers' slogan among worker-leaders today is not quite as "simple as down to that." For most stewards decide on who their political "friends" are by how they "take care" of *working people, as a whole.* That is to say, political friends and enemies are differentiated along clear lines of class, so that the basis for political choice implies a principled concern rather than opportunistic gain.

When grievers emphasized the need to support "the man over the party" they did so in terms of what the candidate "will do for the working man." Thus, a 42-year-old set-up man (IUE 1131) declared:

> That's what I think the whole thing is: How he votes for the working man and the poorer class of people. If a guy is in there and he is for the big shot all the time, why he hasn't got much of a chance with the working class of people.

Most stewards admitted that they vote a split ticket because their main line is to "vote for the man that is qualified for labor." According to these stewards, candidates are "qualified" when "they are out to do things for labor. And out to see that labor gets [a] fair share." At the USA 1258 session, the stewards elaborated a similar theme to which a 31-year-old assembler responded:

> I agree . . . I don't have a certain party. If I find a man in there in the Republican office, Democrat office, or Socialist office who is willing to represent the working group, and to give the working group what their needs are, I will work for that personal man, no matter what party he belongs to.

In the light of this political commitment, the meaning of the old Gomperist slogan "Reward our friends and punish our enemies" is not to be found in a "job conscious" outlook. Stewards approach the issue of political endorsement from a class point of view. They are concerned about what the candidate "will do for the working man." Their focus is not on the job, or plant or union per se, rather they believe candidates should be supported only if they are for the interests of *laboring people as a whole.* While some stewards may follow along strictly opportunistic union paths, i.e., render support to a candidate "friendly" to the international or local union, most stewards viewed the endorsement problem from a principled class outlook. Thus, a 28-year-old assembler (UAW 75) admitted:

> Well, in talking to the men in my department about voting, I tell them "I don't care who you go out and vote for

but make sure who you vote for is going to be for the working man and not for the companies." That's the idea I have.

This class outlook is central to an understanding of the way in which rank-and-file leaders view the two-party system.

It was apparent that the majority of stewards considered the Republican party to be the official political organ of Big Business, whereas the Democratic party was viewed as the party of the working class. Stewards openly acknowledged their political allegiance to the Democratic party because they believed it to be the working-man's party. In the words of a 24-year-old UAW 248 machinist, "Your Democratic party in the United States is more or less your workers' party." At the District 10 Machinists discussion session, a 37-year-old assembler summed up the group sentiment when he declared:

I don't agree with the speaker on why we don't bring a third party in the United States. I think two parties is good enough. [*Laughter.*] The Democratic party has always been the labor party . . . the unions should stick with the Democrats.

The fact that the overwhelming number of industrial workers are likely to vote Democratic is less important than the reasons they advance to explain their position. While workers may have occasionally voted for a Republican "Maverick," they firmly believe that the Republican party is the political vehicle of the "industrialists." At the UAW 438 session, a Catholic steward explained this class difference when she said:

Well, I'll take here in the city of Milwaukee; now your Republican tickets are usually backed by your large industrialists, by money and work. Now, naturally we know your industrialists are not going to be out to help the worker. Their group is going to be out for what's going to help their pockets. Naturally, we have to jump on the other side of the fence and assist the other party that will back the worker, that will help the worker. And that is the Democratic party.

This image of the Democratic party as "the labor party" because "they've always done the most for labor" was repeated over and over again as stewards explained how the Democratic party "supports the labor movement." They presented evidence to suggest that "the Democratic party has been the most liberal for the laboring class of people." They argued that "particularly in this [Milwaukee] area" the difference between the two parties is very great. They stressed that the "Democrats have been more liberal-minded down the road here" on those political issues deemed most important to the working class of people. "Any working man who earns his bread by the sweat of his brow knows that the Democratic party has done more for labor throughout the years than the Republican party has ever done," claimed a 61-year-old packinghouse worker. And this Negro steward added, "that is why the majority of shop stewards lean toward the Democratic party."

In sum, *the dominant view* among union stewards expresses a four-pronged position. It states that, (1) the political home of the organized labor movement belongs in the Democratic party; (2) the difference in class basis and focus between the two parties is markedly apparent in the state; (3) the labor movement has no other political alternative but to wage all-out support for the Democratic party (which has consistently worked in the interests of the poorer class of people); and, (4) most industrial workers view the two-party system in this way.

However, one segment of steward opinion perceived both major parties to be divided along class lines. This *minor but influential* point of view among stewards suggests the following theme:

> There is no real difference between the two parties, possibly, in name only. Therefore, neither party has a right to claim the mantle of liberalism toward the working class. Both parties are beholden to the propertied classes. In fact, the Southern-based, anti-labor, conservative forces in the Democratic party are to be considered as much an enemy of labor as the corporation-supported Republican administration.

Thus, a 34-year-old UAW 438 delegate to the County Council remarked, "I'm a Democrat not by choice but by necessity." And then he continued:

> Frankly speaking, the Democrats today are not the home for labor, they are the lesser of two evils. If anyone

> believes that a Democrat is my mind of thinking, my way
> of thinking . . . he's crazy. If you don't think so, just
> go south of that Mason and Dixon line. Where you
> know what the economic structure and what the political
> structure . . . down there . . . you know what it can
> really be down there. So I don't buy their political
> party—because as far as I'm concerned they are a party of
> prostitution because they have to accept that kind of
> approach . . . [which is] contrary to all my union ideals.

While these stewards appreciate the class basis of political strivings, they were notably reluctant to say that the major parties are clearly divided along class lines. "What is really the difference in your definition between your Republican or your Democrat?" asked a 28-year-old repairman (UE 1111). And he answered, "it's just a belief, actually, that your Republicans are more big shots. What is really the definition? What is the difference between the Republicans and the Democrats? I don't mean the big shot and that. It's the name of a party, that's all. That's all it is to me." Although the Democratic party is supposed to be the "liberal party for the working class of people," these grievers related that there are "some very good liberal Republican Congressmen and Senators right today in office"; so that neither party has a right to claim a "liberal monopoly" toward the working class. As a matter of fact, they argued quite strongly that both parties belong to the men of property and wealth. At the County Council session, a Polish Catholic steward pointedly said:

> A lot of people don't have faith in the Republicans; I
> don't have faith in them. I don't have a heck of a lot
> more faith in the Democrats either. Because I haven't
> seen anything so great that they've done . . . even in the
> past. Frankly, I get nauseated at the bowing and scrap-
> ing that a lot of labor leaders do toward the Democrats.
> They even go back and hold Franklin Roosevelt as an
> idol . . . and from what I've studied on the subject . . .
> there was a lot of things that he done, which if it wasn't
> for Labor's pushing [and] really holding the hammer over
> him, he would have went the other way just as well as
> Eisenhower . . . and the rest of them . . . So it seems
> that the whole "kit and kaboodle" is of one caliber.
> They're not after to help out the working man. Their
> main interest is the money interest. And he who pays
> the piper calls the tune . . . in both parties.

Other grievers noted that while the Republican administration shouldered much responsibility for the recession, "still we got a Democratic-controlled Congress [and] they aren't doing anything either." They saw the inability of the Democrats to effect a comprehensive anti-recession program as a perfect illustration of the influence which anti-labor forces wield within the structure of the Democratic party. Specifically referring to the Southern wing of the party as the base for this political conservatism, a 36-year-old Catholic steward (UAW 438) remarked:

> Well, it has been frequently charged that the Northern Republicans represent nothing but the business interests and their particular district. And I think the same thing can be said of the Southern Democrats. That they are not properly concerned with the interests of the whole group. Rather, they look to the interests of the fewer and more wealthy constituents.

The answer to the present political dilemma for these stewards is to hope for a more rational realignment of class interests within the framework of the two-party system. Briefly stated, these stewards were convinced that the two-party system as it is now constituted merely allows the working class to choose the lesser of two evils. They agreed that the country needs a fundamental political realignment so that the two-party system would, in fact, reflect basic class divisions in society. Until this change comes about, workers should have political protest alternatives available. Otherwise, they will not be stimulated to make the choice between the lesser of two evils. "I personally think that what we should have is two parties, similar to what they have in England," said a 49-year-old press operator (Harvester 22631). However, this Catholic steward did not call for a labor party. Rather, he stated, "You have your conservative party and you have your liberal party. You have it in Canada, too, I believe, a conservative and a liberal. And I think we should have two parties." Personally, he believed "that your Republican is going to be your conservative and the Democrats the more liberal." The big "if," of course, is that "we have a problem in the Southern states to take care of before it happens."

In general, rank-and-file leaders look upon the two-party system as class-conscious workers. The basic outlook is one which sees the Republican party as the political party of "Big Business" while the Democratic party is the "working-men's party."   Most stewards hold to this view which suggests that the political struggle between Republicans and Democrats clearly expresses the class struggle between business and labor.   But a strong undercurrent of opinion among grievers stands opposed to this belief.   Instead, this minority outlook maintains that the structure of vested interests in the two-party system so distorts class lines as to make political choice an irrational process.   These stewards believe that both parties are fundamentally controlled by industrial and land-owning groups who are opposed to the interests and needs of laboring people.   The political demand of these stewards is to force a rational realignment of class and party within the framework of the existing two-party system.   Some stewards merely urge that "we nominate more people, not only a Republican or a Democrat, have a Socialist in there and have a Communist in there even if they don't get nominated or elected.   But have it important and interesting."   And, there are, of course, those stewards who advocate the formation of an independent labor party as an answer to the apparent dilemma of the two-party structure.

3. A LABOR PARTY?

Very few stewards openly advocated the need for an independent labor party.   Of those who did, it is likely that many of them retain organizational connection with "splinter" political sects. Nevertheless, among these stewards were also some who "independently" stressed the desire for an alternative to the two-party system.

In the group discussions some stewards happily recalled the golden times of political yesteryears.   These men remembered the hegemony of the Milwaukee socialist movement and the political achievements of Wisconsin progressivism.   At the Region 9 AIW session, a 42-year-old German Catholic proudly noted:

> I just wanted to say that I was a member of a third party
> in the state, I belonged to the Progressive party at one
> time.   I considered it one of the greatest farmer-labor
> parties of all time.   I think it was one of the greatest
> political parties that actually man could wrought.   It
> was a wonderful party.   It took years and years to build
> the party up, there was no doubt of that.   The U.S.

Senator from Wisconsin was a Progressive at that time, we had a Progressive governor. The state of Wisconsin was one of the most prosperous states in the union. It only took a matter of a few months to tear it down. Of course, it was unfortunate that it was torn down.

In their recall of political glory, these stewards wished to lend favorable support toward the formation of a new party devoted to the interests of laboring and farming people.

Other stewards emphasized the need for competition in the political arena. They argued that "competition makes good business" because it allows people the opportunity to "shop across the street." They explained that political office holders will never respond to the people unless they are threatened by defeat and, therefore, the formation of a labor party would provide a healthy alternative. As a 50-year-old griever (Harvester 22631) stated, "it will wake up the people in office that they either had better start helping the common man along or they'll be the next to get their head lopped off." And, this Polish Catholic steward urged:

I think labor should put out a party of its own. Let the country at wide, let the world know, by God, if the people here are organized and would like to have their speakers and their people in the various offices . . . true, they do run them in some states and they don't get elected . . . But, if you don't succeed at first, try again. Keep on pushing, keep on pushing, sooner or later that will become a reality.

At the Brewery 9 session, a 33-year-old German Catholic worker also expressed the need for political competition. Although he noted that "the Democratic party, more or less, pertains to the working man or tries to represent him in some degree," nevertheless he continued on to say, "I think we should have a third and it should be a labor party, representing strictly labor." These stewards also noted that the need for political alternatives is more apparent on the national rather than the local scene. That is to say, they generally agreed with the idea that the Democratic and Republican parties fairly well follow class lines, interests, and policies in Wisconsin. However, "on the national level," remarked a 53-year-old machine operator (USA 1173), "we don't know any of these fellows." Therefore, he believed that "a labor party on the national level would be quite effective."

In short, this general outlook suggests that a "working-man's party" or "labor party" is vitally needed in order to make the political atmosphere more competitive. If the voting public has more candidates to choose from, then officeholders will become more responsive to the needs of the people. Furthermore, political officials would undoubtedly begin to adhere to their pre-election platforms and would tend to keep their electoral promises.

Thus, labor party "spokesmen" emphasized the need for political alternatives in the form of a party "strictly representing labor," especially on the national level. They also claimed that such a party would come to pass even though the "time is not ripe now." They predicted that a labor party will come into being at (1) the moment of working-class disillusionment with the Democratic party and (2) the moment of independent political initiative by top labor leadership. They asserted that after organized labor tries "the Democrats one more time and the Democrats don't produce . . . labor will find out she will have to do what labor has done [elsewhere]."

These stewards believed that basic class and party realignment in the United States demands the emergence of a labor party whose platform would reflect the general interests of the working class. Some of them recognized that "labor is not ready for their own particular party in this country as yet," but as a 28-year-old Jewish autoworker (UAW 75) noted, "I don't think the stewards are opposed to a labor party. We're in favor of anything that is going to benefit labor. It's just that now . . . it's a question of time, whether we are ready for it." Hence, these men did not doubt the "inevitable" rise of a mass labor party but they did recognize existing obstacles which prevent immediate political organization. First of all, they agreed that the Democratic party commands the political allegiance of most working people; and secondly, they recognized that no one in the higher reaches of labor leadership has "taken the lead to push" a third party movement.

At the Region 9 AIW session, a 38-year-old Catholic machinist confided that he is a "card carrying Democrat." Nevertheless, he added:

But I feel this, if the Democratic party fails to do good for the rest of the land and do for the majority of the people, and the Republican party fails, and it has up to now, that I think if they would put up a farmer-labor bloc and have a farmer-labor party. . . . And, if the farmers ever get together with labor people, instead of going apart from them, then we could actually have a party which would actually rule the land. We could have a third party! In other words, if the Democrats can't do for us what we need, or the Republicans, and they haven't until now, maybe we will have a third party, regardless of the cost.

At the County Council discussion, a 37-year-old communications worker had just concluded an attack against labor leadership for its unqualified support of the Democratic party. Then this Polish Catholic steward added that the political answer for working people "is the labor party" but he did not think that "we'll get it too soon." He explained the dilemma faced by advocates of a labor party and placed the primary responsibility on the shoulders of labor leadership:

> The simple reason is that the higher echelons of labor say that there is no agitation from the fields . . . from the working people. And the working people say, we're not going to stick our necks out with you plugging all these Democrats out there . . . So there it's going to stand. And perhaps things will have to get a lot worse until somebody grabs the bull by the horns and gives a little encouragement. I think that's all it would take . . . is a little encouragement on the behalf of certain people and certainly—my encouragement is next to nothing. I can think about it, and talk about it personally to different people . . . but as far as convincing anybody, I don't think I am capable . . . I don't think they would take my word against as well as to get the blessings they get from the so-called higher ups in the labor movement.

Perhaps the most ardent labor party supporter among these grievers was a 57-year-old press operator (Harvester 22631). This old-time German laborite steward railed against those in the group who maintained that workers and farmers are so thoroughly divided as to be unable to unite politically into a unified farmer-labor party. He pointed out that farmers and laborers "are voting together now." Therefore, he strongly urged the immediate formation of a labor party. In halting English, he exclaimed:

> Why can't we have a third party? Our top labor leaders, they got to come out with this proposition . . . to form a

labor party. Not alone for labor, but for the whole nation as a whole . . . for saving our resources. Them two parties what we have in there now, they are wasting our natural resources so that we are in a short time in a poor house. [*Shouting*] We have to have a labor party in there that will stop the misuse of all our natural resources. And then labor will gain, and even the big shots will gain, see. And it will be good for the whole nation. But, if we keep out and let them two parties run the country it's no good, they are only out for profit!

The fact remains, however, that neither the shouting nor the rationale of this "Milwaukee Socialist" convinced his fellows. Although some stewards did identify with the "wonderful" third party movements of the past and others did recognize the need for an alternative to the "Republocrat" anti-labor coalition, they apparently did not view the formation of an independent working-men's party as the road to political salvation. Arguments against a third party ranged from beliefs that the labor movement is too weak for this move to the fear that the development of a mass labor party in the U.S. would encourage political totalitarianism.

Many stewards argued against the formation of a labor party because they felt that the labor movement was on "pretty thin ice to organize." Pointing to such factors as an inadequate mass voting base, traditional cleavages between industrial workers and family farmers, lack of campaign friends, and the unfortunate "moral" situation of the trade union movement, most grievers hinted that the development of a third party would further weaken labor's position in the U.S. The IUE chief steward warned, "I don't think the labor [movement] is in a position today to sponsor a labor party . . . I don't think they are anywhere near strong enough." A 42-year-old tool and die maker (AIW 9) cautioned that "we haven't got the money." And he predicted, "the laboring class of people, they'll maybe throw out a buck after they are in the bread lines for a while till they're back into harness again, good times and that . . . [but that is it]." A 55-year-old machinist (Harvester 22631) commented on the moral bankruptcy of labor occasioned by public hearings on the alleged racketeering and corruption in the trade union movement. He said that these scandals are "going to hurt labor more than anything." And he noted that, "it is going to be a damn long time before you get to the point where you are going to have anyone qualified by the people to lead a labor party in the U.S. . . . in Reuther's time or Meany's time." To these remarks a 40-year-old steward (Harvester 22631) voiced his agreement on labor's chances to "go it alone" in politics:

> Well, that's true, any presidential election you got now or any election, it seems like you more or less run it as a beauty contest.   If Meany were to run for president or something, somebody would say, "He's a labor man? Well, you can't vote for that son of a bitch, he must know Beck."   Well, you're right, that's the problem you'd have.

While some stewards emphasized the relative weakness of organized labor in political society, others worried about the great power which labor would come to have if they developed a mass party.   That is to say, some stewards warned that American workers would become politically enslaved if they were made to support a workers' party.   A 27-year-old production helper (USA 1258) said, "Well, the worker he got freedom here and votes the way he wants instead of sticking for one party like picking out our own labor party.   I don't think that would be a good idea." At the UE 1111 session, a 31-year-old molding operator registered his opposition to a labor party in this way:

> I think ["Mueller"] is off on the wrong tangent here.   He expects us to have a political business like in Germany. Well, you know, I don't know too much about German history but Nazism started with unionism.   And some of those political outfits . . . I think that's what the American people fear in having a union party.

The real fear of these stewards, however, was based not so much on the potential development of fascism as it was on the more probable emergence of communism.   Thus, some stewards noted that the labor party in England seems like "a bunch of communists.   Everything they say seems to be pro-communist."   A 47-year-old brewhouse worker summarized the logic of this fear when he exclaimed:

> There shouldn't be a . . . union party only.   Having Republicans and Democrats keeps the level so long as one don't go ahead and take advantage of the other.   Say now, that the Democrats would be entirely union and that we had power.   They would snow the capitalists, you know, and it would ruin the capitalist system.   That would be the next thing; it would lead to dictatorship or communism.

In general, one may state that opposition to the formation of a labor party is quite widespread among the union stewards. While a vocal minority of rank-and-file leaders do carry the ideological torch for a labor-centered political movement, they have been unable to transform the main body of political thought on this issue.   Although advocates for a labor party point to the political glories of the past and the need for political alternatives in the present, their opponents argue from a position of strength that: (1) a labor party would eventually engulf trade union activities, (2) the two-party system already provides enough alternatives for organized labor, (3) the trade union movement does not possess the political, financial, or moral strength to embark upon a third party venture, and (4) the development of a mass labor party in the U.S. might lead to political totalitarianism, possibly of a fascist character, but more probably of a communist nature because it would disturb the very balance of capitalism's power structure.   But the most important argument which these stewards offer is that a new party would tend to weaken labor's position in political society.   It would divide the "working-man's vote" and it would lead to "a dominantly Republican party at all times" and then "where would the working-man be?"   The heritage of Gomperism with its emphasis on non-partisanship still informs most rank-and-file leaders.   Although they approach political questions and parties from a class-conscious point of view, rank-and-file leaders generally share in the thought of a 42-year-old shipping clerk (AIW 9) who recalled the classic line:

> Labor has many friends and labor can have more friends by supporting one of the political parties.   They can even do better by supporting both political parties where the members of such political parties are going to do them the most good.   I would like to remind the gathering . . . of a quote from former President Green of the AFL . . . that we should vote for our friends and defeat our enemies.   He didn't say which party, but he did refer to the friends of labor who are in politics.

For class-conscious workers "having a complete labor party would be a detriment," because the game of politics played in the United States is between "friendly enemies."   The major political problem for the working class is to know who its "real friends" are in the "enemy" parties.

AMERICA'S TOP UNION OFFICIALS AND THE ENTIRE LABOR BUREAU-
*cracy of the AFL-CIO are now in danger of a genuine revolt of the
ranks, claims Weir, who is a trade unionist, organizer, and activist.
The central issue is control of the conditions of work, to which top
labor bureaucrats, who left the shops long ago, are not sensitive.
Weir documents his contention by examining the widespread rank-
and-file revolts and "wildcat" (unauthorized) strikes that have been
occurring in the sixties.   Such revolts have occurred in the automobile
industry, among longshoremen on both coasts, among steelworkers,
electricians, oil, gas, and atomic workers, coal miners, seamen and
maritime workers, airline mechanics, painters, paper and pulp
workers, teamsters, and transport workers.   Scarcely a major union
among those that founded the CIO has not experienced a revolt
against its old officialdom.   Usually, and at best, the split is between
the "hard" and "soft" line: between those who ignore or repress the
rank-and-file revolt, and those who maintain that concessions from
the top are the only means by which the revolt can be checked.   A
genuine response to these pressures: the adoption of a new program
dedicated to fundamental changes in work methods and conditions
and opposition to technological disemployment (which would mean
a long and difficult struggle against the largest corporations) has been
almost nonexistent.   These revolts have usually been channeled into
electoral struggles, several of which have resulted in the replacement
of old top bureaucrats by secondary bureaucrats more responsive to
such pressures.   There have also been splits between large locals and
the international union, some of which have resulted in disaffiliations
and the establishment of new unions.   Independent labor leaders are
threatened, assaulted, and even killed.   Disaffiliation may result in
the workers' finding themselves involved in a struggle merely to maintain their new unions, rather than being able to expand and win new
gains.*

*Throughout the country, there are workers whose conditions and
wages are artificially depressed because of captive affiliations with
conservatively-led unions to which there are no progressive alternatives.
The central cause of the rank-and-file revolt is the conditions in the
plants.   Weir points out that this fight for better conditions cannot
be waged at periodic intervals, as can the fight for wage increases; it
must be fought every day inside the plants.   During such fights, the
base and authority of the union would be moved from the union hall
back inside the plant.   Workers who are willing to fight their employer
to obtain a better life on-the-job have to be prepared to fight their union
leaders as well.*

464

The two principal reasons for the new persistence in demands for improved working conditions are postwar automation and its threat to the safety and health of workers. Automation displaces workers, shakes up old patterns of work, and forces severe readjustments. It results in the addition of new machinery and work rules which force a faster, more dangerous pace of work. The material improvements in the lives of organized American workers during and since World War II contrast to the stagnation or deterioration in their working conditions. The major union leaders have ignored these changing conditions, and the workers have responded with a form of in-plant guerrilla warfare: sabotage of production, slow downs, and wildcat strikes. This revolt also led to more changes in the leadership of American labor unions between 1964 and 1967 than had occurred in the previous fifteen years. The Meany-Reuther split is a reflection of this struggle and of Reuther's response to it. A genuine workers' movement would distinguish itself from the old bureaucratic unions by demanding basic social reforms, emphasizing class solidarity, fighting racism, and building a democratic union structure extending into the workplaces, thereby giving the ranks a voice and role in the daily union operation and decision making. It would give top priority, Weir concludes, to the major demand to "humanize working conditions," and end labor's subservience to the existing political parties.

In the brief article following that by Weir, Robert Avakian argues that such a movement among American workers must come into being. His experience in the alliance between student strikers at San Francisco State College and striking oil workers at the Standard Oil plant in Richmond, California strengthened his belief that such alliances between students and workers can spread to other industrial centers where the radical movement among students is already relatively developed. In this way, the basis of a genuine mass movement of the Left could emerge in the United States.

37

U.S.A.: THE LABOR REVOLT

Stanley Weir

The rank-and-file union revolts that have been developing in the industrial workplaces since the early 1950s are now plainly visible. Like many of their compatriots, American workers are faced with paces, methods and conditions of work that are increasingly intolerable. Their union leaders are not sensitive to these conditions. In thousands of industrial establishments across the nation, workers have developed informal underground unions. The basic units of organization are groups composed of several workers, each of whose members work in the same plant-area and are thus able to communicate with one another and form a social entity. Led by natural on-the-job leaders, they conduct daily guerrilla skirmishes with their employers and often against their official union representatives as well. These groups are the power base for the insurgencies from below that in the last three years have ended or threatened official careers of long standing.

During the same period, farm laborers, teachers, professionals, white collar, service and civil service workers, who were not reached by labor's revolt of the 1930s, have demonstrated an adamant desire to organize themselves into unions. For the first time in over three decades the United States faces a period in which the struggles of the unionized section of the population will have a direct and visible effect on the future of the entire population. Because the press coverage of the revolts has been superficial and because they have been ignored by the liberal and a majority of

Reprinted, with author's revisions, from the *International Socialist Journal*, Nos. 20, 21 (April and June 1967), pp. 279–86, 465–73, by permission of the author. Copyright 1967 by Stanley Weir. Footnotes have been renumbered.

radical publications, it is necessary that the major revolts be examined in some detail.

WIDESPREAD REVOLT BEGINS IN AUTO

The General Motors Corporation employs as many workers as all other auto manufacturers combined.   In 1955, United Automobile Workers' president, Walter Reuther, signed a contract with GM which did not check the speedup or speed the settlement of local shop grievances.   Over 70 percent of GM workers went on strike immediately after Reuther announced the terms of his agreement.   A larger percentage "wildcatted" after the signing of the 1958 contract because Reuther had again refused to do anything to combat the speedup.   For the same reason, the auto workers walked off their jobs again in 1961.   The strike closed every GM and a number of large Ford plants.

The UAW ranks' ability to conduct a nation-wide wildcat strike is made possible by a democratic practice that has been maintained by GM workers since the thirties.   Every GM local sends elected delegates to Detroit to sit in council during national contract negotiations.   They instruct their negotiators and confer with them as the bargaining progresses.   Ideally the council and negotiators arrive at an agreement on the package that the latter have been able to obtain from the employer and both the rank-and-file delegates and leaders recommend ratification by the ranks at the local union level.   In 1961, when the council unanimously recommended rejection and strike, Reuther notified the press that the strike was official, that he was leading it and that it would continue until all grievances concerning working conditions had been settled in separate local supplemental agreements rather than in the national contract.   He thus maintained control.   The ranks were outmaneuvered and angered.

Just prior to the negotiation of the 1964 contract, a development took place in the UAW that is unique in American labor history.   Several large Detroit locals initiated a bumper sticker campaign.   In all cities across the country where UAW plants are located the bumpers of auto workers' cars pushed the slogan: "Humanize Working Conditions."   Lacking the support of their official leaders, they were attempting to inform the public of the nature of the struggle they were about to conduct and that its primary goal would be to improve the condition of factory life rather than their wages.

Their attempt to bypass Reuther failed.   Contrary to established practice, he opened negotiations with Chrysler, the smallest of the Big Three auto makers.   He imposed the pattern of this contract on the Ford workers and announced that the Chrysler-Ford agreements would be the pattern for the GM contract.   The dialogue of the GM workers with their president was brief.   They struck every GM plant for five weeks and were joined by thousands of Ford workers.   They returned to work under a national contract no better than those signed with Ford and Chrysler.   Their strike won the settlement of a backlog of local grievances; created pride in the knowledge that it was primarily and publicly directed against Reuther's maneuver; and made possible the further development of rank-and-file leaders.   They demonstrated that they would not give ground in their efforts to make their national contract a weapon against the speedup and to rid themselves of a grievance procedure that allows the settlement of individual grievances to take up to two years.

Aware that the ranks would be continuing their fight and seeking revenge at the UAW's September 1966 convention in Long Beach, California, Reuther sought issues that could be used to divert their wrath.   In early 1965 the ballot count in the election between incumbent International Union of Electrical Workers (IUE) President James B. Carey and his challenger Paul Jennings was in doubt.   Reuther issued a statement to the press announcing his offer to merge the IUE with the UAW.   The merger might have salvaged Carey's reputation and employment in the labor movement.   It could also have been used as a major agenda item necessitating extended discussion at the UAW convention, but Carey rigidly turned down the offer claiming that he had learned of Reuther's offer only hours before it was made public.

The Long Beach UAW convention in May of last year was the first labor convention experience for over 60 percent of the delegates.   Many of the faces that had become familiar to Reuther during previous conventions were absent.   None of the delegates got a chance to discuss what was the main issue of the ranks who elected them—the demands they want to make and win in the negotiations for the 1967 contract; that point on the agenda was postponed to a special conference in April 1967.   Reuther won more than a breathing spell at Long Beach.   In the months preceding the convention the rebellion in the UAW's 250,000 man Skilled Trades Department had reached crisis proportions.   Their wages had fallen behind those of craft union members doing comparable work in other industries.   They threatened to disaffiliate and join the rival International Society of Skilled Trades (independent).   The convention amended the UAW constitution to give the Skilled Trades Department, containing less than 20 percent of the UAW's members, veto power over all national contracts. It is likely that they will get a substantial wage increase in the 1967 contract.   They do not work under the same conditions as the semi-skilled who buck the assembly lines and who are the majority and now second class citizenry of the UAW.   Reuther has obtained an aristocratic power base and laid the foundation for another and more violent rupture in the UAW.

For more than a decade it has been absolutely clear that the UAW ranks demand top priority be given to the fight to improve working conditions.   Their efforts to make Reuther lead this fight have been herculean.   At this late date it is almost paradoxical that he remains rigid in his refusal to make that fight. And so he must try to go into the April conference equipped with a diversionary tactic of gigantic proportions—based on more than a transparent maneuver that will only further enrage his ranks. His recent resignation as first vice president of the AFL-CIO and his open split with that body's president, George Meany, has among other things, armed him with such a diversion.   The question of total withdrawal from the AFL-CIO is the first point on the agenda of the April conference which is now scheduled to last only three days.

Leaflets circulated by UAW members in Detroit auto plants last January and prior to the split, ridiculed Reuther's inability to stand up to Meany.   They were picked up by the national press and significantly hurt Reuther's prestige.   Evidence mounts to indicate that Reuther was finally driven to sever his distasteful relationship with Meany for two principal reasons: (1) the demands of the UAW's revolt and internal struggle, and (2) the widespread revolts throughout the labor movement, particularly in the unions that form Reuther's domain in the AFL-CIO (Industrial Union Department).   The latter may include a third principal factor. The revolts are numerous enough to have given Reuther the vision that the revolts in the 1930s gave to John L. Lewis—the formation of a powerful new labor confederation through the organizational centralization of the unions that are in rebellion—a confederation that could now include white collar, professional, service and farm workers.

The wildcat strike of UAW-GM Local 527 in Mansfield,

Ohio, in February, revealed the depth of the liberal stance Reuther has taken in his fight with Meany. The total walkout at Mansfield occurred because two workers were fired for refusing to make dies and tools ready for shipment to another plant in Pontiac, Michigan. GM has long followed a policy of transferring work out of plants where workers have established better working conditions, or are conducting a struggle to improve them, to other plants with less militant work forces. The Mansfield workers had long observed this practice in silence. To be forced to participate in the transferral and their own defeat was the final indignity.

Mansfield is a key GM parts feeder plant and their strike idled 133,000 men in over 20 shops. Instead of utilizing this power to win his men's demands, Reuther declared the strike illegal. Moreover, he threatened to put the local into trusteeship and suspend local democracy. In an all-day session on February 22, his leadership pressured Local 727 leaders into asking their men to return to work without winning a solution of their grievances. The local leaders were told that the strike was poorly timed because it came on the eve of the UAW's big push for annual salaries and profit-sharing in 1967 bargaining. These two demands are to be given preference over all others. It is probable that the Mansfield strike has prematurely revealed the argument that Reuther will use in the April Conference against rank-and-file demands that the big push be to eliminate the speedup and inoperable grievance machinery.

The above probability is reinforced by the February 8 UAW Administrative Letter issued to elaborate upon Reuther's position on his split with Meany. It contains a long and detailed "Outline of UAW Program for the American Labor Movement." Under its section on collective bargaining it stresses the "development of a sound economic wage policy." No mention or hint is made of the need to improve working conditions which to this moment is the cause of the major crisis for Reuther's leadership.

Under "Aims and Purposes of a Democratic Labor Movement" the February 8 letter stresses collective bargaining and "appropriate progressive legislation" as the methods to be used to advance the interests of union members and their families. But Reuther's current policies insure that direct action, including wildcat strike and minor acts of sabotage in the plants, will daily continue to interrupt production. His program's concessions to the revolt can only encourage the fight against conservative union leadership and does not include goals that will enable him to lead and contain it. His failure to champion an improvement of working conditions will create a consequent dimming of enthusiasm and support for Reuther's new program for American labor, both within the UAW ranks and the ranks of unions whose support he hopes to win. His actions will tend also to undercut the possibility of success for the many good policies the program contains.

LONGSHOREMEN AND STEELWORKERS

In 1964 the ranks of the International Longshoremen's Association (east and Gulf coasts) conducted a strike-revolt against both their employers and union officials that was identical to and almost simultaneous with that accomplished by the UAW rank and file. The stevedoring companies and ILA officials had negotiated what appeared to be an excellent contract. It contained, by past standards, a significant wage increase. It guaranteed every union member a minimum of 1,600 hours of work per year and minor economic fringe benefits. The dockers struck immediately upon the announcement of the terms. Their president, Thomas W. Gleason, hurriedly toured all locals at the request of George Meany on a mission called "Operation Fact." Gleason claimed his ranks wildcatted because they didn't understand the contract. They understood only too well. In return for the recommended settlement the number of men in each work gang was to be cut from 20 to 17. The employers originally demanded a gang size reduction to 14 men, a size more nearly in line with manning scales negotiated by International Longshoremen's and Warehousemen's Union President Harry Bridges for west coast longshoremen. The ILA ranks did not give in to this or the many other undercutting pressures. President Johnson declared a national emergency and invoked the 80-day "cooling off" period under the provisions of the Taft-Hartley Act.

Wildcat strikes resumed on December 21, one day after the "cooling off" period ended and continued through January. All ports were on strike at the same time for over 18 days, and longer in southern and Gulf ports where separate and inferior contracts were offered. Longshoremen in New York and northern east coast ports returned to work, having lost on the main issue of gang size, but their defeat in this battle was not accompanied by a deep demoralization. Their union has long been unofficially divided into separately-led baronies. For the first time in the history of the ILA the entire membership initiated and conducted an all-union strike.

The United Steelworkers' Union revolt deserves special attention because it demonstrates how long it takes in some instances for a revolt to develop. In 1946 the steelworkers conducted a 26-day strike; in 1949, 45 days of strike; in 1952, 59 days; in 1956, 36 days. All of these strikes were conducted with only reluctant or forced support from the international leadership.

In 1957, an obscure rank-and-file leader named Ronald Rarick ran against USW President David MacDonald. Rarick, a conservative who has since become a reactionary, based his entire program on opposition to a dues increase and increase in the salaries of officials. As the campaign for the presidency developed, the rank-and-file could see that Rarick was not a militant unionist. Militants couldn't vote for Rarick with enthusiasm. His candidacy was used in the main to record opposition to MacDonald. He beat MacDonald in the Pennsylvania region by a slight margin, but lost nationally. The vote ran 223,000 for Rarick, 404,000 for MacDonald. I. W. Abel, running for Secretary-Treasurer, got 420,000 and his opposition got 181,000. In effect, Rarick disappeared after the election, but the vote he received alarmed the leaders of the large unions.

Four years later, MacDonald ran unopposed and received only 221,000 votes. It was obvious that MacDonald had been able to win a large vote against Rarick because he was able to utilize the treasury and resources of the International. To beat MacDonald a candidate had to be recruited from inside the International who also had access to its facilities.

As early as the Special Steelworkers Conference of 1952, the regional and local union leaders of the USW had warned MacDonald that he would have to do something about the deterioration of working conditions in the plants. They further warned that the resulting rank-and-file anger was threatening their position and they might have no other alternative than to transmit this pressure to him.

Twelve years later many of these same secondary and tertiary leaders realized that they could not survive under MacDonald's leadership. They picked I. W. Abel, a man who had not worked in a mill for 25 years, to challenge MacDonald. After a long dispute over the ballot count, Abel was declared the winner. Under his leadership a significant democratization of the negotiation process has begun. Delegates to the 1966 USW convention terminated the union's participation in the joint employer-union

Human Relations Committee whose function was to study plant working conditions and to determine how they could be changed in order to cut the costs of production and speed the automation process.   The union's 165 man Wage Policy Committee which had the power to ratify contracts was also completely stripped of its power.   A new and somewhat liberalized method for allowing the ranks a voice in negotiations was instituted.   The policy of last minute "shotgun" bargaining a few days prior to contract expiration was substituted for MacDonald's practice of beginning negotiations a year in advance of deadline.

ELECTRICAL WORKERS AND THEIR SECONDARY LEADERS UNITE

James B. Carey, President of the International Union of Electrical Workers was removed from office in a struggle similar to that which deposed David MacDonald.   By 1953, he had been out of contact with his membership for many years.   He had failed to lead them in a fight for improved working conditions against the General Electric and Westinghouse corporations.   He had been less successful than Reuther or even MacDonald in obtaining wage increases to ease his ranks' anger.   However, he felt the pressure of coming rebellion and sought to oppose rather than appease it.   He proposed a constitutional change for his union that would have had the employers collect union dues and send them directly to the union's Washington, D.C., headquarters, which would in turn dispense to the locals their stipulated share.

The secondary leaders recognized the danger to themselves and in 1964, with the backing of the ranks, organized an opposition to Carey.   In Paul Jennings of the Sperry local in New York they found a candidate with a good union reputation.   Jennings beat Carey, but a majority of the ballot counters were Carey supporters and they declared Carey the winner.   Jennings forces challenged the count and Carey supporters readied a second set of ballots to show the challengers.   They would have given Carey the victory.   Because of the ease with which Carey made enemies, even among men like George Meany, the supporters of Jennings were able to obtain aid in a world unfamiliar to the union's ranks.   The U.S. Department of Labor impounded the original ballots before a ballot switch could be made.

The struggle for rank-and-file autonomy in the IUE did not end with Jennings' 1964 part-coup victory.   In a very short time Jennings did more to improve wages than his predecessor, but he too neglected the fight for working conditions. Under his leadership the IUE engineered a united effort of eleven unions in the 1966 negotiations and subsequent strike against GE. A showdown was long overdue. GE had a 1965 volume of $6.2 billions, up one billion over 1964. It spent $330 million for capital expansion and still netted $355 million after taxes. Profits after taxes for the 1960–1965 period were up 52 percent. They had grown accustomed to docile union negotiators. The IUE-led united front broke GE's Boulwarist approach to bargaining, i.e., GE's practice of making their first settlement offer their last settlement offer under Board President Boulwaris' chairmanship. It also broke President Johnson's 3.2 percent wage guideline and obtained a 5 percent wage increase. However, after the contract was signed, major locals of all unions in the front, including thousands of workers of the IUE, UAW, International Brotherhood of Electrical Workers and the independent United Electrical Workers, stayed out on strike. Jennings and the leaders of the other unions had failed to negotiate an improvement of grievance machinery and working conditions. A Taft-Hartley injunction was necessary to end the strike of those involved in defense production.

Carey and MacDonald were not the only leaders of large industrial unions to be felled since 1964. In that year O. A. "Jack" Knight, President of the Oil, Gas and Atomic Workers retired three years early in the face of a developing rank-and-file revolt. During the Miami convention of the United Rubber Workers' Union in September 1966, the widespread unrest and revolts in the local unions that had preceded the convention forced incumbent President George Burdon to withdraw his candidacy for renomination. In an emotional speech he conceded the "serious mistakes" made during his administration. The major criticisms leveled against him were: loss of touch with the ranks, lack of personal participation in negotiations and an attempt to have the union pay his wife's personal traveling expenses. Veteran vice president Peter Bommarito was swept into office by acclamation. He immediately pledged to take a tougher position against the employers.

COAL MINERS AND THE LEWIS LEGACY

The 1963–1966 and still-continuing revolt in the United Mine Workers' Union did not unseat its president, W. A. "Tony" Boyle, the hand-picked successor of John L. Lewis. However, the insurgent nominees for all top offices at the 1963 UMW convention, standing firm in spite of the violence committed against them, provided the first formal opposition to top UMW incumbents since the 1920s. Steve "Cadillac" Kochis (Boyle's challenger from Bobtown, Pennsylvania) and his supporters lost as they predicted. They knew they had decisive strength in the Ohio-Pennsylvania-West Virginia region, but they also knew the dangers of the very loose UMW balloting system. They knew that the Boyle forces would build up a commanding block of votes in far-away districts that they found impossible to monitor.

Boyle inherited the revolt. Immediately after World War II, John L. Lewis turned from his policy of leading militant strikes for demands closest to the desires of his membership to an all-out program to speed the mechanization of the richest mines. The shift was hailed in the press for its technological progressiveness, but the human cost was staggering. Between 1947 and 1964 the UMW lost over 380,000 members. Lewis retained as members only those who worked in mines that could afford to automate; the rest were cut loose.

The abandoned did not all lose their jobs. More than 100,000 remained in the small mines or after a period of unemployment found work in mines that had been shut down because their veins were near exhaustion. The Lewis shift enabled them to re-open by hiring displaced miners at low pay. In West Virginia, Pennsylvania and Ohio there are now a large number of mines that have a headroom that is often no more than 36 inches. The miners who work them literally spend their lives on their hands and knees. By 1965, the production of coal in the poorer, non-automated and non-union mines accounted for 30 percent of total U.S. coal production. Their owners are again making fortunes. They employ embittered and impoverished former UMW members who have top experience and skill, at $14 a day, little more than half the union rate, and do not have to pay pension or fringe benefits. Thus, a small scale mechanization of the small mines has been made possible.

The increase in the strength of the competitive position of the non-union mines has in turn forced the large mine operators to impose a speedup on their employees. Pressure is applied, resulting in a deterioration of protective working and safety conditions. Fatalities are as high as they were during World War II when 700,000 men were working coal underground.

During the summer of 1965 in the Ireland Mine near Mounds-ville, West Virginia, five local union leaders refused to work under unsafe conditions and were fired. An unauthorized strike ensued which in one week spread over the West Virginia, Ohio and Penn-sylvania region. Roving bands of pickets easily shut down mine after mine, including United States Steel's large captive Robena mine. The UMW International leadership including the griev-ance processors they appoint at the local levels lost all control. The halfhearted legal efforts of the U.S. Department of Labor, that had the year before attempted to increase the democratic rights of the local and regional UMW organizations, had failed. The local leaders, the only authority the rebel ranks would follow in a disciplined and responsible manner, were labeled "instigators of anarchy."

The main reason for this large unauthorized strike was the jam of unsettled grievances in mine after mine; in addition, the rank-and-file miners were angered that their top officials had negotiated a wage increase in the previous contract at the expense of improv-ing working conditions. The main demands of the rebels became the right to elect their own local business agents and a democratized union structure from bottom to top. They felt that only by obtaining these rights could they find ways of helping themselves and their friends, relatives and former union brothers in the small mines. They returned to work only after being promised a greater voice in the negotiation of the next contract. In what was a major departure from past practice in the UMW, Boyle sent out a call for the Contract Policy Committee to meet *before* the opening of formal negotiations with the operators in 1966.

The contract obtained a 3 percent wage increase for the 100,000 soft coal miners who are left in the UMW. Their eco-nomic fringe benefits were slightly improved, but they are still far behind the workers in auto and steel. They won the right of first preference to any job openings in other mines in their district if laid off. During the negotiations they had to conduct a series of wildcat strikes to obtain these gains and their only satisfaction lay in the knowledge that the contract was an improvement over the one negotiated two years earlier. The revolt and the conditions that generate it persist. "Non-union" union men work for poverty level wages under nineteenth century conditions. In this period between contracts, sporadic acts of all forms of sabotage are on the increase.

BRIDGES, AUTOMATION AND B MEN

In 1960 International Longshoremen's and Warehousemen's Union President Harry Bridges negotiated the first six year "Mechanization and Modernization" contract with the Pacific Maritime Association. Like the contract that John L. Lewis negotiated for the automation of Big Coal, Bridges' contract allowed the unrestricted introduction of containerization of cargo, the use of vans, and automated cargo handling machinery. At the same time, it eliminated thousands of jobs. Primarily because of increased maritime activity due to war shipments, widespread unemployment up to now has been avoided.

Just as in coal, however, the human costs have been staggering. In the first year of the contract, the accident rate in what has become the nation's most dangerous industry went up 20 percent.[1] In the same year the longshore accident rate on the east coast declined one-half percent. To obtain this contract Bridges gave in to the employer's request that they be allowed to "buy" the elimination of the major working and safety conditions improvements won in the militant struggles of the 1930s. The long established manning scales and the 2,100 pound sling load limit were eliminated. These provisions were not only eliminated for labor performed on containerized cargo, but on the still very sizeable amount of cargo manhandled piece by piece and sack by sack.

Even more than Lewis, Bridges won the respect of employers everywhere, admiration in many liberal circles, and from the press—the title of "labor statesman." The contract established one gain for only one section of the longshoremen: during the six-year life of the contract those who entered the industry before 1948, had achieved union membership prior to 1960, had reached the age of 65 and who additionally had 25 years of service, could retire with a $7,900 bonus in addition to their unimproved pension. They could retire earlier if disabled and receive a smaller bonus on a pro-rated basis. Or, if they had 25 years in the industry at age 62 they could collect the $7,900 in monthly installments until they reached 65 when the regular pension payments began.

Although the fund that pays the bonuses is created by the tonnage worked by all longshoremen, the recipients are older union members who work little more than half that tonnage. The

[1] *Longshore Bulletin*, ILWU Local 10, February 8, 1962.

balance is moved by B men and casuals working under the jurisdiction of the union and the younger men who became union
members (A men) after 1960, none of whom are allowed to share in
the fund.

The B men are a permanent and regular section of the work
force who get the pick of the dirtiest and heaviest jobs that are
left over after the A, or union, men have taken their pick.   After
the B men, casuals hired on a daily basis get their turn at the
remainders.   The casuals get none of the regular fringe benefits
and are not compensated for that loss.

The B man system was created simultaneously with negotiations for Bridges' automation contract.   The production of B men
is appreciably higher than that of the union men because they lack
union representation on the job.   They pay dues but have no vote.
In Bridges' San Francisco base and home Local (No. 10) they can
attend union meetings providing they sit in a segregated section
of the meeting hall's balcony.   These eager-to-be-organized non-
union men do most of the work that is performed deep in the holds
of the ships, the area of production that produced the militants who
built the ILWU in the thirties.

Bridges fears these young men.   In 1963, in collusion with the
employers, he led the Kafkaesque purge that expelled 82 of them
from the waterfront jobs they had held for 4 years.   (Over 80
percent of the 82 are Negroes.)   They were tried in secret.   The
charges against them were not revealed.   Their number, but not
their identities, was made known to ILWU members.   Bridges'
witch hunt methods and double standards make the bureaucratic
procedures used to expel his union from the CIO, and the insidious
tactics used by the government to prosecute both him and
James Hoffa, bland by comparison.   Hoffa and Bridges at least
had the right to counsel, to produce witnesses, to know the charges
and to formal trial prior to judgment or sentencing.

The atmosphere of intimidation resulting from the framing of
the 82 has, until now, successfully silenced open opposition among
B men and younger men.   However, to Bridges' surprise, a revolt
against his automation contract and leadership has recently
developed among the older men.   Unlike B men and casuals, most
of them work on the ships' decks and the docks rather than down
in the hold where the major burden of the current speedup is being
carried.   It appeared for a time that the prospect of their receiving
a bonus upon retirement and lighter daily labors would conserva-
tize them; but 42 percent of all ILWU longshoremen (union or A

men) on the coast voted against the second six-year "Mechanization and Modernization" Agreement negotiated in July 1966. The speedup had reached these men as well. The contract won a majority in the large San Francisco local where retired members (pensioners) are allowed to vote, but lost in the other three large Pacific coast ports of Los Angeles, Portland and Seattle. Had the B men been allowed to vote, there is little doubt that it would have been overwhelmingly defeated.

The dissension that has developed between Bridges and other top ILWU leaders since last July has become so deep that news of it has appeared in the San Francisco press. Rumors persist that the fall out is over the question of how to handle the growing revolt in the ranks. Whether Bridges continues to pursue the automation policies in which he has staked his entire reputation or abandons it to pursue a re-winning and improvement of the working conditions desired by his ranks, the effect will be to stimulate a continuance of the revolt. He is now plagued by lawsuits, including one filed by the expelled B men and another filed in federal court several years ago by ILWU Local 13 in the name of all members in the large port of Los Angeles. James B. Carey and David McDonald learned, and now Bridges is learning, that the pursuit of policies that alienate the ranks can also isolate a top leader from his co-officials and hasten his fall from power.

MORE TROUBLE IN MARITIME

The accelerated advancement of cargo-handling technology during the last decade has in the last two years created an opposition to the leadership of Joseph Curran, president of the National Maritime Union. There has been a sharp decrease in the time that ships remain in American ports and the seamen are allowed ever shorter time with their families. The seamen's anger has been increased by the small monetary compensation for the special sacrifices of family and social life demanded by their industry. Curran has not responded to these problems, but instead has attempted to improve his position with the large New York membership by announcing plans for the construction of rent-free housing built with the union's pension fund. The announcement—an example of a positive and conservatizing reform initiated from above to quiet dissatisfaction—did not quell the revolt.

An aspirant to office in the NMU must already have served a term as a paid official. James M. Morrissey was one of the few oppositionists who could meet this requirement. The press has done nothing to inform the public of the fight made by Morrissey and his supporters. To this date the only source of printed information about it comes from Issue No. 23 of editor H. W. Benson's respected journal, *Union Democracy in Action*, published in New York. In an election [of questionable] honesty . . . , the incumbent officialdom conceded that Morrissey got 34 percent of the total vote and 14 percent of the New York vote in his struggle to unseat Curran.

Morrissey got close to what is the full treatment risked by rank-and-file opposition leaders in unions, whose democratic practices are limited. Last September three unidentified assailants beat him with metal pipes outside his union hall. No arrests have been made. His skull was shattered in several places and the bone over one eye was crushed. He still lives as does the opposition he leads. Curran is still [involved] in his fight to retain the job that pays him $83,000 annually.

By the autumn of 1966 it was possible to observe that, with the exception of the United Packinghouse Workers (UPW), every major union that contributed to the creation of the CIO in the 1930s had experienced a major revolt. Conditions in the coal, auto, rubber, steel, electric and maritime industries in the sixties are now renovating the unions whose formation they stimulated in the thirties. It should also be observed that most of the unions being renovated belong to and are a majority in the AFL–CIO Industrial Union Department, headed by Walter Reuther. The reasons for the UPW's exemption from the revolt process thus far are apparent: to the credit of its president, Ralph Helstein, the first day of its 1966 convention was thrown open to the delegates to voice their gripes about conditions in both their union and industry.

THE AIRLINE MECHANICS STRIKE

Most of the major industrial union revolts broke into the open prior to last summer. The press reported each as an individual phenomenon, if it reported them at all, and the full significance was missed. It took the five week July–August strike of the airline mechanics, who are affiliated with the International Association of Machinists (IAM), to make the general American public conscious of what *Life* magazine's August 26, 1966 strike-end issue called the "New Union Militancy," and the November issue of *Fortune* documented as a period of "dramatic shift from the familiar faces to the face-lessness of the rank and file."   This strike of less than 30,000 men did what the much larger strike-revolts failed to do.   By stopping 60 percent of the nation's air passenger travel they directly touched the lives of the nation's middle class.

Without advance signalling from liberal social analysts, who are usually among the first to call attention to signs of labor unrest, the daily press gave recognition to labor's new era—and no wonder.   The mechanics made it impossible for reporters to ignore the observation.   But the press stressed wages as the issue. Robert T. Quick, President and General Chairman of IAM District 141, gave an indication of the real issue in one of his strike press releases: "We're working under chain gang conditions for cotton picking wages."

The public had not witnessed a stance like that taken by the mechanics since the 1930s.   They rejected the first contract proposed by their new president P. L. Siemiller.   They rejected a second contract worked out under the direct intervention of the Johnson administration.   Siemiller stated he was sure his ranks could live with this contract, but the strike continued without pause.   They went further: not only did they make plain their opposition to Johnson's intrusion in their affairs, they rejected labor's allegiance to the Democratic party.   The four largest mechanics locals on the Pacific coast—Los Angeles, San Francisco, Portland and Seattle—sent telegrams to George Meany, Walter Reuther, James Hoffa and Harry Bridges asking that "immediate action be taken to form a third political party that will serve the best interests of labor."

The mechanics returned to work, having broken more than the 3.7 percent wage guideline of the nation's chief executive. More than damaging his prestige, they increased their own.   It is certain that back on the job they will be treated with more respect by their immediate supervisors and that it will be easier for them to unofficially institute improvements of their "chain gang" working conditions.

REVOLT AGAINST HOFFA RULE

The revolts have not all been national or union-wide in scope, but this does not diminish their potential or importance.   In the latter months of 1965 James Hoffa's Teamster leadership became unable to restrain the rebellion of the Philadelphia Teamsters.

Local 107, City Freight Drivers, have a long tradition of opposition to their international.   The leader of their local in 1963–1964 was Ray Cohen, a Hoffa supporter.   The ranks were dissatisfied with the representation he supplied.   Two caucuses existed in the local: "The Real Rank-and-File Caucus" (pro-Hoffa) and "The Voice Caucus," so called because of its publication.

The opposition to Cohen became so great that Cohen became a liability to the international.   Hoffa made his first appearance in Philadelphia, after becoming International Brotherhood of Teamsters president, to announce Cohen's demotion.   The elimination of Cohen evidently created no basic changes in the local. In June, 1965, at Roadway Express Incorporated's freight loading dock, a young worker, 18 years old and a son of a night over-the-road teamster's shop steward, was helping to load a big box into a trailer.   He refused to work under conditions he considered unsafe.   The foreman said: "If you don't do it, I'll fire you." The young freight handler answered: "Screw you.   Fire away." He was fired.   Four other men were ordered to do the same job, they said the same and were also fired.   The five men left the job together and went to the union hall.   They told their story to the ranks standing around the hall and to the local leaders.   A meeting was held.   The Voice Caucus took the lead away from its opponent caucus and made a motion for a general strike of all Philadelphia Teamsters; it carried and the strike was on: from five men to a strike of every driver and handler in the city and outlying region in less than 24 hours.   Now to insure that the strike was totally general, the Teamsters patroled the streets, stopped trucks and made out-of-town drivers get off their trucks. As a main location for the latter activity, they chose the area in front of Sears and Roebuck's department store.   There is an immense lawn and the highway widens out allowing room to parallel park trucks and trailers in large numbers.   After several days of this activity, the police attacked the local drivers.   The out-of-town drivers joined the strikers against the police.   A pitched battle ensued.   Within five minutes, the boulevard in front of Sears and Roebuck was impassable due to overturned trailers.   This guerrilla-type warfare continued in many areas of the city for several days.   Finally by injunction and because *both* factions of the leadership backed down, the strikers were forced back to work.   Although none of their strike gains have been contractualized, they are working under better conditions because they are able to express their strike-won strength on-the-job.

At present, both caucuses—Real Rank-and-File and the Voice—are in disrepute among the ranks because both backed down in the face of local authorities. Hoffa has threatened to take the local under trusteeship. The rank-and-file, to demonstrate that it is not defeated, had a meeting and passed a resolution which stated that such an attempt would be met by another strike.

THE PAINTERS AND DOW WILSON

The 1965 Building Trades strike in northern California's giant home-building industry was particularly important because it involved skilled workers with relatively high wage scales. Plumbers, laborers, sheet metal workers and painters struck against the wishes of their international union leaders. All but the painters settled within a few days. Ten thousand painters stayed out for 37 days.

San Francisco Painters' Local No. 4 is the largest local in the International Brotherhood of Painters. It was led by Dow Wilson and Morris Evenson. Its strike demands, including coffee time, were some of the most radical ever made by painters. Painting labor processes, due to the rapid advances in paint chemistry, are more rationalized than those of any other trade in the building industry. Time studies and resulting speedups are the rule. Paint foremen, rushing to make new tracts ready for the developers' sales forces, stand over painters with blank wage checkbooks protruding from their pockets. If a man falls behind he can be summarily fired and paid off in full. Tension of all kinds is high. Unsatisfied, the employers have for some time been pressuring the union to allow them to institute the use of new methods of paint application—the elimination of brushes for rollers, pressure rollers and spray guns.

During the strike the leaders of the international union publicly sided with the employers' automation demands. Local No. 4 and its leadership stood firm. Leaders in several other northern California locals backed down and their ranks rebelled. Less than half way through the strike Dow Wilson, in effect, became the leader of the entire strike and a majority of San Francisco Bay area locals. The painters won their strike, their coffee time, a big wage increase and temporarily checked the advance of technological unemployment.

Wilson knew that the international leaders would be vindictive and that they would try to get at the ranks through him.   The strike filled out his reputation as a model union leader, unique in these times.   He was an independent political radical who was unhampered by dreams of wealth.   He saw himself as a servant of the ranks, had exposed collusion and corruption in the painting of government housing that was cheating the taxpayers of millions of dollars, and had used his prestige to bring Negro workers into the industry.   He was a threat to the international union and employers.   Wilson realized he would have to carry his ranks' fight for union democracy to the international convention.

In the early morning hours of April 6, 1966, Dow Wilson was assassinated in front of the San Francisco Labor Temple—gangster style, by a shot gun blast in the face.   A month later Lloyd Green, president of the nearby Hayward local and a colleague of Wilson's, was killed in an identical manner.   The leaders and ranks of Local No. 4 accompanied by Wilson's widow and children demonstrated on the main streets of San Francisco and in front of the homes of city and federal authorities.   Arrests were made shortly thereafter.

An official of a painting employers' association confessed a major role in authoring the assassinations and driving the murder car.   His trial made it clear that his power in labor relations came from money he stole from the painters' pension fund and by threatening recalcitrants with a visit from his friend Abe "the Trigger" Chapman, whose name was formerly identified with Murder Incorporated.   He also indicated a top regional union official who is a supporter of the international union's policies. The official's guilt has not been proven; legal proceedings continue.

In a matter of weeks after the burial of the assassinated leaders, the international officials of the painters union made their first unsuccessful attempt to take several Bay Area locals into trusteeship and suspend local autonomy.   The courts have refused to grant an injunction against further attempts of the International to take control, but the rank-and-file painters and their remaining leaders, headed by the courageous Morris Evenson, continue to show a willingness to protect their independence in every way.

DISAFFILIATION AS A REVOLT TOOL

The revolt of California, Oregon and Washington pulp and paper workers in 1964 received little publicity.   However, it caught the attention of labor leaders nationally. In compliance with National Labor Relations Board requirements, workers in locals that were affiliated with two aging and eastern based AFL–CIO internationals (International Brotherhood of Pulp Sulphite and Paper Mill Workers and the United Papermakers and Paper-workers) broke away to form the independent Association of Western Pulp and Paper Workers (AWPPW). The old unions lost face and $500,000 a year in dues monies.

The AWPPW members whose work in 49 mills accounts for 90 percent of pulp and paper production on the Pacific coast, set up headquarters in Portland, Oregon. They announced the birth of their union through the publication of a monthly newspaper, *The Rebel*. They elected a president who is typical of the new union's staff; before taking office he was a mill electrician.

Since its initial organization, the AWPPW has had strong support from regional and local unions in areas where they set up locals, but life has been hard for this new union. Its newness and small membership has made it impossible to build the large treasury needed to operate a union today. It is not just the high cost of routine operation, collective bargaining against large corporations and legal costs that have created problems. The AWPPW is continually harassed by the two bureaucratized unions from which it split, both of which have the support of George Meany and the conservative AFL–CIO hierarchy. As their isolation increases and the official support they receive from other unions shrinks, owing to pressure from Meany, their energies are expended in a fight for existence rather than growth.

Throughout the United States there are large numbers of workers in local and regional units whose position is similar to that of the Pacific coast pulp and paper workers, prior to their establishment of independence in 1964. Their working conditions and wages are artifically depressed because of what amounts to captive affiliations with conservatively-led international unions. Their tolerance of their captivity seems unlimited only because at present there is no progressive alternative available.

WHY WORKERS REVOLT

Almost without exception, the revolts were conducted primarily to improve the conditions of life on-the-job. This is absolutely contrary to what the public has been led to believe. Newspaper, television and radio reporting rarely relate the existence, let alone the details, of labor's non-economic demands. The following statement by the Director of Research in Technology and Industrial Relations at Yale University stands as a classic definition of strike causes in American industry:

> In 1936 and 1937, a wave of sit-down strikes swept through the rubber and automobile plants of the United States. The workers on strike wanted higher wages, union recognition, and an organized machinery for the handling of day-to-day grievances, but, above all, they were striking against what they called the "speedup" of work as governed by the assembly line. The causes of every major strike are complex and frequently so interwoven as to be inseparable. But somewhere among the causes (and frequently basic to the others, as in the sit-downs) are work methods and working conditions.
> Two years before the first sit-down strike the country experienced a nation-wide walk-out of textile workers. Here, discrimination against union members, wages, and many other issues were involved, but the dynamic origin of the disturbance (not only in 1934, but through the remaining thirties and after) was the introduction of new work methods and machinery, all of which were generally lumped by the workers and denounced as the "stretch-out." If particular work methods or undesirable working conditions may sometimes cause a national walk-out, they are also the common origin of innumerable lesser conflicts in the world of industry. The net result of a minor conflict over a work method may be a day's slow-down or a grievance fought through the local's plant grievance machinery or, perhaps, hostilities expressed in low-quality work or by a high rate of absenteeism. . . . When neglected or misunderstood, these merely local disturbances can, with surprising rapidity, grow into a national emergency.[2]

Walker does not deny the importance of issues other than those involving working conditions, he simply says that they are secondary. Work methods and conditions are not the only issues in the current revolts. Wage increases have not kept up with price increases since the end of World War II. Americans have

[2] Charles R. Walker, "Work Methods, Working Conditions, and Morals," *Industrial Conflict*, A. Kornhauser, R. Dubin and A. Ross, eds. (New York: McGraw-Hill, 1954).

become accustomed to the pattern and have adjusted to it. Workers have maintained or increased their purchasing power by working long overtime hours, "moonlighting" (working two jobs) or putting their wives to work.   This is not to say that the unusually big jump in the cost of living that occurred last year failed to increase anger, frustration and discontent.   It did, but the American working class has not yet found an effective way to oppose price increases.   Workers in the larger and stronger unions in particular have come to believe that wage increases are a defensive or holding action.   Even when they have won substantial raises, price increases have wiped them out in a matter of months.   They no longer believe that a collective bargaining contract whose major achievement is a wage increase represents a victory of more than temporary progress.

The above belief nothwithstanding, it is always difficult and often impossible for workers to make the improvement of working conditions the formal as well as primary goal of contract negotiation.[3]   It is absolutely impossible for the employed near-poor and poor to do so.   For example, the conditions of work of the farm laborers in California's central valley are brutal and improvements are sorely needed, yet the United Farm Workers Organizing Committee headed by Caesar Chavez continues to give the wage demands top priority.   His ranks would have it no other way. In a sense, the farm worker puts aside his own most immediate need because he has responsibilities to his wife and children.   Then too, it should not be forgotten that workers who have incomes twice as large as the farm workers find it difficult to keep their wives in good spirits or their creditors patient during a strike whose major goal is anything other than a sizable wage increase.

Employers take the attitude that their authority over work methods and conditions is unchallengeable and sacrosanct.   Most of all they fear any kind of employee control over the production process.   No matter that the union sometimes forces them to grant sizeable wage boosts, they cover their increased costs and more by getting more work out of their employees.   American employers have made it clear that they will make a principled stand against any demand that would give a union any authority over the methods, conditions and speed of production.   Union officials fear fighting so determined an enemy, and they fear the new union leaders that would be developed in such a fight.   The

[3] An informative discussion of this point is contained in Alvin W. Gouldner, *Wildcat Strike* (Yellow Springs, Ohio: Antioch Press, 1954).

fight for better conditions cannot be made every one, two or three years like the wage fights; it must be fought every day inside the plants. During such a fight the base and authority of the union would be moved from the union hall back inside the plant. Workers who are willing to fight their employer to obtain a better life on-the-job have to be prepared to fight their union leaders as well.

The struggle of American industrial workers to improve the conditions under which they perform their labors is not an effort simply to obtain a better physical work environment. The goals go far beyond clean air and surroundings. Work paces and safety take higher priority.

Of equal, if not greater importance, is the drive to obtain formal contractual control over the methods whereby they are forced to perform their productive duties and to control their relationship to the machines with which they live. Cheated of the opportunity to make decisions of any kind, they are unable to take responsibility for what they do. In many cases, they are not told the identity of the product part which they help produce, let alone its function. Yet, they may be forced to remain at that labor for years, denied the right to transfer to other jobs that would allow a break in the monotony and increased knowledge of both the end product and total technology involved in its manufacture. Alienated, adjuncts to the machine, they resent the respect the machinery commands from their employers. In a word, industrial workers are fighting for dignity. Without it there is no daily gratification in their lives.

It was precisely this struggle that in the early 1930s caused mass production workers to organize independent local unions on a plant for plant basis without outside help and which inspired John L. Lewis to create the CIO by centralizing the power of those locals in the mid 1930s. But the CIO was not to become a weapon that would win significant improvements of work conditions, methods and controls. Those goals had to be subordinated to more immediate ones. The first priority of the CIO had to be the winning of collective bargaining recognition and the negotiation of corporation or industry-wide contracts so that workers in one plant would not be forced to compete against those in others.

By 1941, the industrial unions had accomplished these immediate goals to a substantial degree. The time had arrived when the workers, through their new unions, could be free to return their attention to the problems of the work process. World War II cheated them from doing so.

The war provided employers with an opportunity to check the momentum of the CIO. With the exception of John L. Lewis, the official labor leadership, especially those who were pro-Communist, pledged that for the "duration," their unions would not strike. The employers responded by trying to win back organized labor's recent gains. Alone, workers were forced to defend just the fundamental victories of the 1930s. The attempts to do so were often branded as "aid to the enemy."

The war, however, by its very totality, had a far more crippling effect on labor's ranks than those directly imposed on them by their employers, the government and their official leaders. Within a year after it had begun, the war atomized the rank-and-file's on-the-job union cadres. It took large numbers of experienced local union leaders and shop stewards from the workplaces. It decimated the personnel of labor's most fundamental organizational unit, the informal work groups created by the productive process. These groups, with their informal leaders, form a social unit able to discipline their members and restrict production. The CIO was born in these groups. They pyramided their power, plant-wide, and an independent local union was formed. The process was called "self organization." A typical example of the effect of World War II on the groups was as follows: A group of ten welders and grinders who worked in close contact with one another were employed in a plant that unionized in the late 1930s. Half of them became employed there in the late 1920s or early 1930s. Others came later, but all participated in a portion of the long fight that brought the union into the plant, and more importantly, to obtain the right to *openly* bargain with their immediate supervisor—the foreman. By 1943, five of them had gone into the armed forces and two had gone to the shipyards on the west coast. They were replaced by two housewives, a draft-exempt youth and four men beyond draft age from farms and marginal jobs. How could the three remaining members of the original group impart to the newcomers the history, tradition and knowledge of their group's struggles or the union lessons learned in years of fighting? They could not. Before it sustained war losses the group was able to conduct actions that would tame a foreman. They could participate in that process which keeps union leaders militant. If they saw a local president softening in his attitude toward management he would be told: "Look, remember when you worked with us and how it was, and how you complained louder than anybody else? And now you're talking out of both sides of your mouth and letting us live under these conditions." Neither did they spare their own members who showed signs of weakening. A failure to attend union meetings brought jibes, serious but with smiles, that reminded the absentees of what they had all been through together and the need to continue. No such pressures could be applied to their group's wartime replacements. To the new members, the union officials were unapproachable "big shots."

When the war was over, the reconversion to peacetime consumer production once again broke up the personnel of the work groups. Large numbers who had entered the armed forces or war industries did not return to their old jobs. The old groups could not re-establish themselves. In plant, after workplace, the workers were divided into segments with three major identities: old timers, vets, and kids, so-called. For a time their attentions focused primarily on stockpiling home furnishings. Who could blame them? For the first time in American history a majority of workers were able to consume a large number of the products made. But the brightness of that goal diminished. The routine drudgery of workers' lives soon re-established its monotonous predictability. Besides, television sets and dishwashers at home did not bring gratification to life on-the-job. And the workers were getting to know one another again. They were learning who, among those near them, liked to bowl, sew, garden, repair cars and fish. The questions had been asked: "How many kids do you have?" and "Where do you want to go next vacation?" The social cohesion and the work eliminated the separate identities. Work groups again attained leaders. The selection, as always, was natural. No formal elections were held. The vote was by a nod, by the raising of a brow, or by a silent consensus that at first is not always conscious. Someone in a group emerges as courageous and articulate, stands up to a foreman, and the rest support him or her, with the result that it is once more a fighting unit involved in guerrilla warfare.

By the mid-1950s, American workers, particularly in the mass production, transportation and maritime industries, were ready once more to resume the struggle that had caused the revolts of the 1930s. They found, however, that the leadership created during the rise of the CIO was not responsive to their desires. There was an unwillingness among the official leaders to give up the control they had so easily attained during the war. The workers had no choice but to conduct a fight on two levels. Inside the workplaces, they fought their employers, and at the same time conducted a campaign to win the in-plant local union officials—the only section of the labor leadership with whom they have daily and direct contact—to their cause.   Officials who identified with them were supported.   Every possible pressure was brought to bear on those who would not.   By 1964, the tactic had achieved enough success to separately pit large numbers of individually unified local unions against their regional leaders who, in turn, were forced to apply pressure on those top leaderships that were not responsive. Thus, the revolts broke into the open.   They were created, grew, and became a fact visible to the public, first because of the need and secondly *because the rank-and-file of American unions had been able to build from their work groups the basic organizational vehicle for them.*

The revolts continue to grow in both depth and magnitude. Wildcat strikes show a steady increase.   Each year the Federal Mediation and Conciliation Service enters nearly 8,000 disputes. Last year union rank-and-file members rejected 11.7 percent of the contracts negotiated with the Service's aid, an all time high that is still rising.   In the first month of fiscal 1967 the rejections rose to 19.3 percent.   There is continued increase in the number of elections in which long-time incumbents are being challenged from below.

The present struggle to improve work conditions, methods, and controls is far more desperate than that of the 1930s, and represents a far deeper potential crisis for the nation.   The productivity of the entire labor force is far higher.   Employers have retained the right to establish the speed at which assembly lines will travel and the methods by which work shall be performed. No major union, including the UAW, has made a concerted effort to restrict that right.   Workers in most modern automobile assembly plants often turn out between 60 and 70 cars an hour. Neither the human anatomy nor mentality was designed to endure such strain or monotony.

A manifestation of this may be the reported increase in the use of drugs within the plants:

> Pep pill use by factory workers draws increasing concern as a hidden hazard.   Plant medical directors and safety specialists fear scattered signs of drug use by production workers are symptomatic of an underground factory safety problem.   A major farm equipment maker, a big food processor, detect increased use of pep pills in

their plants.   One worker's tool box turns up a hundred bennies (benzedrine capsules).   One executive suspects "there are several pushers in our plants."   "The problem is most acute in California," he adds, "but we've found a little of this to be countrywide."

Los Angeles narcotics authorities turn up a well-supplied pusher in an auto plant; they aid big aerospace companies seeking remedies to the problem.   One California narcotics specialist figures pills are pushed in all plants with assembly-line operations.   Some executives blame today's fast production pace and excessive moon-lighting for driving workers to stimulants.   One detective says that employers don't want to attack the problem for fear of stirring unfavorable publicity.[4]

The increased use of speedup methods in industry now threatens the safety and health of workers in the most literal sense. According to the National Safety Council's 1966 report on U.S. industry, "14,500 workers died and another 2.2 million were temporarily or permanently disabled in 1966."   The U.S. Public Health Service recognizes the crisis is greater than at any time in the nation's history and is spending a record $6.6 million on occupational health this year.   Syndicated columnist Sylvia Porter recently discussed a "top level" report to the U.S. Surgeon General that argued that $50 million a year is needed to reduce hazards by 20 percent; she further argued that doing so "would add $11 billion a year to our production."[5]

The problems of speedup and increased safety hazards have been largely ignored by the official union leaders.   Workers have been forced to seek solutions outside official union grievance machinery.   Production, particularly in heavy industry, is plagued by slowdowns and minor acts of sabotage.   Bolts are dropped into the slots in which the chains travel that pull the assembly lines; machinery is not maintained or is handled in a way that will hasten its breakdown.   The quality of the product is harmed by shortcuts that allow a momentary breathing spell; creativity and efficiency are withheld.   The object is revenge, release from boredom, and the rest that results while repairs are awaited.

For brief periods after each guerrilla victory (and under management's increased surveillance) the glee is limitless though

[4] *Wall Street Journal*, November 22, 1966, p. 1.
[5] *San Francisco Chronicle*, April 13, 1967.

no trace of it can be found on the facial expressions of the participants. Nevertheless it is a difficult war. Victories are short-lived. The tension saps energies and the speedup continues. In many plants employees hired as spies openly take notes. While there are few mortalities (firings), there are many casualties. Suspected trouble-makers are sometimes temporarily laid-off for real or for alleged infractions of rules unrelated to the actual charge. Most often they are transferred to other departments of the shop. They sustain no loss in pay, but must accustom themselves to new foremen, new repetitive tasks and undergo a period of initiation in their new work groups.

The widespread introduction of automated machinery since World War II has increased the existing alienation of American workers. When new machines and methods are substituted for the old, new job classifications and rates must be defined. The employers make every attempt to reclassify jobs so as to downgrade wages. Then too, they sometimes meet outbreaks of worker militancy with threats of automating jobs out of existence. It is impossible to measure the anger that results.

Automation qualitatively increases nervous tension on-the-job. A worker at a machine on which he or she can produce one hundred pieces a day, is placed at a machine that can be made to turn out five hundred. A mistake that previously made it necessary to scrap one piece becomes one that necessitates the scrapping of five. At the same time, the new machine cheats the worker of the opportunity to use the skills needed to operate the old one. The deskilled worker loses individual bargaining power, freedom in the job market and a daily loss of work gratification—a damage to self-image.

Even though armament production has absorbed the jobs lost because of automation, workers bitterly hate the automation process. In it they see future joblessness. They reject all claims that it represents progress. They are aware of the human price. It uproots them and requires that they transplant themselves to another workplace and often to another geographic area. If their work area is automated and they are lucky enough to retain their employment, they may face an even more dismal prospect: an on-the-job loneliness for which there is no compensation. The friends that once surrounded them, providing an on-the-job family, disappear or no longer work within earshot. Increased absenteeism and loss of morale are inevitable. What once made the job just bearable has been eliminated. Also, the fighting weapon, the informal work group, has been destroyed; new ones must be built.

The final indignity of the process for the workers is that they and their leaders are seldom if ever consulted before automated change is introduced. They are presented with an accomplished fact—change designed by humans who have no conception of an industrial worker's life experience, on the job or off.

But the consequences of automation give workers weapons they did not previously have. Probably, like the British workers during the beginnings of Luddism in the late eighteenth century, American workers now note the demoralization of industry's middle class. Computerization, automation's companion, is stripping middle executives and immediate management of their power to make decisions. Meaningful decisions are increasingly made at the top.

Automation creates problems for management in still other ways. Automated machines represent a far larger capital investment than their predecessors. They are far more vulnerable to neglectful treatment. Their complexity provides increased opportunities for the minor acts of sabotage that are already widespread and difficult to detect. A slowdown or stoppage of an automated machine causes a production loss several times over the loss caused by a similar crisis involving the machines it replaced. One worker is able to restrict production to a degree that earlier would have involved a half dozen.

The rapid disappearance of family-owned companies and the growing number of corporate mergers contribute to the rank-and-file revolts in a manner similar to that of automation. In industries run from the top by professionals for multi-absentee owners, the symbol of authority is no longer human, with a consequent effect on the contents and enforcement of directives from the main office. Embattled from above and below, the vise on middle and lower management twists tighter. The problem is exaggerated in corporations of the conglomerate type owning factories of productive units in a number of non-related industries. Top managers directing units making steel, candy, silk stockings and chemicals lose contact with the production processes. They are in the business of managing.

The unique character of the comglomerate gives their managers a new weapon in their dealings with organized labor. If a particular union strikes in one of their industries, the others—in different industries under contract to different unions—are free to operate and profit.   It is much easier to pit union against union.

According to Federal Trade Commission figures, over 70 percent of all important mergers and acquisitions (involving $10 million in assets) between 1960 and 1965 were conglomerate.   Only 13 percent of the mergers were with firms producing similar or related products.   The same trend continued into 1967.   (The FTC estimates that at the current merger pace, 75 percent of all corporate assets in the nation will be in the hands of 200 corporations by 1975.)   International unions (so called because they include Canadians) are thus forced to negotiate contracts for larger and larger numbers of their members.   By their very nature, these negotiations become more and more attentive to wage and economic fringe benefit payment patterns, less and less concerned with the working conditions that vary so widely from workplace to workplace.   The condition of daily life in industry degenerates. It is absolutely necessary and proper that American workers permit the top leaders of their international unions more centralized power.   There is no other way to challenge growing corporate power during the negotiation of master collective bargaining agreements.   At the same time, the ranks want to determine the goals of those negotiations and to use their power in the workplace to increase their control over the nature of work.   How to simultaneously centralize labor's total power on the one hand and decentralize it on the other is a decisive issue of the revolts.   No sense can be made of them unless this is recognized.

There is another objective condition in industrial society that affects the revolts and must be mentioned briefly: the labor shortage.   It became a major problem for industry in 1966, or after the revolts began, but this is not to downgrade its effect.   It allowed a greater degree of independence for those already in the workforce when it began.   Probably more important, however, it caused industry to hire hundreds of thousands of youths who would in the past have had to wait years longer to get what has long been considered "adult employment."   The attitudes of the new young workers have been a revelation to the older workers.   They, like their middle class counterparts in the universities, are free of the wounds that the Depression inflicted on previous generations. For large numbers of them a good self-image is not dependent upon having a reverent attitude toward employment.   They rebel against doing what has dulled and shortened the lives of their

parents.   The following experience in today's factories is not un-
common: A young worker is offered a higher paying job, discovers
it requires a faster pace or involves an onerous condition and turns
it down—preferring to live easier at less pay.   The older workers
observe such an action in shocked respect.   They would not have
dreamed of taking such a step.   It reveals to them the sacrifices
they have long endured.   The experience can widen but more often
helps to narrow gaps.   Today's young are armed with mirrors.

The revolt of university students has had a radicalizing effect
on the entire society.   This includes industrial workers.   Many
of them are repulsed by the attire and conduct of some of the
students, but dissent of any kind has a contagion.   Besides, the
repulsion is an initial and surface reaction.   The workers' rebellion
creates tolerances and even feelings of kinship for others doing
the same.

Will the students develop new alliances now that they have
lost a base in the civil rights movement?   Already, radical students
have begun to re-evaluate their attitudes toward unions.   They
have been taught, often by formerly radical social scientists, that
American workers are now fat on beer, barbecue and television,
and no longer capable of struggle for social progress.   The rank-
and-file revolts are destroying the cynical myth and providing
opportunity for alliances.   The initiative will not always be from the
students.   It must not be forgotten that during the Free Speech
Movement's revolt on the Berkeley campus in December, 1964, it
was the San Francisco local of the Service Employees International
Union that provided the FSM with its first public support in the
Bay Area and paved the way for public support from the powerful
San Francisco Central Labor Council.   During the FSM strike
that in the same month closed that campus, rank-and-file Teamsters respected the students picket lines until ordered to cross them
by their leadership.   The Cement Truck Drivers East Bay
Teamsters local, however, officially honored the strike.   Early in
1965, when Mario Savio and the other FSM leaders were under
attack from the entire establishment in the state, Paul Schrade,
the west coast director of the United Automobile Workers visited
the Berkeley campus and before press and public declared that he
would greet the presence of students like Savio inside his union.

The most decisive crisis for American unions is the alienation
that lies between them and members of the black community:
particularly the black youth, but also the black union members.
The main cause of the crisis is twofold: White rank-and-file

workers are, in the main, but to varying degrees, racially preju-
diced; the leadership of labor has generally failed to provide the
leadership that could solve the crisis. In the broadest sense of the
term the crisis is one of leadership. The top officials of labor have
failed to provide adequate leadership for any of the major problems
facing workers. Walter Reuther provides a good example. He
has many times provided segments of the civil rights movement
with valuable aid. Those admirable actions are cheated of their
full educational value for the UAW ranks—both white and black.
"He is helping them, but what about us?" A Reuther who
conducted a more than rhetorical battle against the speedup
in the auto plants could increase his union's support of the black
revolution tenfold without incurring the wrath of the white
workers in his ranks. At first they would forgive him his tres-
passes because he was also delivering for them. Only then could
there be the receptivity that allows for education in the best
sense. Also, the black UAW members, who suffer from the
speedup as much as do the white workers, could begin to take
Reuther seriously.

Almost invariably, when labor leaders make speeches asking
that their white ranks champion the rights of blacks in industry,
they are asking the whites to give up something without offering
them anything in return. White workers involved in the formation of the CIO welcomed the presence of blacks because it won
an industrial union for them. For that time, the appearance of
substantial numbers of blacks in mass production industries with
full union membership was progress. As a result, the prejudice
of the whites who experienced it was diminished. As always,
morality followed necessity. Tragically, the initial progress was
not built upon. The CIO bureaucratized and lost its momentum.
The blacks lost a vehicle for major progress and organized labor
lost a natural ally.

The momentum of the movement for black liberation and
labor's lack of responsiveness dictate that black workers will
organize, as such, within industry and unions. If this attempt at
organization is grounded in demands for an improvement of work
life as well as black freedom it will find sympathies among white
workers. The organizations they form will help stimulate the
formation of internal union opposition movements in general.
The present weakness of the rank-and-file revolts is that they are
localized and isolated from one another. If the revolts continue
to grow in scope, it is likely that it will mean the beginning of the

end of labor's leadership crisis.   Only the failure of the revolts and the consequent demoralization can create the basis for the development of a major racist movement among white industrial workers.

The isolation of labor from its natural allies is closely related to its political failures.   The politics which join the official labor leadership to the Democratic party contribute to its impotency in serving its membership.   There is hardly a major labor negotiation that fails to demonstrate this fact.   There is not one aspect of labor's leadership crisis that has not contributed to the cause of the rank-and-file revolts.

Thus far, these pages have discussed those causes of the revolts that are in some way internal to industry and the unions, due mainly to policies and conditions that affect workers as such. But there are developments in our society that have a radicalizing effect on a major portion of the population—workers included. Although it is difficult to measure the impact of these broader developments, it is doubtless that they are among the principal causes of the revolts.   Or, to put it another way, the rank-and-file union revolts are the industrial workers' expression of a more widespread radicalization process taking place in America.

The active development of the process begins with a question that Americans increasingly ask themselves and each other: "Is this all there is to life?"   The absence of life satisfaction in an era of instant communication and atomic miracles seems a tragic contradiction.   The question was not formulated yesterday, nor inspired by just the experiences of the 1960s.   It reaches much deeper into our past and the institutions, ideas and values on which our society operates.   The conscious pursuit of happiness via government programs is not new to Americans.   We have tried a number of governmentally sponsored attempts at what was claimed would be a new society.   All of these attempts were characterized by an ideological vagueness.   Yet, for a time, they instilled hope.

The New Deal of Franklin Roosevelt instilled more optimism than all its succesors.   However, it was production for World War II, rather than the New Deal, that brought full employment. Regardless of the cause of full employment, there was not a New Deal supporter whose inspiration was not dulled by that program's destruction of food at a time when there were Americans who were starving.

Americans fought World War II with an enthusiasm instilled by the promise of a "better life" after victory.   The Fair Deal of

Harry Truman did no more than provide a faint echo of the New Deal and we marked time until the Korean War—fought with far less enthusiasm than World War II. The New Frontier of John Kennedy gave many Americans a moment of hope. The President was youthful. He surrounded himself with professional intellectuals. No basic change was accomplished. The Great Society has done no more. The impatience of Americans has grown. Lyndon Johnson is no longer a popular president. The impatience is based on more issues than the war in Vietnam.

None of the promises from the top, of a newer and greater society, have been kept. A period of war, hot and cold, H-bombs, nerve gas and bacteriological weapons, is not one in which people can live on hope for the distant future. Americans have more and more sensed that their leaders are without program, answers, or clear idea of where we are headed. This and an increased awareness of corruption in high places has stimulated initiatives from below.

Dissent initiative in the population mystifies many national political figures. They have always operated on the idea that if a majority of the population enjoyed a degree of prosperity, there could be political stability. But the general public has developed an awareness of what it previously paid little attention to. There are millions of Americans who live in material and, therefore, spiritual poverty. Whatever lessons have not been learned from the War on Poverty, have been taught by the struggles of black, Mexican, Indian, and poor white Americans.

It is only since the end of World War II that a majority of Americans have experienced a relatively high standard of consumption. Yet, there exists an uneasiness and an insecurity. How is it possible to enjoy a large well-balanced meal that stimulates overeating when others are denied this right? Guilt can cheat a dinner table of its warmth. And then, how safe is a wealth not enjoyed by all? The problem is not limited to the United States. For the first time in history and in many parts of the world the idea that progress toward happiness can be individually instead of collectively achieved through material plenty is beginning to be challenged— given actual test. It is logical, however, that the major challenge should be made in the most advanced industrial nation.

The problems of an atomic and computer era automatically pose the question of collective solution, in all problem areas. Collective action and the need for decisions made collectively and more democratically immediately follows.   The major factor that propels a society into a period of accelerated social change is the existence of an "ever increasing divorce between reality and the law, between institutions and men's way of living, between the letter and the spirit."[6]   When the divorce becomes wide enough, all practices that oppress and all institutions that are not responsive get challenged.   Blacks, for example, cannot live with racism in any of its forms; students cannot live in multiversities operating on century-old methods; and the new middle class cannot abide the unilateral decisions which factoryize professional work. Industrial workers are unable to utilize unions with aged organizational structures and a low degree of internal democracy.   The broad social action program of the UAW, for example, has wide public appeal.   It is vastly superior to those of most other unions. In contrast, the UAW, like most other unions, is structured so that its power lies outside the factories: in the international headquarters and local union halls rather than primarily on the shop floor.   The auto corporations have a foreman-to-worker ratio of approximately one to fifteen.   The ratio of bargaining UAW shop stewards to workers in most plants is one to 250.   Regardless of the quality of the steward, it is physically impossible to provide adequate representation.   Nevertheless, it is the stewards more than any other section of union officials, who are in constant contact with the ranks and who perform the primary official function of the union.   They are not cut into the official union power structure as an organizational unit; this automatically preserves the open gap between top leadership and ranks.   The gap exists in all American unions.   Long absent from the place of work, the top leaders live in an atmosphere that makes it easy for them to accept or tolerate management philosophies.   For some time, management and top union leaders have operated on the premise that, in order to grant wage increases, the employers must be free to get more production from workers.   It is difficult to find a worker who accepts the idea, but the union provides no built-in vehicle—such as a shop stewards' council system—that allows constant expression of this rejection in top leadership echelons.

What of the future of the rank-and-file union revolts and their ability to wrest change?   Their weakness lies in their lack of more than local level organization or program.   Their main strength is that they do not exist in societal isolation.   They have broken into

[6] Albert Mathiez, *The French Revolution* (New York: Alfred A. Knopf, 1928); (New York: Grosset and Dunlap, 1964), p. 3.

the open in a period when other segments of the population are also in revolt.   This was far less true in the revolts of the 1930s: at that time there were no black or student rebellions.   One other condition is brand new: unlike the 1930s, for the first time, intellectuals have the means to build their own organizational base within labor.   Teachers, professionals of all kinds, white collar workers, and government employees at all levels are forming unions of their own.   In return for the support they are getting from blue collar unions they are bringing to labor's ranks a degree of cultural and technical expertise never before available.*

* In a recent series of articles on the Black Revolutionary Union Movement in Detroit's auto plants, Robert Dudnick (a reporter for the independent radical weekly, The Guardian), argues that the principal purposes of the black workers' movement are quite similar to those advocated by Weir for labor as a whole.   See Dudnick's pamphlet: "Black Workers in Revolt" (The Guardian, 197 E. 4th Street, New York).—M.Z.

38

WORKER–STUDENT ALLIANCE?

Robert Avakian

On Friday, February 7, [1969] Jake Jacobs, Secretary-Treasurer of the Oil, Chemical, and Atomic Workers Union, Local 1–561, in Richmond, California, shook up the media by informing reporters that a "mutual aid pact" had been formed between oil workers on strike against Standard Oil and teachers and students whose combined struggles have shut down San Francisco State College for more than three months. Jacobs echoed the sentiments of many of the top leaders of the SF State student strike when he pointed out that the enemy of the oil workers, the teachers, and the students is the same: the political establishment, acting as the oppressive instrument of the modern-day plantation owners who control the giant monopolies like Standard Oil and the universities and colleges throughout the country.

This mutual aid pact, along with the presence of hundreds of students on the picket lines with oil workers at Standard Oil, has made the possibility of a "worker-student alliance"—which until recently seemed only the dream of a few isolated political sects—appear very real indeed. And it has raised a number of very important questions. What do we mean by "worker-student alliance"? Around what principles must it be built? Why has solidarity between students and workers suddenly become possible, after a relatively long period of not only isolation, but outright hostility between them?

Reprinted from the *Mid-Peninsula Observer* (February 16–23, 1969), pp. 17, 21, by permission of the publisher. The article was originally titled "Oil Strikers, Students Form Mutual Aid Pact."

Students, who make up a very small percentage of the people, are by definition in a transitional state (relative to the means of production): their class status is very unclear. Most students come from sections of the middle classes—and this, of course, is one of the crucial issues raised by the student strike at SF State.

In fact, the SF State student strike represents a new stage in the development of the student movement. Beginning with the Free Speech Movement in Berkeley in 1964, students have gone through a cycle of revolt against the structuring of the colleges and universities. They see that educational institutions are management-training and research-service centers for the ruling class of big businessmen from banks, oil companies, agricultural trusts, and other monopolies.

These student rebellions have been somewhat contradictory: the students fought against the university as a factory, but they also fought against the tide of history. Their response was to say to the rulers of America—the bosses of the university and the corporations—you cannot make *us* into dumb animals or raw materials; we will stop your machinery first.

In much the same way, craftsmen in the seventeenth century fought against the first forms of mass production. In the early stages of their political development the students, too, tried to turn history back to an idealized time when the "higher" educational system was set up to individually pamper each student.

In plain language, while the students first fought against the capitalist bosses who had in fact perverted the university, they fought for more privilege for themselves. And like the handicraft guilds in the seventeenth century, the student movement was bound to move to a higher stage or be crushed.

The basic principle of the Third World Liberation Front strike at SF State was clearly stated time and time again by the leaders of the front at a community rally called by local labor leaders in support of striking teachers and students. "The university should serve the people," the black, brown, and yellow spokesmen for the front told the audience of students, teachers, and other supporters of the State strike, including a number of working people.

In other words, if the capitalist bosses are turning all of society, including the educational system, into one big factory, all right; but then we will fight so the people can control the factory and the goods and services it produces so the factory will benefit the great majority of the people, not a handful of billionaire bankers and business bigshots.

It is in this context that the demand for self-determination—for Third World control of the Third World college—and for open enrollment for Third World people has to be understood. Up until now, the colleges and universities have been reserved almost exclusively for the professionals. In California, for example, the children of those who have plenty of leisure time to read and suck up the so-called "culture" of the rulers of the country make it to one of the campuses of the University of California.

WHO GOES WHERE

The children of the lower middle classes, along with a small number of kids from more privileged working class backgrounds, get into the State colleges (see Table 1); and the sons and daughters of working people, if they get to college at all, find themselves in the junior colleges. All of these institutions are supported by the taxes of the people: taxes that working people pay out of their own wages and their bosses pay out of the profits they extract from the labor of "their" workers.

But the public pays more than twice as much for the education of one university student as for a student at a state college; and the amount spent on each state college student is more than twice the amount spent on the junior college student. In other words, the sons and daughters of the upper and middle classes are worth more to the rulers of the country than the children of working people.

So the demand at SF State (and University of California,

Table 1. Percentages of State College and University Students by Family Income of the Students

Income group	State colleges	University of California
$ 0–1,999	.7%	2.9%
2,000–3,999	3.3	2.0
4,000–5,999	10.0	7.4
6,000–7,999	16.6	11.0
8,000–9,999	16.8	12.9
10,000–11,999	19.5	13.1
12,000–13,999	10.5	11.2
14,000–19,999	12.7	20.0
20,000–24,999	3.2	6.5
25,000 and over	4.4	11.6

Berkeley) to allow open enrollment for the most downtrodden of all working people—black people, Latin Americans, and Asian-Americans—is a basic challenge to the whole system of educational privilege. It is a demand to throw open the doors of the university to the exploited and oppressed, which means white workers as well as their black, brown, and yellow brothers.

It means challenging the whole notion of using the universities and colleges to turn out future foremen, supervisors, and bosses and to preserve a system where a small number of this privileged group control and live off the majority of people who are prevented from acquiring more than the basic necessities of life—and those through soul-stealing and life-stealing struggle.

The SF State student strike has gained more and more support from the people in the community, exactly because the students are fighting for the needs of not only black, brown, and yellow people, but the majority of white working people as well. This makes it very clear that a worker-student alliance, if it is to last and to grow and take in other victims of the ruling class, must always be built on the basic needs of the most oppressed sections of the laboring masses.

The SF State strike represents a great step in this direction. As long as we follow the principle that has been the cornerstone of the SF State strike—that the university and the students should serve the people—we will be able to strengthen and broaden the worker-student alliance.

MANDEL ARGUES THAT SEVERAL TRENDS ARE DEVELOPING IN *American capitalism which, in combination, may destroy the social equilibrium of the past several decades in the United States. Accelerated technological change, or automation, is increasingly eliminating unskilled labor, thereby increasing the rate of chronic unemployment and underemployment—an increase that disproportionately affects black workers, especially young ones, to whom radical and nationalist explanations and appeals become more attractive.*

A similar trend can be seen in results of the expulsion of manual labor from industry. Intellectual labor is drawn into public and private administration and education, where it becomes industrialized—that is, standardized, hierarchical, and mechanized. As salaried labor replaces self-employed and free professional labor, students who will not accept this future for themselves become increasingly alienated and radicalized.

Automation also leads to accelerated depreciation and replacement of fixed capital, a condition that requires increased concentration of capital and diversification of investment in order to minimize the risks of rapid technological change. The coordination of production and investment of several unrelated but financially-integrated industries becomes essential in order to ensure maximum profitability for the large corporation. At the same time, the historic obsolescence of the situation in which those who build the decisive power in directing the economy are those who are remotest from actual productive activity—the owners of capital—becomes more apparent to those who actually direct production, the highly-educated workers, technicians, and administrators (many of whom are recruited from an increasingly radicalized student body.

In addition to these tendencies are the facts of continually-rising private indebtedness and continually-rising inflation—tendencies that (accelerated by the war in Vietnam) have had the effect of causing the real income of American workers in the sixties to stagnate or even to decline for the first time in three decades. This inflationary pressure has created tensions in the world monetary system which also compel solution. Deflationary "solutions" in turn lead to more unemployment, while "growth" policies yield more inflation. Either way, American workers cannot remain quiescent. Inflation further compounds the basic contradiction in the U.S. between so-called "private affluence" and the "public squalor" that makes our cities unlivable. This contradiction is becoming sharper because the number of public employees is rising rapidly, while the indirect costs of

506

production are increasingly borne by the public rather than by the private sector. The capitalists, in resisting increased taxation to pay these indirect production costs, are actually resisting the increasingly unionized employees. The result of this struggle by the public employee to erase the public-private wage differential is likely to be his increased radicalization.

To these interacting tendencies within the system must be added the effects of foreign competition, which, argues Mandel, will in turn have internal consequences: As the productivity differential between the U.S., Europe, and Japan narrows, and as competition for markets grows more intense, the historically great wage differential between workers in the U.S. and the other countries will pose insuperable problems for American capitalism. The capitalists' attempt to impose wage "guidelines" and to increase productivity by the speedup and other means of intensified exploitation of labor must result in heightened combativity in the trade unions. Mandel concludes that, if and when all of these processes converge, socialism will become the next immediate issue on the historical agenda, put there by the mass of American workers.

39

WHERE IS AMERICA GOING?

Ernest Mandel

Today, profound forces are working to undermine the social and economic equilibrium which has reigned in the United States for more than 25 years, since the big depression of 1929–1932 and of 1937–1938. Some of these are forces of an international character, linked with the national liberation struggles of the peoples exploited by American imperialism—above all, the Vietnamese revolution. But from the point of view of Marxist method, it is important in the first place to stress those forces which are at work inside the system itself. This essay will attempt to isolate six of these forces—six historic contradictions which are now destroying the social equilibrium of the capitalist economy and bourgeois order of the United States.

1. THE DECLINE OF UNSKILLED LABOR AND THE SOCIAL ROOTS OF BLACK RADICALIZATION

American society, like every other industrialized capitalist country, is currently in the throes of an accelerated process of technological change. The third industrial revolution—summarized in the catchword "automation"—has by now been transforming American industry for nearly two decades. The changes which this new industrial revolution has brought about in American society are manifold. During the fifties, it created increased unemployment. The annual growth-rate of productivity was

Reprinted, with author's revisions, from the *New Left Review*, No. 54 (March–April 1969), pp. 3–15, by permission of the publisher.

higher than the annual growth-rate of output, and as a result there was a tendency to rising structural unemployment even in times of boom and prosperity.   Average annual unemployment reached 5,000,000 by the end of the Republican administration.

Since the early sixties, the number of unemployed has, however, been reduced somewhat (although American unemployment statistics are very unreliable).   It has probably come down from an average of 5,000,000 to an average of 3,500,000 to 4,000,000; these figures refer to structural unemployment, and not to the conjunctural unemployment which occurs during periods of recession.   But whatever may be the causes of this temporary and relative decline in structural unemployment, it is very significant that one sector of the American population continues to be hit very hard by the development of automation: the general category of unskilled labour.   Unskilled labour jobs are today rapidly disappearing in U.S. industry.   They will in the future tend to disappear in the economy altogether.   In absolute figures, the number of unskilled labour jobs in industry has come down from 13,000,000 to less than 4,000,000, and probably to 3,000,000, within the last 20 years.   This is a truly revolutionary process. Very rarely has anything of the kind happened with such speed in the whole history of capitalism.   The group which has been hit hardest by the disappearance of unskilled jobs is, of course, the black population of the United States.

The rapid decline in the number of unskilled jobs in American industry is the nexus which binds the growing Negro revolt, especially the revolt of Negro youth, to the general socio-economic framework of American capitalism.   Of course it is clear, as most observers have indicated, that the acceleration of the Negro revolt, and in particular the radicalization of Negro youth in the fifties and early sixties, has been closely linked to the development of the colonial revolution.   The appearance of independent states in Black Africa, the Cuban Revolution with its radical suppression of racial discrimination, and the development of the Vietnam War, have been powerful subjective and moral factors in accelerating the Afro-American explosion in the U.S.A.   But we must not overlook the objective stimuli which have grown out of the inner development of American capitalism itself.   The long post-war boom and the explosive progress in agricultural productivity were the first factors in the massive urbanization and proletarization of the Afro-Americans: the Northern ghettoes grew by leaps and bounds.   Today, the average rate of unemployment among the black population is double what it is among the white population, and the average rate of unemployment among *youth* is double what it is among adults, so that the average among the black youth is nearly four times the general average in the country. Up to 15 or 20 percent of young black workers are unemployed; this is a percentage analogous to that of the Great Depression. It is sufficient to look at these figures to understand the social and material origin of the black revolt.

It is important to stress the very intimate inter-relationship between this high rate of unemployment among black youth and the generally scandalous state of education for black people in the ghettoes.   This school system produces a large majority of drop-outs precisely at the moment when unskilled jobs are fast disappearing.   It is perfectly clear under these conditions why black nationalists feel so strongly about the problem of community control over black schools—a problem which in New York and elsewhere has become a real crystallizing point for the black liberation struggle.

2. THE SOCIAL ROOTS OF THE STUDENT REVOLT

The third industrial revolution can be seen at one and the same time as a process of *expulsion* of human labour from traditional industry, and of tremendous *influx* of industrial labour into all other fields of economic and social activity.   Whereas more and more people are replaced by machines in industry, activities like agriculture, office administration, public administration and even education become industrialized—that is, more and more mechanized, streamlined and organized in industrial forms.

This leads to very important social consequences.   These may be summed up by saying that, in the framework of the third industrial revolution, manual labour is expelled from production while intellectual labour is reintroduced into the productive process on a gigantic scale.   It thereby becomes to an ever-increasing degree alienated labour—standardized, mechanized, and subjected to rigid rules and regimentation, in exactly the same way that manual labour was in the first and second industrial revolutions.   This fact is very closely linked with one of the most spectacular recent developments in American society: the massive student revolt, or, more correctly, the growing radicalization of students.   To give an indication of the scope of this transformation in American society, it is enough to consider that the United States, which at

the beginning of this century was still essentially a country exporting agricultural products, today contains fewer farmers than
students. There are today in the United States 6,000,000 students; the number of farmers together with their employees and
family-help has sunk below 5,500,000. We are confronted with
a colossal transformation which upsets traditional relations
between social groups, expelling human labour radically from
certain fields of activity, but reintroducing it on a larger scale
and at a higher level of qualification and skill in other fields.

If one looks at the destiny of the new students, one can see
another very important transformation, related to the changes
which automation and technological progress have brought about
in the American economy. Twenty or thirty years ago, it was
still true that the students were in general either future capitalists,
self-employed or agents of capitalism. The majority of them
became either doctors, lawyers, architects, and so on, or functionaries with managerial positions in capitalist industry or the
State. But today this pattern is radically changed. It is obvious
that there are not 6,000,000 jobs for capitalists in contemporary
American society; neither for capitalists or self-employed professionals, nor for agents of capitalism. Thus a great number of
present-day students are not future capitalists at all, but future
salary-earners, in teaching, public administration and at various
technical levels in industry and the economy. Their status will
be nearer that of the industrial worker than that of management.
For meanwhile, as a result of automation, the difference of status
between the technician and the skilled worker is rapidly diminishing. U.S. society is moving towards a situation in which most
of the skilled workers for whom there remain jobs in industry will
have to have a higher or semi-higher education. Such a situation
already exists in certain industries even in countries other than
the United States—Japanese shipbuilding is a notable example.

The university explosion in the United States has created the
same intense consciousness of alienation among students as that
which is familiar in western Europe today. This is all the more
revealing, in that the material reasons for student revolt are much
less evident in the United States than in Europe. Overcrowding
of lecture halls, paucity of student lodgings, lack of cheap food
in restaurants and other phenomena of a similar kind play a comparatively small role in American universities, whose material
infrastructure is generally far superior to anything that we know
in Europe. Nevertheless, the consciousness of alienation resulting

from the capitalist form of the university, from the bourgeois structure and function of higher education and the authoritarian administration of it, has become more and more widespread.   It is a symptomatic reflection of the changed social position of the students today in society.

American students are thus much more likely to understand general social alienation, in other words to become at least potentially anti-capitalist, than they were 10 or 15 years ago.   Here the similarity with developments in western Europe is striking.   As a rule, political mobilization on the U.S. campus started with aid to the black population within the United States, or solidarity with liberation movements in the Third World.   The first political reaction of American students was an anti-imperialist one.   But the logic of anti-imperialism has led the student movement to understand, at least in part, the necessity of anti-capitalist struggle, and to develop a socialist consciousness which is today widespread in radical student circles.

3. AUTOMATION, TECHNICIANS AND THE HIERARCHICAL STRUCTURE OF THE FACTORY

The progress of automation has also had another financial and economic result, which we cannot yet see clearly in Europe, but which has emerged as a marked tendency in the United States during the sixties.   Marxist theory explains that one of the main special effects of automation and the present technological revolution is a shortening of the life-cycle of fixed capital.   Machinery is now generally replaced every four or five years, while it used to be replaced every ten years in classical capitalism.   Looking at the phenomenon from the perspective of the operations of big corporations, this means that there is occurring a shift of the centre of their gravity away from problems of *production* towards problems of *reproduction*.

The real bosses of the big corporations no longer mainly discuss the problems of how to organize production; that is left to lower-echelon levels of the hierarchy.   The specific objective in which they are interested is how to organize and to ensure reproduction.   In other words, what they discuss is future plans: plans for replacing the existing machinery, plans for financing that replacement, new fields and locations for investment, and so on. This has given the concentration of capital in the United States a new and unforeseen twist.   The process of amalgamation during

the last few years has not predominantly consisted in the creation
of monopolies in certain branches of industry, fusing together
automobile, copper or steel trusts, or aviation factories. It
has instead been a movement towards uniting apparently quite
unconnected companies, operating in completely heteroclite fields
of production. There are some classical examples of this process,
widely discussed in the American financial press, such as the
Xerox-CIT merger, the spectacular diversification of the International Telephone and Telegraph Corporation, or the Ling-
Temco-Vought empire, which recently bought up the Jones and
Loughlin Steel Corporation.

What this movement really reflects is the growing preoccupation with "pure" problems of accumulation of capital. That
is to say, the imperative today is to assemble enough capital and
then to diversify the investment of that capital in such a way as
to minimize risks of structural or conjunctural decline in this or
that branch—risks which are very great in periods of fast technological change. In other words, the operation of the capitalist
system in the United States today shows in a very clear way what
Marxists have always said (and what only economists in the Soviet
Union and some of their associates in east European countries
and elsewhere are forgetting today), namely that real cost reduction and income maximization is impossible if profitability is reck-
oned only at plant level. In fact, it is a truth which every big
American corporation understands, that it is impossible to have
maximum profitability and economic rationality at plant level,
and that it is even impossible to achieve it at the level of a *single
branch of industry*. That is why the prevailing capitalist tendency
in the U.S.A. is to try to combine activities in a number of branches
of production. The type of financial empire which is springing
up as a result of this form of operation is a fascinating object of
study for Marxists.

But the more Big Capital is exclusively preoccupied with
problems of capital accumulation and reproduction, the more it
leaves plant management and organization of production to lower-
echelon experts, and the more the smooth running of the economy
must clash with the survival of private property and of the hierarchical structure of the factory. The absentee factory-owners
and money-juggling financiers divorced from the productive
process are not straw men. The retain ultimate power—the
power to open or to close the plant, to shut it in one town and
relaunch it 2,000 miles away, to suppress by one stroke of their

pens 20,000 jobs and 50 skills acquired at the price of long human efforts. This power must seem more and more arbitrary and absolute in the eyes of the true technicians who precisely do *not* wield the decisive power, that of the owners of capital. The higher the level of education and scientific knowledge of the average worker-technician, the more obsolete must become the attempts of both capitalists and managers to maintain the hierarchical and authoritarian structure of the plant, which even contradicts the logic of the latest techniques—the need for flexible co-operation within the factory in the place of a rigid chain of command.

4. THE EROSION OF REAL WAGE INCREASES THROUGH INFLATION

Since the beginning of the sixties and the advent of the Kennedy administration, structural unemployment has gone down and the rate of growth of the American economy has gone up. This shift has been generally associated with an increased rate of inflation in the American economy. The concrete origins and source of this inflation are to be located not only in the huge military establishment—although, of course, this is the main cause—but also in the vastly increased indebtedness of the whole American society. Private debt has accelerated very quickly; in the last 15 years it has gone up from something like 65 percent to something like 120 percent of the internal national income of the country, and this percentage is rising all the time. It passed the $1,000,000,000 (thousand million) mark a few years ago, in 1966, and is continually rising at a quicker rate than the national income itself. The specific price behaviour of the monopolistic and oligopolistic corporations, of course, interlocks with this inflationary process.

This is not the place to explore the technical problems of inflation. But it should be emphasized that the result of these inflationary tendencies, combined with the Vietnam war, has been that, for the first time for over three decades the growth of the real disposable income of the American working class has stopped. The highest point of that disposable real income was reached towards the end of 1965 and the beginning of 1966. Since then it has been going down. The downturn has been very slow—probably less than 1 percent per annum. Nevertheless it is a significant break in a tendency which has continued practically without interruption for the last 35 years. This downturn in the real income of the workers has been the result of two processes: on the one hand inflation, and on the other a steep increase in taxation since the beginning of the Vietnamese war.   There is a very clear and concrete relation between this halt in the rise of the American working class's real income, and the growing impatience which exists today in American working class circles with the U.S. Establishment as such, whose distorted reflection was partly to be seen in the Wallace movement.

It is, of course, impossible to speak at this stage of any political opposition on the part of the American working class to the capitalist system as such.   But if American workers accepted more or less easily and normally the integration of their trade union leadership into the Democratic party during the long period which started with the Roosevelt administration, this acceptance was a product of the fact that their real income and material conditions, especially their social security, improved during that period. Today that period seems to be coming to an end.   The current stagnation of workers' real income means that the integration of the trade union bureaucracy into the bourgeois Democratic party is now no longer accepted quite so easily as it was even four years ago.   This was evident during the presidential election campaign of 1968.   The UAW leadership organized their usual special convention to give formal endorsement to the Democratic candidates, Humphrey and Muskie.   This time they got a real shock.   Of the thousand delegates who normally come to these conventions, nearly one half did not show up at all.   They no longer supported the Democratic party with enthusiasm.   They had lost any sense of identification with the Johnson administration.   All the talk about welfare legislation, social security, medicare and the other advantages which the workers had gained during the last four years was largely neutralized in their eyes by the results of inflation and of increased taxation on their incomes.   The fact was that their real wages had stopped growing and were even starting to decline a little.

It is well known that dollar inflation in the United States has created major tensions in the world monetary system.   Inside the U.S.A., there is now a debate among different circles of the ruling class, the political personnel of the bourgeoisie, and the official economic experts, as to whether to give priority to restoring the U.S. balance of payments, or to maintaining the present rate of growth.   These two goals seem to be incompatible.   Each attempt to stifle inflation completely, to re-establish a very stable currency, can only be ensured by deflationary policies which create unemployment—and probably unemployment on a considerable scale. Each attempt to create full employment and to quicken the rate of growth inevitably increases inflation and with it the general loss of power of the currency. This is the dilemma which confronts the new Republican administration today as it confronted Johnson yesterday. It is impossible to predict what course Nixon will choose, but it is quite possible that his economic policy will be closer to that of the Eisenhower administration than to that of the Kennedy-Johnson administrations.

A group of leading American businessmen, who form a council of business advisors with semi-official standing, published a study two weeks before the November 1968 election which created a sensation in financial circles. They stated bluntly that in order to combat inflation, at least 6 per cent unemployment was needed. These American businessmen are far more outspoken than their British counterparts, who are already happy when there is talk about 3 percent unemployment. Unemployment of 6 percent in the United States means about 5,000,000 permanently without work. It is a high figure compared to the present level, to the level under "normal" conditions, outside of recessions. If Nixon should move in that direction, in which the international bankers would like to push him, the American bourgeoisie will encounter increased difficulty in keeping the trade-union movement quiescent and ensuring that the American workers continue to accept the integration of their union bureaucracy into the system, passively submitting to both bosses and union bureaucrats.

5. THE SOCIAL CONSEQUENCES OF PUBLIC SQUALOR

There is a further consequence of inflation which will have a growing impact on the American economy and especially on social relations in the United States. Inflation greatly intensifies the contradiction between "private affluence" and "public squalor." This contradiction has been highlighted by liberal economists like Galbraith, and is today very striking for a European visiting the United States. The extent to which the public services in that rich country have broken down is, in fact, astonishing. The huge budget has still not proved capable of maintaining a minimum standard of normally functioning public services. In late 1968, the *New York Times Magazine*, criticizing the American postal services, revealed that the average letter travels between Washington and New York more slowly today that it did a hundred years ago on horseback in the West. In a city like New York, street sweeping has almost entirely disappeared. Thoroughfares are generally filthy; in the poorer districts, streets are hardly ever cleaned. In the richer districts, the burgers achieve clean streets only because they pay private workers out of their own pockets to sweep the streets and keep them in more or less normal conditions. Perhaps the most extraordinary phenomenon, at any rate for the European, is that of certain big cities in the Southwest that do not have any public transport system *whatsoever;* not a broken-down system—just no system at all. There are private cars and nothing else—no buses, no trams, no subways, nothing.

The contradiction between private affluence and public squalor has generally been studied from the point of view of the consumer, and of the penalties or inconveniences that it imposes on the average citizen. But there is another dimension to this contradiction which will become more and more important in the years to come. This is its impact on what one could call the "producers," that is to say, on the people who are employed by public administration.

The number of these employees is increasing very rapidly. Public administration is already the largest single source of employment in the United States, employing over 11,000,000 wage earners. The various strata into which these 11,000,000 can be divided are all chronically underpaid. They have an average income which is lower than the income of the equivalent positions in private industry. This is not exceptional; similar phenomena have existed or exist in many European countries. But the results—results which have often been seen in Europe during the last 10 or 11 years—are now for the first time appearing on a large scale in the United States.

Public employees, who in the past were outside the trade-union movement and, indeed, any form of organized social activity, are today becoming radicalized at least at the union level. They are organizing; they are agitating; and they are demanding incomes at least similar to those which they could get in private industry. In a country like the United States, with the imperial position it occupies on a world scale, the vulnerability of the social system to any increase in trade-union radicalism by public employees is very great. A small example will do as illustration. In New York recently both police and firemen were, not officially but effectively, on strike—at the same time. They merely worked to rule, and thereby disorganized the whole urban life of the city. Everything broke down. In fact, for six days total traffic chaos reigned in New York. Drivers could park their cars anywhere without their being towed away. (Under normal conditions, between two and three thousand cars are towed away by the police each day in New York.) For those six days, with motorists free to park where they liked, the town became completely blocked after an hour of morning traffic—just because the police wanted a 10 percent increase in wages.

The economic rationale of this problem needs to be understood. It is very important not to see it simply as an example of mistaken policy on the part of public administrators or capitalist politicians, but rather as the expression of basic tendencies of the capitalist system. One of the main trends of the last 25 or 30 years of European capitalism has been the growing socialization of all indirect costs of production. This constitutes a very direct contribution to the realization of private profit and to the accumulation of capital. Capitalists increasingly want the State to pay not only for electrical cables and roads, but also for research, development, education, and social insurance. But once this tendency towards the socialization of indirect costs of production gets under way, it is obvious that the corporations will not accept large increases in taxation to finance it. If they were to pay the taxes needed to cover all these costs, there would in fact be no "socialization." They would continue to pay for them privately, but instead of doing so directly they would pay indirectly through their taxes (and pay for the administration of these payments too). Instead of lessening the burden, such a solution would in fact increase it. So there is an inevitable institutionalized resistance of the corporations and of the capitalist class to increasing taxes up to the point where they would make possible a functional public service capable of satisfying the needs of the entire population. For this reason, it is probable that the gap between the wages of public employees and those of private workers in the United States will remain, and that the trend towards radicalization of public employees—both increased unionization and even possibly political radicalization—will continue.

Moreover, it is not without importance that a great number of university students enter public administration—both graduates and so-called drop-outs. Even today, if we look at the last four or five years, many young people who were student leaders or militants three or four years ago are now to be found teaching in the schools or working in municipal social services. They may lose part of their radical consciousness when they take jobs; that is the hope not only of their parents but also of the capitalist class. But the evidence shows that at least part of their political consciousness is preserved, and that there occurs a certain infiltration of radicalism from the student sector into the teaching body— especially in higher education—and into the various strata of public administration in which ex-students become employed.

6. THE IMPACT OF FOREIGN COMPETITION

The way in which certain objective contradictions within the United States' economy have been slowly tending to transform the subjective consciousness of different groups of the country's population—Negroes, especially Negro youth; students; technicians; public employees—has now been indicated. Inflation has begun to disaffect growing sections of the working class. But the final, and most important, moment of a Marxist analysis of U.S. imperial society today has not yet been reached—that is the threat to American capitalism now posed by international competition.

Traditionally, American workers have always enjoyed much higher real wages than European workers. The historical causes for this phenomenon are well known. They are linked with the shortage of labour in the United States, which was originally a largely empty country. Traditionally, American capitalist industry was able to absorb these higher wages because it was practically isolated from international competition. Very few European manufactured goods reached the United States, and United States industry exported only a small part of its output. Over the last 40 years, of course, the situation has slowly changed. American industry has become ever more integrated into the world market. It participates increasingly in international competition, both because it exports more and because the American domestic market is rapidly itself becoming the principal sector of the world market, since the exports of all other capitalist countries to the United States have been growing rapidly. Here a major paradox seems to arise. How can American workers earn real wages which are between two and three times higher than real wages in western Europe, and between four and five times higher than real wages in Japan, while American industry is involved in international competition?

The answer is, of course, evident. These higher wages have been possible because United States industry has operated on a much higher level of productivity than European or Japanese industry. It has enjoyed a productivity gap, or as Engels said of British industry in the nineteenth century, a *productivity monopoly* on the world market. This productivity monopoly is a function of two factors: higher technology, and economy of scale—that is, a much larger dimension of the average factory or firm. Today, both of these two causes of the productivity gap are threatened. The technological advance over Japan or western Europe which has characterized American imperialism is now disappearing very rapidly. The very trend of massive capital export to the other imperialist countries which distinguishes American imperialism, and the very nature of the so-called "multi-national" corporation (which in nine cases out of ten is in reality an American corporation), diffuses American technology on a world scale, thus equalizing technological levels at least among the imperialist countries. At the same time, it tends, of course, to increase the gap between the imperialist and the semi-colonial countries. Today, one can say that only in a few special fields such as computers and aircraft does American industry still enjoy a real technological advantage over its European and Japanese competitors. But these two sectors, although they may be very important for the future, are not decisive for the total export and import market either in Europe or in the United States, nor will they be decisive for the next 10 or 20 years. So this advantage is a little less important than certain European analysts have claimed.

If one looks at other sectors, in which the technological advantage is disappearing or has disappeared—such as steel, automobiles, electrical appliances, textiles, furniture, or certain types of machinery—it is evident that a massive invasion of the American market by foreign products is taking place. In steel, something between 15 and 20 percent of American consumption is today imported from Japan and western Europe. The Japanese are beginning to dominate the west coast steel market, and the Europeans to take a large slice of the east coast market. It is only in the Midwest, which is still the major industrial region of the United States, that imported steel is not widely used. But with the opening of the St. Lawrence seaway, even there the issue may be doubtful in the future. Meanwhile, automobiles are imported into the United States today at a rate which represents 10–15 percent of total annual consumption. This proportion too could very quickly go up to 20–25 percent. There is a similar development in furniture, textiles, transistor radios and portable television sets; shipbuilding and electrical appliances might be next.

So far, the gradual disappearance of the productivity differential has created increased competition for American capitalism in its own home market. Its foreign markets are seriously threatened or disappearing in certain fields like automobiles and steel. This, of course, is only the first phase. If the concentration of European and Japanese industry starts to create units which operate on the same scale as American units, with the same dimensions as American corporations, then American industry will ultimately find itself in an impossible position. It will then have to pay three times higher wages, with the same productivity as the Europeans or the Japanese. That would be an absolutely untenable situation, and it would be the beginning of a huge structural crisis for American industry.

Two examples should suffice to show that this is not a completely fantastic perspective. The last merger in the Japanese steel industry created a Japanese corporation producing 22,000,000 tons of steel a year. In the United States, this would make it the second biggest steel firm. On the other hand, in Europe the recent announcement that Fiat and Citroen are to merge by 1970 has created an automobile corporation producing 2,000,000 cars a year; this would make it the third largest American automobile firm, and it would move up into second place, overtaking Ford, if the momentum of its rate of growth, compared with the current rate of growth in the American industry, were maintained for another three or four years.

These examples make it clear that it is possible for European and Japanese firms, if the existing process of capital concentration continues, to attain not only a comparable technology but also comparable scale to that of the top American firms. When they reach that level, American workers' wages are certain to be attacked, because it is not possible in the capitalist world to produce with the same productivity as rivals abroad and yet pay workers at home two or three times higher wages.

7. THE WAGE DIFFERENTIALS ENJOYED BY AMERICAN WORKERS

The American ruling class is becoming increasingly aware that the huge wage differential which it still grants its workers is a handicap in international competition.   Although this handicap has not yet become a serious fetter, American capitalists have already begun to react to it in various ways over the past few years.

The export of capital is precisely designed to counteract this wage differential.   The American automobile trusts have been investing almost exclusively in foreign countries, where they enjoy lower wages and can therefore far more easily maintain their share of the world market, with cars produced cheaply in Britain or Germany, rather than for higher wages inside the United States. Another attempt to keep down the growth of real wages was the type of incomes policy advocated by the Kennedy and Johnson administrations—until 1966, when it broke down as a result of the Vietnam war.   A third form of counteraction has been an intensification of the exploitation of labour—in particular a speedup in big industry which has produced a structural transformation of the American working class in certain fields.   This speedup has led to a work rhythm that is so fast that the average adult worker is virtually incapable of keeping it up for long.   This has radically lowered the age structure in certain industries, such as automobiles or steel.   Today, since it is increasingly difficult to stay in plants (under conditions of speedup) for 10 years without becoming a nervous or physical wreck, up to 40 percent of the automobile workers of the United States are young workers.   Moreover, the influx of black workers in large-scale industry has been tremendous as a result of the same phenomenon, since they have fewer job opportunities that are better outside the factory compared to white workers.   Today, there are percentages of 35, 40 or 45 percent black workers in some of the key automobile factories.   In Ford's famous River Rouge plant, there are over 40 percent black workers; in the Dodge automobile plant in Detroit, there are over 50 percent. These are still exceptional cases—although there are also some steel plants with over 50 percent black workers.   But the average employment of black workers in United States industry as a whole is far higher than the demographic average of 10 per cent: it is something like 30 percent.

None of these policies has so far had much effect.   However, if the historic moment arrives when the productivity gap between American and west European and Japanese industry is closed, American capitalism will have absolutely no choice but to launch a far more ruthless attack on the real wage levels of American workers than has occurred hitherto in western Europe, in the various countries where a small wage differential existed (Italy, France, West Germany, England and Belgium, at different moments during the sixties). Since the wage differential between Europe and America is not a matter of 5, 10, or 15 percent, as it is between different western European countries, but is of the order of 200–300 percent, it is easy to imagine what an enormous handicap this will become when productivity becomes comparable, and how massive the reactions of American capitalism will then be.

It is necessary to stress these facts in order to adopt a Marxist, in other words, a materialist and not an idealist approach to the question of the attitudes of the American working class towards American society. It is true that there is a very close interrelation between the anti-communism of the Establishment, the arms expenditure which makes possible a high level of employment, the international role of American imperialism, the surplus profits which the latter gets from its international investments of capital, and the military apparatus which defends these investments. But one thing must be understood. The American workers go along with this whole system, not in the first place because they are intoxicated by the ideas of anti-communism. They go along with it because it has been capable of delivering the goods to them over the last 30 years. The system has been capable of giving them higher wages and a higher degree of social security. It is this fact which has determined their acceptance of anti-communism, and not the acceptance of anti-communism which has determined social stability. Once the system becomes less and less able to deliver the goods, a completely new situation will occur in the United States.

Trade-union consciousness is not only negative. Or, to formulate this more dialectically, trade-union consciousness is in and by itself socially neutral. It is neither reactionary nor revolutionary. It becomes reactionary when the system is capable of satisfying trade-union demands. It creates a major revolutionary potential once the system is no longer capable of satisfying basic trade-union demands. Such a transformation of American society under the impact of the international competition of capital is today knocking at the door of U.S. capitalism.

The liberation struggles of the peoples of the Third World, with their threat to American imperialist investment, will also play an important role in ending the long socio-economic equilibrium of American capitalism. But they do not involve such dramatic and immediate economic consequences as the international competition of capital could have, if the productivity gap were filled.

As long as socialism or revolution are only ideals preached by militants because of their own convictions and consciousness, their social impact is inevitably limited.   But when the ideas of revolutionary socialism are able to unite faith, confidence and consciousness with the immediate material interest of a social class in revolt—the working class—then their potential becomes literally explosive.   In that sense, the political radicalization of the working class, and therewith socialism, will become a practical proposition in the United States within the next 10 or 15 years, under the combined impact of all these forces which have been examined here.   After the black workers, the young workers, the students, the technicians and the public employees, the mass of the American workers will put the struggle for socialism on the immediate historical agenda in the United States.   The road to revolution will then be open.

Some works by Mandel which he requested be noted here:
Europe vs America: The Socialist Alternative To The American Challenge.   New Left Books.
Introduction To Marxist Economic Theory.   Beverly Hills, Calif.: Merit Publishers.
Marxist Economic Theory.   2 vols.   New York: Monthly Review Press.
The Development of Marx's Economic Thought.   New York: Monthly Review Press.
The Revolutionary Student Movement—Theory and Practice.   Beverly Hills, Calif.: Merit Publishers.

AUTHOR INDEX